THE EVIDENT MEMORANDUM

THE EVIDENT MEMORANDUM

A Commentary on
Ibn Mulaqqin's

Al-Tadhkirah

MUSA FURBER

ISBN 978-1-944904-14-2 (paper)

Published by:
Islamosaic
islamosaic.com
publications@islamosaic.com

بسم الله الرحمن الرحيم

All praise is to Allah alone, the Lord of the Worlds
And may He send His benedictions upon
our master Muhammad, his Kin
and his Companions
and grant them
peace

TRANSLITERATION KEY

ء	ʾ (A distinctive glottal stop made at the bottom of the throat.)
ا	ā, a
ب	b
ت	t
ث	th (Pronounced like the *th* in *think*.)
ج	j
ح	ḥ (A hard *h* sound made at the Adam's apple in the middle of the throat.)
خ	kh (Pronounced like *ch* in Scottish *loch*.)
د	d
ذ	dh (Pronounced like *th* in *this*.)
ر	r (A slightly trilled *r* made behind the upper front teeth.)
ز	z
س	s
ش	sh
ص	ṣ (An emphatic *s* pronounced behind the upper front teeth.)
ض	ḍ (An emphatic *d*-like sound made by pressing the entire tongue against the upper palate.)
ط	ṭ (An emphatic *t* sound produced behind the front teeth.)
ظ	ẓ (An emphatic *th* sound, like the *th* in *this*, made behind the front teeth.)
ع	ʿ (A distinctive Semitic sound made in the middle of the throat and sounding to a Western ear more like a vowel than a consonant.)
غ	gh (A guttural sound made at the top of the throat, resembling the untrilled German and French *r*.)
ف	f
ق	q (A hard *k* sound produced at the back of the palate.)
ك	k
ل	l
م	m
ن	n
ه	h (This sound is like the English *h* but has more body. It is made at the very bottom of the throat and pronounced at the beginning, middle, and ends of words.)
و	ū, u
ي	ī, i, y
ﷺ	A supplication made after mention of the Prophet Muhammad, translated as "May Allah bless him and give him peace."

CONTENTS

المُحْتَوَيَاتُ

TRANSLITERATION KEY VI

CONVENTIONS VIII

PREFACE IX

INTRODUCTION 1

1 Purification 5

2 Prayer 67

3 Funerals 141

4 Zakat 150

5 Fasting 170

6 Pilgrimage 187

7 Sales & Other Transactions 217

8 Inheritance & Bequests 295

9 Marriage & Divorce 318

10 Injurious Crimes 424

11 Punishments 455

12 Jihad 479

13 Hunting & Slaughtering 501

14 Contests & Marksmanship 517

15 Oaths & Vows 519

16 Courts & Testimony 525

17 Manumission 548

Closing 558

APPENDIX A – CROSS-REFERENCES 559

APPENDIX B – BIOGRAPHIES 567

DETAILED TABLE OF CONTENTS 593

BIBLIOGRAPHY 608

CONVENTIONS

المُصْطَلَحَاتُ

Readers should be familiar with the following terms:

- *wājib* – that which one is rewarded for performing and punished for omitting. It is synonymous with *farḍ* except in a *very* limited set of issues. Throughout this translation, it is usually rendered as "obligatory."
- *sunnah* – that which one is rewarded for performing but *not* punished for omitting. It is synonymous with *mustaḥabb* and *mandūb*. It has been rendered as "recommended."
- *mubāḥ* – that which one is neither rewarded nor chastised for performing or omitting. It has been rendered as "merely permissible."
- *makrūh* – that which one is not punished for performing yet rewarded for omitting. It has been rendered as "offensive."
- *ḥarām* – that which one is punished for performing and rewarded for omitting. It has been rendered as "unlawful."

PREFACE

المُقَدِّمَة

This book is a compromise between needs, plans, possibilities, and realities. When I first set out to translate Abū Shujāʿ al-Aṣfahānī's *Matn al-ghāyat wa al-taqrīb* (*The Ultimate Conspectus*) in 2004, I had a plan to include the legal reasoning and evidences behind its various rulings. I began doing this in the interim between translating the text and publishing it. In the first attempt, I used Dr. Muṣṭafā al-Bughā's *Al-Tahdhīb fi adillat Matn al-ghāyat wa al-taqrīb* but I did not complete it because the presentation of evidence did not match what later Shāfiʿīs tend to include in their books. Dr. al-Bughā's book is excellent, but I had different objectives in mind.

I decided to try again using Taqī al-Dīn Abū Bakr ibn Muḥammad Ḥiṣnī's *Kifāyat al-akhyār fī ḥall Ghāyat al-ikhtiṣār* as a foundation since it was closer to what I had in mind. Its evidences were definitely what the Shāfiʿīs include in their books and the author usually followed them with an underlying legal cause (*ʿillah*) – which facilitates extending the ruling to new cases via legal analogy (*qiyās*). I finished roughly one-eighth of the book before other commitments drew me away. I tried to keep the project alive by adding evidence from whatever books I was reading with my students, but this attempt finally came to a halt in 2008.

In 2012, I decided to publish *The Ultimate Conspectus* on its own. Soon afterwards, a friend introduced me to a copy of Ibn Daqīq al-ʿId's *Tuḥfat al-labīb,* which is the earliest commentary on Abū Shujāʿ's text that I have been able to find. It was an excellent base for what I wanted, since he included arguments and evidences for the basic positions, as well as many presentations and discussions concerning alternative opinions, both within the Shāfiʿī school and in other schools. I jumped into translating the text during the last quarter of 2013 and had a first draft finished by the beginning of 2014. The edition I worked from was full of questionable passages which made me want to hold off on additional work until I could be confident that the text I translated matched Ibn Daqīq al-ʿEid's intent. Although I obtained two other editions of the book and used them for two additional drafts of my translation, I decided that much more work would be needed to give the book its proper due, so it would have to wait for a later day (and that day is still coming, *in shāʾ Allāh*).

I still wanted evidence for *The Ultimate Conspectus,* so I turned again to Dr. al-Bughā's book and did a quick translation. But I still did not have what I wanted.

During a short break that summer, I decided that I wanted to translate another short *fiqh* text. I chose Ibn Mulaqqin's short introduction to Shāfiʿī *fiqh*: *Al-Tadhkirah fī fiqh al-Shāfiʿī.* The text was a few hundred words longer than Abū Shujāʿ's text and covered many more rulings. Although it includes content not found in *The Ultimate Conspectus*, it alone does not provide enough new information to justify adding it to the English Shāfiʿī text library. The book does not have a commentary, so I decided to add commentary drawn from Ibn Mulaqqin's other works. The bulk of the commentary is from his *Mukhtaṣar al-Tabrīzī* – another Shāfiʿī text with content similar to *Al-Tadhkirah*. His commentary includes the evidences and intra-school differences that Ibn Mulaqqin thought every beginning student ought to know. While it does not provide evidence for everything, it does provide readers with a foundation of evidences for basic issues, a taste of Shāfiʿī legal reasoning, and a peek at some major reference works. Ibn Mulaqqin's other works helped fill in the gaps, such as his commentaries on other *fiqh* texts, his exhaustively researched books of *fiqh*-hadiths, his commentaries on hadiths related to legal rulings, and his own collection of evidences for *fiqh* works.

In other words, I shifted the goalposts from *Matn al-ghāyat wa al-taqrīb* to *Al-Tadhkirah*.

ABOUT THE AUTHOR

The author of *Al-Tadhkirah* and the works from which the bulk of the commentary is drawn is ʿUmar ibn ʿAlī ibn Aḥmad ibn Muḥammad al-Miṣrī al-Shāfiʿī (723–804 AH/1323–1401 CE), also known as "Ibn al-Mulaqqin." He was born in Cairo, 23 Rabiʿ al-Awwal, 723 AH (31 March 1323 CE). His father was known as "al-Naḥawī al-Shāfiʿī": "the Shāfiʿī grammarian."

Ibn al-Mulaqqin memorized Imam al-Nawawī's *Minhāj al-ṭālibīn* in fiqh and also al-Ḥāfiẓ ʿAbd al-Ghanī al-Maqdasī's *ʿUmdat al-aḥkām* in legal hadiths at a very early age. He wrote commentaries on both of these works later on in his life.

During his studies, he travelled to Damascus, Mecca, Medina, and Jerusalem. He studied with many of the great scholars of his age, including al-ʿAlāʾī, al-Isnawī, Taqi al-Dīn al-Subkī, Ibn Jamāʿ. Many of his students went on to become the leading scholars of the next generation, including Ḥāfiẓ al-Sibṭ Ibn al-ʿAjamī, Walī al-Din al-ʿIrāqī, al-Maqrīzī, and Ibn Ḥajar al-ʿAsqalānī.

Ibn Mulaqqin authored over seventy books. This book draws on the following:

- *Al-Badr al-munīr* ("*The Radiant Full Moon*") is an exhaustive sourcing of every hadith that Imam al-Rāfiʿī (557–623 AH/1162–1226 CE) mentioned in his commentary on *Al-Wajīz* by Imam al-Ghazālī (450–505 AH/1058–1111 CE).
- *Khulāṣat Al-Badr al-munīr* ("*The Summary Radiant Full Moon*") is an abridgment of his own *Al-Badr al-munīr*. He began the book on 19 Muḥarram 749 AH (31 March 1348 CE) and completed it on 4 Shawwāl (25 December 1348 CE). It contains 2995 hadiths.
- *Tuḥfat al-muḥtāj* ("*Gift for The Needy*") is a collection of hadith evidence for *Minhāj al-ṭālibīn* by Imām Yaḥya ibn Sharaf al-Nawawī (631–676 AH/1233–1277 CE). He started the book at the end of Shaʿbān and finished it on 27 Ramadan 753 AH (5 November 1352 CE). It contains 1825 hadiths.
- *Khulāṣat al-fatāwī* ("*Summary Legal Findings*") is a commentary on *Al-Ḥāwī al-ṣaghīr* by Najm al-Dīn ʿAbd al-Ghaffār

al-Qizwīnī (585–665 AH/1189–1286 CE). He finished it in 756 AH.
- *Mukhtaṣar al-Tabrīzī* ("*Al-Tabrīzī Summarized*") is a fiqh commentary on al-Muẓaffar al-Tabrīzī (558–621 AH/1163–1224 CE)'s short introduction to Shāfiʿī law. In his introduction, he mentioned that his goals included instructing novices in the basic evidence and most important disagreements in the school. He finished on 21 Ramadan 761 AH (5 August 1360 CE).
- *ʿUjālat al-muḥtāj* ("*Quick Compilation For the Needy*") is his shorter commentary on Imam al-Nawawī's *Minhāj al-ṭālibīn*. Although it mentions some of the reasoning behind rulings, it tends to be scant and he refers readers to his larger commentary (which has yet to be published). He finished it on 16 Jumādah 773 AH (24 November 1371 CE).

Ibn al-Mulaqqin passed away in 16 Rabīʿ al-Awwal 804 AH (31 October 1401 CE). May Allah grant him His mercy.

ABOUT THE TRANSLATION
It is not clear when Ibn Mulaqqin finished *Al-Tadhkirah*. In *Kashf al-ẓunūn*, Ḥājī Khalīfah reports that Ibn Mulaqqin composed the book for his son.[1]

The Arabic text of *Al-Tadhkirah* is approximately 8,500 words in length. It is two hundred words longer than Abū Shujāʿ al-Aṣfahānī (b. 433 AH/1042 CE)'s *Matn al-ghāyat wa-l-taqrīb*. Although the two are roughly the same size, Ibn Mulaqqin's style is more economical than Abū Shujāʿ's, allowing him to cover more within the same word count. And while Ibn Mulaqqin discusses more issues, he does occasionally skip a few details that Abū Shujāʿ includes.

I based my initial translation of *Al-Tadhkirah* on the Dār al-Kutub al-ʿIlmiyyah edition. When in doubt, I checked it against a manuscript of the text. If needed, I would also check it against *Al-Ḥāwī al-ṣaghīr*, as its tends to have the same wording.

---

1. Ḥājī Khalīfah, *Kashf al-ẓunūn*, 1:392.

The primary sources for comments in this book are Ibn Mulaqqin's books of fiqh, including *Sharḥ Mukhtasar al-Tabrīzī*, *ʿUjālat al-muḥtāj*, and *Khulāṣat al-fatāwī*. The bulk of the commentary comes from *Sharḥ Mukhtaṣar al-Tabrīzī*; I estimate that over half of that commentary has made it into this book. When I needed additional evidence, I turned to Ibn Mulaqqin's books related to legal hadiths, giving priority to *Tuḥfat al-muḥtāj*, *Mukhtaṣar al-Badr al-munīr*, and then *Al-Badr al-munīr*. There are places where I have drawn from sources by other authors. I indicate this by placing the material between angle brackets (i.e. ‹…›). Some of these additions come from my earlier work with Dr. Muṣṭafā al-Bughā's *Al-Tahdhīb*.

Every comment and hadith in this book can be sourced back to either one of Ibn Mulaqqin's fiqh texts or a Shāfiʿī fiqh text. For the sake of brevity, I did not include specific citations to material from Ibn Mulaqqin's fiqh texts. Instead, I have included an appendix that provides cross-references to his fiqh texts for each chapter and section in this book, which facilitates finding the source material in Ibn Mulaqqin's books.

Each hadith mentioned in the book is traced back to its primary sources, along with a reference to one or more of Ibn Mulaqqin's hadith works. Whenever a hadith is not included in one of Ibn Mulaqqin's works, I have referenced it to a Shāfiʿī text that does. Through this, readers can be assured that the hadiths cited here are ones that Shāfiʿīs themselves use. I do not focus on judgments on the hadiths since their inclusion in Shāfiʿī books – especially those whose authors were also hadith masters – indicates that the hadith is strong enough to be cited for its intended purpose.

While translating hadiths, I have tried to convey what the hadith means on its own without imposing a Shāfiʿī fiqh ruling onto it. This is why linguistic imperatives are translated as obligations, since this is their default according to scholars of jurisprudence. I do this even when a hadith – in light of other evidence and factors – is cited as evidence that something is recommended.

Most Quranic quotations are from Muḥammad Marmaduke Pickthall's *The Meaning of the Glorious Koran*. There are places where I have edited his translation to reflect Shāfiʿī linguistic preferences. I have also done this for reasons similar to the ones stated above with regards to hadith.

Readers should always keep in mind that the commentary tends to focus on what Ibn Mulaqqin considered essential for novices. Consequently, one should not expect the book to provide complete, compelling, or rigorous arguments. What readers will find, though, is a synopsis of the essential evidences behind many core Shāfiʿī fiqh positions.

Citations in footnotes use short-forms for oft-cited hadith compendia, by referring to the author's name without the "al-," e.g. "Bukhāri," and "Tirmidhī" for "*Ṣaḥīḥ al-Bukhāri*," and "*Sunan al-Tirmidhī*." Even shorter forms are used for Ibn Mulaqqin's books: "BM" for *Al-Badr al-munīr*; "KBM" for its abridgment; "KF" for *Khulāṣat al-fatāwī*; "MT" for *Mukhtaṣar al-Tabrīzī*; "TM" for *Tuḥfat al-muḥtāj*; and "UM" for *ʿUjālat al-muḥtāj*.

My commentary is intended to help readers who are already familiar with Shāfiʿī fiqh and its basic methodology learn some of the evidence and reasoning behind the rulings and to get a small taste of how its methods are put into practice. Readers should have read a book in fiqh like Shaykh Nuh Ha Mim Keller's *The Reliance of the Traveller* or my own *The Accessible Conspectus*, and a book on fiqh methodology, like my *Sharḥ al-Waraqāt*.

While this book does not cover everything that is discussed in the aforementioned books, it does cover most of the foundational issues addressed in Shāfiʿī fiqh.

I have taken the liberty of introducing additional sections and section titles into the text to assist readers in finding material. I have also reworded the definitions at the beginning of sections so that the bilingual text flows better.

Since the title *Al-Tadhkirah* means "The Reminder" or "The Memorandum," and the commentary focuses in evidence while also clarifying its meanings, I have titled my book *The Evident Memorandum*.

In summary, *The Evident Memorandum* is aimed at readers already familiar with Shāfiʿī fiqh. Its contents are curated primarily from Ibn Mulaqqin's fiqh and hadith books, with supplementary material from other Shāfiʿī texts. Although the individual passages in this book are not completely original, its composition and arrangement are. My goal is to explain Ibn Mulaqqin's Shāfiʿī fiqh primer as he might have done so himself, though I am certain to have fallen short and erred in places.

CLOSING

Many thanks are owed to the individuals who reviewed drafts of the translation and offered corrections, encouragement, and advice – especially Anaz Zubair and Nabeel Aziz. This text has been markedly improved through Khalid Gonçalves' generous offer to edit the text. Last but not least, I owe much to my wife and children for their constant support and sacrifice over the years.

May Allah reward the Imams, scholars and students of the Shāfiʿī school past, present, and future. May He grant Ibn Mulaqqin and everyone else mentioned in this preface – and us – His mercy, and may He make this work beneficial and make us among its beneficiaries. Where I have succeeded, it is only through the grace of Allah; where I have faltered, it is from my own shortcomings. May Allah forgive the book's author and translator, its owner, its readers, its listeners, and all Muslims – living and dead.

MUSA FURBER
KUALA LUMPUR
JULY 8, 2018

This page left blank

INTRODUCTION

المُقَدِّمَةُ

تصنيف الشّيخ الإمام العلام شيخ الإسلام أبي حفص عمر سراج الدّين ابن الشّيخ العلام عليّ نور الدّين المعروف بـ«النّحويّ» الشّافعيّ الأنصاريّ نفع الله به المسلمين ورحم سلفه آمين، والحمد لله ربّ العالمين، وصلّى الله على سيّدنا محمّد وآله وسلّم.

[This is the] compilation of the Imam and luminary scholar, Sheikh al-Islām Abū Ḥafṣ ʿUmar Sirāj al-Dīn, the son of the luminary Sheikh ʿAlī Nūr al-Din al-Shāfiʿī al-Anṣārī, who is known as "the Grammarian." May Allah make it beneficial for the Muslims, and a mercy for his forefathers. (*Amīn*!) All praise belongs to Allah, the Lord of the Worlds. May the prayers and blessings of Allah be upon our Master Muhammad and his family.

بسم الله الرّحمن الرّحيم

وصلّى الله على سيّدنا محمّد وآله، أحمد الله على توالي الأنعام، وأشكره على مزايد المنن الجسام، وأصلي على محمّد أشرف الأنام، مصباح الظّلام، وعلى آله وصحبه الغرّ الكرام، فبعد: فهذه تذكر ذات أحكام واتّفاق على مذهب الإمام المطّلبيّ ابن عمّ أشرف ولد عدنان، سهّلتها للولد والخلّان لينتفع بها أقرب الأوان، وعلى الله في كلّ الأمور الاعتماد والاتّكال.

In the Name of Allah, the Merciful and Compassionate

May the blessings of Allah be upon our liege lord Muhammad, and upon his pure household. I praise Allah for His continuous generosity and thank Him for his ever-increasing abundant blessings. I pray for blessings upon Muhammad, the noblest of [His] creatures and illuminator of darkness, and upon his ﷺ pure Household and most superior and illustrious Companions.

To commence:

These notes contain rulings and accords with the legal school of [Imam al-Shāfiʿī] the Muṭṭallabī imam and son of the paternal uncle of the best who was ever born to the children of ʿAdnān. I made [this book] easy for children and friends so that it may benefit in the least amount of time. Moreover, it is Allah who is relied upon and trusted in every matter.

OBLIGATORY DOCTRINAL KNOWLEDGE

وأوّل الواجبات معرف الرّبّ – جلّ جلاله – واعتقاد: وجوب وجوده وفردانيّته وقدمه وعدم شبهه ومثله وأنّه لم يزل بأسمائه وصفات ذاته وعلمه بالأمر كلّيّه وجزئيّه، وأنّه تعالى أرسل رسله مبشّرين ومنذرين لتنقطع الحجّ، وتتّضح المحجّ، والإيمان بالقدر خيره وشرّه، حلوه ومرّه، وبالغيب، وهو كلّ ما غاب عنّا وأخبر به الصّادق من أحوال البرزخ والحشر والجزاء والعقاب والجنّ والنّار. ولا نكفّر أحدًا من أهل القبل بذنب، ولا يخلّد. ونمسك عمّا شجر بين الصّحاب، ونؤوّل ما صحّ عنهم بإحسان. بوّأنا الله وإيّاهم الجنان.

The first obligation, above all, is to know the Lord (Exalted is His Majesty) and believe [the following]:

He exists necessarily. He is unique and pre-eternal. Nothing resembles or is like Him. He never ceases to possess His names or attributes of His essence. He knows things as they are – as a whole and their particulars.

He Most High sent His messengers bearing glad tidings and warnings; to give decisive, demonstrative proofs; and to clarify the path to follow.

[These obligations include] belief in destiny – good and evil, sweet and bitter.

[They include belief] in the unseen, which is everything unseen to us that the Truthful [Muhammad ﷺ] has informed us of. It includes life in the grave, the resurrection of the dead, reward and punishment, and Paradise and Hell.

We do not declare anyone who faces our direction of prayer [*ahl al-qiblah,* i.e., Muslims] a disbeliever due to a sin, nor do we say that he will remain eternally [in Hell].

We remain silent concerning the disputes that occurred between the Companions (may Allah be pleased with them one and all). We give the best interpretation to authentic reports concerning them. May Allah place us and them in Paradise.

This page left blank

I

PURIFICATION

كِتَابُ الطَّهَارَةِ

هي النّظافة، قال الله تعالى ﴿وَيُنَزِّلُ عَلَيْكُم مِّنَ السَّمَآءِ مَآءً لِّيُطَهِّرَكُم بِهِۦ﴾ [الأنفال: من الآية ١١].

Purification [*ṭahārah*] is "cleanliness."

This is according to its linguistic meaning. In the context of fiqh, purification is performing that which renders prayer lawful to perform.

Allah Most High said, "He...sent down water from the sky upon you, that thereby He might purify you..." [Q8:11].

Evidence for the possibility of removing ritual impurity [*ḥadath*, *janābah*], and filth [*najis*] is in the Quran and Sunnah. The Quranic evidence includes the verse mentioned above. Additional verses include "And He it is Who sendeth the winds, glad tidings heralding His mercy, and We send down purifying water from the sky..." [Q25:48]. Evidence from the Sunnah includes the Prophet ﷺ saying concerning the sea: "Its water is purifying and its dead are lawful."[1]

Only water lifts ritual impurity, whether minor or major.

Allah Most High says, "...and ye find not water, then go to high clean soil and rub your faces and your hands (therewith)..." [Q4:43, Q5:6]. Here, Allah Most High makes dry ablution obligatory in

1. Abū Hurayrah: Abū Dāwūd, 83; Tirmidhī, 69 – *ḥasan ṣaḥīḥ*; Nasā'ī, 59, 332, Ibn Mājah, 386. Jābir: Ibn Mājah, 388. See: TM, 3.

the absence of water, so using anything else would contravene His command.

Only water removes filth. This is the case whether the filth is *slight* (such as the urine of a male infant who has been fed only milk, *severe* (like the filth of dogs, pigs, and the offspring of both or either of them), or *moderate* (filth other than the above).

Asmā' (may Allah be pleased with her) said a woman came to the Messenger of Allah ﷺ and said, "One of us gets menstrual blood on her garment. What should she do with it?" He ﷺ said, "Scrape it, then rub it using water, pour water over it, and then pray [in it]."[2] The reasoning here is the same as in the Quranic verse above: using anything else would disagree with his ﷺ command.

Abū Hurayrah (may Allah be pleased with him) reported that a Bedouin stood up and started urinating in the mosque. The people grabbed him. However, the Prophet ﷺ ordered them to leave the Bedouin and pour a bucket or tumbler of water over the place where he had urinated. The Prophet ﷺ then said, "You have been sent to make things easy, not to make them difficult."[3]

Dry ablution [*tayammum*], tanning skins, and a large quantity[4] of contaminated water becoming pure on its own do not contradict the command to use water to remove filth. This is because dry ablution does not actually remove impurity (according to the soundest opinion), while the other two are examples of transformation [*iḥālah*].

WATER

المياه أقسام: طهور وهو المطلق المفهوم من قولك: «ماء»، ومكروه وهو المشمّس بقطر حارّ وإناء منطبع، وطاهر فقط وهو المستعمل في فرض ما دام قليلاً والمتغيّر

2. Asmā': Bukhārī, 227, 307; Muslim, 291 #110. See: TM, 7.
3. Abū Hurayrah: Bukhārī, 220. Abū Dāwūd, 380; Ibn Mājah, 629. Anas: Muslim, 285 #100; Abū Dāwūd, 380; Tirmidhī, 147; Ibn Mājah, 629.
4. The definition of "large quantity" is two or more *qullah*s of water, which is approximately 216 liters or 57.1 gallons.

بمخالط طاهر كثير، ونجس وهو ما لاقاه نجس وكان دون قلتين إن لم يكن ميتةً لا دم لها يسيل، أو لا يدركها الطرف، أو بلغ قلّتين وهما خمسمائة رطل بغداديّ تقريبًا وتغيّر.

There are [four] categories of water:

1. Purifying: plain water, understood when one says "water."

2. Offensive [to use]: water irradiated by the sun in hot lands while in a metallic container.

It is considered offensive to use due to fear of [transmitting] leprosy, or as a ritual whose rationale is not known to us [*taᶜbbud*]. However, the preferred opinion is that it is never offensive.

3. Pure [but not purifying]: water that

a. has been used in an obligatory act and whose volume remains small; or

Here, "obligatory act" includes lifting minor or major impurity, and "small volume" is an amount less than two *qullah*s.

Water that has already been used in an obligatory act is not purifying: it does not thereafter raise the state of ritual impurity or remove filth. This is the opinion of Imam al-Shāfiᶜī (may Allah grant him His mercy)'s new school [*al-madhhab al-jadīd*] (in Egypt, after leaving Baghdad). According to his old school [*al-madhhab al-qadīm*] (in Baghdad, before going to Egypt), it remains purifying. Among the evidence that Imam al-Shāfiᶜī used for his opinion in the new school was the fact that the earliest Muslims (may Allah be pleased with them) did not collect water that had been used for ablution in order to use it again, even though they needed water on many occasions during their travels.

There is disagreement concerning the reason why this water ceases to be purifying. One opinion is that it is due to its use within the performance of an obligatory action. Another is that it is due to its use within the performance of an act of worship.[5]

5. In other books, Ibn Mulaqqin presents this second reason as using water within an obligatory act of worship. See *Khulāṣat al-fatāwī,* 1:193.

The ramifications are evident with respect to [the ruling related to] a non-Muslim wife washing to make herself permissible to her Muslim husband [for sexual intercourse], in the second and third washings when making ablution, and in recommended baths.[6] If we take the first opinion, the water only becomes used in the case of the non-Muslim wife. This is the soundest opinion. However, if we take the second opinion, it covers all but her.

The disagreement above concerns whether used water is purifying. There is agreement [*ittifāq*] that used water is pure.

b. has changed significantly through admixture with a pure substance.

Changes caused by stagnation or water moss do not prevent water from being purifying due to the difficulty of their avoidance.

Slight changes do not prevent water from being purifying since they do not remove it from being referred to as "water."

4. Impure: water that

a. has encountered an impurity while being less than two *qullah*s in volume (so long as the impurity was not a dead animal lacking free-flowing blood, or imperceptible); or

The Prophet ﷺ said, "When water reaches two *qullah*s, it does not carry filth."[7] The negative implication of the hadith is that when the water is less than two *qullah*s, it does carry filth.

Animals without free flowing blood [such as flies] do not render water nor other liquids filthy due to the difficulty in avoiding them.

Abū Hurayrah (may Allah be pleased with him) narrated that the Messenger of Allah ﷺ said, "If a fly falls in one of your vessels, immerse all of it and then throw it [the fly] away, for one of its wings

6. See "Recommended Baths" on page 43.

7. Ibn ʿUmar: Abū Dāwūd, 63–65; Nasāʾī, 52; Ibn Mājah, 517–518; Bayhaqī, 1:261–262; Ḥākim, 458. See: TM, 10.

contains healing and the other contains sickness."[8] ‹Immersing the fly is likely to leave it dead by drowning. He ﷺ would not have ordered its immersion if its death would render the water filthy. Animals lacking free-flowing blood are considered analogous to the fly mentioned in this hadith.›

Imperceptible filth is excused because of the difficulty in its avoidance.

b. has reached two *qullahs* in volume (approximately 500 Baghdādī *riṭl*) and has changed.

This is according to consensus. Ibn al-Mundhir (may Allah grant him His mercy) said, "They [i.e., the scholars] have consensus that if a small or large quantity of water changes due to filth falling into it and the water's taste, color, or smell changes, then the water is filthy [so long as it remains that way. Ablution and purificatory baths made with it are invalid]."[9]

In a well-known hadith from Abū Umāmah (may Allah be pleased with him), the Messenger of Allah ﷺ reportedly said, "Allah created water purifying. Nothing makes it filthy except that which changes its smell, taste, or color."[10] The hadith cannot be used [as proof] because it is weak [*ḍaʿīf*]. Imam al-Shāfiʿī (may Allah grant him His mercy) said, "The People of Hadith do not affirm the likes of this hadith. However, it is the opinion of the masses [of scholars] and I do not know of any disagreement among them."[11]

---

8. Abū Hurayrah: Bukhārī, 5782. See: TM, 13.
9. Ibn al-Mundhir, *Al-Awsaṭ fī al-sunan wa al-ijmāʿ wa al-ikhtilāf,* 1:260. The words between parentheses were added from *Al-Awsaṭ*.
10. Abū Umāmah: Ibn Mājah, 521. See: TM, 14.
11. Al-Shāfiʿī, *Ikhtilāf al-ḥadīth,* 8:612. In *Al-Majmūʿ*, Imām al-Nawawī also says that this hadith is not valid to use it as proof, 1:162.

CONFUSING PURE AND FILTHY WATER

(فصل) [اشتباه المياه]

إذا اشتبه طاهر بنجس اجتهد وتطهّر بما ظنّ طهارته بعلامة، ولو أعمى ووجد متيقّنًا.

ويعيد الاجتهاد ما بقي طاهر بيقين ولا ينقض الأوّل بالثاني.

If pure water and filthy water become indistinguishable, one exercises *ijtihād* [informed reasoning]...

Al-Ḥasan (may Allah be pleased with him) said, "I memorized from the Messenger of Allah ﷺ, 'Leave that which confuses you for that which does not confuse you.'"[12]

...and makes purification with whichever one thought was pure based on indicators.

Since water is necessary to fulfill the obligation of prayer and its purity can be ascertained via *ijtihād* [based on physical indicators], *ijtihād* becomes obligatory – just as one must use *ijtihād* to determine the direction of prayer [if one is uncertain] by relying upon physical indicators.

Indicators include changes in color, smell, and a dog's wet footprints leading away from one water source but not the other source.

One exercises *ijtihād* even if one is blind,...

This is because one can still perceive some of the indicators, such as which contains more or less water, a change of smell, or water being disturbed.

12. al-Ḥasan: Aḥmed, 1723, 1724, 1727; Tirmidhī, 2518; Nasā'ī, 5711; Ibn Ḥibbān, 722; Ḥākim, 166, 2169, 2170, 7046. See: TM, 15.

...or if one is certain that an item is pure.

One continues exercising *ijtihād* so long as one is certain that the pure water remains. And one's earlier *ijtihād* is not voided by a later *ijtihād*.

Since *ijtihād* is not voided by *ijtihād*.

CONTAINERS

(فصل) [استعمال أواني الذّهب والفضّة]

واستعمال أواني النّقدين حرام، وكذا الاتخاذ والتّزيين.

و[يحرم] المضبّب به لزينة وكبر، وبواحد مكروه.

It is impermissible to possess or use containers [*awānī*] made of gold and silver, even for decorative purposes.

The Prophet ﷺ said, "The one who eats or drinks from gold and silver containers kindles the fire of Hell in his belly."[13]

Other uses of such containers are analogous to eating and drinking from them.

Solder that is both a large amount and decorative is impermissible. It is offensive if it is just a large amount *or* decorative [but not both].

Imam al-Nawawī (may Allah grant him His mercy) considered gold solder always unlawful.

It is not permissible to perform purification from [water contained in] them. The ablution is valid even though such use is unlawful – just like praying on stolen land.

13. Umm Salamah: Muslim, 2065. See: KBM, 51.

THE TOOTHSTICK

(فصل) [السّواك]

والسّواك سنّة في كلّ حال، ويتأكّد عند الوضوء والصّلاة وتغيّر الفم.

ويكره للصّائم بعد الزّوال.

Using the toothstick [*miswāk*] is recommended at all times.

The Prophet ﷺ said, "The toothstick [*sīwāk*] is a means of purification for the mouth and is pleasing to the Lord."[14]

Its use is especially recommended when making ablution, [before] praying, and whenever the mouth is stale.

The Prophet ﷺ said, "Had I not feared burdening my community, I would have commanded them to use a toothstick for every prayer."[15] The command would have made it an obligation. Since obligation is negated, it remains especially recommended [*sunnatu mu'akkadah*]. Another version has "...with every ablution."[16]

Its use is also especially recommended prior to reciting the Quran, when one's teeth become yellow (even if the mouth does not otherwise change), and when entering one's house.

Its use is offensive after the sun's zenith for someone who is fasting.

The Prophet ﷺ said, "Your Lord said, 'The smell that comes out of the mouth of a fasting person is better to Allah than the smell of musk.'"[17] This smell is particular to after the zenith, since before then, any change would be due to food [not from fasting alone], so there is no offensiveness.

---

14. ʿĀ'ishah: Nasā'ī, 5; Ibn Khuzaymah, 135 – *ṣaḥiḥ*; Ibn Ḥibbān, 1067. See: KBM, 66.
15. Abū Hurayrah: Bukhārī, 887, 7240; Muslim, 252 #42. See: TM, 62.
16. Abū Hurayrah: Bukhārī, before 1934 – *taʿlīqan*; Ibn Khuzaymah, *Al-Musnad*, 140. See: TM, 62.
17. Abū Hurayrah: Bukhārī, 1894; Muslim, 1151 #163–165. See: TM, 68.

OTHER SUNNAS OF THE BODY

Other recommended actions related to the body include clipping nails, trimming the mustache, plucking armpit hair, and shaving pubic hair. He ﷺ said, "The *fiṭrah* is five: circumcision, shaving pubic hair, trimming the mustache, clipping fingernails, and plucking armpit hair."[18]

ABLUTION INVALIDATORS

(فصل) [نواقض الوضوء]

The five invalidators of ablution will soon be mentioned along with the evidence for each one. Ablution is not invalidated by anything else since the default ruling is the absence of its invalidation until something has been established as its invalidator, and there is no textual evidence concerning other things. The use of analogy is barred in this topic since the *ʿillah* [legal cause] of invalidation is not rational.

ويجب الوضوء بالخارج من أحد السّبيلين إلّا المنيّ، وبنوم غير الممكّن وبالغلبة على العقل بسكر، وإغماء، ولمس الكبيرة غير المحرم، وبمسّ فرج الآدميّ بباطن الكفّ.

Ablution is necessitated by

1. **anything exiting from the two waste-passages – other than ejaculate [*manī*];**

Allah Most High says, "...or one of you cometh from the place of relieving thyself..." [Q4:43, Q5:6]

The Prophet ﷺ said, "There is no ablution except due to breaking wind or passing gas."[19]

---

18. ʿĀʾishah: Bukhārī, 5889; Muslim, 257 #49, 50. See: cf BM, 2:5, 2:98.
19. Abū Hurayrah: Tirmidhī, 74 – *ḥasan ṣaḥīḥ*; Ibn Mājah, 515; Ibn Khuzaymah, 27. See: TM, 20.

Ejaculate [*manī*] is an exception since it does not invalidate ablution according to the soundest opinion.[20]

If the natural opening is closed and waste exits through another opening below the stomach [e.g., as with a colostomy], anything exiting from it will have the same ruling as the original opening. This is because a human must have an exit for his waste, so this must be it. If the opening is located above the stomach, it does not have the same ruling as the original opening. Neither does the opening of a new opening while the original remains.

2. **sleeping while one's buttocks are not firmly seated;**

As the Companions (may Allah be pleased with them) of the Prophet ﷺ would wait for Night Prayer [*Ṣalāt al-ʿIshāʾ*], they would sleep while seated and then pray without making ablution.[21]

3. **losing mental control due to intoxication or loss of consciousness;**

This is according to consensus.[22] A weak hadith from Ibn ʿAbbās (may Allah be pleased with him) supports this consensus: "No ablution is required of one who sleeps seated. Ablution is required only from one who sleeps reclined since when he reclines, his joints become relaxed."[23]

---

20. However, it causes one to be in a state of major ritual impurity [*janābah*], which necessitates a full bath [*ghusl*]. See "The Purificatory Bath" on page 36.
21. Anas: al-Shāfiʿī, *Al-Musnad*, 11; cf Muslim, 376 #135. See: KBM (156).
22. Ibn al-Mundhir, *Al-Ijmāʿ*, 31.
23. Ibn ʿAbbās: Aḥmed, 2315; Abū Dāwūd, 202; Tirmidhī, 77; Dāraquṭnī, 596; Bayhaqī, 597. See: KBM, 157.

4. **touching an unrelated woman [if one is a man, and touching an unrelated man if one is a woman]; and**

Allah Most High says, "...or one of you cometh from the place of relieving thyself, or ye have touched[24] women, and ye find not water, then go to high clean soil..." [Q4:43, Q5:6] Here, touching is conjoined with returning from relieving oneself, and dry ablution is commanded for both in the absence of water. This indicates that touching the skin of an unrelated member of the opposite sex causes minor ritual impurity – just like relieving oneself does.

Touching an [unmarriageable] relative[25] does not cause minor ritual impurity since they are not presumed to be a locus for attraction. Neither does touching children, who are too young to be considered attractive.

5. **touching a human's front or rear private parts with one's palm.**

The Prophet ﷺ said, "Whoever touches his genitals is to perform ablution."[26]

He ﷺ said, "If one of you women touches her genitals, you are to make ablution."[27]

The same ruling applies to touching the anus with the palm, since the anus is one of the two waste-passages [*sabīlayn*].

Touching the private parts with the back of the hand does not break ablution. He ﷺ said, "If one of you touches [*afḍā*] his hand to his genitals without there being any cover or barrier between them, [he] is to make ablution."[28] The word "*ifḍā*" indicates an

24. The recitation of Ḥamzah and al-Kisāʾī have "*lamastum*." The recitation of Abū ʿAmr, Ibn ʿĀmir, Ibn Kathīr, and al-Nāfiʿ have "*lāmastum*."

25 For a detailed list of unmarriageable relatives, see page 344.

26. Busrah bint Ṣafwān: Abū Dāwūd, 183; Tirmidhī, 82 – *ḥasan ṣaḥīḥ*; Nasāʾī, 163, 164; Ibn Mājah, 479. See: TM, 25.

27. ʿĀʾishah: Dāraquṭnī, 1:269 #535. See: BM, 2:475 #15.

28. Abū Hurayrah: Ibn Ḥibbān, 1118; Ḥākim, 472; Ibn ʿAbd al-Barr, *Al-Tamhīd*, 17:204. See: TM, 26.

action performed only with the palm of the hand, as agreed upon by linguists.[29]

The person doing the touching does not lose his ablution when he touches using the tips of his fingers or the area between the fingers.

Ablution is invalidated when touching oneself because of the aforementioned. It is also invalidated when touching someone else because Busrah bint Ṣafwān (may Allah be pleased with her) said she heard the Prophet ﷺ command ablution for anyone who touched [anyone's] private parts.[30]

ACTIONS UNLAWFUL DUE TO MINOR RITUAL IMPURITY

(فصل) [ما يحرم بالحدث]

ويحرم به خمسة أشياء: الصّلاة، وخطبة الجمعة، والطّواف، ومسّ المصحف، وحمله إلا أن يكون تابعًا.

Minor ritual impurity renders five things unlawful:

1. **prayer;**

This is according to consensus. ʿAbd Allāh ibn ʿUmar (may Allah be pleased with them both) said, "I heard the Messenger of Allah ﷺ say, 'Allah does not accept prayer without purification nor charity from [an act of] treachery.'"[31]

‹Abū Hurayrah (may Allah be pleased with him) said that the Prophet ﷺ said, "Allah does not accept the prayer of anyone of you if you have minor ritual impurity until you perform ablution."[32]›

29. al-Nawawī, *Sharḥ al-Muhadhdhab,* 2:36. Imām al-Shāfiʿī in *Al-Umm* says that *"ifḍā'"* is only with the palm of the hand (1:34)
30. Busrah bint Ṣafwān: ʿAdb al-Razzāq, *Al-Muṣannaf,* 411. See: cf TM, 25.
31. Ibn ʿUmar: Muslim, 224. See: TM, 344.
32. Abū Hurayrah: Bukhārī, 6954; Muslim, 225 #2. See: al-Damīrī, *Al-Najm al-wahhāj fī sharḥ Al-Minhāj,* 1:277; al-Budhā, *Al-Tadhhīb,* 22.

2. **[delivering] the Friday sermon;**
3. **circumambulating the Kaʿbah;**

Since circumambulating the Kaʿbah is the same as prayer.

The Prophet ﷺ said, "Circumambulating the Kaʿbah is of the same station as prayer, except Allah has permitted speech during it, so whoever speaks is not to speak except what is good."[33]

4. **touching the Quran [*muṣḥaf*]; and**

Allah Most High says, "Which none toucheth save the purified" [Q56:79].

5. **carrying it (except consequentially to another act).**

Such as when one carries luggage that contains a Quran without intending carrying the Qurʾān. This is because carrying involves more than touching.

OBLIGATORY ACTIONS OF ABLUTION

(فصل) [فرائض الوضوء]

وفرائض الوضوء ستّة: نيّة رفع متوقّف على الطّهر مقرونة بغسل جزء من الوجه وهو ما يقع به المواجهة، ويجب إيصال الماء إلى باطن كلّ شعر عليه إلّا اللّحية الكثّة من الرّجل، وغسل يديه مع مرفقيه فإن قطع بعضه وجب ما بقي، ومسح ما ينطلق عليه الاسم من الرّأس، وغسل رجليه مع كعبيه، وترتيبه هكذا.

Six actions are obligatory in ablution.

‹The foundation for these obligatory actions is that Allah Most High says, "O ye who believe! When ye rise up for prayer, wash your faces, and your hands to [*ilā*] the elbows, and lightly rub your

33. Ibn ʿAbbās: Ḥākim, 3056. See: TM, 30.

heads [*bi ru'ūsikum*] and (wash) your feet to [*ilā*] the ankles..." [Q5:6].[34]›

[They are:]

1. Intending to lift whatever depends upon purification, concurrent to washing a part of the face. [The face] is that through which one is faced.

The textual basis for requiring an intention here and elsewhere is the Messenger of Allah ﷺ saying, "Actions are according to intentions."[35] ‹The hadith indicates that actions are not of any consideration unless they are accompanied by an intention.[36]›The intention must be concurrent to washing a part of the face since that is the first obligatory body part washed during ablution.

The intention for performing ablution can be to raise the state of impurification (or one of its causes), to achieve purification from impurification (though not for someone whose impurification is chronic), or to make it permissible to perform something requiring ablution.

2. Washing the entire face.

The face includes the area from the hairline to the bottom of the chin and jaw, and from ear to ear.

The water must reach the interior [root] of all facial hair except for a man's thick beard.

This exception is due to difficulty. As for young men, females, and hermaphrodites: water must penetrate to the skin underneath, even if the beard is thick.

34. al-Bughā, *Al-Tadhhīb,* 10 #2.
35. ʿUmar: Bukhārī, 1; Muslim, 1907 #155. See: TM, 57.
36. al-Bughā, *Al-Tadhhīb,* 16.

3. **Washing the arms [up to and] including the elbows. If a [body] part is severed, then [washing] the remainder is obligatory.**

Allah Most High says, "...When ye rise up for prayer, wash your faces, and your hands to [*ilā*] the elbows, and lightly rub your heads and (wash) your feet to [*ilā*] the ankles..." [Q5:6]. In the verse, "*ilā*" is understood to mean "with [*maʿ*]," just as it does in "Who will be my helpers *ilā* Allah?" [Q3:52].

If the arm is amputated at the elbow, the exposed end must be washed since it is part of the obligatory area. The ruling is the same for the forearm if the arm has been amputated from the wrist.

4. **Wiping what is considered part of the head.**

Al-Mughīrah (may Allah be pleased with him) indicated that the Messenger of Allah ﷺ performed ablution and wiped over his forehead and completed wiping over his turban.[37] If wiping the entire head was obligatory, he ﷺ would not have wiped just the forehead.

‹Additional support comes from within the verse which is the foundation for ablution, wherein Allah Most High says, "...lightly rub your heads [*bi ruʾūsikum*]..." [Q5:6]. Here, the phrase "*bi ruʾūsikum*" means a part of the head.›

5. **Washing the feet including the ankles.**

This is because of Q5:6. According to al-Māwardī, no one disagreed on this except the Rawāfiḍ.[38] As for [evidence for] including the ankles, see the previous explanation concerning elbows.

6. **Doing [the above] in that order.**

Every narration about the Prophet ﷺ's ablution describes it in a specific sequence. If doing it without a specific sequence was per-

37. al-Mughīrah: Muslim, 274 #83. See: TM, 60.

38. al-Māwardī, *Al-Ḥāwī al-kabīr,* 1:123.

missible, he ﷺ would have done it – even if only once – to show its permissibility.

DOUBTS ABOUT PURIFICATION

Doubts about purification are inconsequential once one is certain of having purification. This is because having purification is certain, and certainty is not removed by doubts.

RECOMMENDED ACTIONS OF ABLUTION

(فصل) [سنن الوضوء]

وتسنّ التّسميّة، وغسل الكفين، وكره إدخالها الظّرف قبله إن لم يتيقّن طهرهما، والمضمضة والاستنشاق، والجمع بثلاث غرف أولى، واستيعاب الرّأس بالمسح، ومسح الأذنين مع الصّماخ، وتخليل الأصابع، وتقديم اليمنى على اليسرى، والتّكرار، والموالاة والنّطق بالشّهادتين بعده.

It is recommended to
1. say *"Bismi Llāh"*;

The Prophet ﷺ said, "Every matter of worth that does not begin with *'Bismi Llāh'* is cut off [from blessing]."[39]

The minimum is to say "*Bismi Llāh.*" Its complete form is "*Bismi Llāhi r-Raḥmāni r-Raḥīm.*"

39. al-Khaṭīb al-Baghdādī, *Al-Jāmiʿ li akhlāq al-rāwī* (1209–10). In *Al-Badr al-munīr* (7:530), and *Al-Tawḍīḥ sharḥ Al-Jāmiʿ al-ṣaḥīḥ* (2:121), Ibn Mulaqqin mentions that ʿAbd al-Qādīr al-Rahāwī included the hadith in his collection of forty hadith. See: BM, 2:92.

2. **wash the hands (as it is offensive to put them in the water vessel when one is not certain of their purity);**

The Prophet ﷺ would wash his hands prior to making ablution.[40]

After sleeping, it is offensive to place one's hands in a water vessel before washing them. He ﷺ said, "If one of you wakes from his sleep, he is not to dip his hands into the [water] vessel until he washes them three times, since he does not know where his hands spent the night."[41]

If one is certain that one's hands are pure, it is not offensive to dip them into the water before making ablution. Rather, it is not recommended to wash them first.

3. **rinse the mouth and nose (combining them both with three handfuls of water is best);**

The Prophet ﷺ would rinse both when making ablution.[42]

One should not rinse the mouth and nose vigorously when fasting. He ﷺ said to Laqīṭ ibn Ṣabirah (may Allah be pleased with him), "Be vigorous when rinsing the mouth and nose, unless you are fasting."[43]

4. **wipe the entire head;**

This is to remove oneself from disagreement with those [of other schools] who consider it obligatory.

---

40. ʿUthmān: Bukhārī, 159, 1934; Muslim, 226 #4. See: TM, 71.
41. Abū Hurayrah: Bukhārī, 162; Muslim, 278 #87. See: TM, 71.
42. ʿUthmān: Bukhārī, 159; Muslim, 226. See: BM, 2:98 #21.
43. ʿĀṣim ibn Laqīṭ from his father: Abū Dāwūd, 142, 143; Tirmidhī, 788; Nasāʾī, 87; Ibn Mājah, 407. See: BM, 2:129.

5. wipe the ears (including the ear canal);

The Prophet ﷺ did this.[44]

One uses new water since he ﷺ would wash his ears with water that was different from what he had used to wipe his head.[45]

6. run wet fingers between the fingers and toes;

When a man with a thick beard washes his face, it is also recommended that he run his wet fingers through his beard, since the Prophet ﷺ would run his wet fingers through his noble beard, which was thick.[46]

As for running the fingers between the fingers and toes, he ﷺ said, "go between the fingers and toes."[47] The early Shāfiʿī colleagues[48] did not mention the fingers, though Ibn Kajj (may Allah grant him His mercy) recommended it because of this hadith.

7. wash the right side before the left;

The Prophet ﷺ said, "When you make ablution, begin with your right."[49]

However, the cheeks, ears, and palms are exceptions, since they are washed simultaneously.

---

44. al-Miqdām Muʿdī Karib: Abū Dāwūd, 123. See: BM, 2:143 #31; 2:207 #44.
45. ʿAbd Allāh ibn Zayd: Bayhaqī, 313, 314; Ḥākim, 539. See: TM, 78.
46. ʿUthmān: Tirmidhī, 31 – *ḥasan ṣaḥīḥ*; Ibn Mājah, 429, 430, 433; Ibn Ḥibbān, 1081; Ḥākim, 528. See: TM, 79.
47. Ibn ʿAbbās: Tirmidhī, 39; Ibn Mājah, 429, 430, 433; Ibn Khuzaymah, 151; Ibn Ḥibbān, 1081; Ḥākim, 528. See: TM, 80.
48. "Colleagues" ("*aṣḥāb*") are early *mujtahid*s within the Shāfiʿī school, whose opinions are the sources for "*wujūh*" mentioned in the book.
49. Abū Hurayrah: Abū Dāwūd, 4141; Ibn Khuzaymah, 178. See: TM, 81.

8. repeat [each action three times];

This means washing or wiping each body part three times, except when wiping over *khuffs* [leather socks, which is only done once].

He ﷺ made ablution three by three and said, "This is my ablution and the ablution of the prophets before me."[50]

9. perform the actions consecutively; and,

What is meant by consecutively is that one washes the next limb before the prior one dries, given moderate heat and humidity.

Evidence for this is from the practice of the Prophet ﷺ as shown in the aforementioned hadiths.

10. utter the *shahādatayn* afterwards.

ʿUmar (may Allah be pleased with him) reported that the Prophet ﷺ said, "None of you makes ablution, completes it well, then says 'I testify that there is no deity except Allah and that Muhammad is His Messenger' save that eighty doors to Paradise will open, and he will enter from whichever of them he wishes."[51]

---

50. Ibn ʿUmar: Ibn Mājah, 420; Dāraquṭnī, 1:138 #263. See: TM, 83.
51. ʿUqbah ibn ʿĀmir: Muslim, 234 #17. See: TM, 87.

WIPING OVER KHUFFS

(فصل) [المسح على الخفّين]

والمسح على الخفّ وإن قلّ من الأعلى بدل الغسل مؤقّت للمسافر ثلاثة أيّام ولياليهنّ وللمقيم يوم وليلة من الحدث.

Wiping over *khuffs* [leather socks] instead of washing [the feet] (even if one wipes only a small area on the top) is [permissible] for a limited duration.

Evidence of its permissibility comes from numerous reports indicating that he ﷺ would wipe over his *khuffs*.[52] These reports have been transmitted through numerous hadiths in the books of *ṣaḥīḥ* hadiths and other books.[53]

ʿAlī ibn Abī Ṭālib (may Allah be pleased with him) narrated that the Prophet ﷺ stipulated three days and three nights [of wiping] for a traveller, and one day and one night for a resident.[54]

DURATION

The duration is 72 hours for travelers, and 24 hours for residents.

Shurayḥ ibn Hāniʾ (may Allah grant him His mercy) said, "I came to ʿĀʾishah (may Allah be pleased with her) to ask her about wiping over *khuffs*. She said to go ask ʿAlī (may Allah be pleased with him) since he used to travel with the Messenger of Allah ﷺ.

---

52. A *khuff* is a leather sock. Socks made of other material can be used as *khuffs* provided they meet the conditions listed in this section. The reports related to wiping over *khuffs* do not indicate that a specific amount of wiping is obligatory, so what suffices is whatever is considered wiping.
53. Barīdah, Jarīr ibn ʿAbd Allāh, Bilāl, and ʿUmar: Abū Dāwūd, 150–6; Tirmidhī, 93–99; Ibn Mājah, 545–51. See: TM, 90–96.
54. ʿAlī: Muslim, 276 #85. See: TM, 231.

We asked him and he said, 'The Messenger of Allah ﷺ stipulated three days and three nights for a traveller, and one day and one night for a resident.'"[55]

If one wipes while a resident and then travels, or wipes while a traveler and then becomes a resident before the end of one day and night, one cannot complete the duration of a traveller. This is because the resident status dominates. If one were to wipe [while a resident] and then travel, does one complete the duration of a traveler, or of a resident? There are two opinions from Shāfiʿī colleagues: al-Rāfiʿī (may Allah grant him His mercy) was certain of the first [i.e., as a traveler], while al-Nawawī (may Allah grant him His mercy) authenticated the second [i.e., as a resident].[56] [The latter is the relied-upon opinion.[57]]

The duration begins the moment one's ablution is nullified.

The permissible duration for wiping starts from the time one's ablution is nullified, not from the time the *khuffs* were first worn, nor the time they were [first] wiped. Wiping is a matter of worship that has a limited duration, which begins as soon as it becomes permissible to perform – just like prayer.

---

55. Shurayḥ ibn Hāniʾ: Muslim, 276 #85. See: KBM, 231; cf TM, 90–91.

56. al-Rāfiʿī, *Al-Sharḥ al-kabīr*, 1:286; al-Nawawī, *Rawḍat al-ṭālibīn*, 1:131–2.

57. As a general rule of thumb, when Imams al-Rāfiʿī and al-Nawawī disagree, Imam al-Nawawī's opinion is preferred.

CONDITIONS FOR ITS VALIDITY

[ويصحّ] بشرط لبسهما على الطّهارة وإمكان المشي عليهما ومنع نفوذ الماء من غير الخرز وسترهما لجميع المحلّ.

[Wiping is valid] with the conditions that

1. **both [socks] were put on after [one] achieved a state of [complete] purification;**

Abū Bakrah Nafīʿ ibn al-Ḥārith (may Allah be pleased with him) said that the Messenger of Allah ﷺ authorized travelers [to wipe] for three days and nights, and residents for one day and a night, and that when one performs purification and then wears both *khuffs*, one can wipe over both *khuffs*.[58]

Al-Mughīrah ibn Shuʿbah (may Allah be pleased with him) said, "I was in the company of the Prophet ﷺ one night during a journey. I poured water for him from a skin. He ﷺ washed his face and forearms and wiped his head. I bent down to remove his *khuffs*. He ﷺ said, 'Leave them. I donned them both while they [the feet] were purified.' He ﷺ then wiped his hands over them."[59]

2. **one is able to walk around in them;**
3. **water cannot penetrate them except where they have fasteners; and**
4. **they cover the entire area.**

"The entire area" refers to the area of the feet (and ankles) that one is obligated to wash when making ablution.

---

58. Abū Bakrah Nafīʿ ibn al-Ḥārith: Ibn Khuzaymah, 192, Ibn Ḥibban, 1324. Al-Shāfiʿī (may Allah have mercy on him) said it is an authentic ascription; al-Bukhārī (may Allah have mercy on him) said the hadith is *ḥasan*. See TM, 91.

59. al-Mughīrah ibn Shuʿbah: Bukhārī, 206; Muslim, 274 #79–80. See: KBM, 226.

INVALIDATORS

ويبطل بموجب الغسل وبانقضاء المدّة وبالخلع فيغسل الرّجلين إن خلعهما على طهارة المسح.

[Wiping] is invalidated by
1. the occurrence of whatever necessitates the purificatory bath;

Ṣafwān ibn ʿAssāl (may Allah be pleased with him) narrated: "The Messenger of Allah ﷺ would order us when traveling to wipe over our *khuffs* and, for up to three days, to not remove them due to defecating, urinating or sleep – except due to *janābah*."[60]

2. the duration expiring; and
3. their removal.

Al-Mughīrah ibn Shuʿbah (may Allah be pleased with him) said, "We fought alongside the Prophet ﷺ and he commanded us to wipe over *khuffs* for three days and nights for travelers and one day and night for residents – so long as they are not taken off or removed."[61]

One may wash one's feet if the *khuffs* are removed [while] one is in a state of ritual purity after having wiped over them.

This is permissible because washing the feet is the default action.

---

60. Ṣafwān ibn ʿAssāl: Tirmidhī, 96; Nasāʾī, 126. See: TM, 94–95.
61. al-Mughīrah ibn Shuʿbah: al-Bayhaqī, 1376. See: TM, 96.

RELIEVING & CLEANING ONESELF

(فصل) [آداب قاضي الحاجة]

ويجب الاستنجاء بماء أو حجر، وجمعهما أفضل، يجب ثلاث مسحات فإن لم ينق زيد.

Cleaning oneself [from urine and feces] using water or stones is obligatory.

Either water or three stones are required. The Prophet ﷺ said that "he is to clean his privates with water or three stones." The evident meaning of this command is that it indicates obligation. This is with respect to stones. As for water, it is because it is the foundation [for purification].

The stones [or whatever object takes their place] must be pure. Filthy stones do not suffice since he ﷺ forbade cleaning oneself using dung or old bones.[62]

Other filthy objects do not work for the reason mentioned above.

Liquids other than water do not work since they merely spread the filth.

The stone [or object] must remove the filth, so glass or other smooth surfaces do not work. [If filth is not removed,] the purpose is not met.

The stone [or object] cannot be something with sanctity or venerated, like bones or bread. The Prophet ﷺ forbade cleaning oneself with bones, and said, "They are a provision for your brothers from jinn-kind."[63]

Water is superior to stones [for removing filth], since water removes the substance and its traces, whereas stones only remove the substance.

62. Abū Hurayrah: Abū Dāwūd, 8; Nasā'ī, 40; Ibn Mājah, 313; Ibn Khuzaymah, 80; Ibn Ḥibbān, 1431, 1440. See: BM (2:296 #2; 2:348 #18).

63. Abū Hurayrah: Bukhārī, 155, 3860. Ibn Mas'ūd: Muslim, 450 #150. See: BM, 2:348 #19.

Using water and stones together is superior.

Allah Most High praised the people of Qubāʾ for this. Abū Hurayrah (may Allah be pleased with him) said that the Prophet ﷺ said, "The following verse was revealed in connection with the people of Qubāʾ: '...wherein are men who love to purify themselves...' [Q9:108]." Abū Hurayrah [explained]: "They used to cleanse themselves with water after relieving themselves, and the verse was revealed concerning them."[64]

[When wiping with stones], three wipes are obligatory. More are added if three do not clean the area.

The Prophet ﷺ said, "When one of you cleans himself with stones, he is to do so an odd number of times."[65]

He ﷺ said that "he is to clean his privates with water or three stones."

FACING THE DIRECTION OF PRAYER

ويجتنب في الصّحراء استقبال القبلة واستدبارها بلا حائل.

In vacant areas where there is no barrier, one [obligatorily] avoids facing or turning one's back to the direction of prayer.

The Prophet ﷺ said, "When one of you goes to the lavatory, he is not to face the direction of prayer nor turn his back to it while defecating or urinating."[66]

‹The hadith that Ibn Mulaqqin (may Allah grant him His mercy) mentions in the text concerns areas that are not prepared for use as lavatories and are uncovered. Another hadith concerns covered

64. al-Haytamī, *Kashf al-astār ʿan zawāʾid al-Bazzār,* 247; Abū Dāwūd, 44; Tirmidhī, 3100; Ibn Mājah, 357. See: TM, 530.

65. Abū Hurayrah: Bukhārī, 161, 162; Muslim, 237 #20. See: TM, 54.

66. Abu Ayūb al-Anṣārī: Bukhārī, 144; Muslim, 264 #59. See: TM, 36.

places prepared for relieving oneself:› ʿAbd Allāh ibn ʿUmar (may Allah be pleased with them both) said, "I climbed to the roof of Ḥafṣah's house for some task and I saw the Messenger of Allah ﷺ answering the call of nature facing *Shām* [i.e., the Levant] with his back towards the *qiblah*."[67]

PLACES WHERE RELIEVING ONESELF IS OFFENSIVE

ويكره البول في الثّقب، والماء الرّاكد، ومهبّ الرّيح، وتحت المثمر والظّلّ وقارعة الطّريق، والكلام.

It is offensive to urinate
1. into crevices and burrows,

The Prophet ﷺ forbade urinating into holes. Qatādah (may Allah be pleased with him) was asked, "What's wrong with them?" He replied, "It is said that they are houses for jinn."[68]

2. into stagnant water,

The Messenger of Allah ﷺ forbade urinating into stagnant water.[69]

3. where it is windy,

It is offensive due to the prohibition from doing so.[70]

4. under fruit-bearing trees,

This protects the fruit from becoming filthy when it falls.

---

67. Ibn ʿUmar: Bukhārī, 149; Muslim, 266. See: TM, 37.
68. ʿAbd Allāh ibn Sarjis: Abū Dāwūd, 29; Nasāʾī, 34; Ḥākim, 666, 667. See: TM, 41.
69. Jābir: Muslim, 281 #94. See: TM, 40.
70. See: KBM, 127.

5–6. in shade and on paths, and

The Messenger of Allah ﷺ said, "Be on your guard against the two things that provoke cursing." [The Companions who were present] said, "Messenger of Allah ﷺ, what are those things that provoke cursing?" He ﷺ said, "Relieving oneself on people's paths or under their shade."[71]

The prohibition is not restricted to shade and includes wherever people gather to converse.

7. while speaking or conversing [with others].

The Prophet ﷺ said, "When two men go to the lavatory, each should conceal himself [*falyatawāra*] from the other. They should not converse while relieving themselves, since Allah loathes this."[72]

ENTERING AND EXITING THE LAVATORY

When one intends to use the lavatory, one should divest oneself of anything mentioning Allah Most High since the Prophet ﷺ would remove his ring when entering the lavatory.[73] Engraved upon the ring was "Muhammad is the Messenger of Allah."[74]

One should enter with one's left foot, since it is debasement.

---

71. Abū Hurayrah: Muslim, 269 #68. See: TM, 42.
72. Jābir: Abū Dāwūd, 15; Ibn Khuzaymah, 71; Ḥākim, 560; Bayhaqī, 483. See: TM, 44.
73. Anas: Abū Dāwūd, 19; Tirmidhī, 1746 – *ḥasan gharīb*; Nasā'ī, 2528; Ibn Mājah, 303; Ibn Ḥibbān, 1413; Ḥākim, 670. See: TM, 33.
74. Bukhārī, 3106; Tirmidhī, 1747–48; Ibn Ḥibbān, 1481. See: BM, 2:341–43. Also: Anas: Bukhārī, 65; Muslim, 2091, 2093 #54, 55. See: BM, 2:339, 2:342.

ويسنّ عند الدّخول: «بِاسْمِ اللهِ اللَّهُمَ إِنِّي أَعُوْذُ بِكَ مِنَ الخُبْثِ وَالخَبَائِثِ»، وخروجه: «غفرانك».

Upon entering [the lavatory] it is recommended to say "*Bismi Llāh. Allāhumma innī aʿūdhu bika min al-khubthi wa al-khabāʾith*" ("In the name of Allāh. O Allāh, verily I seek protection through You from male and female devils");...

Anas ibn Malik (may Allah be pleased with him) reported that whenever the Prophet ﷺ went to the lavatory, he used to say: "*Allāhumma innī aʿūdhu bika min al-khubthi wa al-khabāʾith.*"[75]

One should remain fully covered until nearing the ground since The Prophet ﷺ would do this.[76] Concealing one's nakedness is required so one should preserve one's modesty as much as possible.

One should rest one's weight on the left foot; one does not use one's right foot while in that state. It is said that this eases the exit of the waste. Surāqah ibn Mālik (may Allah be pleased with him) said, "The Messenger of Allah ﷺ taught us that if one of us wanted to relieve himself, he is to support himself on the left [foot, i.e., by resting it flat on the ground] and raise up the right [so his toes support his weight]."[77]

When relieving oneself outside, one should distance oneself from others since the Prophet ﷺ would do this whenever he would go to relieve himself.[78]

And one should cover oneself, since he ﷺ said, "Whoever goes to the lavatory is to conceal himself."[79]

---

75. Anas: Bukhārī, 142; Muslim, 375 #122. See: TM, 48.
76. ʿAbd Allāh ibn Jaʿfar: Ibn Ḥibbān, 1411. Support is also found in Muslim, 342 #79; Abū Dāwūd, 2549; Ibn Mājah, 340; Ibn Khuzaymah, 53; Ḥākim, 2485.
77. Surāqah ibn Mālik: al-Bayhaqī, 457. See: TM, 34.
78. al-Mughīrah: al-Tirmidhī, 20. See: TM, 37.
79. Abū Hurayrah: Abū Dāwūd, 35. See: TM, 39.

One should seek a place where the ground is soft, since he ﷺ said, "When one of you wants to urinate, he is to find a place with soft ground."[80]

When finished, one should cough and press lightly [behind the scrotum and then along the shaft of the penis] to remove the remaining urine.[81] Coughing produces the same result, though the matter differs from person to person.

...and upon exiting, to say "*Ghufrānak*" ("Grant me Your forgiveness").

ʿĀʾishah (may Allah be pleased with her) said, "When the Prophet ﷺ would exit the toilet he would say, '*Ghufrānak*.'"[82]

One should exit the lavatory with one's right foot, since one is proceeding to a superior place. One should also say "*Al-ḥamdu li-Llāh illadhi adhhaba ʿannī al-adhā wa ʿāfānī*" ("Praise belongs to Allah, who removed harm from me and cured me") since he ﷺ would say this.[83]

The supplications for entering and exiting the lavatory should be said before one steps in and after one steps out.

---

80. Abū Mūsā: Abū Dāwūd, 3.
81. ʿĪsā ibn Yazdād from his father: Abū Dāwūd in *Al-Marāsīl*, 74 #4; Ibn Mājah, 326. See: BM, 2:344.
82. ʿĀʾishah: Abū Dāwūd, 30; Tirmidhī, 7 – *ḥasan gharīb*; Ibn Mājah, 300; Nasāʾī, *ʿAmal al-Yawm wa l-Layl*, 79; Ibn Ḥibbān, 1444; Ibn Khuzaymah, 90; Ḥākim, 562. See: TM, 49.
83. I did not locate it in al-Nasāʾī's *ʿAmal al-yawm wa l-layl*, however it is mentioned in *Tuḥfat al-ashrāf* (12003). Al-Nasāʾī did transmit it in his *Al-Sunan al-kubrā* (9825), as did Ibn Mājah, 301. See: TM, 50.

THE PURIFICATORY BATH

(فصل) [الغسل]

WHEN IT IS NECESSARY

وموجب الغسل موت وحيض ونفاس وولادة بلا بلل وجنابة بدخول حشفة أو قدرها فرجًا وبخروج منيّ، وخواصّه التّدفّق والتّلذّذ والرّائحة.

The purificatory bath [*ghusl*] is necessitated by
1. death;

Ibn ʿAbbās (may Allah be pleased with him) reported: "A man was killed by his camel while we were with the Prophet ﷺ and he [the man] had been performing Pilgrimage [*Ḥajj*]. So the Prophet ﷺ said, 'Wash him with water and *ṣidr* [lote tree] and shroud him in two pieces of cloth...'"[84]

Umm ʿAṭiyyah al-Anṣāriyah (may Allah be pleased with her) said, "The Messenger of Allah ﷺ came to us when his daughter died and said, 'Wash her thrice.'"[85]

2–3. menstruation and lochia;

This is due to consensus. ‹Its basis is from the Quran and Sunnah. Allah Most High says, "...and go not in unto them till they are cleansed. And when they have purified themselves, then go in unto them as Allah hath enjoined upon you. Truly Allah loveth those who turn unto Him, and loveth those who have a care for cleanness" [Q2:222].[86]›

ʿĀʾishah (may Allah be pleased with her) reported that the Messenger of Allah ﷺ said to Fāṭimah bint Abī Ḥubaysh (may Allah

84. Ibn ʿAbbās: Bukhārī, 1267; Muslim, 1206. See: TM, 97.
85. Umm ʿAṭiyyah al-Anṣāriyah: Bukhārī, 1253; Muslim, 939. See: TM, 769.
86. al-Bughā, *Al-Tadhhīb*, 25 #1.

be pleased with her and her father): "When menstruation starts, cease praying. When it finishes, pray."[87]

ʿĀʾishah (may Allah be pleased with her) narrated that the Prophet ﷺ said, "When menstruation comes, cease praying. When its amount [i.e., its duration] has gone, wash the blood from you."[88]

Lochia [*nifās*] is analogous to menstruation [*ḥayḍ*].

4. **dry birth;**

This is because the child is [composed of] solidified [male and female] ejaculate [*manī*], and childbirth is usually accompanied by bleeding.

5. **a state of major ritual impurity due to insertion of the prepuce [head] of the penis or its length into [the vagina or anus]; and**

The Prophet ﷺ said, "If the two circumcised parts meet, the purificatory bath is obligatory."[89]

Abū Hurayrah (may Allah be pleased with him) narrated that the Prophet ﷺ said, "When a man sits between a woman's four limbs and has sexual intercourse with her, bathing becomes compulsory."[90] and in Muslim's version: "...even if without orgasm."

The purificatory bath is required even if a deceased human or animal is penetrated, though the deceased does not have to be washed due to their cessation of being legally responsible.

87. ʿĀʾīshah: Bukhārī, 320. See: TM, 98.
88. ʿĀʾīshah: Bukhārī, 331, 320; Muslim, 333 #62. See: TM, 98.
89. ʿĀʾishah: al-Shāfiʿī, *Al-Musnad* (p158); Ibn Ḥibbān, 1176, 1177, 1183. See: TM, 99.
90. Abū Hurayrah: Bukhārī, 291; Muslim, 348. See: BM, 2:521.

6. **The emission of [sexual] fluid [*manī*] during orgasm, whose specific properties are its release in pleasurable spurts and its [distinctive] smell.**

The Prophet ﷺ said, "Water is from water."[91] ‹The hadith means that the obligation to wash with water is from seeing ejaculate released during orgasm.›

Umm Salamah (may Allah be pleased with her) said that Umm Sulaym (may Allah be pleased with her) approached the Prophet ﷺ and said, "O Messenger of Allah ﷺ! Verily, Allah does not shy from [telling you] the truth. Is it essential for a woman to bathe after she had an erotic dream?" He ﷺ said, "Yes, if she sees water."[92]

OBLIGATORY ACTS

وفرضه: النّيّة وإيصال الماء إلى الشّعر والبشرة.

Its obligatory actions are

1. **the intention and,**

This is required – as it is with ablution – because of the hadith, "Actions are according to intentions…"[93]

2. **water reaching every part of the hair and skin.**

This is also based on a hadith: "Sexual impurity is beneath every hair, so wet the hair and cleanse the skin."[94]

Water must also reach under the fingernails and toenails, the ears canals, and any cracks in the skin.

---

91. Abū Saʿīd al-Khudrī: Muslim, 343 #80, 81. See: TM, 100.
92. Umm Sulaym: Bukhārī, 282; Muslim, 313. See: KBM, 177.
93. See "Actions are according to intentions" on page 18.
94. Abū Hurayrah: Abū Dāwūd, 258 – *ḍaʿīf*; Tirmidhī, 106 – *gharīb*. See: TM, 104.

RECOMMENDED ACTS

وسننه: الوضوء والتّدلّك والتّكرار والولاء، وتتبّع لحيض أثره مسكًا وإلّا فنحوه.

Its recommended actions are:
1. making ablution [beforehand];

The Prophet ﷺ did it thus.

ʿĀʾishah (may Allah be pleased with her) said, "Whenever the Messenger of Allah ﷺ bathed due to sexual impurity, he would begin by washing his hands and then would pour water with his right hand on his left hand and wash his genitals. He would then perform his ablution for prayer, then take some water and run his fingers through the roots of the hair. Then he would pour three handfuls on his head, then pour water over the rest of his body and subsequently wash his feet." In another version: "he would begin by washing his hands three times" which includes "until he thought that he had completely wet his skin, and then he would pour water over it three times."[95]

Maymūnāh (may Allah be pleased with her) said, "I brought the Messenger of Allah ﷺ water for his bath from sexual impurity. He washed his hands two or three times, rubbing them vigorously. He then made ablution for prayer. Then he poured three handfuls of water on his body. He then washed the rest of his body. Then he slid from where he was standing and washed his feet. I then brought him a towel. He refused it and said, 'This is how water is dried.'" One version has "he made his ablution for prayer – except for his feet."[96]

2. rubbing the hand over the body;

This is understood from "and cleanse the skin" in the earlier hadith.[97]

---

95. ʿĀʾishah: Bukhārī, 248, 272; Muslim, 316 #35. See: TM, 106.
96. Maymūnah: Bukhārī, 249; Muslim, 317 #37. See: TM, 107.
97. Abū Hurayrah: Abū Dāwūd, 258, et al. See: TM, 104.

3. **repeating [each action three times];**

The purificatory bath is analogous to ablution, hence the repetition.

4. **performing the actions consecutively; and**

This is similar to what was mentioned concerning ablution. It is recommended because it is obligatory according to the Mālikīs.

One should begin with the right side first. ʿĀʾishah (may Allah be pleased with her) reported that the Prophet ﷺ "liked starting with the right when wearing sandals, combing his hair, [performing] his purification, and in all of his affairs."[98]

5. **applying musk when possible, or something similar, after menstruation.**

ʿĀʾishah reported that Asmāʾ bint Shakal al-Anṣārī (may Allah be pleased with them) asked the Prophet ﷺ about washing after menstruation. He ﷺ said, "She is to use water [mixed with the leaves of the] lote tree, cleanse herself well, and then pour water on her head and rub it vigorously until it reaches the roots of her hair. Then she is to pour water on [her body]. Afterwards, she is to take a piece of cotton smeared with musk and cleanse herself with it." Asmāʾ said, "How is she to cleanse herself with it?" He ﷺ then said, "Praise be to Allah! She is to cleanse herself with it." ʿĀʾishah said in a subdued tone, "She applies it to the traces of blood."[99]

ʿUmrah ibn Ḥabbān al-Sahamiyyah (may Allah be pleased with her) said, "ʿĀʾishah said to me: 'Is one of you not able to insert something with a bit of incense when she becomes pure from her menses? If you cannot find any, then a bit of basil – meaning myrtle

98. ʿĀʾishah: Bukhārī, 2548; Muslim, 268. See: TM, 109.

99. ʿĀʾishah: Bukhārī, 7357, Muslim, 332 #61. See TM, 112.

[may be used instead]. And if she cannot find any, then some fruit kernels. And if she cannot find any, then a bit of salt.'"[100]

ACTIONS UNLAWFUL DUE TO MAJOR RITUAL PURITY

(فصل) [ما يحرم بالجنابة]

ويحرم بالجنابة ما يحرم بالحدث، وقراءة القرآن، واللّبث في المسجد.

The state of major ritual impurity renders [the following] unlawful: 1–5. everything rendered unlawful by minor ritual impurity,...

Allah Most High says, "...draw not near unto prayer when ye are drunken, till ye know that which ye utter, nor when ye are polluted, save when passing through, till ye have bathed..." [Q4:43].

‹In this verse, "prayer" refers to its location, because one cannot be "passing through" during one's prayer. A fortiori, the prayer is prohibited for those in a state of major ritual impurity. The word "washed" includes purification from the state of minor and major ritual impurity, thus indicating the unlawfulness of people praying while in those states.[101]›

ʿAbd Allāh ibn ʿUmar (may Allah be pleased with them both) said, "I heard the Messenger of Allah ﷺ say, 'Prayer is not accepted without purification, nor is charity from [an act of] treachery.'"[102]

---

100. Abū Naʿīm al-Aṣfahānī, *Al-Ṭibb al-nabawī,* #435.

101. al-Bughā, *Al-Tadhhīb,* 40 #2.

102. Ibn ʿUmar: Muslim, 224. See: TM, 344.

...in addition to

6. reciting the Quran, and

The Prophet ﷺ said, "Someone in the state of major ritual impurity [*junub*] does not recite anything from the Quran." Another version includes "or a woman with menses."[103]

7. remaining within a mosque.

Allah Most High says, "...nor when ye are in the state of ritual impurity..." [Q4:43].

ʿĀʾishah (may Allah be pleased with her) said, "The Messenger of Allah ﷺ said, 'I do not permit the mosque to women who are menstruating nor to those in the state of major ritual impurity.'"[104]

It is unlawful for a woman with menses to pass through the mosque if she fears soiling it. However, it is permissible for someone in the state of major ritual impurity to do so, due to the verse above.

See the previous verses and hadiths regarding touching the Quran [for additional evidence].

103. Ibn ʿUmar: Dāraquṭnī, 2:462 #1879; Tirmidhī, 131; Ibn Mājah, 596. See: TM, 102.

104. ʿĀʾishah: Abū Dāwūd, 232. See: TM, 101, 151.

RECOMMENDED BATHS

(فصل) [الاغتسالات المسنونة]

ويسنّ خمسة عشر غسلاً: غسل الجمعة، والعيدين، والكسوفين، والاستسقاء، والغسل من غسل الميّت، والكافر إذا أسلم ولم يجنب، والمجنون والمغمى عليه إذا أفاقا، وللإحرام، ولدخول مكّة والمدينة، وللوقوف ولرمي أيّام التّشريق.

A purificatory bath is recommended for fifteen occasion:
1. Friday Prayer [*Ṣalāt al-Jumuʿah*];

The Prophet ﷺ said, "Whoever performs ablution on Friday will receive a blessing. And whoever bathes, bathing is more virtuous."[105]

One must bathe after dawn, since a bath before then would not be valid as a bath for the Friday Prayer.

2–3. Eid al-Fiṭr and Eid al-Aḍḥā;

Both are occasions when people gather, so it is recommended to bathe for them – just as one would for the Friday Prayer. It can be done after half of the night has passed (in contrast to the bath for Friday). Since the Eid Prayer is performed at the beginning of the day, it would be a hardship if we were to say that its bath could only be performed after the dawn on that day.

ʿAbd Allāh ibn ʿUmar (may Allah be pleased with them both) would bathe on the day of Eid al-Fiṭr before going out to the place of prayer.[106]

4–5. the Eclipse Prayers [*Ṣalāt al-Kusūf* and *Ṣalāt al-Khusūf*];

Bathing is recommended for the same reasons given for the Eid Prayers.

---

105. Samurah: Abū Dāwūd, 354; Tirmidhī, 497; Ibn Mājah, 1091; Nasāʾī, 1380; Ibn Khuzaymah, 1756, 1757, 1818. See: TM, 644.

106. Ibn ʿUmar: Mālik, 609; al-Shāfiʿī, *Al-Musnad*, 73. See: TM, 689.

6. the Drought Prayer [*Ṣalāt al-Istisqā*ʾ];

These last three prayers might be listed here because, like the Friday and Eid Prayers, they are occasions when people gather.

7. [after] washing the deceased;

Abū Hurayrah (may Allah be pleased with him) reported that the Prophet ﷺ said, "Whoever washes the deceased is to bathe. Whoever carries him is to make ablution."[107]

This washing is not obligatory because of the report from Ibn ʿAbbās (may Allah be pleased with him) in which the Messenger of Allah ﷺ said, "It is not incumbent upon you to bathe after you have washed your dead."[108]

8. when a non-Muslim enters Islam without ever having experienced anything that would necessitate the purificatory bath;

The Prophet ﷺ ordered Qays ibn ʿĀṣim (may Allah be pleased with him) to bathe when he entered Islam.[109] ‹It is not considered obligatory since the Prophet ﷺ did not command everyone who entered Islam to bathe.[110]›

It is obligatory if something occurred prior to Islam that would necessitate taking the purificatory bath, such as sexual intercourse.

9–10. losing sanity and regaining consciousness;

The Prophet ﷺ bathed as a result of losing consciousness. ʿĀʾishah (may Allah be pleased with her) said, "The Prophet ﷺ became seriously ill and asked whether the people had prayed. We replied,

107. Abū Hurayrah: Tirmidhī, 993 – *ḥasan*; Ibn Ḥibbān, 1161; Ibn Mājah, 1463; Ḥākim, 1426. See: TM, 647.

108. Ibn ʿAbbās: Ḥākim, 1426. See: TM, 648.

109. Qays ibn ʿĀṣim: Tirmidhī, 605 – *ḥasan*; Abū Dāwūd, 355; Nasāʾī, 188; Ibn Khuzaymah, 254, 255; Ibn Ḥibbān, 1240. See: TM, 650.

110. al-Bughā, *Al-Tadhhīb,* 28 #2.

'No, O Prophet of Allah! They are waiting for you.' He ﷺ added, 'Put water for me in a trough.'" ʿĀʾīshah added, "We did so. He ﷺ took a bath and tried to get up but fainted. When he ﷺ recovered, he ﷺ again asked whether the people had prayed. We said, 'No, they are waiting for you. O Messenger of Allah.' He ﷺ again said, 'Put water in a trough for me.' He ﷺ sat down and took a bath and tried to get up but fainted again. Then he ﷺ recovered..."[111] If this is legislated for unconsciousness, then it is even more appropriate for insanity, since al-Shāfiʿī (may Allah grant him His mercy) said, "Rarely does someone go insane save that they ejaculate."[112]

11. entering the state of pilgrim sanctity;

The Prophet ﷺ bathed before commencing the Pilgrimage.[113]

12. entering Mecca;

Ibn ʿUmar (may Allah be pleased with him and his father) would not enter Mecca without spending the night at Dhī Ṭūwā until dawn, whereupon he would bathe and then enter Mecca in the day. He mentioned that the Prophet ﷺ did the same.[114]

13. entering Medina;

‹It is even more appropriate to clean and ready oneself when visiting the Prophet ﷺ.[115]›

14. standing [at ʿArafah] and;

People gather on the day of ʿArafah as they do for the Friday Prayer so bathing in preparation for it is recommended.

---

111. ʿĀʾīshah: Bukhārī, 687; Muslim, 418 #90.

112. al-Shāfiʿī, *Al-Umm,* 1:54.

113. Zayd ibn Thābit: Tirmidhī, 830 – *ḥasan gharīb*. See: TM, 1075.

114. Ibn ʿUmar: Bukhārī, 1553, 1573; Muslim, 1259 #127. See: TM, 1077.

115. Walī al-Dīn al-Baṣīr, *Al-Nihāyah,* 34.

15. throwing [stones] at the three pillars during the Days of Tashrīq.

Imam al-Shāfiʿī (may Allah grant him His mercy) said that one does not bathe for throwing stones at Jamrat al-ʿAqabah.[116]

FILTH AND ITS REMOVAL

(فصل) [النّجاسات]

LIQUID INTOXICANTS

وكلّ مسكر نجس.

Every [liquid] intoxicant is filth.

All intoxicants are filth, including wine and other types.

As for wine, Allah most High says, "...strong drink and games of chance and idols and divining arrows are only an infamy [*rijs*]..." [Q5:90]. The word "infamy [*rijs*]" means "filth." That wine is mentioned along with gambling and other sins does not weaken the argument that it is filth even though the others are pure, since these three things are removed [from this ruling] according to consensus, so wine remains [filthy] following the meaning of the words. This is the argument of the Shāfiʿī colleagues. This is questionable, since "infamy [*rijs*]" linguistically is "unclean [*qadhr*]," and this does not entail that it is filth. Neither does the command to avoid it entail that it is filth. The closest thing that can be said is what al-Ghazālī (may Allah grant him His mercy) said: "It is judged to be filth out of vehemence," and as a deterrent – analogous to dogs and what they lap from.[117]

All other [liquid] intoxicants are filthy out of being analogous to wine since they are the same in being unlawful. In *Al-Minhāj,*

116. al-Shāfiʿī, *Al-Umm* (2:160).

117. al-Ghazālī's quote is from *Al-Wasīṭ* (1:140). This paragraph is taken from al-Nawawī, *Al-Majmūʿ* (2:563).

Imam al-Nawawī (may Allah grant him His mercy) added "every liquid intoxicant."[118]

THAT WHICH EXITS FROM THE PRIVATE PARTS

وكذا ما خرج من السّبيلين إلّا المنيّ فيجب غسله، وإلّا بول صبيّ لم يطعم غير لبن فينضح.

Anything that exits from the private parts is filth, except for [male or female] ejaculate [*manī*].

There is consensus that urine from an adult human is filth.[119] By analogy, so is urine from a human infant fed nothing but milk. The urine of all non-edible animals is filth by consensus. So is the urine of edible animals, according to the soundest opinion.

Feces is filth by consensus. So are blood, *madhī* [pre-ejaculate] and *wadī* [prostatic fluid]. ʿAlī (may Allah be pleased with him) said, "I was one who frequently discharged *madhī* and felt ashamed to ask the Messenger of Allah ﷺ about it. So I asked al-Miqdād ibn al-Aswad to ask him. Al-Miqdād asked him and he ﷺ replied, 'One washes one's penis and performs ablution.'"[120]

As for ejaculate, ʿĀʾishah (may Allah be pleased with her) said, "I would scrape ejaculate from the garment of the Messenger of Allah ﷺ and he would then go offer prayer in it."[121]

As for the ejaculate of non-humans, it is filthy according to al-Rāfiʿī (may Allah grant him His mercy) and pure according to al-Nawawī (may Allah grant him His mercy).[122]

---

118. al-Nawawī, *Minhāj al-ṭālibīn,* 15.
119. Ibn al-Mundhir, *Al-Ijmāʿ,* 36.
120. ʿAlī: Bukhārī, 178; Muslim, 303. See: TM, 21, 125.
121. ʿĀʾishah: Ibn Khuzaymah, 288, 290; Abū Dāwūd, 372; Nasāʾī, 296; Ibn Ḥibbān, 1380. See: BM, 1:489 #10.
122. al-Rāfiʿ, *Al-Sharḥ al-kabīr,* 1:41; al-Nawawī, *Rawḍat al-ṭālibīn,* 1:17.

Pus is filth because it is putrefied blood. Blood is filth, a fortiori, so is pus.

Vomit is filth because it is food that has putrefied and become foul, so it is analogous to feces.

Washing [what exits from the private parts] is obligatory.

The filthy substance must be removed, since there can be no purification so long as it remains.

An exception to this is urine from a male infant who has not received any nourishment other than milk, as it is sprinkled with water.[123]

The Prophet ﷺ said, "A male infant's urine is sprinkled [with water]. A female infant's is washed."[124]

LIVING ANIMALS

والحيوان كلّه طاهر إلّا الكلب والخنزير والفرع.

All animals are pure, except for dogs, pigs, and their offspring.

Dogs are filth. Abū Hurayrah (may Allah be pleased with him) reported that the Messenger of Allah ﷺ said, "The purification of utensils belonging to any one of you, after a dog has licked them, is to wash them seven times, using dirt the first time."[125] The argument is that purification is prompted by ritual impurity or filth [*khabath*]. There is no ritual impurity here, so it must be filth. If a dog's mouth is filthy, so are the rest of its parts, since its mouth is its most wholesome part.

123. This suffices once the physical substance itself has been removed.

124. Abū Samḥ: Abū Dāwūd, 376; Nasā'ī, 304; Nasā'ī, *Al-Sunan al-kubrā*, 304; Ibn Mājah, 526; Ibn Khuzaymah, 283; Ḥākim, 589. See: TM, 133.

125. Abū Hurayrah: Muslim, 279 #91. See: TM, 118.

Pigs are worse than dogs, as they are not kept under any circumstances. A fortiori, pigs are filth. Ibn Mundhir (may Allah grant him His mercy) conveyed consensus that pigs are filth,[126] and it is the best evidence to use – provided it is affirmed. However, the Mālikī school considers pigs pure so long as they are alive. Imam al-Nawawī (may Allah grant him His mercy) said, "We do not have a clear proof that pigs are filth while they are alive."[127] Al-Māwardī cited [the verse] "...or the flesh of swine – for indeed, it is infamy [*rijs*]..." [Q6:145] and said, "What is intended by 'flesh of swine' is the entire pig, since its flesh is part of the dead animal. Interpreting it thus is more useful [than interpreting it as repetition]."[128]

Their offspring (even with a pure animal) are also filth, since the filth dominates.

The tears, sweat, and saliva of every pure animal are not filthy.

There is no disagreement concerning their saliva [being pure]. The Prophet ﷺ was asked: "Do we make ablution from water left over from a donkey?" He ﷺ said, "Yes. And from water left over from every predator."[129]

Sweat is pure, since he ﷺ rode a horse bareback while it galloped and did not avoid its sweat.[130]

There is consensus that tears are pure.

There is consensus that milk is pure since it nourishes children.

Eggs and rennet [*infiḥah*] are like milk [in their ruling].

---

126. Ibn al-Mundhīr, *Al-Awsaṭ,* 2:280.

127. Up to here, all of this paragraph is quoted from from al-Nawawī, *Al-Majmūʿ* (2:586).

128. The text between brackets is from al-Māwardī, *Al-Ḥāwī al-kabīr,* 1:315–6.

129. Jābir: al-Shāfiʿī, *Al-Musnad,*8; al-Nawawī, *Al-Majmūʿ*,1:173 – *ḍaʿīf*. See: KBM, 15.

130. ʿAbd Allāh ibn Mughaffal: al-Rūyānī, *Al-Musnad*, 2:90 #876. Bukhārī and Muslim transmitted it without the phrase "bareback," from Anas: Bukhārī, 2627; Muslim, 411 #80. See: KBM, 16.

DEAD ANIMALS

والميتات نجسة إلّا السّمك والجراد والآدميّ.

Dead animals [which have not been slaughtered] are filth, except for fish, locusts, and human beings.

Allah Most High says, "Forbidden unto you (for food) are dead animals..." [Q5:3]. The prohibition of something that is not revered or harmful (like poison), indicates that it is filth.

Humans are not filthy because they are ennobled. ‹Allah Most High says, "Verily we have honoured the Children of Adam..." [Q17:70].[131]›

There is consensus regarding the purity of fish and locusts.[132]

HAIR AND BONES

وشعر الميتة وعظمها نجس إلّا شعر الآدميّ.

The hair and bones of dead animals [which have not been slaughtered] are filth, except for human hair [and bones].

Animal bones are filth because they are [part of and] subordinate to the whole unslaughtered animal, which is now filth.

Human hair [and bone] is not filthy because humans are ennobled.

131. al-Bughā, *Al-Tadhhīb,* 13 #4.

132. For textual evidence, see "Hunting and Slaughtering" on page 501.

WASHING DUE TO DOGS OR PIGS

ويغسل من الكلب أو الخنزير سبعًا إحداهنّ بالتّراب الطّاهر.

Filth from a dog or pig must be washed seven times, with one of the washings accompanied by dirt that is ritually pure.

Abū Hurayrah (may Allah be pleased with him) reported that the Messenger of Allah ﷺ said, "The purification of utensils belonging to any one of you, after a dog has licked them, lies in washing them seven times, using dirt the first time."[133]

Pigs are analogous to dogs but are even more filthy. Other parts of an impure animal are, a fortiori, like its mouths. Similarly, the hadiths indicate that the entire animal is filthy.

All other parts of a dog and its waste are considered analogous to its saliva.

REMOVING OTHER TYPES OF FILTH

وسائر النّجاسات تغسل مرّةً، والتّثليث سنّة.

Other [types of] filth are washed a single time, though three washings are recommended.

Three washings are recommended because of the hadith related to the sunnah of washing one's hands thrice before ablution.

133. Abū Hurayrah: Muslim, 279 #91. See: TM, 118.

VINEGAR AND TANNING OF ANIMAL SKINS

ولا يطهر نجس العين إلّا خمر تخلّلت من غير عين، إلّا جلد نجس بالموت فبالدّباغ.

Physical filth cannot be rendered pure except for wine that turns to vinegar without a foreign substance being added to it.

Wine is considered filth because it is an intoxicant. It ceases being filth once it becomes vinegar because the reason for it being categorized as filth (i.e., its intoxicating properties) is no longer there.

But it remains filth when a foreign substance is added to it since whatever is added becomes filthy through contact with the wine and remains filthy. And if the wine becomes vinegar, that filthy substance causes the vinegar to become filthy.

Exceptions to this include animal skins that became filthy due to death, which are purified via tanning.

The Prophet ﷺ said, "When the skin is tanned, it becomes purified."[134]

Tanning does not purify the skins of dogs and pigs since they were not pure while alive. A fortiori, parts of them cannot become pure after death. (Also, life is a greater means of purification than tanning.)

Dirt and sunlight are not sufficient for tanning since they do not remove the excess tissue.

DRY ABLUTION

(فصل) [التّيمّم]

Dry ablution [*tayammum*], linguistically, is "deliberation" [*qaṣd*]. In the Sacred Law [*Sharᶜ*], it is the act of transferring dirt to the face and hands with particular conditions. Ibn Ḥabīb (may Allah grant him His mercy) said that tayammum was divinely mandated in 4 AH. Others said it was in 6 AH. It is said that tayammum due

134. Ibn ʿAbbās: Muslim, 366 #105. See: TM, 130.

to the absence of water is a base ruling [*ʿazīmah*], but an allowance [*rukhṣah*] if due to an[other] reason.

CONDITIONS

شرط التّيمّم: فقد الماء أو تعذّر استعماله لمرض يخاف معه محذورًا، ودخول الوقت ، وطلب الماء عند التّوهّم، والتّراب الطّهور.

The [four] conditions for dry ablution are:

1. [the] absence of water or being excused from using it due to sickness when one fears harm if [water is] used;

Dry ablution can be made in place of ablution or the purificatory bath. As for being a substitute for ablution, it is due to Him Most High saying, "...and if ye be ill..." [Q4:43, Q5:6].

As for being a substitute for the purificatory bath, it is because of the well-known hadith of ʿAmmār ibn Yāsir (may Allah be pleased with him). He said, "The Messenger of Allah ﷺ sent me on an errand. I was befallen by major ritual impurity. I did not find water so I rolled in the dirt just as a beast rolls in it. I mentioned this to the Prophet ﷺ and he said, 'Indeed, it would have sufficed you to do like this,' and he ﷺ struck his palms upon the ground, shook them, and wiped the back of his hand with his left (or the back of his left hand with his palm), and then wiped them over his face."[135]

‹Additionally, ʿImrān bin Ḥuṣayn (may Allah be pleased with him) said, "We were on a journey with the Messenger of Allah ﷺ. He ﷺ lead people in prayer and saw an isolated individual. He ﷺ said, 'What prevented you from praying?' He said, 'I am befallen by major ritual impurity and there is no water.' He ﷺ said, 'Use clean earth, as it will suffice you.'"[136]›

135. ʿAmmār ibn Yāsir: Bukhārī, 347; Muslim, 368 #110; Abū Dāwūd, 321; Nasāʾī, 316, 320, *Al-Sunan al-kubrā*, 298, 304. See: TM, 138.

136. ʿImrān ibn Ḥuṣayn: Bukhārī, 348; Muslim, 682. See: al-Baghawī, *Al-Tahdhīb fī fiqh al-Imām al-Shāfiʿī*, 1:352.

2. that the time [for prayer] has entered;

It is not permissible to make dry ablution before the prayer time enters. Since it is a purification of necessity, it is not permitted unless there is need, and there is no need before the time has entered.

3. seeking water when it is thought to be present; and

Allah Most High says, "...and ye find not water..." [Q4:43]. One cannot claim to have found no water if one did not first seek it.

4. [using] earth that is purifying.

Nothing else suffices. Allah Most High says, "...then seek clean high ground..." [Q4:43]. Ibn ʿAbbās (may Allah be pleased with him) understood "high ground" to mean "pure earth."[137]

OBLIGATORY ACTIONS

وفرضه: نيّة الفرض، ومسح الوجه واليدين إلى المرفقين، والتّرتيب.

Dry ablution has [three] obligatory actions,...

[A foundation for the obligatory actions is the hadith from] Ibn ʿUmar (may Allah be pleased with them both), who reported that the Messenger of Allah ﷺ said, "Dry ablution is two strikes: one strike for the face and one strike for the two hands up to the elbows."[138]

...which are:
1. intending the obligation [for which it is being performed];

‹Allah Most High said, "...then seek [*fa tayammamu*] clean, high ground and rub your faces and your hands with some of it..."

137. Ibn ʿAbbās: Bayhaqī, 995. See: BM, 2:673.

138. Ibn ʿUmar: Dāraquṭnī, 685 – *mawqūf*, Ḥākim, 634, 636. See TM, 145.

[Q5:6.] The phrase "then seek" [*fa tayammamu*] means "to deliberately seek something." When combined with "actions are according to intentions," it indicates that one's intention is obligatory.[139]›

One intends to make an act of worship permissible to perform (not to lift the state of impurity itself), since the state of impurity remains and one is permitted to perform the act of worship only as an allowance. One must also intend that the dry ablution is for carrying out an obligatory action, though it is not required to specify which one.

One must transfer the earth. It must be done via two strikes according to what Imam al-Nawawī (may Allah grant him His mercy) considered soundest. However, Imam al-Rāfiʿī (may Allah grant him His mercy) said that one strike might suffice if using something like a cloth to transfer the earth.[140]

2. **wiping the face and hands up to and including the elbows; and**
3. **performing the actions in the prescribed sequence.**

When dry ablution is made in place of ablution, it must be repeated each time one intends to perform a personally obligatory action, since it is a deficient form of purification. Because of this deficiency, it cannot be used for more than a single obligatory act. Support for this includes Ibn ʿUmar (may Allah be pleased with both of them) saying that "one makes dry ablution for every prayer, even if one has not invalidated one's [previous] ablution."[141]

Dry ablution does not need to be repeated for communal obligations (like the funeral prayer), or recommended prayers. Dry ablution in place of the purificatory bath does not need to be repeated.

---

139. al-Bughā, *Al-Tadhhīb,* 31 #2.

140. al-Rāfiʿī, *Fatḥ al-ʿazīz,* 2:329; al-Nawawī, *Minhāj al-ṭālibin,*18.

141. Ibn ʿUmar: Bayhaqī, 1054, with an authentic chain. See: TM, 146.

RECOMMENDED ACTIONS

وسننه: التّسميّة، وتقديم اليمنى، والولاء.

Its [three] recommended actions are:
1. **saying "*Bismi llāh*";**
2. **wiping the right side before the left; and**
3. **performing the actions consecutively.**

These actions are recommended when making full ablution and by extension, dry ablution, since the latter is a substitute for the former.

INVALIDATORS

ويبطله كلّما أبطل الوضوء، ووجود الماء في غير الصّلاة، أو في صلاة لا تسقط به، والرّدّة.

Dry ablution is invalidated
1. **whenever ablution is invalidated,**
2. **by water being present**
   a. **outside of prayer, or**

If one discovers water before the prayer, one must perform ablution with it, provided nothing prevents its use, such as thirst.

The Messenger of Allah ﷺ said, "Pure clean earth is a Muslim's purifier, even if he did not find water for ten [lunar] years. When he does find water, he is to use it on his body, as this is better."[142] ‹In the hadith, "use it on his body," means "make ablution with it," since the dry ablution would be invalided [by the discovery of water].[143]›

142. Abū Dharr: Tirmidhī, 124 – *ḥasan ṣaḥīḥ*. Also: Abū Dāwūd, 332; Nasāʾī, 322; Ibn Ḥibbān, 1311–3; Ḥākim, 627. See: TM, 110–11.

143. al-Bughā, *Al-Tadhhīb,* 32 #1.

   b. during a prayer that is not fulfilled when prayed via dry ablution; and
3. by apostasy.

IT IS REPEATED FOR EACH OBLIGATORY ACT

ويتيمّم لكلّ فرض.

Dry ablution is repeated for each obligatory act.

SPLINTS AND BANDAGES

وصاحب الجبائر يمسح عليها مع التيمّم، ولا يعيد إن وضعها على طهر إن لم تكن في أعضاء التيمّم.

Someone with a splint wipes over it while performing dry ablution. He does not repeat [his prayer] if the splint was applied while he was in the state of ablution and if it is not on one of the limbs upon which dry ablution is made.

The Prophet ﷺ commanded ʿAlī (may Allah be pleased with him) to wipe over a splint.[144]

144. ʿAlī: Ibn Mājah, 657; Bayhaqī, 1081, 1086. See: KBM, 200.

IN THE ABSENCE OF WATER OR EARTH

ويعيد فاقد الطّهورين، والمتيمّم للعدم في موضع يندر فيه الإعواز، وللمسافر العاصي وللبرد.

One's prayer must be repeated if one had no access to water or earth, if one made dry ablution in a place where not finding water is rare, or if one was a traveller in disobedience or [subject to intense] cold.

One does not have to repeat prayers prayed with dry ablution unless [the dry ablution] was performed due to intense cold while one was a resident (as this is rare), or a bandage was placed [on one's wound] while one was not in the state of ritual purity. One must repeat prayers if dry ablution was performed while a resident due to lack of water, or during a journey intended for an act of disobedience.

Abū Saʿīd al-Khudrī (may Allah be pleased with him) said that two men set out on a journey. When the time of prayer came, they had no water. They performed dry ablution with clean earth and prayed. Later, they found water. One of them repeated his prayer with ablution but the other did not. Then they came to the Messenger of Allah ﷺ and mentioned that to him. He ﷺ said to the one who did not repeat: "You followed the Sunnah and your prayer suffices you." And to the one who performed ablution and repeated, he ﷺ said, "There is a double reward for you."[145]

145. Abū Saʿīd al-Khudrī: Abū Dāwūd, 338, Nasāʾī, 433, Ḥākim, 1094. See TM, 148.

MENSTRUATION, POSTNATAL & IRREGULAR BLEEDING

(فصل) [الحيض والنّفاس والاستحاضة]

MENSTRUATION

أقلّ الحيض - وهو الخارج على سبيل الصّحّة من غير سبب الولادة - يوم وليلة، بشرط رؤيته بعد تسع سنين تقريبًا، وأكثره خمسة عشر بلياليها، وغالبه ستّ أو سبع.

The minimum duration for menstruation (bleeding that occurs as part of normal health and not due to giving birth) is one day and night [i.e., twenty-four hours].

What is significant here [for determining these durations] is the durations that were actually found.

ʿĀʾishah (may Allah be pleased with her) said, "We set out with the sole intention of performing Ḥajj. When we reached Sarif, I got my menses. The Messenger of Allah ﷺ came to me while I was crying. He ﷺ said, 'What's wrong? Have you got your menses?' I said, 'Yes.' He ﷺ said, 'This is a thing that Allah has ordained for the daughters of Adam. Do all that pilgrims do except for circumambulating the Kaʿbah.'" Another version includes "'...until you become pure.'"[146]

A condition [for the bleeding to be considered menstruation] is that it first occurs after a woman is approximately nine lunar years of age.

Imam al-Shāfiʿī (may Allah grant him His mercy) said, "The earliest I heard of a woman menstruating was from the women of Tuhama, who menstruate at nine [lunar] years."[147]

146. ʿĀʾishah: Bukhārī, 294; Muslim, 1211. See: TM, 150.
147. al-Shāfiʿī, *Al-Umm*, 5:229.

Its maximum duration is fifteen [days] and nights.

ʿAlī (may Allah be pleased with him) said, "any bleeding lasting longer than this is irregular bleeding [*istiḥāḍah*]."[148]

Its average duration is six or seven days.

The Prophet ﷺ said to Ḥamnah bint Jaḥsh (may Allah be pleased with her): "You menstruate – as Allah knows – for six or seven days, just like women menstruate and are pure in their respective times of menstruation and times of purity."[149]

PURITY

وأقلّ طهر فاصل بين الحيضين خمسة عشر، ولا حدّ لأكثره، وغالبه بقيّة غالب الحيض.

The minimum duration of purity between two menstrual cycles is fifteen days.

This is the shortest interval that has been established.

It has no maximum limit.

This is according to consensus.[150]

148. ʿAlī: Bukhārī, with a suspended chain (before 325). See: BM, 3:145.
149. Ḥamnah bint Jaḥsh: Abū Dāwūd, 287; Tirmidhī, 128 – *ḥasan* [*ṣaḥīḥ*]; Ḥākim, 615. See: TM, 155.
150. al-Anṣārī, *Asnā al-Maṭalib,* 1:100; Ibn Ḥajar, *Tuḥfat al-muḥtāj,* 1:385; al-Ramlī, *Nihāyat al-muḥtāj,* 1:327.

Its average duration is related to the average duration for menstruation.

That is, twenty-three or twenty-four days [for six- or seven-day menses].

Moments of purity that occur during menstrual flow are given the ruling of menstruation. So if [during menstruation,] one has a day of purity and then a day of bleeding, both days are considered menstruation. Otherwise, if the times when no blood is seen were considered pure, the post-marital waiting period would end after just three of these occurrences. Al-Ghazālī (may Allah grant him His mercy) said in *Al-Basīṭ*: "The Ummah has consensus that each individual day cannot be made a complete duration of purity."[151]

If the duration of purity is not preceded by and followed by bleeding, the interval without bleeding is not considered menstruation. It is also a condition that the total duration of bleeding not be less than one day and night.

PREGNANCY

وأقلّ الحمل ستّة أشهر، وأكثره أربع سنين.

The minimum duration for pregnancy is six [lunar] months. Its maximum is four [lunar] years.

‹The minimum duration for pregnancy is understood from Allah Most High saying: "...and the bearing of him and the weaning of him is thirty months..." [Q46:15], and "...and his weaning is in two years..." [Q31:14]. If pregnancy and weaning combined is thirty lunar months, and weaning alone is two lunar years (twenty-four months), pregnancy must then be [at least] six lunar months.

The maximum duration is based upon a partial census.[152]›

151. I could not source this as *Al-Basīṭ* is not yet published at this time. However, al-Nawawī quotes the same text in *Al-Majmūʿ* (2:502). In *Al-Wasīṭ*, Imām al-Ghazāli says, "There is no disagreement..." (1:412).

152. al-Bughā, *Al-Tadhhīb*, 38 #1.

POSTNATAL BLEEDING

وأقلّ النّفاس - وهو الخارج عقيب الولد - لحظة، وأكثره ستّون يومًا، وغالبه أربعون.

The minimum duration for lochia (bleeding after giving birth) is a single instant.

This is according to a census. The soundest opinion is that lochia [*nifās*] includes the blood that exits with the child, but not the blood that precedes it after contractions begin.

Its maximum duration is sixty days.

This is according to a census. If the bleeding exceeds sixty days, one refers back to one's habitual cycle, if it is known, or one notes any distinctions between bleeding. But if it is the first occurrence, the duration is assumed to be the shortest possible duration.

The average duration is forty days.

Umm Salamah (may Allah be pleased with her) said, "During the time of the Messenger of Allah ﷺ, women with lochia would sit [refraining from prayer] for forty days."

This duration [forty days] is understood to be the average; it does not negate the possibility of it being longer.

153. Umm Salamah: Abū Dāwūd, 311; Tirmidhī, 139; Ḥākim, 648. See: TM, 162.

IRREGULAR BLEEDING

والاستحاضة: الخارج في غيرهما، فإن كانت مبتدأةً ردّت إلى يوم وليلة في الحيض وباقي الشّهر في الطّهر، أو معتادةً فالعادّة، أو مميّزةً فالتّمييز، أو متحيّرةً فتحتاط.

Irregular bleeding is [bleeding] other than menstruation or lochia.

ʿĀʾishah (may Allah be pleased with her) reported that Fāṭimah bint Abī Ḥubaysh (may Allah be pleased with her) came to the Prophet ﷺ [to inquire] about irregular bleeding.[154]

If it is one's first period ever, one's menstruation is assumed to be a single day and night, and one is assumed to be pure the rest of the month.

If one [already] has a habit[ual cycle], one follows it.

So if one menstruates for fifteen days and then is pure for a [lunar] month, and then menstruates for fifteen days and is pure for another [lunar] month (or more or less), and then one's bleeding is excessive in the following month, one refers to one's habit[ual cycle: fifteen days of menstruation and then purity for a [lunar] month]. A single occurrence is enough to establish a habit[ual cycle].

If one's bleeding is distinctive [i.e., it can be divided into heavy or dark, and light], then one follows it [with the heavy or dark bleeding assumed to be menses, and the light bleeding to be purity].

Umm ʿAṭiyyah (may Allah be pleased with her) said, "We did not consider yellow or murky [discharge] as anything significant. Another version adds "...after purity."[155]

Women would send little boxes to ʿĀʾishah (may Allah be pleased with her) containing pieces of cotton cloth covered with yellow

---

154. ʿĀʾīshah: Bukhārī, 228; Muslim, 333. See: al-Baghawī, *Al-Tahdhīb,* 1:445.

155. Umm ʿAṭiyyah: Bukhārī, 326; Abū Dāwūd, 307. See: TM, 156.

[blood]. She would say, "Do not be hasty until you see a white discharge." By that she meant purity from menses.[156]

Fāṭimah bint Abi Ḥubaysh (may Allah be pleased with her) suffered from irregular vaginal bleeding. The Messenger of Allah ﷺ said to her, "When it is menstrual blood, the blood is black and recognizable. When it is this, stop praying. And when it is the other, perform ablution, for it is hemorrhage."[157]

If one is confused, one must follow precaution.

If one forgets the place within the month or the duration, her menstruation is considered whatever is certain or possible, except with respect to obligatory actions, and she takes the purificatory bath whenever it is possible that the bleeding has stopped.

An example of forgetting the place within the month is if someone with irregular bleeding says, "My menstruation occurs during one of the three thirds of the month but I forget which one it is." In such a case, she will make ablution for each obligatory act during the first third of the month, make the purificatory bath at the end of each ten days, and make ablution for each obligatory act during each of the sets of ten days. This is because she has no menstruation or purity with certainty.

If she says, "My menstruation is ten days during the last twenty days," then the first ten days of the month are purity with certainty. During the second ten days, she makes ablution for each obligatory act. At the end of the third set of ten days, she makes the purificatory bath.

An example of forgetting the duration is her specifying thirty days and then saying, "I know that my bleeding would start at the beginning of the thirty days." Here, the first day and night are menstruation with certainty, and it may end at any time within

---

156. Bukhārī, before 320. See: TM, 157.

157. Abū Dāwūd (286); Nasā'ī (215–216, 362–363); Ibn Ḥibban (1348); Ḥākim (618). See TM (158).

fifteen days. So she bathes for each obligatory act up to the end of those fifteen days. After that, she is pure until the end of the month.

If she forgets both the place within the month and the duration (like if she says, "I do not know the place of my menstruation nor its amount"), then the sound opinion is that she employs precaution by praying and fasting (since it is possible that she is pure) and avoiding intercourse with her husband (since it is possible that she is menstruating). She fasts all of Ramadan, then thirty days, and then two more days. When she fasts Ramadan and the month is full, she achieves fourteen days [of valid fasting]. This is because for each day of the month, it is possible that bleeding will begin during that day and end during the next. If the month was short, she will have achieved thirteen days. The same happens when she fasts thirty days, which is why she fasts thirty days instead of a lunar month. And she will still need to fast two more days after that – whether Ramadan was full or short.

If she does not have a habitual cycle and does not have distinctive bleeding, she returns to one day and one night of menstruation and twenty nine days of purity. This is because it is certain that she is not required to pray during this amount of time, while there is doubt concerning anything else. And doubt is not removed except with certainty or with an indicator – like distinctive bleeding or a habitual cycle.

If she does not have a habitual cycle but does have distinctive bleeding (such as her bleeding becoming lighter after passing the minimum duration of menstruation and before reaching the maximum), then she is referred back to her cycle for that month. She continues to refer back to it in future months until the duration of the stronger bleeding is identified.

So, if a girl during her first menses sees dark blood for a day and a night, and then has lighter bleeding until the end of the month, she is referred back to the dark blood for her menstruation. It is the same if she sees dark blood up to fifteen days and then red blood for the rest: her menstruation is the dark. And if she were to see in the next month five days of dark bleeding and the rest red, we would refer her back in this month to the five dark days. If she sees one day and one night of dark blood and then the rest is red, and then the next month she sees five dark and the rest red, she is referred back to the dark [e.g., five days]. This is what is meant by "until the duration of the stronger bleeding is identified" at the end of the previous paragraph.

Note that the duration of the red (weaker) blood must not be shorter than the minimum duration of purity between two menstruations [i.e., fifteen days].

ACTIONS UNLAWFUL DUE TO MENSTRUATION & LOCHIA

(فصل) [ما يحرم بالحيض]

ويحرم بالحيض والنّفاس ما حرم على الجنب، والصّوم، ودخول المسجد إن خافت التّلويث، والوطء، والاستمتاع بما بين السّرّة والرّكبة، والطّلاق.

The things that menstruation and lochia render unlawful are

1–7. those that are unlawful for someone in the state of major ritual impurity, in addition to...

The scholars have consensus that lochia is analogous to menstruation with respect to everything that is lawful or prohibited, and what is offensive or recommended.

As for evidence specific to menstruation and lochia, prayer is unlawful because Q2:222 ("They question thee (O Muhammad) concerning menstruation...") was revealed concerning them. There is also the case of Fāṭimāh bint Abī Ḥubaysh (may Allah be pleased with her), whose blood kept flowing, so the Prophet ﷺ said to her: "When it is menstrual blood, the blood is black and recognizable. When it is this, stop praying. And when it is the other, perform ablution, for it is hemorrhaging."[158]

---

158. Abū Dāwūd (286); Nasā'ī (215–216, 362–363); Ibn Ḥibban (1348); Ḥākim (618). See: TM (158).

Quranic recitation is unlawful because the Messenger of Allah ﷺ said, "No one in the state of major ritual impurity is to read anything from the Quran." Another transmission has "nor a woman who is menstruating."[159]

8. fasting;

This is according to consensus. Fasting is unlawful until the bleeding stops. [Fasting becomes permissible once the bleeding stops, even before making a purificatory bath.]

Fasts missed due to menstruation and lochia must be made up. Prayers are not made up.

Concerning menstruation, ʿĀʾishah (may Allah be pleased with her) said, "We were ordered to make up fasts, but we were not ordered to make up prayers."[160]

Lochia is analogous to menstruation because it is [similar to] an accumulation of menstrual blood.

9. entering the mosque, if one worries one will soil it;

ʿĀʾishah (may Allah be pleased with her) said, "The Messenger of Allah ﷺ said, 'I do not permit the mosque to women during menstruation nor to those in the state of major ritual impurity.'"[161]

Other hadiths indicate the permissibility of entering and passing through the mosque. ʿĀʾishah (may Allah be pleased with her) reported: "The Messenger of Allah ﷺ said to me, 'Get me the mat from the mosque.' I said, 'I am menstruating.' He ﷺ then said, 'Your menstruation is not in your hand.'"[162]

---

159. Ibn ʿUmar: Dāraquṭnī, 1:124 #413; Tirmidhī, 131. See: TM, 102.

160. ʿĀʾishah: Bukhārī, 321; Muslim, 335 #69. See: TM, 152.

161. ʿĀʾishah: Abū Dāwūd, 232; Ibn Khuzaymah, 1327. See: TM, 101, 151.

162. ʿĀʾishah: Bukhārī, 298. See: BM, 2:565.

10. **intercourse;**

Intercourse remains impermissible until the purificatory bath is performed. Allah Most High says, "...so let women alone at such times and go not in unto them till they are cleansed. And when they have purified themselves, then go in unto them as Allah hath enjoined upon you..." [Q2:222]. ‹In this verse, "so let women alone" and "go not in until them" mean "abstain from intercourse"; "purified themselves," refers to taking the purificatory bath after menstruation has ended; and "then come to them," refers to intercourse.[163]›

11. **seeking sexual enjoyment from the area between the [woman's] navel and knees; and**

ʿAbd Allāh ibn Saʿd al-Anṣārī (may Allah be pleased with him) asked the Messenger of Allah ﷺ, "What is lawful for me to do with my wife when she is menstruating?" He ﷺ replied, "Whatever is above the waist-wrapper is lawful for you."[164]

11. **divorce.**

Divorce is [unlawful at this time, though] still effective.

---

163. al-Maḥallai and al-Suyūṭī, *Tafsīr al-Jalālayn*.

164. ʿAbd Allāh ibn Saʿd al-Anṣārī: Abū Dāwūd, 212. See: TM, 153.

2

PRAYER

كِتَابُ الصَّلَاةِ

هي الدّعاء.

Prayer [*ṣalāh*] is "supplication."

This is according to its linguistic meaning.

‹The textual foundation for prayer comes from the Quran and hadith. Allah Most High says, "...Prayer at fixed times hath been enjoined on the believers" [Q4:103].[1]›

The hadith concerning the Night Ascent [*al-Miʿrāj*] includes "Allah enjoined fifty prayers upon my community... So I returned to Him [repeatedly] and He Most High said, 'Five [prayers], and they are [equal to] fifty, and My word does not alter.'"[2]

Ibn ʿUmar (may Allah be pleased with them both) reported that the Messenger of Allah ﷺ said, "Islam is based on five [principles]: testifying that there is no deity except Allah and that Muhammad is the Messenger of Allah, establishing prayer, offering zakat, performing Hajj, and fasting the month of Ramadan."[3]

PRAYER TIMES

والمكتوبات خمس: الظّهر، وأوّل وقته زوال الشّمس، وآخره مصير ظلّ الشّيء مثله سوى ظلّ الاستواء، وبه يدخل العصر، والمختار إلى مصير الظّلّ مثليه، والجواز

1. al-Bughā, *Al-Tadhhīb,* 41 #1.
2. Abū Dharr: Bukhārī, 349; Muslim, 163, and others. See: TM, 163.
3. Ibn ʿUmar: Bukhārī, 8; Muslim, 16. See: KBM, 1088, 1183.

إلى الغروب وبه يدخل وقت المغرب، ويبقى إلى مضيّ قدر طهارة، وستر عورة، وأذانين، وخمس ركعات، وله الاستدامة إلى مغيب الشّفق الأحمر، وبه يدخل وقت العشاء، والمختار الثّلث، والجواز إلى طلوع الفجر الثاني، وهو الصّادق وبه يدخل وقت الصّبح، والمختار الإسفار، والجواز إلى طلوع الشّمس.

Five prayers are obligatory.

Their number is established through textual evidence and consensus.

The textual foundation for the prayer times is a well-known, *ṣaḥīḥ* hadith involving Jibrīl (peace be upon him). Ibn ʿAbbās (may Allah be pleased with them both) said that the Messenger of Allah ﷺ said, "Jibrīl (peace be upon him) led me in prayer at the House [the Kaʿbah] twice. He prayed the Noon Prayer [*Ẓuhr*] with me when the sun had passed its zenith the length of a sandal strap. He led me in the Afternoon Prayer [*ʿAṣr*] when a[n object's] shadow was like itself [in length]. He led me in the Sunset Prayer [*Maghrib*] when someone fasting would break the fast. He led me in the Night Prayer [*ʿIshāʾ*] when the [sky's] red glow had disappeared. He led me in the Morning Prayer [*Fajr*] when food and drink become unlawful to someone who is fasting. The next day, he led me in the Noon Prayer when a[n object's] shadow was like itself [in length]. He led me in the Afternoon Prayer when a[n object's] shadow was twice itself [in length]. He led me in the Sunset Prayer when someone fasting would break their fast. He led me in the Night Prayer until the end of the first third of the night. He led me in the Morning Prayer when the horizon had yellowed. He then turned to me and said, 'O, Muhammad. This is the time of the prophets before you. The time is between these two times."[4]

4. Ibn ʿAbbās: Abū Dāwūd, 393; Tirmidhī, 149 – *ḥasan ṣaḥīḥ*; Ibn Khuzaymah, 325 – *ṣaḥīḥ*; Ḥākim, 693 – *ṣaḥīḥ al-isnād*. See: TM, 164, 165.

[1] The [time for the] Noon Prayer begins when the sun has passed its zenith. Its time ends when [the length of] an object's shadow, minus its shadow's length at the sun's zenith, is the same as its height...

This is because of Jibrīl's hadith concerning times (peace be upon him).[5]

... – whereupon the time for [2] the Afternoon Prayer begins. Its preferred time ends when an object's shadow is twice its height. [Its] permissible time extends until sunset...

This is also because of Jibrīl's hadith concerning times (peace be upon him).[6] Also, the Prophet ﷺ said, "The time for the Afternoon Prayer endures so long as the sun has not set."[7]

... – whereupon the time for [3] the Sunset Prayer begins. Its time lasts long enough to make ablution, cover what must be covered for prayer, perform the call to prayer [*adhān*] and the call to commence the prayer [*iqāmah*], and pray five prayer cycles [*rakʿāt*].

That is, three prayer cycles for the obligatory prayer, two for the voluntary cycles after it, or – according to another opinion – the two before it. This is the opinion of the new school of Imam al-Shāfiʿī (may Allah grant him His mercy). However, the opinion of the old school, as explained below, is preferred in the *madhhab*. Imam al-Shāfiʿī (may Allah grant him His mercy) also has an opinion in the new school that its time continues until twilight disappears, and that one can begin one's prayer at any time in between.

The opinion of the old school is that the time for the Sunset Prayer extends until the sun's red glow disappears [and the Night Prayer begins]. This opinion is considered preponderant due to the

5. Ibn ʿAbbās: Abū Dāwūd, 393, et al.
6. Ibn ʿAbbās: Abū Dāwūd, 393, et al.
7. ʿAbd Allāh ibn ʿAmr: Muslim, 612 #171, et al. See: TM, 167.

weight of its evidence, such as the Prophet ﷺ saying, "The time for the Sunset Prayer is until the red glow disappears."[8]

‹There is also the Medinan narration:›

Abū Mūsā al-Ashʿarī (may Allah be pleased with him) said a person came to the Messenger of Allah ﷺ to question him about the times of the prayers. He ﷺ did not reply. The call to [commence] the Morning Prayer was made when dawn appeared and people were barely able to recognize one another. He ﷺ later commanded [Bilāl] and he made the call to [commence] the Noon Prayer when the sun had passed its zenith, and someone would say that it is midday; but he ﷺ was more knowledgeable than they. He ﷺ commanded him and he made the call to [commence] the Afternoon Prayer while the sun was high. He ﷺ commanded him and he made the call to [commence] the Sunset Prayer when the sun set. He ﷺ then commanded him and he made the call to [commence] the Night Prayer when the twilight had disappeared. The next day, he ﷺ delayed the Morning Prayer until it had passed and someone would say that the sun has risen or is on the verge. Then he ﷺ delayed the Noon Prayer until it was near the time of the Afternoon Prayer from the previous day. Then he ﷺ delayed the Afternoon Prayer until people would say that the sun has reddened. Then he ﷺ delayed the Sunset Prayer until [near] the end of twilight. He ﷺ then delayed the Night Prayer until a third of the night had passed. He ﷺ then got up in the morning, called for the questioner and said, "The time [for prayers] is between those two."[9]

‹This hadith is preponderant over the hadith of Jibrīl (peace be upon him), which took place in Mecca,[10] because greater consideration is given to what came later. This hadith mentions the Prophet ﷺ delaying the Sunset Prayer until twilight disappeared.›

8. ʿAbd Allāh ibn ʿAmr ibn al-ʿĀṣ: Ibn Khuzaymah, 354. See: TM, 167.

9. Abū Mūsā al-Ashʿarī: Muslim, 614. See: KBM, 264.

10. Ibn ʿAbbās: Abū Dāwūd, 393, et al. See: TM, 164, 165.

And he ﷺ said, "The time for the Sunset Prayer endures so long as twilight has not ended."[11]

One can continue [praying] until the red in the sky disappears, whereupon the time for [4] the Night Prayer begins. Its preferred time extends until the end of the first third of the night. Its permissible time extends to the second dawn (true dawn)...

This is because of the hadith: "A prayer's time [endures] so long as the next prayer's time does not enter."

... – whereupon the time for the [5] Morning Prayer begins. Its preferred time extends until the yellow glow [appears on the horizon]. Its permissible [time extends to] the rising of the sun.

The Prophet ﷺ said, "The time for the Morning Prayer is from dawn onwards, so long as the sun does not rise."[12]

The beginning of a prayer's time is best, since He Most High says, "...so vie with one another in good works..." [Q2:148]. Though this is not the case for the Noon Prayer when it is intensely hot, for then it is best to wait for it to cool (provided its conditions are met).[13]

Whoever delays a prayer beyond its time is to make it up. He ﷺ said, "Whoever slept through a prayer or forgets it is to pray it when he remembers it."[14]

There are exceptions to this, including a non-Muslim who was never a Muslim. This is because Allah Most High says, "Tell those who disbelieve that if they cease (from persecution of believers) that which is past will be forgiven them; but if they return (thereto) then the example of the men of old hath already gone (before them, for

---

11. ʿAbd Allāh ibn al-ʿĀṣ: Muslim, 612 #171. See: TM, 167; cf al-Bughā, *Al-Tadhhīb fī adillat Matn al-ghāyat wa al-taqrīb*, 43 #2.
12. ʿAbd Allāh ibn ʿUmar: Muslim, 612 #174. See: TM, 167.
13. Ibn Mulaqqin mentions many other exceptions in *ʿUjālat al-muḥtāj*, 1:166–7.
14. Anas: Bukhārī, 597; Muslim, 684 #314–316. See: cf TM, 185.

a warning)" [Q8:38]. Also, he ﷺ did not command anyone who entered Islam to make up the prayers.

It is an act of disobedience to delay making up a missed prayer. Exceptions to this include the case of someone under compulsion, asleep, oblivious of the time, or intending to combine while traveling – as all of these are excusable. Similarly, someone who is not aware that it is obligatory and was not negligent in learning it, like someone who enters Islam in the distant wilderness or in lands hostile to Islam and cannot emigrate, is excused.

CONDITIONS OBLIGATING PRAYER

(فصل) [شروط وجوب الصّلاة]

وشرط وجوبها الإسلام والبلوغ والعقل والطّهارة، فلا وجوب على حائض ونفساء.

The obligation of prayer is conditional upon [the person being]:

There is consensus that it is obligatory when these conditions are met.

1. a Muslim;

Ibn ʿAbbās (may Allah be pleased with them both) said, "The Prophet ﷺ sent Muʿādh (may Allah be pleased with him) to Yemen and said, 'Invite people to testify that there is no deity other than Allah and that I am the Messenger of Allah. If they obey you in doing so, teach them that Allah has enjoined upon them five prayers in every day and night...'"[15]

Non-Muslims who have never been Muslims are not required to pray. This is because prayer is invalid for them while they are disbelievers, and due to the absence of their being commanded to make up prayers upon entering Islam. The aforementioned indicate that they are not required to pray – similar to women with respect to making up prayers missed during menstruation.

15. Ibn ʿAbbās: Bukhārī, 1395; Muslim, 19. See: TM, 440.

Apostates [who return to Islam] are obligated and commanded to make up missed prayers upon returning.

2. **mature;**
3. **of sound mind; and**

Prayer is not an obligation for youths or the insane due to the well-known authentic hadith in which the Prophet ﷺ said, "The pen [that records deeds] has been lifted from three: a sleeper until he wakes, a boy until he reaches puberty, and a lunatic until he comes to reason."[16]

4. **ritually pure (so there is no obligation for a woman during menses or postpartum bleeding).**

Prayer is not an obligation for women during menstruation or lochia, according to consensus.

ويؤمر بالصّلاة لسبع، ويضرب على تركها لعشر، كالصّوم إذا أطاقه.

At seven years [of age, children] are ordered to pray. At ten, they are disciplined for neglecting it. The same applies to fasting once they are able [to perform it].

He ﷺ said, "Command youths to pray when they reach seven years. When they reach ten, discipline them for it."[17]

16. ʿĀʾishah: Abū Dāwūd, 4398, 4401–3; Tirmidhī, 1423; Nasāʾī, 3432; Ibn Mājah, 2041; Ibn Ḥibbān, 142, 143; Ḥākim, 2350. See: TM, 192, 1004, 1281, 1476, 1626.
17. Saburah: Abū Dāwūd, 495; Tirmidhī, 407 – *ḥasan*; Ḥākim, 708, 948; Ibn Khuzaymah, 1002. See: TM, 194–5.

RECOMMENDED PRAYERS

(فصل) [الصّلوات المسنونة]

RECOMMENDED IN CONGREGATION

والمسنونات خمس، العيدان، والكسوفان، والاستسقاء.

There are five recommended prayers:
1–2. the two Eid Prayers;
3–4. the solar and lunar Eclipse Prayers; and
5. the Drought Prayer.

The Eid Prayers [*Eid al-Fiṭr* and *Eid al-Aḍḥā*] are the most emphatically recommended prayers since they have a specific time for their performance – just like the obligatory prayers.

The solar and lunar Eclipse Prayers [*Ṣalāt al-Kusūf* and *Ṣalāt al-Khusūf*] are the next-most emphatically recommended since it is feared that their time will end with the reappearance of the sun or moon – like how it is feared that the appointed time for time-specific prayers will exit. Also, the Prophet ﷺ never omitted them, whereas he ﷺ would perform the Drought Prayer [*Ṣalāt al-Istisqā'*] and sometimes omit it at other times.

While all of these prayers resemble obligatory prayers in that they are performed in congregation, perhaps the Eclipse Prayers follow the Eid Prayers [in order of recommendation] because the Eid Prayers are the only ones that must be performed within a defined time.

It is best to perform these three [the Eid, Eclipse, and Drought Prayers] in congregation.

Even though *Tarawīḥ* Prayer is also performed in a group, it is not mentioned here since recommended prayers tied to the obligatory daily prayers [*rawātib*] are emphasized more than these.

Evidence for these prayers will come in their respective sections.

EMPHASIZED RAWĀTIB

والرّاتبة المؤكّدة عشر: ركعتا الفجر، وركعتان قبل الظّهر، وبعدها، وبعد المغرب والعشاء.

There are ten prayer cycles [*rakʿāt*] of emphasized prayers associated with the obligatory daily prayers:
1–2. two before the Morning Prayer;

The Prophet ﷺ encouraged them. ʿĀʾishah (may Allah be pleased with her) said the Prophet ﷺ was never more consistent and particular in offering any voluntary prayers than [he was with] the two prayer cycles [before] the Morning Prayer.[18]

3–4. two before the Noon Prayer;
5–10. two after the Noon, Sunset, and Night Prayers [i.e., six total].

The Prophet ﷺ performed all of them.

Ibn ʿUmar (may Allah be pleased with them both) said, "I remember ten voluntary prayer cycles from the Prophet ﷺ: two before the Noon Prayer prayer and two after it; two after the Sunset Prayer in his house; two after the Night Prayer in his house; and two before the Morning Prayer, which was at a time during which no one would enter upon the Prophet ﷺ."[19]

‹The ten prayer cycles mentioned in the above hadith are more emphatically recommended than the others. The other recommended prayer cycles are mentioned in other narrations.›

18. ʿĀʾishah: Bukhārī, 1123; Muslim, 724 #94.
19. Ibn ʿUmar: Bukhārī, 1180; Muslim, 729 #104, 730 #105. Others include Tirmidhī, 436; Nasāʾī, 873. See: TM, 421.

NON-EMPHASIZED RAWĀTIB

وسنّ أربع قبل الظّهر وبعدها، وقبل العصر، والوتر وأقلّه ركعة، وأدنى الكمال ثلاث مفصولة، وغايته إحدى عشرة.

Also recommended are:
1. four prayer cycles before the Noon Prayer and after it,...

The Prophet ﷺ said, "Whoever offers four prayer cycles before the Noon Prayer and four after, Allah makes [him] unlawful to the fire."[20]

‹The Friday Prayer [*Ṣalāt al-Jumuʿah*] is like the Noon Prayer in what was previously mentioned since it is [performed] in its place.[21]› Abū Hurayrah (may Allah be pleased with him) said the Messenger of Allah ﷺ said, "When any one of you observes the Friday Prayer, he is to offer four prayer cycles afterwards."[22]

Ibn Masʿūd (may Allah be pleased with him) would offer four [prayer cycles] before the Friday Prayer and four after it.[23] It is evident that Ibn Masʿūd (may Allah be pleased with him) knew this from the actions of the Prophet ﷺ.

...and before the Afternoon Prayer; and...

Ibn ʿUmar (may Allah be pleased with them both) reported that the Prophet ﷺ said, "May Allah have mercy upon a man who offers four [prayer cycles] before the Afternoon Prayer."[24]

‹These four [prayer cycles] should be performed in pairs.[25]›

---

20. Umm Ḥabībah: Abū Dāwūd, 1269; Tirmidhī, 427 – *ḥasan gharīb*, 428 – *ḥasan ṣaḥīḥ gharīb*; Nasāʾī, 1816; Ḥākim, 1175. See: TM, 424.
21. al-Bughā, *Al-Tadhhīb,* 45 #3.
22. Abū Hurayrah: Muslim, 881. See: TM, 428.
23. Ibn Masʿūd: Tirmidhī, 523. See: al-Nawawī, *Sharḥ Al-Muhadhdhab,* 4:10; Zakariyā al-Anṣārī, *Sharḥ Al-Buhjah,* 1:396.
24. Ibn ʿUmar: Abū Dāwūd, 1271; Tirmidhī, 430 - *gharīb ḥasan*; Ibn Ḥibbān, 2453. See: TM, 426.
25. al-Bughā, *Al-Tadhhīb,* 46 #1.

ʿAlī (may Allah be pleased with him) reported that the Messenger of Allah ﷺ would offer four prayer cycles before the Afternoon Prayer, separating between them by saying "*Al-salāmu ʿalaykum...*"[26]

2. *Witr.*

Ṭalḥah ibn ʿUbayd Allah (may Allah be pleased with him) asked [the Prophet ﷺ], "Am I required to perform [other prayers]?" He ﷺ said, "No, not unless you volunteer."[27]

ʿAlī (may Allah ennoble his face) said, "*Witr* is not incumbent, however it is a sunnah that the Messenger of Allah ﷺ established."[28]

Its minimum number of prayer cycles is one.

This is due to the hadith: "Whoever wishes to perform *Witr* with one [prayer cycle] is to do so."[29]

Its minimum complete form is three prayer cycles [i.e., two, followed by one]. Its upper limit is eleven prayer cycles.

This is due to authentic reports. ʿĀʾishah (may Allah be pleased with her) reported that the Messenger of Allah ﷺ used to offer eleven prayer cycles between the Night Prayer and Morning Prayer. He ﷺ would say "*Al-salāmu ʿalaykum...*" between every two prayer cycles, and would perform *Witr* as one [cycle]. When the muezzin was silent after [calling to] the Morning Prayer and dawn became apparent, and the muezzin came to him, he ﷺ stood, offered two

---

26. ʿAlī: Tirmidhī, 429. See: TM, 425.
27. Ṭalḥah ibn ʿUbayd Allāh: Bukhārī, 46; Muslim, 11 #8, 9. See: TM, 439.
28. ʿAlī: Tirmidhī, 453 – *ḥasan*; Nasāʾī, 1676; Ibn Mājah, 1169; Ibn Khuzaymah, 1067.
29. Abū Ayyūb: Abū Dāwūd, 1422; Nasāʾī, 1670, 1712; Ibn Mājah, 1190; Ibn Ḥibbān, 2407, 2411; Ḥākim, 1128, 1130. See: TM, 443.

light prayer cycles, and then lay down on his right side until the muezzin came to make the call to commence prayer.[30]

Abū Ayyūb al-Anṣārī (may Allah be pleased with him) reported the Prophet ﷺ said, "*Witr* is a duty. Anyone who wishes to observe it with five prayer cycles is do to so, and whoever wishes to observe it with three is to do so, and whoever wishes to observe it with one is to do so."[31]

It is best to group them [by praying two cycles and then one cycle as separate prayers], since he ﷺ would group them into even-numbered [cycles] and [end with an odd cycle i.e.], *Witr*.[32]

EMPHASIZED SUPEREROGATORY PRAYERS

وثلاث نوافل مؤكّدة: التّهجّد – وهو الصّلاة بالليل وإن قلّ – والضّحى – وأقلّها ركعتان وأكثرها ثمان – والتّراويح وهي عشرون – لغير أهل المدينة – بعشر تسليمات.

Three supererogatory prayers are emphasized:

1. **The Night Vigil Prayer [*Tahajjud*], which is prayed at night [after the Night Prayer], is recommended, even if a small quantity.**

Abū Hurayrah (may Allah be pleased with him) reported that the Messenger of Allah ﷺ was asked which prayer is most superior after the prescribed prayers. He ﷺ said, "Prayer at night."[33]

‹This prayer is known as "*Qiyām al-Layl*" and "*Tahajjud*." The latter is mention in the Quran [Q17:79].[34]›

30. ʿĀʾishah: Bukhārī, 994; Muslim, 736. See: TM, 444.
31. Abu Ayyūb al-Anṣārī: Abū Dāwūd, 1422. See: BM, 4:294–300.
32. Ibn ʿUmar: Aḥmed, 5461; Ibn Ḥibbān, 2433, 2434. See: *TM*, 446.
33. Abū Hurayrah: Muslim, 1163. See: TM, 480.
34. al-Bughā, *Al-Tadhhīb*, 48 #2.

2. **The Mid-morning Prayer [*Ḍuḥā*].**

The Mid-morning Prayer is what is intended by "sunrise [*al-ishrāq*]" in the verse "...exalting [Allah] in the nightfall and sunrise..." [Q38:18].

Its minimum number of prayer cycles is two.

Abū Hurayrah (may Allah be pleased with him) said, "My intimate friend ﷺ advised three things: to fast three days every month; to offer two prayer cycles of the Mid-morning Prayer; and to pray *Witr* before sleeping."[35]

Its maximum number is eight.

The Prophet ﷺ prayed them this way on the day of Mecca's conquest. Umm Hāni' (may Allah be pleased with her) said that the Messenger of Allah ﷺ performed the Mid-morning Prayer as eight prayer cycles, saying "*Al-salāmu ʿalaykum...*" after every two cycles.[36] ‹In addition to indicating that praying eight prayer cycles [is preferable], this hadith shows that it is best to divide them into sets of two.[37]›

There is another variation of this hadith, in which Umm Hāni' bint Abī Ṭālib (may Allah be pleased with her) reports that during the year of the conquest [of Mecca], she went to the Messenger of Allah ﷺ while he was staying in the upper part of Mecca. The Messenger of Allah ﷺ got up for his bath. Fāṭimah (may Allah be pleased with her) held a curtain around him. He ﷺ then put on his garments, wrapped himself with [the curtain], then offered eight prayer cycles of the Mid-morning Prayer.[38]

---

35. Abū Hurayrah: Bukhārī, 1981. See: TM, 456.
36. Umm Hānī': Abū Dāwūd, 1290; Ibn Mājah, 1323; Ḥākim, 1183. See: TM, 466–467.
37. al-Bughā, *Al-Tadhhīb,* 38 #3.
38. Umm Hānī': Bukhārī, 357; Muslim, 336. See: TM, 466.

Al-Rāfiʿī (may Allah grant him His mercy) said that the maximum [number of prayer cycles] is twelve,[39] because of a hadith to this affect.[40]

3. *Tarāwīḥ* Prayer, which is twenty prayer cycles (if prayed outside Medina) with ten instances of "*Al-salāmu ʿalaykum.*"

The Messenger of Allah ﷺ said, "Whoever establishes prayers faithfully during the nights of Ramadan, out of conviction and sincerity, will have all of his past sins forgiven."[41]

Tarawīḥ Prayer should consist of twenty prayer cycles, since this is what the people did during the time of ʿUmar (may Allah be pleased with him).[42]

MAXIMUM NUMBER OF VOLUNTARY PRAYERS

There is no limit to non-*rawātib* voluntary prayers. He ﷺ said, "Prayer is the best of subjects: whoever wishes can perform a little, and whoever wishes can perform a lot."[43]

It is best for voluntary prayers to be performed two prayer cycles at a time, due to the hadith: "Prayer during the night and day are two by two."[44]

---

39. Al-Rāfiʿī, *Al-Muḥarrar* (p49).
40. Abū Hurayrah: Tirmidhī, 473 – *gharīb*; Ibn Mājah, 1380. See: TM, 456, 466.
41. Abū Hurayrah: Bukhārī, 37, 2009; Muslim, 759 #173, 174. See: TM, 478.
42. Jubayr ibn Muṭʿim: Bayhaqī, 4288.
43. Abū Hurayrah: Ibn Ḥibbān, 631; Ḥākim, 4166. See: TM, 479.
44. Ibn ʿUmar: Abū Dāwūd, 1295; Tirmidhī, 424, 597; Nasāʾī, 1666; Ibn Khuzaymah, 1210, 1211, Ibn Ḥibbān, 2453, 2482–2483, 2494; Ibn Mājah, 1322. Without "day": Bukhārī, 990; Muslim, 749. See: TM, 486.

REPUDIATING PRAYER AND NEGLECTING ITS PERFORMANCE

(فصل) [تارك الصّلاة جحودًا أو كسلاً]

من جحد فرضًا مجمعًا عليه ظاهرًا كفر، أو تركه كسلاً قتل إذا أخرجه عن وقت الضّرورة، وفي الصّوم يحبس ويمنع المفطر.

Anyone who [had previously affirmed but later] openly denies an obligatory prayer, over which there is consensus, has disbelieved.

Such a person is given the opportunity to repent by praying and announcing that he believes the prayer to be obligatory. If he does not repent, he is executed as a disbeliever: he is not washed, prayed over, or buried in the Muslim graveyard.

Jābir (may Allah be pleased with him) said, "I heard the Prophet ﷺ say, 'Verily between man and polytheism and unbelief is the omission of prayer.'"[45]

Ibn ʿUmar (may Allah be pleased with them both) reported that the Messenger of Allah ﷺ said, "I was ordered to fight people until they testify that there is no deity save Allah and that Muhammad is the Messenger of Allah; to offer prayers; and to give zakat. If they do this, then their lives and property are inviolate to me except by a right of Islam, and their accounting is with Allah."[46] ‹The hadith indicates that someone who affirms the two testifications of faith is fought if he does not offer prayer, even though he is not a disbeliever.[47] (The reason for this is clarified in Ibn Mulaqqin's text and in the next hadiths.)›

[Anyone] who omits a prayer out of laziness is killed if he delays it beyond the time [when it can be delayed] out of necessity. [Any-

45. Jābir: Muslim, 82. See: TM, 749.
46. Ibn ʿUmar: Bukhārī, 25; Muslim, 22. See: TM, 748.
47. al-Bughā, *Al-Tadhhīb,* 224 #3.

one who omits an obligatory fast] is detained and prevented from breaking his fast.

This is due to the negative implication of the hadith, "I was prohibited from killing those who pray,"[48] and him ﷺ saying, "Whoever omits prayer has freed himself of the protection [granted by Islam]."[49]

Some Shāfiʿī colleagues considered delaying prayers out of laziness to be disbelief. But the majority are of the opinion that it is not.

The Prophet ﷺ said, "Allah has enjoined five prayers upon His slaves. Whoever performs them without negligently omitting anything, Allah will make a covenant with him that He will admit him to Paradise on the Day of Resurrection. But whoever performs them negligently and omits something from them will not have such a covenant with Allah: if He wills, He will punish them; and if He wills, He will forgive them."[50] ‹The hadith indicates that someone who omits prayer is not a disbeliever. If he were, the statement "if He wishes, He will admit him into Paradise" would not apply to him since disbelievers never enter Paradise. After the evidences are combined, the hadith is understood to apply to someone who has omitted a prayer out of laziness.[51]›

Someone who omits an obligatory prayer out of laziness is asked to repent. He is not worse than an apostate, and apostates are asked to repent.

[If such a person is executed,] he is washed, shrouded, prayed over, and buried in a Muslim graveyard – just like other [Muslims] who have committed enormities – because he is still a Muslim.

---

48. Abū Hurayrah: Abū Dāwūd, 4928. See: BM, 8:632.
49. Abū al-Dardā': Ibn Mājah, 4034. See: KBM, 989.
50. ʿUbādat ibn al-Ṣāmit: Abū Dāwūd, 425, 1420; Nasā'ī, 461; Ibn Mājah, 1401; Ibn Ḥibbān, 1732, 2417. See: TM, 753.
51. al-Bughā, *Al-Tadhhīb,* 224 #3.

PREREQUISITES FOR PRAYER

(فصل) [شروط الصّلاة]

شروط الصّلاة ستّة: معرفة فرض الصّلاة وسننها، ومعرفة الوقت، واستقبال القبلة إلّا في الخوف ونفل السّفر، وطهارة الحدث والخبث، وستر العورة.

There are six prerequisites for prayer:

1. **knowing which acts of prayer are obligatory and which are recommended;**
2. **knowing its time [has entered];**

‹Allah Most High says, "...Prayer at fixed times hath been enjoined on the believers." [Q4:103]. Since the times are specified, one must have knowledge of their entry.›

3. **facing the direction of prayer...**

Allah Most High says, "We have seen the turning of thy face to heaven (for guidance, O Muhammad). And now verily We shall make thee turn (in prayer) toward a *qiblah* which is dear to thee. So turn thy face toward the Inviolable Place of Worship [*al-Masjid al-Ḥarām*], ..." [Q2:144].

Abū Hurayrah (may Allah be pleased with him) narrates in the well-known hadith concerning the person who prayed poorly [*al-masīʾ ṣalātihi*]: "If you stand to pray, perform ablution properly, face the direction of prayer [*qiblah*], and say '*Allāhu akbar...*'"[52] ‹The hadith will be quoted in full in the next section.›

...– except during peril...

Peril includes fighting and other dangers. [Not facing the *qiblah* is excused] if the peril is the result of a permissible act. Allah Most High says, "And if you fear [an enemy, then pray] on foot

52. Abū Hurayrah: Bukhārī, 757; Muslim, 397. See: TM, 260.

or riding..." [Q2:239] [that is,] facing towards or away from the *qiblāh*.[53] ‹The verse is understood to mean "if you are not able to offer a complete prayer due to fear of harm from an enemy (or a flood, a predator, or the like), then pray however is easiest for you, whether walking on foot, or riding on your animal."›

...or during non-obligatory prayers while traveling;

The Prophet ﷺ would do this. Jābir (may Allah be pleased with him) reported that the Messenger of Allah ﷺ used to pray while riding on his mount, wherever it faced. According to another narration, he would dismount and pray facing the *qiblah* whenever he wanted to offer the obligatory prayer.[54]

Ibn ʿUmar (may Allah be pleased with him and his father) reported that he would pray while traveling by nodding in whichever direction his riding animal faced. Ibn ʿUmar mentioned that the Prophet ﷺ did this.[55]

If it is possible for the rider to face the *qiblah* while on his saddle[56] and to complete his bowing and prostration, then he must. Otherwise, if facing the *qiblah* is easy, he must do it; otherwise [if it entails hardship], he doesn't have to.

Deviating from the *qiblah* while traveling is permissible only when the journey is lawful. Thus, it is not permissible during journeys that are [intended for] disobedience.

---

53. Ibn ʿUmar: Bukhārī, 4535. Al-Nāfiʿ commented: "I do not think Ibn ʿUmar would say that except from the Messenger of Allāh ﷺ."
54. Jābir: Bukhārī, 400. See: TM, 228.
55. Ibn ʿUmar: Bukhārī, 1096. See: TM, 230.
56. The original has "*markad*," which is a berth. Other books mention hawdaj and ship. Ibn Mulaqqin mentions that in such cases, facing the *qiblah* is possible. See Ibn Mulaqqin, *Khulāṣat al-fatāwī*, 1:475.

4–5. absence of ritual impurity…

This is due to consensus.[57]

‹Absence from impurity here includes minor and major ritual impurity. Evidence for this includes Allah Most High saying, "O ye who believe! When ye rise up for prayer, wash your faces, and your hands up to the elbows, and lightly rub your heads and (wash) your feet up to the ankles. And if ye are in a state of major ritual impurity, purify yourselves…" [Q5:6].›

…and filth; and

This includes being free of filth on one's body, due to the hadith, "Clean it…" – meaning purify – "…from urine, since most of the torture in the grave comes from it."[58]

Filthy garments must be avoided, due to Him Most High saying, "And your clothing purify," [Q74:4], and due to the hadith: "Wash yourself from the blood and pray."[59]

And it includes the place of prayer being free from filth, due the hadith regarding pouring water on the place where the bedouin urinated in the mosque.[60]

Filth on the ground where one prostates that does not touch the body is not harmful according to the soundest opinion.

Exceptions to this prerequisite include blood from pimples, wounds, flea bites, irregular vaginal bleeding [*istiḥāḍah*], or incontinence that is difficult to avoid. These are excused due to the difficulty and hardship in avoiding them [though some require special provisions].

---

57. Ibn Mundhir, *Al-Ijmāʿ*, 33.
58. Ibn ʿAbbās: Dāraquṭnī, 1:231 #459; 1:232 #464 – with a *ḥasan* chain. See: TM(124, 346).
59. Fātimah bint Abī Ḥubaysh: Bukhārī, 228, 320; Muslim, 333 #62. See: TM, 98, 345.
60. Anas: Bukhārī, 221; Muslim, 284 #98, 99. See: TM, 347, 1769.

Other types of filth that are excused include what is imperceptible to the unaided, naked eye, and mud in the street that one is certain contains filth but is typically unavoidable. This ruling differs from time to time, where the filth is located on the garment or body, and the locale [where one is offering the prayer].

It is offensive to pray in graveyards, bathhouses, camel stables, and in the middle of a path due to the prohibitions concerning praying in such locations.[61]

It is offensive to pray in a slaughterhouse, even if one is certain that [the area set aside for prayer] is pure.

It is also prohibitively offensive to pray in a house that was stolen or [(for males) to offer prayer while wearing] a silk garment. Concerning the first situation, one is occupying someone else's property without their permission. Concerning the second, one is committing an unlawful act, though only when the silk garment is unlawful for one to wear. Nonetheless, the prayer is still valid, since the prohibition is not related to the prayer itself, but rather due to an external factor, which is what we have mentioned.

5. **covering one's nakedness.**

[One's prayer clothing] must conceal the color of the skin underneath it.

61. Ibn ʿUmar: Tirmidhī, 346–7 – the chain is not that strong; Ibn Mājah, 746, 747. See: TM, 395.

NAKEDNESS DURING PRAYER

وعورة الرّجل والأمة ما بين السّرّة والرّكبة، والحرّة ما سوى الوجه والكفّين.

The nakedness of an adult male and an adult female slave is what lies between the navel and the knees.

Concerning a male's nakedness, the Prophet ﷺ said: "A believer's nakedness is what lies between his navel and his knees."[62]

A female slave's nakedness is established via the hadith narrated by ʿAmr ibn Shuʿayb, from his father, from his grandfather [ʿAbd Allāh ibn ʿAmr ibn al-ʿAṣ] (may Allah be pleased with them), from the Prophet ﷺ who said: "If one of you marries your female slave to a male slave or to his hireling, you are not to look at her nakedness [*ʿawrah*]. Her nakedness is what lies between the navel and the knees."[63]

This is regarding her nakedness during prayer. With respect to being looked at, it is the same as a free woman's, according to Imam al-Nawawī. This is the soundest opinion amongst the critical experts [*muḥaqiqīn*]. Al-Rāfiʿī, however, considered the sound opinion to be that it is only unlawful to look at what is between the navel and the knees. (May Allah grant them His mercy.).[64]

The nakedness of an adult free female is everything besides the face and hands.

This is what is meant by Allah Most High saying, "…to display of their adornment only that which is apparent…" [Q24:31].

62. *Musnad al-Ḥārith,* 143 – but with "A man's nakedness…" See: TM, 338.
63. ʿAmr ibn Shuʿayb, from his father, from his grandfather [ʿAbd Allāh ibn ʿAmr ibn al-ʿĀṣṣ]: Abū Dāwūd, 4113–4; Bayhaqī, 3219, 4114, 13537. See: KBM, 1919.
64. al-Nawawī, *Rawḍat al-Ṭālibīn,* 7:23; al-Rāfiʿī, *Al-Muḥarrar,* 288.

‹The well-known opinion amongst the masses of scholars is that "adornment" here is the parts of a woman's body that are adorned and visible, which are the face and hands.[65]

This understanding is confirmed by ʿĀʾīshah (may Allah be pleased with her), who reported that the Messenger of Allah ﷺ said, "The prayer of a woman who has reached the age of menstruation is not accepted without a head covering [*khimār*]."[66]

If covering the head is obligatory, then the obligation to cover the rest of the body is even greater. ʿAʾīshah (may Allah be pleased with her) reported that the Messenger of Allah ﷺ would offer the Morning Prayer and the women in attendance would conceal themselves with their veiling sheets and return home unrecognized.[67]

Umm Salamah (may Allah be pleased with her) asked the Prophet ﷺ, "Can a woman pray in a long shirt and long head covering, without wearing a waist wrapper [*izār*]?" He ﷺ said, "If the shirt is ample and covers the tops of her feet."[68]

If [a garment] is long enough to cover a woman's feet while standing and bowing, it would drape down during prostration – since she draws herself together – and thus, cover her feet.[69]›

65. Ibn Kathīr, 6:45.

66. ʿĀʾīshah: Tirmidhī, 377. See: TM, 337.

67. ʿĀʾīshah: Bukhārī, 372. See: BM, 3:222–3.

68. Umm Salamah: Abū Dāwūd, 640. See: BM, 4:162–4.

69. al-Bughā, *Al-Tadhhīb,* 66 #4.

ESSENTIAL ELEMENTS OF PRAYER

(فصل) [أركان الصّلاة]

‹Evidence for most of these essential elements [*arkān*] comes from the hadith about the man who performed his prayer poorly.›

Abū Hurayrah (may Allah be pleased with him) reports that a man entered the mosque and started praying while the Messenger of Allah ﷺ was sitting somewhere in the mosque. Then [after finishing his prayer] he came to the Prophet ﷺ and greeted him. The Prophet ﷺ said to him, "Go back and pray, for you did not pray." He went back, and having prayed, came and greeted the Prophet ﷺ again. The Prophet ﷺ returned his greetings and said, "Go back and pray, for you did not pray." After the third time, the man said, "By Him who sent you with the truth, I can do no better, so teach me." The Prophet ﷺ said, "When you get up for the prayer, perform ablution properly, then face the *qiblah* and say "*Allāhu akbar.*" Then recite what is easy for you from the Quran. Next, bow until you repose in bowing, then raise your head and stand straight. Then prostrate until you repose in prostration, sit up until you repose in sitting. Then prostrate again until you repose in prostration. Then rise and stand up straight. Do all this in all your prayers."[70]

وأركانها عشر:

١. النّيّة – وهي قصد الفعل والفرض والتّعيين – ولا يشترط في النّفل المؤقّت قصد النّفل، ويشترط في غيره قصد الفعل فقط.

٢. والقيام في فرض القادر، فإن عجز فعلى حاله، وللقادر النّفل قاعدًا، ومضطجعًا لا موميًا ومستلقيًا.

٣. وتكبيرة الإحرام «الله أكبر» أو «الله الأكبر».

70. Abū Hurayrah: Bukhārī, 757; Muslim, 397. See: TM, 260.

٤. وقراءة الفاتحة في كلّ ركعة إلّا ركعة مسبوق والبسملة منها وتشديداتها ويراعى حروفها، وكذا بدلها.

٥. والرّكوع والرّفع منه.

٦. والسّجود والرّفع منه.

٧. ثمّ السّجود.

٨. والطّمأنينة بعدم الصّارف في الكلّ.

٩. والجلوس الأخير والتّشهّد فيه.

١٠. والصّلاة على النّبيّ ﷺ.

١١. والتّسليمة الأولى.

There are ten integrals [*arkān*] for prayer [mentioned in their order of occurrence]:...

‹These integrals apply whether one is the imam, praying behind him, or praying alone.›

1. **Intention, which is resolving to perform the action, affirming it being an obligation, and identifying the action itself. However, it is not a prerequisite to resolve to perform a voluntary action for voluntary prayers tied to a specific time. For actions related to other prayers, only intending its performance is required.**

There is agreement [*ittifāq*][71] that one's intention is essential, though al-Ghazālī (may Allah grant him His mercy) said that it is more akin to being a condition.[72]

71 Agreement [*ittifāq*] tends to refer to opinions held by a majority of scholars. Although their agreement suggests the strength of the opinion, the opinion is not binding on others, nor does it exclude the possibility of other current or future disagreement. Agreement should not be taken lightly, but it also should not be confused with consensus [*ijmā*ʿ].

72. al-Ghazālī, *Al-Wasīt*, 2:82.

The prayer is identified by intending it to be the obligatory Noon Prayer or the obligatory Afternoon Prayer, or a voluntary prayer associated with an obligatory prayer, or a prayer that is occasioned by an event.

2. **Standing in obligatory prayers, when one is able. If one is unable to stand, one does whatever one's situation allows. Someone able to stand may perform voluntary prayers sitting, lying on his side (but not by nodding), or lying on his back.**

The Prophet ﷺ said to ʿUmrān ibn Ḥuṣain (may Allah be pleased with him), "Pray standing. If you cannot, then sitting. And if you cannot, then on your side," [al-Bukhāri]. Another version adds: "And if you are not able, then on your back: 'Allah tasketh not a soul beyond its scope' [Q2:286].'"[73]

Concerning nodding, there is a hadith in al-Dāraquṭnī with a chain that cannot be cited as proof.[74]

3. **Saying the opening *"Allāhu akbar,"* or *"Allāhu al-akbar"*;**

There is agreement on this. It is to be concurrent with the intention, not before it or after it.

4. **Reciting *Al-Fātiḥah* in every prayer cycle.**

The Prophet ﷺ said, "A prayer wherein the person did not recite *Fātiḥat al-Kitāb* is not sufficient."[75]

‹This is also indicated in the hadith of the man who performed his prayer poorly, wherein the Prophet ﷺ said to him "recite what is easy for you from the Quran." This means *Al-Fātiḥah,* as one

73. ʿImrān ibn Ḥuṣayn: Bukhārī, 1117; Nasāʾī, 1660. See: TM, 239.

74. Jābir: Dāraquṭnī, 1320. See: BM, 3:646.

75. ʿUbādat ibn al-Ṣāmit: Ibn Ḥibbān, 1789; Dāraquṭnī, 1225; and Ibn Khuzaymah, 490. See also Bukhārī, 756; Muslim, 394 #34, #37. See: TM, 246.

variation of the hadith has instead: "Then read *Umm al-Qur'ān*," which is *Al-Fātiḥah*.[76, 77]

An exception is made for a latecomer's [first] prayer cycle.. "*Bismi llāhi r-raḥmāni r-raḥīm*" is part of *Al-Fātiḥah*,...

The Prophet ﷺ recited it at the beginning of *Al-Fātiḥah* in prayer and considered it a verse.[78]

...as are its doubled letters [*shaddahs*]. All of its letters are carefully observed and similarly, [the letters of] its substitute [for one who has not yet memorized *Al-Fātiḥah*].

5. Bowing...

This is according to consensus.[79]

...and rising from it.

The Prophet ﷺ said to the person who was deficient in his prayer, "then rise until you stand upright."[80]

---

76. al-Bughā, *Al-Tadhhīb*, 54 #1.
77. See "The man who performed his prayer poorly" on page 89.
78. Umm Salamah: Ḥākim, 848; judged authentic by Ibn Khuzaymah, 493. See: TM, 249.
79. Ibn Ḥazm, *Marātib al-ijmāʿ*, 1:26.
80. This phrase is found in the following narrations of this hadith: Abū Hurayrah: Bukhārī, 757, 793; Muslim, 397 #45; Abū Dāwūd, 856; Nasā'ī, 884, 1053, 1313, 1314; Tirmidhī, 303; Ibn Mājah, 1060. See: TM, 260. See "The man who performed his prayer poorly" on page 89.

6. Prostrating.

By consensus, "prostrating" includes the two prostrations and the seated posture between them.[81]

7. Reposing in every position, when there is no cause to turn away from it.

This is because it is mentioned in the hadith of the Prophet ﷺ [presented in the following paragraphs]. The exception is standing upright, which is [deduced] by analogy [*qiyās*].[82]

8. The final sitting, and saying the *tashahhud* therein.

Ibn Masʿūd (may Allah be pleased with him) said, "Before the *tashahhud* was made obligatory, we used to say, '...peace be upon Allah before His servants, peace be upon Jibrīl, peace be upon Mikāʾīl, peace be upon so-and-so.' So then the Messenger of Allah ﷺ said, 'Do not say "peace upon Allah" for verily Allah is Peace. Rather, say "Greetings to Allah, and prayers and goodness. Peace be upon you, O Prophet, and the mercy of Allah and His blessings. Peace be upon us and upon the righteous servants of Allah. I testify that there is no deity except Allah, and I testify that Muhammad is the Messenger of Allah."'"[83]

The shortest version is "Greetings to Allah. Peace be upon you, O Prophet, and the mercy of Allah and His blessings. Peace be upon us and upon the righteous servants of Allah. I testify that there is no deity except Allah, and I testify that Muhammad is the Messenger of Allah," ("*Al-taḥiyyāt li-Llāh salāmun ʿalayk ayyuhā al-nabī wa raḥmatu Llāhi wa barakātuhu, salāmun ʿalaynā wa ʿalā ʿibādi Llāhī al-ṣāliḥīn, ashhadu an lā ilāha illā Allāh, wa ashhadu*

---

81. Ibn Ḥazm, *Maratib al-ijmāʿ*, 1:26.

82. See "The man who performed his prayer poorly" on page 89.

83. Ibn Masʿūd: Daraquṭnī, 1327; Bayhaqī, 2843. See: BM, 4:12 #106, TM, 296.

anna Muḥammadan rasūlu Llāh") since it incorporates the meanings from the various transmissions.[84]

Imam al-Rāfiʿī (may Allah grant him His mercy) considered this version to be soundest.[85] Imam al-Nawawī (may Allah grant him His mercy) said that it is soundest to omit the phrase "I testify" and to say, "and that Muhammad is the Messenger of Allah" since they are omitted in Muslim's narration.[86] (Also, Imam al-Rāfiʿī did omit it in *Al-Sharḥ al-Ṣaghīr*.)

9. Saying the prayers upon the Prophet ﷺ [therein].

Abū Masʿūd [ʿUqbah ibn ʿĀmir al-Anṣārī] al-Badrī (may Allah be pleased with him) said, "O Messenger of Allah ﷺ, how do we pray upon you when we pray upon you in our prayers?" He ﷺ said, "Say, '*Allāhumma ṣali ʿalā Muḥammad....*"[87] It is also because of the command in Allah Most High saying, "Lo! Allah and His angels shower blessings on the Prophet. O ye who believe! Ask blessings on him and salute him with a worthy salutation" [Q33:56]. The hadith indicates obligation. There is consensus that the obligation is not outside of prayer, so it must be within prayer.

Its obligatory formulation is "*Allāhumma ṣali ʿalā Muḥammad*," because of the hadith of Abū Masʿūd (may Allah be pleased with him) mentioned above.

Its complete form is "*Allāhumma ṣali ʿalā Muḥammadin wa ʿalā ālī Muḥammad, kamā ṣalayta ʿalā Ibrāhīma wa ʿalā ālī Ibrāhīm, wa bārik ʿalā Muḥammadin wa ʿalā ālī Muḥammadin kamā barakta ʿalā Ibrāhīma wa ʿalā ālī Ibrāhīm, fi-l-ʿālamīna innaka ḥamīdun majīd*," which is established by *ṣaḥīḥ* hadiths.[88]

84. Ibn Masʿūd: Bukhārī, 831; Muslim, 402 #55. See: TM, 296.

85. al-Rāfiʿī, *Al-Muḥarrar*, 37.

86. al-Nawawī, *Minhāj al-.ṭālibīn*, 29.

87. Ibn Masʿūd: Dāraquṭnī, 1339; Ibn Ḥibbān, 1958; Ḥākim, 988; Bayhaqī, 3965. See: TM, 306.

88. Bukhārī, 3370, 4794, 6357; Muslim, 405 #65, 406 #66, 403 #60. Other transmissions include: Abū Dāwūd, 978, 1504; Tirmidhī, 483, 3220;

10. Saying the first "*Al-salāmu ʿalaykum.*"

The Prophet ﷺ said [about the prayer]: "Its opening is '*Allāhu akbar*' and its release is '*Al-salāmu ʿalaykum.*'"[89]

‹These integrals must be performed in a certain order since, in the hadith of the man who performed his prayer poorly,[90] they are conjoined with "and then" [*thumma*]. This is confirmed by the various *ṣaḥīḥ* hadiths detailing how the Prophet ﷺ prayed.[91]›

ACTIONS RECOMMENDED BEFORE AND DURING PRAYER

(فصل) [سنن الصّلاة]

PRIOR TO PRAYER

وسننها قبل الدّخول فيها الأذان والإقامة، وهما سنّة كفاية في المكتوبات.

The actions recommended prior to the commencement of prayer are:
1–2. the call to prayer [*adhān*]; and the call for its commencement [*iqāmah*].

Based on authentic reports, the call to prayer is recommended for a group of men, prior to their performance of an obligatory prayer in its current time.[92]

It is not valid to perform the call to prayer before the prayer's time has entered. The call for the Morning Prayer is an exception, since it is permissible after the middle of the night because of the report concerning it.[93]

Nasāʾī, 1285, 1287–88, 1290–92; Ibn Mājah, 900, 902, 904, 906; Ibn Ḥibbān, 912, 1957–58, 1964–65; Ḥākim, 991, 4710. See: TM, 306–9.

89. ʿAlī: Tirmidhī, 3. See: TM, 27, 235.

90. See "The man who performed his prayer poorly" on page 89.

91. al-Bughā, *Al-Tadhhīb,* 57 #2.

92. Like Ibn Masʿūd: Bukhārī, 621; Muslim, 1093 #39–40. See: TM, 197.

93. Ibn Masʿūd: Bukhārī, 621; Muslim, 1093 #39–40. See: BM, 3:196–7.

According to the new *madhhab,* the call to prayer should not be performed for makeup prayers.[94]

Women are recommended to perform the call to commence prayer. However, performing the call to prayer is not recommended for them.[95]

The rulings for individuals are the same as the rulings for a group (given above).

Performing the call to prayer is valid only if [the individual is] a Muslim (since a disbeliever is not qualified to perform an act of worship); has reached discernment (since those without it also lack the qualifications); and is male (so a call to prayer by a woman is not valid for men since it is analogous to her leading them in prayer). It is the same if the caller is a hermaphrodite.

Abū Maḥdhūrah Samurah (may Allah be pleased with him) said that the Prophet ﷺ taught him this call to prayer: "*Allāhu akbar, Allāhu akbar. Ashhadu an lā ilāha ill Allāh, ashhadu an lā ilāha ill Allāh. Ashhadu anna Muḥammad rasūl Allāh, ashhadu anna Muḥammad rasūl Allāh.*" Then one returns and says, "*Ashhadu an lā ilāha ill Allāh, ashhadu an lā ilāha ill Allāh. Ashhadu anna Muḥammad rasūl Allāh, ashhadu anna Muḥammad rasūl Allāh. Ḥay ʿala l-ṣalāt, ḥay ʿala l-ṣalāt. Ḥay ʿala l-falāḥ, ḥay ʿala l-falāḥ. Allāhu akbar, Allāhu akbar. Lā ilāha ill Allāh.*"[96]

Anas (may Allah be pleased with him) said, "It is from the Sunnah that, [after] the muezzin says '*Ḥay ʿala l-falāḥ*' during the call for Morning Prayer, he says '*Aṣ-ṣalātu khayrun mina n-naum, Allāhu akbar, Allāhu akbar. Lā ilāha ill Allāh.*'" One version has "*aṣ-ṣalātu khayrun mina n-naum*" repeated twice.[97]

---

94. al-Nawawi, *Rawḍat al-ṭālibīn* 1:197. Imām al-Nawawī mentions this, but then says that the most evident [*aẓhar*] is to make the call to prayer, since it was established in authenticated reports that the Messenger of Allah ﷺ did it, and because many Shāfiʿī colleagues have authenticated this opinion. And Allāh knows best.

95. al-Nawawī, *Rawḍat al-ṭālibīn,* 1:196.

96. Abū Maḥdhūrah: Muslim, 379 #6. See: TM, 208.

97. Anas: Ibn Khuzaymah, 386; Dāraquṭnī, 944–45; Bayhaqī, 1984. See: TM, 209.

It is recommended that the call to commence prayer be made rapidly. This is because of the hadith: "When you make the call to commence prayer, be swift. When you make the call to prayer, do it slowly."[98]

The phrases of the call to commence prayer are singular except for the two phrases of the call to prayer. This is because of the hadith: "Bilāl (may Allah be pleased with him) was commanded to make the call to prayer odd numbered, and the call to commence prayer even numbered."[99]

The call to prayer is made melodically because of what preceded.

The community as a whole is recommended to perform both calls for obligatory prayers.

Performing them is considered a group obligation because of the hadith: "When the prayer is due, one of you is to make the call to prayer, and the eldest of you is to lead it."[100] However, the soundest opinion according to al-Rāfiʿī and al-Nawawī (may Allah grant them His mercy) is that the call to prayer is recommended [and not a group obligation].[101]

DURING THE PRAYER

و[سننها] بعده:

١. رفع اليدين عند الإحرام، والرّكوع، والرّفع منه،

٢. ووضع اليمين على الشّمال،

٣. ودعاء الاستفتاح،

٤. والتّعوّذ كلّ ركعة،

98. Jābir: Tirmidhī, 195; Ḥākim, 732. See: TM, 207.

99. Anas: Bukhārī, 603; Muslim, 378 #2, 3, 5. See: TM, 206.

100. Mālik ibn al-Ḥuwayrith: Bukhārī, 631, 658; Muslim, 674 #292. See: TM, 197.

101. al-Rāfiʿī, *Al-Sharḥ al-kabīr,* 3:136; al-Nawawī, *Rawḍat al-ṭālibīn,* 1:195.

٥. والجهر والإسرار في موضعهما،

٦. والتّأمين،

٧. وقراءة السّورة،

٨. والتّكبير عند كلّ خفض ورفع،

٩. وقول «سمع الله لمن حمده»

١٠. [و] «ربّنا لك الحمد»،

١١. والتّسبيح في الرّكوع والسّجود،

١٢. ووضع اليدين على الفخذين في الجلوس يبسط اليسرى ويقبض اليمنى إلّا المسبّحة، ويرفعها عند قوله «إلّا الله»،

١٣. والتّشهّد الأوّل،

١٤. والافتراش في سائر الجلسات خلا الأخيرة فالتّورّك،

١٥. والقنوت في الصّبح، وفي الوتر في النّصف الأخير من رمضان،

١٦. والجلسة الأولى.

[The actions recommended] during prayer are:

1. Raising the hands concurrently with the opening "*Allāhu akbar,*" [before] bowing, and [after] rising.

ʿAbd Allāh ibn ʿUmar (may Allah be pleased with them both) reported: "I saw the Messenger of Allah ﷺ begin the prayer with '*Allāhu akbar.*' He ﷺ raised hands to the level of his shoulders when saying [this] '*Allāhū akbar.*' He ﷺ did the same when he said it for bowing. When he ﷺ said, '*Samiʿ Allāhu li-man ḥamidah,*' he ﷺ did the same and then said, '*Rabbana lak al-ḥamd.*'"[102]

102. Ibn ʿUmar: Bukhārī, 735; Muslim, 390 #21. See: TM, 237.

2. Placing the right hand over the left.

The hands should be placed that way on the [lower] chest. Wā'il ibn Ḥujr (may Allah be pleased with him) said, "I saw the Prophet ﷺ pray. He ﷺ placed his right hand over his left, on his chest."[103] Another narration has "at his chest," as though what is intended is placing them at the bottom of the chest.

3. Saying the opening supplication.

Our master Muhammad ﷺ would begin his prayer with "I turn my face in complete devotion to One Who is the Originator of the heavens and the earth and I am not of the polytheists. Verily my prayer, my sacrifice, my living, and my dying are for Allah, the Lord of the worlds; There is no partner with Him and this is what I have been commanded (to profess and believe) and I am of the believers. O Allah, Thou art the King, there is no god but Thee, Thou art my Lord, and I am Thy slave."[104]

The phrasing of this supplication is: "*Wajahtu wajhī lilladhī faṭara al-samāwāti wa-l-arḍa ḥanīfan wa mā anā min al-mushrikīn, inna ṣalāt wa nusukī wa maḥyāya wa mamātī li-Llāhi rabbi l-ʿālamīn, lā shar ka lahu, wa bidhālik umirtu wa anā min al-muslimīn, Allāhumma anta al-malik lā ilāha illā anta, anta rabb wa ana ʿabduka.*"

4. Seeking protection from Satan [*Shayṭān*] in every prayer cycle [before reciting *Al-Fātiḥah*].

The Prophet ﷺ would seek protection from Satan in his prayer before reciting.[105] It is recommended in every prayer cycle. The supplication for seeking protection from Satan is said silently to oneself, as is the opening supplication.

---

103. Wā'il ibn Ḥujr: Ibn Khuzaymah, 479. See: TM, 323.

104. ʿAlī: Muslim, 771 #201, 202; Ibn Ḥibbān, 1771. See: TM, 243.

105. Jubayr ibn Muṭʿim: Abū Dāwūd, 764. See: TM, 245.

5. Making utterances audible and quiet when [each is] appropriate.

Reciting is audible in the Morning Prayer, since Abū Hurayrah and Ibn ʿAbbās (may Allah be pleased with them both) said, "The Prophet ﷺ would recite in the Morning Prayer on Friday '*Alif Lām mīm. Tanzīl...*' [Q32], and '*Hal atā ʿalā al-insān...*' [Q76]"[106]

It is also audible in the Friday prayer, since Abū Hurayrah and Ibn ʿAbbās (may Allah be pleased with them both) said that the Prophet ﷺ would recite *Al-Jumuʿah* [Q62] and *Al-Munāfiqūn* [Q63];[107] during the first two prayer cycles of the Sunset Prayer, since Zayd ibn Thābit (may Allah be pleased with him) reported that *Al-Aʿrāf* [Q7] and *Al-Māʾidah* [Q5] are recited during the Sunset Prayer because he heard the Messenger of Allah ﷺ recite them;[108] and during night prayers,[109] since it is authenticated that the Prophet ﷺ would do that.

6. Saying "*Āmīn.*"

One says this after one's recitation and after the imam's recitation of *Al-Fātiḥah,* since this has been established by the Messenger of Allah ﷺ through authentic hadiths which include "When the imam says, '*Amīn,*' say, '*Amīn,*' for if one's saying of '*Amīn*' coincides with that of the angels, one's prior sins will be forgiven."[110]

Its place [within the prayer] is mentioned in a hadith from Abū Hurayrah (may Allah be pleased with him) who reported that

---

106. Abū Hurayrah and Ibn ʿAbbās: Bukhārī, 288; Muslim, 880 #66. See TM, 259.

107. Ibn ʿAbbās: Muslim, 874 #64. See: TM, 632–33.

108. Zayd ibn Thābit: Bukhārī, 754. See: TM, 168.

109. al-Barāʾ: Bukhārī, 767; Muslim, 464 #175–177.

110. Abū Hurayrah: Bukhārī, 780, 782, 4475; Muslim, 410 #72, 73 – in addition to the previous. See: TM, 252.

when the Messenger of Allah ﷺ finished reciting *Umm al-Qur'ān* [*Al-Fātiḥah*], he raised his voice and said, "*Āmīn*."[111]

Also, Abū Hurayrah (may Allah be pleased with him) reported that when the Messenger of Allah ﷺ recited the verse "Not the (path) of those who earn Thine anger nor of those who go astray," [Q1:7] he ﷺ would say "*Āmīn*" so it would be audible to those behind him in the first row.[112] Another narration includes, "...and the mosque would shake with it."[113]

7. Reciting a chapter [of the Quran after reciting *Al-Fātiḥah*].

Abū Qatādah (may Allah be pleased with him) said, "The Prophet ﷺ would recite *Al-Fātiḥah* and two chapters during the first two prayer cycles of the Noon and Afternoon Prayers. In the last two [prayer cycles] he ﷺ would recite *Al-Fātiḥah* [only]. We would occasionally hear a verse. He ﷺ would prolong the first prayer cycle, making it longer than the second; and likewise in the Afternoon Prayer." One variation also mentions that he ﷺ did the same thing in the Morning Prayer.[114]

‹Additional evidence comes from the hadiths concerning audible recitation.[115]›

8. Saying "*Allāhu akbar*" with every rise and descent.

Because the Prophet ﷺ would say "*Allāhu akbar*" with every descent and [every] rise.[116]

---

111. Abū Hurayrah: Dāraquṭnī, 2452, Ibn Ḥibbān, 1806, Ḥākim, 812, Ibn Khuzaymah, 571. See: TM, 253.
112. Abū Hurayrah: Abū Dāwūd, 934. See: BM, 3:586.
113. Abū Hurayrah: Ibn Mājah, 853. See: BM, 3:585.
114. Abū Qatādah: Bukhārī, 759; Muslim, 451. See: BM, 3:591 #41.
115. al-Bughā, *Al-Tadhhīb,* 62 #2.
116. Abū Hurayrah: Bukhārī, 784; Muslim, 392 #31, 32. See: TM, 263.

9. **Saying "*Samiʿa Allāhu li man ḥamidah*" [as one begins to rise from bowing].**
10. **Saying "*Rabbanā laka al-ḥamd*" [after one has straightened up].**

This is because of a prior hadith from Ibn ʿUmar (may Allah be pleased with them both).[117]

11. **Saying "*Subḥāna rabbī... [al-ʿaẓīm]*" when bowing and ["*Subḥāna rabbī al-ʿalā*"] when prostrating.**

Ḥudhayfah (may Allah be pleased with him) reported that the Messenger of Allah ﷺ would say "*Subḥāna rabbī al-ʿaẓīm wa biḥamdihi*" three times during his bowing, and "*Subḥāna rabbī al-aʿlā wa biḥamdihi*" three times during his prostration.[118] Another version has, "he ﷺ said during his bowing, '*Subḥāna rabbī al-ʿaẓīm*' and during his prostration, '*Subḥāna rabbī al-aʿlā.*'"[119]

12. **Placing one's hands upon one's thighs when sitting.**

One supplicates while sitting between the two prostrations.

Ibn ʿAbbās (may Allah be pleased with them both) said that the Prophet ﷺ would say between the two prostrations, "*Allāhumma ighfir lī wa-rḥamnī wa-jburnī wa-rzuqnī wa-hdinī wa-ʿāfinī wa-rfaʿnī*" ("O, Allah forgive me, give me mercy, rectify me, sustain me, guide me, pardon me, raise me").[120]

---

117. Ibn ʿUmar: Bukhārī, 736. See: TM, 275, 528.
118. Ḥudhayfah: Dāraquṭnī, 1292. See: TM, 264–5.
119. Ḥudhayfah: Nasāʾī, 1046. Also: Tirmidhī, 262 – *ḥasan ṣaḥīḥ*. See: BM, 3:610–11.
120. The phrasing combined reports from Ibn ʿAbbās: Abū Dāwūd, 850; Tirmidhī, 284; Ibn Mājah, 898; Bayhaqī, 2749, 2751; Ḥākim, 964, 1004. See: TM, 294.

One extends the fingers of the left hand and closes the right except for the index finger. One raises the index finger when saying "*illā Allāh*" [during the *tashahhud*].

Ibn ʿUmar (may Allah be pleased with them both) said that when the Messenger of Allah ﷺ sat for *tashahhud,* he would place his right hand on his right knee, clench all of his fingers, and point with the finger next to the thumb. He ﷺ would place his left hand [with fingers extended] on his right thigh.[121]

ʿAbd Allāh ibn al-Zubayr (may Allah be pleased with him) mentioned that when the Prophet ﷺ supplicated, he would point with his finger without moving it. In another narration, he said that he saw the Prophet ﷺ that way, [and that he] ﷺ would brace himself with his left hand on his left knee. And in another narration, his gaze would not go beyond his index finger.[122]

Concerning the sitting for rest [*jalsat al-istirāhah*], al-Rāfiʿī (may Allah grant him His mercy) says that the Sunnah when one stands from the sitting for rest [performed after the second prostration and before standing up] is to prop oneself up with one's hands like an "*ʿājin*" (with a *nūn*) – meaning someone kneading dough. This is done by clenching one's hands shut.[123] Ibn al-Ṣalāḥ (may Allah grant him His mercy) conveyed that al-Ghazālī (may Allah grant him His mercy) understood this from similar issues and stated it explicitly in one of his lessons.[124] Al-Nawawī (may Allah grant him His mercy) rejected this and said, "What is correct is that one opens one's hands [by extending one's fingers]," and that "linguistically, '*ʿājin*' means 'an elderly man.'"[125]

---

121. Ibn ʿUmar: Muslim, 580. See: TM, 298.
122. ʿAbd Allāh ibn al-Zubayr: Abū Dāwūd, 989; al-Nasāʾī, 1270. See: TM, 301.
123. al-Rāfiʿ, *Al-Sharḥ al-kabīr,* 3:491.
124. Ibn Ṣalāh, *Sharḥ mushkal Al-Wasīṭ,* 2:141–4.
125. The closest I could find is in al-Nawawī's *Sharḥ Al-Muhadhdhab,* 3:442. Most of al-Nawawī's text is taken from Ibn Ṣalāh. See: BM, 3:678.

13. The first *tashahhud.*

The Prophet ﷺ rectified it[s omission] via a prostration of forgetfulness. ʿAbd Allāh ibn Buḥaynah (may Allah Most High be pleased with him) said that the Prophet ﷺ led them in the Noon Prayer. He ﷺ stood after the first two prayer cycles and did not sit, so the people stood with him. When the prayer finished, people waited for him to say "*Al-salāmu ʿalaykum.*" He ﷺ said "*Allāhu akbar*" while sitting down and then prostrated twice before saying "*Al-salāmu ʿalaykum*," and then he ﷺ said "*Al-salāmu ʿalaykum.*"[126] If the *tashahhud* was obligatory, he ﷺ would have performed it.

One should pray for the Prophet ﷺ at this point [after the first *tashahhud*]. One is recommended to make remembrance of Allah Most High during this time, so it is also recommended to mention His Messenger ﷺ.

14. Sitting in the manner of *iftirāsh* whenever one sits during the prayer – other than the final sitting, during which one sits in the manner of *tawarruk*;

Abū Ḥumayd al-Sāʿidī (may Allah be pleased with him) said, "I remember the prayer of the Messenger of Allah ﷺ better than you...and when he ﷺ sat [after] two prayer cycles, he sat on his left foot and propped up the right one. And when he ﷺ sat in the final prayer cycle, he pushed his left foot forward, propped up the other, and sat on his buttocks."[127]

ʿAbd Allāh ibn al-Zubayr (may Allah be pleased with him) said that when the Messenger of Allah ﷺ sat in prayer, he placed his left foot between his thigh and shin, and stretched the right foot...[128]

126. ʿAbd Allāh ibn Buḥaynah: Bukhārī, 830; Muslim, 570 #86. See: KBM, 558.

127. Abū Ḥumayd al-Sāʿidī: Bukhārī, 828. See: TM, 287.

128. ʿAbd Allāh ibn al-Zubayr: Muslim, 579 #112. See: TM, 300.

15. Making the [*Qunūt*] supplication during the Morning Prayer...

The Prophet ﷺ did not cease performing the *Qunūt* supplication during the Morning Prayer until he ﷺ died (or until he departed this world).[129]

It is performed after rising from bowing in the second prayer cycle of the Morning Prayer because the narrators affirming this are greater in number and have better memory, according to al-Bayhaqī (may Allah grant him His mercy).[130]

The well-known supplication is: "O Allah, guide me among those You have guided..." Al-Ḥasan ibn ʿAlī (may Allah be pleased with them both) said, "The Messenger of Allah ﷺ taught me the words to say in *Witr*: 'O Allah, guide me among those You have guided, grant me security among those You have granted security, take me into Your charge among those You have taken into Your charge, bless me in what You have given to me, guard me from the evil of what You have decreed, for You do decree, and nothing is decreed for You. He whom You befriend is not humbled. Blessed and Exalted are You, our Lord.'"[131]

Its phrasing is: "*Allāhumma ihdinī fī man hadayt, wa ʿāfinī fī man ʿāfayt, wa tawallanī fī man tawallayt, wa bārik lī fī mā aʿtayt, wa qinī sharra mā qaḍayt, innaka taqḍī wa lā yuqḍā ʿalayk, wa innahu lā yadhillu man wālayta, wa lā yaʿizzu man ʿādayta, tabārakta rabbanā wa taʿālayta.*"

...and in *Witr* Prayer during the second half of Ramadan.

ʿUmar (may Allah be pleased with him) gathered the people to pray *Ṭarawīḥ* behind Ubay ibn Kaʿb (may Allah be pleased with him). He did not perform the *Qunūt* Supplication except during

129. Anas: Ḥākim – Ibn Ḥajar in *Al-Talkhīṣ al-ḥabīr* (1:443 #371 mentions that this is in a monograph related to the *Qunūt* Supplication); Bayhaqī, 3104, 3105; Dāraquṭnī, 1692–4, 1703. See: TM, 269.

130. Anas: Bayhaqī, 3131.

131. al-Ḥasan ibn ʿAlī: Abū Dāwūd, 1425, Bayhaqī, 3138. See: TM, 454.

the second half [of Ramadan].[132] There was no objection, so it became consensus.

It is also recommended to perform the supplication during the five obligatory prayers whenever there is a calamity, following the example of the Prophet ﷺ with the people who were killed at Biʾr Maʿūnah.[133]

16. The first sitting [during three- or four-*rakʿāt* prayers].

Included with this is the *tashahhud,* since the Prophet ﷺ rectified it[s omission] by making a prostration of forgetfulness. If it had been obligatory, he would have performed it. ʿAbd Allāh ibn Buḥaynah (may Allah be pleased with him) said, "The Messenger of Allah ﷺ stood up during the Noon Prayer while he should have sat. When he finished his prayer, he prostrated twice." Another version has: "The Messenger of Allah ﷺ lead us for two prayer cycles in one of the prayers and rose without sitting..."[134]

Supplicating for him ﷺ is recommended since it is a sunnah to make remembrance of Allah Most High during this time, so it is also a sunnah to make remembrance of His Messenger ﷺ.

‹It is also recommended to say a second "*Al-salāmu ʿalaykum.*"›

Saʿd ibn Abī Qawwās (may Allah be pleased with him) said, "I would see the Messenger of Allah ﷺ say '*Al-salāmu ʿalaykum*' to his right and to his left until I would see the whiteness of his cheek."[135]

ʿAbd Allāh ibn Masʿūd (may Allah be pleased with him) reported that the Prophet ﷺ would repeat "*Al-salāmu ʿalaykum*" to his right and to his left until the whiteness of his cheek was seen, [saying]: "*Al-salāmu ʿalaykum wa raḥmatu Llāh.*"[136]

---

132. Ubay ibn Kaʿb: Abū Dāwūd, 1429. See: TM, 453.

133. Anas: Bukhārī, 4095; Muslim, 677 #297; Abū Dāwūd, 1425; Tirmidhī, 464; Ibn Mājah, 1178. See: BM, 3:620.

134. ʿAbd Allāh ibn Buḥaynah: Bukhārī, 830; Muslim, 570 #85–87. See: TM, 297.

135. Saʿd ibn Abī Qawwās: Muslim, 582. See: TM, 312.

136. Abū Dāwūd, 996; Tirmidhī, 295 – *ḥasan ṣaḥīḥ*. See: TM, 313.

DIFFERENCES BETWEEN MEN & WOMEN DURING PRAYER

(فصل) [صلاة المرأة]

والمرأة تخالف الرّجل في التّجافي في الرّكوع والسّجود فتضمّ، والجهر فتخفت بحضرة الرّجال، والتّسبيح عند العارض فتصفّق بضرب اليمين على ظهر اليسار، والعورة وقد سلفت.

Women differ from men [during prayer in several ways].

1. **Men spread their limbs when bowing and prostrating, whereas women draw themselves together.**

ʿAbd Allāh ibn Mālik ibn Buḥaynah (may Allah be pleased with him) said that when the Prophet ﷺ prostrated, he would spread out his arms so that the whiteness of his armpits was visible.[137]

Abū Ḥumayd (may Allah be pleased with him) reported that he ﷺ spread his forearms away from his sides and placed his hands parallel to his shoulders.[138]

When describing the prayer of the Messenger of Allah ﷺ, Abū Ḥumayd (may Allah be pleased with him) said that when he ﷺ prostrated, he would keep his thighs wide apart without letting his stomach touch any part of his thighs.[139]

A woman draws herself together because it is more concealing.[140]

The Prophet ﷺ passed by two women who were praying. He ﷺ said, "When you two prostrate, gather some of your flesh to the ground, for indeed in this, women are not the same as men."[141]

---

137. ʿAbd Allāh ibn Mālik ibn Buḥaynah: Bukhārī, 390; Muslim, 495. See: BM, 3:665.
138. Abū Ḥumayd: Abū Dāwūd, 734; Tirmidhī, 270. See: BM, 3:660.
139. Abū Ḥumayd: Abū Dāwūd, 735. See: BM, 3:660, 3:665. TM, 288.
140. al-Shāfiʿī, *Al-Umm,* 1:138; al-Nawawī, *Sharḥ Al-Muhadhdhab,* 3:409–410.
141. Yazīd ibn Abī Ḥabīb: Abū Dāwūd, *Al-Marāsil*, 87; Bayhaqī, 3201. See: TM, 293.

2. **Men recite audibly, whereas women lower their voices in the presence of men [who are not close relatives].**

‹This is done as a precaution against temptation. Allah Most High says, "O ye wives of the Prophet! Ye are not like any other women. If ye keep your duty (to Allah), then be not soft of speech, lest he in whose heart is a disease aspire (to you), but utter customary speech," [Q33:32]. This indicates that a woman's voice can incite temptation, so she is asked to lower her voice in the presence of men who are not related.[142]›

3. **Men say "*Subḥān Allāh*" if something occurs during prayer, whereas women clap their right hand over the back of their left.**

Sahl ibn Saʿd (may Allah be pleased with him) said that the Messenger of Allah ﷺ said, "If something unusual occurs during prayer, say '*Subḥān Allāh*' since [the imam] will take heed if one says this, whereas clapping is [the way] for women [to alert the imam]."[143]

4. **Their nakedness during prayer differs, as previously mentioned.**[144]

---

142. al-Bughā, *Al-Tadhhīb,* 66 #2.

143. Sahl ibn Saʿd: Bukhārī, 684; Muslim, 421. See: TM, 355.

144. See "Prerequisites for Prayer" on page 77.

INVALIDATORS OF PRAYER

(فصل) [مبطلات الصّلاة]

ويبطل الصّلاة الكلام العمد، والعمل الكثير، والحدث، وحدوث النّجاسة من غير إزالة حالًّا، وانكشاف العورة، وتغيير النّيّة، واستدبار القبلة، والأكل، والشّرب والقهقهة بالصّوت، والرّدّة.

Prayer is invalidated by
1. intentional speech;

Muʿawiyah ibn al-Ḥakam al-Sulamī (may Allah be pleased with him) said that the Messenger of Allah ﷺ said, "Human speech is not appropriate during prayer. Rather, [one's words] consist of glorifying Allah, declaring His greatness, and reciting the Quran."[145]

‹Zayd ibn Arqam (may Allah be pleased with him) reported that he and other Companions "would talk during prayer. One of us would speak to his brother concerning his needs, until this verse was revealed: 'Be guardians of your prayers, and of the midmost prayer, and stand up with devotion to Allah,' [Q2:238] whereupon we were commanded to remain silent."[146]›

2. excessive motion;

For example, taking three continuous steps – even unintentionally – [is excessive]. The difference between minimal and excessive motion is that excessive motion is avoidable, whereas minimal motion is not. Discontinuous motion does not invalidate the prayer since the Prophet ﷺ would pray while carrying Umāmah bint Zaynab (may Allah be pleased with her); whenever he ﷺ prostrated, he ﷺ

145. Muʿawiyah ibn al-Ḥakam al-Sulamī: Muslim, 537; and others. See: TM, 350.

146. Zayd ibn Arqam: Bukhārī, 1200, 4534; Muslim, 539. See: al-Nawawī, *Sharḥ Al-Muhadhdhab*, 4:86.

would place her on the ground, and whenever he ﷺ stood, he ﷺ would carry her.[147]

Additionally, excessive motion negates the overall organization and system [*niẓām*] of prayer.

3. **ritual impurity;**
4. **the occurrence of filth without its immediate removal;**
5. **exposure of one's nakedness;**
6. **a change of intention;**

One example is intending to exit prayer.

7. **turning away from the direction of prayer;**

This is because the previous five points involve omitting a condition or an essential element of prayer.

8. **eating;**

Eating invalidates the prayer unless it is done accidentally or without one knowing that it is unlawful. In such [exceptional] cases, eating a small amount does not invalidate the prayer.

9. **drinking;**
10. **audibly cackling; and**
11. **apostasy.**

These factors invalidate the prayer because they negate its general form and its conditions.

Intentionally adding or omitting an essential element also invalidates the prayer, since it is misbehavior. Ibn Mulaqqin (may Allah grant him His mercy) knew of no disagreement concerning this.

---

147. Abū Qatādah al-Anṣārī: Bukhārī, 516; Muslim, 543 #41–43. See: TM, 357.

QUANTITIES OF PRAYER ELEMENTS

(فصل) [عدد الرّكعات والأركان]

ركعات الصّلاة المفروضة سبع عشرة ركعةً، فيها أربع وثلاثون سجدة، وأربع وتسعون تكبيرة، وتسع تشهّدات، وعشر تسليمات.

The obligatory prayers include seventeen prayer-cycles, thirty-four prostrations, ninety-four occurrences of "*Allāhu akbar,*" nine *tashahhuds*, and ten utterances of "*Al-salāmu ʿalaykum.*"

وجملة الأركان في الثّنائيّة أحد وعشرون ركنًا وفي الثلاثيّة ثمانية وعشرون، وفي الرّباعيّة خمسة وثلاثون.

The total number of integrals is twenty-one during a two-cycle prayer, twenty-eight in a three-cycle prayer, and thirty-five in a four-cycle prayer.

FORGETFULNESS DURING PRAYER

(فصل) [السّهو]

OMITTING AN OBLIGATORY ACT

ومن ترك فرضًا فلا بدّ من الإتيان به، فإن تذكّره على قرب بنى، وإلّا استأنف.

Whoever omitted an obligatory act must perform it. If one remembers it soon after [omitting it], one performs the action and continues the prayer. Otherwise, one restarts the prayer.

Abū Hurayrah (may Allah be pleased with him) said, "The Prophet ﷺ led us in one of the afternoon prayers. He prayed two prayer cycles and said '*Al-salāmu ʿalaykum.*' He then stood and leaned against a piece of wood in the front of the mosque and placed his hand upon it. Abū Bakr and ʿUmar (may Allah be pleased with them) were amongst the people [of the congregation], but they did not dare speak to him. The people left in a hurry, saying 'Has the prayer been shortened?' Among the people was a man called Dhu l-Yadayn (may Allah be pleased with him). He asked him ﷺ, 'O Messenger of Allah, has the prayer been shortened or did you forget?' He ﷺ said, 'I did not forget nor was it shortened.' He said, 'Rather, you forget.' So the Prophet ﷺ prayed two prayer cycles, then said '*Al-salāmu ʿalaykum,*' then said '*Allāhu akbar*' and prostrated as he does during prostration or longer, then he raised his head and said '*Allāhu abkar,*' then he raised his head while saying '*Allāhu akbar,*' and then he said '*Al-salāmu ʿalaykum.*'"[148]

OMITTING A LESSER RECOMMENDED ACT

وإن ترك سنّةً لم يعد إليها بعد فوات محلّها.

If one omits a lesser recommended action, one does not return to it after passing its place [in the prayer].

One does not return to a recommended action after performing an obligatory one unless it is due to following the imam, since the omitted action is not obligatory.

The soundest opinion is that one does not return to a missed recommended action after engaging in another recommended action. This is because they are not emphasized, and there is no mention of [the Prophet ﷺ] making the prostration of forgetfulness for them.

OMITTING AN EMPHATICALLY RECOMMENDED ACT

وإن ترك بعضًا كالقنوت سجد للسّهو.

If one omits an emphatically recommended action [*baʿḍ*] (like the *Qunūt* Supplication), one performs the prostration of forgetfulness.

Examples [of emphatically recommended actions] include the first *tashahhud* and praying upon the Prophet ﷺ therein. This is due to the well-known *ṣaḥīḥ* hadiths concerning them.

---

148. Abū Hurayrah: Muslim, 573 #97; Bukhārī, 482, 1227. See: TM, 398.

Other actions are analogous to these, including the supplication upon his ﷺ household in the final *tashahhud,* and the supplication for the Messenger of Allah ﷺ during the *Qunūt* Supplication.

The omission of the prayer upon his ﷺ household during the final *tashahhud* and the prayer upon him ﷺ during the *Qunūt* Supplication is rectified by the prostration of forgetfulness.

Some scholars include standing for the *Qunūt* Supplication and sitting for the *tashahhud* among the things that are rectified through the prostration of forgetfulness.

ʿAbd Allāh ibn Buḥaynah (may Allah be pleased with him) said, "The Messenger of Allah ﷺ once led us for two prayer cycles in one of the prayers..." – (in one narration: "...and got up after two prayer cycles of the Noon Prayer...") – ..."and rose without sitting. The people rose with him. When he finished his prayer and we were waiting for him to finish with '*Al-salāmu ʿalaykum.*' He said '*Allāhu akbar,*' performed two prostrations while sitting, then finished with '*Al-salāmu ʿalaykum.*'"[149]

Al-Mughīrah ibn Shaʿbah (may Allah be pleased with him) said that the Messenger of Allah ﷺ said, "If any of you stands after two prayer cycles and has not completely stood up, he is to sit. And if he completely stood up, he does not sit, and he is to perform two prostrations for forgetfulness."[150]

DOUBTING PERFORMANCE OR NUMBER OF PRAYER ELEMENTS

ومتى شكّ في عدد بنى على الأقلّ، ويسجد للسّهو.

When one has doubts concerning how many [prayer cycles one has performed], one takes the least possible number, prays the remainder, then performs the prostration of forgetfulness.

If one is unsure whether one has omitted an emphatically recommended action [during the prayer], one performs the prostration of

149. ʿAbd Allāh ibn Buḥaynah: Bukhārī, 1224; Muslim, 570. See: TM, 558.

150. al-Mughīrah ibn Shaʿbah: Ibn Mājah, 1208, Abū Dāwūd, 1036. See: TM, 402; cf KBM, 552.

forgetfulness, since the default assumption is that one has omitted [the action].

If one is unsure whether one has done something forbidden [during prayer], one does not make the prostration of forgetfulness for the same reason.

But when it comes to [doubts about] the number of prayer cycles [performed], one takes the least number, completes the prayer, and then makes the prostration of forgetfulness. This is due to the *ṣaḥīḥ* hadith from Abū Saʿīd al-Khudrī (may Allah be pleased with him) who said that the Prophet ﷺ said, "When one of you has doubt during his prayer and he does not know how much he has prayed – three [prayer-cycles] or four – he is to cast aside his doubt and base his prayer on what he is sure of. Then [he can] perform two prostrations before saying '*Al-salāmu ʿalaykum.*' If he has prayed five prayer cycles, they make his prayer an even number. And if he has prayed completely, they are in defiance of Satan."[151]

One does the same thing if one has doubts about the performance or omission of essential elements, like prostrating and bowing.

ITS PROPER PLACE WITHIN THE PRAYER

ومحلّه قبل السّلام.

The prostration of forgetfulness is performed prior to saying "*Al-salāmu ʿalaykum.*"

This is because it the more complete of the two ways the Prophet ﷺ performed it. And it has been established in the previous hadiths.

The prostration itself is recommended since it is not legislated for the omission of an obligatory act.

151. Abū Saʿīd al-Khudrī: Muslim, 571 #88. See: TM, 403.

TIMES DURING WHICH PRAYER IS UNLAWFUL

(فصل) [أوقات النّهي]

وتحرم صلاة لا سبب لها عند الطّلوع والغروب والاستواء إلّا يوم الجمعة، وبعد فعل الصّبح والعصر إلى الطّلوع والغروب، وتبطل.

It is unlawful to perform a prayer that lacks a cause...

‹It is permissible and valid to pray during the forbidden times when the reason for performing the prayer exists prior to or during its performance, such as the recommended two-cycle prayers upon entering the mosque or after performing ablution, or the Eclipse and Drought Prayers. This is in contrast to when the reason for making the prayer comes after the prayer itself, such as the Prayer of Guidance [*Ṣalāt al-Istikhārah*], which is prayed for the sake of the supplication that follows it.

The evidence for this includes the following:

Anas (may Allah be pleased with him) reported that the Prophet ﷺ said, "If anyone forgets a prayer, he is to pray it when he remembers it. There is no expiation except to pray the same." Then he recited: "...and establish worship for My remembrance" [Q20:14].[152]›

Umm Salamah (may Allah be pleased with her) reported that the Prophet ﷺ offered two prayer cycles after the Afternoon Prayers: [She said,] "I asked him about that and he ﷺ said, 'O Bint Abī Umayyah, you asked about two prayer cycles after the Afternoon Prayer. Some people from ʿAbd al-Qays came and kept me occupied, causing me to miss the two prayer cycles that follow the Noon Prayer. These are those two [prayer cycles].'"[153]

152. Anas: Bukhārī, 597; Muslim, 684 See: TM, 185; al-Shāfiʿī, *Al-Umm*, 1:97.

153. Umm Salamah: Bukhārī, 1233; Muslim, 834. See: TM, 476; BM, 3:256–63.

...when

1. **the sun is rising or setting;**
2. **[the sun is] at its zenith (except on Friday); and**
3. **after performing the Morning or Afternoon Prayers until the sun has risen or set [respectively].**

Prayer is invalid [during those times].

This is due to the authentic reports establishing this prohibition.

The bulk of evidence includes reports in al-Bukhārī and Muslim from ʿUmar, Abū Hurayrah, Abū Saʿīd al-Khudrī, Ibn ʿUmar, Abū Baṣrah al-Ghaffārī, and ʿUqbah ibn ʿĀmir (may Allah be pleased with them).[154] Examples include the following:

Abū Saʿīd al-Khudrī (may Allah be pleased with him) said, "I heard the Messenger of Allah ﷺ say, 'There is no prayer after the Morning Prayer until the sun rises, and there is no prayer after the Afternoon Prayer until the sun sets.'"[155]

ʿUqbah ibn ʿĀmir (may Allah be pleased with him) said, "There were three times during which the Messenger of Allah ﷺ forbade us to pray or bury our dead: when the sun begins to rise until it has fully risen; when the sun is at the height of its midday heat until it passes its zenith; and when the sun draws near to setting."[156]

‹The negation here indicates prohibition, and prohibition means invalidity. Thus, one is not to pray during these times and if one does, it is invalid.[157]›

ولا يكره شيء من ذلك بمكّة.

None of the aforementioned are offensive [or invalid] in Mecca.

---

154. Bukhārī, 581–9, and Muslim, 825 #285–831 #293. See: TM, 187–9.
155. Abū Saʿīd al-Khudrī: Bukhārī, 581; Muslim, 827. See: BM, 2:243.
156. ʿUqbah ibn ʿĀmir: Muslim, 831. See: TM, 187.
157. al-Bughā, *Al-Tadhhīb,* 70 #3.

CONGREGATIONAL PRAYER

(فصل) [صلاة الجماعة]

The textual foundation for the legislation of prayer in congregation – prior to consensus – is Allah Most High saying, "And when thou (O Muhammad) art among them and arrangest (their) prayer for them..." [Q4:102]. He Most High commanded it in times of peril, so it is even more appropriate in times of safety. Further evidence for it will be mentioned [in this section].

والجماعة سنّة في المكتوبات.

Congregational prayer is recommended for obligatory prayers.

This is for both men and women. He ﷺ said, "Prayer in congregation is twenty-seven times superior to prayer offered by an individual."[158]

Imam al-Rāfiʿī (may Allah grant him His mercy) considered it recommended. However, the soundest opinion is that it is a group obligation for men. Evidence for this includes the statement from the Prophet ﷺ: "If three men are in a village or in the desert and prayer is not offered in congregation, Satan has mastery over them."[159]

ولا بدّ من نيّة الإئتمام.

One must intend to follow the imam.

The imam must intend to lead in order for his leadership to be valid and for him to obtain the reward for praying in congregation, in accordance to the hadith: "Actions are according to intentions..."

Similarly, if an individual follows the motions of someone else without intending him to be the imam, the prayer is not valid.

158. Ibn ʿUmar: Bukhārī, 645; Muslim, 650 #249. See: TM, 492.

159. Abū Dardāʾ: Abū Dāwūd, 547, Nasāʾi, 847, Ibn Ḥibbān, 2101. See: TM, 495.

ولا يصحّ اقتداء رجل ولا خنثى بامرأة ولا خنثى، ويؤتمّ بالعبد والمراهق، والحرّ والبالغ أولى منهما.

It is not valid for a man or hermaphrodite to be led by either a woman...

Jābir (may Allah be pleased with him) said that the Prophet ﷺ said, "No woman is to lead a man in prayer."[160]

‹Mālik ibn al-Ḥuwayrith (may Allah be pleased with him) said, "I heard the Messenger of Allah ﷺ say, 'Whoever visits a people is not to lead them [in prayer]. One of their men is to lead them.'"[161] The negative implication is that women do not lead a group of people that includes men.›

...or a hermaphrodite.

This is because of the possibility that the follower is a male and the one being followed is a female.

It is valid to follow a slave...

Anas (may Allah be pleased with him) narrated that the Messenger of Allah ﷺ said, "Listen and obey, even if the one appointed over you is an Ethiopian slave with a head like a raisin."[162]

...or an adolescent...

ʿAmr ibn Salamah (may Allah be pleased with him) lead his people in prayer when he was six or seven years of age.[163]

---

160. Jābir: Ibn Mājah, 1081. See TM, 527.
161. Mālik ibn al-Ḥuwayrith: Abū Dāwūd, 596, Tirmidhī, 356, Bayhaqī, 5324. See: al-Bughā, *Al-Tahdhīb fi adillat Matn al-ghāyat wa al-taqrīb*, 72.
162. Anas: Bukhārī, 7142. See: TM, 531.
163. ʿAmr ibn Silamah: Bukhārī, 4302. See: TM, 529.

...– but following [an imam] who is free or mature is better than [following] either of those two.

ولا يصّحّ الاقتداء بالأمّيّ، وهو من يخلّ بحرف من الفاتحة.

It is not valid to be led by an illiterate [*ummī*] who recites *Al-Fātiḥah* incorrectly – even if the error is a [single] letter.

Since reciting *Al-Fātiḥah* in its entirety is an essential element [of prayer] (as is already known), the prayer of someone who makes mistakes in *Al-Fātiḥah* is valid [only] for himself out of necessity, due to his inability to learn.

وإذا جمعهما مسجد صحّ الاقتداء ما لم يتقدّم عليه.

If two people are together in a mosque, it is valid [for one of them] to follow [the other (i.e., the imam)] provided that he does not advance closer [to the direction of prayer than his imam].

Departing from the imam's actions invalidates one's prayer, so standing closer to the direction of prayer is even more excessive. There is no harm in standing parallel to the imam.

وإذا صلّى خارجه بصلاته جاز إذا لم يحلّ بينهما حائل، اللّهمّ إلّا إذا زاد ما بينهما على ثلثمائة ذراع.

It is permissible to follow the imam while one is praying outside of the mosque, provided there is no barrier between [the follower and the prayer line within the mosque] – unless the distance between them exceeds 300 *dhirā*ʿ [approximately 144 meters or 472 feet].

The follower must be aware of the imam's prayer, either by hearing or seeing him. The follower must neither advance closer [towards the *Ka*ʿ*bah*] than the imam nor inexcusably lag behind him (by two essential prayer elements). If he does so, his prayer is invalid due to intentional disharmony.

Whoever performs the bowing of a prayer cycle has caught that cycle, because the Prophet ﷺ said, "Whoever catches a prayer cycle from a prayer has caught that prayer."[164] However, the merit of the group prayer is obtained by even less, such as the *tashahhud*, since one has caught a portion of the prayer.

SHORTENING & COMBINING PRAYERS

(فصل) [صلاة المسافر]

SHORTENING

The textual foundation for shortening prayers, before consensus, is Allah Most High saying, "And when ye go forth in the land, it is no sin for you to curtail (your) prayer if ye fear that those who disbelieve may attack you..." [Q4:101]. He Most High permitted it during travel, provided there was danger from disbelievers. The Sunnah established its permissibility in times of safety.

Yaʿlā ibn Umayyah (may Allah be pleased with him) reports that he said to ʿUmar ibn al-Khaṭṭāb (may Allah be pleased with him), "Allah has said, 'And when you travel throughout the land, there is no blame upon you for shortening the prayer, [especially] if you fear that those who disbelieve may disrupt [or attack] you,' but the people are now safe [so how can they shorten]?" He replied, "I also wondered about this in the same manner that you have, so I asked the Messenger of Allah ﷺ about it. He ﷺ said, 'It is an act of charity that Allah has given you, so accept His charity.'"[165]

وقصر الرّباعيّات جائز في السّفر الطّويل المباح، وهو مرحلتان بسير الأثقال.

Shortening four-cycle [i.e., four *rakaʿāt*] prayers is permissible during a journey...

This is because of authentic reports [including the previous one].

164. Abū Hurayrah: Bukhārī, 580; Muslim, 607 #161. See: TM, 184; cf 570; 666.

165. Yaḥyā ibn Umayyah: Muslim, 686. See: TM, 581.

Four-cycle prayers that one missed while one was a resident cannot be shortened when one travels. If a prayer is missed while traveling, the soundest of the two opinions according to al-Rāfiʿī (may Allah grant him His mercy) is that one must complete it as four,[166] since shortening is due to the hardship of traveling, and the hardship ceases once one becomes a resident.

...that is itself permissible...

Shortening prayers is not valid for an impermissible journey, such as a wife traveling against her husband's wishes. Shortening is meant to facilitate reaching one's destination, not to enable disobedience. And it is not what is intended by the verse.

If a permissible journey becomes an act of disobedience, shortening is no longer permissible.

If during an unlawful journey, one repents from its unlawful aspect, the journey's length is based on the place of repentance.

...and long – meaning two *marḥalah* [two days' distance] of travel with heavy loads [approximately 50 miles or 81 kilometers].

Ibn ʿUmar and Ibn ʿAbbās (may Allah be pleased with them and their fathers) would shorten prayers upon reaching a distance of four *burud*, which is sixteen *farsakh*.[167, 168] ‹Neither of them would have done this without knowledge from the Prophet ﷺ.[169]›

166. al-Rāfiʿī, *Al-Muḥarrar,* 61; al-Nawawī, *Minhāj al-ṭālibīn,* 44; ibid., *Rawḍat al-ṭālibīn,* 1:389.

167. 1 *farsakh* is approximately 5 kilometers or 3.125 miles.

168. ʿUmar and Ibn ʿAbbās: al-Bayhaqī, 5392–5404; Bukhārī, before 1086; al-Dāraquṭnī, 1477. See: TM, 578.

169. al-Bughā, *Al-Tadhhīb,* 73 #1.

ولا بدّ من نيّة القصر عند الإحرام، والتّحرز عن المنافي في الدّوام.

One must intend to shorten the prayer while one is making the opening "*Allāhu akbar,*" and then avoid anything that negates its continuation [for the duration of the prayer].

If one forgets to intend to shorten, intends to perform the full prayer, or is indecisive, one must perform the prayer in its entirety.

COMBINING

والجمع تقديمًا وتأخيرًا جائز إلا بالمطر فيمتنع التأخير.

Combining (whether by preempting or delaying) is permissible,...

It is permissible (thought not best) for someone on a lawful journey to combine the Noon and Afternoon Prayers, and the Sunset and Night Prayers, at either of their times, once he has reached a distance of two days of traveling. The conditions for doing so include that he has passed the walls of his people [i.e., his locale's city limits] (or buildings, in the absence of walls; or tents, in the absence of walls and buildings); he has made the intention to delay the prayer during the first prayer's time, or the intention to combine before finishing the first prayer; and he does not separate the two prayers with speech or the like (other than with the call to prayer, call to commence, light speech, or by making purification). All of this is due to the well-known hadiths on the topic.

Concerning combining the Sunset and Night Prayers, Ibn ʿUmar (may Allah be pleased with them both) would combine the Sunset and Night Prayers (after the red glow [of the sun] disappeared) whenever he was travelling. He would say, "When the Messenger of Allah ﷺ was in the midst of travel, he would combine the Sunset and Night Prayers."[170]

170. Ibn ʿUmar: Bukhārī, 1106, 1805, 3000; Muslim, 703 #42–44; Nasāʾī, 598–600, *Al-Kubrā,* 1572, 1577. See: TM, 588.

The general evidence for combining the Noon and Afternoon Prayers comes from Anas ibn Mālik (may Allah be pleased with him) who said, "When the Messenger of Allah ﷺ wanted to depart before the sun reached its zenith, he would delay the Noon Prayer until the time of the Afternoon Prayer. He ﷺ would then descend [from his mount] and combine them. And if the sun passed its zenith before he ﷺ departed, he would pray the Noon Prayer and then ride."[171]

Other Companions (may Allah be pleased with them) also narrated evidence permitting combining prayers at either of these times. Ibn ʿAbbās (may Allah be pleased with them both) said that the Messenger of Allah ﷺ would combine the Noon and Afternoon Prayers, and combine the Sunset and Night Prayers when travelling.[172]

Another example comes from Muʿādh (may Allah be pleased with him) who said, "At the Battle of Tabūr, if the Prophet ﷺ wanted to depart before the sun's decline, he ﷺ would delay the Noon Prayer so he ﷺ could pray it with the Afternoon Prayer. And if he ﷺ wanted to travel after the sun's decline, he ﷺ would pray the Noon and Afternoon Prayers together, and then travel. If he ﷺ departed before sunset, he ﷺ would delay the Sunset Prayer so he could pray it with the Night Prayer."[173]

...except delaying for rain, which is excluded.

The conditions for joining prayers due to rain include that the prayer be performed in congregation in a mosque or in a remote area [relative to one's location]. It is not permissible to delay combining the prayers until the time of the second prayer since the rain might stop by then and, thus, the first prayer would be performed outside its time without a valid excuse.

171. Anas ibn Mālik: Bukhārī, 1111–1112; Muslim, 704 #46–48; Abū Dāwūd, 1211–1212; Nasāʾī, *Al-Kubrā,* 1062, 1066. See: TM, 587.

172. Ibn ʿAbbās: Bukhārī, 1107. See: al-Bughā, *Al-Tadhhīb,* 73 #4.

173. Muʿādh: Abū Dāwūd, 1208, Tirmidhī, 553. See: TM, 589.

Ibn ʿAbbās (may Allah be pleased with them both) said, "While in Medina, the Prophet ﷺ prayed seven and eight prayer-cycles: the Noon and Afternoon Prayers, and the Sunset and Night Prayers…." (Muslim's transmission includes "…without being in a state of fear or on a journey.") Ibn ʿAbbās (may Allah be pleased with them both) was asked, "Perhaps it was during a rainy night?" He replied, "Perhaps."[174]

FRIDAY PRAYER

(فصل) [صلاة الجمعة]

‹The textual foundation for Friday Prayer [*Ṣalāt al-Jumuʿah*] is "O ye who believe! When the call [*adhān*] is heard for the prayer of the day of congregation, haste unto remembrance of Allah and leave your trading. That is better for you if ye did but know" [Q62:9].[175]›

ʿAbd Allāh ibn ʿUmar and Abū Hurayrah (may Allah be pleased with them) heard the Messenger of Allah ﷺ say [while] on the planks of his pulpit: "People are to cease missing the Friday Prayers or Allah will seal their hearts, and then they will be among the negligent."[176]

WHO IS OBLIGATED TO ATTEND

الجمعة فرض عين بشرط الإسلام والبلوغ والعقل والحرّيّة والذّكورة والصّحّة والاستيطان.

The Friday Prayer is a personal obligation, provided that one [is]:

1. **a Muslim;**
2. **mature;**
3. **of sound mind;**
4. **free;**

---

174. Ibn ʿAbbās: Bukhārī, 543; Muslim, 705 #49–50. See: TM, 591.

175. al-Bughā, *Al-Tadhhīb,* 74 #2.

176. ʿAbd Allāh ibn ʿUmar and Abū Hurayrah: Muslim, 865. See: KBM, 718.

5. male;
6. of sound health; and
7. a resident.

Anyone who is required to pray the Noon Prayer is required to attend the Friday Prayer, except for women, male slaves, those who are immature, the sick, and anyone who is otherwise excused from congregational prayers. He ﷺ said, "The Friday Prayer is an obligation upon every Muslim, in congregation, except for four: owned slaves, women, youths, and the sick."[177]

Someone attending a sick person is not required to go, since he is occupied with attending the sick.

A person who is ill and inside the mosque when the time for Friday Prayer enters must attend, unless he is harmed by waiting.

Fear of a tyrant or [excessive] water [on the path to the mosque] that wets one's clothing are excuses for missing congregational prayer, so they are also excuses for missing the Friday Prayer.

Someone who cannot hear the [unamplified] call to prayer being made from a place where its performance is obligatory is not required to attend. The Prophet ﷺ said, "The Friday Prayer is a duty for those who hear its call."[178]

CONDITIONS FOR ITS PERFORMANCE

وشرط فعلها: البلد، وأربعون من أهلها لا يظعنون إلّا لحاجة، والوقت.

The performance of the Friday Prayer is subject to certain conditions, namely that:

1. [it is performed] in a permanent settlement;

The Prophet ﷺ and his Companions (may Allah be pleased with them) only prayed it this way. Arab tribes staying around Medina did not pray it, and the Prophet ﷺ did not order them to pray it.

---

177. Ṭāriq ibn Shihāb: Abū Dāwūd, 1067; Ḥākim, 1062. See: TM, 592–3.

178. ʿAbd Allāh ibn ʿĀmr: Abū Dāwūd, 1056, 1069. See: TM, 595.

2. **[the congregation includes] forty of those who are required to attend and who do not reside elsewhere part of the year except out of need; and...**

Jābir (may Allah be pleased with him) said, "The Sunnah has been that... in every [group of] forty and above, there is a Friday Prayer."[179]

3. **its time [remains].**

The Friday Prayer's time is the same as that of the Noon Prayer.

Salamah ibn al-Akwaʿ (may Allah be pleased with him) said, "We would offer the Friday Prayer with the Prophet ﷺ and then depart while the walls provided no shade for us to screen ourselves."[180]

Sahl ibn Saʿd (may Allah be pleased with him) said, "We did not have a midday nap [*qaylūlah*] or lunch except after the Friday Prayer."[181]

‹The two hadiths indicate that the Friday Prayer was not prayed except during the time of the Noon Prayer and at its start.[182]›

OBLIGATORY ELEMENTS

وفرضها: تقدّم خطبتين بالقيام والجلوس بينهما، وإسماع أربعين كاملين.

The following elements are obligatory for the Friday Prayer:

The prayer itself is two prayer cycles in length, according to consensus.

ʿUmar (may Allah be pleased with him) said, "The Friday Prayer is two prayer cycles... as stated by Muhammad ﷺ."[183]

---

179. Jābir: Dāraquṭnī, 1579; Bayhaqī, 5607. See: TM, 721.

180. Salamah ibn al-Akwaʿ: Bukhārī, 4168; Muslim, 860. See: TM, 600.

181. Sahl ibn Saʿd: Muslim, 897, 859. See: TM, 602.

182. al-Bughā, *Al-Tadhhīb,* 76 #1.

183. ʿUmar: Nasā'ī, 1420. See: TM, 686. Al-Rūyānī, *Baḥr al-madhhab*, 2:390.

1. **two sermons preceding the prayer, both of which are delivered by the imam while he is standing and between which he sits;**

Ibn ʿUmar (may Allah be pleased with them both) reported that the Prophet ﷺ did not pray the Friday Prayer except with two sermons.[184]

The sermons should include praise of Allah, prayers upon the Prophet ﷺ, admonitions inspiring Godfearingness, and recitation of the Quran – following the example of the Prophet ﷺ.

ʿUmar (may Allah be pleased with him) said that the Prophet ﷺ delivered a sermon on Friday. He ﷺ praised Allah and extolled Him.[185]

Jābir (may Allah be pleased with him) reported that during his sermons, the Prophet ﷺ advised people to have Godfearingness.[186]

Umm Hishām bint Ḥārithah (may Allah be pleased with her) said, "I did not memorize *Qāf* [Q50] except from the mouth of Allah's Messenger ﷺ, who included it in each Friday's sermon."[187]

The Quran must be recited in at least one of the sermons.

The supplication is required in the second sermon, since it is more appropriate as a conclusion.

Standing and sitting are based on the Prophet's actions ﷺ.

Jābir ibn Samurah (may Allah be pleased with him) said, "The Messenger of Allah ﷺ would deliver the [first] sermon while standing, then would sit, and then would stand and deliver the [second] sermon. Whoever told you that he ﷺ would deliver the sermon seated has lied. By Allah, I prayed more than two thousand prayers with him ﷺ," (which means two thousand prayers other than the Friday Prayer). Another version of the hadith has "The Messenger of Allah ﷺ had two sermons; he would sit between them reading Quran and reminding the people." Yet another has "He ﷺ would deliver the sermon standing, then sit without speaking."[188]

---

184. Ibn ʿUmar: Bukhārī, 928; Muslim, 862 #34. See: KBM, 731.

185. ʿUmar: Ibn Mājah, 1014. See: KBM, 733.

186. Jābir: Muslim, 867. See: BM, 4:609.

187. Umm Hishām bint Ḥārithah: Muslim, 873 #52. See: BM, 4:610.

188. Jābir ibn Samurah: Muslim, 862 #35, 867 #34 [respectively], Abu Dāwūd, 1095. See: TM, 608.

Ibn ʿUmar (may Allah be pleased with them both) said, "The Prophet ﷺ used to deliver the sermon while standing and then he would sit, then stand again, just as you do now."[189]

The sequence of the essential elements is not required. However, consecutiveness, ritual purity, purity from filth, and covering one's nakedness all are.

2. the presence of forty congregants [all of whom meet the conditions mentioned above] to hear the sermons.

Jābir (may Allah be pleased with him) said, "The precedent of the Sunnah is that in every forty and above, there is a Friday Prayer."[190]

According to the old school, three congregants suffice.[191]

The Friday Prayer is not valid for people who live in encampments or similar temporary settlements.

It is best that the Friday Prayer be held in a single mosque – following the example of the Prophet ﷺ and the Rightly Guided Caliphs (may Allah be pleased with them) – unless there are too many congregants for one mosque.[192]

RECOMMENDED ACTS

وسننها: الغسل، والتّطيّب، ولبس البياض والإنصات، والمشي بسكينة ووقار، ومن دخل والإمام يخطب صلّى ركعتين خفيفتين ثمّ يجلس.

The recommended actions associated with the Friday Prayer include:

1. performing the purificatory bath;

---

189. Ibn ʿUmar: Bukhārī, 920; Muslim, 861 #33. See: BM, 4:606.

190. Jābir: Dāraquṭnī, 1579; Bayhaqī, 5607. See: KBM, 721.

191. al-Nawawī, *Rawḍat al-ṭālibīn,* 2:7. However, Imām al-Nawawī mentions that most of the colleagues did not confirm it as an opinion.

192. Ibn al-Mundhir, *Al-Awsaṭ,* 4:116.

The Prophet ﷺ said, "Whoever [wishes to] attend the Friday Prayer is to bathe."[193]

It is not obligatory because Samurah ibn Jundab (may Allah be pleased with him) reported that the Prophet ﷺ said, "Whoever performs ablution on Friday is upon it [i.e., the Sunnah] and will receive a blessing. And as for whoever bathes, bathing is more virtuous."[194]

It is recommended to depart for the prayer early.

The Prophet ﷺ said, "Whoever bathes on Friday and then goes [to the mosque] in the first hour, it is as though he has offered a camel as a sacrifice. Whoever goes during the second hour, it is as though he has offered a cow as a sacrifice. Whoever goes in the third hour, it is as though he has offered a horned ram as a sacrifice. And whoever goes in the fourth hour, it is as though he offered a chicken as a sacrifice. Whoever goes in the fifth hour, it is as though he has offered an egg as a sacrifice. And when the imam goes forth [to perform his sermon], the angels attend and listen to the remembrance."[195]

2. **applying perfume;**
3. **wearing white;**

The Prophet ﷺ said, "Wear your white garments since they are among your best garments."[196]

It is also recommended to remove any hair [that is recommended to remove], trim one's nails, remove offensive odors, apply scent, and use a toothstick.

---

193. Ibn ʿUmar: Bukhārī, 877; Muslim, 844 #2; Ibn Ḥibbān, 1227. See: TM, 634, cf 644.
194. Samurah: Abū Dāwūd, 354; Tirmidhī, 497; Ibn Mājah, 1091; Nasāʾī, 1380; Ibn Khuzaymah, 1756, 1757, 1818. See: TM, 644.
195. Abū Hurayrah: Al-Bukhārī, 881 and Muslim, 850 #10.
196. Ibn Abbās: Abū Dāwūd, 3878, 4061; Tirmidhī, 994 – *ḥasan ṣaḥīḥ*; Ibn Mājah, 3566; Ḥākim, 1308, 7375, 7378; Ibn Ḥibbān, 5423. See: TM, 778, 1081.

Abū Hurayrah (may Allah be pleased with him) reported that the Prophet ﷺ would trim his nails and mustache on Fridays before going out to the prayer.[197]

4. listening attentively;...

Abū Hurayrah (may Allah be pleased with him) reported that the Prophet ﷺ said, "On Friday, if you tell your companion to keep quiet and listen while the imam delivers his sermon, surely you have uttered wrongly."[198]

5. walking to the prayer with calmness and dignity; and...

Abū Qatādah (may Allah be pleased with him) reported that the Messenger of Allah ﷺ said, "When one of you comes to the prayer, he is to arrive with composure. Pray whatever you reach; complete whatever you miss."[199]

6. Offering two brief prayer cycles when entering the mosque during the imam's sermon, then sitting.

Jābir ibn ʿAbd Allāh (may Allah be pleased with him) narrated: "The Messenger of Allah ﷺ said, 'When one of you comes to the Friday Prayer while the imam is delivering the sermon, he is to pray two prayer cycles and make them short.'"[200]

---

197. Abū Hurayrah: al-Bazzār, 8291; Bayhaqī, 5964. See: TM, 657.
198. Abū Hurayrah: Bukhārī, 934; Muslim, 851. See: TM, 617.
199. Abū Qatādah: Bukhārī, 635; Muslim, 603 #155. See TM, 651. Also from Abū Hurayrah, agreed upon. See TM, 652–53.
200. Jābir: Bukhārī, 931; Muslim, 875 #55. See: BM, 4:618; Ibn Rifʿat, *Kifāyat al-nabīh fī sharḥ Al-Tanbīh,* 4:395.

THE TWO EIDS

(فصل) [صلاة العيدين]

THEIR RULINGS

وصلاة العيدين سنّة.

The Eid Prayers are recommended.

They each consist of two prayer cycles.

This is according to consensus,[201] and ‹affirmed by› ʿUmar (may Allah be pleased with him) who said "The [Eid] al-Fiṭr Prayer is two prayer cycles, the prayer of [Eid] al-Aḍḥā is two prayer cycles… from the mouth of Muhammad ﷺ."[202]

Their times begin when the sun has risen and end when it reaches its zenith.

THEIR PERFORMANCE

يكبّر في الأولى سبعًا سوى تكبيرة الإحرام، وفي الثانيّة خمسًا سوى تكبيرة القيام، ويخطب بعدها خطبتين.

In the first prayer cycle [*rakʿah*], [the imam] says "*Allāhu akbar*" seven times, in addition to the opening "*Allāhu akbar*." In the second cycle, he says it five times, in addition to the one for rising [from prostration].

ʿAmr bin ʿAuf al-Muzanī (may Allah be pleased with him) reported that the Prophet ﷺ pronounced *takbīr*s in the two Eid prayers: [there were] seven in the first [prayer cycle] before recitation, and five in the second [prayer cycle] before recitation.[203]

---

201. Ibn Ḥazm, *Marātib al-Ijmāʿ*, 32.
202. ʿUmar: Nasāʾī, 1420, Ibn Mājah, 1064, Ibn Khuzaymah, 1425, Ibn Ḥibbān, 2784; al-Bayhaqī, 5719. See: TM, 686.
203. ʿAmr ibn ʿAuf al-Muzanī: Tirmidhī, 536 – *ḥasan*; Ibn Mājah, 1277; Dāraquṭnī, 1727; Bayhaqī, 6178, Ḥākim, 6554. See: TM (687).

[The imam] delivers two sermons after the prayer.

Ibn ʿUmar (may Allah be pleased with them both) said, "The Prophet ﷺ Abū Bakr, and ʿUmar (may Allah be pleased with them both) would offer the Eid [prayers] before giving the sermons."[204]

‹ʿUbayd Allah ibn ʿAbd Allāh ibn ʿUtbah (may Allah be pleased with him) said that the Sunnah is the imam giving two sermons for the two Eids and separating them by sitting.[205]›

[The imam] says *"Allāhu akbar"* nine times before the first [sermon], and seven times before the second. This is in accordance with the actions of the Prophet ﷺ.

‹Imam al-Shāfiʿī (may Allah grant him His mercy) said that the Sunnah is to begin the first sermon with nine consecutive *takbīr*s, and the second with seven consecutive *takbīr*s.[206]›

CUSTOMARY LITANIES

ويكبّر من غروب الشّمس ليلتي العيد إلى أن يدخل في الصّلاة، وفي الأضحى خلف كلّ صلاة مفعولة فيه من ظهر يوم النّحر إلى الصّبح من آخر أيّام التّشريق، والمختار من صبح عرفة، ويختم بعصر آخر التّشريق.

[One] recites the customary litanies [*takbīr*s] from sunset [on the night before] Eid until commencing the Prayer.

‹Allah Most High says, "...and (He desireth) that ye should complete the period, and that ye should magnify Allah for having guided you, and that peradventure ye may be thankful," [Q2:185]. The scholars have said that this refers to the *takbīr*s of Eid al-Fiṭr. And the *takbīr*s of Eid al-Aḍḥā are analogous to them.›[207]

---

204. Ibn ʿUmar: Bukhārī, 963, Muslim, 888 #8. See: TM, 693.
205. al-Shāfiʿī, *Al-Umm,* 1:272.
206. al-Shāfiʿī, *Al-Umm,* 1:273.
207. al-Bughā, *Al-Tadhhīb,* 79 #1.

During Eid al-Aḍḥā, one recites them after every performed prayer, from the Noon Prayer on the Day of ʿArafah until the Morning Prayer on the last of the Days of Tashrīq [13 Dhi al-Ḥijjah]. The best is to begin reciting after the Morning Prayer on the Day of ʿArafah, and conclude with the Afternoon Prayer on the last of the Days of Tashrīq.

It is reported that the Prophet ﷺ would recite the *takbīr* litanies from the Morning Prayer on the Day of ʿArafah until the Afternoon Prayer on the last of the Days of Tashrīq..[208]

ʿUmar, ʿAlī, Ibn ʿAbbās, and Ibn Masʿūd (may Allah be pleased with them) reportedly performed these litanies starting with the Morning Prayer on the Day of ʿArafah until sometime during the last of the Days of Tashrīq.[209]

THE ECLIPSE PRAYERS

(فصل) [صلاة الكسوفين]

ويصلّى للكسوف ركعتان، في كلّ ركعة قيامان وركوعان يطيل القراءة والتّسبيح، ويخطب بعدها، ويسرّ في الكسوف، ويجهر في الخسوف.

The Eclipse Prayers are offered as two prayer cycles [*rakʿatayn*]. Each prayer cycle contains two periods of standing and [two] periods of bowing wherein [the times for] recitation and saying "*Subḥān Allāh*" are prolonged.

One would be following the example of the Prophet ﷺ in all of these [actions]. ʿAʾishah (may Allah be pleased with her) said that during the lifetime of the Messenger of Allah ﷺ, the sun was eclipsed. So

---

208. ʿAlī and ʿAmmār: al-Ḥākim, 1111; al-Dāraquṭnī, 1734; al-Bayhaqī, 6278. See: TM, 709.

209. ʿUmar, ʿAlī, Ibn ʿAbbās, Ibn Masʿūd: al-Ḥākim, 1112, 1115, 1116; al-Bayhaqī, 6273, 6277. See: BM, 5:91–92

he ﷺ led the people in prayer. He stood and performed an extended period of standing, then bowed for extended period. He ﷺ then stood up again and performed a second period of standing but this time, it was shorter than the first. Then he ﷺ bowed again for an extended period, but for a shorter time than the first bow. Then he ﷺ fell into a prolonged prostration. He ﷺ performed the second prayer cycle just as he had performed the first, and then concluded the prayer. By then, the sun (eclipse) had cleared so he ﷺ delivered the sermon. After praising and glorifying Allah, he ﷺ said, "The sun and moon are two of Allah's signs: they do not eclipse for the death or life of anyone. When you witness them [i.e., the eclipses], supplicate to Allah and pray until they have passed."[210]

The imam delivers two sermons after the prayer.

This is based on the previous hadith.

The prayer for the solar eclipse is silent. The prayer for the lunar eclipse is audible.

Samurah ibn Jundab (may Allah be pleased with him) said, "The Prophet ﷺ led us in prayer during a solar eclipse [*kusūf*] and we did not hear his voice."[211]

ʿĀʾishah (may Allah be pleased with her) said that the Prophet ﷺ recited audibly in the lunar eclipse [*khusūf*] prayer.[212]

‹The first hadith applies to praying during the solar eclipse, which occurs during the day, while the second applies to praying during the lunar eclipse, which occurs in the evening.[213]›

210. ʿĀʾishah: Bukhārī, 1044; Muslim, 901. See: TM, 721, cf 714, 716–18.

211. Samurah ibn Jundab: Tirmidhī, 562 – *ḥasan ṣaḥīḥ*. See: TM, 720.

212. ʿĀʾishah: Bukhārī, 1066; Muslim, 901. See: TM, 719.

213. al-Bughā, *Al-Tadhhīb,* 80 #1.

THE DROUGHT PRAYER

(فصل) [صلاة الاستسقاء]

وصلاة الاستسقاء متأكّدة عند الحاجة إليها بعد أمر الإمام بالخروج من المظالم والصّيام ثلاثًا، ويخرج بهم في الرّابع صيامًا في ثياب بذلة واستكانة، ويصلّي ركعتين كالعيد، ويخطب، ويحوّل رداءه وينكس، ويكثر من الدّعاء والاستغفار.

The Drought Prayer is emphatically recommended...

ʿAbd Allāh ibn Zayd (may Allah be pleased with him) said that the Prophet ﷺ left to the place of prayer to pray for rain. He faced the direction of prayer, wore his cloak inside out, and offered two prayer cycles.[214]

...whenever there is need for [rain], and after the imam has [ordered the people] to cease oppression and fast for three days.

These matters have an influence on the acceptance of supplications, as has been established in hadiths.

Abū Hurayrah (may Allah be pleased with him) said, "There are three whose supplications are not rejected: someone who is fasting until he breaks his fast, a just Imam, and the oppressed."[215]

Here, the phrase "to cease oppression" refers to those who have enmity concerning worldly affairs [and must desist from it].

[The imam] leads the people out [to the prayer area] on the fourth day, while all are still fasting. They wear shabby clothes,...

‹...ordinary clothing, free of conceit or pride...›[216]

---

214. ʿAbd Allāh ibn Zayd: Bukhārī, 1012; Muslim, 894. See: TM, 723.
215. Abū Hurayrah: al-Tirmidhī, 3598; Ibn Mājah, 1752; Ibn Ḥibbān, 3428. See: TM, 725.
216. al-Bughā, *Al-Tadhhīb,* 81 #2.

...and are quiet and humble.

Ibn ʿAbbās (may Allah be pleased with them both) said that the Messenger of Allah ﷺ went out humbly, wearing work clothes, walking with a moderate gait, and beseechingly. He ﷺ offered two prayer cycles, just as he would for the Eid Prayer.[217]

The imam offers two prayer cycles, similar to the Eid Prayer.

ʿAbd Allāh ibn Zayd al-Anṣārī (may Allah be pleased with him) said, "The Messenger of Allah ﷺ went out to the prayer area [*muṣallā*]. He ﷺ asked for rain, faced the *qiblah,* inverted his cloak, and then prayed two prayer cycles. ."[218]

When asked about how the Prophet ﷺ prayed the Drought Prayer, Ibn ʿAbbās (may Allah be pleased with him) said, "...and he ﷺ offered two prayer cycles, just as he would for the Eid prayer."[219]

After the prayer, he delivers a sermon. He reverses his cloak, turning it inside out.

Abū Hurayrah (may Allah be please with him) said, "The Messenger of Allah ﷺ went out one day to pray for rain. He ﷺ led us in offering two prayer cycles without any call to prayer or call to commence prayer. Then he ﷺ addressed us and supplicated to Allah. He ﷺ turned to face the *qiblah,* raising his hands. Then he ﷺ turned his cloak around, putting its right on the left and its left on the right."[220]

---

217. Ibn ʿAbbās: Ibn Mājah, 1266. See: TM, 727.

218. ʿAbd Allāh ibn Zayd al-Anṣār: Bukhārī, 1012; Muslim, 894 #3. See: TM, 723.

219. Ibn ʿAbbās: Abū Dāwūd, 1165, Tirmidhī, 558; al-Bayhaqī, 6402. See: TM, 727.

220. Abū Hurayrah: Ibn Mājah, 1268. See: TM, 732.

He supplicates abundantly and asks for forgiveness.

During his sermons and supplications, the imam asks for forgiveness, as this is more appropriate for the situation than the *takbīr*s that are recited in the Eid sermons.

‹Evidence for this includes Allah Most High saying, "And I have said: Seek pardon of your Lord. Lo! He was ever Forgiving. He will let loose the sky for you in plenteous rain...'" [Q71:10–11].[221]›

Ibn ʿUmar (may Allah be pleased with them both) said that when the Prophet ﷺ would supplicate for rain, he would say: "O Allah, send us rain – wholesome, healthy, torrential, wide-spread, pouring in sheets, drenching rain – continuously until Judgment Day. O Allah, give us rain and make us not of those who despair. O Allah, your servants and their cities are in distress with hunger and want, from which we can ask none but You for relief. O Allah, make the crops grow and the milk of the livestock flow. Send down the blessings of the sky upon us and bring forth for us the blessings of the earth. O Allah, remove from us our troubles, hunger, and nakedness. O Allah, remove the afflictions that none but You can lift. O Allah, we seek forgiveness from You since You are Oft-Forgiving, so let loose the [rain from the] sky upon us in torrents."[222]

PRAYER DURING PERIL

(فصل) [صلاة الخوف]

The textual foundation for prayer during peril is Allah Most High saying, "And when ye go forth in the land, it is no sin for you to curtail (your) prayer if ye fear that those who disbelieve may attack you..." [Q4:101]. Also, the Companions (may Allah be pleased with them) performed it after this verse was revealed.

221. al-Bughā, *Al-Tadhhīb,* 71 #5.

222. al-Shāfiʿī, *Al-Umm,* 1:287; al-Muzanī, *Al-Mukhtaṣar,* 8:128. See: TM, 733.

وصلاة الخوف جائزة على أنحاء بطن نخل وذات الرّقاع وعسفان، والمسايفة فيصلّي على حسب حاله إلى القبلة وإلى غيرها.

Prayer during peril [*Ṣalāt al-Khawf*] is permissible according to the ways performed at Baṭn Nakhl, Dhāt al-Riqāʿ, ʿUsfān, and al-Musāyifah – where one prays however they can, facing the direction of prayer or turned away.

[1] Baṭn al-Nakhl is when the enemy is not in the direction of prayer or there is a [visual] obstruction. In either case, [the Muslims] break into two groups, so that one group can stand guard while the other one prays. The imam prays twice [once with each group].

Jābir (may Allah be pleased with him) said, "We went forward with the Prophet ﷺ..." and he mentioned the whole hadith, which included "The call to prayer was given. He ﷺ prayed two prayer cycles with one group. They then withdrew. And then he ﷺ prayed two prayer cycles with the other group." He said, "The Prophet ﷺ prayed four prayer cycles, while the people prayed two prayer cycles [each]." Another version has "...so the Prophet ﷺ prayed two prayer cycles of peril."[223] Abū al-Zubayr (may Allah grant him His mercy) reported that Jābir (may Allah be pleased with him) said, "We were with the Prophet ﷺ at the date palms [*al-nakhl*] and he prayed [the prayer of] peril."

[2] Dhāt al-Riqāʿ is when the enemy is not in the direction of prayer. [During a two *rakʿah* prayer], the imam prays one prayer cycle with each group. The imam breaks them into two groups. One group faces the enemy [while the other group stands behind him, facing the *qiblah*]. He prays a single prayer cycle with this group (which remains armed). When he stands for the [prolonged] second prayer cycle, they complete their prayer on their own. When they finish, they exchange places with the group that has been guarding. The group that has been guarding joins the imam's prayer. When the imam sits to make [a prolonged] *tashahhud,* they

223. Jābir: Bukhārī, 4136; Muslim, 843 #311; Ibn Ḥibbān, 2884. See: TM, 671, KBM, 789.

stand and continue their prayer and catch up to him before he says "*Al-salāmu ʿalaykum*" and they then [sit and] say it with him. This is how he ﷺ prayed at Dhāt al-Riqāʿ.

Concerning those who witnessed the prayer of peril led by the Messenger of Allah ﷺ at the battle of Dhāt al-Riqāʿ, Ṣāliḥ bin Khawwāt (may Allah be pleased with him) said, "One group lined up behind him ﷺ while another group faced the enemy. The Prophet ﷺ led the first group in one prayer cycle, then remained standing while that group completed their prayer by themselves. Then they went away and lined up to face the enemy while the second group came [to pray]. He ﷺ offered his remaining prayer cycle with the second group and then remained seated while they continued their prayer by themselves. [Once they caught up to him ﷺ], he ﷺ ended the prayer with them, with a *taslīm*."'[224]

[3] ʿUsfān is when an enemy (against whom fighting is permissible) is in the direction of prayer, there is no barrier between them [and the believers], and the Muslims are numerous. The imam forms the Muslims into two lines so that the enemy cannot surprise them. The imam prostrates with one line while the other stands guarding. When he rises from prostration, the line of guards takes their turn to prostrate. The Prophet ﷺ prayed this way in ʿUsfān.[225]

[4] Al-Musāyifah is referred to in the Quran: "...And if ye go in fear, then (pray) standing or on horseback..." [Q2:239] – meaning facing the *qiblah* or facing away from it.

Nāfiʿ (may Allah be pleased with him) reported that Ibn ʿUmar (may Allah be pleased with them both) described the prayer during which the peril was far greater, saying: "They prayed walking upright on their feet, or riding – facing the [proper] direction of prayer or not. Nāfiʿ (may Allah be pleased with him) did not think that Ibn ʿUmar (may Allah be pleased with them both) would have mentioned this unless it was from the Messenger of Allah ﷺ.[226]

---

224. Ṣāliḥ ibn Khawwāt: Bukhārī, 4129; Muslim, 842 #310. See: TM, 672.

225. Abū ʿAyyāsh al-Zuraqī: Abū Dāwūd, 1236. See: TM, 670.

226. Ibn ʿUmar: Bukhārī, 4535. See: TM, 673.

CLOTHING

(فصل) [اللباس]

ويحرم على الرّجل استعمال الحرير وما أكثره حرير، وكذا الذّهب إلّا لضرورة، أما المرأة فلها لبس ذلك وافتراشه.

It is unlawful for men to wear silk or that which contains silk as its majority fabric, and likewise gold – except out of necessity. As for women, they can wear these and use them for bedding.

The Prophet ﷺ said, "These two [silk and gold] are unlawful for the men of my community, and permissible for their womenfolk."[227]

227. ʿAlī: Tirmidhī, 1720 – *ḥasan ṣaḥīḥ*; Ibn Mājah, 3595, 3597; Nasāʾī, 5159, 5160 – without "permissible for their females." See: TM, cf 677; KBM, 54, 1059.

3

FUNERALS

الجَنَائِز

(فصل) [الجنائز]

PREPARING FOR DEATH

It is recommended to instruct the dying to say "*Lā ilāha illā Allāh.*" The Prophet ﷺ said, "Coach those among you who are dying to say '*Lā ilāha illā Allāh.*'"[1] And he ﷺ said, "Whoever's final words are '*Lā ilāha illā Allāh*' enters Paradise."[2]

FUNERARY PREPARATIONS

وغسل الميّت وتكفينه والصّلاة عليه ودفنه فروض كفاية.

Washing, shrouding, praying over, and burying the dead are communal obligations.

Washing, shrouding, praying over, and burying the deceased are, by consensus, communal obligations. The expenses are paid from the deceased's estate, before paying those to whom he is in debt. This is because of the well-known hadith of Khabbāb (may Allah be pleased with him) concerning inheritance.

---

1. Abū Saʿīd al-Khudrī: Muslim, 916, 917. See: TM, 758.
2. Muʿādh: Abū Dāwūd, 3116; Ibn Ḥibbān, 3116; Ḥākim, 1299, 1842. See: TM, 759.

Khabbāb ibn al-Aratt (may Allah be pleased with him) said, "We migrated with the Messenger of Allah ﷺ in the path of Allah and seeking Allah's pleasure, so our reward was assured with Allah. Amongst us were those who spent their lives without consuming any of their reward. Muṣʿab ibn ʿUmair (may Allah be pleased with him) was one of them. He was killed on the Day of ʿUḥud and nothing but a woolen cloak was found to shroud him. When we covered his head with it, his feet were exposed; when we covered his feet, his head was exposed. So the Messenger of Allah ﷺ said, 'Place it from the direction of his head and cover his feet with grass.' And there are some amongst for whom the fruit has ripened and they enjoy it."[3] ‹The last part of the hadith refers to how their worldly condition changed once Islam had spread.›

However, if someone has a claim to a specific item in the deceased's estate (such as [an item meant for] personal injury recompense or collateral), he has priority with respect to that item.

A husband is required to cover his wife's funerary expenses if he can afford to do so – just as he was required to cover her expenses while she was alive. If he cannot afford it, the expenses are paid from her own estate.

If the husband or the estate of the deceased cannot cover the expenses, they are paid from the Muslim treasury [*bayt al-māl*], since the deceased is among the needy.

ولا يغسّل الشّهيد ولا يصلّى عليه، وكذا الطّفل الّذي لم يستهلّ.

Martyrs are not washed or prayed over,...

Jābir ibn ʿAbd Allāh (may Allah be pleased with them both) reported that the Prophet ﷺ ordered that the dead from [the Battle of] Uḥud be buried with their blood on their bodies]; they would not be washed or prayed upon.[4]

3. Khabbāb ibn al-Aratt: Bukhārī, 1276; Muslim, 940 #44. See: TM, 775, 813.
4. Jābir ibn ʿAbd Allāh: Bukhārī, 1343. See: TM, 809.

...nor is a fetus that did not show signs of life.

Jābir ibn ʿAbd Allāh (may Allah be pleased with them both) narrated the Messenger of Allah ﷺ said, "If a miscarried fetus shows signs of life, he inherits and is prayed over."[5]

THE FUNERAL BATH

والواجب إمرار الماء عليه بعد إزالة النّجس، ويستحب وترًا بماء وسدر، ويجعل في الأخيرة كافورًا.

It is obligatory that water flow over [the deceased] after any filth has been removed. It is recommended to wash the deceased an odd number of times, and for the washing be accompanied by lote tree [leaves], with [a bit of] camphor in the last [washing].

It is best for the washing to be preceded by ablution, due to the *ṣaḥīḥ* hadith "Start with her right and the places where she makes ablution."[6]

Lote tree [leaves] and camphor should be used.

Umm ʿAṭiyyah (may Allah be pleased with her) said, "The Prophet ﷺ came to us while we were washing his daughter [Zaynab or Umm Kalthūm (may Allah be pleased with them both)]. He said, 'Wash her three, five, or more times than this if you deem it necessary, and add camphor to the last one' – or he said, 'or something with camphor' – 'and start with her right side and her limbs of ablution. When you finish, inform me.' When we finished, we informed him and he tossed us his waist-wrapper and said, 'Wrap her in it first.' We braided her hair into three plaits, and let them fall behind her back."[7]

---

5. Jābir ibn ʿAbd Allāh: Ibn Mājah, 1508; Nasāʾī, *Al-Sunan al-kubrā,* 6324; Ibn Ḥibbān, 6032; Ḥākim, 1345; al-Bayhaqī, 6782–83. See: TM, 808.
6. Umm ʿĀṭiyyah: Bukhārī, 1255; Muslim, 939 #42, 43. See: TM, 769.
7. Umm ʿĀṭiyyah: Bukhārī, 1253; Muslim, 939 #36. See: TM, 769.

The hair should be brushed gently, so none is pulled out.

The body should be dried after washing, so [the moisture] does not destroy the shroud.

FUNERAL SHROUDS

ويكفّن في ثلاثة أثواب بيض ليس فيها قميص ولا عمامة.

The deceased is shrouded in three white garments, which do not include a long shirt or turban.

The minimum amount according to Imam al-Ghazālī is covering the entire body. Imam al-Nawawī considered covering the person's nakedness the sound opinion.[8]

Three white shrouds comprise the complete amount. The Messenger of Allah ﷺ was shrouded in three white cotton cloths from Yemen. They did not include a shirt or a turban.[9]

Women are also shrouded with an *izār* [a long garment worn from the waist] and a *khimār* [a woman's long head covering] out of observing additional covering.

Laylā bint Qānif al-Thaqafiyyah (may Allah be pleased with her) said, "I was among those who washed Umm Kulthūm, daughter of the Prophet ﷺ after she died. The first thing that the Messenger of Allah ﷺ gave us was the lower garment [*ḥiqā'*], then the shirt [*dirʿ*], then the head covering [*khimār*], then the cloak [*milḥafah*]. She was then shrouded in another garment." She said, "The Messenger of Allah ﷺ was sitting at the door with her shrouds, giving [them to] us garment by garment."[10]

Using more than five garments is offensive, as it is wasteful.

---

8. al-Ghazālī, *Al-Wasīṭ*, 2:370; al-Nawawī, *Rawḍat al-ṭālibīn*, 2:110.
9. ʿĀ'ishah: Bukhārī, 1271–1273, 1387; Muslim, 941 #45–47. The phrase used here is from Abū Dāwūd, 3151; Tirmidhī, 996; Ibn Mājah, 1469. See: TM, 776.
10. Laylā bint Qānif al-Thaqafīyyah: Abū Dāwūd, 3157. See: TM, 777.

THE FUNERAL PRAYER

ويكبّر عليه أربعًا، يقرأ بعد الأولى، ويصلّي على النّبيّ ﷺ عند الثّانية. ويستحبّ قبلها «الحمد لله»، وبعدها الدّعاء للمؤمنين والمؤمنات، ويدعو للميّت بعد الثّالثة ويسلّم بعد الرّابعة.

[During the prayer,] "*Allāhu akbar*" is said over the deceased four times.

Abū Hurayrah (may Allah be pleased with him) said that the Prophet ﷺ informed his companions about the death of al-Najāshī the day he died. He went to the place of prayer, lined people up, and made four *takbīr*s.[11]

Intention is required.[12]

After saying the first *takbīr*, one recites [*Al-Fātiḥah*].

After the second [*takbīr*], one sends prayers upon the Prophet ﷺ – with it being recommended that "*Al-ḥamdu li-Llāh*" precede them – and then supplicates [for all] Muslims, male and female.

After the third [*takbīr*], one supplicates for the deceased.

After the fourth [*takbīr*], one says [a single] "*Al-salāmu ʿalaykum.*"

Abū Umāmah ibn Sahl (may Allah grant him His mercy) said that one of the companions of the Prophet ﷺ informed him that the Sunnah for the funeral prayer is that the imam makes *takbīr* and then reads *Al-Fātiḥah* after the first *takbīr,* silently to himself. He then supplicates upon the Prophet ﷺ. The *takbīr*s of the funeral prayer are only for supplicating for the deceased. Noth-

11. Abū Hurayrah: Bukhārī, 1245, 1333; Muslim, 951 #62. See: TM, 854.
12. ʿUmar: Bukhārī, 1; Muslim, 1907 #155. See: TM, 1, 57, 234; al-Māwardī, *Al-Ḥāwī al-kabīr,* 3:55.

ing [else] is recited after the *takbīrs*. He [the imam] then gives the *taslīm* silently.[13]

After the fourth *takbīr*, one says, "*Allāhumma lā taḥrimnā ajrahu wa la taftinā ba'dahu wa-ghfir lanā wa lahu*" ("O Allah, do not deprive us of his reward, nor afflict us after him. [O Allah,] grant us and him forgiveness.")[14] [One says, "*ba'dahā*" and "*lahā*" if the deceased is female.]

Adding a fifth [saying of "*Allāhu akbar*"] does not invalidate the prayer, according to the soundest opinion.

Zayd ibn Arqam (may Allah be pleased with him) said, "The Prophet ﷺ would say '*Allāhu akbar*' four and five times for funerals."[15]

After the prayer, when the deceased is carried to be buried, it is best to walk ahead of the deceased.

Ibn 'Umar (may Allah be pleased with them both) saw the Prophet ﷺ, Abū Bakr, and 'Umar (may Allah be pleased with them) walk ahead of the deceased.[16]

It [the burial] should be hastened due to the authentic hadith: "Hurry with [burying] the dead. If he was pious, you speed him to goodness. If he was otherwise, you remove an evil from your necks."[17]

---

13. Abū Umāmah ibn Sahl: Al-Shāfi'ī, *Al-Musnad*, 1:359; Nasā'ī, 1989; al-Bayhaqī, 6959, 6961, 6962. See: TM, 785, 788.
14. Abū Hurayrah: Abū Dāwūd, 3201. See: TM, 796.
15. Muslim, 957 #72; Abū Dāwūd, 3197; Nasā'ī, 4:72; Tirmidhī, 1023; Ibn Mājah, 1505. See TM, 783.
16. Ibn 'Umar: Ibn Mājah, 1482; Abū Dāwūd, 3179; Tirmidhī, 1007–8; Nasā'ī, 1944; Ibn Ḥibbān, 3045–47. See: TM, 780.
17. Abū Hurayrah: Bukhārī, 1315; Muslim, 944 #50, 51. See: TM, 781.

BURIAL

ويدفن في اللّحد مستقبل القبلة، ويسطّح القبر، ولا يجصّص.

The deceased is buried in a niche [*laḥd*] facing the direction of prayer.

Hishām ibn ʿĀmir (may Allah be pleased with him) reported that the Messenger of Allah ﷺ said, concerning the dead from the Battle of Uḥud: "Dig. Make it wide. And do it well."[18]

Saʿd ibn Abī Waqqāṣ (may Allah be pleased with him) said, during the illness from which he died: "Make a niche for me [in the side of the grave], and cover me with bricks, as was done with the Messenger of Allah ﷺ."[19]

The deceased should be placed in the grave head first, entering from the direction where his feet will be.

ʿAbd Allāh ibn Yazīd (may Allah be pleased with him) placed al-Ḥārith in his grave from the side where the legs would be and said, "This is a sunnah."[20]

The person placing the deceased in the grave should say "*Bismillāh wa ʿalā sunnati rasūli llāh*" ("In the name of Allah, and according to the Sunnah of the Messenger of Allah"). Ibn ʿUmar (may Allah be pleased with them both) narrated that "whenever the deceased was placed in his grave, the Prophet ﷺ would say 'In the name of Allah, and according to the Sunnah of the Messenger of Allah.'"[21]

Two individuals should not be buried in the same grave unless there is a need.

Jābir ibn ʿAbd Allāh (may Allah be pleased with them both) said that the Prophet ﷺ buried the martyrs from the Battle of Uḥud in pairs [i.e., two in each grave].[22]

18. Hishām ibn ʿĀmir: Abū Dāwūd, 3215, Tirmidhī, 1713 – *ḥasan ṣaḥīḥ*. See: TM, 814.
19. Saʿd ibn Abī Waqqāṣ: Muslim, 966. See: TM, 816.
20. ʿAbd Allāh ibn Yazīd: Abū Dāwūd, 3211 – with a *ṣaḥīḥ* chain. See: TM, 817.
21. Ibn ʿUmar: Abū Dāwūd, 3213; Tirmidhī, 1046 – and he said it is *ḥasan*. See: TM, 879.
22. Jābir: Bukhārī, 1280. See: TM, 824.

The grave is made flat [i.e., raised one handspan above the surrounding ground].

Jābir ibn ʿAbd Allāh (may Allah be pleased with them both) said that "a niche [in the side of the grave, a *laḥd*] was made for the Messenger of Allah ﷺ and unburnt [sun-dried] bricks were placed [to cover it]. The grave was raised one hand-span from the ground."[23]

It should not be covered with gypsum.

Jābir (may Allah be pleased with him) said that the Messenger of Allah ﷺ forbade that graves be plastered, sat upon, or built over.[24]

CRYING OVER THE DECEASED

ولا بأس بالبكاء عليه من غير ندب ولا نياحة.

There is no harm in crying over the deceased, provided one does not bemoan or wail.

The permissibility of crying is due to a *ṣaḥīḥ* hadith which includes "Indeed, the eyes shed tears and the heart grieves."[25]

Anas (may Allah be pleased with him) said, "I attended the burial for [Umm Kalthūm (may Allah be pleased with her)] a daughter of the Prophet ﷺ. He was sitting at the grave and I saw his eyes wet with tears."[26] Also, Abu Hurayrah (may Allah be pleased with him) said that the Prophet ﷺ visited the grave of his mother. He wept and moved those around him to weep.[27]

23. Jābir: Ibn Ḥibbān, 6635. See: TM, 822.
24. Jābir: Muslim, 970. See: TM, 828.
25. Anas: Bukhārī, 1303; Muslim, 2315 #15, Abū Dāwūd, 3126, Ibn Ḥibbān, 2902. See: TM, 833.
26. Bukhārī, 1285, 1342.
27. Abū Hurayrah: Muslim, 976 #108. See: TM, 885.

Bemoaning and wailing are unlawful because the Messenger of Allah ﷺ cursed wailing women,"[28] and he ﷺ said, "He who slaps his cheeks, tears his clothes and laments according to ways of the Days of Ignorance is not one of us."[29]

Bemoaning and wailing negate yielding and submitting to the decree of Allah. Ripping garments and slapping one's cheeks are similar [in character].

OFFERING CONDOLENCES

ويعزّى أهله إلى ثلاثة أيّام من دفنه.

Condolences are offered to the family of the deceased for up to three days after the burial.

The Prophet ﷺ said, "Whoever consoles someone stricken by a calamity receives the same rewards that he does."[30]

The Prophet ﷺ said, "No Muslim consoles his brother for his calamity save that Allah will clothe him with noble garments on the Day of Resurrection."[31]

28. Abū Saʿīd al-Khudrī: Abū Dāwūd, 3128. See: BM, 5:362; TM, cf 833.
29. Ibn Masʿūd: Bukhārī, 1297–8; Muslim, 165 #103. See: TM, 835.
30. Ibn Masʿūd: Tirmidhī, 1073; Ibn Mājah, 1602. See: TM, 829.
31. Ibn Mājah, 1601; Bayhaqī, 7087. See: TM, 831.

4

ZAKAT

كِتَابُ الزَّكَاةِ

هي النّماء.

Zakat [*zakāt*] is "growth."

This is according to its linguistic meaning. Legally, it is an amount of property that Muslims extract at a particular time to give to a particular group.

Its textual foundation (prior to consensus) is that Allah Most High says, "...pay the poor-due [zakat]..." [Q2:43] and other verses; in addition to well-known and well-transmitted reports.

‹Additional evidence for the general obligation of zakat includes Allah Most High saying, "Take alms of their wealth, wherewith thou mayst purify them and mayst make them grow..." [Q9:103].›[1]

Muʿādh (may Allah be pleased with him) said that when the Prophet ﷺ sent him as governor to Yemen, he ﷺ said, "Tell them that Allah has made a charity obligatory upon them that is collected from their rich and given back to their poor."[2]

Ibn ʿUmar (may Allah be pleased with them both) reported that the Messenger of Allah ﷺ said, "Islam is based on five... offering zakat...."[3]

1. al-Bughā, *Al-Tadhhīb,* 92 #1.
2. Ibn ʿAbbās: Bukhārī, 1395; Muslim, 19. See: TM, 904.
3. Ibn ʿUmar: Bukhārī, 8; Muslim, 16. See p# for the full hadith. See: KBM (1088); al-Māwardī, *Al-Ḥāwī al-kabīr*, 3:72.

PROPERTIES SUBJECT TO ZAKAT

لا تجب الزّكاة إلّا في النّعم، والذّهب، والفضة، والزّرع، والثّمار، وعرض التّجارة والمعدن والرّكاز.

Zakat is not owed except on...
1. livestock [*niʿam*];
2. gold and silver;
3. agriculture;
4. fruit;
5. trade goods;
6. ore; and
7. treasure.

[Evidence for the aforementioned categories of wealth is presented throughout this chapter. The exclusion of other categories is based on hadiths, including:]

Abū Hurayrah (may Allah be pleased with him) reported that the Messenger of Allah ﷺ said, "No charity is incumbent upon a Muslim for his slave or horse."[4]

LIVESTOCK

(فصل) [زكاة بهيمة الأنعام]

أما النّعم، وهو الإبل والبقر والغنم.

Zakat is owed on the following types of livestock:
1. camels;
2. cows; and
3. sheep [and goats].

4. Abū Hurayrah: Bukhārī, 1463–63, Muslim, 982 #8. See: TM, 900.

CAMELS

ففي الإبل شاة في كلّ خمس إلى خمس وعشرين، فبنت مخاض – لها سنة – إلى ستّ وثلاثين، فبنت لبون – لها سنتان – إلى ستّ وأربعين، فحقّة – لها ثلاث سنين – إلى إحدى وستّين، فجذعة – لها أربع – وفي ستّ وسبعين بنتا لبون، وفي إحدى وتسعين حقّتان، وفي مائة وإحدى وعشرين ثلاث بنات لبون، ثمّ يتغيّر الواجب بزيادة تسع، ثمّ عشر، في كلّ أربعين بنت لبون، وفي كلّ خمسين حقّة.

One *shāh* [a one-year-old sheep or a two-year-old goat] is owed for every multiple of 5 camels up to 24.

[On 25 camels,] one *bint makhāḍ* (a one-year-old female camel) is owed for up to 35 camels.

[On 36 camels,] one *bint labūn* (a two-year-old female camel) is owed for up to 45 camels.

[On 46 camels,] one *ḥiqqah* (a three-year-old female camel) is owed for up to 60 camels.

[On 61 camels,] one *jadhʿah* (a four-year-old female camel) is owed [for up to 75 camels].

On 76, two *bint labūns* are owed; on 91, two *ḥiqqahs*; and on 121, three *bint labūns*.

Anas (may Allah be pleased with him) said that when Abū Bakr (may Allah be pleased with him) was appointed as caliph [*khalīfah*], Abū Bakr wrote him [a zakat schedule] when sending him to Bahrain [which read]: "In the name of Allah, the Beneficent, the Merciful. This is the obligatory charity that the Messenger of Allah ﷺ made obligatory for every Muslim, and which Allah had ordered His Messenger to observe: Whoever amongst the Muslims is asked to pay it accordingly is to do so, and whoever amongst the Muslims is asked to pay more than it is not to give it. Camels: for 24 camels or fewer, four *shāh*s are to be paid. For every five camels, one *shāh* is to be paid. If there are between 25 to 35 camels, one *bint makhāḍ* is to be paid; but if they do not have a *bint makhāḍ*, then an *ibn labūn*. If they are between 36 to 45, one *bint labūn* is to be paid. If they are between 46 to 60, one *ḥiqqah* is to be paid. If the number is between 61 to 75, one *jadhʿah* is to be paid. If the number is between 76 to 90, two *bint labūn*s are to be paid. If they are from 91 to 120, two *ḥiqqah*s are to be paid.[5]

Thereafter, the amount owed changes with the addition of 9, and then 10: for every 40 there is one *bint labūn*, and for every 50, one *ḥiqqah*.

‹So, for 140 camels, 2 *ḥiqqah*s and 1 *bint labū*n are owed; for 150 camels, 3 *ḥiqqah*s are owed; and for 200 camels, either 4 *ḥiqqah*s or 5 *bint labūn*s are owed.›

The zakat document from Abū Bakr (may Allah be pleased with him) included: "If they are over 120, for every 40, one *bint labūn* is to be paid, and for every 50, one *ḥiqqah* is to be paid."[6]

Whenever the type of animal required for payment is not found, the owner can give a type that is higher or lower in value, with the difference being paid as two *shāh*s or 20 *dirham*s [approximately 59.29 grams of silver].

The zakat document from Abū Bakr (may Allah be pleased with him) included: "If a man has camels on which the *ṣadaqah* is one *jadhʿah* and he does not have a *jadhʿah* but does have a *ḥiqqah*, then the *ḥiqqah* should be accepted from him. Two *shāh*s should be given [in addition], if they are readily available, or twenty *dirham*s. Whoever is obligated to pay a *ḥiqqah* as *ṣadaqah* and does not have a *ḥiqqah* but does have a *jadhʿah*, the *jadhʿah* is accepted from him and he is given 20 *dirham*s or two *shāh*s."[7]

5. Anas: Bukhārī, 1454. Fragments of this hadith are cited repeatedly throughout this chapter. See: TM, 901.
6. Anas: Bukhārī, 1454. See: TM, 901.
7. Anas: Bukhārī, 1454. See: TM, 901.

COWS

وأما البقر: فتبيع - ابن سنة - في كلّ ثلاثين، ومسنّة - بنت سنتين - في أربعين وهكذا.

One *tabīᶜ* (a one-year-old male calf) is owed for every 30 cows.

One *musinnah* (a two-year-old cow) is owed for every 40 cows.

(And so forth.)

Muᶜādh ibn Jabal (may Allah be pleased with him) narrates: "The Messenger of Allah ﷺ sent me to Yemen and ordered me to collect a *tabīᶜ* or a *tabīᶜah* on every thirty cows, a *musinnah* on every forty, and a *dīnār* for every adult [as *jizyah*] or its equivalent in *maᶜāfir*."[8] ‹The word "*maᶜāfir*" refers to a type of Yemeni garment.[9]›

So for every 30 cows, a *tabīᶜ* is owed and for every 40, a *musinnah*. When there are 120 cows, then either 3 *musinnah*s or 4 *tabīᶜ*s are owed. The collector takes whichever is most beneficial for the poor.

8. Muᶜādh: Abū Dāwūd, 1576, 3038; Tirmidhī, 623 – *ḥasan*; Nasā'ī, 2450–2, Ibn Mājah, 1803, Ibn Ḥibbān, 4886, Ḥākim, 1449. See: TM, 905.
9. al-Bughā, *Al-Tadhhib*, 86 #1.

SHEEP

وأما الغنم: فشاة في أربعين جذعة ضأن ذات سنة، أو معز ذات سنتين، وشاتان في مائة وإحدى وعشرين، وثلاث في مائتين وواحدة، ثمّ في كلّ مائة شاة.

One *shāh* is owed for 40 sheep: either a one-year-old sheep or a two-year-old goat.

Two *shāh*s are owed for 121.

Three are owed for 201.

Thereafter, on every [multiple of] 100, one *shāh* is owed.

After 300 sheep, one *shāh* is owed for each 100. ‹So, for 500 sheep, 5 *shāh*s are owed.›

The zakat document from Abū Bakr (may Allah be pleased with him) included: "...Concerning the *ṣadaqāh* on grazed sheep: from 40 to 120 sheep, one *shāh* is owed. From 121 to 200, two *shāh*s are owed. From 201 to 300, three *shāh*s are owed. If there are more than 300, then one *shāh* is owed for every 100. If a man's grazed [sheep] are fewer than 40 by a single sheep [i.e., 39], nothing is owed on them – unless their owner so wishes."

A *jadhʿah* has completed one year and a *thaniyyah* two.

MIXED PROPERTIES

(فصل) [الخلطة]

FLOCKS

والخليطان ما اجتمعا في الفحل، والحوض، والرّاعي، والمسرح المراح، وموضع الحلب، فيزكّيان زكاة المنفرد.

Two flocks are [considered] mixed if they use the same stud, watering area, and shepherd; and if they are penned, bedded, and milked in the same places.

[In such a case], zakat is extracted as though they are a single flock.

MONEY

وتجري الخلطة أيضًا في النّقود.

Gold and silver [currency] may also be mixed.

The zakat document from Abū Bakr (may Allah be pleased with him) included: "One should not combine or separate [animals] out of fear of paying zakat. When a mix of cattle is shared between two partners and zakat is paid jointly between them, they have to calculate it equally among them."[10]

10. Anas: Bukhārī, 1454, 1448. See: TM, 901.

GOLD & SILVER

(فصل) [زكاة الذّهب والفضّة]

‹The textual foundation for zakat being obligatory on gold and silver is Allah Most High saying, "...They who hoard up gold and silver and spend it not in the way of Allah, unto them give tidings (O Muhammad) of a painful doom" [Q9:34].

The "hoarding" mentioned here occurs when zakat is not paid on a property. This is how Ibn ʿUmar (may Allah be pleased with them both) explained the meaning of the verse: "Whoever hoarded them and did not pay the zakat thereof, then woe to him."[11]›

MINIMUM AMOUNTS

وأما الذّهب: فنصابه عشرون مثقالاً.

The minimum amount of gold requiring a zakat payment is twenty *mithqāls* [85 grams, 2.37 troy ounces, one *dīnār*].

ʿAlī (may Allah ennoble his face) said, "Nothing is owed on less than twenty *dīnārs*, and in twenty there is half a *dīnār*, and any addition is according to that."[12]

والفضّة ونصابها مائتا درهم.

The minimum amount of silver is 200 *dirhams* [595 grams or 19.13 troy ounces].

This is due to the ḥadīth, "No zakat is due on less than five *ūqiyyahs* of silver."[13]

An *ūqiyyah* equals forty *dirhams*, according to Meccan weights.

11. Ibn ʿUmar: Bukhārī, 1404. See: al-Bughā, *Al-Tadhhīb*, 93 #4.
12. ʿAlī: Abū Dāwūd, 1573. See: MT, 125.
13. Abū Saʿīd al-Khudrī: Bukhārī, 1405; Muslim, 979 #5. See: TM, 925.

WHAT IS OWED

وزكاتهما ربع العشر، وفيما زاد بحسابه.

A zakat of 2.5% is owed on the minimum amount. Anything above the minimum amount is calculated according to the same proportion.

Gold is [subject to zakat] because of the hadith from ʿAlī (may Allah ennoble his face) mentioned earlier, and silver because of a hadith that includes: "In silver there is one quarter of a tenth."[14]

JEWELRY

ولا زكاة في الحليّ المباح.

There is no zakat [owed] for lawful jewelry.

"Lawful" means silver rings for men and gold bracelets and the like for women.

Jābir (may Allah be pleased with him) said that the Messenger of Allah ﷺ said, "There is no zakat on jewelry."[15]

Similarly, this category of zakat does not apply to anything that circulates as currency (other than gold or silver) since the default is that zakat is not owed. This is also because of how easy it is for gold and silver to earn a profit – in contrast to other things.

---

14. Anas: Bukhārī, 1454. See: TM, 928.
15. Jābir: Bayhaqī, 7537. See: TM, 1058; KBM, 1058

AGRICULTURE & FRUIT

(فصل) [زكاة الزّروع]

The textual foundation for zakat being owed on agriculture and fruit is consensus and what will be mentioned in this chapter from the Quran and Sunnah.

THE MINIMUM AMOUNT

وأما الزّروع والثّمار: فنصابها خمسة أوسق، وذلك ألف وستّمائة رطل بالبغداديّ، وفيما زاد بحسابه.

The minimum amount for agriculture and fruit is five *wasaq*s (1,600 ʿIrāqī *riṭls*) [609.84 kilograms or 1,344.5 pounds]. Anything additional is calculated according to its proportion.

The Prophet ﷺ said, "No zakat is due on less than five *wasaq*s."[16]

WHAT IS OWED

وواجبه العشر إن إن سقي بلا مؤنة، كماء السّماء، وإلّا فنصفه.

A zakat of 10% is owed if the crop was watered without labor (i.e., via rainfall). Otherwise, [the amount owed is] half [5%].

The Prophet ﷺ said, "On land watered by rainfall or [other] natural water channels or if the land is wet due to a nearby water channel, one-tenth [is due on its yield]; and on the land watered via animal labor, half of one-tenth [is due on its yield]."[17]

16. Abū Saʿīd al-Khudrī: Bukhārī, 1447; Muslim, 979 #1, 3. See: TM, 935.
17. Ibn ʿUmar: Bukhārī, 1483. See: TM, 920.

CONDITIONS

وتختصّ بالقوت الغالب، ومن الثّمار بالرّطب والعنب. وتجب ببدوّ صلاح الثّمر، واشتداد الحبّ.

[The obligation of zakat on non-fruit] is limited to dominant staple food crops; and [for] fruits, [it is limited] to dates and grapes.

Zakat becomes obligatory once the crop's soundness becomes apparent and its grains become strong.

"Staple food crops" are food items that can be stored without spoiling and are the dominant nutritional components in the land. Thus, what is intended is wheat, barley, chickpeas, beans, and the like.

TRADE GOODS

(فصل) [زكاة التّجارة]

The textual basis for zakat being owed on trade goods comes from what is mentioned elsewhere in this chapter.

وأما عروض التّجارة: ففيها ربع العشر، ويقوّم آخر الحول.

The amount owed on trade goods is one-quarter of a tenth [2.5%]...

This is due to the hadith, "From camels there is *ṣadaqah,* and from dry goods [*bazz*] there is *ṣadaqah*."[18]

The zakat amount is 2.5% since this is what is owed on currency.

The amount is paid with the currency used to appraise its value. If it was purchased in gold, it is appraised in gold. If it was purchased in silver, it is appraised in silver, and so forth. Goods

18. Abū Dharr: Dāraquṭnī, 1932–4; Bayhaqī, 7598, 7599, 7602; Ḥākim, 1433. See: TM, 942.

are not appraised using trade goods if they are acquired through barter of other trade goods.

To be considered a trade good, trade must have been intended when obtaining the good through an exchange. If the good was obtained without any intention to use it in trade and one later intends to use it for trade, it is not [considered] a trade good [and thus not subject to its zakat]. (This is contrary to al-Karābīsī, who said that intention makes it so.)[19] Items acquired as inheritance, gifts, or bequests are not [considered] trade goods as they were acquired without an exchange.[20]

...appraised at the end of a [lunar] year.

Offspring [of trade animals] and profit [from sales] are combined with the original goods [for zakat assessment] – provided the goods have not been liquidated.

ʿUmar (may Allah be pleased with him) said, "Yes, you include a lamb [*sakhlah*] the shepherd is carrying, but you do not take it."[21]

MINES & TREASURE

وأما المعدن: ففيه ربع عشره حالًّا وفي الرِّكاز الخمس.

[A zakat of] 2.5% is taken from [gold and silver] ore immediately [after separating the ore from the dirt].

This is because of the hadith mentioned earlier: "On silver there is one quarter of a tenth."[22]

19. al-Nawawī, *Rawḍat al-ṭālibīn,* 2:266.
20 Contemporary currencies (e.g., the US dollar), and digital currencies and assets (e.g., bitcoin), are subject to zakat under this category. A simplified way of doing this is, once the conditions are met, one calculates the minimum amount that one has kept throughout the lunar year and pays 2.5% on any amount that is above the *niṣāb*. (And Allah knows best.)
21. ʿUmar: Mālik, 909. See: KBM, 1000.
22. Anas: Bukhārī, 1454.

Reaching the minimum amount [*niṣāb*] is a condition. The passing of a lunar year is not. Consecutive yields are combined.

[A zakat of] 20% is taken from [gold and silver] treasures.

Abū Hurayrah (may Allah be pleased with him) said that the Messenger of Allah ﷺ said, "On buried treasure: when it reaches the *niṣāb,* one-fifth [is due]."[23]

Treasure refers to buried pre-Islamic gold and silver.

The Messenger of Allah ﷺ said about a treasure a man had found: "If you found it in an inhabited village or [on] a traveled path, announce it. And if you found it in an uninhabited [village] or [on] an untraveled path, then from it – and from treasure – is one fifth."[24]

Its zakat is extracted upon its acquisition, provided it has reached the minimum amount [*niṣāb*].

CONDITIONS OBLIGATING ZAKAT

(فصل) [شروط وجوب الزّكاة]

وشرائط وجوبها الإسلام، والحريّة، والملك التّامّ، والنّصاب، والحول إلّا فيما سلف، والسّوم إلّا أن تكون عاملة.

The conditions whereby zakat becomes obligatory are:
1. [that the owner] is a Muslim;

Zakat is owed on a Muslim's property even if he is a child or insane. This [condition] is based upon analogy to adults and upon his ﷺ saying, "Strive to increase an orphan's wealth. Do not leave it until zakat [*ṣadaqah*] consumes it."[25]

23. Abū Hurayrah: Bukhārī, 1499; Muslim, 1710 #45. See: TM, 938, 940, 1561.
24. al-Ḥākim, 2374. See TM, 940.
25. Yūsuf ibn Māhak: Al-Shāfiʿī in *Al-Musnad,* 92. See: TM, 952.

2. free;

Jābir (may Allah be pleased with him) said, "Zakat is not owed from the property of a slave buying his freedom[26] until he is free."[27]

3. **possesses complete ownership [over the item];**[28]

It is not obligatory to pay the zakat before the property is present, since it is not available.

It is permissible to pay zakat early. The Prophet ﷺ gave an allowance to ʿAbbās (may Allah be pleased with him) to do so.[29]

If any of the conditions obligating one to pay zakat is absent before it becomes due, the payer can ask the recipient to return it since he is not yet required to pay it. However, this is contingent upon the payer informing the recipient that it is advanced zakat.

Debts do not prevent zakat from being owed. This is according to the narrated texts pertaining to zakat, which do not qualify it [as an excuse].

4. **possesses the minimum amount [*niṣāb*];**
5. **that a [lunar] year has passed (except regarding what was previously mentioned [mines and treasure]); and**

The Prophet ﷺ said, "No zakat is owed on property until a [lunar] year passes on it."[30]

---

26. See "Kitābah" on page 553.
27. Jābir: Dāraquṭnī, 1960, Bayhaqī, 7352. See: TM, 951.
28. According to the old Shafiʿi school. This is not a condition according to the new school.
29. ʿAbbās: Abū Dāwūd, 1624; Tirmidhī, 678; Ibn Mājah, 1795; Ḥākim, 5431. See: KBM, 1020.
30. ʿAlī: Abū Dāwūd, 1573, Ibn Mājah, 1792. See: TM, 911, 937.

6. **that the animals are grazed [on herbage that grows without human intervention] (unless they are work animals).**

If a free Muslim owns the minimum amount [*niṣāb*] of camels, sheep, or cows that graze, gold or silver, or trade goods – for one whole lunar year – then zakat is owed from it. Ibn Mulaqqin (may Allah have mercy upon him) said that he did not know of any disagreement on this.

ZAKĀT AL-FIṬR

(فصل) [الفطرة]

تجب زكاة الفطر بغروب الشّمس ليلة العيد على من ملك صاعًا – وهو أربعة أمداد والمدّ رطل وثلث بالبغداديّ، وهو مائة وثلاثون درهمًا – من قوت بلده بشرط أن يفضل عن قوته وقوت من يقوته ليلة العيد ويومه.

Zakāt al-Fiṭr is obligatory, upon sunset on the night of Eid, for anyone who owns one *ṣāʿ* (1⅓ Baghdādī *riṭl*s, which is 130 *dirham*s [or 4 *mudd*s or 2.03 liters]) of their region's stored staple foods, provided that the amount given is in excess of his needs and the needs of his dependents for the night and day of Eid.

Ibn ʿUmar (may Allah be pleased with them both) said, "The Messenger of Allah ﷺ prescribed the payment of Zakāt al-Fiṭr of Ramadan for the people: one *ṣāʿ* of dried dates or one *ṣāʿ* of barley for every freeman or slave, male or female, among the Muslims."[31]

It is owed by any Muslim alive at sunset on the last day of Ramadan. Ibn ʿUmar said, "Zakāt al-Fiṭr is part of Ramadan."[32]

One must pay it for one's Muslim dependents, including wives, children, parents, and slaves. This because of the hadith, "Give

31. Ibn ʿUmar: Bukhārī, 1503; Muslim, 984 #12–16. See: TM, 943.
32. Ibn ʿUmar: Bukhārī, 1503; Muslim, 984 #12–16. See: TM, 943.

Zakāt al-Fiṭr for those you support."[33] Another transmission has: "...of the Muslims."[34]

It is permissible to pay it early during (but not before) Ramadan.

One has sinned if its payment is delayed past the day of Eid, according to a hadith which includes: "Free them [of begging] during this day."[35]

ولا فطرة على كافر إلّا في قريبه وعبده المسلم.

Zakāt al-Fiṭr is not owed by a non-Muslim except on behalf of his [dependent] Muslim relatives or slaves.

A Zakāt al-Fiṭr that has been missed is made up – just like prayers that are delayed outside their time.

ELIGIBLE RECIPIENTS

(فصل) [صرف الزّكاة]

The textual foundation for rulings related to eligible recipients is Allah Most High saying, "Alms are only for the poor..." [Q9:60].

CATEGORIES OF RECIPIENTS

ويجب صرف الزّكاة إلى الموجود من الأصناف الثمانيّة المذكورة في قوله تعالى: ﴿إِنَّمَا الصَّدَقَاتُ لِلْفُقَرَاءِ وَالْمَسَاكِينِ وَالْعَامِلِينَ عَلَيْهَا وَالْمُؤَلَّفَةِ قُلُوبُهُمْ وَفِي الرِّقَابِ وَالْغَارِمِينَ وَفِي سَبِيلِ اللهِ وَابْنِ السَّبِيلِ * فَرِيضَةً مِنَ اللهِ * وَاللهُ عَلِيمٌ حَكِيمٌ﴾.

Zakat must be given to whichever exist of the eight categories [of people] mentioned by Allāh Most High: "The alms are only for

33. Ibn ʿUmar: al-Shāfiʿī, *Al-Musnad,* 93; Dāraquṭnī, 2077, 2078; Bayhaqī, 7682, 7685. See: KBM, 1084.

34. Ibn ʿUmar: Dāraquṭnī, 2073, 2074. See: KBM, 1084.

35. Ibn ʿUmar: Dāraquṭnī, 2133; Bayhaqī, 7739. See: KBM, 1083.

[*lām*] the poor and [*wāw*] the needy, and [zakat] collection workers, and those whose hearts are to be reconciled, and to free the captives and the debtors, and for the cause of Allah, and (for) the wayfarer..." [Q9:60].

Zakat is given to these eight categories of people because of this verse. Here, charity is attributed to them via the "*lām* of ownership" which is then conjoined using the "*wāw* of partnership." Whenever anything that is legally valid to own is attributed to someone via a legitimate cause, that attribution establishes his ownership. [Thus, once zakat is owed, it becomes the property of the individuals within these categories – even if its specific owners have not yet been determined.]

"Poor" here means someone who does not possess anything to meet his needs, such as someone who needs a single [dollar] and cannot even find change. Having a place to live or wealth somewhere else does not prevent someone from being poor.

"Needy" does not mean someone who cannot meet any of their needs, since that is "poor." [Rather, it means someone who can fulfill part of what they need.]

The poor and needy are given enough for their lifespan, according to Imam al-Nawawī (may Allah grant him His mercy). According to Imam al-Rāfiʿī (may Allah grant him His mercy), they are given enough for one year.[36]

Zakat workers are given wages for their work but no more.

Slaves ["captives"] buying their freedom are given enough to pay off what they still owe to obtain their freedom.

Zakat is given to debtors who went into debt to prevent [Muslims from] fighting [one another] (since we have a need for this); or who went into debt for personal reasons and cannot pay it off – so long as those reasons were not acts of disobedience from which they have not repented.

Wayfarers (travelers) are given enough to cover their round trip expenses.

36. al-Nawawī, *Rawḍat al-ṭālibīn*, 2:324.

MINIMUM DISTRIBUTION

ولا يقتصر على أقلّ من ثلاثة من كلّ صنف إلّا العامل.

One does not give to fewer than three recipients from each category – except for zakat collection workers [who can be fewer].

Allah Most High speaks of each category using the plural, and the minimum plural [in Arabic] is three.

An equal amount [of zakat] needs to be given to each category [of individuals]. Allah Most High commanded that zakat be distributed among them, and the default is that none is to be given preference. It is similar to someone saying, "This house now belongs to Zayd and ʿAmr," which means each would own half.

It is permissible to differentiate between individuals within the same category.

It is best to give the zakat to the Imam [for distribution] if he is upright since he is more knowledgeable of who deserves it. Another opinion is that it is best to distribute it oneself so one can be assured of its utilization. It can also be distributed by one's agent.

One must make the intention [to give zakat] when distributing it. This is because it is an act of worship like any other, so it requires the intention. The intention does not have to be concurrent to giving: it suffices to make the intention beforehand.

INELIGIBLE RECIPIENTS

ولا تدفع الزّكاة لغنيّ بمال أو كسب، وعبد، وكافر، وبني هاشم، والمطّلب ومولاهم، ومن تلزمه نفقته.

Zakat is not given to someone who is:

1. self-sufficient through savings or work;

2. a slave;

3. a non-Muslim;

Zakat can only be given to a Muslim. Muʿādh (may Allah be pleased with him) reported that the Prophet ﷺ said, "It is taken from their rich and returned to their poor."[37] Here, "poor" means the poor Muslims.

4. **a descendant of Banī Hāshim or Banī al-Muṭṭalib and their affiliates [*mawlāhum*]; and...**

The Messenger of Allah ﷺ said, "These *ṣadaqāt* are people's filth. They are not permissible for Muhammad ﷺ nor for the family of Muhammad ﷺ."[38]

5. **the zakat giver's dependents.**

Zakat cannot be given to individuals one is required to support even if they fall within in the category of poor or needy since the obligatory support they are already owed should free them of needing zakat. However, it is permissible to give them zakat under one of the other categories, such as if they are in debt, on jihad, or the like.

It is unlawful to transport zakat to another land when deserving recipients are present. Muʿādh (may Allah be pleased with him) reported that the Prophet ﷺ said, "It is taken from their rich and returned to their poor."[39]

37. Ibn ʿAbbās: Bukhārī, 1395, 1496, 4347; Muslim, 19 #29–31. See: TM, 904, 1387.
38. ʿAbd al-Muṭṭalib ibn Rabīʿah: Muslim, 1072 #167. See: TM, 1388.
39. Ibn ʿAbbās: Bukhārī, 1395, 1496, 4347; Muslim, 19 #29–31. See: TM, 904.

VOLUNTARY CHARITY

(فصل) [صدقة التّطوّع]

صدقة التّطوّع سنّة.

Voluntary charity is a sunnah.

It is recommended. Allah Most High says, "Who is it that will lend unto Allah a goodly loan" [Q2:245]. ‹In the verse, "lend unto Allah" means spending money for His sake; "a goodly loan" means doing it willingly.[40]›

ودفعها سرًّا، وفي رمضان، وقريب، وجار أولى كالإظهار في الفرض.

Giving it secretly, during Ramadan, to relatives, and to neighbors is superior – like giving obligatory zakat openly is superior.

It is permissible to give to the rich and to non-Muslims.

It is not recommended for someone who is in debt or who has dependents to give charity until he pays what he owes of his debts.

ويستحبّ التّصدّق بكلّ ماله إن قوي صبره، ويتأكّد على الموسر المواساة بما زاد على كفاية سنة.

It is recommended to donate all of one's wealth if one has strong patience. It is emphatically recommended for the affluent to share whatever they have in excess of their needs for a year.

40. al-Maḥallī and al-Suyūṭī, *Tafsīr al-Jalālayn.*

5

FASTING

كِتَابُ الصِّيَامِ

هو الإمساك.

Fasting [*ṣawm*] is "restraint."

This is according to its linguistic meaning.

Technically, its meaning is a particular type of restraint, by a particular person, with intent. The foundation for fasting comes from the Quran, Sunnah, and consensus. Fasting was made obligatory during the month of Shaʿbān in 2 AH, the same year that Zakāt al-Fiṭr was made obligatory.

‹The Quran initially mentioned a general obligation to fast but without restricting it to a particular time. Allah Most High says, "O ye who believe! Fasting is prescribed for you, even as it was prescribed for those before you, that ye may ward off (evil)" [Q2:183]. Later, another verse clarified that the obligation is specific to Ramadan. Allah Most High says, "The month of Ramadan in which was revealed the Quran, a guidance for mankind, and clear proofs of the guidance, and the Criterion (of right and wrong). And whosoever of you sights [the new moon], let him fast the month..." [Q2:185].[1]›

A Bedouin said to the Prophet ﷺ: "Inform me regarding which fast Allah has made compulsory upon me." The Prophet ﷺ replied, "The fast of Ramadan."[2]

1. al-Bughā, *Al-Tadhhīb,* 102 #1.
2. Ṭalḥah ibn ʿUbayd Allāh: Bukhārī, 1891; Muslim, 11. See: KBM, 1089.

Ibn ʿUmar (may Allah be pleased with them both) reported that the Messenger of Allah ﷺ said, "Islam is based on five... fasting Ramadan..."[3]

CONDITIONS AND INVALIDATORS

CONDITIONS OBLIGATING THE FAST OF RAMADAN

وشرائط وجوبه: الإسلام، والبلوغ، والعقل، والإطاقة.

The obligation to fast the month of Ramadan is conditional upon the person being:

1. **a Muslim;**
2. **mature;**
3. **of sound mind; and...**

One who lacks any of the above is not obligated to fast.

4. **able to fast.**

Every mature Muslim who is of sound mind, pure [i.e., free of menstrual and postpartum bleeding], and knows that Ramadan has begun, must fast.

The start of Ramadan is known by completing Shaʿbān; sighting the new moon by oneself or others; or, if one is unable [to confirm it via the above], *ijtihād*.

Sighting the new moon establishes the obligation because the Prophet ﷺ said, "Fast when you sight it and break your fast when you sight it. But if the sky is cloudy, complete Shaʿbān as thirty [days]."[4]

A single witness suffices, as will be discussed later.[5]

Completing the [month's full] number [thirty days] is like witnessing [the new moon], because of the same hadith..

3. Ibn ʿUmar: Bukhārī, 8; Muslim, 16. See: TM, 1041.
4. Abū Hurayrah: Bukhārī, 1909; Muslim, 1081 #18, 19. See: TM, 957.
5. See: "What Constitutes Testimony and Evidence" on page 537

A person (such as a prisoner) who cannot sight [the moon] or complete the month uses *ijtihād,* by analogy to prayer [times].

CONDITIONS FOR RAMADAN BEING VALID

و[شرائط] صحّته: الإسلام، والعقل، والنّقاء عن الحيض والنّفاس كلّ يوم.

The validity of fasting Ramadan is conditional upon [the person being]:

1. a Muslim;

This is according to consensus.

2. of sound mind; and

The legal status of someone who is insane or lacks discernment is analagous to that of animals in being free of responsibility.

3. free of menstruation and lochia the entire day.

This is according to consensus.

INVALIDATORS

ولا بدّ من الإمساك عن الجماع، وخروج المنيّ بلمس ونحوه، والإستقاءة، وعن وصول عين إلى ما يسمّى جوفًا عمدًا مختارًا.

One's fast is invalidated by:

1. intercourse;

There is consensus about this.

‹Allah Most High says, "...and eat and drink until the white thread becometh distinct to you from the black thread of the dawn. Then strictly observe the fast till nightfall and touch them not while you are at devotions in the mosques..." [Q2:187].

In this verse, "the white thread" refers to the light of dawn; "the black thread" is the darkness of the night; "touch them not" refers to intercourse, and "while you are at devotions in the mosques" means "*iʿtikāf*."[6]›

2. ejaculation as a result of skin contact or the like;

An example of such contact is kissing. Ejaculate exiting is one of the two causes of major ritual impurity.

3. vomiting intentionally;

The Prophet ﷺ said, "Whoever is overcome by vomiting is not required to make it up. Whoever intentionally vomits is to make it up."[7]

4. [consuming] any substance intentionally and voluntarily…

The Prophet ﷺ said, "Whoever forgot and ate or drank is to complete his fast, since Allah has fed him and given him drink."[8]

If one were to forgetfully eat [what is customarily considered] a large amount, it would not break one's fast according to al-Nawawī (may Allah grant him His mercy). However, it would according to al-Rāfiʿī (may Allah grant him His mercy).[9]

Doing any of the aforementioned out of forgetfulness, compulsion, or involuntarily will often be excused. This is because of the hadith, "Mistakes, forgetfulness, and what one is compelled to do have been lifted from my Community."[10]

---

6. al-Bughā, *Al-Tadhhīb,* 103 #2.
7. Abū Hurayrah: Abū Dāwūd, 2380; Nasāʾī in *Al-Sunan al-kubrā,* 8025–7; Ibn Mājah, 1676; Tirmidhī, 720 – *ḥasan gharīb*; Dāraquṭnī, 2276. See: TM, 964.
8. Abu Hurayrah: Bukhārī, 1933, 6669; Muslim, 1155 #171. See: TM, 967.
9. al-Nawawī, *Rawḍat al-Ṭālibīn,* 2:363; al-Rāfiʿī, *Al-Sharḥ al-kabīr,* 3:203.
10. Ibn ʿAbbās: Ibn Mājah, 2043, 2045; Ibn Ḥibbān, 7219; Ḥākim, 2801 – and al-Dhahabī concurred. Al-Nawawī considered *ḥasan* in *Al-Rawḍah* (8:193). See: TM, 1486, 1542, 1576.

One's fast is not broken by swallowing dust, saliva, or flies because of the difficulty in avoiding them.

It is also not broken by applying oil or kohl, or by swimming. This is because these acts do not cause a substance to enter into an internal cavity, and something entering through the pores of the skin is not significant enough to break the fast.

...[and that substance] reaching what is considered a body cavity.

Body cavities include the brain, chest, abdomen, and head.,

‹Intentionally doing any of the above will break one's fast.›

One who intentionally breaks his fast has sinned; there is no known scholarly disagreement concerning this. His fast must be made up, without anything else being required [such as an expiation]. ‹Fasts broken via intercourse are an exception.›

INTENTION

وتجب النّيّة فيه، ففي الفرض يبيت، وفي النّفل قبل الزّوال.

It is obligatory to intend the fast.

This applies to current performances and makeup fasts. The Prophet ﷺ said, "Actions are by intentions."

One must identify the fast in one's intention. (For example, "I intend to fast tomorrow as an obligatory Ramadan fast.") It is more complete to also include in one's intention whether it is a current performance or a makeup, and that it is for the sake of Allah Most High.

[Intention must be made] during the night for obligatory fasts, and before the [sun's] zenith for voluntary fasts.

One's intention must be made before dawn. The Prophet ﷺ said,

"Whoever does not form his intention to fast before dawn has no fast."[11]

It does not suffice to make the intention as the sun rises, according to the soundest opinion.

Other obligatory fasts (like an expiation or a vowed fast) are given the same ruling as [fasting days of] Ramadan.

RECOMMENDED ACTIONS

ويستحبّ تعجيل الفطر، وتأخير السّحور، وترك الهجر من الكلام.

It is recommended to hasten to break the fast;...

Sahl ibn Saʿd (may Allah be pleased with him) said that the Messenger of Allah ﷺ said, "People will remain on goodness so long as they hasten the breaking of the fast."[12]

‹When the Prophet ﷺ was fasting, he would not pray [the Sunset Prayer] until he was given a fresh date or water and had consumed it. If it was winter, he ﷺ would not pray until we brought him a dried date or water.[13]›

...to delay the [pre-dawn] meal prior to fasting;...

The Prophet ﷺ said, "My community will remain upon goodness so long as they hasten to break their fast and delay their pre-dawn meal."[14]

‹Anas ibn Mālik (may Allah be pleased with him) said that the Prophet ﷺ and Zayd ibn Thābit (may Allah be pleased with him)

---

11. Ḥafṣah and ʿĀʾishah: Abū Dāwūd, 2454; Tirmidhī, 730; Nasāʾī, 2331–43; Ibn Mājah, 1700; Ibn Khuzaymah, 1933; Dāraquṭnī, 2213–18; Bayhaqī, 7907, 7988. See: TM, 961–2.
12. Sahl ibn Saʿd: Bukhārī, 1957; Muslim, 1098. See: TM, 979.
13. Anas: Ibn Khuzaymah, 2065. See: al-Anṣārī, *Asnā al-maṭālib,* 1:419.
14. Abū Dharr: Aḥmed, 5:147. See: TM, 989.

ate their pre-dawn meal together. When they finished, the Prophet ﷺ stood for the prayer and prayed it. We asked Anas, "What was the interval between their finishing the pre-dawn meal and the starting the morning prayer?" Anas replied, "It was equal to the time one takes to recite fifty verses."[15]›

...and to avoid unpleasant speech.

Abū Hurayrah (may Allah be pleased with him) reported that the Messenger of Allah ﷺ said, "Whoever does not leave falsehoods and evil actions, Allah is not in need of his leaving his food and drink."[16] ‹This hadith is understood to mean that such abstention from food is not correlated with any rewards, even if one has carried out the obligation.›

DAYS UNLAWFUL TO FAST

وستّة أيّام يحرم صيامها، العيدان، وأيّام التّشريق، ويوم الشّكّ بلا سبب.

Fasting is unlawful on six days:
1–2. the two Eids;

This is because of the *ṣaḥīḥ* hadiths concerning fasting on these days. Abū Hurayrah, ʿUmar and Abū Saʿīd (may Allah be pleased with them) said, "These two days the Messenger of Allah ﷺ forbade you to fast: the day you break your fast [Eid al-Fiṭr] and the other day wherein you eat from your rites [Eid al-Aḍḥā]."[17]

---

15. Anas: Bukhārī, 576. See: BM, 5:700; al-Rūyānī, *Baḥr al-madhhab,* 3:269.
16. Abū Hurayrah: Bukhārī, 1903. See: TM, 990.
17. Abū Hurayrah: Bukhārī, 1991; Muslim, 1138 #139. Also: ʿUmar and Abū Saʿīd: Bukhārī, 1990, 1991, 1994; Muslim, 1138 #141. See TM, 974.

3–5. the Days of Tashrīq [the three days immediately after Eid al-Aḍḥā]; and...

This is because of the *ṣaḥīḥ* hadiths concerning fasting on these days. ʿĀʾishah and Ibn ʿUmar (may Allah be pleased with them) reported that nobody was allowed to fast on the Days of Tashriq except those who could not afford the *ḥadī* sacrifice.[18]

6. the Day of Doubt [*Yawm al-Shakk*], if one does not have a reason [such as it coinciding with one's habitual fast].

The Day of Doubt is the thirtieth of Shaʿbān if the previous night was cloudy and no one reported sighting the new moon; or if people speak about it being seen but the witnesses do not meet the necessary conditions for giving testimony.

It is not permissible to voluntarily fast on this day due to reports indicating its prohibition.

ʿAmār ibn Yāsir (may Allah be pleased with him) said that the Messenger of Allah ﷺ said, "Whoever fasts on the Day of Doubt has disobeyed Abu l-Qāsim ﷺ."[19]

It is not offensive to fast on this day if doing so conforms to one's habit or one's ongoing fast, or if one is making up a missed fast. This is because of reports indicating its permissibility.

Abū Hurayrah (may Allah be pleased with him) reported that the Messenger of Allah ﷺ said, "No one is to precede Ramadan by fasting a day or two, unless he is observing a [particular] fast, in which case he is to observe it."[20]

---

18. Nubayshah al-Hudhalī: Muslim, 1141 #144, 145. ʿĀʾishah and Ibn ʿUmar: Bukhārī, 1997. See: TM, 975–6.
19. ʿAmāar ibn Yāsir: Bukhārī *muʿallaq* (*Fatḥ al-Bārī*, 4:119); Abū Dāwūd, 2334; Nasāʾī, 2188; Tirmidhī, 686 – *ṣaḥiḥ*; Ibn Mājah, 1645; Ibn Khuzaymah, 1914; Ibn Ḥibbān, 3585, 3596; Dāraquṭnī, 2150; Ḥākim, 1542; Bayhaqī, 7952. See: TM, 977.
20. Abū Hurayrah: Bukhārī, 1914; Muslim, 1082. See: TM, 979.

‹It is also unlawful to fast from the middle of Shaʿbān onward. Abū Hurayrah (may Allah be pleased with him) reported that the Messenger of Allah ﷺ said, "When it is the middle of Shaʿbān, you are not to fast."[21] And he ﷺ said, "When it is the middle of Shaʿbān, there is no fasting until Ramadan arrives."[22]›

INTERCOURSE IN THE DAYTIME DURING RAMADAN

(فصل) [كفارة إفساد صوم يوم من رمضان بالجماع]

ومن أفسد يومًا من رمضان بجماع أثم بسبب الصّوم كفّر بعتق رقبة، فإن عجز فبصيام شهرين متتابعين، فإن عجز فبإطعام ستّين مسكينًا.

If one has nullified a day of [fasting] Ramadan by having intercourse and was sinful in doing so due to the fast, one must perform an expiation by emancipating a Muslim slave. If no slave is found, one must fast consecutively for two months. If one is unable to do so, one feeds sixty people who are poor.

This is because of the reports concerning the individual who had intercourse with his wife during Ramadan.

Abū Hurayrah (may Allah be pleased with him) reported that "A bedouin man came to the Prophet ﷺ and said, 'O Messenger of Allah, I am ruined! I have had intercourse with my wife during the month of Ramadan.' He ﷺ said, 'Can you find a slave to set free?' He replied, 'No.' He ﷺ said, 'Can you observe fast for two consecutive months?' He replied, 'No.' He ﷺ said, 'Can you feed sixty poor people?' He replied, 'No.' A basket containing dates was brought to the Prophet ﷺ. He ﷺ said, 'Give these in charity.' He replied, 'Am I to give to one who is poorer than I? By God [I swear] there is no family poorer than mine between the two lava

---

21. Abū Hurayrah: Abū Dāwūd, 2337; Tirmidhī, 738 - authentic. See: al-Rūyānī, *Baḥr al-madhhab,* 3:312.
22. Abū Hurayrah: Ibn Mājah, 1651. See: al-Bughā, *Al-Tadhhīb,* 105 #3.

plains of Medina.' The Messenger of Allah ﷺ laughed and said, 'Feed them to your family.'[23]

The expiation is only required of the husband, according to the soundest opinion.[24]

ISSUES RELATED TO FASTING

(فصل) [كفّارة الإفطار في رمضان]

THE DECEASED WHO OWES FASTS

ومن مات وعليه صيام تمكّن منه أطعم عنه لكلّ يوم مدًّا، والمختار أنّ وليّه يصوم عنه إن شاء.

If someone dies while still owing fast days that he had the opportunity to perform, one *mudd* [0.51 liters] of food is given away [on his behalf, for each fast day missed].

Ibn ʿUmar (may Allah be pleased with them both) reported that the Prophet ﷺ said, "If someone died while owing a month of fasting, a poor person is to be fed on his behalf for each day."[25]

The preferred opinion is that his guardian can fast on his behalf, if he wishes.

‹It is better that a relative or someone authorized by the deceased or his heirs fast on his behalf.›

ʿĀʾishah (may Allah be pleased with her) reported that the Messenger of Allah ﷺ said, "If someone dies while fast [days] are incumbent upon him, his guardian fasts on his behalf."[26]

23. Abū Hurayrah: Bukhārī, 1936; Muslim, 1111 #81. See: TM, 1010.
24. al-Nawawī, *Rawḍat al-ṭālibīn,* 2:374.
25. Ibn ʿUmar: Tirmidhī, 817 – *ṣaḥīḥ*. See: TM, 1006.
26. ʿĀʾishah: Bukhārī, 1952; Muslim, 1147. See: TM, 1007.

Ibn ʿAbbās (may Allah be pleased with them both) reported that a man came to the Prophet ﷺ and said, "O Messenger of Allah, my mother died while owing a month of fasting. Should I observe it on her behalf?" He ﷺ replied, "Yes, as debts to Allah have more right to be paid."[27]

THE ELDERLY AND THOSE UNABLE TO FAST

والشّيخ العاجز عن الصّوم يفطر ويفدي عن كلّ يوم مدًّا.

If someone is elderly and unable to fast, he breaks his fast and gives away one *mudd* of food for each fast day missed.

PREGNANCY, ILLNESS, AND TRAVEL

والحامل والمرضع، إذا خافتا على أنفسهما يقضيان من غير فدية، وعلى الولد فالفدية أيضًا.

When a woman who is pregnant or nursing fears for herself, she [breaks her fast and] makes it up without an expiation.

[If she fears only] for her child, then she also owes an expiation.

Ibn ʿAbbās (may Allah be pleased with them both) said concerning the verse, "...and for those who can afford it [i.e., are able to fast, but with hardship] there is a ransom [as a substitute]..." [Q2:184] that "it is abrogated except concerning pregnant and nursing women who fear for their child: they break the fast and pay an expiation. If they fear for themselves, they break the fast and make it up, and there is no expiation owed."[28]

Anas ibn Mālik al-Kaʿbī (may Allah be pleased with him) reported that the Messenger of Allah ﷺ said, "Allah Most High has lifted

27. Ibn ʿAbbās: Bukhārī, 1953; Muslim, 1148 #154, #155. See: TM, 963.
28. Ibn ʿAbbās: Abū Dāwūd, 2318. See: TM, 1008.

the [obligation of] fasting and half the prayer from travelers, and [only] fasting from women who are pregnant or nursing."[29] ‹The hadith indicates that during journeys, it is permissible to defer fasting to a later time and that four-*rakʿāt* prayers can be prayed as two-*rakʿat*s. It also indicates that pregnant and nursing women can defer their fast but not their prayer.[30]›

والمريض والمسافر سفر القصر، يفطران ويقضيان.

Someone who is ill or on a journey whose distance warrants the shortening of prayers can break their fast and make it up later.

As for people on a journey or nursing, Allah Most High says, "... and whosoever of you is sick or on a journey, (let him fast the same) number of other days..." [Q2:185]. Pregnant and nursing women are analogous [to them].

VOLUNTARY FASTING

(فصل) [صوم التّطوّع]

RECOMMENDED FASTING DAYS

ويسنّ صوم الإثنين والخميس وعرفة إلّا للحاجّ، ويوم التّروية وعاشوراء، وتاسوعاء، وأيّام البيض، وأيّام السّود وهي أواخر الشّهر، وستّ من شوّال.

It is a sunnah to fast on the following days:
1–2. Mondays and Thursdays;

The Prophet ﷺ would strive to fast [on those days].[31]

29. Anas ibn Mālik al-Kaʿbī: Tirmidhī, 715; Abū Dāwūd, 2408. See: BM, 5:712.
30. al-Bughā, *Al-Tadhhīb*, 108 #2.
31. ʿĀʾishah: Tirmidhī, 745 – *ḥasan gharīb*; Nasāʾī, 2360; Ibn Mājah, 1739; Ibn Ḥibbān, 3643. See: TM, 1012.

He ﷺ said, "Deeds are shown to Allah on those days, and I like that my deeds are presented while I am fasting."[32]

3. **the Day of ʿArafah [9th of Dhi l-Ḥijjah] – for those not making Pilgrimage;**

The Prophet ﷺ said, "Fasting on the day of ʿArafah expiates the [sins of the] past year and the next."[33]

He ﷺ did not observe the fast while at ʿArafah.[34]

4. **the Day of Tarwīyah [8th of Dhi l-Ḥijjah];**
5. **ʿĀshūrā [10th of Muḥarram]ʾ;**

He ﷺ said, "Fasting on ʿAshūrāʾ expiates the past year['s sins]."[35]

6. **Tāsūʿā [9th of Muḥarram]ʾ;**

The Prophet ﷺ said, "If I live to the next year, verily I will fast on the ninth."[36]

7. **the white days [of every lunar month];**

These are the thirteenth, fourteenth, and fifteenth days of each lunar month. The Prophet ﷺ advised Abū Dharr (may Allah be pleased with him) to fast them.[37]

---

32. Abū Hurayrah: Tirmidhī, 747 – *ḥasan gharīb*. See: TM, 1013.
33. Abū Ayyūb al-Anṣārī: Muslim, 1162 #196, 197. See: TM, 1015.
34. Umm Faḍl and Maymūnah: Bukhārī, 1988, 1989; Muslim, 1123 #110–11, 1124 #112. See: KBM, 1159.
35. ʿUmar: Muslim, 1162 #197. See: TM, 1015.
36. Ibn ʿAbbās: Muslim, 1134 #134. See: KBM, 1162.
37. Abū Dharr: Tirmidhī, 761 – *ḥasan*; Nasāʾī, 2422–7, 4311; Ibn Ḥibbān, 3656, 3667. See: TM, 1021.

8. the black days – the last days of the month; and

‹The wisdom of fasting is in seeking perpetual removal of darkness or, in another opinion, the removal of darkness from the heart.[38]›

9. six days in Shawwāl.

The Prophet ﷺ said, "If someone fasted Ramadan, then followed it with six days in Shawwāl, it is as if he fasted the entire year."[39]

OFFENSIVE FASTING DAYS

ويكره إفراد الجمعة والسّبت والأحد.

It is offensive to single out Friday, Saturday, or Sunday [for fasting].

Abū Hurayrah (may Allah be pleased with him) reported that the Messenger of Allah ﷺ said, "None of you is to fast on Friday unless he fasts [a day] before it or after it."[40]

Al-Ṣammā' bint Busr (may Allah be pleased with her) reported that the Messenger of Allah ﷺ said, "Do not fast on Saturday except what was made obligatory for you. If one of you finds nothing but a grape peel or a tree's twig, he is to chew it [to prevent fasting]."[41]

---

38. Sulaymān ibn ʿUmar al-Jamal, *Futūḥāt al-Wahhāb,* 2:350.
39. Abū Ayyūb al-Anṣārī: Muslim, 1164 #204. See: TM, 1023.
40. Abū Hurayrah: Bukhārī, 1985, Muslim, 1144 #147. See: TM, 1024.
41. al-Ṣammā' bint Busr: Abū Dāwūd, 2421; Tirmidhī, 744. See: TM, 1026.

SPIRITUAL RETREAT

(فصل) [الاعتكاف]

IT IS A SUNNAH

و الاعتكاف سنّة.

Spiritual retreat [*iʿtikāf*] is a sunnah.

There is consensus that it is recommended.

It is emphatically recommended during Ramadan since Ramadan is distinguished among other months.

It is emphasized even more during the last ten days of Ramadan, in anticipation of Laylat al-Qadr, since the Prophet ﷺ did this habitually.

ʿA'ishah (may Allah be pleased with her) said that the Messenger of Allah ﷺ used to perform a spiritual retreat during the last ten days of Ramadan until he ﷺ died. His wives (may Allah be pleased with them) continued to perform it after his ﷺ death.[42]

Laylat al-Qadr is expected to occur during the odd nights. He ﷺ said, "Seek Laylat al-Qadr during the last ten odd nights of Ramadan."[43]

According to Imam al-Shāfiʿī (may Allah grant him His mercy), the most likely nights are the twenty-first and the twenty-third.[44]

CONDITIONS FOR A VALID RETREAT

لا يصحّ إلّا بنيّة في مسجد.

A retreat is not valid unless done with intention and in a mosque.

42. ʿĀ'ishah: Bukhārī, 2026; Muslim, 1172 #5. See: TM, 1002.

43. ʿĀ'ishah: Bukhārī, 2017; and Muslim, 1169 #219. See: KBM, 1173.

44. Al-Muzanī, *Al-Mukhtaṣar,* 8:156; al-Nawawī, *Rawḍat al-ṭālibīn,* 2:389.

One must remain in the mosque (even if for just an hour), since being in the mosque cannot be considered a retreat ["*iʿtikāf*"] without one remaining there.

The intention is required, since there is no act without it.

Fasting is not required. ʿUmar (may Allah be pleased with him) said, "O Messenger of Allah, [prior to entering Islam,] I had vowed to make a spiritual retreat for a night in the Mosque of the Sacred Precinct." He ﷺ said, "Fulfill your vow."[45]

INVALIDATORS

ويبطل بالجماع والإنزال مع المباشرة.

One's spiritual retreat is invalidated by intercourse or ejaculation resulting from touching.

Allah Most High says, "...and touch them not while you are at devotions in the mosques..." [Q2:187].

CONDITIONS FOR THE ONE INTENDING RETREAT

وشرطه: الإسلام والعقل والنّقاء عن الحيض والجنابة.

The conditions for one who intends a retreat include [being] Muslim, sane, and free of menstrual or postpartum bleeding.

INTERRUPTION OF CONSECUTIVE PERFORMANCE

ويقطع التّتابع بخروج بلا عذر.

The consecutiveness of one's retreat is interrupted by exiting [the mosque] without having an excuse.

ʿĀʾishah (may Allah be pleased with her) said, "The Messenger of

---

45. ʿUmar: Bukhārī, 2032, 2042; Muslim, 1656 #27. See: TM, 1035.

Allah ﷺ would extend his head into my house while he was in the mosque and I would comb his hair. And when he would make a spiritual retreat, he ﷺ would not enter the house except for a human need [i.e., to relieve himself]."[46]

46. ʿĀʾishah: Bukhārī, 1925; Muslim, 297. See: TM, 1039.

6

PILGRIMAGE

كِتَابُ الْحَجِّ

The foundation for the Hajj pilgrimage is found in the Quran, Sunnah, and consensus.

Ibn ʿAbbās (may Allah be pleased with him) reported that the Prophet ﷺ said, "When Ibrāhīm (peace be upon him) finished building the House [the *Kaʿbah*], he said, 'Lord, I have finished.' Allah said, 'Announce Hajj to the people.' He said, 'Lord, my voice does not reach.' Allah said, 'Announce and I will make it reach them.' He said, 'Lord, how do I say it?' Allah said, 'Say, "O people! Hajj has been made obligatory upon you. Make pilgrimage to the Ancient House."' [His call] was heard by everything between the heaven and the earth. Do you not see that they come from the furthest reaches of the earth saying '*Labbayk*' ['(I am) at Your service']?"[1] Another version has "Your Lord has taken a house and commanded you to make pilgrimage to it. Every stone, tree, hill, and dirt that heard [the announcement] said, '*Labbayk, Allāhumma labbayk* ['(I am) at Your service. O Allah, (I am) at Your service.']'"[2]

وهو القصد، وهو فرض، والعمرة أيضًا.

Hajj [*ḥajj*] is "aiming for a destination."

This is according to its linguistic meaning.

1. Ibn ʿAbbās: Ḥākim, 3464. See: KBM, 1184.
2. Ibn ʿAbbās: Ḥākim, 4026.

Hajj is a personal obligation, as is Umrah.

[The obligation of] Hajj need not be fulfilled immediately; it may be performed later in life. Hajj was made obligatory in 6 AH, and Mecca was not conquered until 8 AH. The Messenger of Allah ﷺ sent Abū Bakr (may Allah be pleased with him) with the people to make Hajj in 9 AH, while he ﷺ performed it in 10 AH. He ﷺ had not been occupied [the previous year] with war or fear of enemies, which indicates that delaying is permissible. However, if one fears becoming too weak to perform it, the obligation is lifted.

‹The textual foundation for Hajj being obligatory is that Allah Most High says "...And Hajj to the House is a duty unto Allah for mankind, for him who can find a way thither..." [Q3:97]. There are also hadiths affirming it.[3]›

Abū Hurayrah (may Allah be pleased with him) said, "The Messenger of Allah ﷺ addressed us and said, 'O people! Allah has made Hajj obligatory for you, so perform Hajj.'"[4]

Ibn ʿUmar (may Allah be pleased with them both) reported that the Messenger of Allah ﷺ said, "Islam is based on five... performing Hajj to the House..."[5]

It must be performed a single time in one's life, since he ﷺ said, "Hajj is one time. Whoever adds [another Hajj] does so voluntarily."[6]

Umrah is also a personal obligation once in a lifetime. It is obligatory because he ﷺ said, "Make Hajj and make Umrah."[7]

ʿĀʾishah (may Allah be pleased with her) reported that she said, "O Messenger of Allah, is jihad incumbent upon women?" He ﷺ said, "Yes, a jihad free of fighting: Hajj and Umrah."[8]

---

3. al-Bughā, *Al-Tadhhīb,* 110 #1.
4. Abū Hurayrah: Muslim, 1337. See: TM, 1043.
5. Ibn ʿUmar: Bukhārī, 8; Muslim, 16. See: TM, 1041.
6. Ibn ʿAbbās: Ḥākim, 3155. See: KBM, 1184.
7. ʿUmar: Ibn Khuzaymah, 1, 3065; Dāraquṭnī, 2708; Bayhaqī, 8537; Ḥākim, 8755. See: TM, 1045.
8. ʿĀʾishah: Ibn Mājah, 2901. See: TM, 1042.

As for it being required only once, it is due to the hadith of Surāqah (may Allah be pleased with him): "Is this Umrah of ours [only] for this year or is it forever?" He ﷺ said, "Rather, it is forever."[9]

It is lawful to delay Umrah, as it is analogous to Hajj.

It is possible for Hajj or Umrah to be required immediately or more than once if one needs to make up for an invalidated Hajj or Umrah or fulfill a vow.

Concerning conditions for Hajj or Umrah, one must be a Muslim (for it to be valid); be of sound mind (in order to perform its rites); be mature, free, and capable of fulfilling obligations; and possess the minimum resources necessary to make it obligatory.

CONDITIONS OBLIGATING PILGRIMAGE

وشرط الوجوب: الإسلام، والعقل، والبلوغ، والحريّة، والاستطاعة، وأمن الطّريق، وإمكان المشي شرط لاستقراره.

Hajj becomes obligatory upon someone who is:

1. **a Muslim;**

It is neither obligatory nor valid for non-Muslims to perform it because they are not qualified to perform acts of worship.

2. **sane;**

It is likewise not obligatory or valid for the insane to perform it.

3. **mature;**

Maturity is a condition that makes it obligatory, though it is valid for a youth who has reached the age of discernment provided that

9. Surāqah: Dāraquṭnī, 2709. See: BM, 6:119; cf TM, 1093.

he has permission from his guardian, as it requires money. [The act is supererogatory and would need to be repeated when the child reaches maturity.]

4. free;

Maturity and freedom are both required to fulfill the obligation of Hajj and Umrah. The Prophet ﷺ said, "Any slave who performs Hajj while not being free must make another Hajj. Any youth who makes Hajj and then becomes mature must make another Hajj."[10]

5. **able to travel; and**

The wherewithal to travel is a condition, according to consensus, because of the explanation for "*sabīl*[*an*]" ["way"] in the Quranic verse "...And Hajj to the House is a duty unto Allah for mankind, for him who can find a way thither..." [Q3:97]." Anas (may Allah be pleased with him) said concerning it: "The Prophet ﷺ was asked 'What is "way"?' He ﷺ said, 'Provisions and a means to travel.'" "The Prophet ﷺ was asked 'What is "way"?' He ﷺ said, 'Provisions and a means to travel.'"[11]

For those who are within the distance for shortening prayers, being able to walk that distance suffices to establish that they have "a means to travel."[12]

6. **[assured] safe passage.**

This means the path should be free of inconveniences and one should be able to reach Mecca within the time that such a journey typically takes.

10. Ibn ʿAbbās: Bayhaqī, 8613, 9849; Ibn Khuzaymah, 3050; Ḥākim, 1769. See: TM, 1051.
11. Anas: Dāraquṭnī, 2413, 2417; Ḥākim, 1613, 1614. See: TM, 1052.
12. See "Shortening & Combining Prayers" on page 120..

The ability to walk is a condition that establishes [the obligation].

Someone who is able to perform it himself cannot delegate it to someone else, since it is a physical act of worship.

It is permissible for someone who is physically unable or elderly to delegate the performance of Hajj [or Umrah] to someone else on his behalf because of the *ṣaḥīḥ* hadith concerning it.[13]

Someone who died without making Hajj [or Umrah] is similar to the above if they left behind money. This is because of the hadith "Perform Hajj for your mother."[14]

INTEGRALS OF HAJJ

وأركان الحجّ خمسة: الإحرام والوقوف، والطّواف، والسعي، والحلق.

The integrals of Hajj are five [in the following order]:
1. entering the state of *iḥrām* [accompanied by intention];

The Prophet ﷺ said, "Actions are according to intentions."[15]

2. standing [on the plane of ʿArafah];

ʿAbd al-Raḥmān ibn Yaʿmar (may Allah be pleased with him) said, "Some people from Najd came to the Messenger of Allah ﷺ while he was standing at ʿArafah and asked him about Hajj. He ﷺ commanded an announcer to proclaim, 'Hajj is ʿArafah. Whoever comes to *Jamʿ* [Muzdalifah] during the night before dawn has reached Hajj...'"[16] ‹Muzdalifah is also known as "*Jamʿ*" since it is a place

13. Ibn ʿAbbās: Bukhārī, 1513; Muslim, 1334 #407. See: TM, 1055.
14. Buraydah: Bukhārī, 1852, Tirmidhī, 929. See: KBM, 1191.
15. ʿUmar: Bukhārī, 1513; Muslim, 1334 #407.
16. ʿAbd al-Raḥmān ibn Yaʿmar: Abū Dāwūd, 1949; Tirmidhī, 899; Nasāʾī, 3044; Ibn Mājah, 3015; Ibn Khuzaymah, 2822; Dāraquṭnī, 2516; Ḥākim, 1703, 3100; Bayhaqī, 9812. See: TM, 1122.

where people gather.[17]›

The standing must occur between the sun's zenith [on the 9th] and dawn [on the 10th]. He ﷺ stood after the zenith;[18] and he ﷺ said "Take your rites from me!"[19]

One must stand there, even if only for an instant. This is because of the previous hadith from ʿAbd al-Raḥmān (may Allah be pleased with him).[20]

It is not a condition that one be aware of standing at ʿArafah or that one be awake, though one cannot be insane or unconscious.

3. **circumambulating [the House];**

Allah Most High says, "...and circumambulate [perform *ṭawāf* around] the ancient House," [Q22:29]. ‹It is referred to as the ancient House since it was the first house [of worship] built for humankind.[21]› Al-Qāḍi Abu al-Ṭayyib (may Allah grant him His mercy) said Muslims have consensus that this refers to circumambulation after standing at ʿArafah [*ṭawāf al-ifāḍah*].

The time for this [circumambulation] enters after the middle of the night of Eid.

Its conditions are the same as the conditions for entering prayer (i.e., having ritual purification, being free of filth, covering one's nakedness) except that speaking is permitted. He ﷺ said, "Circumambulating the House is like prayer, except that you can speak during it. So whoever speaks is not to speak except something good."[22]

---

17. al-Bughā, *Al-Tadhhīb,* 111 #1.
18. Jābir: Muslim, 1218 #147. See: BM, 6:245 #58.
19. Jābir: Muslim, 1297 #310. See: KBM, 1269.
20. ʿAbd al-Raḥmān ibn Yaʿmar: Abū Dāwūd, 1949; Tirmidhī, 899; Nasāʾī, 3044; Ibn Mājah, 3015; Ibn Khuzaymah, 2822; Dāraquṭnī, 2516; Ḥākim, 1703, 3100; Bayhaqī, 9812. See: TM, 1122.
21. al-Bughā, *Al-Tadhhīb,* 111 #2.
22. Ibn ʿAbbās: Tirmidhī, 960; Ibn Ḥibbān, 3836; Ḥākim, 1687, Ibn Khuzaymah, 2739. See: TM, 29, 1101.

Seven circuits are performed. The Prophet ﷺ circumambulated seven times.[23] And he ﷺ did say, "Take your rites from me!"[24]

The circuits do not have to be consecutive, according to the sound opinion.

The circuits must be performed outside the House, since the Prophet ﷺ did them thus. A circuit is not valid if someone treads upon the *shādharwan,* since this would be a circumambulation within the house, not around it. Nor is a circuit valid if one enters through an entrance to the Station [of Ibrahīm (peace be upon him)] and exits from the other, or if one touches the House's walls while circumambulating.

Each circuit begins at the Black Stone, with the House on one's left. The Prophet ﷺ circumambulated and the House was on his left.[25] And he ﷺ did say, "Take your rites from me!"[26]

It is a sunnah to follow circumambulation with two prayer cycles, since he ﷺ prayed them.[27]

One intends them as the two prayer cycles of circumambulation [*rakʿatayn al-ṭawāf*].

4. traversing [between Ṣafā and Marwah seven times];

The Prophet ﷺ faced the people during traversal [*saʿy*] and said, "Traverse, since Allah Most High has made traversal incumbent upon you."[28]

Traversal is performed after any circumambulation, whether upon one's arrival at the Sacred Precinct [*ṭawāf al-qudūm*] or after standing at ʿArafah [*ṭawāf al-ifāḍah*].

---

23. ʿUmar: Bukhārī, 1603; Muslim, 1261 #230–232. See: TM, 1093.
24. Jābir: Muslim, 1297 #310. See: TM, 1153; al-Nawawī, *Sharḥ Al-Muhadhdhab*, 8:78, 8:119, 8:282.
25. Ibn Masʿūd: Bukhārī, 1748–49; Muslim, 1296 #307. See: BM, 6:288.
26. Jābir: Muslim, 1297.
27. Ibn ʿUmar: Bukhārī, 1627; Muslim, 1234 #189. See: TM, 116.
28. Ḥabībah bint Abī Tajrāh: Aḥmed, 27367; Dāraquṭnī, 2582–2585 – with a *ṣaḥīḥ* chain.

It is [performed] seven times, since this is how he ﷺ did it. Ibn ʿUmar (may Allah be pleased with them both) said, "The Prophet ﷺ arrived in Mecca and circumambulated the House. He ﷺ then prayed two prayer cycles. Then he ﷺ traversed between Ṣafā and Marwah. He ﷺ then recited, 'Verily in the messenger of Allah ye have a good example...'" [Q33:21].[29] And he ﷺ did say, "Take your rites from me!"[30]

Going [one direction from Ṣafā to Marwah] is one traversal, and returning [from Marwah to Ṣafā] is a second. One must begin with Ṣafā, since he ﷺ said, "Begin with what Allah began with."[31]

One need not fulfill the conditions of prayer to perform the traversal, so even if one is in a state of major ritual impurity or menstruating while performing it, the traversal is valid.

5. **shaving or trimming [the hair].**

Trimming the hair is better for women as it is offensive for them to shave it. The Prophet ﷺ said, "[Shaving] is not incumbent upon women. Only trimming is incumbent upon women."[32]

Shaving or trimming is done after throwing stones at Jamrat al-ʿAqabah or after making circumambulation. Anas ibn Mālik (may Allah be pleased with him) reported that "the Messenger of Allah ﷺ came to Minā. He ﷺ approached the Jamrah and threw stones at it. He ﷺ then came to his spot in Minā and slaughtered there. Then he ﷺ said to the barber, 'Take.' (And in another version, 'Shave.') He ﷺ pointed to his right side, then his left. Then he ﷺ gave it [the shorn hair] to the people."[33]

---

29. Ibn ʿUmar: Bukhārī, 1623; Muslim, 1234 #189. See: TM, 1116.
30. Jābir: Muslim, 1297.
31. Jābir: Muslim, 1218 #148; Abū Dāwūd, 1905; Tirmidhī, 862; al-Nasāʾī, 2961–4; Ibn Mājah, 3074; Ibn Khuzaymah, 2757; Ibn Ḥibbān, 3943, 3944. See: TM, 61, 1093, 1115.
32. Ibn ʿAbbās: Abū Dāwūd, 1984, 1984. See: TM, 1135.
33. Anas: Bukhārī, 171; Muslim, 1305. See: TM, 1129.

INTEGRALS OF UMRAH

وأركان العمرة: ذلك ما عدا الوقوف.

The integrals of Umrah are [the same as those of Hajj] – other than standing [at ʿArafah].

‹Its integrals consist of entering *iḥrām* from one's designated place of entry [*mīqāt*], circumambulating the Kaʿbah, and traversing between Ṣafā and Marwah. It is required to trim one's hair afterwards.

Jābir (may Allah be pleased with him) said, "The Prophet ﷺ commanded his companions to intend it [the Pilgrimage] as Umrah, to circumambulate, shave, and then be released from *iḥrām*."[34]

An alternate narration from Ibn ʿAbbās (may Allah be pleased with them both) includes "...to circumambulate the House, then [traverse] Ṣafā and Marwah, then to trim the hair on their heads, and then be released from *iḥrām*."[35]

Yet another narration includes "...then release [yourselves] from *iḥrām*, and shave or trim."[36]

A narration from Ibn ʿUmar (may Allah be pleased with them both) includes "...then be released from *iḥrām*, and shave or trim."[37]›

---

34. Jabir: Bukhārī, 1651. See: KBM, 1217; al-Nawawī, *Sharḥ Al-Muhadhdhab*, 7:154–55.
35. Ibn ʿAbbās: Bukhārī, 1545.
36. Ibn ʿAbbās: Bukhārī, 1731.
37. Ibn ʿUmar: Muslim, 1227 #174. See: KBM, 1217; al-Nawawī, *Sharḥ Al-Muhadhdhab*, 7:154–55.

OBLIGATORY ACTS OF HAJJ

وواجباته: الإحرام من الميقات، ورمي الجمار، ومبيت مزدلفة، وليالي التّشريق، وطواف الوداع.

The obligatory actions [of Hajj] are:

1. entering *iḥrām* at the proper place and time [*mīqāt*];

The proper places for entering *iḥrām* [*mīqāt*s] are those that the Messenger of Allah ﷺ designated for people coming from each direction. One does not enter *iḥrām* before passing one's *mīqāt* when coming to Mecca for the purpose of Hajj or Umrah.

As for the places, Ibn ʿAbbās (may Allah be pleased with him) said, "The Messenger of Allah ﷺ designated Dhu l-Ḥulayfah as the *mīqāt* for the people of Medina; al-Juḥfah for the people of Shām; Qarn al-Manāzil for the people of Najd; and Yalamlam for the people of Yemen. These are the *mīqāt*s for the people living in those places and for those who come through those places with the intention of performing Hajj and Umrah. And whoever lives within these places should assume *iḥrām* from his dwelling place, and similarly, the people of Mecca can assume *iḥrām* from Mecca.""[38]

ʿĀʾishah (may Allah be pleased with her) said that the Messenger of Allah ﷺ designated Dhu l-Ḥulayfah for the people of Medina, and al-Juḥfah for the people of Shām, Egypt, and the west [*al-maghrib*].[39] There is another version without "the west [*al-maghrib*]," but with "and Dhāt al-ʿIrq for the people of Iraq" added.[40]

The places mentioned above are for their inhabitants and anyone who passes through those places. This is because of the [earlier] hadith from Ibn ʿAbbās (may Allah be pleased with him).[41]

People who are closer to Mecca than to the aforementioned places enter *iḥrām* from their location, also due to the hadith from Ibn

38. Ibn ʿAbbās: Bukhārī, 1524; Muslim, 1181 #11, 12. See: TM, 1060.
39. al-Shāfiʿī, *Al-Umm,* 2:150 – but Jābir and ʿAṭāʾi; *Al-Musnad*, p114.
40. ʿĀʾishah: Abū Dāwūd, 1739; Nasāʾī, 2653, 2656. See: TM, 1061.
41. Ibn ʿAbbās: Bukhārī, 1524; Muslim, 1181 #11, 12. See: TM, 1060.

ʿAbbās (may Allah be pleased with him), which includes "And whoever is closer than that [enters *iḥrām*] from wherever they begin."[42]

2. throwing stones at the three pillars;

Throwing stones at *Jamrat al-ʿAqabah* is done [after Morning prayer] on the Day of Sacrifice [Eid al-Aḍḥā], in accordance with the Sunnah of the Prophet ﷺ.

Ibn ʿUmar (may Allah be pleased with them both) would throw seven small pebbles at *al-Jamrat al-Duniyā* and recite *takbīr* after throwing each pebble. Then he would proceed until reaching the bottom of the valley, where he would stand for quite a long time, facing the direction of the *qiblah* and supplicating to Allah with his hands raised. Then he would throw seven pebbles at *al-Jamrat al-Wusṭā* in the same manner. He would then turn left at the base of the valley and stand facing the *qiblah,* again supplicating to Allah with hands raised. Then he would proceed to *al-Jamrat Dhāt al-ʿAqabah,* in the middle of the valley, and throw seven pebbles at it, without pausing [at it]. He would then say, "This is how I saw the Prophet ﷺ perform [these rites]."[43]

‹*Jamrat al-Duniyā* [*al-Ṣughrā*], is the smallest pillar and the one closest to Minā, near Masjid al-Khayf.

Jamrat al-ʿAqabah [*al-Kubrā*] is the largest pillar.[44]›

The time for throwing stones enters after half the night [of Sacrifice] has passed. From that point on, one may depart from Muzdalifah and commence throwing at any time, such as [before or] after the Morning Prayer. This is because, on the night [preceding] the Day of Sacrifice [the night before Eid al-Aḍḥā], he ﷺ commanded Umm Salamah (may Allah be pleased with her) to throw pebbles at Jamrat al-ʿAqabah before Morning Prayer.[45]

---

42. Preceded.

43. Ibn ʿUmar: Bukhārī, 1752. See: TM, 1127.

44. al-Bughā, *Al-Tadhhīb,* 113 #1.

45. ʿĀʾishah: Abū Dāwūd, 1942; Bayhaqī, 9571. See: BM, 6:272 #77.

Pebbles are thrown at all three pillars during the Days of Tashrīq. One begins with the pillar next to Masjid al-Khayf [*Jamrat al-Ṣughrā*], then moves to the middle one [*Jamrat al-Wusṭā*], and then ends at *Jamrat al-ʿAqabah*.

Throwing during the Days of Tashrīq is only valid after the sun has passed its zenith. Jābir (may Allah be pleased with him) said that the Messenger of Allah ﷺ threw after sunrise [*ḍuḥā*] on the Day of Sacrifice. On all other days, he ﷺ threw after the sun had passed its zenith.[46]

Seven pebbles are thrown, in accordance with the Sunnah of the Prophet ﷺ. ʿĀʾishah (may Allah be pleased with her) said that he ﷺ "then returned to Minā and remained there overnight on [the Days of] Tashrīq, and threw pebbles when the sun had passed its zenith – [pelting] each pillar with seven pebbles..."[47]

The pebbles must be thrown one at a time and conveyed in a way that can be called "throwing." Placing them does not suffice.

The Sunnah is for the pebbles to be the size of [fava] beans or, it is said, date stones.[48]

3. staying the night at Muzdalifah...

One stays there during the night of Eid. This is what al-Nawawī (may Allah grant him His mercy) considered soundest. Al-Rāfiʿī (may Allah grant him His mercy) was of the opinion that it is not an obligation (like staying the night at ʿArafah), so a blood sacrifice is recommended but not required. Ibn Khuzaymah (may Allah grant him His mercy) and others said that it is an essential

46. Jābir: Muslim, 1299 #314. See: TM, 1142.
47. ʿĀʾishah: Abū Dāwūd, 1973. See: TM, 1141.
48. Jābir: Muslim, 1299 #313; Abū Dāwūd, 1905, 1944, 1966; Tirmidhī, 886, 897; Nasāʾī, 3054, 3057, 3059, 3074, 3075, 3076. Sulaymān ibn ʿAmr bin al-Aḥwaṣ from his mother, and from Ibn ʿAbbās: Ibn Mājah, 3023, 3028, 3029, 3074. See: TM, 1093, 1128.

element. The well-known opinion is that it is obligatory.[49] Among the evidence for this is that Jābir (may Allah be pleased with him) said that the Prophet ﷺ reached al-Muzdalifah and prayed the Sunset and Night Prayers there. Then he ﷺ lay down until dawn and prayed the Morning Prayer.[50]

There are three opinions concerning what fulfills the obligation of staying the night. The soundest is that one must remain for a single hour during the second half of the night. The second is that one must remain for most of the night. The third is that one must remain there for an hour, sometime between the second half of the night and sunrise.[51]

...and the nights of Tashrīq [at Minā]; and...

This is what Imam al-Nawawī (may Allah grant him His mercy) considered sound,[52] based upon the actions of the Prophet ﷺ.[53]

According to Imam al-Rāfiʿī (may Allah grant him His mercy), the sound opinion is that it is not obligatory.[54] This is because Ibn ʿAbbās (may Allah be pleased with him) said, "When you throw stones at the pillar, stay the night wherever you wish."[55]

‹However, hadiths indicate that it is not permissible to omit staying the night, except for those who have an excuse to omit it.› Ibn ʿUmar (may Allah be pleased with them both) reported that al-ʿAbbās ibn ʿAbd al-Muṭṭalib (may Allah be pleased with him) asked permission from the Messenger of Allah ﷺ to stay in

---

49. al-Nawawī, *Rawḍat al-ṭālibīn,* 3:99; al-Rafiʿī, *Al-Sharḥ al-kabīr,* 3:421; ibid., *Al-Muḥarrar,* 129.
50. Jābir: Muslim, 1218. See: TM, 109.
51. al-Nawawī, *Rawḍat al-ṭālibīn,* 3:99.
52. al-Nawawī, *Rawḍat al-ṭālibīn,* 3:104.
53. ʿĀʾishah: Abū Dāwūd, 1973; Ibn Khuzaymah, 2956, 2971; Dāraquṭnī, 2680; Ḥākim, 1756; Bayhaqī, 9661. See: TM, 1141.
54. al-Rāfiʿī, *Al-Sharḥ al-kabīr,* 3:431, 3:435 onwards.
55. Ibn ʿAbbās: Ibn Abī Shaybah, *Al-Muṣannaf,* 3:298 #14379. See: MT, 155.

Mecca during the nights of Minā to provide drinking water [to the pilgrims]. He ﷺ allowed him [to do so].[56]

There are two opinions [from Imam al-Shāfiʿī (may Allah grant him His mercy)] concerning the period of time that fulfills the obligation of spending the night. The first and most sound opinion is that one spends most of the night. The second is that one need only be present at sunrise.

The obligatory amount of time one must remain at Muzdalifah differs from that at Minā. One reason for this is that staying at Muzdalifah is connected to circumambulation and throwing stones at the pillars – in contrast to staying at Minā, which has no such rites associated with it.

One who is present on the second day and remains until sunset must stay that night and then throw stones during the third day. This is due to ʿUmar (may Allah be pleased with him) saying, "Whoever is there at night on the second day is to stay until the next day so he can go forth with the masses."[57]

4. **performing the Farewell Circumambulation.**

Ibn ʿAbbās (may Allah be pleased with them both) said, "The people used to depart through every way [imaginable]. So the Messenger of Allah ﷺ said, 'None of you is to depart until his final rite is [performed] at the House.'"[58]

The obligation is lifted from women during menstruation and lochia. Ibn ʿAbbās (may Allah be pleased with them both) said, "People were commanded to perform their last rite at the House – except menstruating women, for whom the command was lifted."[59] Lochia is considered analogous to menstruation.

56. Ibn ʿUmar: Bukhārī, 1634. See: TM, 1139.

57. Ibn ʿUmar: Mālik, 1531; Bayhaqī, 9468. See: BM, 6:310.

58. Ibn ʿAbbās: Muslim, 1327. See: TM, 1143.

59. Ibn ʿAbbās: Bukhārī, 1755; Muslim, 1328. See: TM, 1144.

‹Other hadiths clarify that what is intended by "his final rite" is circumambulation of the House.[60]›

RECOMMENDED ACTS OF HAJJ

وسننه: الإفراد وهو الإحرام بالحجّ والفراغ منه ثمّ بالعمرة والفراغ منها، عكس التّمتّع، والقران جمعهما، والتّلبيّة، وطواف القدوم، وركعتا الطّواف.

The recommended actions [of Hajj] are:

1. performing *Ifrād*, which is entering *iḥrām* for Hajj and completing it, then entering *iḥrām* for Umrah and completing it,...

This is the optimal way, according to the Shāfiʿī school, due to the long hadith narrated by Jābir (may Allah be pleased with him) which mentions that the Messenger of Allah ﷺ did this.[61]

Others also mention this. ‹ʿĀʾishah (may Allah be pleased her) said, "We left Medina with the Messenger of Allah ﷺ to perform the Farewell Hajj. Some of us entered *iḥrām* to perform Umrah, while others entered *iḥrām* to perform both Hajj and Umrah. Yet others entered *iḥrām* to only perform Hajj. The Prophet ﷺ entered *iḥrām* for [the latter]. Those who entered *iḥrām* for Hajj alone or Hajj with Umrah did not exit their *iḥrām* until the Day of Sacrifice [Yawm al-Naḥr]."[62]›

[*Ifrād*] is best when Umrah will be made the same year. Otherwise, *Tamattuʿ* is better.

... – [as opposed to] *Tamattuʿ* [Umrah before Hajj],...

Tamattuʿ [Umrah before Hajj] requires a blood sacrifice, as Allah Most High says, "...And if ye are in safety, then whosoever con-

60. Ibn ʿAbbās: Abū Dāwūd, 2002. See: BM, 6:292.

61. Jābir: Bukhārī, 1568; Muslim, 1218. See: KBM, 1219.

62. ʿĀʾishah: Bukhārī, 4408. See: KBM, 1215; al-Bughā, *Al-Tadhhib*, 114 #2).

tenteth himself with the visit for the Hajj (shall give) such gifts as can be had with ease…" [Q2:196].

The sacrifice is obligatory when certain conditions are met, namely that [1] one does not reside in the vicinity of the Sacred Precinct (as stated in the verse); [2] one's Umrah takes place during the months of Hajj, and [3] during the same year; and [4] one does not return to one's *mīqāt* to enter *iḥram* for Hajj.

…[or] *Qirān*, which is performing them simultaneously;

A sacrifice is obligatory for one who performs *Qirān*.

2. saying "*Labbayk Allāhummah labbayk…*";

‹It is recommended to adhere to the invocation that the Prophet ﷺ. recited.[63]› Ibn ʿUmar (may Allah be pleased with them both) reported that when the Prophet ﷺ reached the mosque at Dhi l-Ḥulayfah he would enter *iḥrām* and say, "*Labbayk Allāhumma labbayk, labbayka lā sharīka laka labbayk, inn al-ḥamada wa al-niʿmata laka wa-l-mulka lā sharīka lak.*"[64]

3. performing the Arrival Circumambulation and;

ʿĀ'ishah (may Allah be pleased with her) said that the first thing the Prophet ﷺ did when arriving in Mecca was to make ablution and then circumambulate the House.[65]

4. performing the two-*rakʿat* Circumambulation Prayer.

Ibn ʿUmar (may Allah be pleased with them both) said that the Messenger of Allah ﷺ arrived [at Mecca] and circumambulated

63. al-Bughā, *Al-Tadhhīb*, 114 #3.
64. Ibn ʿUmar: Bukhārī, 1549; Muslim, 1184. See: TM, 1089.
65. ʿĀ'ishah: Bukhārī, 1614; Muslim, 1235. See: TM, 1097.

the House seven times, then prayed two prayer cycles behind the Station [of Ibrāhīm (peace be upon him)].[66]

ENTERING IḤRĀM

(فصل) [الإحرام]

ويتجرّد لإحرامه من مخيط الثّياب، ويلبس إزارًا ورداء أبيضين، ونعلين، ويصلّي ركعتين، ويحرم إذا قامت راحلته أو توجّه لطريقه ماشيًا.

One divests himself of stitched garments to enter *iḥrām* [if male].

One can enter *iḥrām* to perform Umrah at any time of the year.

The Prophet ﷺ said, "Umrah during Ramadan has the magnitude of Hajj."[67]

The Prophet ﷺ performed Umrah during Shawwāl.[68]

Anas (may Allah be pleased with him) said that "he ﷺ performed Umrah four times, and all were during Dhi l-Qaʿdah except for the one he ﷺ performed with his Hajj."[69]

Jābir (may Allah be pleased with him) said that "he ﷺ commanded ʿAbd al-Raḥmān to take ʿĀʾishah (may Allah be pleased with them) on Umrah from al-Tanʿīm on the 14th night of Dhi l-Ḥijjah."[70]

The aforementioned hadiths indicate that there is no specific time [for Umrah].

An exception to this is someone who is making Hajj while they are at Minā, since they are occupied with the rites of staying there and throwing pebbles at the pillars.

---

66. Ibn ʿUmar: Bukhārī, 1623, Muslim, 1234 #189. See: TM, 1116.
67. Ibn ʿAbbās: Bukhārī, 1782; Muslim, 1256 #221. See: TM, 1059.
68. ʿĀʾishah: Abū Dāwūd, 1991. See: TM, 1058.
69. Anas: Muslim, 1253 #217. See: TM, 1069.
70. Jābir: Bukhārī, 7230; Muslim, 1211.

It is not valid to enter *iḥrām* for Hajj except during the months of Shawwāl, Dhi l-Qaʿdah, and the first ten nights of Dhi l-Ḥijjah. This is how Ibn ʿAbbās (may Allah be pleased with them both) explained Allah Most High saying, "Hajj is (in) the well-known months..." [Q2:197]. Many exegetes also mentioned this.[71]

One wears a white waist-wrapper, mantle, and sandals [if male].

One offers two prayer cycles, then enters *iḥrām* when one's riding animal rises [or when one's vehicle departs] or, if traveling on foot, when one sets out upon one's path.

71. Including al-Ṭabarī, 4:115.

THINGS UNLAWFUL DURING PILGRIMAGE

(فصل) [محرّمات الإحرام]

ويحرم عليه بالإحرام:

١. ستر بعض رأس الرّجل بما يسمّى لبسًا ولبس المخيط في باقي بدنه إلّا لحاجة فيهما،

٢. ووجه المرأة ويديها كرأسه،

٣. واستعمال الطّيب في ثوبه أو بدنه،

٤. ودهن شعر الرّأس واللّحية،

٥. وإزالة الشّعر والظّفر،

٦. وعقد النّكاح ولا ينعقد،

٧. والجماع وتفسد به العمرة - وكذا الحجّ قبل التّحلّل الأوّل - وعليه بدنة والمضيّ في الفاسد والقضاء على الفور،

٨. واصطياد كلّ مأكول بريّ، أو متولّد بينه وبين غيره،

٩. وقطع نبات الحرم إلّا الإذخر ونحوه، وصيد المدينة حرام من غير ضمان والمختار سلبه.

The state of *iḥrām* renders the following unlawful:

1. Covering any part of the head with something that could be called clothing or wearing stitched garments on the rest of one's body [if one is male] – unless done out of need.

Ibn ʿUmar (may Allah be pleased with them both) reported that a man asked the Prophet ﷺ, "What garments does someone in *iḥrām* wear?" He ﷺ replied, "Do not wear a shirt, turban, hooded cloak [*burnūs*], pants, garments dyed [yellow] with saffron or *wars* [a type of Yemeni perfume], or leather socks [*khuff*]. But someone who does not find sandals is to wear his leather socks, and he is to cut them below the ankle."[72]

---

72. Ibn ʿUmar: Bukhārī, 1542; Muslim, 1177 #1. See: TM, 1162.

The hadith above mentioned turbans. Things that are not considered a head covering are fine, such as awnings and parasols.

2. **Covering one's face or hands [if one is female], as these are analogous to a man's head.**

Ibn ʿUmar (may Allah be pleased with them both) said, "A woman's *iḥrām* is in her face."[73]

A woman can wear whatever garments she wants – sewn or not, [provided she] does not show anything of herself other than her face and hands. One version of the previous hadith includes "A woman is not to cover her face or wear gloves."[74]

If she fears [causing] temptation, she covers her hands and face, then makes a blood sacrifice.

3. **Applying perfume to one's clothing or body.**

This [prohibition] includes scents such as saffron, rose, jasmine, and narcissus, and is based on the previous hadith from Ibn ʿUmar (may Allah be pleased with them both).[75]

4. **Applying oil to one's hair or beard.**
5. **Removing one's hair or trimming one's nails.**

Removing hair is unlawful since Allah Most High says, "...And shave not your heads until the gifts [i.e., sacrificial animals] have reached their destination..." [Q2:196]. ‹In this verse, "destination" refers to Minā, on the Day of Sacrifice [Yaum al-Naḥr].›[76]

Burning hair is analogous to shaving and plucking it.[77]

---

73. Ibn ʿUmar: Daraquṭnī, 2761; Bayhaqī, 9048. See: BM, 6:329.
74. Ibn ʿUmar: Bukhārī, 1838. See: TM, 1370.
75. Ibn ʿUmar: Bukhārī, 1542, and Muslim, 1177 #1. See: TM, 1162.
76. al-Bughā, *Al-Tadhhīb,* 118 #1.
77. Combing hair is unlawful if one is certain it will cause hair to be plucked out. Otherwise, it is offensive since will likely cause the hair to fall out.

Trimming nails is analogous to [cutting] hair, since they are removed for the sake of hygiene and vanity.

Applying oil is unlawful because it is a form of beautification, while pilgrims are commanded to have unkempt hair and be dusty.

6. **Contracting a marriage (as it would not be legally valid).**

The Messenger of Allah ﷺ said, "Someone in *iḥrām* is to neither marry [himself] nor contract a marriage [for someone else]."[78]

There is no expiation for this, since it is not legally effective and the default ruling is that there is no obligation without evidence.

It is offensive to witness a marriage while in the state of *iḥrām*.

It is not unlawful while in *iḥrām* to return to one's wife, who one has divorced and is still within her waiting period.[79]

7. **Intercourse. It invalidates Umrah. It also invalidates Hajj if it occurs before the first release [*al-taḥallul al-ūlā*];[80] one must make a blood sacrifice [*badanah*], continue in his Hajj, and make it up immediately.**

Allah Most High says, "Hajj is (in) the well-known months, and whoever is minded to perform the pilgrimage therein (let him remember that) there is (to be) no lewdness nor abuse nor angry conversation on the pilgrimage…" [Q2:197].

‹And Allah Most High says, "Perform Hajj and the visit (to Mecca) for Allah…" [Q2:196].

---

78. ʿUthmān: Muslim, 1409 #41–45. Did not find from Bukhārī. See: TM, 1435.
79. See "The ʿIddah Waiting Period" on page 394.
80. The initial release occurs after one has stood at ʿArafah and completed one of the following: throwing stones at the ʿAqabah pillar, circumambulating the House, or shaving or trimming one's hair. After this partial release, acts that are unlawful during Hajj become lawful – except for intercourse and foreplay. The second release occurs when one is standing at ʿArafah and has performed all of the other three rites.

In spite of having to remain in *iḥrām* and complete the rites, one must also make it up, whether the Hajj is obligatory or voluntary.[81]

ʿUmar ibn al-Khaṭṭāb, ʿAlī ibn Abī Ṭālib, and Abū Hurayrah (may Allah be pleased with them) were asked about a man who had intercourse with his wife while in the state of *iḥrām* for Hajj. They said, "The two carry on and complete [the rites] for their sake until they finish Hajj, then they must do a future Hajj and sacrifice..[82]

Touching or kissing with arousal and foreplay are also unlawful. This is because they lead to intercourse.

8. Hunting edible land animals or their offspring (from mating with a [non-edible] animal).

Allah Most High says, "...Kill no wild game while ye are on the pilgrimage..." [Q5:95], and "...but to hunt on land is forbidden you so long as ye are on the pilgrimage..." [Q5:96]. What is intended is edible land animals, like cows and rabbits.

It is not unlawful to defend oneself against an edible land animal, even if doing so will lead to its death. This is due to necessity. It is analogous to a human attacker who cannot be stopped except by being killed: he can be killed without liability.

It is unlawful to eat prey that has been captured with [a pilgrim's] assistance. In a well-known hadith, Abū Qatādah (may Allah be pleased with him) reported that he was not making Hajj while two of his friends were. They saw wild asses, so Abū Qatādah attacked them and slaughtered one of them. They ate from it. When they asked the Messenger of Allah ﷺ he said, "Did any of you command him to attack them or point to them?" They said, "No." He ﷺ said, "Eat." So they ate what remained of it.[83]

---

81. al-Bughā, *Al-Tadhhīb,* 120 #3.

82. ʿUmar, ʿAlī, Abū Hurayrah: Mālik, 1421; Bayhaqī, 9779, 9803. See: KBM, 6:384–5.

83. Abū Qatādah: Bukhārī, 1824; Muslim, 1196. See: BM, 6:353.

9. **Cutting vegetation within the Sacred Precinct (other than *idhkhir* and the like).**

The Prophet ﷺ said on the day Mecca was conquered: "This land is a sanctuary by Allah's ordination. Its shrubs are not uprooted, its game are not chased. Lost properties found within it are not picked up except by someone who announces it. And its vegetation should not be cut." Al-ʿAbbās (may Allah be pleased with him) said, "O Messenger of Allah [ﷺ], except for *idhkhir* [lemongrass] since it used in our smithies and in our homes?" He ﷺ said, "Except for *idhkhir*."[84]

It is unlawful [to hunt or kill] game animals in Medina if one is not required to replace them.

ʿAbd Allāh ibn Zayd ibn ʿĀṣim (may Allah be pleased with him) reported that the Prophet ﷺ said, "Verily Ibrāhīm made Mecca inviolable and supplicated for its inhabitants. And verily I have made Medina inviolable just as Ibrāhīm made Mecca inviolable."[85]

Jābir (may Allah be pleased with him) said the Messenger of Allah ﷺ said, "Verily, Ibrāhīm made Mecca inviolable. And verily, I have made Medina (the area between its two lava fields) inviolable: its trees are not cut and its game are not hunted."[86]

The preferred opinion is that the perpetrator's personal possessions are confiscated.

The ruling attributed to the Prophet ﷺ applies to trees and game.[87]

---

84. al-ʿAbbās: Bukhārī, 1834; Muslim, 1353. See: TM, 1166.
85. ʿAbd Allāh ibn Zayd: Bukhārī, 2129; Muslim, 1360 #454. See: TM, 1167.
86. Jābir: Muslim, 1362 #458. See: TM, 1168.
87. Trees are mentioned in Muslim; game in Abū Dāwūd.

OMITTING STANDING AT ʿARAFAH

(فصل) [ما يفوت المحرم في إحرامه]

ومن فاته الوقوف تحلّل بطواف وسعي وحلق، وعليه دم والقضاء.

Someone who misses standing at ʿArafah is released from performing Hajj by performing circumambulation, traversal, and by shaving [or trimming].

Ibn ʿUmar (may Allah be pleased with them both) said, "We set out with the Prophet ﷺ but the disbelievers of Quraish blocked us from the House. So the Prophet ﷺ slaughtered his sacrificial camels and shaved [his head]. His Companions (may Allah be pleased with them) trimmed [their hair]."[88]

ʿĀʾishah (may Allah be pleased with her) said, "The Messenger of Allah ﷺ entered [the house of] Ḍubāʿah bint al-Zubayr (may Allah be pleased with her) and said to her, 'Did you want to make Hajj?' She said, 'By Allah, I am always sick.' He ﷺ said to her, 'Make Hajj and make a stipulation saying, "O Allah, my place of release [from *iḥrām*] is wherever You detain me."'"[89]

Ibn ʿAbbās (may Allah be pleased with him) has a similar hadith, which includes "and she completed it [without being detained]."[90]

Such a person must make a blood expiation and perform a make-up Hajj.

Habbār ibn al-Aswad (may Allah be pleased with him) arrived on the day of slaughtering while ʿUmar ibn al-Khaṭṭāb (may Allah be pleased with him) was slaughtering his animal. ʿUmar said, "Go to Mecca. You and those accompanying you should circumambulate the House, slaughter your sacrifices if you have them, then shave or trim [your hair]. After that, return. Next year, perform Hajj and

88. Ibn ʿUmar: Bukhārī, 4185. See: TM, 1171.
89. ʿĀʾishah: Bukhārī, 5089; Muslim, 1207 #104. See: TM, 1171, 1173.
90. Ibn ʿAbbās: Muslim, 1208 #106. See: TM, 1173.

bring a sacrifice. Whoever does not find [a sacrifice] is to fast three days during Hajj and seven upon returning."[91]

Someone who missed any other essential element [*rukn*] is not released from *iḥrām* until performing it.

EXPIATIONS

THE HADI SACRIFICE FOR OMITTING A NON-INTEGRAL OBLIGATION

(فصل) [الدّماء الواجبة في الإحرام]

والدّم الواجب بترك نسك شاة، فإن لم يجد فصيام عشرة أيّام، ثلاثةً في الحجّ، وسبعةً إذا رجع إلى أهله.

The expiation required for omitting a[n obligatory, non-integral] rite is one *shāh* [a one-year-old sheep]. If none is found, then one fasts ten days: three during Hajj and seven after returning to one's family.

This is because of what has been transmitted: "Whoever omits a rite must perform [a] blood [sacrifice]."[92] ‹Here, "rite" refers to an act that is obligatory but not an integral.›

---

91. Ḥabbār ibn al-Aswad: Mālik, 1429. See: KBM, 1443.

92. Ibn ʿAbbās: I only found it *maqwūfan*. Mālik, 240; Bayhaqī, 8925, 9688; cf BM, 6:91; Ibn Ḥajar, *Al-Talkhīṣ al-ḥabīr*, 972, 973. See: KBM, 1205.

THE EXPIATION FOR SHAVING OR USING LUXURIES

و[الدّم الواجب] بالحلق والتّرفّه شاة، أو صوم ثلاثة أيّام، أو التّصدّق بثلاثة آصع على ستّة مساكين.

[The expiation required for] shaving or [the use of] luxuries is [one of the following]:
1. **sacrificing one *shāh*;**
2. **fasting three days; or**
3. **giving three *ṣāʿ*s [of food; 6.09 liters] in charity, distributed among six of the poor.**

‹Allah Most High says, "...and shave not your heads until the gifts have reached their destination. And whoever among you is sick or hath an ailment of the head must pay a ransom of fasting or almsgiving or offering..." [Q2:196].[93]›

Kaʿb ibn ʿUjrah (may Allah be pleased with him) said that when the Messenger of Allah ﷺ saw him in Ḥudaybiyah and lice were spread all over his face, he ﷺ asked, "Do the pests from your head harm you?" Kaʿb replied, "Yes." He ﷺ said, "Shave your head and sacrifice a sheep, or fast three days, or give a *furuq* [6 *sāʿ*s] of food to six needy people.[94]

Other unlawful indulgences (such as using perfume, oiling one's hair and body, wearing sewn clothing, trimming one's nails, and foreplay) are analogous to shaving since all of them are luxuries.

93. al-Bughā, *Al-Tadhhīb,* 121 #1.

94. Kaʿb ibn ʿUjrah: Bukhārī, 1814, 1815; Muslim, 1201. See: TM, 1165; BM, 6:334.

THE EXPIATION FOR BEING RESTRAINED

و[الدّم الواجب] بالإحصار شاة ونيّة التّحلّل والحلق، فإن فقد الشّاة فطعام بقيمتها، فإن عجز فعن كلّ مدّ يومًا.

[The expiation required for] being restrained from [from completing one's Hajj] is:

1. **One *shāh*, and [then one is released from Hajj via one's] intention and shaving.**
2. **If no *shāh* is found, one gives away food of the same value.**
3. **If unable to give food, [one fasts] a day for each *mudd* [0.51 liters].**

‹Allah Most High says, "Perform the Hajj and the visit (to Mecca) for Allah. And if ye are prevented, then send such gifts as can be obtained with ease..." [Q2:196].[95]›

The Prophet ﷺ released [himself] from *iḥrām* at Ḥudaybiyah when the polytheists prevented him [from proceeding]. He ﷺ had been in *iḥrām* for Umrah.[96]

The minimum is a single sheep that suffices for an *uḍhiyah* [Eid] sacrifice.[97]

Slaughtering must be done before shaving, since Allah Most High says (in the same verse), "...and shave not your heads until the gifts [i.e., sacrificial animals] have reached their destination..." [Q2:196].

Ibn ʿUmar (may Allah be pleased with them both) said, "We set out with the Prophet ﷺ to perform Umrah. Polytheists from Quraysh prevented us from reaching the House. So the Messenger of Allah ﷺ slaughtered a *badanah* and shaved his head."[98] ‹A "*badanah*" is a camel sent to the Sacred Precinct for sacrifice.[99]›

---

95. al-Bughā, *Al-Tadhhīb,* 121 #2.
96. Ibn ʿUmar: Bukhārī, 1639; Muslim, 1230. See: BM, 6:102, 6:377.
97. See "The Hadi Sacrifice for omitting non-integral obligation" on page 211.
98. Ibn ʿUmar: Bukhārī, 1812. See: al-Bughā, *Al-Tadhhīb,* 121 #2.
99. al-Bughā, *Al-Tadhhīb,* 121 #1.

THE EXPIATION FOR KILLING GAME

و[الدّم الواجب] بقتل الصّيد المثل في المثليّ، أو قوّمه وأشترى بقيمته طعامًا، وتصدّق به، أو صام عن كلّ مدّ يومًا، والقيمة في غيره، أو صام عن كلّ مدّ يومًا.

[The expiation required for] killing a game animal is:

1. **replacing it with a similar animal if one exists, or**
2. **appraising its value and buying food of the same value, which is then given away as charity, or**
3. **fasting one day for each *mudd* [0.51 liters] of food [that the amount would have purchased].**

If a similar animal does not exist, one must give its value or fast one day for each *mudd* [0.51 liters] of food [that the amount would have purchased].

Allah Most High says, "O ye who believe! Kill no wild game while ye are on the pilgrimage. Whoso of you killeth it of set purpose he shall pay its forfeit in the equivalent of that which he hath killed, of domestic animals, the judge to be two men among you known for justice, (the forfeit) to be brought as an offering to the Kaʿbah; or, for expiation, he shall feed poor persons, or the equivalent thereof in fasting, that he may taste the evil consequences of his deed..." [Q5:95].

THE EXPIATION FOR INTERCOURSE

وبالجماع قبل التّحلّلين بدنة، كما سلف، فإن لم يجد فبقرة، فإن لم يجد فسبع من الغنم، فإن لم يجد قوّم البدنة واشترى به طعامًا وتصدّق به، فإن لم يجد صام عن كلّ مدّ يومًا.

[The expiation required for] intercourse [that occurred] before completing both releases from Hajj is:

1. **A camel [suitable for sacrifice].[100]**
2. **If none is found, then one cow.**
3. **If none is found, then seven sheep [or goats].**
4. **If sheep [or goats] cannot be found, the value of a camel [suitable for sacrifice] is appraised and one uses the value to buy food, which one gives in charity.**
5. **If unable to give away food, one fasts a day for each *mudd* [0.51 liters] of food [that the amount would have purchased].**

Ibn ʿAbbās (may Allah be pleased with them both) reported that he was asked about a man who had intercourse with his wife while in Minā and before he had performed the essential circumambulation. He commanded the man to sacrifice an animal.[101] The same was related from ʿUmar, his son ʿAbd Allāh, and Abū Hurayrah (may Allah be pleased with them all). No one is known to have objected to this ‹so it is a consensus›.

Substituting a cow or seven sheep for a camel is valid because they all have the same sacrificial value.

Reverting to feeding the poor and then fasting is prescribed because the Sacred Law offers options for one who needs to atone for hunting animals, but does not specify which. The same is done here since a specific order is not possible.

---

100. See "Sacrifices for Eid al-Aḍḥā" on page 506.

101. Ibn ʿAbbās: Mālik, 1432; Bayhaqī, 9800. See: BM, 6:387.

THE LOCATION FOR EXPIATION

والهدي والإطعام مختصّان بالحرم، بخلاف الصّوم.

The expiatory sacrifice and distribution of food must be done in the Sacred Precinct, in contrast to [expiatory] fasting.

Since slaughtering is associated with a ritual sacrifice, it is restricted to the Sacred Precinct.

‹Allah Most High said, "...to be brought as an offering to the Kaʿbah..." [Q5:95].›

VISITING THE GRAVE OF THE PROPHET ﷺ

(فصل) [زيارة قبر النّبيّ ﷺ]

وزيارة قبره عليه أفضل الصّلاة والسّلام مستحبّة من أهمّ القربات.

Visiting the grave of the Prophet ﷺ [in Medina] is recommended and is among the most important acts of devotion [*qurabāt*] that one can perform. [It can be done at any time of the year.]

The Prophet ﷺ said, "Whoever of you is able to pass away in Medina is to do so, for my intercession is obligatory for whomever visits my grave."[102]

102. Ibn ʿUmar: Ibn Mājah, 3112. See: TM, 1149

7

SALES AND OTHER TRANSACTIONS

كِتَابُ الْبُيُوعِ وَغَيْرِهَا مِنَ الْمُعَامَلَاتِ

SALES

A sale [*bay*ʿ], linguistically, is "an exchange of one property for another." Ibn al-Rifʿah (may Allah grant him His mercy) defined it as an exchange of one [lawful] property for another – both subject to disposal [by their rightful owners], with an offer and an acceptance, in a manner authorized [by the Sacred Law].[1]

The foundation is Allah Most High saying, "...whereas Allah permitteth trading and forbiddeth usury [*ribā*]..." [Q2:275] and includes other well-known verses, which will be mentioned in this chapter, as well as the consensus of the Muslim community.

CONDITIONS FOR VALIDITY

إنّما يصحّ بإيجاب وقبول، في عين مشاهدة، طاهرة، منتفع بها مملوكة، مقدور على تسليمها، معلومة.

A sale is valid with an offer and acceptance,...

The requirement for an offer and acceptance is analogous to that of a marital contract. So it is not valid to exchange by simple stating the specific price without there being a verbal offer and acceptance. According to another opinion, this type of exchange is acceptable

1. Ibn al-Rifʿah, *Kifāyat al-nabīh fī sharḥ Al-Tanbīh*, 8:367.

in transactions wherever this is customary. Many scholars preferred this opinion (including Imam al-Nawawī[2] [may Allah grant him His mercy]), since there is no *ṣaḥīḥ* text establishing that a verbal phrase is required. Given this absence, it is necessary to return to custom [*ʿurf*] – just like for other phrases.

Offers include phrases like "I sell to you," and "I give ownership to you." Acceptances include phrases like "I bought it," "I take ownership," and "I accept."

The acceptance needs to be immediate since a delay indicates an aversion to the transaction.

The acceptance needs to match the offer. A sale is not valid when the response to "I sell for ten partial dirhams" is "I accept for ten complete *dirhams*." And the opposite is also invalid.

Both the offer and acceptance need to be final and unconditional. So a sale is not valid if the seller says, "When the new month comes, I will have sold it," and the buyer says, "When the new month comes, I will have bought it."

It is not permissible to sell all of something while excluding a part that is connected to it, such as selling a sheep except for its leg. This is due to the *ṣaḥīḥ* hadith in which the Messenger of Allah ﷺ forbade selling exceptions [*bayʿ al-thunyā*].[3] So if someone says, "I sell you this slave except for her fetus," it is not valid, since her fetus is part of her.

It is not permissible to sell all of something while excluding an unspecified part of it, like "I sell you this house except for a room." This is because of the inherent risk of fraud and deceit.

Nor is it permissible to exclude one of the sale item's benefits, such as [prohibiting] use of the item for a month. This is because of the earlier hadiths.[4]

---

2. al-Nawawī, *Rawḍat al-Ṭālibīn,* 3:339; *Al-Majmūʿ,* 9:162–3.
3. Jābir: Muslim, 1536 #85; Abū Dāwūd, 3404–5; Tirmidhī, 1290 – *ḥasan ṣaḥīḥ gharīb*; Nasāʾī, 3880, 4633; Ibn Ḥibbān, 4971; Dāraquṭnī, 2990–1; Bayhaqī, 10618, 10621, 10832. See: KBM, 1456.
4. Jābir: Muslim, 1536 #85, et al. See: KBM, 1456.

It is not valid to stipulate a condition that undermines the sale. Examples include someone selling with the condition that the seller does not have to surrender the item; that the buyer cannot make use of it; and that the buyer cannot sell or rent it. These conditions all void the sale.

It is not valid to stipulate a purpose that is not entailed by the contract. Examples include someone selling with the condition that the buyer sell him his house, or with the condition that the buyer give him a loan. This is because he ﷺ forbade selling with a condition.

However, it is valid to stipulate deferring payment to a known time, since Allah Most High says, "...When ye contract a debt for a fixed term, record it in writing..." [Q2:282]. And he ﷺ said, "Whoever pays for something in advance is to pay it in advance for a specified measure and specified weight, for a specified period."[5] Also, transactions generally have a need for it.

It is also valid to stipulate collateral or a guarantor, since they may be needed to ensure a [bona fide] transaction. Both must be identified, either by seeing the collateral or naming the guarantor.

It is also valid to stipulate that the transaction be witnessed because [additional] security may be needed – like with collateral.

It is valid to stipulate that a slave being sold will be set free. This is because of the hadith of Barīrah (may Allah be pleased with her), in which the Messenger of Allah ﷺ said to ʿĀʾishah (may Allah be pleased with her): "Buy her and stipulate that they [the former owners] receive *walāʾ* [affiliation],[6] as *walāʾ* belongs to whomever set [her] free."[7]

It is also valid to stipulate things that can be known through their qualities. Examples include writing, sewing, trade, and the like. This is because of the need for identifiable and desirable goods to circulate [in the marketplace]. This is in contrast to things that cannot be known through their qualities (such as a sheep that

5. Ibn ʿAbbās: Bukhārī, 2239–41; Muslim, 1604 #127, 128. See: TM, 1248.

6. See "Walāʾ" on page 551.

7. ʿĀʾishah: Bukhārī, 2168; Muslim, 1504. See: TM, 1206.

gives a specified amount of milk every day). This is because these cannot be precisely measured, and one is not able to provide them.

However, it is not valid to stipulate pregnancy. Thus, it is not valid to sell a slave or animal with the condition that it is pregnant. This is a *qawl* [an opinion from Imam al-Shāfiʿī] (may Allah grant him His mercy) or a *wajh* [an opinion from the early colleagues of the Shāfiʿī school]. The sound opinion is that the sale and condition are valid. There is an opinion that it is certainly valid with respect to a slave. This disagreement is based upon whether pregnancy can be known or not. If we say it cannot be known, then the transaction is invalid; if we say it can be known, then it is valid.[8]

...for something that is seen first hand,...

Sales transactions involving items which have not been seen or that are absent are invalid because of the inherent risk of fraud and deceit. The Messenger of Allah ﷺ forbade all sales transactions involving risk.[9] ‹Risk [*gharar*] is any sale involving an unknown that makes it waver between being beneficial and harmful, and which has unknown outcomes. Examples include selling an unborn animal while in its mother's womb, milk in the udder, [an item] of unknown category, and the like.›

...pure,...

It is not valid to sell dogs, wine, or filth that cannot be purified. This is because there is agreement that it is unlawful to eat filth, and whatever is unlawful to eat is unlawful to sell. The Prophet ﷺ said, "When Allah declares something unlawful to a people, He makes its price unlawful to them."[10]

---

8. al-Rāfiʿī, *Al-Sharḥ al-kabīr*, 4:117; al-Nawawī, *Rawḍat al-ṭālibīn.*, 3:406.
9. Abū Hurayrah: Muslim, 1513 #4. See: TM, 1186, 1202.
10. Ibn ʿAbbās: Abū Dāwūd, 3488. See: TM, 1177.

...useful,...

It is not valid to sell insects (except for leeches), predatory animals (unless they are useful), two grains of wheat, or musical instruments. The reason is that exchanging money for these things is foolish and an unjust consumption of wealth. Allah Most High said, "And eat not up your property among yourselves in vanity..." [Q2:188]. ‹Here "in vanity" includes consumption that is unlawful, such as theft.›

Sales transactions involving items or services that the Sacred Law considers unlawful or filthy are invalid, such as wine, swine, musical instruments, and the like.

...fully-owned,...

It is not valid for someone to buy or sell on another's behalf without his permission, since the Prophet ﷺ said, "Do not sell what you do not possess."[11]

The seller must be the owner who has unrestricted disposal and management of his property.

Sales are also not valid from a youth, someone insane, or someone who is suspended from transactions.[12]

It is valid for an individual's agent to sell on his behalf.

It is also valid for guardians to sell on behalf of their wards, provided they exercise precaution.

The authorities can also sell on behalf of a debtor who refuses to pay, though the sale must be at the fair market price.

...deliverable,...

It is not valid to sell something lost, that has run away, or that was stolen. This is because it forfeits the intended purpose [i.e., ownership].

11. Ḥakīm ibn Ḥazzām: Ibn Mājah, 2187; Abū Dāwūd, 3503; Tirmidhī, 1232; Nasā'ī, 4613. See: TM, 1183.

12. See "Suspension" on page 241.

Selling one's stolen property to someone who can recover it is valid since the purpose is achievable.

...and known.

It is not valid to sell one of two things, due to the lack of specificity – just as it is not permissible [for a father] to marry one of his two daughters to someone without identifying which daughter.

Specificity is required for both items being exchanged – unless the item is known through its quantity, type, or qualities. Specificity occurs by explicit mention (e.g., "I sell you this garment for ten complete *dirhams*"), or through custom (e.g., "I sell you this garment for ten *dirhams*" when only one type of *dirham* is used in the land).

NON-MUSLIMS BUYING THE QURAN OR A MUSLIM SLAVE

ولا يصحّ شراء الكافر المصحف، والمسلم إلّا أن يعتق عليه.

It is not valid for a non-Muslim to buy a Quran [*mushaf*] or a Muslim [slave] (unless the Muslim is automatically set free).

This is because of the shame involved, as it exposes the Quran to disrespect and the slave to humiliation. The sale is not valid – just as it is not valid for a disbeliever to marry a Muslim woman.

SEPARATING A MOTHER FROM HER CHILD

ويحرم التّفريق بين الأصل والفرع إلى التمييز، ويبطل.

It is unlawful to separate a parent from their child – up to the age of discernment [*tamyīz*] – and [such a sale] is void.

The Prophet ﷺ said, "Whoever separates a mother from her child, Allah will separate him from his loved ones on the Day of Judgment."[13]

UNLAWFUL GAIN

(فصل) [الرّبا]

The foundation for unlawful gain [*ribā*] being prohibited includes verses, hadiths, and scholarly consensus.

Allah Most High says, "...whereas Allah permitteth trading and forbiddeth usury [*ribā*]..." [Q2:275].

Jābir (may Allah be pleased with him) reported that the Messenger of Allah ﷺ cursed any individual who consumes *ribā*, pays it, records it, and the two who witness it.[14]

Muslims have consensus that *ribā* is unlawful and that it is among the enormities [*kabā'ir*]. It is said to be unlawful in all Divine Laws.[15]

Technically, *ribā* is the exchange of certain items [i.e., gold, silver, foodstuffs] which are either not known to be equal according to the Sacred Law's standard measurements at the time of the contract, or whose delivery is delayed.

GOODS SUBJECT TO UNLAWFUL GAIN

والرّبا في النقّدين والمطعومات.

[Transactions involving] gold and silver [*naqdayn*], or foodstuffs [*maṭʿūmāt*] have the potential to incur unlawful gain [*ribā*].

This is because the legal concept of *ribā* occurs in these things.

13. Abū Ayyūb: Tirmidhī, 1566. See: TM, 1217.
14. Jābir: Muslim, 1598 #106. See: TM, 1465.
15. al-Māwardī, *Al-Ḥāwi al-kabīr,* 5:74.

TRANSACTIONS INVOLVING A SINGLE USURIOUS CATEGORY

فمتى باع النّقد بالنّقد، أو المطعوم بجنس المطعوم فلا بدّ من الحلول، والمماثلة، والتّقابض قبل التّفرق.

Whenever gold is sold for gold, silver for silver, or a foodstuff for another of the same kind, it must be paid for on the spot, be of equal quantity, and exchanged before parting company.

These conditions are required because ʿUbādah ibn al-Ṣāmiṭ (may Allah be pleased with him) said, "I heard the Messenger of Allah ﷺ forbid selling gold for gold, silver for silver, wheat for wheat, barley for barley, dates for dates, and salt for salt – unless it is equal for equal, identical item for identical item. Whoever gives more or asks for more has engaged in *ribā*."[16] These conditions are also required because Muʿmar ibn ʿAbd Allāh (may Allah be pleased with him) said, "I heard the Messenger of Allah ﷺ say, 'Food is exchanged for food, like for like.'"[17] This hadith indicates that the underlying legal cause [*ʿillah*] is its being food, according to the new *madhhab*. In the old *madhhab*, being measured or weighed is a condition in addition to being food.[18]

Al-Māwardī (may Allah grant him His mercy) said that potable water is subject to *ribā* according to the soundest of two opinions, since it is a foodstuff as Allah Most High says, "...and whosoever tasteth it not he is of me..." [Q2:249]. However, brackish water is not subject to *ribā*.[19]

Concerning gold and silver: one opinion is that their *ribā* is due to their essence and not due to an underlying cause. The soundest opinion is that their underlying cause is that they are the kinds of items by which other items are evaluated.

---

16. ʿUbādah ibn al-Ṣāmiṭ: Muslim, 1587 #80. See: TM, 1187, 1190.
17. Muʿmar ibn ʿAbd Allāh: Muslim, 1592. See: KBM, 1463.
18. al-Nawawī, *Rawḍat al-Ṭālibīn*, 3:379.
19. al-Māwardī, *Al-Ḥāwī al-Kabīr*, 5:126.

Equality in measure is for things that are measured, and equality in weight is likewise for things that are weighed. These are conditions because the Messenger of Allah ﷺ said, "Do not sell gold for gold, nor silver for silver, except one weight for [its] weight."[20] And, Anas (may Allah be pleased with him) reported that the Prophet ﷺ said, "Whatever is weighed is sold for its equal (when it is of one type). And whatever is weighed is treated the same way. If the types differ, there is no harm in them [differing]."[21]

If something typically measured is sold by weight, or something typically weighed is sold by measure, its sale is not valid.

The weights and measures from the time of the Prophet ﷺ are of primary consideration since it is evident that he ﷺ would have known and affirmed them. Gold and silver are weighed. The other four items [wheat, barley, dates, and salt] mentioned in the hadith of ʿUbādat ibn al-Ṣāmiṭ (may Allah be pleased with him)[22] are measured. When the custom of the Hejaz at the time of the Prophet ﷺ is not known, the custom of the land where the sale takes place is used instead. This is the soundest of seven *wajh*s.

TRANSACTIONS INVOLVING DIFFERENT USURIOUS CATEGORIES

فإن كان بغير جنسه جاز التّفاضل فقط.

If [any of the above is] sold for a different kind [but of the same category], only the quantity can differ [and the other conditions remain].

This is because of the hadith of ʿUbādah ibn al-Ṣāmiṭ (may Allah be pleased with him), which includes the Messenger of Allah ﷺ saying, "If these kinds differ, then sell as you wish if payment is

20. Abū Saʿīd al-Khudrī: Bukhārī, 2177; Muslim, 1584 #75–77. See: KBM, 1461.
21. Anas : Dāraquṭnī, 2853.
22. ʿUbādah ibn al-Ṣāmiṭ: Muslim, 1587 #80. See: TM, 1187, 1190.

made hand to hand."[23] And this requires that it be done on the spot. Ibn ʿUmar (may Allah be pleased with them both) said that the Prophet ﷺ was asked about buying gold for silver and silver for silver. He ﷺ said, "If you take one [type] for the other, do not leave your companion while [a debt remains] between you and him."[24]

A type [*jins*] is the answer to "What's that?" – except when one asks about subtypes [*furūʿ al-ajnsās,* i.e., kinds]. If one points to some fruit and asks "What's that?" and the answer is "apples," and then points to other fruit and the answer is also "apples," then they are the same *jins*. But if one points to some grain and asks "What's that?" and the answer is "wheat," and then points to other grain and the answer is "barley," then they are not the same *jins* because the answer to "What's that?" is different. Sub-type includes things like kinds of vinegar, flour, and meat.

EXCHANGING MEAT FOR ANIMAL PRODUCTS

ويحرم بيع اللحم بالحيوان، ولو كان غير مأكول.

It is not permissible to sell [edible] meat for a live animal – even if the animal is inedible.

Samurah (may Allah be pleased with him) said that the Prophet ﷺ forbade selling a sheep for meat.[25]

Saʿid ibn al-Musayyib (may Allah grant him His mercy) said that the Prophet ﷺ forbade selling animals for meat.[26]

It is valid to sell via an *ʿarāyā* transaction, which is when unripe dates are sold in exchange for dried dates. This is due to the hadith from Sahl ibn Abī Ḥathmah (may Allah be pleased with him) in which the Prophet ﷺ forbade selling dates for dates but

23. ʿUbādah ibn al-Ṣāmiṭ: Muslim, 1587 #80. See: TM, 1187, 1190.
24. Ibn ʿUmar: Abū Dāwūd, 3354; Nasāʾī, 4582, 4589; Ibn Ḥibbān, 4920; Dāraquṭnī, 2875; Ḥākim, 2285. See: KBM, 1529.
25. Samurah: Ḥākim, 2251. See: TM, 1194.
26. Saʿid ibn al-Musayyib: Mālik,2414 – *mursal.* See: TM, 1194; al-Shafiʿī, *Al-Umm,* 3:82.

sanctioned *ʿarāyā*: selling an estimated yield of [unripe] dates so that its owners can eat dried dates."[27]

The quantity must weigh less than five *wasaq*s [609.84 kilograms or 1,344.5 pounds], because Abū Hurayrah (may Allah be pleased with him) said that "the Messenger of Allah ﷺ sanctioned selling *ʿarāyā* for its estimated yield in what is five *wasaq*s or less."[28] Dāwūd ibn al-Ḥuṣṣayn – Imam Mālik's sheikh (may Allah grant them His mercy) – had doubts about the specific amount. The most sound opinion is that it must be less than five *wasaq*s due to the doubt regarding five itself.

It is also possible to sell grapes on the vine for dried raisins.

CHOOSING TO RESCIND

(فصل) [الخيار]

DURING THE TRANSACTION

والمتبايعان بالخيار ما لم يفترقا.

The transactors are entitled to choose [to rescind the sale]...

This is according to consensus, and because of the well-known hadith concerning Ḥabbān ibn Munqadh (may Allah be pleased with him) on the topic: A man mentioned to the Prophet ﷺ that he is always cheated in transactions. The Prophet ﷺ said, "Whenever you transact [a sale], say, 'No cheating.'"[29] Another variation of the narration continues: "...then in everything you transact, you have an option [to cancel] for up to three nights."[30]

---

27. Sahl ibn Abī Ḥathmah: Bukhārī, 2191; Musim, 1540 #67–70. See: KBM, 1543.
28. Abū Hurayrah: Mālik, 2297; Bukhārī, 2190; Muslim, 1541 #71. See: TM, 1243.
29. Ibn ʿUmar: Bukhārī, 2117; Muslim, 1533 #48. See: TM, 1222.
30. Bayhaqī, 5:273 – *ḥasan* chain. See: TM, 1223.

Either or both transactors can choose this. It is also valid to give the decision to a third party, according to the soundest of two opinions.

...so long as they have not parted company.

ʿAbd Allāh ibn ʿUmar (may Allah be pleased with them both) transmitted that the Messenger of Allah ﷺ said, "Each of the transactors has the option [to rescind] until they separate or until one tells the other to choose."[31] ‹In the hadith, either of the transactors "has the option" to cancel the sale and return the item "until they separate," meaning until one of them leaves the location of the transaction; and "until one tells the other to choose" is one of them saying to the other, "Affirm the sale or cancel it." Thus, if one of them affirms it, the sale becomes final.[32]›

STIPULATING RETURN

ويصحّ شرط الخيار ثلاثًا.

It is valid to stipulate rescission of the sale for up to three days.

The stipulation to rescind cannot exceed three days, since three days is usually enough time to fulfill the need the item serves. Also, the option to rescind diverges from the general foundation for sales transactions, so it must be limited to what was mentioned in the textual evidence. Durations shorter than the three-day limit are, a fortiori, permissible since they are even closer to finality.

The duration must be connected to the contract. It is not possible to stipulate that the option to rescind commences tomorrow: the stipulation must also include today.

The item must remain unchanged during the stipulated period.

31. Ibn ʿUmar: Bukhārī, 2109, 2112; Muslim, 1531 #44. See: TM, 1221.

32. al-Bughā, *Al-Tadhhīb*, 129 #1.

The period begins once the contract has been made – not from the time the transactors separate.

It is valid to stipulate the sale item be free of defects, in which case the seller is absolved of an animal's internal defects that he is not aware of.

DEFECTIVE GOODS

وإذا خرج المبيع معيبًا – وهو ما يعدّه النّاس عيبًا – فللمشتري ردّه.

If the sold item is found to be defective (i.e., what is customarily considered flawed), the buyer is entitled to return it.

The transaction can be voided if it is found to have been defective prior to [the buyer] taking possession. ʿĀʾishah (may Allah be pleased with her) said that a man bought a young male slave and put him to work. He then found that the slave had a flaw and returned him because of the flaw. The seller said, "You earned from my slave." The Prophet ﷺ said, "Proceeds come with accountability."[33] Another variation has "Earnings come with accountability."[34]

One can return an animal before milking it if one learns that the previous owner had not been milking it prior to selling it. The Prophet ﷺ said, "Don't leave camels and sheep without being milked. Whoever buys such an animal and then milks it has the option of either keeping it if he wants, or returning it with a *ṣāʿ* [2.03 liters] of dates if he wants."[35] This option applies to all edible animals.

This hadith is also evidence for establishing the option to return because of defects.

---

33. ʿĀʾishah: Abū Dāwūd, 3508, 3510; Tirmidhī, 1285, 1286; Nasāʾī, 4490; Ibn Mājah, 2442, 2443; Ibn Ḥibbān, 4490, 4928; Ḥākim, 2176, 2178, 2179, 2180, 2181. See: TM, 1225.
34. ʿĀʾishah: Ḥākim, 2177. See: TM, 1225.
35. Abu Hurayrah: Bukhārī, 2148; Muslim, 1524 #23–28. See: TM, 1228.

There is also an option to rescind the transaction if the goods are found to differ from their description, such as if the seller claims that a slave can write and it turns out that he cannot. This is because of the resultant fraud, and it is similar to returning an animal that had been left without being milked. It suffices that the specified quality is present, and it need not be the utmost extent of that quality.[36] The buyer cannot return the item if it possesses qualities superior to the ones he specified.

Choosing to rescind because of one of the above three options must be done immediately. If one chooses to rescind and another defect occurs, one has the right to compensation for the difference but not to return the item. This is because of the increased harm to the seller and the impossibility of returning the item free of the defect, and compensation is the way to repel injustices to both the seller and the buyer. The compensation is a portion of the price that is proportional to the decrease in value resulting from the defect. If the value is 100 without a defect and 90 with it, the compensation will be one-tenth of the sale price. The value is based on the lowest value of the item from the day it was sold to the day the buyer took possession of it.

A merchant also has the option to rescind a transaction if intercepted by a trader while on his way to the market. He ﷺ forbade intercepting them, saying: "Do not meet merchants en route and transact with them." Some versions include: "Whichever of them is met and bought from has the option to rescind upon arrival at the market."[37] But there is no option to rescind if the price the merchant received from the intercepting trader is equal to or higher than the price found in the market.

36. An example is a "fast car" that can go 80 miles per hour but not 120.

37. Abū Hurayrah: Bukhārī, 2150; Muslim, 1515 #11; 1519. See: TM, 1208.

VARIOUS ISSUES RELATED TO SALES

(فصل) [الأصول والثّمار]

FRUIT AND CROPS

ولا يجوز بيع الثّمرة مطلقًا، إلّا بعد بدو صلاحها، ولا الزّرع الأخضر في الأرض إلا بشرط قطعه، إلّا أن يبتاع معها.

It is not permissible to sell fruit unconditionally, except after ripeness becomes apparent,...

The Messenger of Allah ﷺ forbade the sale of fruits until their ripeness was evident.[38]

...[or to sell] unripe crops [*zarᶜ akhḍar*] that are unharvested, unless immediate harvest is stipulated – [or] unless the fruit or crops are being sold with the tree or land.

It is permissible to sell unripe fruit still on the tree if their immediate harvest is stipulated. This is according to consensus, and because it avoids what is prohibited.

TAKING POSSESSION

ولا بيع ما ابتاعه قبل قبضه، ويرجع فيه إلى العرف، ولا يدخل في الضّمان ولا يستقر إلّا به.

It is not permissible to sell something one has purchased until taking possession of it. [Taking possession] is determined by common custom.

For movable items, possession entails moving them. Ibn ᶜUmar (may Allah be pleased with them both) said, "We would buy food from camel-riders at random and the Messenger of Allah ﷺ would

38. Ibn ᶜUmar: Bukhārī, 2194; Muslim, 1534 #51, 52. See: TM, 1237.

forbid us from selling it until we moved it from its spot [i.e., its point of purchase]."[39]

For properties and fruit, the buyer takes possession once the seller abandons or relinquishes them. While the Sacred Law mentions taking possession, it does not define it and since there is no linguistic definition, it is determined by custom (just like custom defines what is considered a secure spot when it comes to theft, reviving abandoned lands, and their like).

For a property, possession is transferred when the seller vacates it for the buyer and allows him to dispose of it – provided that it is free of the seller's goods. If the two transactors are not present at the location of the sold property, the condition [for a valid transfer of possession] is that enough time has passed for the buyer to have reached it.

An item does not become a liability [*ḍamān*] or final [*yastaqarr*] without it.

So a seller cannot utilize the compensation he received for his item so long as the sale can be rescinded since the compensations does not actually belong to him yet. The seller also cannot dispose of the sold item while he possesses it and the buyer has a right associated with it. Similarly, the buyer's [right to its] disposal is not executed during the time when the sale can be rescinded for the same reasons.[40]

Once the possibility to rescind is gone, neither one can dispose of an item until they have taken possession of it (even if the second sale mirrors the first).

---

39. Ibn ʿUmar: Muslim, 1527. See: TM, 1233.

40. Simply put, one cannot sell an item so long as the transaction is still open to cancellation (i.e., because one of the transactors has a right to cancel the sale) or someone else has a claim against the item (e.g., the item is used as collateral).

ORDERING GOODS

(فصل) [السّلم]

The linguistic basis of "*salam*" is putting something forward. Its textual foundation is Allah Most High saying, "O ye who believe! When ye contract a debt for a fixed term, record it in writing..." [Q2:282]. Ibn ʿAbbās (may Allah be pleased with them both) said that the verse refers to buying goods in advance.[41]

Ibn ʿAbbās (may Allah be pleased with them both) said that when the Prophet ﷺ came to Medina, people would buy dates two or three years in advance. He ﷺ said, "Whoever pays for a thing in advance, is to pay it in advance for a specified measure and specified weight, for a specified period."[42]

CONDITIONS FOR THE GOODS

ويحل السّلم حالًّا ومؤجلًا في كلّ مضبوط بالصّفة، جنسًا ونوعًا معلوم [القدر] لم يختلط بغيره، ولم تدخله النّار لغير التّمييز.

It is permissible to order goods [*salam*], [deliverable] immediately or deferred.

[It is permissible to do so] for everything that is defined by its type and kind,...

Since sales are invalid when the items for sale are not specified, a fortiori, buying in advance is invalid when the [unspecified] item of the sale is owed as a debt.

41. al-Shāfiʿī, *Al-Musnad*, p138; Ḥākim, 3130; Bayhaqī, 11081, 11087. See: BM, 6:616.
42. Ibn ʿAbbās: Bukhārī, 2239, 2240; Muslim, 1604. See: TM, 1248.

...of known [quantity],...

It cannot be a specific item that one can point to, since the transaction is a debt [because the item is not present].

...not mixed with another [type and kind];

This is because of the lack of consistency and its combined risk since the quantities of its individual components are not known.

...and which was not touched by fire except for separation [as with honey].

This is because the purpose [and quality] of the item will be affected by the fire. It is permissible with honey and sugar, since the fire is very mild.

CONDITIONS FOR THE TRANSACTION

ولا بد من وجود عند الاستحقاق غالبًا، ومن بيان محلّ التّسليم إذا أسلم بموضع لا يصلح، أو يصلح ولحمله مؤنة، ومن تسلّم رأس المال في المجلس.

The goods must typically be available at the time the transaction becomes due.

This is because the item being sold must be deliverable. If it is not, one can choose to annul the transaction or to wait until the item becomes available.

The [expected] goods cannot be exchanged for something else. This is because Abū Saʿīd al-Khudrī (may Allah be pleased with him) reported that the Messenger of Allah ﷺ said, "Whoever buys something in advance is not to divert it to something else."[43]

43. Abū Saʿīd al-Khudrī: Abū Dāwūd, 3468. See: KBM, 1528.

Another transmission has: "Whoever buys something in advance is not to accept anything other than what he bought in advance or his capital [i.e., his refunded payment]."[44] Such an exchange is invalid because it would be a sale, and selling an item purchased in advance is not permissible – just like selling an item before taking possession of it is impermissible.

The place of delivery must be mentioned if the transaction occurs in a place unsuitable for delivery, or if it is suitable but there is a considerable cost for transport.

The capital must be paid at the venue wherein the contract is made.

Otherwise, it becomes akin to selling one deferred debt for another, since deferred delivery has the status of debt in currency exchanges and other transactions.

The transaction must be final, without an option to rescind. This is because the transaction involves risk: it is a contract for something absent. An option to rescind also involves risk since the contract may be fulfilled or voided. Two risks are not to be combined, so the option to cancel cannot be combined with purchasing in advance.

PERSONAL LOANS

(فصل) [القرض]

القرض مندوب إليه في كلّ ما يسلم فيه إلّا جارية تحلّ للمقترض، ويردّ المثل.

Lending [*qarḍ*] is recommended...

This is because it is a form of assistance and removing difficulties from a Muslim.

The lender must have free disposal of his property, since lending is a form of charity or closely resembles it.

44. Abū Saʿīd al-Khudrī: Dāraquṭnī, 2977. See: BM, 6:563.

...[and valid] for any item that can be ordered in advance [*salam*] – except a female slave with whom the borrower can legally have intercourse.

An item's equivalent [not the lent item itself] is returned [to the lender].

A similar item must be returned if it is fungible, otherwise its value is returned.

Any personal loan that provides [worldly] benefit to the lender is *ribā*.

CONTRACTUAL DISAGREEMENT

(فصل) [اختلاف العاقدين]

إذا اتّفقا على صحّة عقد ثمّ اختلفا في كيفيّته تحالفا، ويكفي كلّ واحد يمين يجمع نفيًا وإثباتًا، ثمّ لا ينفسخ بمجرد ذلك، بل بالفسخ بعده.

If the contractors agree that a transaction is valid but then disagree over its particulars, they are both asked to swear an oath.

The seller swears first, since his case is stronger.

What suffices is each swearing an oath that combines negation and assertion.

For example, saying, "I did not sell in exchange for this. Rather, I sold in exchange for that."

The transaction is not annulled solely on the basis of this [oath], but by voiding afterwards.

It is not voided if both parties consented [to the transaction]. Otherwise, one or both of them, or the judge, can void it. Once it is voided, the buyer returns the item. If he had endowed it, freed it, sold it, or it died, then he returns its value – which is its value on the day he relinquished possession of it or on the day it died.

SLAVES WHO HAVE PERMISSION TO TRADE

(فصل) [معاملات الرّقيق]

العبد المأذون تصرّفه صحيح على حسب ما أذن له مع مراعاة النّظر والاحتياط، ويؤدي دين التّجارة من مالها ومن كسبه، ولا يملك ولو ملّك.

Transactions by slaves who have permission to trade are valid provided they are in accordance with the permission [the slaves] were given [by their owners], and [that the slaves] employ good judgment and precaution.

There is consensus that their transactions are valid if their owner has given them permission. A slave cannot marry, hire himself out, give to charity, or engage in transactions with his owner. His owner's silence as the slave transacts is not considered permission.

Whoever knows that an individual is a slave is not to transact with him until knowing that he has permission. Permission is known by hearing it from the owner, through witnesses, or it being common knowledge. The slave's word is not sufficient.

Trade loans are reimbursed from his trade and his own income.

A slave cannot assume ownership – even if it is given to him.

OFFERING COLLATERAL

(فصل) [الرّهن]

Linguistically, collateral [*rahn*] is making something secure. Legally, it is making an item of wealth security for a debt, from which the debt will be paid if the borrower is not able to pay.

The textual foundation (in addition to consensus) is the Quran and Sunnah. Allah Most High says, "If ye be on a journey and cannot find a scribe, then a pledge in hand (shall suffice)" [Q2:283]. The Messenger of Allah ﷺ purchased food from a Jew on credit and gave him his iron armor as collateral.[45]

GOODS OFFERABLE AS COLLATERAL

وما جاز بيعه جاز رهنه – إلا المدبّر والمعلّق عتقه على صفة يمكن سبقها حلول الدّين – بدين ثابت لازم بإيجاب وقبول، ولا يلزم إلّا بالقبض.

Anything that can be sold can be offered as collateral...

It is valid to put up collateral whether one is a traveller or resident (as indicated in the aforementioned verse and hadith, respectively).

The collateral must be an item. It cannot be a debt, since collateral must be deliverable.

...(except for a slave who will be set free upon his owner's death [*mudabbar*] or whose freedom is contingent upon something that could occur before the debt is paid)...

Since it is not permissible to sell these, offering them as collateral would undermine its purpose, which is that the item can be sold to pay off the debt when the need arises.

...for loans that have become irrevocably established.

[Collateral is established] via an offer and acceptance,...

A collateral agreement is analogous to a sale. It applies here, a fortiori, due to the legal deficiency of collateral.

The owner of the collateral must have unrestricted disposal of his property. This is because it is a donation involving the debt's type in exchange for a specific item.

---

45. ʿĀ'ishah: Bukhārī, 2068; Muslim, 1603 #124–126. See: KBM, 1651.

...and does not become final until [the lender] takes possession of the item.

The collateral agreement does not become final for the one offering it until the person who will hold it takes it into their possession. This is because it is a contract for convenience that requires an acceptance, so it resembles a gift.

The lender for whom the loan is being secured through the collateral is never required to accept the contract, since it is purely for his benefit. He can forfeit it at any moment, such as by absolving the debt altogether.

TRANSACTIONS ON COLLATERAL

وليس له تصرّف يزيل الملك، أو ينقضه، نعم إن أعتق نفذ إن كان موسرًا، وكانت قيمته رهنًا مكانه.

[The owner of the item established as collateral] cannot do anything that removes or voids his ownership of the item. However, if he frees a slave [whom he had offered as collateral], the manumission is carried out if the owner is affluent and the slave's value replaces the slave as collateral.

Freeing the slave is valid since the Sacred Law encourages it. The value [for the substitute collateral] is based on the slave's value at the time of manumission, since that was the value of the collateral at the time it was destroyed.

UPKEEP AND LIABILITY

ومؤنة المرهون على الرّاهن، وهو أمانة في يد المرتهن، لكن لا يقبل قوله في ردّه.

The owner of the collateral is responsible for its maintenance.

This is because it is his property.

The collateral is an item entrusted with the person holding it [*amānah*] [so he is not liable for damages except for transgression].

The person holding the collateral cannot use it since the contract does not entail anything other than him securing the item.

The owner of the item who put it up for collateral can continue to make use of it in ways that do not harm it, such as riding it. The Prophet ﷺ said, "The back [of an animal] is ridden when it is placed as collateral. Whoever rides it must pay its upkeep."[46]

However, his claim to have returned the collateral is not accepted [without corroborating evidence].

RELEASING COLLATERAL

وينفك بفسخ المرتهن وبالبراءة من الدّين.

The person holding the collateral releases it if he voids the collateral agreement or the debt is paid.[47]

46. Abū Hurayrah: Bukhārī, 2512. See: TM, 1256.

47. See "The Insolvent" on page 230.

SUSPENSION

(فصل) [الحجر والتّفليس]

Linguistically, suspension [*ḥajr*] means "to inhibit." Legally, it is defined as inhibiting financial transactions.

Insolvency is a type of suspension.

PEOPLE WHO ARE SUSPENDED FROM TRANSACTIONS

والحجر أنواع.

[١] صبي وجنون وتبذير: ووليهم الأب، ثمّ الجدّ، ثمّ الوصي، ثّم القاضي، يتصرّف بالمصلحة، ويرتفع ببلوغه رشيدًا في ماله ودينه، وبالإفاقة.

Different types of people are suspended from transactions. They are
1. Minors, the insane, and spendthrifts.

Allah Most High says, "...But if he who oweth the debt is of low understanding, or weak, or unable himself to dictate, then let the guardian of his interests dictate in (terms of) equity..." [Q2:282].

[Ibn Mulaqqin (may Allah grant him His mercy) explains:] In the verse, "low understanding," refers to wasting money; "weak" refers to the youth; and "unable himself to dictate" means lacking mental capacity.

Their guardianship goes to their father, grandfather, an executor [*waṣī*], or (finally) the judge.

Guardians act according to [their ward's] interests.

The suspension is lifted once [the minor] reaches adolescence and [he and the spendthrift] demonstrate sound judgment [*rashīd*] towards their property and debts; and [when the insane] regains sanity.

This is because the reason for suspension (i.e., being a minor or insane) has ceased. Allah Most High says, "Prove orphans till they reach the marriageable age; then, if ye find them of sound judgment, deliver over unto them their fortune..." [Q4:6]. ‹In this verse, "orphan" refers to any minor lacking a father; "reach the marriageable age," according to Imam al-Shāfiʿī (may Allah grant him His mercy) means becoming eligible for marriage by attaining sexual maturity or reaching fifteen [lunar] years of age. The verse indicates that individuals who do not show sound judgment are not given their property, and are thus suspended from transactions.[48]›

Maturity occurs through:

1. Ejaculation. Allah Most High says, "And when the children among you come to puberty..." [Q24:59]. He ﷺ said, "The pen [that records deeds] is lifted from three..." and mentioned, "a youth until reaching puberty."[49]

2. Menstruation. The Prophet ﷺ said, "Allah does not accept prayer from a woman who menstruates unless she is wearing a head covering [*khimār*]."[50] [The hadith] suggests that by menstruating, she has become responsible. He ﷺ said to Asmāʾ bint Abī Bakr (may Allah be pleased with them both): "If a woman reaches menarche [i.e., her first menstruation], it is not acceptable for any of her to be seen except this and this," and he ﷺ pointed to the face and hands."[51] [The hadith] indicates the obligation to cover is due to menstruation, and this obligation is a type of responsibility.

3. Pregnancy. There is no certainty of maturity until a child is delivered, whereupon maturity is judged to have occurred six months before delivery.

4. Reaching fifteen lunar years of age. Ibn ʿUmar (may Allah be pleased with them both) said [regarding participating in battle]: "I was presented to the Prophet ﷺ when I was fourteen years old

48. al-Bughā, *Al-Tadhhīb*, 132 #3.
49. ʿĀʾishah: Abū Dāwūd, 4398, 4401–3; Tirmidhī, 1423; Nasāʾī, 3432; Ibn Mājah, 2041; Ibn Ḥibbān, 142, 143; Ḥākim, 2350. See: BM, 3:225–8.
50. ʿĀʾishah: Abū Dāwūd, 641; Tirmidhī, 377 – *ḥasan*; Ibn Mājah, 655; Ibn Khuzaymah, 775; Ibn Ḥibbān, 1711; Ḥākim, 917. See: TM, 337.
51. Asmāʾ bint Abī Bakr: Abū Dāwūd, 4104. See: KBM, 1582.

and he did not permit me [to attend]. I was presented to him when I was fifteen years old and he accepted me."[52]

5. Pubic hair (for non-Muslims). Saʿd ibn Muʿādh (may Allah be pleased with him) passed a verdict [on this basis] concerning Banī Qurayẓāh: their combatants were to be executed and their children enslaved.[53]

[٢] ومرض: لورثة، ونافذ في ثلثه، والزّائد موقوف على إجازة الوارث الخاصّ.

2. **The terminally sick, for the sake of inheritors. [The transactions of the terminally sick are] executed until reaching one third of their wealth. Anything in excess is suspended pending permission from the heirs who actually inherit.**

Here "the sick" refers to those suffering from a terminal illness.

[٣] ورق: للسّيّد، وإذا تصرّف ففي ذمّته يتبع به إذا عتق.

3. **Slaves, for the sake of their owners. The transactions of a slave are his personal debt [*dhimmah*] and follow him when he is freed.**

[٤] وفلس: في حقّ من ركبته ديون حالة زائدة على ماله، ويصحّ تصرّفه في ذمّته، وإذا لم يعرف له مال فالقول قوله في الإعسار مع يمينه، والحاكم بعد الحجر يبيع ما وجد ويقسمه على قدر الدّيون.

4. **The insolvent, who have incurred debts that are due and in excess of their wealth.**

If it is proven that the borrower cannot pay back his debt, it is better to delay the transaction until he is able to do so. Allah Most

52. Ibn ʿUmar: Bukhārī, 2664, 4097; Muslim, 1868 #91. See: TM, 1263.

53. Saʿd ibn Muʿādh: Bukhārī, 4122; Muslim, 1768 #64, 1769 #65. See: KBM, 1580.

High said, "And if the debtor is in straitened circumstances, then (let there be) postponement to (the time of) ease..." [Q2:280].

The transactions of someone insolvent are valid as personal debt. If he is not known to have wealth, then his inability to pay is accepted when accompanied by his sworn oath.

The oath is required because the default assumption is that one is in a state of good financial health.

If the debtor is known to possess wealth, his claim of insolvency is accepted only when accompanied by proof of his condition [because of the default assumption]. The default is that one is in a state of good financial health, so there is no escaping verification of his alleged lack of funds and his assertion of poverty. Two witnesses suffice, as with all rights.

Someone who claims to be insolvent can be asked to swear an oath (in addition to presenting proof) that he is insolvent and has no wealth. This is because it is possible that he possesses hidden wealth. He is imprisoned until his insolvency becomes evident because his claim disagrees with what is apparent (i.e., him continuing to have wealth).

If his current debts are in excess of what he possesses, his lenders can petition the judge to suspend him from transactions. The Prophet ﷺ suspended Muʿādh ibn Jabal (may Allah be pleased with him) from transactions when he was afflicted by debts and his lenders spoke to him ﷺ about it. He ﷺ sold some of Muʿādh's property on his behalf.

There are four conditions to suspension: [1] that it is requested; [2] that the lenders make the request; [3] that the debts are due; and [4] that the debts exceed the debtor's wealth.

Once suspended,...

The debtor's disposal over his present wealth is not executed, as that is the objective of suspension.

Also, he cannot dispose of what he earns before paying off his debt, as that is also the objective of suspension.

The suspension is not lifted if the lenders consent [to its being lifted]. Suspension occurs through a judge's decree, so it is not lifted except through another decree. Neither is it lifted if the lenders absolve the debts, since it is possible that another lender will appear.

...the authorities sell whatever property the spendthrift has and distributes it to the lenders in proportion to the debt they are owed.

If one of the lenders finds the specific item that he is owed before the property is sold, he has more right to it and can take it. Abū Hurayrah (may Allah be pleased with him) said that the Prophet ﷺ said, "If a man dies or becomes insolvent, whoever owns goods [possessed by that man] has a greater claim to his goods if they themselves are [ever] found."[54] This is provided that the specific items are not associated with preemption, collateral, or payment for personal injuries since in such cases, the items are already associated with someone else's right, which supersedes the owner's right to have them returned.

A lender who finds his specific property is still entitled to participate in the pool of lenders to collect the amount he is owed.

The insolvent person is left with suitable clothing and enough wealth to cover his and his dependents' expenses for the day. His house and servant are sold.

Once the debtor clears his debt, a judge is required to lift the suspension.

54. Abū Hurayrah: Bukhārī, 2402; Muslim, 1559 #22–25. cf Ibn Mājah, 2360. See: TM, 1262.

SETTLEMENTS

(فصل) [الصّلح]

Linguistically, a settlement [*ṣulḥ*] is the resolution of a dispute. Legally, it is a proceeding that leads to a settlement between two disputants.

The textual foundation is that the Prophet ﷺ said, "Settlements between Muslims are allowed, except for a settlement that makes the lawful unlawful, or the unlawful lawful. Muslims are held to their conditions, except conditions that make the lawful unlawful, or the unlawful lawful."[55] Also, Allah Most High says, "...and settlement is best...." [Q4:128]

Al-Rāfiʿī (may Allah grant him His mercy) said that, legally, a settlement is a contract through which a dispute is ended.[56]

والصّلح جائز مع الإقرار، وسبق الخصومة.

A settlement is permissible when there is an admission[57] [concerning wealth or what has the potential to be converted into wealth],[58] and there has already been a dispute.

An admission might come from the defendant and be related to what is being reconciled.

فإن كان على بعضه فإبراء، أو على غيره فبيع، أو بعضه فهبة.

A settlement is a release from liability [*ibrāʾ*] when it is for part [of a debt]; or a sale [*bayʿ*] when it is [in exchange] for something else;...

Thus, [like sales,] settlements include the option to cancel before departing the place of contract, the option to cancel for up to three days, the ability to return an item due to a defect, and other [sale-related] stipulations.

---

55. Abū Hurayrah: Abū Dāwūd, 3594, Ibn Ḥibbān, 5091, Dāraquṭnī, 4472, Bayhaqī, 11352. See: TM, 1268.
56. Al-Rāfiʿī, *Al-Sharḥ al-kabīr*, 5:84.
57. See "Admissions" on page 262.
58. An example of the latter is claims for personal injuries.

...or a gift [*hibah*] when it is for a part [of something that is owed].

‹It is considered a rental when the settlement involves its utility.›

PROPERTY-RELATED SETTLEMENTS

THOROUGHFARES

والطّريق النّافذ: لا يتصرّف فيه بما يضرّ المارة، وغيره متوقّف على الإذن.

Thoroughfares cannot be used in any way that hampers traffic.

It is permissible to extend a part of one's roof beyond one's walls and over a [public or shared] path, since it is a harmless convenience. Thus, it is similar to walking through the path, or sitting in the market in a place prepared for sitting.

Evidence for its permissibility is that the Prophet ﷺ personally erected a rain spout in the house of his paternal uncle ʿAbbās (may Allah be pleased with him), and over the path leading to the mosque of the Messenger of Allah ﷺ.[59]

An extension is prohibited if it harms anyone, like passersby, or if it rests upon the wall of one's neighbor, since the Prophet ﷺ said, "There is no harming and no reciprocating harm."[60]

Use of cul-de-sacs is suspended pending permission [from those who share their usage].

This is because the cul-de-sacs are owned [by the residents]. Thus, one cannot do anything to them that will restrict their utility without permission from their owners.

59. ʿUbayd Allāh ibn ʿAbbās: Aḥmed, 1790. See: BM, 6:689.

60. ʿUbādat ibn al-Ṣāmit: Ibn Mājah, 2340, 2341. See: TM, 1308.

WALLS

والجدار المشترك والمختصّ: لا يجبر على وضع الجذوع عليه.

One cannot be forced to allow beams to be placed upon the walls of one's property if those walls are shared or privately owned.

It is permissible to accept compensation in exchange for allowing water to flow through one's property, granting the right to build on one's property, or for placing beams [on one's walls]. This is because such compensation involves the exchange of things that are permissible and intended. One does not have to agree to the above for free, since the Prophet ﷺ said, "A Muslim's property is not licit except for what he gives willingly."[61]

In the old *madhhab,* Imam al-Shāfiʿī (may Allah grant him His mercy) considered it obligatory to allow [a neighbor] to place beams [on one's walls], because the Prophet ﷺ said, "One is not to prevent his neighbor from placing [a beam of] wood on one's wall."[62] In the new *madhhab,* Imam al-Shafiʿī interpreted it to be recommended because of the first hadith. According to the old *madhhab,* there were conditions for it being obligatory: that the owner not need the location for himself; that the neighbor['s proposed construction] not exceed the height of one's own wall; that the neighbor not place anything harmful on the wall [or beam]; and that the neighbor not own more than one wall – if he owns two then [allowing] it is not obligatory.[63]

However, it is not valid to accept compensation in exchange for permitting an extension over one's land, since air alone cannot be singled out in a contract.

---

61. Anas, Ibn ʿAbbās, Abū Ḥurrah al-Raqqāshī: Dāraquṭnī, 2885, 2886; Bayhaqī, 11545, 16756; Ḥākim, 318. See: KBM, 1591.

62. Abū Hurayrah: Bukhārī, 2463; Muslim, 1609 #136; Abū Dāwūd, 3629; Tirmidhī, 1353; Ibn Mājah, 2335. See: KBM, 1590.

63. al-Rāfiʿī, *Al-Sharḥ al-kabīr,* 5:104.

DEVELOPMENT

ولا يجبر الشّريك على العمارة، فإن أراد إعادته بماله لنفسه لم يمنع.

Partners cannot be forced to develop [jointly-owned lands or buildings].

Just as a partner is not required to plant on jointly-owned land, he is not obligated to build on it since forcing him to do so would cause him harm.

Thus, he [the developer] is not prevented from restoring [the property] to its original condition at his own expense.

Since developing the property allows him to exercise his right [to make use of it], he is free to do so.

ASSIGNMENT OF DEBT

(فصل) [الحوالة]

Assignment of debt [*ḥawālah*] is derived, linguistically, from "transformation" [*taḥwīl*] and "transfer" [*intiqāl*]. Legally, it is reassigning the right to collect a debt from one individual to another. [In the following example, in which a creditor is also a debtor,] it is as though he is transferring the debt owed to him in order to pay his own debt [by transferring its collection from himself to his creditor].

‹At the start of this transaction, we have A, B and C. A owes B, and B owes C. B removes himself by giving C the right to collect the debt A owes him. In such a scenario, A is the *muḥāl ʿalayhi,* B the *muḥīl,* and C the *muḥtāl.*›

The legislative foundation for this (after consensus) is from Abī Hurayrah (may Allah be pleased with him): The Messenger of Allah ﷺ said, "The wealthy person's procrastination is injustice. Thus, if your debt is transferred from your [original] creditor to a [new,] rich creditor, you are to [agree to the] transfer."[64] Another transmission has: "If your debt is transferred to someone who is wealthy, you are to transfer."[65] The command here is understood to indicate that transferring a debt is recommended.

Al-Māwardī (may Allah grant him His mercy) said the command indicates permissibility, since it was preceded by a prohibition (e.g., the prohibition of selling one debt for another).[66, 67]

والحوالة بيع لكن لا خيار فيها، برضى المحيل والمحتال لا المحال عليه - على من عليه دين لازم أو آيل إليه، وعليه، معلوم القدر والصّفة، والتّساوي وتبرأ بها ذمّة المحيل.

An assignment of debt is a sale,...

This is the soundest opinion because it involves exchanging one property for another.

...except that it is devoid of the option to rescind, with consent from B and C...

This is because B can fulfill his right from wherever he wishes, and he is not required to do so from some ways and not others.

This is because C's right is owed by B, and it cannot be transferred except with C's consent.

...(A's consent is not needed),...

This is because A is the locus of the debt owed and the transaction. Thus, A is like a slave whose consent is not required when he is sold.

64. Abū Hurayrah: Aḥmed, 9973, Bayhaqī, 11389. See: TM, 1272.
65. Abū Hurayrah: Bukhārī, 2287; Muslim, 1564 #33. See: TM, 1272.
66. Ibn ʿUmar: ʿAbd al-Razzāq, Al-Muṣannaf, 14440; Bayhaqī, 5:290. See: KBM, 1530, 1594.
67. al-Māwardī, *Al-Ḥāwī al-kabīr,* 6:418.

...between someone who owes a debt that has or will become irrevocably established, and someone with the like, where the items owed are of known quantity and quality – and are equal.

The amounts owed must be equal in kind, quantity, and quality.

They must be equal in kind, since it is an exchange of convenience and not an actual exchange.

They must be equal in quantity, also because it is an exchange of convenience. There is an opinion that it is possible to transfer to a higher quantity, where the excess is considered a donation.[68]

They must also be equal in quality, which includes being due concurrently (i.e., both to be paid now or later), and the quality of the items.

Through the transaction, B's debt is absolved.

This is because B has essentially paid C by transferring the debt A owed him to C.

If A is ultimately unable to pay, C cannot seek reimbursement from B, just as if B had repaid his debt to C but the item was destroyed as soon as C took possession of it.

PROVIDING SURETY OF PAYMENT

(فصل) [الضّمان]

The legal meaning of providing surety of payment [*ḍamān*] is lumping one's obligation with another person's obligation.

The foundation for this (before consensus) is the hadith of Abū Umāmah (may Allah be pleased with him) attributed to the Prophet ﷺ: "The guarantor is responsible,"[69] and, because of the hadith of Abī Qatādah (may Allah be pleased with him) in which

68. al-Nawawī, *Rawḍat al-ṭālibīn,* 4:231.

69. Abū Umāmah al-Bahilī: Abū Dāwūd, 3565; Tirmidhī, 1265, 2120 – *ḥasan ṣaḥīḥ*; Ibn Mājah, 2405; Dāraquṭnī, 2960, 4066. See: TM, 1273.

he agreed to guarantee the debt of the deceased. In the beginning of Islam, the Prophet ﷺ would not lead the funeral prayers of those who passed away while in debt, since his prayer would have been an intercession for them.[70]

ويصحّ ضمان الدّين المعلوم الثّابت اللازم أو الآيل إليه كالثّمن في مدّة الخيار.

It is [only[valid to guarantee payment of debts of a known amount...

This is because guaranteeing something of unknown quantity and quality is a risk. Risk is not allowed when giving and gifting is not a binding contract. A fortiori, it is not allowed here.

The debtor who is being guaranteed must also be identified, since people differ in their ability to pay, and not knowing the debtor's identity is a risk.

The debtor's consent is not required.

...that are or have the potential to become irrevocably established, such as the price during the duration wherein there is an option to rescind.

This is because it is a security. What cannot be irrevocably established cannot be guaranteed, since the person who is owed something irrevocably established can forgive that debt at any time. Thus, there is no need for it.

ولا خيار فيه، ولا تأقيت، ولا تعليق.

There is no option to rescind, set a duration, or make the guarantee conditional.

70. Abū Qatādah: Bukhārī, 2289. See: KBM, 1597.

وللمستحقّ مطالبته مع الأصيل، فإن شرط براءته فسد، فإن أبرأ الأصيل برىء الضّامن من غير عكس، ومن مات منهما حلّ عليه فقط.

The creditor is entitled to seek fulfillment from the guarantor and the debtor for whom he guarantees.

If the creditor stipulates release of liability, the surety is invalid. If the debtor pays, the guarantor is absolved...

This is because the guarantor is the debtor's delegate.

...(though not the opposite).

The debtor is not absolved if the guarantor pays. This is because the guarantor's payment only removes the bond, and removing the bond does not imply removing the debt altogether – just like removing an item from being collateral does not absolve a debt.

If either the debtor or the guarantor dies, the obligation is reassigned to the other [remaining person].

وللضّامن الرّجوع على الأصيل إذا طولب إن ضمن بالإذن، أو أدى بشرط الرّجوع، ويرجع بما غرمه إلا إذا وقع تقاصّ أو باع بما ضمن به.

If the guarantor is asked to pay, he can seek reimbursement from the debtor if the surety was made with his [i.e., the debtor's] permission, or if he paid with the condition of being reimbursed.

If the guarantor paid without the debtor's permission, he does not have the right to reimbursement, since he volunteered to donate. If he paid with the debtor's permission, he can seek reimbursement – even if he did not stipulate it.

The guarantor's payment is reimbursed – unless it involved a mutual cancellation of liability, or he sold what was used as its guarantee.

SURETY OF PHYSICAL PRESENCE

والكفالة ببدن من عليه دين لازم أو عقوبة جائزة.

It is permissible to guarantee a debtor's physical presence...

Surety of physical presence [*kaffālah al-badan*] is permissible because people agree to it and there is a dire need for it. ‹Support for it is found in the verse, "...so take one of us instead of him. Lo! we behold thee of those who do kindness..." [Q12:78].[71]›

...who owes an irrevocable debt, or is owed a punishment.

This is limited to punishments owed to specific individuals because it is an irrevocable right (like money), so its owner is entitled to demand the transgressor's presence.

It also includes crimes such as murder and [insufficiently proven] accusations of illicit sex. But it does not include theft, consuming intoxicants, or fornication.

وتسلّم في موضعها إلّا أن يعين مكانا، ويبرأ به بلا حائل، وبحضور المكفول، وتسليم نفسه عنها.

The debtor is delivered to the location where the guarantee was made (unless another location was specified). The guarantor is absolved by delivering the debtor without any obstacle, or by the debtor presenting himself.

وإن مات سقطت الكفالة. وإن انقطع خبره لم يطالب به حتى يعرف.

If the debtor dies, the surety contract ceases. If the debtor's whereabouts are unknown, the guarantor is not required to present him until the debtors is located.

The guarantor is not required to surrender the debtor unless it is actually possible, which is analogous to paying debts only if one

71. al-Bughā, *Al-Tadhhīb*, 136 #1.

is able. He is not required to surrender the debtor if he has disappeared and there is no news concerning his whereabouts. But if it is possible for the guarantor to present the debtor, he must do so – even if it involves difficulty.

PARTNERSHIPS

(فصل) [الشّركة]

Linguistically, partnership [*sharikah*] is "mixing things together." Legally, it is establishing a right for two or more individuals within a single entity.

The foundation for the permissibility of partnerships is indicated by what Abū Hurayrah (may Allah be pleased with him) said: "The Messenger of Allah ﷺ said, 'Allah Most High says, "I am a third for two partners so long as one does not defraud the other. If he does cheat him, I depart from them."'"[72] It is also indicated in what al-Sā'ib ibn Abī al-Sā'ib (may Allah be pleased with him) related, which is that he was the partner of the Prophet ﷺ before revelation, and he boasted of his partnership afterwards. He said [to the Prophet ﷺ], "You were my partner in *Jāhiliyyah* [i.e., "the Age of Ignorance"] and you were a good partner: you did not contend or dispute."[73] Also, al-Barā' and Zayd ibn Arqam were partners (may Allah be pleased with them).[74]

Partnership contracts have three essential elements: the two transactors, the verbal phrase, and the capital.

72. Abū Hurayrah: Abū Dāwūd, 3383; Dāraquṭnī, 2933; Ḥākim, 2322; Bayhaqī, 11424. See: TM, 1277.

73. Al-Sā'ib ibn Abī al-Sā'ib: Abū Dāwūd, 4836; Ibn Mājah, 2287; Ḥākim, 2357; Bayhaqī, 4836. See: KBM, 1600.

74. Abū al-Minhāl: Aḥmed, 19307; Bukhārī, 2497, 2498. See: KBM, 1601.

CONDITIONS FOR VALID PARTNERSHIPS

ولا يصحّ من الشّركة إلّا شركة العنان، بلفظ دالّ على التّصرّف، وأهليّة، ونقد، ولو كان مغشوشًا وخلط بحيث لا تميّز.

The only type of partnership that is valid is *Sharikat al-ʿanān* [i.e., a partnership of two or more persons in the ownership of gold or silver, fungibles, mixed goods that are no longer distinct, or shared goods],...

This type of partnership is valid because it gives [the partners] authority to manage and dispose of one another's property, even if that property is something that will be owned through a sale, just like [earnings from] financing a profit venture.

...with [the following conditions:] a phrase indicating freedom to act according to one's judgment in the disposal and management of the property [*taṣarruf*]; the capacity to do so; and [the capital contributions from both partners based on] gold or silver (even if it is not pure) that have been combined together whereby they are indistinguishable.

It is certainly permissible on gold and silver that have been minted.

There are two opinions regarding [the validity of a partnership in which the capital contribution includes] fungibles. If we do allow it, the items must be of equal genus [*jins*] and quality [*waṣf*] [and therefore indistinguishable from one another when combined]. Mixing red and white wheat is not sufficient, since they are distinguishable. Rather, red and white wheat [and other unequal items used as capital] must be mixed before the contract is made. Mixing different capital is invalid if done afterwards, since there is no actual joint ownership over the goods at the time of the contract.

Partners are not required to provide equal capital.

PROFIT AND LOSS, AND LIABILITY

والرّبح والخسر على قدر المالين، ويده أمانة.

Profit and loss is commensurate with each partner's contribution [to the capital].

This is true whether they stipulated it or not, or whether they worked the same amount or not. They act according to what is implied by their ownership [of the original capital].

His hand is trustworthy [i.e., a partner is not liable for losses unless he negligently allowed them or maliciously caused them].

Each [partner] must act with precaution and with the other's interest in mind. This is because one must behave this way when transacting on someone else's behalf.

PARTNERSHIP NULLIFIERS

وتنفسخ بموت أحدهما وجنونه وإغمائه وبطرو السّفه، وبفسخهما، فإن فسخ أحدهما انعزل فقط.

The partnership is voided if one of the partners dies, becomes insane, loses consciousness, is a spendthrift, or by both partners voiding it.

The same ruling applies when commissioning others.[75]

If one of them voids it, it voids only his engagement in transaction.

Each partner is the other's commissioned agent, so if one voids his own agency, he does not void the other's. Thus, each has his own ruling.

75. See "Commissioning Others" on page 258.

COMMISSIONED TRANSACTIONS

(فصل) [الوكالة]

Commissioning [*wakālah*], linguistically means "authorization." Legally, it is an agent taking the place of a principal in performing what he has been authorized to perform.

Its foundation includes well-known reports from the Prophet ﷺ and consensus. It is also hinted at in the Quran, when Allah Most High says, "Now send one of you with this your silver coin unto the city..." [Q18:19]

CONDITIONS FOR COMMISSIONERS AND AGENTS

من صحّ تصرّفه بنفسه صحّ أن يوكّل أو يتوكّل فيه.

Whatever is valid for one to perform for oneself, one can commission another to perform...

The need for this is apparent. [And it is supported by hadiths.]

The Prophet ﷺ commissioned people [to assess and collect] zakat,[76] and ʿUrwah al-Bāriqī to buy two sheep (may Allah be pleased with him).[77]

He ﷺ also commissioned ʿAmr ibn Umayyah and Abū Rāfiʿ to contract his marriage to Umm Ḥabībah[78] and Maymūnah [respectively] (may Allah be pleased with them).[79]

And when Jābir (may Allah be pleased with him) was preparing to leave for Khaybar, the Prophet ﷺ said to him: "When you reach my agent, you should take fifteen *wasaq*s [of dates] from him. If

76. Ibn ʿUmar: Bukhārī, 1473; Muslim, 1045 #110, 111. Abī Ḥumayd: Bukhārī, 1500; Muslim, 1832 #26. Others: Bukhārī, 1468; Muslim, 983 #11. See: KBM, 1602.

77. ʿUrwah al-Bāriqī: Bukhārī, 3642. See: TM, 1278.

78. al-Bayhaqī, in his *Khilāfiyāt*. See: KBM, 1604.

79. Sulaymān ibn Yasār: Mālik, 1267. See: KBM, 1605.

he asks you for a sign, then place your hand on his collarbone."[80] (May Allah be pleased with them all.)

...or one can be commissioned to perform [on another's behalf].

It is recommended to accept a request to be an agent.

THE BLIND

ويصحّ توكيل الولي والأعمى في تصرّفاته.

It is valid for a guardian or someone who is blind to commission another to engage in transactions on his behalf.

Even though he cannot engage in these himself, it is valid out of necessity.

YOUTH AND SLAVES

ويعتمد الصّبي في الإذن وإيصال الهديّة ودفع الزّكاة، والعبد يوكّل في قبول نكاح دون إيجاب.

Youths can be relied upon for conveying permission, delivering gifts, and paying zakat.

A youth can be relied upon since the Forebearers [*salaf*] permitted it (may Allah be pleased with them).

Slaves [can be commissioned] to accept marriage offers but not to initiate them.

A slave can accept a marriage offer [on someone else's behalf] since it is harmless to his master. He cannot initiate an offer

80. Jābir: Abū Dāwūd, 3632. See: TM, 1279.

since he cannot do this for his own daughter, a fortiori, he cannot represent someone else for their daughter.

CONDITIONS FOR COMMISSIONED TRANSACTIONS

وشرط المؤكل فيه أن يملكه المؤكل، وقبوله للنّيابة، فتخرج العبادات إلّا الحجّ والعمرة، والأيمان لا يصحّ التوكيل فيها، والظّهار والإقرار.

ويصحّ في استيفاء عقوبة الآدميّ، وفي المحصور دون المطلق كـ«وكلتك في كلّ شيء».

The conditions of the task being commissioned are that the commissioner owns it, and that it is valid for someone else to perform (thus excluding acts of worship...

This is because devotional acts are a test for the person responsible for performing them.

...other than Hajj and Umrah).

[Also excluded are] zakat, slaughtering sacrifices, expiations, and voluntary charity because all of these are financial acts of worship.

It is not valid to commission someone to perform acts of disobedience since everyone is specifically commanded to avoid them.

It is not valid to commission sworn vows,...

The is because their rulings are associated with venerating Allah Most High.

...likening one's wife to one's mother,...[81]

Because this is a form of disobedience.

81. See "Likening One's Wife to One's Mother" on page 386.

Imprecation[82] is also invalid since it is somewhere between making a vow and testifying. Swearing to forgo intercourse [*īlāʾ*][83] is likewise invalid since it is a vow.

...or admissions [*iqrār*].[84]

This is because an admission is a declarative statement, thus resembling witnessing.

It is also not valid to commission someone to give testimony, since it is subsumed within acts of worship.

It is valid to commission someone to carry out a punishment for violating a right owed to a human. [It is also valid] for commissions to be specified but not general, such as "I commission you for everything."

This is because of the enormous risk inherent in an unrestricted commission.

ولا بدّ من الإيجاب.

There must be an offer.

WHAT VOIDS OR INVALIDATES THE CONTRACT

وهي جائزة كعقد الشّركة، ولا يصحّ تعليقها.

It is a permissible contract [*jāʾizah*], just like a partnership.[85]

---

82. See "Charging One's Wife With Adultery" on page 364.
83. See "Forswearing One's Wife" on page 385.
84. See "Admissions" on page 262.
85. See "Partnerships" on page 255. Additionally, *jāʾiz* refers to a contract that either party can cancel. This is in contrast to contracts that only one party can cancel, or neither.

This means that it is cancelled if either the principal or the agent wishes to cancel it, if either of them dies, becomes insane, or loses consciousness.

A contract is invalid when it is contingent upon something else.

THE AGENT

وهو أمين، فيقبل قوله في التلّف والرّدّ، ولا يتصرّف إلا على وجه الاحتياط، فلا يبيع عند الإطلاق إلا حالًّا، بنقد البلد، وبغير غبن فاحش، ولا يبيع من نفسه وولده الصغير.

The commissioned agent is trusted, so his word is accepted [implicitly] regarding the destruction or [safe] return of property.

He must always exercise caution when engaging in transactions. Unless otherwise specified, transactions must include immediate payment, use local currency, and be negotiated at a fair market price.

One may not purchase from oneself or one's child who is a minor.

Such purchases are prohibited due to the conflict of interest.

ADMISSIONS

(فصل) [الإقرار]

Linguistically, an admission [*iqrār*] is "establishing something." Legally, it is when someone acknowledges that they owe a right to someone else.

The foundation for the legality of admissions is found in the Quran and Sunnah. Allah Most High says, "O ye who believe! Be ye staunch in justice, witnesses for Allah, even though it be against yourselves…" [Q4:135]. The exegetes say that witnessing against oneself is an admission.[86]

86. al-Māwardī, *Al-Nukat wa-l-ʿuyūn,* 1:535

Also, the Prophet ﷺ said, "O Unays! Go to the wife of this [man] and if she confesses, stone her."[87]

WHO CAN CONVEY AN ADMISSION

ويصحّ الإقرار من مطلق التّصرّف - إلا المكره - لكلّ من يثبت له الاستحقاق.

An admission is valid from someone who has the unrestricted right to manage and dispose of his own property (unless compelled to do otherwise). He can make an admission related to any individual who can be owed.

Admissions from minors and the insane are not valid – just as with their other transactions. Admissions given under compulsion are not valid – just as are other coerced transactions.

RETRACTIONS

ولا يصحّ رجوعه بعده إلّا في حقّ الله تعالى.

It is not valid to retract an admission once it has been made, unless it concerns rights owed to Allāh Most High.

This is indicated in the hadith about Māʿiz (may Allah grant him His mercy and be pleased with him), who fled upon being touched by the stones [thrown at him as punishment for fornication], so the Companions (may Allah be pleased with them) caught up to him and stoned him [to death]. When the Messenger of Allah ﷺ was informed of this, he ﷺ said, "Why didn't you leave him be?"[88]

87. Abū Hurayrah: Bukhārī, 2314, 6827; Muslim, 1697 #25, 1698. See: TM, 1582.
88. Yazīd ibn Naʿīm from his father: Abū Dāwūd, 4419; Nasāʾī, *Al-Sunan al-kubrā,* 7167; Ḥākim, 8082; Bayhaqī, 16958, 17001. Abū Hurayrah: Tirmidhī, 1428; Ḥākim, 8081. See: TM, 1584–85.

MISCELLANEOUS ISSUES

وإذا أقرّ بمجهول طولب ببيانه، وإذا استثنى جاز بشرط اتّصاله وعدم استغراقه.

والإقرار بظرف ليس إقرار بالمظروف ولا عكسه.

والإقرار في الصّحّة والمرض سواء للوارث وغيره.

وإذا أكذب المقرّ له المقرّ لا ينزع المال منه، فإن رجع وقال غلطت نزعه منه.

If one vaguely admits to something, one is required to clarify it.[89] One may withhold part of one's admission so long as the omission is directly connected to the admission and is not exhaustive.

An admission related to a container is not an admission to its contents, nor the opposite.

Admissions while one is healthy or sick have the same legal status, whether to an heir or a non-heir.

If the rightful owner mentioned in an admission doubts the admission's veracity, the property is not taken from the one who made the admission.

NULL ADMISSIONS

وإذا عقّب الإقرار بما يرفعه – كـ«عليّ ألف لزيد» ثم قال: «من ثمن خمر»، لا يقبل رجوعه.

If one follows the admission with something that nullifies (like saying "I owe 1,000 to Zayd" and then saying "...from [selling] wine") the nullification is not accepted.

This is because the nullifier is a denial after one has made an ad-

89. Since he has already acknowledged a right that can be known only from him.

mission; the nullifier cannot be accepted since it would render the admission inconsistent.

ATTRIBUTIONS OF PATERNITY

وإذا ألحق النّسب به - بأن قال: «هذا ابني»، مع الإمكان - لحق، إلّا أن يكون الملحق بالغًا، فلا بدّ من تصديقه، أو بغيره كـ«هذا أخي»، فإن كان وارثًا حائزًا، والملحق به ميتًا وأمكن، لحق.

If one ascribes a relation to oneself (such as by saying [about another person] "This is my son"), and the relationship is plausible, kinship is established. But, if the one named [as the relation] is mature, he must first be convinced [of the relationship and believe the ascription to be true]. In that case, the one named must believe it to be true.

If one ascribes a relation to someone else (like [attributing a person's paternity to one's own father, by] saying [about that person] "This is my brother"): the relation is establish only if the one making the ascription is an heir entitled to inheritance, the one to whom he is making the ascription is dead, and the relationship is plausible.

[In this case, where one ascribes a relation to someone else, the one who ascribes] must be entitled to inheritance since someone who is not entitled to inheritance cannot be the deceased's successor.

According to the sound *wajh,* the husband and wife [i.e., both parents] must confirm the ascription.

According to the soundest *wajh,* the one being ascribed does not inherit.

LENDING

(فصل) [العارية]

Linguistically, lending [*ʿāriyah*] is derived from "wandering," like when a horse wanders and returns [to its owner]. In a legal context, it entails allowing someone to make use of an item that contains a lawful benefit which can be utilized without being consumed, and is eventually returned to its owner.

The foundation for lending is the Quran and Sunnah. Allah Most High says, "...Yet refuse small kindnesses!" [Q107:7]. A multitude of scholars have explained that this refers to what neighbors lend to one another.[90]

Abū Umāmah (may Allah be pleased with him) reported that the Prophet ﷺ said, "Loans are paid back, guarantors are held responsible, and what is lent must be returned."[91]

The Prophet ﷺ borrowed coats of mail from Ṣafwān ibn Umayyah (may Allah be pleased with him).[92]

Al-Rūyānī (may Allah grant him His mercy) said that [lending] was obligatory and then later became recommended.[93]

A loan has four essential elements: a lender, a borrower, an item to be borrowed, and a verbal phrase.

---

90. al-Māwardī, *Al-Nukat wa-l-ʿuyūn,* 6:353; Ibn Kathīr,8:495.
91. Abū Umāmah: Abū Dāwūd, 3562; Nasāʾī, *Al-Sunan al-kubrā,* 5749–50; Tirmidhī, 1266; Ibn Mājah, 2400; Ḥākim, 2302. See: KBM, 1593, 1615, 1617.
92. Ibn ʿAbbās: Abū Dāwūd, 2562; Nasāʾī, *Al-Sunan al-kubrā,* 5744, 5745, 5747; Ḥākim, 2300, 2301. See: TM, 1283.
93. al-Rūyānī, *Baḥr al-madhhab,* 6:391. Evidence for this comes from Allāh Most High saying, "Ah, woe unto worshippers, Who are heedless of their prayer; Who would be seen (at worship) Yet refuse small kindnesses!" [Q107:4–7].

CONDITIONS FOR LENDERS AND BORROWED ITEMS

من صحّ تبرعه فله إعارة كلّ ما ينتفع به مع بقاء عينه، ويكفي لفظ أحدهما مع فعل الآخر.

Whoever can make valid donations is entitled to lend...

This excludes the borrower because he is only granted the right to utilize the item: he cannot rent out the utility or lend it since he does not own it.

...anything from which benefit can be derived, as long as the item itself is not consumed.

The Prophet ﷺ borrowed a horse from Abū Ṭalḥah (may Allah be pleased with him) and rode it.[94]

Food cannot be lent because its use cannot be obtained without its consumption.

Usage must be specified for multipurpose items, such as land. Otherwise, it is sufficient and valid to say, "[This is to be used] however you wish." Whenever usage is specified, the borrower may make use of the item in a way that is less damaging.

Clothing and residential properties are [presumed] to be used according to whatever is customary.

If one party speaks of lending and the other acts upon it, this suffices [as a verbal phrase].

94. Anas: Bukhārī, 2627; Muslim, 2307. See: KBM, 16; al-Rūyānī, *Baḥr al-madhhab*, 6:397.

LIABILITY

ومتى تلفت لا باستعمال ضمنها وإن لم يفرط بقيمة يوم التّلف.

If the loaned item becomes destroyed through means other than its [typical] usage, the borrower is liable for it (even if he was not negligent)...

The Prophet ﷺ said, “The hand is liable for what it takes until it returns it.”[95]

...based on the item’s value [not its price] the day it was destroyed [not the day it was lent].

OPEN-ENDED OR TIME-LIMITED LOANS

وتصحّ مطلقة ومؤقّتة.

It is valid for the loan to be open-ended or for a set duration.

SUB-LENDING

والمستعير لا يعير خلاف المستأجر، وهي جائزة إلّا إذا أعار للدّفن.

The borrower cannot lend [or rent] the item to someone else (in contrast to the lender [or renter]).

This is because the borrower has only been granted the [limited] right to utilize the item: he does not own the utility itself, so he cannot rent it out.

95. Ḥasan ibn Samurah: Abū Dāwūd, 3561; Tirmidhī, 1266; Ibn Mājah, 2400; Nasā’ī in *Al-Sunan al-kubrā,* 5751; Ḥākim, 2302. See: TM, 1286, 1368, 1598.

Lending [to a third party] is permissible [*jā'iz*][96] – except if the item is lent for a burial.

This is because doing so would violate the sanctity of the deceased [since returning the item would entail disinterment of the body].

DISAGREEMENTS

وإذا اختلف في الإعارة وعدمها فالمصدّق المالك إذا ادعى الإجارة أو الغصب، وكذا إذا اختلفا في الرّدّ.

If the two parties disagree whether an item was lent, the owner's word takes precedence – if he claims it was a rental or stolen. The same is true if they disagree whether it was returned.

DEPOSITS FOR SAFEKEEPING

(فصل) [الوديعة]

A deposit [*wadīʿah*] is the name for an item its owner (or his agent) has placed with another for its safety. Linguistically, it comes from stasis – its as though it is stationary in the depository.

Its legal foundation comes from Quranic verses and hadiths. Allah Most High says, "Lo! Allah commandeth you that ye restore deposits to their owners..." [Q4:58]. And the Messenger of Allah ﷺ said, "Fulfill trusts for those who entrusted you with them; do not cheat those who cheated you."[97]

---

96. Here, *jā'iz* refers to a contract that either party can cancel. This is in contrast to contracts that one party can cancel, or neither.

97. Abū Hurayrah and Anas: Abū Dāwūd, 3534, 3535; Tirmidhī, 1264; Ḥākim, 2296, 2297. See: TM, 1367.

من وثق بأمانة نفسه استحب له قبول الوديعة، وهي أمانة فيقبل قوله في ردها،
وعليه حفظها في حرز مثلها، ودفع متلفاتها، ويلزمه تخليتها عند الطّلب.

It is recommended for someone who considers himself trustworthy to accept items deposited for safekeeping.

The depositee's word is accepted [implicitly] concerning the item's return.

His word is also accepted concerning the item's destruction. However, this is contingent upon the destruction not being attributable to an apparent cause. If it is, then that cause must be established. If the cause is known to the general public, the depositee is not required to swear an oath. Otherwise, he must swear that the item was destroyed by that cause.

This is because a depositee is in a position of trust. A hadith ascribed to the Prophet ﷺ includes: "There is no liability placed upon the depositee."[98]

The depositee must safeguard the property in a manner typical for the property, and protect it from destruction. He must produce it when asked.

The deposit is annulled if either party dies, becomes insane, or loses consciousness. This is because it is a type of agency, and agencies are annulled if either the principal or agent dies.

WRONGFULLY SEIZED PROPERTY

(فصل) [الغصب]

The unwarranted seizure of another's property [*ghasb*] is unlawful according to the Quran, Sunnah, and consensus.

---

98. ʿAmr ibn Shuʿayb from his father from his grandfather: Dāraquṭnī, 2961. See: KBM, 1800.

Allah Most High says, "Squander not your wealth among yourselves in vanity…" [Q4:29]. And the Prophet ﷺ said [in his sermon at Minā during the Farewell Pilgrimage]: "Your blood, property, and honor are sacred to one another, just like the sanctity of this day of yours, in this land of yours."[99] He ﷺ also said, "Whoever wrongly took a handspan of land will have seven earths wrapped around his neck on Judgment Day." And there are also authentic hadiths concerning it.[100] He ﷺ said, "The hand is responsible for anything it takes until it is paid back."[101]

Its preferred definition is "unjust seizure of a right (which is not limited to just property) belonging to someone else." This definition allows for the inclusion of items that are not property per se, such as the skins of unslaughtered animals, dogs, and rights owed to individuals.[102]

ومن استولى على حقّ الغير عدوانًا جهرًا لزمه ردّه وأرش نقصه وأجرة مثله.

Whoever wantonly takes control of something that rightfully belongs to another is required to return it, along with compensation for any damages incurred, and a payment equal to its rental value [for the duration it was taken].

فإن تلف ضمنه بالمثل - إلا الماء في المفازة فبقيمتها - فإن تعذر فبالقيمة أكثر ما كانت من وقت الغضب إلى تعذّره، وإن كان متقوّمًا فبالأكثر من الغضب إلى التّلف.

If the property is destroyed [and is fungible], one replaces it with an identical item (though water in places of scarcity is remunerated according to its value). If one is unable to replace the property,

---

99. Abū Bakrah: Bukhārī, 67; Muslim, 1679 #30. See: TM, 1093.

100. Abū Hurayrah: Muslim, 1611 #141. See: TM, 1287–8.

101. Samurah: Abū Dāwūd, 3561, Tirmidhī, 1266, Ibn Mājah, 2400, al-Nasā' in *Al-Sunan al-kubrā,* 5751; Ḥākim, 2302, etc. See: TM, 1286, 1368, 1598.

102. al-Nawawī, *Rawḍat al-ṭālibīn,* 5:3.

one is liable for its maximum value from the time it was wrongly taken until it was ruined.

If the property is appraised by its value [since it is non-fungible and no identical item exists], then one is liable for its maximum value from the time it was taken until it was destroyed.

ولا يضمن المسكر، ولا يراق على ذمّي إلّا أن يظهرها، والصّلبان وآلات الملاهي تفصل فقط إن قدر عليه.

There is no liability for [destroying] intoxicants.

Since intoxicants are not property, there is no liability for them – just as with carrion.

A *dhimmī*'s intoxicants are not poured out unless they are displayed publicly. [Openly displayed] crucifixes and musical instruments are likewise disassembled, if possible.

Wine intended for vinegar production, untanned skins of carrion [and improperly slaughtered animals], and dogs must be returned because they are items which are permissible to keep, so they must be returned – just like property. However, there is no liability if they are destroyed since [according to the Sacred Law], they are not actually property.

والقول قول الغاصب في القيمة، والمغصوب منه في الرّدّ.

The thief's word is accepted concerning [a stolen item's] value, and the word of the person from whom it was stolen is accepted concerning its return.

PREEMPTION

(فصل) [الشّفعة]

Linguistically, preemption [*shufʿah*] is derived from a word meaning "to lump or increase," or "to bolster and aid," or "to intercede." Legally, it is an existing partner's automatic right of ownership [of a property] over that of a new partner whose status is the result of an exchange [or sale of that property]. Its purpose is to repel any harm [that may affect the original partner as a result of the exchange], such as the expense of dividing the property or extending amenities.

The foundation for preemption comes from *ṣaḥīḥ* hadiths. The Prophet ﷺ said, "Preemption occurs with every property that has not been demarcated. Thus, when boundaries are made and paths are fixed, there is no preemption."[103]

لا تثبت الشّفعة في المنقولات استقلالًا ولا بالجوار بل في المنقسم الّذي لا تبطل منفعته المقصودة، فيما ملك معاوضة ملكًا لازمًا متأخّرًا عن ملك الشّفيع، ويؤخذ إذا شرط الخيار للمشتري وحده.

Preemption is not established for movable properties [independent of immovable real estate], nor is it established through ownership of a neighboring property.

Preemption is restricted to immovable properties like houses, orchards, and land. This is because of the hadith, "There is no preemption except in dwellings or gardens."[104]

Rather, it is established for [jointly owned] divisible properties that do not lose their intended purpose when divided, and only if irrevocable ownership occurred through an exchange [or sale]

103. Jābir: Bukhārī, 2257; Muslim, 1608 #135. See: TM, 1294.
104. Jābir: al-Bazzār, *Al-Musnad*, 7887. See: KBM, 1629.

that took place after the preemptor acquired ownership. One may preempt the sale if the buyer alone has the option to rescind.

ولا بدّ من لفظ، وتسليم العوض إلى المشتري، أو رضاه ببقائه في ذمّته، أو قضاء القاضي له به.

There must be a phrase [to indicate the preemption]. The buyer must be compensated with something equivalent in value or consent to a deferred payment [i.e., a debt]; or a judge must decide that it is a debt owed to the buyer.

فإن اشتراه بمثلي أخذه بمثله، وإلا فبقيمة يوم البيع، وإن كان ممهورًا أخذه بمهر المثل.

If the buyer purchased the property using fungible goods, then the preemptor pays him with the same. Otherwise, the preemptor pays the property's [market] value on the day of the sale. If the preemption involves a marriage payment, the preemptor pays her [the bride] an amount similar to what other women [of her status] receive.

وهي على الفور، فيبادر على العادة.

Preemption must be declared immediately, so one hastens [to finalize it] according to what is customary.

It must be done immediately since preemption is analogous to returning defective items: both were legislated in order to mitigate harm. Also, Ibn ʿUmar (may Allah be pleased with them) reported that the Messenger of Allah ﷺ said, "Preemption is like undoing the tether,"[105] which means that preemption is lost when one does not immediately seek it – just like a camel flees when its tether is untied and one does not immediately set after it.

Delaying preemption after knowing about the sale and its price indicates declining it.

105. Ibn ʿUmar: Ibn Mājah, 2500. See: KBM, 1634, 1636.

وإن استحقّها جمع أخذوها على قدر الحصص، قال في «الأمّ»: «وبالرّؤوس أقول».

If a group of people has the right to preemption, each individual is entitled according to the proportion of his share.

For example, A, B, and C [are co-owners of a property]: A owns one-half, B owns one-third, and C owns one-sixth. If A sells [his share to an outside buyer] and B and C preempt, B will end up with two-thirds of the total property, and C with one-third. [Thus, their respective ownership ratios remain unchanged:] B owns twice that of C before and after preemption.

[Imam al-Shāfiʿī (may Allah grant him His mercy) said in] *Al-Umm*: "My opinion is according to the number of heads."[106]

وإن مات الشفيع انتقل حقه إلى ورثته.

If the preemptor dies, his right transfers to his heirs.

Preemption is an established right, so it is passed on to one's heirs – just like all other rights.

وإن اختلف المشتري والشّفيع في قدر الثّمن، فالقول قول المشتري، وكذا إذا ادّعى الجهل بالثّمن.

If the buyer and preemptor disagree about the price, the buyer's word is accepted. It is likewise accepted if the buyer claims to be ignorant of the price.

106. al-Shāfiʿī, *Al-Umm*, 4:3.

FINANCING A PROFIT-SHARING VENTURE

(فصل) [القراض]

Financing a profit-sharing venture [*qirāḍ*] is when someone funds another individual to engage in trade with the profits split between them.

The foundation for this is the consensus of the Companions (may Allah be pleased with them).

القراض جائز - بدفع نقد خالص معلوم معيّن مسلم إلى العامل ليتّجر فيه مطلقًا، أو في نوع لا يندر وجوده، والربح بينهما بالجزئيّة - بإيجاب وقبول، ولا يشترط بيان مدّته.

Financing profit-sharing ventures is permissible, by giving gold or silver that is pure,...

Trade goods cannot be used as capital since their value fluctuates. Also, if trade goods were made the source of financing, some would consume profit as their value rises while others would become profit due to their loss in value.

...known, and specified...

Thus, it is not valid for the capital to be one of two bags of an unspecified amount of gold. This is because if the capital is not known, the profit will not be known.

...to a worker...

It must be given to a worker because otherwise, he might not be available when needed and thus miss the opportunity for profit. And profit is the objective of the contract.

...to engage in trade that is unrestricted or restricted to items that are not rare;...

The investor(s) cannot restrict trade to a specific task (such as lending the worker wheat to grind). This is because such a restriction is not among the activities of trade.

The investor(s) also cannot restrict trade to rare items since they might not be able to sell them, buy them, or profit from them.

...with the profit split between them [the investors];...

It is a contract for exchange, so the exchange must be known – just like with sales and rentals. It must be a specific portion, such as half or a third.

...and with an offer and acceptance.

The offer should indicate permission for the worker to engage in trade on behalf of the investors. The acceptance must be temporally connected to the offer. It is a contract for an exchange, so this is significant – just like in sales.

It is not required to clarify the duration.

It is valid to set a duration for the assignment after which the worker can no longer purchase on behalf of the investors, since they can prevent him from conducting transactions whenever they like. Thus, it is permissible to mention it in the contract.

وهو أمين، ويجبر الخسران بالرّبح.

The worker is trusted [*amīn*].

The worker's word is accepted when it comes to profit, loss, destruction, and returning the capital. His word is accepted with an oath – just as the word of a depositee is accepted regarding deposits for safekeeping.

He is not liable so long as he did not act maliciously or negligently in the tasks he was required to perform.

Losses are compensated by profits.

وإن اختلفا في قدر الرّبح المشروط تحالفا، وله أجرة المثل، ويقدم العامل على سائر الغرماء.

If the investors disagree about the stipulated portion of profit [each receives], they are [asked] to swear an oath. The worker is entitled to wages typical [for the work involved]. The worker is given priority over lenders [in the event of bankruptcy].

WATERING CROPS FOR A PORTION OF THE YIELD

(فصل) [المساقاة]

The linguistic root of "watering grapes for a stipulated portion" [*musāqah*] comes from "watering," which is the most beneficial work in this type of contract. Typically, it is a contract where a tree's owner enlists a worker to water and care for his [fruit-bearing] tree and then the fruit is shared between them.

The textual foundation is agreement among the Companions and what has been established in the *ṣaḥīḥ* hadiths, such as the Messenger of Allah ﷺ giving [the people of] Khaybar half of its yield of dates and crops.[107]

ولا تصحّ المساقاة إلّا على النّخل والعنب أصالة، وعلى غيرهما إذا كان بينهما تبعًا، ولا بدّ من التّقدير بمدّة معلومة، وبجزء معلوم.

Watering crops in exchange for a portion is not permissible except when it is for dates or grapes [exclusively],...

This is based on the aforementioned hadith. Khaybar only produced dates and grapes, and these fruit require work to grow – in contrast to other types of trees.

---

107. Ibn ʿUmar: Bukhārī, 2329, 2338, 3125; Muslim, 1551 #1–6. See: TM, 1297.

...or [for dates or grapes] principally and other crops interspersed among the spaces in between them secondarily.

The owner must provide the seeds.

The specific duration of the agreement must be known [to both parties],...

This type of contract is analogous to a rental agreement, so the duration must be stated.

...as does the portion [of the crops for the worker].

A specific quantity, such one-third or one-fourth, must be stated.

وما قصد به حفظ الأصل، ولم يتكرّر، فعلى المالك، وما لا فعلى العامل.

Work that is intended to benefit the land and is not repeated is required from the owner. Otherwise it is required from the worker.

والمزارعة والمخابرة باطلتان، والمختار جوازهما للحاجة إليهما.

***Muzāriʿah* and *Mukhābarah* are both invalid.**

But the preferred opinion is that they are permissible due to [general] need.

Muzāriʿah is working the land in exchange for some of its crop, with the seeds coming from the owner.

Mukhābarah is working the land in exchange for some of its crop, with the seeds coming from the worker.

Imam al-Nawawī (may Allah grant him His mercy) said that the preferred opinion is that they are both permitted, and that the hadiths forbidding them are interpreted to refer to when the yield of one plot is specified for one individual, and the yield of another plot is specified for the other.[108]

---

108. al-Nawawī, *Rawḍat al-ṭālibīn,* 5:168.

RENTING GOODS & HIRING SERVICES

(فصل) [الإجارة]

The legal definition of renting goods and hiring services [*ijārah*] is "a contract for a lawful intended benefit, which is open to being given to others and permissible, for a known compensation."

Its legal foundation is indicated in Quranic verses, such as Allah Most High saying "...Then, if they give suck for you, give them their due payment..." [Q65:6], and the story [of the agreement] between Prophets Mūsā and Shuʿayb (peace be upon them both) [Q28:26–28].

It is also indicated in the Sunnah. Its foundation includes a hadith that Ibn ʿUmar (may Allah be pleased with them both) attributed to the Prophet ﷺ: "Give the employee his wages before his sweat dries."[109] And ʿAlī (may Allah ennoble his face) hired himself out to a Jew.[110]

There is also consensus.

وكلّ ما أمكن الانتفاع به مع بقاء عينه صحّت إجارته إذا قدرت بمدّة أو عمل، وإذا أطلقت الأجرة تعجّلت.

Any item from which benefit may be derived...

Because utility is the purpose of the rental, and there is no benefit in renting something that has no use.

The benefit must be intended and must also be permissible, otherwise it would not be legally valid to provide it.

...without the item being consumed, is valid to rent out as long as the duration of the rental or work to be performed is specified. If the [time for payment of the] wage is left unspecified, it is owed in advance.

---

109. Ibn ʿUmar: Ibn Mājah, 2443. See: KBM, 1653.

110. Ibn ʿAbbās: Ibn Mājah, 2446; Tirmidhī, 2473; Bayhaqī, 11649, 11650. See: KBM, 1658.

وهي لازمة فلا تنفسخ بموت المتعاقدين، وتنفسخ بتلف العين المستأجرة لا بانقطاع ماء الأرض، وحدوث العيب، ووجدانه.

The contract is binding [*lāzimah*], so it is not nullified by the death of [one of] the parties.

This is analogous to a sales agreement.

The contract is voided if the [rented] item is destroyed, except for land that ceases to have water, or...

This is because the land's purpose is not lost with the absence of water.

...if a new defect occurs or is discovered.

والعقد على العين يثبته، والأجير أمين، فالقول قوله في التلّف بلا تعد.

A contract for a specific item establishes [the rental].

The renter is trusted [implicitly],...

This is because the renter handles the item with the owner's permission – not for the sake of the item itself but out of necessity for fulfilling its uses – so he is not liable unless he is negligent.

...so he is believed if he affirms that the item was destroyed without transgression [on his part].

ويصحّ بيع العين المستأجرة ولو من غير المستأجر، ولا تنفسخ الإجارة، وإن كان عبدًا فأعتقه عتق ولا تنفسخ.

It is valid to sell an item that has been [or is being] rented – even to someone other than the renter – and [its sale] does not void the rental. If the rented item is a slave whom the owner later sets free, the slave is manumitted but the rental contract is not voided.

WAGES

(فصل) [الجعالة]

Wages [*juʿālah*] refers to rewarding someone for performing a task.

Some of the basis for wages is found in Allah Most High saying, "...and he who bringeth it shall have a camel-load, and I (said Joseph) am answerable for it." [Q12:72], since nothing mentioned in the Sacred Law contradicts it. Rather, it is affirmed in our legal texts, such as the hadith in which wages were paid for a *ruqyā*.[111] ‹A *ruqyā* is the reading of Quran or *adhkār* for the sake of protection and healing.›

Some books place this section after "Rentals" since the two are analogous. Others books place it after "Found Items" since wages are typically needed for their recovery.

والجعالة جائزة، وهي أن يجعل لمن عمل له عملاً عوضًا معلومًا، فإذا عمله استحقّه، ولا أجرة لعمل دون شرط كالغسال ونحوه.

Wages are permissible [*jāʾizah*].[112]

However, if the person who made the offer withdraws it and the worker proceeds without being aware of its cancellation, he is still owed wages typically given for similar work.

[For example,] one stipulates that whoever performs a task will be given a specific reward.

If someone performs it, he deserves the stipulated reward.

This is provided that the worker heard the offer. If he performs the work without having heard it, he is not entitled to the wages because he [willingly] performed the work for free.

---

111. Abū Saʿīd al-Khudrī: Bukhārī, 2276; Muslim, 2201 #65, 66. See: TM, 1336. TM, 265.

112. Here, *jāʾiz* refers to a contract that either party can cancel. This is in contrast to contracts that one party can cancel, or neither.

Another condition is that the person who heard the offer is someone who is legally responsible.

No wages are owed for work performed without a stipulated wage, such as laundry and the like.

In the absence of stipulated wages, such work is an act of charity.

RECLAMATION AND USE OF UNCLAIMED RESOURCES

(فصل) [إحياء الموات]

Wastelands [*mawāt*] are lands that no one has claimed by means of development and the like.

The foundation for the reclamation of wastelands [*iḥyā al-mawāt*] [being permissible] is that the Prophet ﷺ said, "Whoever revives dead land becomes its owner and unjust roots have no right."[113] There is general consensus about this, despite disagreement about its details.

Reclamation is recommended because of the hadith: "Whoever revives dead land receives a reward from it, and whatever forages [*ʿāfiyah*] or benefits from it is charity."[114]

والأرض التي لم تعمر قط، للمسلم إحياؤها، وللكافر في دارهم، وهو التّهيئة لما يريد.

Land that has never been developed can be reclaimed by a Muslim.

It is restricted to Muslims because he ﷺ said, in reference to abandoned lands, "It is yours from me, O Muslims!"[115]

113. Saʿīd ibn Zayd: Abū Dāwūd, 3073; Tirmidhī, 1378 – *ḥasan gharīb*; Nasāʾī, *Al-Sunan al-kubrā*, 5729, 5730, 11538, 11539, 11772, 11781; al-Bazzār, 1256. See: TM, 1292.

114. Jābir: Nasāʾī, *Al-Sunan al-kubrā*, 5724–5726; Ibn Ḥibbān, 5205. See: TM, 1303.

115. Ibn Ṭāwūs: Bayhaqī, 11783 – however the phrase "O Muslims!" is not in any of the narrations. See: KBM, 1664; cf TM, 1303.

Non-Muslims can do so in their own lands [i.e., lands not under Islamic rule].

Reclamation takes place by making [the land] suitable for its intended purpose.

Reclamation is mentioned in Sacred Law without qualifiers. Thus, it occurs according to the demands of custom and, thus, depends upon what it is intended for.

By default, streets are means to be used as passageways. [However,] no one is prevented from sitting in them so long as doing so does not obstruct the passage of others. If someone sits therein intending to sell, he has a right to claim the spot so long as he does not leave the trade, become sick, or travel. If he leaves with the intention of returning, his right is not voided unless he leaves for a long enough period that his work is interrupted and others desire the spot, in which case and it does not matter whether he left without an excuse [i.e., he loses his spot].

Exposed minerals [and other natural resources] are owned simply by collecting them, including water, water from an uninterrupted source, petroleum, phosphate [though it is filthy if derived from the bones of unslaughtered animals], rocks, and salt. "Exposed" means they are plainly visible without excavation, and the only toil involved is gathering them.

Everyone is entitled to flow water onto his land since water is communal property [*mubāḥāt*]. If someone upstream needs the entire river, those downstream must remain patient until his needs are met. It is not permissible to withhold the water from him by using it to revive land above him, since the person below already has the right to it.

Hidden minerals are owned by exposing them, including gold and silver, and everything that is below the earth's surface. None of these are owned until they are revived via excavation – like exposed ore. Unlike reviving abandoned lands, whose revival eliminates the need for daily work on them, ore [and other minerals] embedded in the layers of the earth require excavation and daily effort.

The first to arrive has priority for water and minerals when there is high demand [for the resources]. The Prophet ﷺ said, "Whoever reaches something that was not reached before him has more right to it."[116]

WATER RIGHTS

ويجب بذل الماء للماشية للحاجة دون الزّرع.

One is obliged to give [one's excess] water to others when it is needed for their livestock – but not for their crops.

Abū Hurayrah (may Allah be pleased with him) said that the Messenger of Allah ﷺ said, "Three things are not withheld: water, pasture, and fire."[117]

Abū Hurayrah (may Allah be pleased with him) also said that the Messenger of Allah ﷺ said, "[There are] three people Allah will not look at on the Day of Resurrection nor purify, and who will have a painful punishment: a man on a pathway who possessed excess water and barred travelers from using it…"[118] ‹In the hadith, "will not look at" means to look at them with mercy and honor; and "purify them" means to cleanse them of the sins of their bad deeds.[119]›

Jābir ibn ʿAbd Allāh (may Allah be pleased with them both) said that the Messenger of Allah ﷺ forbade the sale of excess water.[120]

‹There are conditions that make the water obligatory to share and unlawful to withhold. Among them are that the water replenishes itself, and that the excess water not be stored in a container.›

116. Asmar ibn Muḍarris: Abū Dāwūd, 3071; Dāraquṭnī, 11779, 11836–7. See: TM, 1034.

117. Abū Hurayrah: Ibn Mājah, 2473. See: TM, 1310.

118. Abū Hurayrah: Bukhārī, 2358; Muslim, 108 #173. See: BM, 8:192.

119. al-Bughā, *Al-Tadhhīb,* 146 #1.

120. Jābir: Muslim, 1565. See: BM, 7:92.

ENDOWMENTS

(فصل) [الوقف]

An endowment [*waqf*] is the retention of a beneficial, non-consumable asset [or property] that becomes unlawful to trade, and whose benefits are used exclusively for pious deeds.

The textual foundation for endowments includes the hadith in which ʿUmar ibn al-Khaṭṭāb (may Allah be pleased with him) sought advice from the Prophet ﷺ for what to do with land he obtained in Khaybar. ʿUmar (may Allah be pleased with him) made its fruit an endowment and gave it as charity. [He stipulated] that it was never to be sold, gifted, or inherited.[121] ‹Concerning the meaning of the hadith: "obtained" refers to lands obtained when Khaybar was conquered and its lands divided; "keep it" means to make it an endowment; and "use it as charity" means through its fruits and yield.[122]›

Its foundation also includes his ﷺ saying, "When a person dies, his deeds end except for three: ongoing charity, beneficial knowledge, or a pious child who prays for him."[123] The scholars understood "ongoing charity" to refer to endowments.

---

121. Ibn ʿUmar: Bukhārī, 2764, 2772; Muslim, 1632 #15, 1633; Nasāʾī, *Al-Sunan al-Kubrā,* 6431. See: BM, 7:99.

122. al-Bughā, *Al-Tadhhīb,* 146 #5.

123. Abū Hurayrah: Muslim, 1631 #14. See: TM, 893, 1314.

وكلّ ما أمكن بيعه والانتفاع به دوامًا – مع بقاء عينه – صحّ وقفه في غير محظور
وغير منقطع الأوّل
بصريح وكناية، ويتبع شرطه.

Anything that provides ongoing benefit (without being consumed) is valid as an endowment...

Exceptions to this includes someone who is free, a slave who has borne her master's child,[124] and something put up as collateral. [125]

...provided it is not for something unlawful...

An endowment cannot be used for something unlawful according to the Sacred Law, as that would aid in performing acts of disobedience.

...and its initial recipients exist.

The specific individuals or members of a specific category must be alive at the time the endowment is made, and the intended [subsequent] recipients will continue to benefit from it in perpetuity. For example, one may establish an endowment for one's descendants and, thereafter, for the poor.

If a specific individual is named, he must accept the endowment [for it to be effective]. This is because it is unlikely that something can come into someone's possession without his consent.

[It is valid whether the language is] explicit or vague.

This is because an endowment is a transferral of ownership of a utility, or a good and a utility. Thus, it resembles all other transferals of ownership.

124. See "Ummahāt al-Awlād" on page 555.

125. See "Offering Collateral" on page 237.

The endowment's conditions must be followed.

The asset [or property] is managed by either the one who made the endowment (since he donated it in charity and is therefore most entitled to administer it) or by the person to whom he assigned it. ʿUmar (may Allah be pleased with him) initially managed his own charity. He then assigned it to Ḥafṣah (may Allah be pleased with her), and after her, to members of her family who were known to be circumspect.[126]

The administrator of the endowment is not entitled to wages unless the donor has stipulated it.

GIFTS

(فصل) [الهبة]

Part of the legal foundation for giving gifts [*hibah*] is found in Allah Most High saying, "When ye are greeted with a greeting, greet ye with better than it or return it..." [Q4:86]. [Some scholars] consider "greeting" to mean "giving gifts." Also, Allah Most High says, "... and giveth wealth, for love of Him..." [Q2:177]. [Some scholars consider] "greeting" to mean "give gifts and charity." There is also a hadith, which includes the phrase: "Exchange gifts and you will love one another."[127]

وما جاز بيعه جاز هبته ولا تلزم إلا بقبض وإذن فيه، مع إيجاب وقبول.

Whatever is permissible to sell is permissible to offer as a gift.

Gift-giving transfers ownership while one is still alive. It is not valid except with sellable items.

126. Yaḥyā ibn Saʿīd: Abū Dāwūd, 2879, Bayhaqī, 11893. See: KBM, 1692.

127. Bayhaqī, 6:169; ibid., *Shuʿab al-īmān*, 8976. See: KBM, 1696.

The gift is not binding except if the recipient takes possession of it while having permission to do so,...

ʿĀʾishah reported: "Abū Bakr the Truthful gave me palm trees from his property at al-Ghābah whose produce was twenty *wasaq*s. When he was dying, he said, 'By Allah, little daughter, there is no one I would prefer to be wealthy after I die than you. Nor is there anyone whose poverty would be harder on me after I'm gone than you. I gave you palm trees whose produce is twenty *wasaq*s. Had you cut them and taken possession of them, they would have been yours, but today they are the inheritance of your two brothers and two sisters, so divide according to the Book of Allah.'" ʿĀʾishah continued, "I said, 'My father! By Allah, even if it had been more, I would have left it. There is only Asmāʾ. Who is my other sister?" Abū Bakr replied, 'What is Bint Khārijah carrying in her womb? I think that it is going to be a girl.'" (May Allah be pleased with them all.)[128]

...with an offer and acceptance.

Just like sales and all other transferals of ownership, both the offer and acceptance are required.

The offer cannot be contingent upon some condition, nor can it be temporary.

The acceptance must occur immediately after the offer, as with sales.

However, this [offer and acceptance] is not a requirement for a *hadiyah*. This is because the gift being delivered is like an offer from the sender, and taking possession of it is like an acceptance from its recipient. Charity is the same.

128. ʿĀʾishah: Mālik (2783). See: KBM, 1708.

WITHDRAWING A GIFT

ولا رجوع إلّا لأصل ما دامت باقية في يد الموهوب.

A gift cannot be withdrawn, except in the case of a parent [taking back a gift the parent gave to their child], provided the gift is still in the recipient's possession.

Ibn ʿAbbās (may Allah be pleased with them both) reported that the Messenger of Allah ﷺ said, "It is not permissible for a man to give a grant and then retract it, except for a father in what he gives his son," and Abū Dāwūd includes "or to give a gift" after "a grant."[129]

Ibn ʿAbbās (may Allah be pleased with them both) also reported that the Messenger of Allah ﷺ said, "Someone who retracts a gift is like a dog who vomits and then takes back his own vomit."[130]

A parent may only reclaim their gift if it is still in their child's possession. The parent cannot reclaim the gift's value if it has been sold, nor can they reclaim the gift itself if their child sold it and then reacquired it, or if it is [now] associated with someone else's rights.

LIFE AND SURVIVOR GRANTS

وإذا أرقبه شيئًا، أو أعمره كان هبة.

When a [property] owner says "If I die first, this is yours" or "It is yours as long as you live," the property is [considered] a gift [to the person whom he addressed].

In *ʿumrā* ["life grant"]: X gives Y the property so long as X lives, and it then returns to X.

---

129. Ibn ʿAbbās: Abū Dāwūd, 3539; Tirmidhī, 1299, 2131–2 – *ḥasan ṣaḥīḥ*; Nasāʾī, 3690, 3694, 3703; Ibn Mājah, 2377; Ibn Ḥibbān, 5123; Dāraquṭnī, 2967; Ḥākim, 2298. See: TM, 1325.

130. Ibn ʿAbbās: Bukhārī, 2589; Muslim, 1622. See: BM, 7:136. al-Shafiʿī, *Al-Umm*, 2:64.

In *ruqbā* ["survivor grant"]: X gives Y the property, and if X dies first, Y becomes the owner, or if Y dies first, ownership reverts back to X.

Jābir (may Allah be pleased with him) said that the Messenger of Allah ﷺ said, "Any person who confers a life grant [*ʿumrā*] upon a[nother] person and his progeny by saying, 'I confer this upon you, upon your descendants, and upon anyone who survives you' relinquishes ownership of that property to the recipient and his posterity. It will not return to its original owner since he has given a gift that is inheritable." It is inheritable and the recipient's heirs have a right to it.[131]

Jābir (may Allah be pleased with him) also said that the Messenger of Allah ﷺ said, "Life grants [*ʿumrā*s] are lawful to whomever they are given, and survivor grants [*ruqbā*s] are lawful to whomever they are given."[132] ‹In the hadith, "lawful" means that they are executed and carried out.[133]›

FOUND ITEMS

(فصل) [اللقطة]

Found items [*luqaṭah*] refers to taking an unprotected item in order to preserve it for its owner.

Several hadiths establish the textual foundation for found items and their pertinent rulings. Zayd ibn Khālid al-Juhanī (may Allah be pleased with him) said that a man asked the Prophet ﷺ about picking up stray gold or silver. He ﷺ said, "Make note of its strap and its bag, then announce it for a year. If it is not recognized [by its owner], spend it and it will be entrusted to you. If someone demands it one day, return it to him." He then asked him ﷺ about a stray camel. He ﷺ said to him, "What business is it of yours? Leave it, as it has its feet and water: it will drink from the water and eat of trees until its owner finds it." He asked him ﷺ about

131. Jābir: Muslim, 1625. See: TM, 1317.

132. Jābir: Abū Dāwūd, 3558, Tirmidhī, 1351 - *ḥasan ṣaḥīḥ*. See: TM, 1321.

133. al-Bughā, *Al-Tadhhīb*, 148 #1.

[a stray] sheep and he ﷺ said, "Take it, as it's either for you, your brother, or the wolf."[134]

الواثق بأمانة نفسه التقاطه مستحب.

Picking up lost items is recommended...

It is not obligatory, even if one believes that the item will most likely disappear [if one leaves it].

...for an individual who considers himself trustworthy.

It is also valid for non-Muslims, people who are morally corrupt, youths, and the insane [to pick up lost items].

The guardian of a youth or of one who is insane announces the discovery of the lost property and take it from their possession, since neither a youth's announcement nor that of an insane person is trustworthy.

The authorities remove the property from the possession of someone who is morally corrupt. This is because his own child's property cannot be left in his possession, so how can he be given possession of a stranger's property? The authorities assign someone to witness his announcement.

فإن أخذ لحفظ استحبّ التعريف، والمختار وجوبه، أو للتملّك – وكان قليلًا – عرّفه ما يليق به، فإن كان كثيرًا عرّفه سنّة ثمّ تملّكه، فإن جاء صاحبها أداها إليه.

If one takes the lost item for safekeeping, it is recommended that one announce that a lost item has been found. However, the preferred opinion is that it is obligatory to announce it.

134. Zayd ibn Khālid al-Juhanī: Bukhārī, 91; Muslim, 1722 #61. See: TM, 1328.

[If one wants to] assume ownership (and the item's value is relatively low), one announces, for an appropriate period of time,[135] that a lost item has been found. If it is valuable, one announces it for the duration of one [lunar] year.

[Once the duration is over] one can assume ownership of the item but must return it if its owner appears.

Both conditions are based on the hadith of Zayd ibn Khālid (may Allah be pleased with him): "And if its owner comes [return it], otherwise it is your affair."[136]

FOUNDLINGS

(فصل) [اللقيط]

The word "*laqīṭ*" refers to finding an unclaimed, abandoned child.

Some of the legal basis for assuming guardianship of an abandoned child is found in Allah Most High saying, "...but help ye one another unto righteousness and pious duty..." [Q5:2]. ‹Also, it is done to save an inviolate soul from destruction and to preserve life, concerning which Allah Most High says, "...whoso saveth the life of one, it shall be as if he had saved the life of all mankind..." [Q5:32][137]›

والتقاط المنبوذ فرض كفاية.

Sheltering an abandoned child is a communal obligation.

---

135 "An appropriate period of time" is based upon the value of the item, one's distance from the rest of the population, and the accessibility of one's location.

136. Zayd ibn Khālid al-Juhanī: Bukhārī, 91; Muslim, 1722. See: BM, 7:151, 7:163.

137. al-Bughā, *Al-Tadhhīb,* 150 #2.

ويجب الإشهاد عليه، بخلاف اللقطة، ولا يقرّ إلّا في يد أمين.

It must be witnessed, in contrast to picking up lost items. The child is not to be left in anyone's custody unless that person is trustworthy.

ثمّ نفقته في ماله، وإلّا ففي بيت المال.

The child's expenses are paid from his [own] property;...

This applies only if any property is found with him. The guardian must have permission from the authorities to use the foundling's property. Otherwise, the guardian must reimburse the foundling [for using his property].

...otherwise they are paid from the Muslim treasury [*bayt al-māl*].

ʿUmar (may Allah be pleased with him) sought advice from the Companions (may Allah be pleased with them all) concerning upkeep for a foundling. They were in consensus that it comes from the Muslim treasury.[138]

An impoverished adult can receive funds from the Muslim treasury. A fortiori, so can a foundling. If the treasury is depleted, the affluent must lend money that the child later reimburses.

138. Sunayn Abī Jamīlah: Bayhaqī, 12133. See: KBM, 1724.

8

INHERITANCE AND BEQUESTS

كِتَابُ الْفَرَائِضِ وَالْوَصَايَا

The word for inheritance [*farā'iḍ*] is the plural of "*farīḍah,*" which means a "portion," "segment," "obligation," or "commitment."

The foundation for the rulings on inheritance comes from the Quran and Sunnah. Allah Most High says, "Allah chargeth you concerning (the provision for) your children..." [Q4:11], "And unto you belongeth a half of that which your wives leave..." [Q4:12], and "They ask thee for a pronouncement. Say: Allah hath pronounced for you concerning distant kindred..." [Q4:176].

Numerous hadiths encourage the study and teaching of inheritance laws. The Prophet ﷺ said, "Learn inheritance laws and teach them to the people, since I am a mortal individual. Knowledge will be taken away and strife will appear, such that even two individuals will disagree concerning inheritance and not find anyone to resolve their dispute."[1]

The Prophet ﷺ said, "Learn inheritance laws, as they are part of your religion. They are half of knowledge and the first thing that will be removed from my nation."[2] The phrase "half of knowledge" refers to the two stages of a human being: life and death. Most of the knowledge related to death concerns inheritance.

1. Ibn Masʿūd: Tirmidhī, 2091; Nasā'ī, *Al-Sunan al-kubrā,* 6305, 6306; Ḥākim, 7951. See: TM, 1337, 1726.
2. Abū Hurayrah: Ibn Mājah, 2719; Dāraquṭnī, 4069; Bayhaqī, 12175, 12177; Ḥākim, 7948. See: KBM, 1727.

ʿUmar (may Allah be pleased with him) said, "When you converse, speak about inheritance law. When you entertain yourself, do so with marksmanship."[3]

In pre-Islamic Arabian culture, men inherited but women did not. Instead, wives would be given up to one year of expenses from their husbands' estates. This was justified using the rationale that it is men who bear the burden of providing, hosting guests, and engaging in warfare. Inheritance went to the older children but not the younger ones. Brothers, sons of brothers, the wives of brothers, and paternal uncles were also regarded as heirs.

This tradition was abrogated when Allah Most High revealed, "Unto the men (of a family) belongeth a share of that which parents and near kindred leave, and unto the women a share of that which parents and near kindred leave, whether it be little or much – a legal share" [Q4:7].

In the beginning of Islam, inheritance would take place via adoption and brotherhood. Later, it occurred through succession and alliances, which was understood from "...and as for those with whom your right hands have made a covenant, give them their due..." [Q4:33]. (It is reported that this also happened before Islam.) This was later abrogated, at which point one inherited upon emigrating [to Medina] and [accepting] Islam, so if a group of Muslims emigrated but another did not, the latter would no longer inherit. This is the meaning of Allah Most High's Words, "Lo! those who believed and left their homes and strove with their wealth and their lives for the cause of Allah, and those who took them in and helped them: these are protecting friends one of another. And those who believed but did not leave their homes, ye have no duty to protect them till they leave their homes; but if they seek help from you in the matter of religion then it is your duty to help (them) except against a folk between whom and you there is a treaty. Allah is Seer of what ye do" [Q8:72].

This, too, was abrogated and inheritance was then established via kinship. Allah Most High said, "And those who afterwards

---

3. ʿUmar: Ḥākim, 7952, Bayhaqī, 12178. See: BM, 7:229.

believed and left their homes and strove along with you, they are of you; and those who are akin are nearer one to another in the ordinance of Allah..." [Q8:75].

An alternative opinion suggests that it was abrogated by the verse of bequests: "It is prescribed for you, when death approacheth one of you, if he leave wealth, that he bequeath unto parents and near relatives in kindness. (This is) a duty for all those who ward off (evil)" [Q2:180], which was obligatory for parents and kin.

THE ESTATE

(فصل) [الحقوق المتعلّقة بالتّركة]

CLAIMS AGAINST THE ESTATE

يبدأ من تركة الميّت بمؤنة تجهيزه إن لم يتعلّق بعينها حقّ، ثمّ بدين الله، ثمّ بدين الآدميّ، ثمّ بالوصايا من ثلث الباقي، ثمّ يقسم الباقي بين الورثة.

The estate is first used to cover funerary expenses...

This is because the deceased needs it, and he does not pass to his heirs save whatever is in excess of his needs.

...as long as no specific right is claimed against it. Then [the estate is used to pay] debts owed to Allah, then to human beings. Next, up to one-third of what remains is used to fulfill bequests. Finally, the remaining property is divided amongst the heirs.

Allah Most High says, "...after any bequest you [may have] made or debt..." [Q4:11, 12]. ʿAlī (may Allah be pleased with him) said, "You read this verse '...after any legacy he may have bequeathed, or debt (hath been paid)...' [Q4:11, 12]. Indeed, the Messenger of Allah ﷺ settled debts before fulfilling bequests."[4]

4. ʿAlī: Tirmdidhī, 2094, 2122; Bayhaqī, 12561, 12562; Ḥākim, 7967. See: TM, 1338.

REASONS FOR INHERITANCE

وأسباب الإرث أربعة، قرابة، ونكاح وولاء وإسلام، فيرثه أهل بلده الّذي مات فيه نصّ عليه في «الأمّ».

The four reasons for inheritance are kinship, marriage, freeing the deceased, and Islam (whereby the heirs are the Muslims of the land where the deceased passed away, as stated in *Al-Umm.*[5]

MALE HEIRS

والوارثون الآن من الرّجال: البنوّة، والأبوّة، والأخوّة وبنوهم إلّا للأمّ، والعمومة إلّا للأمّ، وكذا بنوهم، والزّوج، والمعتق.

The males who inherit are:

1. sons,
2. fathers,
3. brothers,
4. sons of paternal brothers,
5. paternal uncles,
6. sons of paternal uncles,
7. husbands, and
8. a male who freed the deceased.

This is according to consensus.

5. al-Shāfiʿī, *Al-Umm,* 4:80; al-Nawawī, *Rawḍat al-ṭālibīn,* 6:3.

FEMALE HEIRS

ومن نساء: البنت وبنت الابن، وإن سفل، والأمّ والجدةّ والأخت، والزّوجة، والمعتقة.

The females who inherit are:

1. daughters,
2. sons' daughters,
3. female descendants with one male between them and the deceased,
4. mothers,
5. grandmothers,
6. sisters,
7. wives, and
8. a female who freed the deceased.

This is by consensus.

PEOPLE WHO ALWAYS OR NEVER INHERIT

(فصل) [الحجب]

ولا يسقط بحال الأبوان والزّوجان والابن والبنت.

Parents, spouses, sons, and daughters [of the deceased] are never excluded [from inheritance].

وتسقط الجدّات بالأمّ، وولد الأمّ بالآباء والأبناء، وولد الأبوين بالأب والإبن وابن الإبن، وولد الأب بهؤلاء وأخ لأبوين.

The [maternal] grandmother is excluded by the presence of the mother.

This is because anyone connected to the deceased through an intermediary is superseded if that intermediary is present.

The [deceased's] mother's child is excluded by the presence of a male ascendant or descendant.

Allah Most High says, "And if a man or a woman have a distant heir (having left neither parent nor child), and he (or she) have a brother or a sister (only on the mother's side)..." [Q4:12].

This is because he is an heir only when the deceased has no ascendant or descendant [*kalālah*]. Thus, he does not inherit when either is present.

The full brother [of the deceased] is excluded by the presence of the father, a son, or a son's son.

This is according to consensus.

The father's son is excluded by the presence of those three, or by a full brother.

The first three exclude a full brother, so it is more appropriate that they exclude a half brother. A full brother excludes a half brother due to his stronger bond.

PREVENTERS OF INHERITANCE

(فصل) [موانع الإرث]

وموانع الإرث: رقّ وقتل، وردّة، واختلاف دين ودار، واستبهام موت ودور.

Inheritance is prevented by:
1. slavery;

Slaves who are totally owned, who are buying their freedom, or who had a child with their master do not inherit or pass inheritance.[6] This is because they do not own anything to begin with.

6. See "Manumission" starting with page 548 for more details.

2. murder;

This is because of numerous hadiths (although they are of contentious authenticity). Abū Hurayrah (may Allah be pleased with him) said that the Prophet ﷺ said, "Murderers are not heirs."[7] The wisdom is that, if we allow a killer to inherit, we will never be secure from those who wish to hasten their inheritance by killing their benefactors. Thus, general welfare calls for its proscription.

3. apostasy;
4. difference of religion or abode; and...

The Prophet ﷺ said, "A Muslim is not the heir of a disbeliever, nor is a disbeliever the heir of a Muslim."[8]

Disbelief [of all types, except for apostasy] is considered a single sect, so non-Muslims inherit to and from one another. But they do not inherit if there is hostility between their respective abodes.

An apostate neither inherits from nor passes inheritance to anyone.

5. uncertainty about death having occurred and [if it has], which of the inheritors died first.

This is because, in cases where the order of death [of individuals who could inherit from one another] is unknown, we do not know who deserves what. It would be arbitrary if one inherits but not the other. It would certainly be wrong if they both inherit.

ويورّث المبعّض بما ملكه بحرّيّته.

Whatever a partially-free slave comes to own through his free portion is passed as inheritance

---

7. Abū Hurayrah: Tirmidhī, 2109, Ibn Mājah, 2645, 2735, Dāraquṭnī, 4147, Bayhaqī, 12243. See: BM, 7:228; al-Māwardī, *Al-Ḥāwī al-kabīr,* 8:84, 13:71.

8. Usāmah ibn Zayd: Bukhārī, 4283, 6764; Muslim, 1614 #1. See: TM, 1354.

SHARES

(فصل) [الفروض]

‹The following verses will be quoted throughout this chapter so they are placed here in full as a convenience. Allah Most High says:

"Lo! Those who devour the wealth of orphans wrongfully, they do but swallow fire into their bellies, and they will be exposed to burning flame" [Q4:10].

"Allah chargeth you concerning (the provision for) your children: to the male the equivalent of the portion of two females, and if there be women more than two, then theirs is two-thirds of the inheritance, and if there be one (only) then the half. And to each of his parents a sixth of the inheritance, if he have a son; and if he have no son and his parents are his heirs, then to his mother appertaineth the third; and if he have brethren, then to his mother appertaineth the sixth, after any legacy he may have bequeathed, or debt (hath been paid). Your parents and your children: Ye know not which of them is nearer unto you in usefulness. It is an injunction from Allah. Lo! Allah is Knower, Wise" [Q4:11].

"And unto you belongeth a half of that which your wives leave, if they have no child; but if they have a child then unto you the fourth of that which they leave, after any legacy they may have bequeathed, or debt (they may have contracted, hath been paid). And unto them belongeth the fourth of that which ye leave if ye have no child, but if ye have a child then the eighth of that which ye leave, after any legacy ye may have bequeathed, or debt (ye may have contracted, hath been paid). And if a man or a woman have a distant heir (having left neither parent nor child), and he (or she) have a brother or a sister (only on the mother's side) then to each of them twain (the brother and the sister) the sixth, and if they be more than two, then they shall be sharers in the third, after any legacy that may have been bequeathed or debt (contracted) not injuring (the heirs by willing away more than a third of the heritage) hath been paid. A commandment from Allah. Allah is Knower, Indulgent" [Q4:12].

"They ask thee for a pronouncement. Say: Allah hath pronounced for you concerning distant kindred. If a man die childless and he have a sister, hers is half the heritage, and he would have inherited from her had she died childless. And if there be two sisters, then theirs are two-thirds of the heritage, and if they be brethren, men and women, unto the male is the equivalent of the share of two females. Allah expoundeth unto you, so that ye err not. Allah is Knower of all things" [Q4:176].›

والفروض المقدّرة في كتاب الله تعالى ستّة: النّصف، ونصفه، ونصف نصفه، والثّلثان ونصفهما ونصف نصفهما.

Six shares are mentioned in the Book of Allah Most High:

1. **one-half,**
2. **its half [one-fourth],**
3. **half its half [one-eighth];**
4. **two-thirds,**
5. **its half [one-third], and**
6. **half its half [one-sixth].**

فالنّصف فرض خمسة: بنت وبنت ابن وأخت شقيقة، ولأب منفردات، وزوج عند عدم ولد وولد ابن.

One-half is the obligatory share for five [categories of people]:

1. **a daughter;**

Allah Most High says, "...and if there be one (only) then the half. ..." [Q4:11].

2. **a son's daughter**

She is analogous to the daughter, according to consensus.

3. **a full sister;**
4. **a consanguine[9] sister, when the above have no siblings; and...**

9. The term "consanguine" indicates a half-sibling from the same father but a different mother.

Allah Most High says, "...If a man die childless and he have a sister, hers is half the heritage..." [Q4:176].

What is intended here is a full or a consanguine sister.

A full sister receives one-half in the absence of a daughter or son's daughter. A fortiori, so does the consanguine sister. Her share is deferred if there is a full sister because the full sister['s relationship] is stronger [than the consanguine sister's].

5. **a husband, when no male descendant is present.**

Allah Most High says, "And unto you belongeth a half of that which your wives leave, if they have no child..." [Q4:12].

والرّبع فرض اثنين: زوج محجوب بما سلف، وزوجة غير محجوبة بذلك.

One-fourth is the obligatory share for two [categories of people]:
1. **the husband, when he has been [partially] excluded (as mentioned above); and...**

Allah Most High says, "...but if they have a child then unto you the fourth..." [Q4:12].

2. **a wife who has not been [partially] excluded (as above).**

Allah Most High says, "...but if they have a child then unto you the fourth of that which they leave, after any legacy they may have bequeathed, or debt (they may have contracted, hath been paid). And unto them belongeth the fourth of that which ye leave if ye have no child..." [Q4:12].

والثّمن فرض واحد: الزّوجة أو الزّوجات مع الحجب بها سلف.

One-eighth is the obligatory share for one [category]: the wife or wives, when [partially] excluded (as mentioned above).

Allah Most High says, "...but if ye have a child then the eighth of that which ye leave..." [Q4:12].

والثّلثان فرض أربعة: بنتين، وبنتي ابن فأكثر، وأختين فأكثر لأبوين أو لأب.

Two-thirds is the obligatory share for four [categories of people]:
1. **two daughters;**

Allah Most High says, "Allah chargeth you concerning (the provision for) your children: to the male the equivalent of the portion of two females, and if there be women more than [*fawq*] two, then theirs is two-thirds of the inheritance..." [Q4:11].

In the verse, "more than [*fawq*] two" means two or more. Some scholars consider "more than [*fawq*]" to be linguistically superfluous, similar to "so strike above [*fawq*] the necks" [Q8:12].

2. **two daughters of a direct son, or more than two of either of the aforementioned;**

Allah Most High says, "and if there be women more than two, then theirs is two-thirds of the inheritance" [Q4:11].

3–4. **two or more full or consanguine sisters.**

Allah Most High says, "And if there be two sisters, then theirs are two-thirds of the heritage" [Q4:176].

والثّلث فرض اثنين: أم ليس لميتها ولد ولا ولد ابن ولا اثنان من الأخوة والأخوات، واثنين فأكثر من ولد الأمّ، وقد يفرض للجدّ مع الأخوة.

One-third is the obligatory share for two [categories of people]:

1. **the mother, provided that the deceased does not have a son, a son's son, or two brothers or sisters and;**

Allah Most High says, "...and if he have no son and his parents are his heirs, then to his mother appertaineth the third..." [Q4:11].

2. **two or more uterine siblings.**[10]

Allah Most High says, "...and if they be more than two, then they shall be sharers in the third..." [Q4:12].

One-third can be given to the grandfather when there are siblings.

والسّدس فرض سبعة: أب وجدّ لميّتهما ولد أو ولد ابن، وأمّ لميّتها ذلك أو اثنان من الأخوة والأخوات، وجدّة، ولبنت ابن مع بنت صلب، ولأخت أو أخوات لأب مع أخت لأبوين، ولواحد من ولد الأمّ.

One-sixth is the obligatory share for seven [categories of people]:

1. **the father and [paternal] grandfather, if the deceased has a[n immediate] descendant or a son's descendant;**

Allah Most High says, "...And to each of his parents a sixth of the inheritance, if he have a son..." [Q4:11]. Refer back to the previous ruling in this section regarding two or more siblings.

The grandfather is analogous to the father, according to consensus.

---

10. The term "uterine" indicates a half-sibling from the same mother but a different father.

2. **the mother who has the same [circumstances as the aforementioned];**

Allah Most High says, "...And to each of his parents a sixth of the inheritance, if he have a son..." [Q4:11].

3. **the mother, when there are two or more siblings;**

Allah Most High says, "...and if he have brethren, then to his mother appertaineth the sixth..." [Q4:11].

4. **the [paternal] grandmother;**

Buraydah (may Allah be pleased with him) said that the Prophet ﷺ gave a grandmother one-sixth when there was no mother between her [and the deceased].[11]

5. **the son's daughter, provided the deceased's daughter is present;**

Huzail ibn Shuraḥbīl said that Abū Mūsā (may Allah be pleased with them both) was asked regarding [inheritance when the survivors are] a daughter, a son's daughter, and a sister. "He [Abū Mūsā] said, 'The daughter will take one-half and the sister will take one-half. If you go to Ibn Masʿūd (may Allah be pleased with him), he will tell you the same.' Ibn Masʿūd was asked and was told of Abū Mūsā's verdict. Ibn Masʿūd then said, 'If I give the same verdict, I would have strayed and not be of the rightly-guided. The verdict I will give in this case will be the same as what the Prophet ﷺ gave: one-half is for the daughter, and one-sixth for the son's daughter (with both shares equaling two-thirds of the total property); and the rest is for the sister.' Afterwards, we came to Abū Mūsā and informed him of Ibn Masʿūd's verdict, whereupon he said, 'Do not ask me for verdicts, as long as this learned man is among you.'"[12] (May Allah be pleased with them.)

---

11. Buraydah: Abū Dāwūd, 2895. See: TM, 1346.
12. Huzail ibn Shiraḥbīl: Bukhārī, 6736, 6742. See: BM, 7:214.

6. one or more consanguine sisters, provided a full sister is present; and...

This is analogous to the son's daughter when the daughter is present.

7. the mother's only child.

Allah Most High says, "...And if a man or a woman have a distant heir (having left neither parent nor child), and he (or she) have a brother or a sister (only on the mother's side) then to each of them twain (the brother and the sister) the sixth..." [Q4:12].

The Companions (may Allah be pleased with them) explain that here, "brother or sister" means "from his mother."

UNIVERSAL INHERITANCE

(فصل) [العصبة]

والعاصب: من ليس له سهم مقدر، فيرث المال أو ما فضل بعد الفروض.

The universal inheritor[13] [*ʿāṣib*] is anyone who does not receive a limited share, so he inherits all of the estate or whatever remains after the obligatory shares [have been distributed].

وأقربهم: الابن، ثمّ ابنه، ثمّ الأب، ثمّ أبوه، ثمّ الأخ لأبوين، ثمّ لأب، ثمّ ابن الأخ لأبوين، ثمّ لأب، ثمّ العمّ، ثمّ ابنه كذلك.

[Universal inheritors, in order of closeness to the deceased, are:]
1. **a son;**
2. **his son;**
3. **the father;**
4. **his father;**
5. **a full brother;**
6. **a consanguine brother;**

13. Also known as an agnate inheritor.

7. a full brother's son;
8. a son of a consanguine brother;
9. a paternal uncle; and
10. his son – similarly [following the order above].

Ibn ʿAbbās (may Allah be pleased with them both) reported that he ﷺ said, "Give the obligatory shares to those who are entitled to them. Then give whatever remains to the closest male relative."[14]

وإن فقدوا فعصبات الولاء بالتّرتيب، إلّا أن أخ المعتق وابن أخيه يقدمان على الجدّ.

If all of the above are absent [and if the deceased was a slave, the estate is given to] the universal inheritors of the manumitter [*walāʾ*], according to the order [listed above], except that the brother of the manumitter and his brother take precedence over the grandfather.[15]

ولا ترث امرأة بولاء إلّا معتقها أو منتميًا إليه بنسب أو ولاء.

A woman does not inherit as a result of manumission [*walāʾ*] except from a slave she [herself] set free or someone related to the slave or someone the former slave set free [*walāʾ*].[16]

وأربعة يعصبون أخواتهم: الابن وابنه وأخ لأبوين ولأب.

Four males are universal inheritors with their sisters:

1. a son;
2. his son;
3. a full brother; and
4. a consanguine brother.

---

14. Ibn ʿAbbās: Bukhārī, 6732; Muslim, 1615. See: TM, 1351.
15 In this case, if the deceased was not a freed slave, the estate is distributed among extended family members according to the percentages previously mentioned and based on their relationship to the deceased.
16. See "Women Do Not Inherit Walāʾ" on page 552.

Allah Most High says, "Allah chargeth you concerning (the provision for) your children: to the male the equivalent of the portion of two females..." [Q4:11]. Here "children" includes sons and their sons.

Allah Most High says, "...and if they be brethren, men and women, unto the male is the equivalent of the share of two females..." [Q4:176].

BEQUESTS & EXECUTORS

(فصل) [الوصيّة]

A bequest [*waṣiyyah*] is the establishment of a right, owed upon one's death.

Its legal basis is derived from Quranic verses and the Sunnah. The verses include, "...after any bequest he [may have] made or debt..." [Q4:11, 12].

The Sunnah includes the well-known hadith of Saʿd bin Abī Waqqāṣ (may Allah be pleased with him) and is established by other authentic hadiths. Saʿd bin Abī Waqqāṣ (may Allah be pleased with him) narrates: "I said, 'O Messenger of Allah! I have wealth. I have no heirs except one daughter. Shall I give two-thirds of my wealth in charity?' He ﷺ said, 'No.' I said, 'Shall I give half in charity?' He said, 'No.' I said, 'Shall I give one-third in charity?' He said, '[Give] one-third, [though] a third is ample. Better to leave your heirs wealthy than leaving them destitute, begging from people.'"[17] Also, Ibn ʿUmar (may Allah be pleased with them both) reported that the Messenger of Allah ﷺ said, "It is not right for any Muslim who has something to bequeath to sleep two nights without recording it and keeping it with him."[18]

Bequests are recommended because of the hadith: "Allah Most High has allotted a third of your wealth at the end of your life for increasing your deeds."[19]

17. Saʿd ibn Abī Waqqāṣ: Bukhārī, 1295; Muslim, 1628. See: TM, 1360.

18. Ibn ʿUmar: Bukhārī, 2738; Muslim, 1627. See: TM, 1357.

19. Abū Hurayrah: Ibn Mājah, 2709; Dāraquṭnī, 3289; Bayhaqī, 12571. See: KBM, 1760.

وصيّة المكلّف صحيحة في غير المعصية، في الجهة العامّة، وفي المعيّن تصوّر الملك، وتصحّ بالمعدوم والمجهول..

The bequest of a responsible individual is valid when it is not for an act of disobedience;

Bequests are meant to obtain good deeds that were missed, so it is not permissible for them to involve disobedience. If a bequest is made for something permissible without being an apparent act of obedience, it is valid – like endowments[, which are only valid for permissible things].

...whether the recipient is unspecified or is specified and can conceivably own property.

It is valid to bequeath something that is nonexistent or unspecified.

An example of a "nonexistent" bequest would be the bequeathal of a future crop from a particular tree.

An example of an "unspecified" bequest would be the bequeathal of a garment without specifying which one.

Bequests can include pure or impure items (such as dogs and manure), since the primary requirement of a bequest is that the bequeathed item be useful and intended for that use.

وهي من الثّلث، فإن زاد وقف على إجازة الوارث الخاصّ كما سلف في الحجر.

[The bequest] is taken from one-third [of the total estate].

If it exceeds [one-third], the consent of the deceased's specific heirs is required – similar to what was mentioned earlier for suspensions.[20]

This is because the right of the heirs is associated with what exceeds one-third. If there is no specific heir, the bequest is invalid, as there is no one to permit its execution.

20. See "Suspension" on page 241.

وتصحّ لقاتل ولوارث إن أجاز باقيهم.

Bequests to the deceased's killer are valid,...

Such a bequest is valid even if the heirs do not consent to it since it is a transference of ownership which has an offer and acceptance, so it resembles transference of ownership via sales and gifting.

...as are bequests to heirs, if the other heirs permit it.

Ibn ʿAbbās (may Allah be pleased with them both) said that the Messenger of Allah ﷺ said, "It is not permissible to make a bequest to an heir unless the [other] heirs consent."[21]

EXECUTORSHIP

وشرط الوصي: تكليف وحرية وعدالة وهداية إلى التّصرّف، وإسلام في المسلم.

The executor of an estate must be:

1. responsible;

Children and the insane do not have freedom to dispose of or manage their own affairs, so they cannot manage the affairs of others.

2. free;

A slave does not oversee the affairs of his own children. Thus, he cannot be an executor for someone else. (This is similar to someone who is insane.) Also, being an executor requires having free time, while a slave is occupied with serving his master.

3. upright;

This is because it is a position of trust with authority over others.

---

21. Ibn ʿAbbās: Dāraquṭnī, 4150, 4153, 4295. See: BM, 7:269.

4. **someone with good judgment regarding management and disposal of property; and...**

Thus, it cannot be given to someone who is suspended from transactions for being a spendthrift.

5. **a Muslim, if the ward is a Muslim.**

ويجوز تعليقها على شرط في الحياة، وبعد الموت، ويجوز الرجوع فيها، ولا تتمّ إلّا بالقبول بعد الموت.

It is permissible to make [executorship] contingent upon the occurrence of some condition while [the benefactor is] still alive, or after their death.

For example, "I appoint you as executor for these children until the eldest reaches adulthood," or "until Zayd arrives."

It is permissible to retract executorship.

Executorship does not become final except upon its acceptance after [the benefactor's] death.

This is required when it is intended for a specific individual – just as gifts [*hibah*] require an acceptance.

ولكلّ منهما العزل متى شاء، إلّا أن يغلب على الظّنّ تلف المال باستيلاء ظالم، فلا يجوز للوصي عزل نفسه.

Either of them [the benefactor or executor] can remove himself whenever he wishes,...

This is because executorship is a type of agency.

...unless he believes that the property will most likely be damaged by an oppressor's usurpation, in which case it is not permissible for the executor to remove himself.

TRIBUTE & SPOILS OF WAR

(فصل) [الفيء والغنيمة]

TRIBUTE

يخمس الفيء، فأربعة أخماسه للمرتزقة، والخمس الباقي يخمّسه للمصالح الأهمّ منها فالأهمّ، ولذي القربى، وهم بنو هاشم والمطلّب، ولليتامى - وهو صغير فقير لا أب له - والمساكين، وابن السّبيل،

Tribute [*fay*ʾ] is divided into five parts.

Allah Most High says, "That which Allah giveth as spoil unto His messenger from the people of the townships, it is for Allah and His messenger and for the near of kin and the orphans and the needy and the wayfarer..." [Q59:7]. ‹In the verse, "near of kin," refers to his ﷺ relatives from Banī Hāshim and Bani al-Muṭṭalib.[22]›

Tribute [*fay*ʾ] is what is taken from non-Muslims without fighting. It is distinct from spoils [*ghanīmah*], which are seized by force.

Four-fifths are given to soldiers who receive periodic allowances;

This amount was originally set aside for the Prophet ﷺ whenever he achieved victory and frightened the non-Muslim aggressors into submission. After the Prophet ﷺ, the armies of Islam were awarded this tribute for similar accomplishments.

The remaining fifth is split into fifths:
1. one-fifth for public welfare, in order of importance;

The first share originally went to the Messenger of Allah ﷺ, who would spend it on his family's yearly expenditure and spend what remained on arms and horses to be used for the sake of Allah.[23] After the Prophet ﷺ, it was diverted to public welfare.

22. al-Maḥallī and al-Suyūṭī, *Tafsīr al-Jalālayn*.

23. Ibn ʿUmar: Bukhārī, 2904; Muslim, 1757 #48. See: KBM, 1807.

2. **one-fifth for relatives (Banū Hāshim and Banu al-Muṭṭalib);**

The Prophet ﷺ said, "We and Banū al-Muṭṭalib are one" and laced his fingers together.[24]

It goes to their rich and poor, since al-ʿAbbās (may Allah be pleased with him) would receive from it and he was affluent.[25]

It also goes to their young and old, and to their women, since al-Zubayr would take some for his mother (may Allah be pleased with them).[26]

3. **one-fifth for orphans – fatherless poor youth;**
4. **one-fifth for the poor; and**
5. **one-fifth for wayfarers.**

Allah Most High says, "That which Allah giveth as spoil unto His messenger from the people of the townships, it is for Allah and His messenger and for the near of kin and the orphans and the needy and the wayfarer..." [Q59:7].

SPOILS OF WAR

والغنيمة: أربعة أخماسها للغانمين - يقدّم فيها السّلب للقاتل - للرّاجل سهم وللفارس ثلاثة أسهم،

ويرضخ للعبد والصّبي والمرأة والذّمّي إذا حضر بلا أجرة وبإذن الإمام،

والخمس الباقي يخمّس خمسة، ويقسم كما سلف.

[As for] the spoils of war, four-fifths are given to those who participated in the battle.

The Prophet ﷺ would divide it among them. ‹A man asked the

24. Jubayr ibn Mutʿim: Bukhārī, 3140. See: TM, 1369, 1389.
25. al-Shāfiʿī, *Al-Umm*, 4:157.
26. al-Māwardī, *Al-Ḥāwī*, 4:416, 8:435.

Prophet ﷺ, "What do you say about the spoils of war?" He ﷺ replied, "A fifth belongs to Allah and four-fifths belong to the army."[27]›

First, whoever kills or disables an enemy is given his personal belongings.

This is restricted to those who did so while exposing themselves to danger while facing the enemy. Abū Qatādah (may Allah be pleased with him) reported: "The Messenger of Allah ﷺ said, 'Whoever kills an enemy and has proof will receive his spoils.'"[28] Here "proof" means some sort of indication or witnesses.

Also, beating an enemy into submission is like killing him, due to the story of Ibn Masʿūd (may Allah be pleased with him) who came upon the two Anṣārīs (may Allah be pleased with them) beating Abū Jahl to death. The Prophet ﷺ gave Abū Jahl's belongings to the two Anṣārīs and withheld them from Ibn Masʿūd.[29]

[After that,] infantry soldiers receive a single share, while cavalry soldiers receive three shares.

The Messenger of Allah ﷺ divided [the spoils of war] from the battle of Khaybar thus: two shares for horsemen and one for the foot soldier. Another narration states: one share for the man, two shares for his horse.[30]

---

27. ʿAbd Allāh ibn Shafīq: Bayhaqī, 12862, 12931, 18012. See: al-Anṣārī, *Asnā al-maṭālib*, 3:93.
28. Abū Qatādah: Bukhārī, 3142; Muslim, 1851. See: TM, 1371.
29. Anas: Bukhārī, 4020; Muslim, 1800, 118. See: BM, 7:341.
30. Ibn ʿUmar: Bukhārī, 4228; Muslim, 1762 #57; Abū Dāwūd, 1303. See: TM, 1376.

Slaves, youths, women, and *dhimmīs* who attended [the battle] without receiving any wages can be given a token payment at the Imam's discretion.

They are not entitled to spoils of war since they are not among those who are required to participate in jihad.

Concerning women, the Prophet ﷺ would give female participants a token payment.[31]

With regard to slaves, he ﷺ offered them a payment that was commensurate with their actions.[32]

As for disbelievers, he ﷺ sought assistance from the Jews of Banī Qaynuqāʿ and gave them a token payment.[33]

The remaining fifth is distributed according to what has already been mentioned.

31. Najdah ibn ʿĀmir: Abū Dāwūd, 2728; Tirmidhī, 1556. See: TM, 1378.
32. ʿUmayr the freed slave of Ibn al-Laḥam: Abū Dāwūd, 2730; Tirmidhī, 1557 – *ḥasan ṣaḥīḥ*; Nasāʾī, *Al-Sunan al-Kubrā,* 7493; Ḥākim, 1224; Bayhaqī, 17968. See: TM, 1377.
33. Ibn ʿAbbās: Bayhaqī, 17970. See: BM, 9:72.

9

MARRIAGE AND DIVORCE

كِتَابُ النِّكَاحِ وَمَا يَتَعَلَّقُ بِهِ مِنَ الْأَحْكَامِ وَالْقَضَايَا

هو الضمّ.

Marriage is "joining together."

This is according to its linguistic meaning; it does not mean intercourse.

The legal foundation for marriage [*nikāh*] is from the Quran, Sunnah, and consensus. Among the evidence establishing it is Allah Most High saying, "...marry of the women, who seem good to you..." [Q4:3] and "And marry such of you as are solitary..." [Q24:32]. The second verse [Q24:32] is said to abrogate "The fornicator shall not marry save an adulteress or a fornicator..." [Q24:3].

RULINGS UNIQUE TO THE PROPHET ﷺ

وخصّ نبيّنا ﷺ فيه بتخيير نسائه بين المقام معه والمفارقة فاخترنه، فحرم عليه أن يتبدّل بهنّ ثمّ نسخ، وطلاق مرغوبته على الزّوج، ووجوب إجابته على المصلّي ولا تبطل، ويزوّج من نفسه ومن شاء بغير إذن، وبتزويج الرّبّ جلّ جلاله، ويزيد على تسع، وينكح بالهبة من جهة الرّاغبة، وأما من جهته فلا بدّ من لفظ، وينكح أيضًا بلا مهر وبلا ولي ولا شهود، ومع الإحرام.

Our Prophet ﷺ was exceptional [in many ways, especially with respect to marriage].

His ﷺ wives were given the option of staying with him or separation, and they chose to stay with him.

Allah Most High says, "O Prophet! Say unto thy wives: If ye desire the world's life and its adornment, come! I will content you and will release you with a fair release" [Q33:28].

It was unlawful for him ﷺ to replace them [with other wives] but this ruling was later abrogated.

Allah Most High says, "It is not allowed thee to take (other) women henceforth, nor that thou shouldst change them for other wives…" [Q33:52]. This was abrogated with the verse where Allah Most High says, "O Prophet! Lo! We have made lawful unto thee thy wives unto whom thou hast paid their dowries…" [Q33:50].[1]

[That] a woman he ﷺ desired would be divorced from her husband [upon his ﷺ request].

‹Allah Most High says, "O ye who believe! Obey Allah, and the Messenger when he calleth you…" [Q8:24].[2]›

It was obligatory for someone making prayer to reply to him ﷺ and doing so did not break the prayer.

When the Prophet ﷺ called Abū Saʿīd ibn al-Muʿallā and he did not reply, he ﷺ asked, "What prevented you from replying? You have heard Allah Most High say, 'O ye who believe! Obey Allah, and the Messenger when he calleth you…' [Q8:24]?"[3]

---

1. Ibn Mulaqqin, *Khulāṣat al-fatāwī,* 4:164; cf al-Nawawī, *Rawḍat al-ṭālibīn,* 7:5.
2. al-Anṣārī, *Asnā al-maṭālib,* 3:101.
3. Abū Saʿīd ibn al-Muʿallā: Bukhārī, 4474.

He ﷺ could marry a woman to himself or to another man without permission.

The Prophet ﷺ could do this without permission from her or her guardian. ‹Allah Most High says, "the Prophet is closer to the believers than their selves" [Q33:6].[4]›

Allah Mighty and Majestic contracted his ﷺ marriage.

‹Allah Most High says, "So when Zayd had performed that necessary formality (of divorce) from her, We gave her unto thee in marriage" [Q33:37].[5]›

He ﷺ could marry more than nine wives simultaneously.

This is because there was no risk that the Prophet ﷺ would be unfair, in contrast to everyone else.

Allah Most High says, "It is not allowed for thee to take (other) women henceforth, nor that thou shouldst change them for other wives..." [Q33:52]. This was abrogated with the verse where Allah Most High says, "O Prophet! Lo! We have made lawful unto thee thy wives unto whom thou hast paid their dowries..." [Q33:50].[6]

He ﷺ could marry a woman interested in him who offered herself as a gift [based on the offer alone] – though he ﷺ had to pronounce [it as marriage].

Allah Most High says, "...and a believing woman if she gives herself unto the Prophet and the Prophet desires to ask her in marriage – a privilege for thee only, not for the (rest of) believers..." [Q33:50].

4. al-Anṣārī, *Asnā al-maṭālib,* 3:101.
5. al-Nawawī, *Rawḍat al-ṭālibīn,* 7:10.
6. al-Anṣārī, *Asnā al-maṭālib,* 3:100.

He ﷺ could also marry without a marriage payment [*mahr*],...

Since the bride offering herself in marriage without a marriage payment is similar to gifting.

...without a guardian, and without witnesses.

The guardian is [normally] necessary in order to ensure suitability, but the Prophet['s status] ﷺ is beyond those who are the most suitable. And witnesses are to prevent [the groom] from denying [that the marriage took place], and this was not a risk with him ﷺ. And a woman's claim contrary to his ﷺ would not be of consideration.

It was unlawful for him ﷺ to keep a wife who disliked being married to him.

[He ﷺ could also marry] while in the state of pilgrimage [*iḥrām*].

‹Ibn ʿAbbās (may Allah be pleased with him) reported that the Prophet ﷺ married Maymūnah (may Allah be pleased with her) while in *iḥrām*.[7] However, the majority of transmitters from Ibn ʿAbbās (may Allah be pleased with him) report that he ﷺ was not in *iḥrām*.[8] And Abū Rāfiʿ (may Allah be pleased with him) said, "He ﷺ married her while he was outside the state of pilgrim sanctity. I was the messenger between them."[9] But Imam al-Shāfiʿī (may Allah grant him His mercy) rejected this because of Ibn ʿAbbās' first narration.[10]›

7. Ibn ʿAbbās: Bukhārī, 1837, 4258; Muslim, 1410 #46–47; Nasāʾī, 2837–41, 3271–74.
8. Ibn ʿAbbās: Muslim, 1410 #46; Abū Dāwūd, 1844; Tirmidhī, 844
9. Abū Rāfiʿ: Tirmidhī, 841.
10. al-Anṣārī, *Asnā al-maṭālib*, 3:100–101.

ISSUES RELATED TO MARRIAGE

(فصل) [حكم النّكاح]

WHO SHOULD MARRY

وهو مستحبّ لذي أهبة محتاج إليه وسليم دون تعبّد.

Marriage is recommended for someone who can provide support, needs it,...

Allah Most High says, "...marry of the women, who seem good to you..." [Q4:3] and "And marry such of you as are solitary..." [Q24:32]. The second verse [Q24:32] is said to abrogate "The fornicator shall not marry save an adulteress or a fornicator..." [Q24:3].

ʿAbd Allāh ibn Masʿūd (may Allah be pleased with him) said, "We were with the Prophet ﷺ when we were young and had no wealth whatsoever. The Messenger of Allah ﷺ said, 'O young people! Whoever among you is able to marry is to do so, since it helps him lower his gaze and be more protective of his genitals. Whoever is not able to marry must fast, as it diminishes his sexual desires.'"[11]

...is healthy, and is not busy with acts of worship.

It is similar for women, minus the condition related to providing support.

Marriage is offensive for those lacking both the ability to support and the need to marry. Allah Most High says, "And let those who cannot find a match keep chaste till Allah gives them independence by His grace" [Q24:33].

11. ʿAbd Allāh ibn Masʿūd: Bukhārī, 5066; Muslim, 1400. See: TM, 1412.

CHARACTERISTICS DESIRABLE IN A BRIDE

وصفتها ديّنة عاقلة بكر رأى وجهها وكفيها بعد العزم على خطبتها.

[It is recommended that the prospective bride be] religious, intelligent, and a virgin.

Abū Hurayrah (may Allah be pleased with him) said that the Prophet ﷺ said, "A woman is married for four things: her wealth, her lineage, her beauty, and her piety. Choose the pious woman and may your hands be rubbed with dust!"[12] ‹The phrase "may your hands be rubbed with dust" is a blessing, i.e. "may you be blessed."›

Know that the Prophet ﷺ was not married to any virgin other than ʿĀʾishah (may Allah be pleased with her and her father).

Jābir (may Allah be pleased with him) related that he married a non-virgin. The Prophet ﷺ said, "Why not a virgin, so you could play with her and she could play with you?"[13] ‹The narrations clarify that Jābir (may Allah be pleased with him) married a non-virgin because he was responsible for caring for his young sisters after her father passed, and he wanted to marry someone who was not similar to them and could help with raising them.›

12. Abū Hurayrah: Bukhārī, 5090; Muslim, 1466 #53; Abū Dāwūd, 2047. See: TM, 1413.

13. Jābir: Bukhārī, 5079–5080, 5367; Muslim, 715; Abū Dāwūd, 2048; Tirmidhī, 1100. See TM, 1414.

LOOKING BEFORE ENGAGEMENT

[It is also recommended that] he sees her face and hands after resolving to engage her.

Al-Mughīrah (may Allah be pleased with him) got engaged to a woman. So the Prophet ﷺ said, "Look at her, for that is more likely to make things better between you both."[14]

Also, Jābir (may Allah be pleased with him) said that the Messenger of Allah ﷺ said, "If one of you engages a woman and is able to look at what will induce you to marry her, you are to do it."[15]

Looking is restricted to the hands and face, since Allah Most High says, "...and to display of their adornment only that which is apparent..." [Q24:31].

MAXIMUM NUMBER OF WIVES

ويجمع الحرّ بين أربع، والعبد بين اثنتين.

[It is permissible for] a freeman to marry four [wives],...

Ghaylān (may Allah be pleased with him) said that he entered Islam while having ten wives. The Prophet ﷺ said to him, "Select four and separate from the rest."[16] ‹Allah Most High says, "...marry of the women, who seem good to you, two or three or four..." [Q4:3].[17]›

Al-Asadī (may Allah be pleased with him) said, "I embraced Islam while I had eight wives. I mentioned it to the Prophet ﷺ, whereupon the Prophet ﷺ said, 'Select four of them.'"[18]

---

14. al-Mughīrah: Tirmidhī, 1087, 1866; Nasāʾī, 3235; Ibn Mājah, 1087. See TM, 1416.
15. Jābir: Abū Dāwūd, 2082. See KBM, 1913.
16. Ibn ʿUmar: Tirmidhī, 1128; Ibn Mājah, 1953; Ibn Ḥibbān, 4156, 4158; Dāraquṭnī, 3683–6; Ḥākim, 2779–83. See: TM, 1441, 1488.
17. al-Bughā, *Al-Tadhhīb,* 159 #2.
18. Wahb al-Asdī: Abū Dāwūd, 2241. See: BM, 7:603; al-Māwardī, *Al-Ḥāwī al-kabīr,* 9:257.

...and for a slave to marry two.

A slave cannot marry three [or four] wives. Evidence for this comes via Layth ibn Abī Salīm from al-Ḥakam ibn ʿUtaybah (may Allah grant them His mercy), who reported that the Companions (may Allah be pleased with them) of the Messenger of Allah ﷺ had consensus that a slave does not marry more than two.[19]

INTERCOURSE WITH SLAVES

ويطأ بملك اليمين ما شاء.

One may engage in sex with as many of his slaves as he wishes.

A Muslim can engage in sex with his female slave who is from Ahl al-Kitāb but not if she is a Zoroastrian or an idol worshiper – out of consideration for what is permissible through marriage.

‹Allah Most High says, "...or (the captives) that your right hands possess..." [Q4:3] without restricting the number. This is in contrast to wives, since the objective in marriage is affection and companionship, for the wife has the option to annul the marriage if she finds her husband to be impotent or insane.[20]›

19. Layth ibn Abī Salīm from al-Ḥakam ibn ʿUtaybah: Bayhaqī, 13676. See: al-Shāfiʿī, *Al-Umm,* 8:269; KBM, 1973.

20. Ibn al-Rifʿah, *Kifāyat al-nabīh fī sharḥ Al-Tanbīh,* 13:137.

MARRYING MINORS AND THOSE WITH DIMINISHED CAPACITY

ويزوّج الأب أو الجدّ الصّغير بالمصلحة ولو أربعًا، والمجنون الكبير بالحاجة فواحدة، والحاكم أيضًا، فإن كان له حال إفاقة انتظرت، والسّفيه عند الحاجة بعد إذنه لهم فواحدة، ولهم أن يأذنوا له أيضًا.

Fathers and grandfathers can contract a marriage for [their ward who is]:

1. a youth – for his welfare [*maṣlaḥah*], even [marrying him to] four wives;

Since the underlying reason for marriage is welfare and his welfare and interests may depend on contracting more than one.

2. an adult who is insane and in need of marriage, though only to one wife.

When there is need [*ḥājah*], such as showing signs of arousal or expecting recovery after having consulted with physicians.

The governor [*ḥākim*] can also contract the marriage on his behalf, but if the ward has periods of sanity, then those are awaited [before a marriage is contracted];

3. a spendthrift [*safīh*] who is in need of marriage, after he has given his guardians permission [to contract the marriage on his behalf, but to only one wife]. They can also give him permission [to contract his own marriage].

It is not valid for the spendthrift to marry without the guardian's permission as he may exhaust his wealth in marital expenses.

MALE SLAVES

والعبد الصّغير لا يجبر كالكبير، ولا يجبر سيّده، نعم ينكح بإذنه.

A young male slave is not forced to marry, just as an adult [is not forced].

This is because the slave's owner cannot terminate the slave's marriage through divorce, so how can he compel something that he cannot terminate?

A slave cannot compel his master [to consent to his marriage by marrying without his master's permission].

Since marriage diminishes some of the objectives and benefits of ownership, and reduces the value [of the slave].

He can, however, marry with his owner's permission.

LOOKING AT MEMBERS OF THE OPPOSITE SEX

(فصل) [النّظر]

ADULT MALES AND UNRELATED ADULT WOMEN

ويحرم نظر فحل بالغ ومراهق إلى عورة كبيرة أجنبيّة ووجهها وكفيها لغير حاجة.

It is unlawful for an adult male or a youth nearing adolescence to look at the *ʿawrah* of an unrelated adult woman – as well as her face or hands – without need.

Allah Most High says, "Tell the believing men to lower their gaze and be modest" [Q24:30].

Looking at a woman's face and hands is permissible for common needs, which include engaging in trade, receiving medical treatment, and seeking engagement.

During medical treatment, it is permissible for [a male physician] to look at any part of his [female] patient's body provided the patient's husband or a close male relative is present and there is no female physician available. Additionally, one does not receive treatment from a non-Muslim if a Muslim is available.

Jābir (may Allah be pleased with him) reported that Umm Salamah (may Allah be pleased with her) sought permission from the Messenger of Allah ﷺ to receive cupping therapy. The Prophet ﷺ asked Abū Ṭaybah (may Allah be pleased with him) to cup her.[21]

When seeking engagement, it is permissible for a man to look at the hands and face of a prospective fiancée.

Sahl ibn Saʿd (may Allah be pleased with him) said that a woman came to the Messenger of Allah ﷺ and said, "O Messenger of Allah ﷺ! I have come to you to offer myself to you." He ﷺ looked towards her and looked at her from head to foot, and then lowered his gaze and did not look back.[22] ‹In the hadith, "offer myself to you" means "I put my affair in your hands: to marry me without a marriage payment, or to marry me off to whomever you see fit."[23]›

Abū Hurayrah (may Allah be pleased with him) said, "I was with the Messenger of Allah ﷺ when a man came and informed him ﷺ that he had contracted to marry a woman of the Anṣār. The Messenger of Allah ﷺ said, 'Did you look at her?' He said, 'No.' He ﷺ said, 'Go look at her, for there is something in the eyes of the Anṣār.'"[24] ‹In the hadith, "something in the eyes" means their eyes differ from others, and might not be pleasing.[25]›

Al-Mughīrah ibn Shuʿbah (may Allah be pleased with him) narrates that he became engaged to a woman, and the Prophet ﷺ said to him, "Look at her since it is more likely to make things better between you both."[26]

---

21. Jābir: Muslim, 2206. See: TM, 1419.
22. Sahl ibn Saʿd: Bukhārī, 5126; Muslim, 1425. See: BM, 7:537.
23. al-Bughā, *Al-Tadhhīb,* 121 #1.
24. Abū Hurayrah: Muslim, 1424 #75. See: al-Shīrāzī, *Al-Muhadhdhab,* 2:424.
25. al-Bughā, *Al-Tadhhīb,* 121 #1.
26. al-Mughīrah ibn Shuʿbah: Tirmidhī, 1087. See: TM, 1416.

SEXUAL PARTNERS

أما نظره لموطوءته فإنّه حلال حتى الفرج.

It is permissible for him [an adult male or a youth nearing adolescence] to look at [the entire body of] a female sexual partner – even the genitals.

It is permissible because one's spouse is intended for licit enjoyment, and looking is one way to enjoy one's spouse.

It is not unlawful to look at the genitals; one can enjoy them, a fortiori one can look at them. But it is offensive to look without need since it is contrary to etiquette.

‹Concerning seeing the genitals, ʿĀʾishah (may Allah be pleased with her) said, "I never, ever saw his ﷺ, and he ﷺ never saw mine."[27]›

CLOSE RELATIVES AND OTHER ADULT MALES

ولا ينظر من المحرم والرّجل العورة كنظرهما إليه.

[An adult male or a youth nearing adolescence] does not look at the *ʿawrah* of close relatives or males...

Allah Most High says, "...and to display of their adornment only that which is apparent, and to draw their veils over their bosoms, and not to reveal their adornment save to their own husbands or fathers or husbands' fathers, or their sons or their husbands' sons, or their brothers or their brothers' sons or sisters' sons..." [Q24:31]. ‹In this verse, "adornment" is explained as the places of adornment – above the navel and below the knees.›

It is the same for them looking at him.

It is not unlawful for a man to see of another man's body except what lies between the navel and the knees.

27. ʿĀʾishah: Ibn Mājah, 662, 1922; Ibn Abī Shaybah, *Al-Muṣannaf,* 1130; Bayhaqī, 13539. See: al-Anṣārī, *Asnā al-maṭālib,* 3:113.

SLAVES AND EUNUCHS

والعبد والممسوح كالمحرم.

Male slaves and eunuchs have the same rulings as near relatives.

Allah Most High says, "or their slaves, or male attendants who lack vigour" [Q24:31].

BEARDLESS YOUTHS

ونظر الأمرد بشهوة حرام.

Looking lustfully at a beardless youth is unlawful.

BETWEEN WOMEN

والمرأة مع المرأة كرجل مع رجل، لا ذمّيّة مع مسلمة.

The ruling of women with women is the same as the ruling of men with men – ...

It is not unlawful for a woman to see another woman's body except for what lies between the navel and the knees.

...but not the ruling of a female *dhimmī* with a female Muslim.

This opinion that Imam al-Rāfiʿī judged to be sound,[28] the soundest in Imam al-Nawawī's *Rawḍat al-Ṭālibīn*,[29] and the most precautionary of two *wajh*s in Imam al-Rāfiʿī's *Al-Muḥarrar*[30] states that it is unlawful for a non-Muslim female citizen of the Islamic State [*dhimmiyah*] to look at [any part of] a female Muslim. The

28. al-Rāfiʿī, *Al-Sharḥ al-kabīr*, 7:477.
29. al-Nawawī, *Rawḍat al-ṭālibīn*, 7:25.
30. al-Rāfiʿī, *Al-Muḥarrar*, p289.

opinion that Imam al-Ghazālī[31] judged to be sound is that such a non-Muslim's gaze is the same as a female Muslim gazing at a female Muslim.

WOMEN AND UNRELATED ADULT MALES

وحرمة نظرها إلى ما عدا العورة من الأجنبيّ.

[It is unlawful] for a woman to look at an unrelated man's body [even] aside from his *ʿawrah*.

It is lawful for a woman to see of a man except for what lies between the navel and the knees. However, al-Nawawī (may Allah grant him His mercy) validated the opinion that a woman cannot see of a[non-maḥram] man except what he can [lawfully] see of her [i.e., the face and hands].

‹Allah Most High says, "And tell the believing women to lower their gaze and be modest..." [Q24:31].[32]›

TOUCHING WHAT IS UNLAWFUL TO SEE

وكلّ موضع حرم فيه النّظر حرم المسّ.

Every part of the body that is unlawful to look at is [also] unlawful to touch.

If looking is unlawful, it is even more appropriate that touching is unlawful since touching is more pleasurable than looking.

31. al-Ghazālī, *Al-Wasīṭ,* 5:30.
32. al-Bughā, *Al-Tadhhīb,* 160 #2.

ENGAGEMENT

(فصل) [الخطبة]

ولا يحلّ التّصريح بالخطبة لمعتدة ويحرم التعريض للرجعية فقط.

It is unlawful to explicitly propose to a woman during her waiting period.

It is unlawful to make an explicit proposal to a woman during her waiting period regardless of whether the waiting period is from a non-finalized and revocable divorce or a finalized (threefold) divorce, and whether the duration is determined by purity, months, or giving birth.[33] It is also unlawful for her or her guardian to respond to the individual making such a proposal.

It is only unlawful to allusively propose to a woman during a waiting period that is revocable.

This is because [a woman during a revocable waiting period] is the same as a married woman – in contrast to a woman whose waiting period is due to a threefold divorce or [her husband's] death. Explicit proposals are unlawful out of fear that she will lie about her waiting period having ended.

Allah Most High says, "There is no sin for you in that which ye proclaim or hide in your minds concerning your troth with women. Allah knoweth that ye will remember them. But plight not your troth with women except by uttering a recognised form of words. And do not consummate the marriage until (the term) prescribed is run..." [Q2:235]. ‹In the verse, "recognised form of words" means what conforms to the Sacred Law, which entails that the offer be phrased allusively.[34]›

‹Fāṭimah bint Qays (may Allah be pleased with her) was divorced by her husband irrevocably, so the Prophet ﷺ said to her, "Inform

33 See "The Waiting Period" on page 394.

34. al-Bughā, *Al-Tadhhīb,* 163 #4.

me when your waiting period is over."[35] When her waiting period was over, the Prophet ﷺ advised her to marry Usāmah ibn Zayd (may Allah be pleased with him).›

It is unlawful to propose to a woman who is known to be engaged – unless one has permission from her fiancé. This is because the Prophet ﷺ said, "A man is not to propose to a woman if his brother has already proposed to her."[36]

Whoever is asked to advise about a prospective spouse is to truthfully mention his shortcomings, since this is part of giving sincere advice [*naṣīḥah*].

THE MARRIAGE CONTRACT

(فصل) [عقد النّكاح]

ELEMENTS AND CONDITIONS FOR A VALID CONTRACT

ولا يصحّ النّكاح إلا بإيجاب وقبول بلفظ التّزويج أو الإنكاح غير مؤقّت ولا معلّق، بحضور ولي مرشد، وشاهديَ مقبول شهادة نكاح، لا مستور إسلام وحرّيّة.

A marriage contract is not valid except with:

1. an offer [from the bride's guardian] and an acceptance [from the bridegroom], using the phrase "marry" or "wed" [*tazwīj* or *inkāḥ*]...

Other phrases are not valid because marriage is an act of worship [*ʿibādah*]. It is an act of worship because texts have been transmitted indicating that it is recommended. Utterances associated with acts of worship are taken from the Sacred Law, and the Quran mentions those two phrases but not others.

A marriage contract is not valid with allusive phrases since the witnesses cannot ascertain their intended meaning.

35. Fāṭimah bint Qays: Muslim, 1480 #147. See: BM, 7:521.

36. Ibn ʿUmar: Bukhārī, 5142; Muslim, 1408 #38. See: KBM, 1942.

...that is neither temporary...

Marriage for a specified or unspecified duration is *mutʿah,* which has been prohibited.[37]

...nor conditional;...

This sort of condition is not valid for contracts to exchange property so there is more reason for it to be invalid in marriage contracts.

2. **the presence of a guardian who is astute [*murshid*]; and**
3. **two individuals who are qualified to be marriage witnesses – not those who are not known to be Muslim or free.**

The Prophet ﷺ said, "There is no marriage except with a guardian and two upright witnesses [*shāhidayn*]. Any marriage performed another way is invalid."[38] Witnesses are required in order to protect women and prevent marriages from being contested.

The witnesses must be free, Muslim, upright, and possess hearing and eyesight since the objective is establishing the marriage.[39]

WOMEN CANNOT ENGAGE DIRECTLY IN THE CONTRACT

It is also invalid for women to engage directly in the marriage contract. Allah Most High says, "...place not difficulties in the way of their marrying their husbands..." [Q2:232]; "Men are in charge of women..." [Q4:34]; and "...so wed them by permission of their folk..." [Q4:25]. Imam al-Shāfiʿī (may Allah grant him His mercy) mentioned these three verses. Evidence for this from the Sunnah includes Abū Hurayrah (may Allah be pleased with him) saying that the Prophet ﷺ said, "A woman does not marry off another

37. See "Temporary Marriage" on page 348.
38. Ibn ʿAbbās: Ibn Ḥibbān, 4075. See: TM, 1427.
39 See "Witnesses" on page 534.

woman, nor marry herself off. We would consider whoever married herself off to be a fornicator [*zāniyah*]."[40]

THE WITNESSES

‹Witnesses must be Muslim, since Allah Most High said, "And the believers, men and women, are protecting friends [*awliyā'*] one of another..." [Q9:71]. Witnessing is a type of alliance, so a non-Muslim's testimony is not accepted against a Muslim.[41]›

The witnesses cannot be morally corrupt since the word of the morally corrupt is not accepted as testimony.

They must also be male, since the phrase "*shāhidayn*" [in the hadith] refers to two male witnesses or two females with one male. The second is not intended here, so it must be the first.

WHEN THE BRIDE IS A DHIMMĪ OR A SLAVE

ولا يفتقر نكاح الذّمّيّة إلى إسلام الولي، ولا نكاح الأمة إلى عدالة السّيّد.

When marrying a female *dhimmī*, her guardian is not required to be a Muslim.

Allah Most High says, "And those who disbelieve are protectors one of another" [Q8:73].

When marrying a female slave, her master need not be upright.

---

40. Abū Hurayrah: Dāraquṭnī, 3536. See: TM, 1428.

41. al-Bughā, *Al-Tadhhīb*, 163 #1.

THE BRIDE'S GUARDIANS

(فصل) [الولي في النّكاح]

وأحق الأولياء أب، ثمّ جدّ لأب، ثمّ أخ لأبوين، ثم لأب، ثمّ ابناهما على هذا الترّتيب، ثّم عمّ، ثم سائر العصبة كالإرث.

The most rightful guardian is:

1. **the father;**

This is because of his abundant compassion for his daughter.

2. **the paternal grandfather;**

This is because he has guardianship and is a universal inheritor,[42] so he is put before those who are not universal inheritors.

3. **a full brother;**
4. **a consanguine brother;**

The full brother comes first because of his increased kinship and compassion.

5. **their sons (in that order);**

Meaning, the son of a full brother, then a son of a consanguine brother.

6. **a paternal uncle; and then,**
7. **the remaining universal male inheritors (as with inheritance).**[43]

---

42. See "Universal Inheritance" on page 308.
43. See "Universal Inheritance" on page 308.

فإن فقدوا زوج المعتق، ثم عصبته كالإرث.

If [the above] are absent, then [if she was once a slave] whoever freed her, followed by the emancipator's universal male inheritors.

فإن فقدوا زوّج الحاكم.

Then, if [all of the above] are absent, the Islamic magistrate [i.e. judge] contracts her marriage [in place of her guardian].

This is because he has general guardianship. ʿĀʾishah (may Allah be pleased with her) said that the Prophet ﷺ said, "The Sultan is the guardian of one who has none."[44]

THOSE BARRED FROM BEING GUARDIANS

(فصل) [سوالب الولاية]

THOSE STRIPPED OF GUARDIANSHIP

ولا ولاية لفاسق غير الإمام، ومحجور عليه بسفه، ومجنون، فيزوّج الأبعد.

Guardianship is not given to someone who is:

1. **morally corrupt – except in the case of the Imam;[45]**
2. **suspended from transactions due to being a spendthrift; or**
3. **insane.**

[If the guardian is one of the above], the next nearest guardian performs her marriage.

---

44. ʿĀʾishah: Abū Dāwūd, 2083, Tirmidhī, 1102. See: TM, 1427, 1429.

45 This is not required of the Imam, his appointed representative, or whoever takes his place since one of his duties is obtaining welfare for the masses. If moral uprightness were a condition, we would risk making this duty practically impossible to fulfill.

WHEN GUARDIANS REJECT A WOMAN'S SELECTION WITHOUT RIGHT OR ARE ABSENT

وإن عضل القريب أو غاب مسافة القصر زوّج الحاكم.

If a [guardian who is a] relative rejects [her choice, repeatedly and without right]...

When a woman who is mature and of sound mind asks to be married to a suitable man, her guardian must comply. Allah Most High says, "...place not difficulties in the way of their marrying their husbands..." [Q2:232]. ‹In the verse: "place not difficulties," addresses their guardians; "their husbands," refers to their former husbands, since the reason for its revelation is that the sister of Ma^cqal ibn Yasār was divorced by her husband (may Allah be pleased with all of them). Her former husband wanted to remarry her but Maʿqal prevented it.[46]›

The Prophet ﷺ said, "[There are] three you are not to delay: prayer when it is due..." and then mentioned "...and (marriage) for the single woman when someone compatible is found."[47] There is no difference here between a virgin and non-virgin, and whether it is for a typical *mahr* [dower] or less.

...or has travelled beyond the distance for shortening prayers, the hakim contracts her marriage.

This is because the governor [as mentioned earlier] has general authority.

46. al-Ḥasan: Bukhārī, 4529, 5130, 5331. See: al-Shafiʿī, *Al-Umm,* 5:13.
47. ʿAlī: Tirmidhī, 171, 1075. See: KBM, 1943.

SUITABILITY

(فصل) [الكفاءة في النّكاح]

FACTORS FOR SUITABILITY

والكفاءة في الدّين والنّسب والصّنعة والحرّيّة، وفقد العيوب المثبتة للخيار.

Suitability is based upon religion,...

A non-Muslim is not suitable for a female Muslim, nor is someone immoral suitable for a chaste woman.

Allah Most High says, "The fornicator shall not marry save a fornicator or an idolatress" [Q24:3].

...lineage,...

Since the Arabs took utmost pride in lineage.

The Prophet ﷺ said, "People are [like] ore: the best of them in the time of [pre-Islamic] ignorance are the best of them in Islam – if they have deep understanding [in the religion]."[48]

...vocation,...

Allah Most High says, "And Allah hath favoured some of you above others in provision" [Q16:71].

The soundest opinion is that suitability is not based upon wealth, since wealth comes and goes.

...freedom,...

Since a freewoman is shamed by being subordinate to a slave.

Barīrah was given a choice when she was manumitted whether to remain with her husband, who was a slave (may Allah be pleased

48. Abū Hurayrah: Bukhārī, 3383, 3493; Muslim, 2526 #199.

with them both).[49] Another narration adds: "If he had been free, he would not have given her a choice."[50]

...and being free of a defect that offers the option to void the marriage.[51]

Since the ego finds it difficult to accompany those who have these defects and they undermine the objectives of marriage.

The Prophet ﷺ said, "Flee from the leper like you flee from a lion."[52]

He ﷺ said, "Someone who is sick is not put alongside someone who is well."[53]

CONSENTING TO MARRY A LESS THAN SUITABLE GROOM

فإن رضيت هي وسائر الأولياء في الدّرجة بترك ذلك صحّ.

If the bride and all of her guardians of the [highest] rank are satisfied with forgoing this [criteria], [the marriage] is valid.

Suitability is not a condition for the validity of a marriage. Rather, it is a right of the bride and her guardians. So there is no objection if they consent to forgo it.

49. Bukhārī, 2536, 5279, 5430, 6758; Muslim, 1504 #11, 14. See: TM, 1449.
50. ʿĀʾishah: Abū Dāwūd, 2233.
51. See "Spousal Defects Permitting Annulment" on page 354.
52. Abū Hurayrah: Bukhārī, 5707.
53. Abū Hurayrah: Bukhārī, 5771; Muslim, 2221 #104.

A HUSBAND'S RIGHTS

(فصل) [حقق متعلّقة بالاستمتاع]

ويجب تسليم المرأة في بلد العقد، وتسلم الأمةبعد ثلث الليل.

It is obligatory to present the wife to her husband in the land where the contract took place, and to deliver a [married] slave after a third of the night has passed.

ويملك الاستمتاع بها من غير إضرار.

A husband is entitled to enjoy his wife without causing her harm.

وله أن يسافر بها إن شاء، والأمة بالإذن.

If he wishes, he brings his wife with him when he travels. He can bring his [wife who is a] slave with [her owner's] permission.

ولا يجوز وطؤها في الحيض وبعده ما لم تغتسل ولا في الدّبر.

It is not permissible for them to have intercourse while she is menstruating and before she has taken her post-menstrual purificatory bath.[54] Anal intercourse is also forbidden.

"Verily, Allah does not shy from the truth: Do not come to women from their anuses."[55]

والعزل جائز.

Withdrawing before ejaculation [coitus interruptus] is permissible.

Jābir (may Allah be pleased with him) said, "We would practice coitus interruptus throughout the revelatory period of the Quran."[56] ‹The Prophet ﷺ would have been aware of this and did not prohibit it, and he ﷺ would have not remained silent about such a matter if

54. See "Actions Unlawful Due to Menstruation & Lochia" on page 60.
55. al-Shāfiʿī, *Al-Umm,* 5:186. See: KBM, 1990.
56. Jābir: Bukhārī, 5208; Muslim, 1440 #136. See: KBM, 1994.

it was prohibited. Thus, the absence of textual evidence indicating its prohibition indicates that it is permissible – even if offensive.›

ويجبرها على ما يقف الاستمتاع أو كماله عليه.

The husband may compel her to do whatever is required to fulfill his sexual needs.

COMPELLING WOMEN TO MARRY

(فصل) [أحكام النّساء في إجبارهن وأخذ رأيهنّ]

وللأب والجدّ إجبار البكر بمهر المثل بنقد البلد من موسر بصداقها.

The father or paternal grandfather can compel a virgin to marry someone who is wealthy enough to provide her with a marriage payment whose value is typical for women of her status and in the local currency.

The Prophet ﷺ said, "A non-virgin [*thayyib*] has more right to her person than her guardians. A virgin is consulted, and her silence is her assent."[57]

This is valid only when the girl is a virgin, the husband is a suitable match, the bride's marriage payment is at least equal to that of similar women, and it is paid using the predominant local currency. However, it is still recommended that her guardian marry her only after obtaining her consent.

The husband must be a suitable match unless she consents, because suitability is her right and she can waive it.

Suitability is not a condition for the validity of the marriage contract. The Prophet ﷺ said to Fāṭimah bint Qays, "Marry Usāmah."[58] Fāṭimah was a Qureshi while Usāmah was a freed slave. Abū Ḥudhayfah married his freed slave Sālim to the daughter of his

57. Ibn ʿAbbās: Muslim, 1421 #66–67. See: TM, 1430.
58. Fāṭimah bint Qays: Muslim, 1480 #36. See: KBM, 1925.

brother al-Walīd ibn ʿUtbah.[59] Al-Miqdād ibn al-Aswad al-Kindī married Ḍubāʿah bint al-Zubayr ibn ʿAbd al-Muṭṭalib.[60] [Hālah] the sister of ʿAbd al-Raḥmān ibn ʿAuf was married to Bilāl.[61] (May Allah be pleased with them all.)

والثّيّب لا تزوّج إلا بعد البلوغ والإذن، إلّا في المجنونة والأمة.

Non-virgins are not married off until they reach maturity and give their permission,...

This is because of the earlier hadith.[62]

Their permission prior to adulthood is not sufficient, since someone who is immature cannot give permission.

...except in the case of a woman who is insane or a slave.

‹If a woman is insane and immature, it is permissible for her father or grandfather to marry her off – but not anyone else. This is because guardianship is emphasized when insanity is combined with immaturity. There are no circumstances in which her permission is sought since both men have a type of guardianship that allows them to compel [her to marry]; and her welfare requires it. Her welfare is a sufficient reason – even if she does not have a need to marry – since marriage benefits her with a dowry and support.[63]›

---

59. ʿĀʾishah: Bukhārī, 4000. See: TM, 328.
60. ʿĀʾishah: Bukhārī, 5089; Muslim, 1207 #104.
61. Abū Sufyān al-Jumaḥī from his mother: Dāraquṭnī, 3797. See: KBM, 1960.
62. Ibn ʿAbbās: Muslim, 1421. See: TM, 1430.
63. Taqi al-Dīn al-Ḥusnī al-Ḥussayni, *Kifāyat al-Akhyār,* 361.

UNMARRIAGEABLE WOMEN

(فصل) [المحرّمات من النّساء]

‹The general evidence for the subject of unmarriageable women comes from Q4:22–23. Allah Most High says:

"And marry not those women whom your fathers married, except what hath already happened (of that nature) in the past. Lo! it was ever lewdness and abomination, and an evil way" [Q4:22].

"Forbidden unto you are your mothers, and your daughters, and your sisters, and your father's sisters, and your mother's sisters, and your brother's daughters and your sister's daughters, and your foster-mothers, and your foster-sisters, and your mothers-in-law, and your step-daughters who are under your protection (born) of your women unto whom ye have gone in – but if ye have not gone in unto them, then it is no sin for you (to marry their daughters) – and the wives of your sons who (spring) from your own loins. And (it is forbidden unto you) that ye should have two sisters together, except what hath already happened (of that nature) in the past. Lo! Allah is ever Forgiving, Merciful" [Q4:23].›

BLOOD RELATION

ويحرم بالنّسب سبع: الأمّ وإن علت، والبنت وإن سفلت، والأخت، والعمّة، والخالة، وبنت الأخ، وبنت الأخت.

Seven are unlawful as a result of kinship:[64]

1. **one's mother and her ancestors;**
2. **one's daughters and their descendants;**
3. **one's sisters;**
4. **one's maternal aunts;**
5. **one's paternal aunts;**
6. **the daughters of one's brother; and**
7. **the daughters of one's sister.**

---

64. Similar rulings exist for women. See *The Accessible Conspectus*, §9.2

Allah Most High says, "Forbidden unto you are your mothers, and your daughters, and your sisters, and your father's sisters, and your mother's sisters, and your brother's daughters and your sister's daughters,..." [Q4:23].

MARRIAGE

و[يحرم] بالمصاهرة أربع: أمّ الزّوجة، والرّبيبة إذا دخل بالأمّ، وزوجة الأب، وزوجة الابن.

Four are unlawful as a result of marriage:

1. the wife's mother;

Allah Most High says, "...your wives' mothers..." [Q4:23].

2. the wife's daughter from a previous marriage when one has consummated the marriage to her mother;

Allah Most High says, "...and your step-daughters under your guardianship [born] of your wives unto whom you have gone in..." [Q4:23].

3. the wife of one's father; and

Allah Most High says, "And marry not those women whom your fathers married..." [Q4:22].

4. the wife of one's son.

Allah Most High says, "...and the wives of your sons who (spring) from your own loins..." [Q4:23].

It is also unlawful to marry [or have intercourse with] a slave with whom one's father or son had intercourse, since intercourse during slavery is given the status of intercourse during marriage.

NURSING

ويحرم هؤلاء بالرّضاع أيضًا.

Those four [who are unlawful through marriage] are also unlawful as a result of nursing.[65]

Nursing also renders unlawful whatever is unlawful through kinship. The Messenger of Allah ﷺ said, "Nursing makes unlawful what consanguinity makes unlawful."[66] ‹Also, Allah Most High says, "...and your foster [milk] mothers, and your foster sisters [through nursing]..." [Q4:23].›

SISTERS AND AUNTS

والجمع بين المرأة وأختها أو عمّتها أو خالتها حرام.

It is unlawful to marry both a woman and her sister,...

‹Allah Most High says, "...And (it is forbidden unto you) that ye should have two sisters together, except what hath already happened (of that nature) in the past..." [Q4:23].[67]›

...or her paternal aunt, or her maternal aunt.

Abū Hurayrah (may Allah be pleased with him) reported that the Messenger of Allah ﷺ said, "A woman and her paternal aunt are not to be joined to the same man; neither is a woman and her maternal aunt."[68]

It is not permissible to marry a woman to anyone other than her husband during her divorce waiting period.[69] Allah Most High

---

65. See "Wet-Nursing" on page 405.
66. Ibn ʿAbbās: Bukhārī, 2465; Muslim, 1446. See: TM, 1439, 1511.
67. al-Bughā, *Al-Tadhhīb*, 165 #1.
68. Abū Hurayrah: Bukhārī, 5109; Muslim, 1408. See: TM, 1440.
69. See "The Waiting Period" on page 394.

says, "...And do not consummate the marriage until (the term) prescribed is run..." [Q2:235].

It is not permissible to remarry one's former wife if one accused her of committing adultery.[70] The Prophet ﷺ said, "Those who have cursed one another are never conjoined."[71]

TRIPLY-DIVORCED FORMER WIFE

It is not permissible to remarry one's former wife if one divorced her three times. Allah Most High says, "And if he hath divorced her, then she is not lawful unto him thereafter until she hath wedded another husband..." [Q2:230]. What is intended in the verse is a woman divorced three times – or twice, if the husband is a slave, as he has half the number of divorces as a freeman. The triply-divorced wife remains unlawful to him until she has consummated another marriage, because of the previous verse.

A FIFTH WIFE

It is not permissible for one to marry a fifth wife. Ghaylān (may Allah be pleased with him) entered Islam with ten wives. The Prophet ﷺ said to him, "Choose four and separate from the rest."[72]

A FREEMAN MARRYING A SECOND SLAVE

It is not permissible for a freeman to marry two slaves, since his marriage to one is permissible out of fear of fornication, and fear of fornication is removed by marrying her.[73]

---

70. See "Charging One's Wife With Adultery" on page 364.
71. Ibn ʿUmar: Dāraquṭnī, 3704–7, Bayhaqī, 15131, 15322. See: KBM, 2105.
72. Ibn ʿUmar: Tirmidhī, 1128; Ibn Mājah, 1953; Ibn Ḥibbān, 4156, 4158; Dāraquṭnī, 3683–6; Ḥākim, 2779–83. See: TM, 1441, 1488.
73. See "Freemen Marrying Slaves" on page 351.

A SLAVE MARRYING A THIRD WIFE

It is not permissible for a slave to marry three wives, since the Companions of the Messenger of Allah ﷺ were of the consensus that a slave does not marry more than two (may Allah be pleased with them).[74]

SHIGHĀR

Shighār marriage is not valid. ʿUmar (may Allah be pleased with him) said that it is forbidden.[75] *Shighār* marriage is saying, "I will marry my daughter to you on the condition that you marry your daughter to me, and each will be the other's marriage payment." However, if each woman is not made the other's marriage payment, it is valid.

TEMPORARY MARRIAGE

Temporary marriage [*mutʿah*] is not valid because "on the Day of Khaybar, the Messenger of Allah ﷺ forbade temporary marriage and the consumption of domestic donkey meat."[76]

---

74. al-Ḥakam ibn ʿUtabah: Bayhaqī, 13898. See: KBM, 1973.

75. ʿUmar: Bukhārī, 5112, 6960; Muslim, 1415 #57–60. See: TM, 1426.

76. ʿAlī ibn Abī Ṭālib: Bukhārī, 4216; Muslim, 1407 #29–32. cf 1939 for Ibn ʿAbbās; 2718. See: TM, 1425.

MARRYING A NON-MUSLIM WOMAN

(فصل) [نكاح الكتابيّات]

IDOLATRESSES AND REVELATIONLESS WOMEN

ويحرم نكاح من لا كتاب لها كوثنيّة.

It is unlawful to marry a woman who [follows a religion that] lacks a book of revelation – just as it is with an idolatress.

This is because of the evident meaning of the verse "Wed not idolatresses [*mushrikāt*] till they believe..." [Q2:221]. ‹In the verse, "idolatresses [*mushrikāt*]" refers to female non-believers [*kafirāt*] in general.[77]›

The Prophet ﷺ said concerning Zoroastrians, "Do with them as is done with Ahl al-Kitāb, other than marrying their women and eating meat they slaughter."[78]

JEWISH AND CHRISTIAN WOMEN

وتحلّ كتابيّة إن علم دخول أوّل آبائها في ذلك الدّين قبل نسخه وتحريفه، اللّهمّ إلا أن تكون إسرائيليّة فتحلّ مطلقًا.

It is permissible to marry a woman who [follows a religion that] has a book of revelation [i.e., Judaism or Christianity] if it is known that her ancestors entered that religion before it was abrogated and corrupted. This is, unless she is an Israelite, in which case marriage to her is lawful without restriction.

The general permissibility was established when Allah Most High revealed "...And so are the virtuous women of the believers and

77. al-Maḥallī and al-Suyūṭī, *Tafsīr al-Jalālayn*.
78. ʿAbd al-Raḥmān ibn ʿAuf: Mālik, 968; al-Shāfiʿī, *Al-Musnad*, p209. See: KBM, 1971.

the virtuous women of those who received the Scripture before you (lawful for you)..." [Q5:5].

It is not permissible to marry a Christian or Jewish woman if her ancestors entered their religion after the arrival of our Prophet Muhammad ﷺ.[79]

If a woman's ancestors entered [Judaism] after the arrival of ʿĪsā (peace be upon him) and before the arrival of our Prophet ﷺ, it is not permissible to marry her because the soundest opinion is that the Sacred Law of ʿĪsā (peace be upon him) abrogated the Sacred Law of Mūsā (peace be upon him).

However, if a woman's ancestors entered their religion before its corruption and abrogation, the soundest opinion is that it is permissible to marry her.

If a woman's ancestors entered their religion after its corruption but before its abrogation yet still clung to the truth and avoided the corruption, then it is like the previous scenario [it is permissible to marry her]. Otherwise it is not permissible to marry them according to the soundest opinion.[80]

If it is not known when a woman's ancestors entered their religion, one may not marry her, according to the soundest opinion, unless she is an Israelite.[81]

If she is an Israelite (i.e., a descendant of Yaʿqūb (peace be upon him]), it is permissible to marry her without qualification – without checking when her ancestors entered that religion and whether it was before or after its corruption due to the nobility of their lineage.[82]

79. al-Nawawī, *Rawḍat al-ṭālibīn,* 7:138.

80. al-Nawawī, *Rawḍat al-ṭālibīn,* 7:137.

81. al-Nawawī, *Rawḍat al-ṭālibīn,* 7:138.

82. c.f. al-Nawawī, *Rawḍat al-ṭālibīn,* 7:137–38.

APOSTATE WOMEN

ولا تحلّ مرتدة لأحد.

A female apostate is not lawful for anyone.

Allah Most High says, "Wed not idolatresses [*kāfirāt*] till they believe..." [Q2:221].

She is not lawful for a Muslim because she is a disbeliever who is not allowed to remain in her current condition.[83] She is not lawful for a non-Muslim either because she continues to have an attachment to Islam.

FREEMEN MARRYING SLAVES

ولا ينكح الحرّ أمة مسلمة ابتداء إلا إذا عدم طول حرّة وخاف العنت - أي الزنا - ولا ينكح من يملكها كعكسه.

A man who is free does not marry a female Muslim slave initially unless he lacks the wherewithal to marry a freewoman and fears committing fornication.

Allah Most High says, "And whoso is not able to afford to marry free, believing women [*muḥṣināt*], let them marry from the believing maids [*fatayātikum*] whom your right hands possess" followed by Him saying, "...This is for him among you who feareth to commit sin..." [Q4:25]. ‹In this verse, "not able to afford" means excess of money; "*muḥṣināt*" means free; "believing maids" means female slaves; and "feareth to commit sin" means committing fornication.[84]›

A non-Muslim slave is not lawful for a Muslim. Allah Most High says, "And whoso is not able to afford to marry free, believing women [*muḥṣināt*], let them marry from the believing maids

83 See "Apostasy" on page 452.

84. al-Bughā, *Al-Tadhhīb,* 160 #1.

[*fatayātikum*] whom your right hands possess" [Q4:25]. But she is lawful for a non-Muslim.

He does not marry someone he owns – just like its opposite [i.e., a freewoman does not marry her male slave].

A man cannot marry his slave because the relationship of slavery outweighs the relationship of marriage. Through slavery, one owns the body and its benefits, whereas through marriage, one owns nothing except a portion of its benefits, so the weaker relationship falls in the presence of the stronger one.

A woman cannot marry her slave because the authority each person would have over the other would be nullified.[85]

AN INDIVIDUAL SPOUSE ENTERING ISLAM

(فصل) [إسلام أحد الزّوجين]

أسلم كتابيّ وتحته كتابيّة دام نكاحه، أو وثنيّة أو مجوسيّة فتخلف قبل دخول تنجزت الفرقة، أو بعده وقفت الفرقة على انقضاء العدة، فإن أسلم الآخر قبل انقضائها استمر.

A male who is a Jew or Christian enters Islam. If he is married to a woman of either faith, the marriage continues.

This is because of the permissibility of initiating a marriage with a woman from a community that possess revelation while he is a Muslim.

85. Her authority over him as an owner and his authority over her as a husband cancel one another.

But [if he is married to] an idolatress or a Zoroastrian and enters Islam before consummation, they are immediately separated.

This is because such a marriage is not fully affirmed, as indicated by its revocability through a single divorce.

If [his conversion] happened after consummation, separation is delayed until the waiting period ends. If the his wife enters Islam before [the end of the waiting period], the marriage continues.

ʿAbd Allāh ibn Shubramah (may Allah be pleased with him) reported: "During the time of the Messenger of Allah ﷺ, a man would enter Islam before his wife, or his wife before him. If either of them would enter Islam before the wife's waiting period expired, she would remain his wife. And if he or she entered Islam after the waiting period expired, there would be no marriage between them."[86]

Ibn ʿAbbās (may Allah be pleased with them both) said, "A woman entered Islam during the time of the Messenger of Allah ﷺ, and then married [a second husband]. Her [first] husband came to the Messenger of Allah ﷺ and said, 'I had already entered Islam and she knew about my Islam.' So the Messenger of Allah ﷺ separated her from her second husband and returned her to her first."[87]

According to Ibn Yūnus (may Allah grant him His mercy), the rulings [related to conversion within a marriage] are analogous to those of divorce.

---

86. Ibn al-Mulaqqin mentions this in *ʿUjālat al-muḥtāj* (331) without attribution to a source. Later in the same book (1265), he mentions that there is a report concerning the issue but he has not been able to find it. He did name a narrator. The editor of UM suggests that the next report from Ibn ʿAbbās is it – and the report does appear in Ibn al-Mulaqqin's *Tuḥfat al-muḥtāj* – but what he mentioned in MT suggests otherwise. I was able to find ʿAbd Allāh ibn Shabramah's report in several books, including al-Shirazī, *Al-Muhadhdhab,* 2:456.

87. Ibn ʿAbbās: Abū Dāwūd, 2239; Ibn Mājah, 2008; al-Ḥākim, 2810. See: TM, 1445.

MARRIAGE BETWEEN NON-MUSLIMS

Marriage between non-Muslims is considered valid. This is because Allah Most High says [concerning Abū Lahab], "And his wife, the wood-carrier" [Q111:4], "And the wife of Pharaoh said..." [Q28:9]. Additionally, if non-Muslims were to bring a case to us [i.e., Muslim authorities] involving non-Muslim marriage, we would not invalidate it.

SPOUSAL DEFECTS PERMITTING MARRIAGE ANNULMENT

(فصل) [خيار النّكاح]

يثبت الخيار بالجنون والجذام والبرص المستحكم والرّتق والقرن والجب والعنة بالحاكم على الفور.

Annulment is an option when there is
1. insanity,
2–3. *jadhdhām* or *baraṣ* [two types of leprosy],
4. vaginal constriction because of flesh or bone,
5. a severed penis, or
6. impotence.

What is intended through marriage is enjoyment via intercourse. That is the primary objective; everything else is secondary. These defects prevent one's complete enjoyment. Impotence and vaginal constriction prevent intercourse. Intercourse is not possible with insanity without it becoming difficult in some circumstances and dangerous in others. Leprosy [*jadhdhām* or *baraṣ*] is extremely repulsive out of fear that it might spread. Since these defects prevent the main objective of marriage, the Sharīʿah gives one the option to annul. By contrast, since an amputated hand or foot, or blindness do not prevent intercourse but rather lead to a slight decrease in pleasure for some people we [Shāfiʿī scholars who champion this opinion] say that there is no option to annul, as the objective is still obtained. There is also consensus that these [six] defects are grounds for canceling a sale [of a slave who possesses them], since they slightly decrease the slave's financial value. A fortiori, they diminish [one's ability to attain] the primary objective of marriage.

According to Imam al-Nawawī (may Allah grant him His mercy) in *Ru'ūs al-Masā'il,* the above explanation is the best that can be used as evidence. Our scholars cite as evidence the well-known hadith that the Prophet ﷺ married a woman from Ghaffār. When he ﷺ entered upon her he saw a white patch of skin and said, "Dress and return to your family."[88] But this hadith does not indicate annulment for the sake of defects, since it is possible that it was a divorce [using an allusive phrase].

The option exists even if the defect occurred after marriage – with the exception of impotence after the marriage has been consummated.

The option does not exist if the defects were known prior to marriage (even if the known defect worsens), since accepting a thing is acceptance of its consequences. There is also no option if the defects became known after the spouse died or after the defect has been cured, since marriage ends with the spouse's death and the harm is gone once it is cured.

[The decision to annul must be taken] immediately, in the presence of a judge.

The decision must be taken immediately, since one is annulling for the sake of a defect. It must be taken in the presence of a judge because it requires the exercise of *ijtihād*.

والقول قول الزّوج في نفي العنّة، وفي وطء الثّيّب، وفي المجبوب إذا بقي ما يمكن الجماع به، وقولها فيما إذا اختلفا في إمكانه، وفيما إذا كانت بكرًا وأنكرت الوطء.

The husband's word is accepted if he denies that he is impotent, [affirms] having had intercourse with his wife (if she is a non-virgin), or [asserts] that what remains of his severed penis suffices for intercourse.

88. Ka'b ibn 'Ujrah: Ḥākim, 6808. See: KBM, 1985.

The wife's word is accepted if they disagree about his ability [to perform intercourse] or if she denies that they have had intercourse [provided that she was known to be a virgin at the time of marriage].

There is neither a marriage payment nor an amenity [*mutʿah*] payment[89] if the marriage is annulled before consummation. This is because, if the defect is his, she is annulling the marriage; and if the defect is hers, she is the cause for the annulment. Thus, it is as though she is annulling it in both instances.

But if the marriage is consummated, the husband must give the wife a typical marriage payment [*mahr al-mithl*]– like if it is annulled due to an event that occurs between the drafting of the marriage contract and its consummation that the spouse was not aware of. This is because the husband gave the named marriage payment thinking that the wife was free of defects while she actually was not. Thus, it is as though the contract was finalized without any marriage payment being named – so a typical marriage payment [*mahr al-mithl*] would be required.

If the defect occurs after intercourse, nothing other than the named marriage payment is obligatory. This is because intercourse made the marriage payment binding before the reason for annulment existed.

PROVIDING A WIFE FOR ONE'S FATHER

(فصل) [إعفاف الأصل]

يلزم الولد إعفاف أصله، وعليه مؤنتها إذا كان فاقد مهر محتاج إلى النّكاح.

Sons must ensure the chastity of their fathers [by providing the means for them to get married]. They must provide for their expenses when the father lacks a bride's marriage payment and needs to be married.

89. See "Amenity Payment" on page 364.

This is because leaving the father without a means to chastity exposes him to [the risk of committing] fornication. That is not appropriate given the sanctity of fatherhood, nor is it consistent with accompanying them with goodness. Allah Most High said, "Consort with them in the world kindly..." [Q31:15]. It is obligatory only if the father has sexual needs.

THE WIFE'S MARRIAGE PAYMENT

(فصل) [الصّداق]

The word for a wife's marriage payment "*ṣadāq*" comes from "*ṣidq*," which means truth, since it indicates that the groom is truly interested in the bride.

The foundation for the marriage payment is from the Quran, Sunnah, and consensus. Allah Most High says, "And give unto the women (whom ye marry) free gift of their marriage portions..." [Q4:4], and "...on [the condition] that you serve me for eight years..." [Q28:27]. (In religions prior to Islam, the marriage payment was given to the bride's guardian.) And, the Prophet ﷺ said, "Find something, even if only an iron ring." There is consensus that whatever can be a marriage payment becomes set once it has been validly specified.

IT IS RECOMMENDED

تسنّ تسميّة الصّداق في العقد.

It is recommended to state the marriage payment in the contract.

‹Allah Most High says, "And give unto the women (whom ye marry) free gift of their marriage portions..." [Q4:4].[90]›

Sahl ibn Saʿd (may Allah be pleased with him) said that a lady came to the Prophet ﷺ and said, "I have given myself as a gift to

---

90. al-Bughā, *Al-Tadhhīb,* 167 #1.

Allah and His Messenger ﷺ." The Prophet ﷺ said, "I am not in need of women." A man said, "Marry her to me." The Prophet ﷺ said, "Give her a garment." The man said, "I cannot afford it." The Prophet ﷺ said, "Give her anything – even an iron ring." The man apologized again. The Prophet ﷺ then asked him, "What do you have [memorized] from the Quran?" He replied, "Such-and-such." The Prophet ﷺ said, "Then I marry her to you for what you have from the Quran."[91]

A marriage is still valid without a named marriage payment. Allah Most High says, "It is no sin for you if ye divorce women while yet ye have not touched them, nor appointed unto them a portion…" [Q2:236]. ‹In this verse, "appointed unto them a portion" means a specific bridal payment. The verse indicates that marriage contracts are valid even when the bridal payment is not specified, since divorce cannot occur except after a valid contract.[92]› And while the marriage is valid, it is offensive.

WHAT IS VALID AS A PAYMENT

وما جاز أن يكون مبيعًا جاز أن يكون صداقًا، ويجوز أن يكون عينًا ومنفعة.

Whatever is permissible as a sale item is permissible as a marriage payment.

ʿĀmir ibn Rabīʿah (may Allah be pleased with him) said that a woman from Banu Fazārah was married for two sandals. The Messenger of Allah ﷺ said to her, "Do you approve of [submitting] yourself and your wealth for two sandals?" She said, "Yes." He ﷺ permitted it.[93]

It is recommended that the marriage payment not be less than ten *dirhams*, since Abū Ḥanīfah (may Allah grant him His mercy) did not permit less than this. And it is recommended that the payment

---

91. Sahl ibn Saʿd: Bukhārī, 5029; Muslim, 1425. See: TM, 1454.

92. al-Bughā, *Al-Tadhhīb*, 167 #2.

93. ʿĀmir ibn Rabīʿah: Tirmidhī, 1113. See: TM, 1454.

not exceed 500 *dirhams*, since this is what was transmitted regarding the dowries for the daughters and wives of the Prophet ﷺ.[94]

‹ʿUmar ibn al-Khaṭṭāb (may Allah be pleased with him) said: "Do not exaggerate in women's dowries. If doing so were honorable in the world or *taqwā* before Allah, then the Messenger of Allah ﷺ would have been the first of you to do it. The Messenger of Allah ﷺ did not give a dowry to any of his wives, nor did any of his daughters receive more than twelve *ūqiyyah*s."[95]

One *ūqiyyah* equals forty *dirhams*, so the maximum reported from the Prophet ﷺ is a total of 480 *dirhams*.[96]›

The marriage payment can be a known utility, such as teaching something from the Quran, or performing a specific task. This was affirmed in the aforementioned hadith from Sahl ibn Saʿd (may Allah be pleased with him).[97]

OWNERSHIP AND ESTABLISHMENT

وتملك بالتّسمية، ويستقرّ بالدّخول والموت.

The marriage payment becomes owned upon being stated and becomes irrevocably established upon consummation...

‹Allah Most High says, "If ye divorce them before ye have touched them and ye have appointed unto them a portion, then (pay the) half of that which ye appointed..." [Q2:237]. The verse indicates that the dowry is due upon consummation since nothing of the dowry is reduced if divorce occurs after consummation.[98]›

94. ʿĀʾishah: Muslim, 1426 #78; Abū Dāwūd, 2105; Ibn Mājah, 1886; al-Ḥākim, 2740. See: TM, 1451.
95. ʿUmar: Abū Dāwūd, 2106; Tirmidhī, 1114; Nasāʾī, 3349.
96. al-Bughā, *Al-Tadhhīb,* 167 #1.
97. Sahl ibn Saʿd: Bukhārī, 5029; Muslim, 1425. See: TM, 1454.
98. al-Bughā, *Al-Tadhhīb,* 168 #3.

ʿUmar (may Allah be pleased with him) said: "Any man who marries a woman and has intercourse with her must give her the entire dowry."[99]

...or the death [of either spouse].

ʿAbd Allāh ibn Masʿūd (may Allah be pleased with him) was asked about a man who married a woman but did not specify the dowry for her and passed away without having sex with her. Ibn Masʿūd said, "She gets the same dowry as women of her status, no less and no more. She has to observe the waiting period, and she receives inheritance." So Maʿqil ibn Sinān al-Ashjaʿī (may Allah be pleased with him) stood and said, "The Messenger of Allah ﷺ judged the same as you have judged regarding Birwaʿ bint Wāshiq (may Allah be pleased with her), a woman of ours." This made Ibn Masʿūd happy.[100]

THE BRIDE'S RIGHT TO ITS DISPOSAL

وتملك التّصرّف فيه بالقبض.

The bride owns the right to dispose of the marriage payment upon taking possession of it.

WHEN THE PAYMENT IS HALVED

ويتشطّر قبل الدّخول إن لم تكن الفرقة بسببها أو منها.

The marriage payment is reduced by half [upon the couple's separation if the separation occurs] before consummation [and] if the separation is not caused by her or on her behalf.

99. Al-Shāfiʿī, *Al-Umm*, 7:249.

100. Ibn Masʿūd: Abū Dāwūd, 2144, Tirmidhī, 1145 – *ḥasan ṣaḥīḥ*. See: TM, 1452.

‹Allah Most High says, "If ye divorce them before ye have touched them and ye have appointed unto them a portion, then (pay the) half of that which ye appointed..." [Q2:237].[101]›

WITHHOLDING ITS PAYMENT

ولها حبس نفسها حتى تقبض المهر المعيّن والحالّ، ولو تمانعا أجبرا.

The bride can withhold herself from her husband until she takes possession of the specified marriage payment that is currently owed.

It is a right owed to her, so she can withhold herself until it is delivered. But she cannot withhold herself for a deferred portion, since she already consented to its delay.

If both of them withhold from one another, they are each compelled [to acquiesce].

He places what he owes her with someone trustworthy, and she is ordered to present herself to him. Once she does, she is given what she is owed. Each one deserves what they are owed, so each delivers it to the other.

DISAGREEMENTS CONCERNING PAYMENT

وإن اختلفا في قبضه، فالقول قولها.

If they disagree as to whether she took possession of the marriage payment, her word is accepted.

101. al-Bughā, *Al-Tadhhīb,* 168 #3.

WHEN THE WIFE DECLINES SPECIFYING AN AMOUNT

وتستحقّه المفوّضة، بالفرض أو الموت.

A woman who declined specifying a marriage payment in the contract [a *mufawwiḍah*] is entitled to a marriage payment specified by the husband [prior to consummation] or upon his death.

This is because the rights related to her body are not purely hers; rather, Allah has rights related to it. Do you not see that it cannot be made freely available to others, thus, it is protected from such scenarios?

Prior to intercourse, she can demand that the husband specify a marriage payment and she can withhold herself from him if she does not accept it.

INVALID OR UNSTATED AMOUNTS AND MAHR AL-MITHL

وحيث فسد فلها مهر المثل – وهو ما يرغب به في مثلها.

Whenever the marriage price is invalid [or left unstated], the woman is entitled to *mahr al-mithl*: whatever payment women of similar status receive.

WHAT IS OWED FOR INVALID OR DUBIOUS INTERCOURSE

وفي وطء في نكاح فاسد أو شبهه مهر مثل، وإن تكرّر إلّا يتعدّد جنسها وكذا إذا كرّر وطء مغصوبة، أو مكرهة على الزّنا.

She is entitled to a [single] *mahr al-mithl* for intercourse that takes place in a marriage that is invalid [*fāsid*] or dubious [*shubhah*],...

She is owed her *mahr* because her husband has achieved fulfillment and has derived benefit from her body.

...even for repeated acts of intercourse...

Just as repeated acts of intercourse in a valid marriage do not merit multiple *mahr*s.

... – unless there are multiple types [of dubiousness].

For example, if a man has intercourse with a woman thinking she is his wife and then determines that she is not – and later has intercourse with her again thinking she is his wife. Or if a man has intercourse with a woman thinking she is his wife, and another time thinking she is his slave. Or he has intercourse with her in an invalid marriage and – after they are separated – he marries her again with an invalid marriage and consummates it.

Because numerous types have occurred, each act of intercourse receives its own ruling.

The ruling is similar for repeated acts of intercourse with a stolen slave or multiple incidents of rape [involving the same woman].

Because the payment is required out of consuming the benefit, and it has happened repeatedly. This is when he is aware [that she is not his licit sexual partner] and she deserves her payment out of being compelled. If he does not know, then he owes a single payment – since ignorance resembles a single, consistent dubiousness, so it resembles repeated acts of intercourse in an invalid marriage.

GUARDIANS CANNOT WAIVE IT

وليس للولي عفو عن الصّداق.

The woman's guardian [*walī*] does not [have the authority to] waive the marriage payment.

No one except a woman of sound mind can waive her marriage payment.

AMENITY PAYMENT

(فصل) [متعة المطلّقات]

وللمطلّقات والمفارقات - لا يمسّها - متاع بالمعروف، إلّا أن يجب شطر مهر، ويستحبّ أن لا ينقص عن ثلاثين درهما.

Women who have been divorced or separated – without their marriage having been consummated – are entitled to provision in kindness on what is acceptable [*matāʿun bi-l-maʿrūf*]...

Allah Most High says, "For divorced women a provision in kindness: a duty for those who ward off (evil)" [Q2:241].

... – except in cases where half of the marriage payment is required.

Such as, while alive, they separate before consummating the marriage for reasons returning to the husband – but not for reasons returning to the wife.

It is recommended that the provision amount be no less than thirty *dirhams* [in value].

If the two parties disagree as to what the amount should be, the judge sets the amount, taking into account both spouses' financial circumstances. Allah Most High says, "...Provide for them, the rich according to his means..." [Q2:236], and, "For divorced women a provision in kindness..." [Q2:241].

THE WEDDING FEAST

(فصل) [الوليمة]

HOLDING THE FEAST

ووليمة العرس سنّة

A wedding feast [*walīmah*] is sunnah.

Anas ibn Mālik (may Allah be pleased with him) said that the Prophet ﷺ saw a yellow trace [of perfume] on ʿAbd al-Raḥmān ibn ʿAwf (may Allah be pleased with him) and said, "What's this?" ʿAbd al-Raḥmān said, "I have married a woman with a marriage payment [*mahr*] of gold equal to a date-stone." The Prophet ﷺ said, "May Allah bless you. Hold a wedding banquet, even with one sheep."[102]

ATTENDING THE FEAST

والإجابة فرض عين بشرط أن يعيّنه بالدّعوة وألّا يخصّ الأغنياء، وأن يكون الدّاعي مسلما، وأن لا يكون هناك عذر مرخّص، وبقصد التودّد.

Answering an invitation is a personal obligation...

The Prophet ﷺ said, "Whoever of you is invited [to a wedding feast] is to comply."[103]

102. Anas: Bukhārī, 5155; Muslim, 1427. See: TM, 1458.
103. Ibn ʿUmar: Bukhārī, 5173; Muslim, 1429 #96, 100. See: TM, 1459.

...provided that the invitee was specifically invited and the invitation is not restricted to the rich,...

The Prophet ﷺ said, "The worst food is the food of a wedding feast to which the rich are invited and the poor are left out. He who rejects an invitation disobeys Allah and His Messenger."[104]

...that the inviter is a Muslim, and that there is no dispensation due to an excuse.

An excuse would be the presence of something blameworthy that the invitee would not be able to change.

[One attends] with the intention of fostering mutual affection [*tawaddud*].

THROWING AND COLLECTING SWEETS

ويحلّ النّثر في الإملاك وغيره، وترك التّقاطه أولى.

It is permissible to throw [sweets and the like] during wedding arrangements and other occasions. It is best not to pick them up.

104. Abū Hurayrah: Bukhārī, 5177; Muslim, 1432 #110; Ibn Mājah, 1913; Abū Dāwūd, 3742. See: TM, 1460.

GIVING WIVES EQUAL TIME

(فصل) [القسم]

وإذا بات عند بعض نسوته، وجب عند الباقي.

When one spends the night with some of one's wives, it is obligatory [to do so] with the others.

The Prophet ﷺ said, "When a man has two wives and is not just between them, he will come on the Day of Resurrection with one side [of his body] hanging inclined or hanging down."[105] Various transmissions include: "...one side hanging inclined," and "...one side hanging down." ‹In this hadith, "not just" refers to their expenses and staying the night with them.[106]›

Equality does not refer to [degrees of one's] affection or [frequency of] intercourse, as alluded to in the hadith of ʿĀʾishah (may Allah be pleased with her): "The Prophet would divide [his time] and do it equally. He ﷺ would say, 'O Allah! This is my division in what I have control over, so do not punish me for what You have control over which I do not have control over.'"[107]

One is not obligated to spend time with one's female slaves – even those who have borne one's children.[108] Allah Most High says, "...and if ye fear that ye cannot do justice (to so many) then one (only) or (the captives) that your right hands possess..." [Q4:3], which suggests that this sort of equity is not required with female slaves. ‹In the verse: "cannot do justice (to so many)" means their financial support and giving them equal time; "(the captives) that your right hands possess" refers to female slaves, who do not have the same rights as wives who are free.[109]›

105. Abū Hurayrah: Abū Dāwūd, 2133; Tirmidhī, 1141; Nasāʾī, 3942; Ibn Mājah, 1969; Ibn Ḥibbān, 4207; Ḥākim, 2759. See: TM, 1467.

106. al-Bughā, *Al-Tadhhīb,* 170 #3.

107. ʿĀʾishah: Abū Dāwūd, 2134; Tirmidhī, 1140. See: BM, 7:481–2, 8:38.

108. See "Ummahāt al-Awlād" on page 555.

109. al-Maḥallī and al-Suyūṭī, *Tafsīr al-Jalālayn.*

This obligation applies equally to wives who are menstruating, in post-natal bleeding, or who have vaginal constriction. This is because the objective is affection, which all of them are in need of. The obligation also includes a wife with whom the husband has sworn not to have intercourse[110] or has likened to his mother.[111]

Other exceptions to this obligation include a disobedient wife and a wife who is undergoing a waiting period due to dubious intercourse (since it is unlawful to be alone with her).

وأقلّه ليلة، ويضعّف للحرّة.

The minimum duration [one must spend with each wife] is one night. Wives who are free are given double [that of wives who are slaves].

The evidence for this comes from two sources. The first is the hadith from al-Ḥasan al-Baṣrī (may Allah grant him His mercy) in which he states that the Messenger of Allah ﷺ forbade marrying a slave when one already has a wife who is free,[112] and that the free wife gets two thirds of the division [of time].[113] The second source is Sulaymān ibn Yasār (may Allah grant him His mercy) who said, "It is from the Sunnah that when a man marries a freewoman when he [already] has a wife who is a slave, the free wife is given two nights while the slave is given one."[114]

ولا يدخل على غير المقسوم لها إلّا لحاجة.

The husband does not visit a wife [at night] if it is not her turn, except when there is need [to do so, e.g., delivering medicine].

---

110. See "Forswearing One's Wife" on page 385.

111. See "Likening One's Wife to One's Mother" on page 386.

112. al-Ḥasan: Dāraquṭnī, 4002. See: TM, 1444.

113. Bayhaqī, 14001–3, 14011, 5169. See: KBM, 2038.

114. Salmān ibn Yasār: ʿAlī: Dāraquṭnī, 3738. Other reports without Ibn Abī Laylā include: Dāraquṭnī, 3737, Bayhaqī, 14003. See: BM, 8:41.

TRAVEL

ويقرع عند إرادته السّفر.

Lots are drawn if he plans to travel.

This is because of the hadith of ʿĀʾishah (may Allah be pleased with her): "Whenever the Messenger of Allah ﷺ wanted to travel, he would draw lots between his wives. Whoever's name was chosen would accompany him on the trip."[115]

The husband does not have to make up missed days [with his other wives] if he is traveling, but he does need to make up any days he unjustly misses while a resident (to fulfill the neglected wife's rights).

If he does not draw lots [to choose which wife will travel with him], he has sinned and must make up the missed days (both while traveling and while a resident).

If he travels to change his place of residence, it is unlawful to draw lots to take some of his wives with him and leave the others behind. It is also unlawful to leave them all behind. Rather, he either takes all of them himself or through an agent, or he divorces all of them since leaving them behind is harmful [for them].

NEW BRIDES

ويخصّ الجديدة البكر بسبع، والثّيّب بثلاث بلا قضاء.

A new, virgin wife is given seven [nights] while a non-virgin is given three, and the husband need not make up these nights with his other wives.

Anas (may Allah be pleased with him) said: "I heard the Messenger of Allah ﷺ say, 'A virgin gets seven nights and a matron gets three. He [the husband] then returns to his [other] wives.'"[116] Another

115. ʿĀʾishah: Bukhārī, 2593; Muslim, 2770 #56. See: TM, 1473.

116. Anas: Dāraquṭnī, 3730. See: TM, 1471.

version includes the phrase "part of the Sunnah,"[117] but in truth, this hadith is *marfūʿ*. We preferred the first narration since it is more explicit and clarifies what is narrated in the two *Ṣaḥīḥ*s [of al-Bukhārī and Muslim]. The purpose of this [extended] period is to remove the alienation between them and nurture intimacy and mutual affection. The virgin is given additional days since her reticence is greater than that of the other wives.

It is recommended that a non-virgin bride be given the choice of three days with her husband [which he need not make up with his other wives] or seven days [which he will need to make up] – as the Messenger of Allah ﷺ did with Umm Salamah (may Allah be pleased with her).[118]

DISOBEDIENCE

(فصل) [النّشوز]

A DISOBEDIENT WIFE

وإذا ظهر أمارات النّشوز وعظها، فإن تحقّقه ولم يتكرّر زاد الهجر في المضجع، فإن تكرّر ضرب.

When there are signs of disobedience from his wife, [the husband] first warns her. If he confirms the disobedience but she doesn't repeat it, he refuses to sleep with her. If the disobedience continues, he strikes her [lightly].[119]

Allah Most High says, "...As for those from whom ye fear rebellion, admonish them and banish them to beds apart, and scourge them.

117. Anas: Bukhārī, 5214; Muslim, 1461; Ibn Ḥibbān, 4208. See: BM, 8:43.

118. Umm Salamah: Muslim, 1460 #41–43; Abū Dāwūd, 2122; Nasā'ī, *Al-Sunan al-Kubrā*, 8876; Ibn Mājah, 1917; Ibn Ḥibbān, 4065. See: TM, 1472.

119. This is solely for the sake of discipline, not injury. If the husband knows that striking his wife is pointless, it is unlawful for him to do so. If striking results in injury, he must pay her compensation.

Then if they obey you, seek not a way against them…" [Q4:34]. ‹In the verse, "fear rebellion," means that there are clear indicators; one may "banish them to beds apart," if they actually show disobedience; then one may "scourge them," non-violently if they do not cease after shunning their bed.[120]›

A HARMFUL OR NEGLIGENT HUSBAND

If a husband denies his wife one of her rights [like neglecting to visit her during her turn or refusing to support her financially], a judge can compel him to fulfill it. If he displays bad behavior and harms her without cause, the judge forbids it; and if the husband harms her repeatedly, the judge gives him a disciplinary punishment. If each spouse accuses the other of being a transgressor, the judge sends a trustworthy person to investigate the matter and restrain the actual transgressor.

ARBITRATION

فإن اشتد الشّقاق بعث حكمًا من كلّ وهما وكيلان لهما.

If their discord becomes severe, an arbitrator for each spouse is sent who acts as their agent.

Allah Most High says, "And if ye fear a breach between them twain (the man and wife), appoint an arbiter from his folk and an arbiter from her folk…." [Q4:35].

‹In the verse: "appoint," is understood to require their consent. The husband authorizes his arbitrator to issue a divorce or accept compensation for the wife's release; and the wife authorizes her arbitrator to seek release for compensation. Each side must expend all efforts. The arbitrators order the transgressor to cease and separate the couple if they feel that it is the best solution.[121]›

---

120. al-Maḥallī and al-Suyūṭī, *Tafsīr al-Jalālayn.*

121. al-Maḥallī and al-Suyūṭī, *Tafsīr al-Jalālayn.*

RELEASE FOR COMPENSATION

(فصل) [الخلع]

The word "*khul*ᶜ" is taken from a word that means divestment. Legally, it is a marriage separation involving an exchange, using a word denoting divorce or divestment.

Its foundation is Allah Most High saying, "...it is no sin for either of them if the woman ransom herself..." [Q2:229]. Also, Ibn ᶜAbbās (may Allah be pleased with him) said that the wife of Thābit ibn Qays (may Allah be pleased with them both) came to the Prophet ﷺ and said, "O Messenger of Allah! I do not blame Thābit for his character or his religion, but I dislike disbelief in Islam." The Prophet ﷺ then said, "Will you give back his garden [that he had given her as *mahr*]?" She said, "Yes." Then the Prophet ﷺ said to Thābit, "O Thābit! Accept your garden, and divorce her once."[122] It is said that Thābit's divorce was the first to take place in Islam. ‹The phrase "I dislike disbelief in Islam" means "I dislike that if I stay with him, I will commit something that leads to disbelief."›

يصحّ الخلع على عوض متموّل معلوم، وتملك نفسها، ولا رجعة له عليها، ولا يلحقها طلاق، ويجوز في الحيض كالطّهر، ومع الأجنبيّ، وبلفظ الخلع والطّلاق والمفاداة.

It is valid for a husband to release his wife in exchange for financial compensation of a known value.

Allah Most High says, "...it is no sin for either of them if the woman ransom herself..." [Q2:229]. And because the marital contract pertains to intercourse, such an exchange is permissible with what we mentioned – just like marriage.

Separation using the phrase "*khul*ᶜ" counts as a single divorce and it diminishes the number of divorces he possesses by one. This is because it is a phrase that no one but the husband can use, so it

122. Ibn ᶜAbbās: Bukhārī, 5273. See: TM, 1475.

must count as a divorce. Separation using the phrase "*mufādāh*" is similar to "*khul*ᶜ" because of the previous verse [Q2:229].

Through this action, the woman regains sole control of herself.

This means that the husband no longer has any control over her since *khul*ᶜ is a final divorce. She has spent money to regain ownership over the right to have intercourse with her, so the husband must relinquish it – just as when he gives her a marriage payment in exchange for the right to intercourse, the woman does not have authority to take back this right.

Separation is permissible during times of menstruation, just as it is permissible during a time of purity. [It is also permissible] when a third party is involved, and when using phrases indicating release for compensation [*khul*ᶜ], divorce [*ṭalāq*], or ransom [*mufādāh*].

Once the release is accepted, no other pronouncement of divorce is effective since she has become foreign to him.

DIVORCE

(فصل) [الطّلاق]

Linguistically, the word "*ṭalāq*" means to undo a knot and to free something, such as a camel. Legally, it denotes undoing marriage – and nothing else.

The textual foundation for divorce comes from the Quran. Allah Most High says, "Divorce must be pronounced twice..." [Q2:229]. Its foundation is also from the Sunnah (as we will see). And Muslims have a consensus concerning its foundation.

يصحّ طلاق المكلّف بصريح «طلقت،» و«فارقت» و«سرحت»، و«خالعت بكذا»، وكناية: كل ما احتمل الطّلاق وعدمه احتمالاً ظاهرًا بنيّة،

A divorce must be issued by a husband who is [legally] responsible.

Divorce is not effected when it is initiated by someone who is a youth, insane, asleep, or compelled. The words of youths and the insane are of no consequence in sales, marriage, and other contracts, so it is the same when it comes to divorce. Divorce is effected – as a form of punishment – when it comes from someone who is intoxicated.

It is valid if he uses explicit statements [like] "I divorce [you]," "I separate from you," "I part from you," and "I release you for such-and such"...

These phrases are acceptable because they are used throughout the Quran as synonyms for divorce:

ṭ-l-q: "It is no sin for you if ye divorce women [*ṭallaqtumūhunna*] while yet ye have not touched them..." [Q2:237], and "O Prophet! When ye (men) put away women, put them away [*ṭalliqūhunna*] for their (legal) period ..." [Q65:1].

s-r-ḥ: "...But content them and release them [*sarriḥūhunna*] handsomely..." [Q33:49].

f-r-q: "...or part from them [*fāriqūhunna*] in kindness..." [Q65:2], and "But if they separate [*yatafarraqā*]..." [Q4:130].

...or uses allusive statements (which is any phrase that has a clear possibility of indicating [both] divorce and its absence) when intended.

An example would be him saying to her, "Return to your family," "You are not my woman," or "You are free."

If he says an allusive phrase intending it as a divorce, then the divorce has happened.

There is consensus that allusive phrases combined with intention are like explicit phrases. However, the intention must accompany the entire utterance.

Divorce before consummation is a complete, irrevocable separation. Allah Most High says, "O ye who believe! If ye wed believing women and divorce them before ye have touched them, then there is no period that ye should reckon" [Q33:49].

Divorce after consummation is suspended pending completion of the waiting period. Allah Most High says, "Women who are divorced shall wait, keeping themselves apart, three (monthly) courses..." [Q2:228]. There are two exceptions to this. The first is when the separation is in exchange for compensation,[123] in which case it is a complete, irrevocable separation without return. This is because the wife gave the husband compensation to regain authority over herself, so if the husband still had the right to take her back, there would be no benefit in compensating him.

The second exception is when it is the final divorce, meaning the third utterance for a husband who is a freeman, or the second for a husband who is a slave. Such a divorce is [also] irrevocable.

UNLAWFUL, INNOVATED DIVORCE

Divorces are either innovated [*bidʿah*] or according to the Sunnah ‹or neither›. Sunnah divorces are known to us because scholars have described them as such for centuries. *Bidʿah* divorces are unlawful since they lead to harm.

وهو بدعيّ حرام: في الطّلاق، والنّفاس، وآخر الطّهر لا الحيض، وطهر وطيء فيه من قد تحبل، أو في حيض قبله، أو استدخلت ماءه ولم يظهر حملها لا اختلاعها، وندبت الرّجعة إلى الطّهر.

An unlawful *bidʿah* divorce occurs when [1] a woman is experiencing postpartum bleeding; [2] at the end of a period of purity (though not at the end of menstruation); or [3] if intercourse has taken place during a period of purity and she can become pregnant...

Also, if the husband divorces his wife after intercourse, she might already be pregnant and he would not desire to divorce her while she is pregnant as he would be saddened.

123 See "Release for Compensation" on page 372.

...or [4] during a period of menstruation, before purity;...

Allah Most High says, "O Prophet! When ye (men) put away women, put them away for their (legal) period..." [Q65:1], which means "for their waiting period" since it is in this condition that a woman begins her waiting period from the time of her divorce.

During the time of the Messenger of Allah ﷺ, ʿAbd Allāh bin ʿUmar divorced his wife while she was menstruating. ʿUmar bin al-Khaṭṭāb asked him ﷺ about it and he ﷺ said, "Order him to take her back and keep her until she is clean, then wait until she gets her next period and becomes clean again. If he wishes to keep her, he may do so; and if he still wishes to divorce her, he may divorce her before having sexual intercourse with her. That is the prescribed period in which Allah commanded that women be divorced."[124] (May Allah be pleased with them all.)

This is because a woman's waiting period does not begin until her menstruation ends, so if she is divorced while she is menstruating, she would have to wait even longer for her waiting period to end.

...or [5] when she could have inseminated herself with her husband's sperm...

Because it is possible that she will become pregnant. The same is true if they engaged in anal intercourse.

...and it is not apparent [in scenarios 3–5] that she is already pregnant – though it is not unlawful when offering her release for compensation.[125]

It is permissible for a husband to release his wife for compensation or to divorce his visibly pregnant wife since his [surprise] sadness is negated [by his awareness of her pregnancy and his willingness to divorce her despite it].

---

124. Ibn ʿUmar: Bukhārī, 5261; Muslim, 1471 #1. See: TM, 1484.

125. See "Release for Compensation" on page 372.

A divorce is not *bidʿah* or unlawful when it occurs via release for compensation. Allah Most High says, "...then there is no blame upon either of them concerning that by which she ransoms herself..." [Q2:229]. ‹In the verse, "she ransoms herself..." means the wife offers compensation for her release from the marriage, so there is no blame on the husband for accepting it nor on her for offering it.[126]› Also, the Prophet ﷺ gave Thābit ibn Qays (may Allah be pleased with him) unrestricted permission to release his wife for compensation without asking Thābit for details about her state."[127] [The Prophet ﷺ did not ask or give details] and menstruation is not something that occurs only rarely for women.

Divorce during postpartum bleeding is like divorce during menstruation.

It is recommended that the husband take the wife back to [postpone divorce until a time of] purity.

Because of the hadith concerning Ibn ʿUmar (may Allah be pleased with them both).[128]

Also, it is sinful if one divorces one's wife intentionally (when she is in such a state), though there is no sin if one did not know that she was menstruating.

It is also unlawful to divorce a woman when she is owed her share of equal time.

SUNNAH DIVORCE

وإلّا فسنّيّ.

Otherwise, [if a divorce isn't effected in the manners previously described,] it is according to the Sunnah.

126. al-Bughā, *Al-Tadhhīb,* 173 #1.

127. Ibn ʿAbbās: Bukhārī, 5273. See: TM, 1475.

128. Ibn ʿUmar: Bukhārī, 5261; Muslim, 1471 #1. See: TM, 1484.

NEITHER OF THE ABOVE

ولمن لا تعتد بالطّهر وفسخ النّكاح لا سني ولا بدعيّ.

Divorcing a wife whose waiting period is not determined by purity[129] and marriage annulment are neither [according to the] Sunnah nor *bidʿah*.

MAXIMUM NUMBER OF DIVORCES FOR FREEMEN

ويملك الحرّ ثلاث تطليقات.

A freeman possesses three [pronouncements of] divorce.

This is according to agreement.

The Prophet ﷺ was asked about Allah Most High saying, "Divorce must be pronounced twice" [Q2:229]: "Where is the third, O Messenger of Allah?" He ﷺ replied, "or released in kindness" [Q2:229].[130]

‹Evidence for this includes Allah Most High saying, "Divorce must be pronounced twice and then (a woman) must be retained in honour or released in kindness..." [Q2:229], and "And if he has divorced her [for the third time], then she is not lawful to him afterward until [after] she marries a husband other than him..." [Q2:230].[131]›

129. See "The Waiting Period" on page 394.

130. Abū Dāwūd, *Al-Marāsil* (220). KBM, 2053; UM(1357).

131. al-Bughā, *Al-Tadhhīb*, 174 #1.

NUMBER OF DIVORCES FOR SLAVES

و[يملك] العبد طلقتين.

A slave possesses two [pronouncements of divorce].

Jābir (may Allah be pleased with him) reported that "A slave's divorce is twice." (In some transmissions, this is attributed to the Prophet ﷺ.)[132]

EXCEPTIONS AND CONTINGENCIES WHEN PRONOUNCING DIVORCE

ويصحّ الاستثناء فيه بشرطه، وتعليقه بالصّفة والشّرط.

It is valid to make an exception when pronouncing divorce provided its conditions are met.[133]

The use of exceptions is a linguistic convention and it is found in the Quran and Sunnah.[134] It is valid provided that there are no interruptions [between the exception and the statement it excepts], that one intends the exception before finishing the statement [it excepts], and that the excepted amount not equal or exceed the number [of remaining divorces].

---

132. Jābir: Dāraquṭnī, 4003; Bayhaqī, 14137, 15142, 15143. See: KBM, 2126.

133. The exception must be connected to the pronouncement and the excepted number must not equal or exceed the original number. So while "I divorce you three times except for two" results in a single divorce, "I divorce you three times minus three" results in the original number, which invalidates the exception.

134 An example is "none save themselves" in the verse where Allah Most High says, "They think to beguile Allah and those who believe, and they beguile none save themselves" [Q2:9]. c.f. Imām al-Juwaynī and Jalāl al-Maḥallī, *Sharḥ Al-Waraqāt: Al-Maḥallī's notes on Imām al-Juwaynī's Islamic Jurisprudence Pamphlet* (Islamosaic, 2014), 27.

It is also valid to make divorce contingent upon [the occurrence of] an attribute or condition.

An example of a divorce contingent upon an attribute is the husband saying to his wife, "You are divorced in such-and-such month," or "...if it rains." She is divorced once the attribute is present.

An example of a divorce contingent upon a condition is the husband saying to the wife, "If you enter the house, you are divorced." She is divorced upon her entry.

PRONOUNCEMENT OF DIVORCE PRIOR TO MARRIAGE

ولا طلاق قبل نكاح.

No divorce is effective prior to the marriage contract.

The Messenger of Allah ﷺ said, "There is no divorce in what one does not possess."[135]

DOUBTS ABOUT OCCURRENCE OR NUMBER OF DIVORCES

وإذا شك في الطلاق فالأصل عدمه، أو في العدد، فالأقل، ولا يخفى الورع.

If there is doubt whether a divorce has occurred, the default is that it has not.

This is according to consensus.

[If there is doubt] about the number [of pronouncements], the default is the lowest possible number...

Since the default is the absence of pronouncements.

135. ʿAmr ibn Shuʿayb: Abū Dāwūd, 2190; Tirmidhī, 1181; Ibn Mājah, 2047, 2190; Ḥākim, 2819. See: TM, 1483.

...and one should err on the side of caution.

Caution is recommended in both scenarios ‹The Prophet ﷺ said, "Leave that which leaves you uncertain for that which leaves you certain."[136]›

In the first scenario [when there is doubt as to whether the divorce has occurred], the husband takes back the wife, if possible;[137] otherwise, he renews the marriage (if he desires staying with her) or lets the divorce stand. In the second scenario [concerning the number of pronouncements], he assumes that two – not three – divorces have occurred.

GIVING A WOMAN THE OPTION TO PRONOUNCE DIVORCE

ويصحّ تفويض الطّلاق إليها، وهو تمليك.

It is valid to give her the option to divorce.

This is because the Prophet ﷺ gave his wives the choice between staying with him and separation after Allah Most High revealed "O Prophet! Say unto thy wives: If ye desire the world's life and its adornment, come! I will content you and will release you with a fair release" [Q7:28].

[The option to divorce] is a transferral of authority.

It is associated with her goals and interests, and it is analogous to him saying "I give the authority to you."

136. Tirmidhī: (2518). See: TM, 15; al-Damīrī, *Al-Najm al-wahhāj*, 7:540.

137 See "Taking Back One's Wife" on page 382.

DIVORCING PART OF A WOMAN

و[يصحّ] إضافته إلى جزء منها.

[It is valid] to attribute divorce to a part of her.

Like saying "Some of you is divorced," or "Part of you is divorced," or "Your hand is divorced."

TAKING BACK ONE'S WIFE

(فصل) [الرّجعة]

Linguistically, taking back one's wife [*rajʿah*] means a single return. Legally, it means returning to marriage after an irrevocable divorce.

The basis for this (before consensus) includes the command of Allah Most High: "...And their husbands would do better to take them back in that case..." – meaning during the waiting period – "...if they desire a reconciliation..." [Q2:228] via taking them back. (This is what al-Shāfiʿī said [may Allah grant him His mercy].) And the Prophet ﷺ divorced Ḥafṣah (may Allah be pleased with her) and took her back.[138]

إذا لم تستوف عدد الطّلاق بغير عوض بعد الدّخول فله مراجعتها، ما دامت العدّة قائمة بـ«راجعتُ» و«رددتُها إليّ» و«أمسكتُها»، والإشهاد مندوب، وإذا جدّد بعد الانقضاء – عادت إليه بما بقي من الثّلاث.

If [the husband] has not exhausted his number [of divorces] and [the release] occurred without compensation...

The compensation is meant to be in exchange for the wife regaining authority over herself, so if the husband still had the right to take her back, there would be no benefit in compensating him.

---

138. ʿUmar: Abū Dāwūd, 2283; Ibn Mājah, 2016; Nasāʾī, 3560; Ibn Ḥibbān, 4275; Ḥākim, 2797; Bayhaqī, 14892. See: TM, 1487.

...and after consummation,...

Returning to one's spouse requires a waiting period, and there is no waiting period for a divorce enacted prior to consummation.

...he may take his wife back (so long as her waiting period has not expired) by saying "I took you back," "I returned her to myself," and "I have kept hold of her."

The wife's consent is not required. Allah Most High says, "...And their husbands would do better to take them back in that case..." [Q2:228]. ‹In the verse: "in that case" refers to the waiting period; "if they desire a reconciliation" is between the husband and wife in order to avoid harming her. This part of the verse encourages reconciliation as the goal; it does not indicate that it is a condition for the permissibility of return.[139]›

The Prophet ﷺ said to ʿUmar regarding his son ʿAbd Allāh (may Allah be pleased with them both), who was divorcing a woman during her menses: "Order him to take her back."[140]

The return does not occur through actions, such as intercourse.

It is recommended that [the reconciliation] be witnessed.

A witness is not required since a wife returning to her husband is like a continuation of their marriage, which is why it does not require her or her guardian's consent. And Allah Most High says, "...take them back in kindness or part from them in kindness..." [Q65:2]. This verse can be understood to indicate recommendation, just as with "And call to witness, from among your men, two witnesses" [Q2:282].

139. al-Maḥallī and al-Suyūṭī, *Tafsīr al-Jalālayn.*

140. ʿUmar: Bukhārī, 5251; Abū Dāwūd, 2179, 2182; Nasāʾī, 3390. TM, 1484.

If the marriage is renewed after the waiting period has expired, she returns with whatever number of divorces remains of the three [original divorces].

‹ʿUmar (may Allah be pleased with him) was asked about someone who had divorced his wife once or twice: the wife had completed her waiting period and married someone else. She later separated from him and then her first husband remarried her. ʿUmar said, "She is with him with whatever remains of her [original] divorces."[141]›

و[إن] استوفى العدد لم تحلّ إلّا بعد انقضاء العدّة منه، وتزوّجها لآخر نكاحًا صحيحًا، ويدخل حشفته بقبلها وتبين منه، وتنقضي عدّتها منه.

If a husband's total number of divorces has been exhausted, his wife remains unlawful for him until her waiting period from him expires, then another man marries her with a valid contract and penetrates her vagina with the glans [or an equivalent length] of his penis, and then she becomes irrevocably separated from the new husband...

Their marriage must have ended through divorce, annulment, or death.

...and completes her waiting period [from the new husband].

‹Allah Most High says, "And if he hath divorced her (the third time), then she is not lawful unto him thereafter until she hath wedded another husband. Then if he (the other husband) divorce her it is no sin for both of them that they come together again if they consider that they are able to observe the limits of Allah..." [Q2:230].

In this verse, "divorced her" means for the third time; "come together again" would be with a new contract; and "observe the limits of Allah" refers to the marital duties required of each one.

141. ʿUmar: Mālik (2180). See: al-Ḥusaynī, *Kifāyat al-akhyār* (409).

The requirement for penetration is established in the narration from ʿĀʾishah (may Allah be pleased with her) in which [Umaymah] the wife of Rifaʿah al-Quraẓī (may Allah be pleased with them both) came to the Prophet ﷺ and said, "I was Rifaʿah's wife, but he divorced me and it was an absolute divorce. Then I married ʿAbd al-Raḥmān ibn al-Zabīr but he's like a garment's fringe." The Prophet ﷺ said, "Do you want to return to Rifaʿah? You cannot until you have tasted [ʿAbd al-Raḥmān's] honey."[142] Here, "garment's fringe" is a euphemism for impotence and "taste his honey" is a euphemism for intercourse – meaning that the enjoyment of sex resembles the enjoyment of tasting honey.[143]›

FORSWEARING ONE'S WIFE

(فصل) [الإيلاء]

Linguistically, forswearing one's wife [*īlāʾ*] means to swear a vow. Technically, it means forswearing intercourse with one's wife without restriction or for a period exceeding four months. Prior to Islam, it was considered a form of divorce. Later, the Sacred Law changed its legal status.

The textual foundation for a man swearing to give up sexual relations with his wife is Allah Most High saying, "Those who forswear their wives must wait four months..." [Q2:226]. And the Prophet ﷺ foreswore his wives for a month.

وإذا حلف ألّا يطأها مطلقًا، أو فوق أربعة أشهر، فهو مول، فيمهل إن سألت أربعة أشهر، ثمّ يخيّر بعدها بين الفيئة والتّكفير، أو الطّلاق، فإن امتنع منه فالحاكم.

If a husband forswears having intercourse with his wife without restriction or for a period exceeding four [lunar] months, he has [indeed] forsworn her.

142. ʿĀʾishah: Bukhārī, 2639; Muslim, 1433. See: KBM, 1968.

143. al-Bughā, *Al-Tadhhīb*, 176 #3.

Forswearing is only valid from a husband who can issue a divorce since the verse says "their wives." It is not valid from children or and the insane because the intended purpose of restraining oneself is not applicable to them.

If she requests [separation],...

According to consensus, she can demand that he either have intercourse with her or divorce her.

...he is left [with her] for four months. He must then choose between breaking his oath and making an expiation, or divorcing her.

‹Allah Most High says, "Those who forswear their wives must wait four months; then, if they change their mind, lo! Allah is Forgiving, Merciful. And if they decide upon divorce (let them remember that) Allah is Hearer, Knower" [Q2:226–227].[144]›

If he refuses [both options], the judge [issues a divorce for him].

This is in order to remove the wife from harm, which cannot be done except by divorcing her from him. The judge can do this, since issuing a divorce is something that can be done by a substitute. So if the husband refuses, the judge becomes his substitute – just like a judge can substitute for another by paying his debts on his behalf.

LIKENING ONE'S WIFE TO ONE'S MOTHER

(فصل) [الظّهار]

The foundation for the impermissibility of likening one's wife to one's mother [*ẓihār*] is found at the beginning of *Sūrat al-Mujādilah* [Q58], whose occasion is documented in the hadith from Aws ibn al-Ṣāmit. He had made *ẓihār* from his wife Khuwaylah bint

144. al-Bughā, *Al-Tadhhīb*, 177 #2.

Thaʿlabah (may Allah be pleased with them both), whereupon she went to the Messenger of Allah ﷺ to complain. Thereafter, Allah Most High revealed: "Allah hath heard the saying of her that disputeth with thee (Muhammad) concerning her husband, and complaineth unto Allah..." [Q58:1].[145]

وإذا قال المكلّف لزوجته: «أنتِ عليّ كظهر أمّي»، ولم يتبعه بطلاق، كفر بعتق رقبة مؤمنة سليمة من عيب يخلّ بالعمل والكسب، فإن عجز فبصوم شهرين متتابعين، فإن عجز عنه فبإطعام ستّين مسكينًا أو فقيرًا كلّ مسكين مدًّا، ويحرم وطؤها قبل التّكفير.

If a [legally] responsible man says to his wife, "To me, you are akin to my mother's back,"...[146]

This is unlawful since Allah Most High says, "...they indeed utter an ill word and a lie..." [Q58:2]. *Ẓihār* was considered a form of divorce prior to Islam, but the Sharīʿah changed its rulings. It was also said that through *ẓihār,* the wife would become unlawful to her husband without becoming lawful to others.

It is possible to pronounce *ẓihār* for a set duration (like "for this month") because of an authentic hadith concerning it.[147]

...and does not follow it with a divorce, [he has reneged on his oath].

By not divorcing her, he has repudiated his declaration that she is unlawful for him.

---

145. Aws ibn al-Ṣāmit: Abū Dāwūd, 2214; Ibn Ḥibbān, 4279; Dāraquṭnī, 3853 transmitted this with the name "Khuwaylah" (i.e., "little Khawlah"). Ḥākim, 3791 transmitted it with the name "Khawlah." See: KBM, 2090.
146. The same applies when the wife is likened to any other of his female kin. These rulings do not apply if the comparison was intended as praise.
147. Salamah ibn Ṣakhr al-Bayāḍī: Abū Dāwūd, 2208; Tirmidhī, 1198 – *ḥasan gharīb*; Ibn Mājah, 2064; Aḥmed, 1642; Ibn Khuzaymah, 2378; Ḥākim, 2815. See: TM, 1011, 1492.

He must expiate...

Allah Most High says, "Those who put away their wives (by saying they are as their mothers [*ẓihār*]) and afterward would go back on that which they have said, (the penalty) in that case (is) the freeing of a slave before they touch one another..." [Q58:3]. This is because likening his wife to his mother entails that he not keep her as a wife. So if he does keep her, he has reneged on what he said, since reneging on an oath is violating it [and violating it requires expiation].

...by emancipating a Muslim slave who is free from any defects that would impede [his ability to] work and earn a living.

Because of the verse [Q58:3], a non-Muslim slave does not suffice since every unqualified statement related to expiations is interpreted according to the qualifications given for the expiation for killing. It is just like how Imam al-Shāfiʿī (may Allah grant him His mercy) understood the unqualified statement in "...And call to witness, from among your men, two witnesses..." [Q2:282] to be qualified by "...and call to witness two just men among you..." [Q65:2].

If he is unable to [free a slave], he expiates by fasting two months consecutively.

Allah Most High says, "And he who findeth not (the wherewithal), let him fast for two successive months before they touch one another..." [Q58:4]. He needs to make the intention to fast each night – just as he would for Ramadan. Additionally, the fast day must be intended as an expiation. It is not required that one intends to fast consecutively.

The two months must be restarted if the fast is broken for reasons other than insanity or sickness. This is because of the verse [Q58:4, which includes "two successive months"].

If he is unable [to fast],...

Reasons for being unable to fast include advanced age, sickness from which he is not expected to recover, extreme hardship resulting from fasting, or fear that fasting will exacerbate or prolong sickness.

...he expiates by giving sixty poor or destitute one *mudd* of food each.

Allah Most High says, "...and for him who is unable to do so (the penance is) the feeding of sixty needy ones..." [Q58:4].

It does not suffice to feed one person sixty *mudd*s of food over sixty days. This is because Allah Most High says, "...the feeding of sixty needy ones..." [Q58:4].

It is unlawful for him to have intercourse with his wife before [completing the] expiation.

Allah Most High says, "...before they touch one another..." [Q58:3].

CHARGING ONE'S WIFE WITH ADULTERY

(فصل) [القذف واللعان]

Legally, charging one's wife with adultery [*liʿān*] is a series of verbal imprecations that serves as legal proof when it is necessary for a husband to accuse his wife of adulterously conceiving a child.

The foundation for this is the verse in which Allah Most High says, "As for those who accuse their wives..." [Q24:6]. This verse was revealed in 9 AH concerning either ʿUwaymir al-ʿAjalānī or Hilāl ibn Umayyah (there are two opinions about the person's identity). After the Prophet ﷺ passed, there was no occurrence of *liʿān* until the era of ʿUmar ibn ʿAbd al-ʿAzīz [more than eighty years later].

وإذا قذف المكلّف زوجته بالزّنا صريحًا وكناية، لاعن لدفع حدّ القذف، بقوله عند الحاكم، على منبر الجامع، في جمع، بعد العصر جمعة، في أشرف بلدة: «أشهد بالله

إنّي لمن الصادقين فيما رميتها به من زنا، وإن الولد المذكور ليس منّي» أربع مرات، وفي الخامسة بعد وعظ الحاكم وعليه لعنة الله إن كنت من الكاذبين فيما رميتها به.

If a [legally] responsible man accuses his wife of adultery – whether explicitly or allusively – he makes a public imprecation [curse] to remove the [prescribed] punishment [from himself] for making such an accusation [without witnesses].

[He does this] in the presence of the judge, while standing on the minbar of the mosque [where Friday prayers are held], in front of a crowd,...

There must be at least four other people present, since this is the number required for establishing proof of fornication. One of those four should be the governor.

...after the Afternoon Prayer [*ʿAṣr*] on Friday, in the noblest part of the land.

In Mecca, he stands between the Kaʿbah and the Station of Ibrahīm [*Maqām Ibrahīm*] (peace be upon him). In Medina, he stands on the minbar [in the Mosque of the Prophet ﷺ]. And in Jerusalem, at the rock [within the Dome of the Rock]. Elsewhere, he stands at the minbar of the mosque where Friday Prayer is held.

He says, "I bear witness to Allah that I am truthful in charging my wife so-and-so with adultery, and that this child is not mine" four times. The fifth time, after the judge warns him [of the consequences of lying],...

Ibn ʿAbbās said that Hilāl ibn Umayyah accused his wife of adultery and came to bear witness (may Allah be pleased with them all). The Prophet ﷺ said, "Indeed Allah knows that one of you is lying.

Will either of you repent?"[148] Another version includes that he ﷺ repeated this three times, and then she stood and bore witness.[149]

...he says: "...and may the curse of Allah be upon me if I am a liar concerning what I have accused her of."

Because of the verses [Q24:6–7], it is recommended that he point to her if she is present. Otherwise, he mentions her lineage [in order to identify her].

ويسقط عنها الحدّ بأن تلتعن فتقول على الوصف السالف: «أشهد بالله إنّه لمن الكاذبين فيما رماني به من الزّنا»، وفي الخامسة بعد وعظها إن عليها غضب الله إن كان من الصّادقين،

She ceases being subject to punishment [for adultery] if she performs a counter-imprecation by saying (following the earlier description): "I bear witness that so-and-so is a liar in his [statement] charging me with adultery" [four times].

The fifth time, after she is warned [by the judge about the consequences of lying],...

Another hadith mentions that the Prophet ﷺ called for [a woman accused of adultery], cautioned her, reminded her [of the consequences], and informed her that the punishment of this life is easier than the punishment of the afterlife.[150]

...she says: "...and may the wrath of Allah be upon me if he is telling the truth."

---

148. Ibn ʿAbbās: Bukhārī, 5307. See TM, 1493.

149. Ibn ʿAbbās: Bukhārī, 5312. See: TM, 1493.

150. Saʿīd ibn Jubayr: Muslim, 1493. See: TM, 1499.

Allah Most High says, "And it shall avert the punishment from her if she bear witness before Allah four times that the thing he saith is indeed false. And a fifth (time) that the wrath of Allah be upon her if he speaketh truth" [Q24:8–9].

ويتعلّق بلعانه: فرقة، وحرمة مؤبّدة، وسقوط حدّ، ووجوب حدّ زناها إن كان القذف بزنا مضاف إلى حال الزّوجيّة، وانتفاء نسب نفاه بلعان.

The consequence of his public imprecation is that they are permanently separated and eternally unlawful [to one another],...

They can never remarry. This is because the Prophet ﷺ said, "Those who have cursed one another are not ever conjoined."[151]

...and he is no longer subject to punishment [for accusing his wife of adultery] but the wife is subject to punishment for her adultery [if the accusation refers to an act that occurred while she was married], and the paternity of the child, which had been denied by the husband, is legally negated.

وإنّما يحتاج إلى نفي ممكن منه وهو على الفور حيث لا عذر.

Imprecation is needed only to negate [the paternity of] a child that could possibly be his.

It is not permissible for him to accuse her of adultery unless he confirms it (by seeing her fornicate) or is overwhelmingly confident because of clear indicators (such as her admitting to adultery and his believing her), or if he hears of it from someone he considers truthful, or if knowledge of her adultery with a specific individual is widespread in addition to being corroborated by others who have seen her alone with another [non-maḥram] man.

151. Ibn ʿUmar: Abū Dāwūd, 2250; Dāraquṭnī, 3704, 3705, 3707; Bayhaqī, 15318, 15321, 15354, 15356, 15357. See: KBM, 2105.

He cannot negate paternity unless they have not had intercourse, the duration of the pregnancy is too short (less than six months), or she had a period after their last intercourse.

The child's paternity must be negated in such a case since the lack of a negation would lead to the assumption that the child is his. It is unlawful for him to claim the child as his own because it is not possible.

[A child's] lack of a resemblance [to oneself] is not enough to accuse one's wife of adultery, because of the hadith: "...perhaps this is just hereditary."[152]

[Denial of paternity] must be done immediately whenever there is no excuse for delay.

ESTABLISHING PATERNITY

(فصل) [إلحاق نسب ولد الأمة]

وطء الأمة ملحق للولد الممكن، إلا أن يدّعي استبراء ويحلف عليه.

Intercourse with a slave establishes paternity for any child that could possibly be from the slave owner – unless he claims that he has established her lack of pregnancy [after the intercourse] and swears to it.[153]

The child may belong to him if the owner is at least nine years old, the child was born at least six months after he took ownership [of its mother], and there is a possibility that the owner and slave had sex.

والاشتراك في الوطء مع الإمكان من كلّ منهما يرجع إلى القائف - وهو مسلم، عدل، مجرب، حرّ والأولى أن يكون مدلجيا.

When two men have had intercourse with the same woman and both could be the father, a *qāʾif* [someone who affirms lineage

152. Abū Hurayrah: Bukhārī, 5305; Muslim, 1500 #18–20. See: KBM, 2102.

153. See "Ensuring Lack of Pregnancy" on page 402.

through physical resemblance] is relied upon. A *qāʾif* [must be] a free, upright Muslim with a reputation for accuracy. It is best that the *qāʾif* be from the Mudlajī tribe.

The use of a *qāʾif* is a way to determine evidential preponderance. The foundation for this is the hadith from ʿAʾishah (may Allah be pleased with her) in which the Messenger of Allah ﷺ came to her in a happy mood, with his features glittering with joy, and said, "Have you not heard what [al-Mujaziz] al-Mudlijī [the *qāʾif*] has said about Zayd and Usāmah? He saw their feet and remarked: 'These belong to each other.'"[154] (May Allah be pleased with them all.)

فإن فقد، أو أشكل، أو ألحقه بهما، أو نفاه عنهما، ترك إلى البلوغ لينتسب بميل الطّبع.

In the absence of [a *qāʾif*] or [when the resemblance assessment] is inconclusive, paternity is either attributed to both men or left undetermined until the child reaches maturity, at which point it can be ascribed via his natural inclination [toward one of the men].

THE WAITING PERIOD

(فصل) [العدد]

The word for the waiting period [*ʿiddah*] comes from "*ʿaddad*," meaning number, since it involves intervals of cleanliness or months of a certain duration. Legally, it refers to the finite period [after divorce or the death of her husband] wherein a woman confines herself to ascertain whether she is pregnant, which ends after intervals of ritual cleanliness, months, or [if pregnant] her child's birth.

The foundation for the waiting period is consensus as well as the Quranic verses and hadiths mentioned in this section.

---

154. ʿĀʾishah: Bukhārī, 3555. See: TM, 1807.

WIDOWS

عدة المتوفّى عنها: إن كانت حاملًا - منسوبًا إليه - فبوضعه، وإلّا فبأربعة أشهر وعشر.

The waiting period for a widow who is pregnant with [her husband's] child [ends with] the delivery [of that child];...

Allah Most High says, "...And for those with child, their period shall be till they bring forth their burden..." [Q65:4]. ‹In this verse, "their period" refers to the duration of their waiting period.[155]›

Al-Miswar ibn Makhramah (may Allah be pleased with him) said that Subayᶜah al-Aslamiyyah (may Allah be pleased with her) gave birth to a child a few days after the death of her husband. She came to the Prophet ﷺ and asked permission to remarry. He ﷺ gave her permission, and she married.[156]

...otherwise, it is four [lunar] months and ten [days].

Allah Most High says, "Such of you as die and leave behind them wives, they (the wives) shall wait, keeping themselves apart, four months and ten days. And when they reach the term (prescribed for them) then there is no sin for you in aught that they may do with themselves in decency. Allah is informed of what ye do" [Q2:234]. ‹In this verse, "reach the term" means to conclude the aforementioned waiting period; "do with themselves" includes beautification and [accepting] allusive proposals for engagement or marriage; and "in decency" means engaging in anything the Sacred Law does not forbid.[157]›

155. al-Bughā, *Al-Tadhhīb,* 171 #2.
156. al-Miswar ibn Makhramah: Bukhārī, 5320. See: TM, 1501.
157. al-Bughā, *Al-Tadhhīb,* 182 #1.

NON-WIDOWS

و[عدّة] غيرها: إن كانت حاملًا، هكذا، وإلّا فإن كانت من ذوات الأقراء فبانقضاء ثلاثة أقراء – أيّ أطهار – تحتوّش بالدّم، وإلّا فبثلاثة أشهر.

[The waiting period] of a non-widow...

This includes women who have been divorced or who have separated from their husbands via imprecation, annulment after intercourse, and the like.

...who is pregnant [from her husband] is the same [as that if a widow: delivery]. Otherwise, if she has menstrual periods, it is three [complete] periods of purity surrounded by bleeding;...

Allah Most High says, "Women who are divorced shall wait, keeping themselves apart, three (monthly) courses [*qurū'*]. And it is not lawful for them that they should conceal that which Allah hath created in their wombs if they are believers in Allah and the Last Day..." [Q2:228]. The phrase "*qurū'*" refers to cleanliness. ‹This is because Allah Most High says, "...put them away for [*li*] their (legal) period..." [Q65:1], meaning during the time of their waiting period. The word "for [*li*]" functions as "in [*fī*]" like in "And We set a just balance for [*li*] the Day of Resurrection..." [Q21:47], meaning "in the Day of Resurrection." And [in another Quranic recitation style], it was also read "For the beginning of their waiting period."[158] So if this is the meaning, then the verse grants permission to divorce in the time of the waiting period. Thus, if she is divorced while pure, she finishes her waiting period upon beginning the third cycle of menstrual bleeding. Or if she is divorced while menstruating, upon beginning the fourth.›

The end of purity is considered a *qur'*. So if a woman is divorced while pure then begins her menses one hour later, the time before the menses is considered a *qur'* so she needs two more cycles after that.

158. Ibn ʿUmar: Muslim, 1471 #14. See: KBM, 2049, 2125.

...otherwise, it is three [lunar] months.

Allah Most High says, "And for such of your women as despair of menstruation, if ye doubt, their period (of waiting) shall be three months, along with those who have it not..." [Q65:4]. ‹In this verse, "ye doubt" means have doubts about their legal status and are not sure what to do; and "have it not" refers to females who have not yet menstruated and are thus given the same ruling as menopausal women.[159]›

If a woman has stopped menstruating because of a change in her physiological condition (due to nursing or sickness), she must wait until her menstruation resumes [before continuing her waiting period].

The waiting period is required even if one is certain that one is not pregnant, because it is a ritualistic practice [*taʿabbud,* as opposed to having a known rationale]. Thus, it is required for an immature bride once the marriage has been consummated.

There is no waiting period for a woman who is divorced before the marriage is consummated. Allah Most High says, "...and divorce them before ye have touched them, then there is no period that ye should reckon. But content them and release them handsomely..." [Q33:49]. ‹In this verse, "touched them" means had intercourse with them; "content them" refers to giving them something they will enjoy; and "release them handsomely" refers to letting them go without harming them.[160]›

159. al-Bughā, *Al-Tadhhīb,* 182 #5.

160. al-Bughā, *Al-Tadhhīb,* 183 #1.

SLAVES

والأمة على النّصف في الأشهر، وتعتدّ بقرأين.

A slave's waiting period is [either] half the number of months [of a freewoman],...

The waiting period of a slave girl can be one and a half months, though two months is better.

It can be one and a half months out of analogy to the time typical for freewomen who menstruate. It can be two months, since months are a substitute for periods of purity, and a freewoman's waiting period of three months is in place of three periods of purity. Thus, it is better that a slave girl's waiting period be two months in place of two periods of purity.

...or two periods of purity.

The Prophet ﷺ said, "A slave woman remains [in her waiting period] two *qur'* [periods of cleanliness]."[161, 162]

SUPPORT DURING THE WAITING PERIOD

A woman whose husband can take her back without a new marriage contract is entitled to housing and support – with the exception of expenses related to purification and cleanliness. She is entitled to this because the husband still has authority over her. ‹Allah Most High says, "Lodge them where ye dwell, according to your wealth, and harass them not so as to make life difficult for them. And if they are with child, then spend for them till they bring forth their burden. Then, if they give suck for you, give them their due payment and consult together in kindness; but if ye make difficulties

161. Due to a hadith from Jābir (may Allah be pleased with him) mentioned earlier. See: TM, 1522.

162. See "Number of Divorces for Slaves" on page 354.

for one another, then let some other woman give suck for him (the father of the child)" [Q65:6].

Additional evidence comes from the story of Fāṭimah bint Qays (may Allah be pleased with her). When her husband divorced her while she had a single divorce remaining, the Prophet ﷺ said to her, "Provision and housing is for whoever possesses return."[163]›

Irrevocably divorced women are entitled to housing without support. ‹Allah Most High says, "Lodge them where ye dwell" [Q65:6].›

A woman whose marriage was annulled – whether by apostasy,[164] entering Islam,[165] nursing,[166] or a defect[167] – is entitled to housing. This is because she has a waiting period occasioned by a separation while alive.

A widow is not entitled to support during her waiting period, even if she is pregnant. The evidence for this is the hadith of Jābir (may Allah be pleased with him) which is attributed to the Prophet ﷺ: "There is no support for a pregnant widow."[168] Imam al-Shāfiʿī (may Allah grant him His mercy) said: "I do not know of any disagreement concerning that."

---

163. Fāṭimah bint Qays: Dāraquṭnī, 3952–4, 3957–8, Nasāʾī, 3403. See: al-Shāfiʿī, *Al-Umm,* 5:117; Ibn Rufʿat, *Kifāyat al-nabīh,*15:209; al-Bughā, *Al-Tadhhīb,* 184 #5.

164 See "Apostate Women" on page 351.

165 See "An Individual Spouse Entering Islam" on page 352.

166 See "Wet-Nursing" on page 405.

167 See "Spousal Defects Permitting Marriage Annulment" on page 354.

168. Jābir: Dāraquṭnī, 3950; al-Shāfiʿī, 4:104. See: TM, 1522.

MOURNING

(فصل) [الإحداد]
وتترك المتوفّى عنها التزيّن بما صبغ للزينة، والتّحلي، والتّطيّب بما يحرم في الإحرام، ودهن الشعر، والاكتحال إلا للرمد.

[For the duration of her waiting period], a widow must refrain from adorning herself with decoratively dyed clothing, wearing jewelry, using perfume that is unlawful when in the state of pilgrim sanctity [*iḥrām*], applying oil to her hair, and applying kohl [to her eyes] – except to treat conjunctivitis.

Umm Ḥabībah (may Allah be pleased with her) said, "I heard the Messenger of Allah ﷺ say, 'It is not permissible for a woman who believes in Allah and the hereafter to mourn a deceased person for more than three nights, except for her husband, [for whom she must mourn] four months and ten [days].'"[169]

Umm ʿAṭiyyah al-Anṣāriyyah (may Allah be pleased with her) said, "We were prohibited from mourning a deceased person for more than three days, except for a husband [for no more than] four months and ten [days]. We would not apply kohl or wear dyed clothes – except for *ʿaṣb*. But we were permitted to use a small amount of perfume after our post-menstrual purificatory bath. And we were forbidden from following funeral processions."[170]

‹In this hadith, "dyed" is understood to mean dye that is typically considered decorative; and "*ʿaṣb*" is a type of Yemeni cloth in which the threads are dyed before being woven.[171]›

169. Ḥabībah: Bukhārī, 5334; Muslim, 1486 #58, 1490. See: TM, 1502.
170. Umm ʿAṭiyyah al-Anṣāriyyah: Bukhārī, 313; Muslim, 938. See: TM, 1503.
171. al-Bughā, *Al-Tadhhīb,* 184 #1.

REMAINING IN ONE'S RESIDENCE

(فصل) [تلازم المسكن]

وتلازم المعتدات مسكن الفراق إلّا لعذر، وإن لم يلق بها فما قرب منه.

During her waiting period, a woman must remain in the house where the separation occurred unless there is an excuse [to go out].

She can leave when there is an excuse, in order to remove any harm caused by her remaining. Allah Most High says, "...Expel them not from their houses nor let them go forth unless they commit open immorality..." [Q65:1]. "Open immorality" means her being abusive to in-laws or other members of the household.

Jābir (may Allah be pleased with him) said, "My maternal aunt was divorced and wanted to [go outside to] pluck dates [from her date palm trees]. A man scolded her for leaving [her marital house], so she came to the Prophet ﷺ and he said, 'Certainly pluck your dates, for perhaps you will give [them in] charity or do a good deed [with them].'"[172]

If [the house] is not appropriate for her, [she moves] to [an appropriate] one nearby.

172. Jābir: Muslim, 1483. See: TM, 1506.

ENSURING LACK OF PREGNANCY

(فصل) [الاستبراء]

The word "*istibrāʾ*" refers to ensuring that a woman is not pregnant.

ويحرم تزويج موطوءة وزائلة فراش من غير الواطىء، ومن غير من زال فراشه عنها، وبحصول ملك غير الزّوجة، وزوال الرّدّة والزّوجيّة.

It is unlawful to marry the following [without first ensuring that they are not pregnant]:

1–2. a female slave who has had intercourse with her master [*mawṭūʾah*] or who is no longer a licit sexual partner – when the groom is not the one who had intercourse with her or the one who is no longer her licit sexual partner,

It is unlawful to marry off a female slave who engaged in intercourse or who is no longer a licit sexual partner [i.e., by the owner who had intercourse setting her free or an *umm walad*'s owner setting her free or dying while she is not married or in a waiting period][173] before ensuring her lack of pregnancy when the groom is not the one who engaged in intercourse with the slave or the one for whom she ceased being a licit sexual partner. If an individual purchases a slave he had had intercourse with or a master frees a slave he had had intercourse with or who bore him a child and then married her: the marriage is valid without ensuring her lack of pregnancy.

3. a newly-owned female slave who is not one's wife,
4. [a slave] who has recanted apostasy,

Because of losing entitlement to sexual enjoyment with her.

173 Ibn al-Muqriʾ, *Ikhlāṣ al-nāwī,* 3:377–378

5. [a slave] who is no longer married.

To someone else, since the reason for it being obligatory has occurred.

و [يحرم] الاستمتاع بغير المسبيّة، أما المسبيّة: فيحرم الوطء فقط.

Intimate behavior [e.g., embracing, touching, kissing] with a female slave who is not a prisoner of war is unlawful.

The Prophet ﷺ said, "Do not have intercourse with one who is pregnant until she gives birth, nor with one who is not pregnant until she menstruates."[174]

As for other intimate behavior, it is unlawful because she might be pregnant from her previous master or from dubious intercourse and thus be someone else's *umm walad*,[175] making it impossible for anyone else to now own her.

As for a female slave who is a prisoner of war, only intercourse is unlawful.

Ibn ʿUmar (may Allah be pleased with him) embraced a female slave he received as part of his spoils of war on the day of Jalūlāʾ.[176]

If she is pregnant, then it is with the enemy's child, which makes intercourse with her unlawful to prevent the possibility of one's sperm mixing with his. Her pregnancy does not, however, prevent one from assuming ownership of her and her child.

---

174. Abū Saʿīd al-Khudrī: Abū Dāwūd, 2157; Ḥākim, 2790. See: TM, 161, 1509, 1649.

175. See "Ummahāt al-Awlād" on page 555.

176. Ibn ʿUmar: Ibn Abī Shaybah, *Al-Muṣannaf*, 3:516. See: BM, 8:262; KBM, 2164; Ibn Ḥajar, *Al-Talkhīṣ al-ḥabīr*, 4:5 #1833.

ويستمر التحريم إلى مضي حيض كامل أو شهر، أو وضع الحمل بعد لزوم الملك، وعدة المعتدة، وطلاق المزوجة وإسلام المحرم نكاحها.

The above remain unlawful until a complete menstruation, the passing of one [lunar] month, or giving birth occurs...

The menstruation is due to the hadith, and the month is in place of it. The remaining portion of a menstruation does not suffice.

...after [her new master] has assumed ownership [of her];...

This is because of the prior hadith, and because it has been established that she is not pregnant.

Ensuring lack of pregnancy must occur after the sale has become final. It is not valid for it to occur while there is an option to cancel.

...after completing a waiting period...;

Ensuring lack of pregnancy must occur after a waiting period has completed. If someone purchases a slave who is undergoing a waiting period for her husband or after dubious intercourse, ensuring her lack of pregnancy must be done after the waiting period has finished.

...a married woman being divorced; or...

Ensuring lack of pregnancy must occur after a married woman is divorced. When a married slave is purchased, ensuring her lack of pregnancy must occur after she is divorced. It can occur immediately after divorce if the marriage was not consummated. But if the marriage was consummated, it must occur after the waiting period.

...entering Islam for a woman who is unlawful to marry [due to her religion].

Ensuring lack of pregnancy must occur after entering Islam. When a slave who is a Zoroastrian, idolatress or apostate is purchased and her lack of pregnancy is ensured before she enters Islam, her lack of pregnancy must be ensured again after she enters Islam. It must be repeated since ensuring lack of pregnancy is for the sake of it being permissible to engage in intercourse with her, and ensuring this is not of consideration unless it is followed by permissibility of intercourse.

WET-NURSING

(فصل) [الرّضاع]

The foundation for the legal rulings pertaining to wet-nursing [*riḍāʿ*] is Allah Most High saying, "...and your foster-mothers, and your foster-sisters..." [Q4:23]. And the Prophet ﷺ said, "Nursing makes unlawful what consanguinity makes unlawful."[177] There is also consensus over this.

CONDITIONS FOR PREVENTING AND NULLIFYING MARRIAGE

يحرّم حصول لبن امرأة حلب حياتها [وما حصل منه] وإن غلب، إن حصل كلّه في معدة حيه – لا بحقنة – خمس رضعات في العادة على من ينتسب إليه من درّ عليه اللبن، ومرضعة زوجته – وإن بانت – ويدفع النّكاح ولزوجتَيْهِ كيف ارتضعتا[١٧٨] .

Milk and its products [i.e. cheese, dough] extracted from a living woman – even if the milk makes up less than half of a mixture – reaching the stomach of a living child younger than two [lunar] years [is legally significant].

177. ʿĀʾishah: Bukhārī, 6156; Muslim, 1445 #9. See: TM, 1511, 1516.

178. Corrected against Ibn Mulaqqin's *Khulāṣat al-fatāwī*, 5:131.

The Messenger of Allah ﷺ said, "There is no nursing except what occurs within two years."[179]

But it being injected through the anus is not [significant].

Since that would be intended as a laxative, not for nourishment.

[Legally significant nursing] on five separate occasions (according to what is usually [considered an individual nursing]),...

ʿĀʾishah (may Allah be pleased with her) said, "Among what was revealed in the Quran is that ten known sucklings make the marriage unlawful. It was then abrogated with five sucklings. The Messenger of Allah ﷺ died and some people were still reciting [the ten known sucklings] as Quran since its abrogation had not yet reached them."[180] This is interpreted as meaning that its ruling was recited.

The Prophet ﷺ said, "One of two nursings, or one suckling or two, do not make marriage unlawful."[181]

...renders [the child] unlawful to the male who is responsible for the milk. And [it renders his infant] wife's wet nurse [unlawful to him] – even after the infant is irrevocably divorced.

It nullifies marriage...

Just as nursing prior to marriage prevents marriage, nursing that occurs within marriage nullifies it. If a man's biological mother nurses his infant wife, they become siblings through nursing and unlawful to one another as spouses.

---

179. Ibn ʿAbbas: Dāraquṭnī, 4364, 4365; Bayhaqī, 15665, 15668. See: TM, 1512.

180. ʿĀʾishah: Muslim, 1452 #24, 25. See: TM, 1514.

181. Umm Faḍl: Muslim, 1451 #20. See: TM, 1515.

...even if one has two [infant] wives [who nursed from the same nurse] no matter how the two nursed.

Through nursing, the infant wives have become milk sisters to one another and therefore unlawful to him, since one may not be married to sisters simultaneously.[182]

The ruling is the same whether the two infant wives nursed simultaneously or serially.

وتثبت بشهادة المرضعة مع غيرها إن لم تطلب أجرة.

Nursing is confirmed [to have occurred] via testimony of the wet nurse with someone else – so long as the nurse did not claim wages [for the nursing].

Since she neither draws benefit or repels harm through her testimony.[183]

SPOUSAL SUPPORT

(فصل) [نفقة زوجة]

DEFINITION AND BASIS

The word for support [*nafaqah*] comes from "*infāq*" which means disbursement. Three things cause it to be obligatory: marriage, blood relation, and ownership.

Support for wives is obligatory according to consensus. Allah Most High says, "...The duty of feeding and clothing nursing mothers in a seemly manner is upon the father of the child..." [Q2:233].

‹Also, Allah Most High says, "Men are in charge of women, because Allah hath made the one of them to excel the other, and because they spend of their property (for the support of women)..."

182 See "Sisters and Aunts" on page 346.

183 See "Things Typically Known Only to Women" on page 538, and "Witnesses" on page 534.

[Q4:34]. This verse indicates that husbands are responsible for support.[184]›

Evidence for the consensus also comes from hadiths. The Prophet ﷺ said, "A wife's right upon her husband is that you feed her when you feed yourself, and clothe her when you clothe yourself."[185]

Hind bint ʿUtbah, the wife of Abū Sufyān (may Allah be pleased with them both) said, "O, Messenger of Allah [ﷺ]! Abū Sufyān is a miserly man and does not give me and my children adequate provisions for maintenance unless I take something from his possession without his knowledge. Is there any sin on me?" Thereupon the Messenger of Allah ﷺ said, "Take from his property what is customary and which may suffice you and your children."[186]

OBLIGATORY AMOUNTS

يجب للممكّنة صبيحة كلّ يوم تمليك مدّي حبّ بمؤنته على الموسر، ومدّ على المسكين، ومدّ ونصف على المتوسّط، واللحم والأدم على العادة، وإخدام حرة تخدم، وكسوة تكفيها بالعادة، وسكنى تليق بها، وإمتاع غطاء ووطاء، وآلة طبخ وشرب ومؤنته، وأجرة الحمام لأهل الحضر.

A wife who makes herself available [to her husband] must be given the following:

1. **Each morning, two *mudds* [1.02 liters] of grain with its [requisite] supplies [*muʾnah*] if the husband is well-off; one *mudd* [0.51 liters] if he is poor; or one and a half *mudd* [0.765 liters] if he is between the two.**

---

184. al-Bughā, *Al-Tadhhīb,* 190 #1.

185. Muʿāwiyah al-Qushayrī: Abū Dāwūd, 2142. See: KBM, 2180.

186. Hind: Bukhārī, 5364; Muslim, 1714. See: TM, 1524, 1777, 1801. KBM, 2178.

We find that the Sacred Law specified the quantity of food that is given in expiations. The most that it made obligatory for a single poor person is two *mudds*, which is the expiation for violating *iḥrām* during Hajj.[187] The least obligatory for a single individual is one *mudd,* for *ẓihār*[188] and for intercourse [while fasting] during Ramadan.[189] We based support on these since each one of them is food that the Sacred Law makes obligatory and establishes against one's debt. We consider the most to be required of someone well-off, and the least required of someone poor, and we made what's between them for someone in the middle.

2. **Meat and savory, as is usual.**

Oil, ghee, cheese, and dates are included as savory since these are part of good cohabitation.

3. **A servant, if a freewoman of her status typically has one.**

If she asks for one, he must provide one since this is part of kind and just cohabitation.

4. **Sufficient clothing, according to whatever is usual.**

Allah Most High says, "...The duty of feeding and clothing nursing mothers in a seemly manner is upon the father of the child..." [Q2:233].

5. **Lodgings appropriate for [someone of] her [status].**
6. **Furniture, blankets, and ground coverings [rugs].**

---

187. See "Expiations" on page 211.
188. See"Likening One's Wife to One's Mother" on page 386.
189. See "Intercourse In Ramadan During the Daytime" on page 168.

7. **Utensils for cooking, [eating,] and drinking, along with their [requisite] supplies [*mu'nah*].**
8. **[Coverage of] bathing expenses, if a city dweller.**

The husband must cover the expenses for her purificatory bath if it is necessitated by intercourse or giving birth, since these are occasioned by him. He is not responsible for expenses related to her purification after menstruation or erotic dreams, since they occurred solely because of her.

WAIVED FOR DISOBEDIENCE

وتسقط بالنّشوز.

The above are withheld if she is disobedient.

She is entitled to support in exchange for making herself available to him and forgoing other activities. Thus, if she is disobedient, support is withheld from her because she has ceased making herself available to him.

INABILITY TO PROVIDE

وإن عجز عن واجب المعسر أمهل ثلاثة، وتفسخ في صبيحة الرابع.

If he is unable to provide the minimum required of a poor husband, he is given three days [to provide] then the marriage is annulled the morning of the fourth.

In a narration from Abū Hurayrah (may Allah be pleased with him), there was a man who did not find enough to support his wife so the Prophet ﷺ said, "Separate them."[190]

---

190. Abū Hurayrah: Dāraquṭnī, 3783; Bayhaqī, 15707, 15708. See: KBM, 2184–5.

Another [weaker] opinion is that there is no annulment for her, since someone without funds is to be waited for. Al-Rūyānī said, "My grandfather told me, 'This what I give as *fatwā*.'"[191]

This annulment requires a judge, since it requires exercising *ijtihād*.

SUPPORTING RELATIVES

(فصل) [نفقة أصل وفرع]

وعلى من فضل عن قوته وقوت زوجته ليوم وليلة كفاية أصل أو فرع لا شيء له ولو كسوبًا.

فيقدّم عند الاجتماع الفرع ثمّ الأصل، ثمّ الأقرب، ثمّ الوارث.

وقدم الأب وآباؤه على الأمّ، وفي الأخذ يعكس.

Whoever has provisions in excess of what is needed for himself and his wife for that day must provide sufficient support for his ancestors or descendants who have nothing – even if they are capable of earning.

The poor are not required [to do this] as they are not among those who must share with others.

If one's descendant is mature, of sound mind, and has an appropriate means of earning, one is not required to support him according to the strongest of two *qawl*s.

When several [relatives are in need], priority is given to descendants, then ancestors, then the closest of the aforementioned kin, then heirs.

One's father and his fathers are given priority over one's mother.

191. al-Rāfiʿī, *Al-Sharḥ al-kabīr*, 10:49; al-Damīrī, *Al-Najm al-wahhāj*, 8:267.

‹This is with respect to who is responsible for providing support to needy offspring.›

It is the opposite for those receiving [support].

‹This is with respect to a needy relative receiving support from a more affluent individual. In such a case, one's mother and one's small children have priority over one's father and one's [older] children, who have the potential to provide for themselves.[192]›

One's mother and her mother are given priority over one's father [with respect to which of one's needy ascendants has priority] due to the increased vulnerability and weakness of women.

Unlike support for one's wives, support for one's kin does not have a specific, legislated quantity. Instead, it is whatever suffices.

The obligation to support one's descendants comes from the Prophet ﷺ, who told Hind (may Allah be pleased with her): "Take from his property what is customary and which may suffice you and your children."[193] ‹In this hadith, "customary" means what people typically provide for someone of similar status, taking the husband's financial circumstances into consideration, and without overspending.

Additional support comes from the verses in which Allah Most High says, "Mothers shall suckle their children for two whole years; (that is) for those who wish to complete the suckling. The duty of feeding and clothing nursing mothers in a seemly manner is upon the father of the child" [Q2:233] and "...Then, if they give suck for you, give them their due payment..." [Q65:6].

---

192 Ibn Mulaqqin, *Khulāṣat al-fatāwī,* 5:174–175; Ibn Ḥajar al-Haytamī, *Fatḥ al-jawwad bi sharḥ Al-Irshād,* 3:262; Ibn al-Muqri', *Ikhlāṣ al-nāwī,* 3:418–419; al-Muzajjad, *Al-ʿUbāb,* 3:202–203; al-Qizwīnī, *Al-Ḥāwī al-ṣaghīr,* 544–545.

193. Hind: Bukhārī, 5364; Muslim, 1714. See: TM, 1524, 1777, 1801; KBM, 2178.

These two verses state that the father is obligated to support his child's wet nurse, and this is even stronger evidence for the obligation of supporting one's children.[194]›

The obligation towards ancestors is analogous to one's obligation to one's descendants since they are also blood relatives. Indeed, it is even more appropriate since the sanctity of one's parents is even greater.

‹Allah Most High says, "...Consort with them in the world kindly..." [Q31:15]. Providing for them is part of appropriate kindness.[195]›

ʿĀʾishah (may Allah be pleased with her) said that the Messenger of Allah ﷺ said, "The most wholesome thing a man eats is from what he earns. And his children are amongst what he earns."[196]

ʿAbd Allāh ibn ʿAmr ibn al-ʿĀṣ (may Allah be pleased with him) said that the Messenger of Allah ﷺ said, "You and your property belong to your father. Your children are amongst the most wholesome of your earnings, so eat from the earnings of your children."[197]

Ṭāriq al-Muḥārabī (may Allah be pleased with him) said, "I came to Medina and the Messenger of Allah ﷺ was standing on the minbar addressing the people, saying 'The hand which gives is the higher hand. Start with those upon whom you depend: your mother, father, sister, brother, and then your closest and then next closest relatives.'"[198]

Kulayb ibn Manfaʿah said that his grandfather (may Allah be pleased with them both) told him that he went to the Prophet ﷺ and said, "Messenger of Allah, to whom should I show kindness?" He ﷺ said, "Your mother, your sister, your brother and the slave

194. al-Bughā, *Al-Tadhhīb,* 188 #1.
195. al-Bughā, *Al-Tadhhīb,* 187 #6.
196. ʿĀʾishah: Abū Dāwūd, 3528, Tirmidhī, 1358. See: KBM, 2187.
197. ʿAbd Allāh ibn ʿAmr ibn al-ʿĀṣ: Abū Dāwūd, 3530. See: cf TM, 1450.
198. Ṭāriq al-Muḥārabī: Nasāʾī, 2532; Ibn Ḥibbān, 3340; Dāraquṭnī, 2976; Ḥākim, 4219; Bayhaqī, 11096. See: al-Bughā, *Al-Tadhhīb,* 187 #6.

whom you set free and who is your relative: it is an obligatory duty and a joined familial relation."[199]

NURSING ONE'S CHILD

(فصل) [إرضاع اللبأ]

وعلى الأمّ إرضاع ولدها اللبأ، ثمّ إن تعيّنت، فيجب عليها أيضًا، وإلّا فبالأجرة إن لم تتبرّع غيرها.

A mother is required to nurse her child with the first milk that she produces upon delivery.

This is because, typically, a newborn will not live without it.

Thereafter, if she is the only one who can nurse him, it becomes obligatory for her [to continue feeding the child]. Otherwise, she is hired if no one volunteers.

This ruling is based upon what preceded [in the previous section on supporting one's descendants].

---

199. Kulayb ibn Manfaʿah from his grandfather: Abū Dāwūd, 5140. See: KBM, 2187; BM, 8:314.

SUPPORTING SLAVES, ANIMALS AND IMMOVABLE PROPERTY

(فصل) [نفقة المملوك]

SLAVES

ويجب للرّقيق قدر الكفاية بالعادة، ويكلفه ما يطيق.

Slaves must be provided with a sufficient amount of whatever is typical. They are held responsible for work that is within their ability to perform.

Abū Hurayrah (may Allah be pleased with him) said that the Messenger of Allah ﷺ said, "Slaves are entitled to their food and their clothing, and they are not burdened with work except that which they are able [to perform]."[200] In one version: "It is sin enough for an individual that he withholds sustenance from those he possesses."[201]

Abū Dharr (may Allah be pleased with him) said that the Messenger of Allah ﷺ said, "Your servants are your brothers. Allah placed them under your authority. Whoever has his brother under his authority is to feed him from what he [himself] eats, and is to clothe them from what he [himself] wears. Do not burden them with what is beyond their capacity. When you burden them, assist them in it."[202]

Imam al-Shāfiʿī (may Allah grant him His mercy) explained that this means work that they can do day after day – not work that they can do one day but not the next.

If an owner does burden a slave with more than he can bear, the slave is forcibly sold (i.e. without the owner's consent).

---

200. Abū Hurayrah: Muslim, 1662 #41. See: TM, 1530.
201. Abū Hurayrah: Muslim, 996 #40. See: TM, 1406.
202. Abū Dharr: Bukhārī, 30; Muslim, 1661 #40. See: TM, 1533.

LIVESTOCK

و[يجب] علف السّائمة بالجدب.

Fodder must be provided to livestock who graze when there is a drought.

This is due to the sanctity of their lives. Allowing animals that graze access to pasture and water takes the place of providing fodder when those are sufficient.

Kept animals that are not able to provide for themselves (i.e., through grazing or hunting vermin) must be provided for.

Ibn ʿUmar (may Allah be pleased with him) reported that the Messenger of Allah ﷺ said, "A woman was punished because of a cat that she had confined until it died and [for this,] she entered Hellfire. She did not provide it with food or drink as it was confined, nor did she free it so that it might eat the vermin of the earth."[203]

PROPERTY DEVELOPMENT

لا [يجب] عمارة العقار.

Developing immobile properties is not required.

However, it is offensive to leave them until they become destroyed.

It is not offensive to build houses and other properties that are needed. However, it is best not to overbuild and it may even be offensive because of the authentic hadith in which the Prophet ﷺ says, "A man is given rewards for all that he spends – save on this dirt."[204] ‹Another narration ends with "...save on building."[205]› Ibn Ḥibbān [quoting Abū Ḥātim]'s explanation (may Allah grant

203. Ibn ʿUmar: Bukhārī, 2365, 3482; Muslim, 2242–43. The phrasing here is from Muslim. See: TM, 1535.

204. Qays ibn Abī Ḥāzim: Ibn Ḥibbān, 3243.

205. Ḥārithah ibn Muḍuarrib: Ibn Mājah, 4163.

him His mercy) said, "One is not rewarded if one spends to build more than one needs. And Allah knows best."

NEGLIGENT OWNERS

فإن امتنع من ذلك بيع عليه، أو أؤجر، ثمّ من بيت المال.

If an owner refuses [to fulfill any of] the [obligations] above, the slave or animal is sold, rented out, or [provided for] by the Muslim treasury [*bayt al-māl*].

This is to protect their lives. When the owner does not give them their rights, the judge takes his place.

MILKING

ولا يحلب إلّا ما فضل عن ولدها.

An animal is not milked except what is in surplus of her baby's needs.

Ḍirār ibn al-Azwar (may Allah be pleased with him) said, "I gifted a female sheep to the Messenger of Allah ﷺ. He ﷺ ordered me to milk it, so I milked it vigorously and then he ﷺ said, 'Leave [the remainder of the milk in the udder].' That is, 'draw the milk [that comes after it],' meaning 'do not exhaust it entirely.'"[206]

CUSTODY

(فصل) [الحضانة]

Custody [*ḥaḍānah*] is protecting and raising someone who is not independent.

206. Ḍirār ibn al-Azwar: Ibn Ḥibbān, 5283; Ḥākim, 5041, 6603. See: TM, 1537.

شرط الحاضن ستّ: عقل، وحريّة وإسلام للمسلم، وأمانة، وإرضاع الرضيع وبصر.

The conditions of the custodian are six. [The custodian must be]:

1. **of sound mind;**
2. **free;**

The custodian must be free because custody is a form of guardianship and slaves are not qualified. Also, a slave is occupied with serving his master.

3. **a Muslim – for a Muslim ward;**

The custodian should be upright and of the same religion as the child. This is because only someone who is upright can be trusted not to deceive when it comes to protection and upbringing.

4. **trustworthy;**
5. **able to nurse a child who is still nursing; and**
6. **perceptive.**

وإن نكحت من لا حق له في الحضانة، بطل حقّها، وإن طلقت عاد كعود شرطها.

A woman loses her right to custody if she marries someone...

This is because she will be occupied with her husband.

...who has no right to custody.

Suppose that a man marries a woman, and his son [from another woman] marries her daughter from another man. The son has a son and his wife then dies. In such a case, custody would go to the mother's mother [the first one mentioned in this paragraph], who is the grandfather's wife.

If she divorces, she regains custody – just as when one of its conditions returns.

Custody is returned to her because the reason for its loss has ended.

وشرط المحضون عدم الاستقلال.

The condition of the ward is the absence of independence.

وتقدّم [١] الأمّ، ثمّ أمّهاتها بإدلاء الإناث القربى فالقربى، ثمّ الأب ثمّ أمّهاته، كذلك، ثمّ أبوه ثمّ أمّهاته كذلك، ثمّ ولد الأبوين، ثمّ لأب، ثمّ لأم، [٩] ثمّ الخالات لأبوين، ثمّ لأب، ثمّ لأمّ، [١٢] ثمّ ولد ولد الأبوين، ثمّ الأب إلا ابن الأخت، [١٤] ثمّ بنت ولد الأم، [١٥] ثمّ ولد الجد لأبوين، ثمّ لأب، [١٧] ثمّ العمّة لأم، [١٨] ثمّ بنات الخالات، ثمّ بنات العمّات بترتيب أصولهنّ، [٢٠] ثمّ ولد العمّ الوارث.

[Custodians are chosen in the following order:]
1. the mother;...

The mother is first because of her abundant compassion. Her mother, and her mother's mother come next because of their share in inheritance and birth.

One of the foundations for this section is the narration of ʿAbd Allāh ibn ʿAmr ibn al-ʿĀṣ (may Allah be pleased with him): "A woman said, 'O Messenger of Allah, this is my son. My womb was a vessel for him, my breasts were a watering-skin for him [to nurse from], and my lap a guard for him. His father has divorced me and wants to take him away from me.' The Messenger of Allah ﷺ said, 'You have more right to him as long as you do not marry.'"[207]

---

207. ʿAbd Allāh ibn ʿAmr ibn al-ʿĀṣ: Abū Dāwūd, 2276; Dāraquṭnī, 3808; Ḥākim, 2830; Bayhaqī, 15763. See: TM, 1526.

This narration is also the foundation for the ruling that the mother is given first priority of guardianship until the child reaches the age of discernment [seven years], and that she loses this right if she remarries.

...the mother's mothers – through her uninterrupted female line, in order of closeness;...

2. **the father;**
3. **the father's mothers – through his uninterrupted female line, in order of closeness**

The father is more rightful than his mothers since they are related to the child through him, so it is unlikely that they would have priority over him. But if the father is missing, priority is given to his mothers through their uninterrupted female line, in order of closeness.

4. **the father's father;**
5. **the father's father's mother – through his uninterrupted female line, in order of closeness;**

When the father's father is missing, priority is given to his mothers through their uninterrupted female line, in order of closeness.

6. **a full sibling;**
7. **a sibling from the same father;**
8. **a sibling from the same mother;**
9. **the mother's full sister;**
10. **the mother's sister from the same father;**
11. **the mother's sister from the same mother;**
12. **a full siblings's son;**
13. **a paternal sibling's son – but not a sister's son;**
14. **a maternal sibling's daughter;**
15. **the father's full sibling;**
16. **the father's sibling from the same father;**
17. **the mother's father's sister;**

18. the mother's sister's daughters;
19. the father's sister's daughters – following the order of their ancestors; and
20. the child of a paternal uncle who inherits.

تقدّم أنثى كلّ رتبة على الذّكر منها.

The female of each rank is given priority over its males.

Just as the mother has priority over the father, so: a full sister has priority over a full brother, a sister from the same father has priority over a brother from the same father – and their children are prioritized in the same manner. And the mother's full sister has priority over the mother's full brother, and the mother's sister from the same father has priority over the mother's brother from the same father – and their children are prioritized in the same manner.

ISSUES RELATED TO CUSTODY

(فصل) [المحضونة]

وقدم مختار المميّز بشرط كون المختار محرم للمحضونة، وله الرّجوع عنه. فإن اختار الأب فللأم الزّيارة، أو الأمّ علّمه حرفة، وله أخذ الصّغير إن سافرت، أو الأب لنقلة.

The preference of a child who has discernment...

Discernment typically occurs around seven years of age.

...is given priority [according to the previous schedule] upon the condition that the preferred person is a *maḥram* for a female charge.

Abū Hurayrah (may Allah be pleased with him) said that the Prophet ﷺ gave a boy the choice between his father and his mother.[208]

208. Abū Hurayrah: Abū Dāwūd, 2277; Tirmidhī, 1357 – *ḥasan ṣaḥīḥ*; Ibn Mājah, 2351. See: TM, 1529.

Another version states that a woman came and said, "O Messenger of Allah. My husband wants to take my son away but he [her son] draws water for me from the well of Abī ʿInabah and has benefited me." The Messenger of Allah ﷺ said, "Cast lots for him." The father said, "Who is disputing with me about my son?" The Prophet ﷺ said, "This is your father and this is your mother. Take the hand of whichever one you want." He took the hand of his mother and went with her.[209] ‹In the hadith, "the well of Abī ʿInabah" refers to a specific well that appears to be distant, indicating that her son has grown and has been helping her with things after she took care of him in his infancy. But if she loses custody, he would no longer be available to help her.[210]›

The child can retract his preference.

If the ward chooses the father, the mother may visit.

The mother cannot be barred from visiting her child. This is in order to prevent breaking family ties.

A male ward cannot be prevented from visiting his mother – also in order to prevent breaking family ties.

A female ward can be prevented from visiting her mother. This is to shield her from public exposure and to help her become accustomed to protective seclusion. One of Ibn Ṣalāḥ's fatwas is that a mother can request her daughter, and the daughter is brought to her for the duration of the visit. (May Allah grant him His mercy.)

In the event of the ward's sickness, the mother is preferred for nursing because she is more capable of this and her compassion is more complete.

If the ward chooses the mother, the father teaches him a trade.

Since this is in his best interest.

209. Abū Hurayrah: Abū Dāwūd, 2277. See: KBM, 2198.

210. al-Bughā, *Al-Tadhhīb,* 192 #1.

The father can assume [temporary] custody of the child while the mother travels, and is entitled to [permanent] custody if he moves.

If one of them wants to take a temporary trip, the child remains with the custodian who is not travelling.

If one of the parents is permanently relocating, the father has priority. This is in order to protect the ward's lineage and welfare. This applies whether the father married the mother in his own land or a foreign land. However, it is conditional upon the passage and destination being safe and free of extreme heat or cold.

10

INJURIOUS CRIMES

كِتَابُ الْجِنَايَاتِ

هي من «جنى الثّمر» إذا قطعه.

[The word for injurious crimes (*jināyāt*) comes] from [the phrase] "the fruit was picked," [and refers to] when fruit has been harvested.

The foundation for the rulings on injurious crimes [*jināyāt*], before consensus, is found in the words of Allah Most High: "...retaliation is prescribed for you in the matter of the murdered..." [Q2:178]. There are also other verses and well-known hadiths.

Abū Hurayrah (may Allah be pleased with him) said that the Prophet ﷺ said: "Avoid the seven destructive things." It was asked: "What are they, O Messenger of Allah?" He ﷺ replied, "Associating anyone or anything with Allah in worship, practicing sorcery, unjustly killing someone Allah has declared inviolate, devouring the property of an orphan, consuming usury, fleeing from the battlefield, and slandering chaste women who never have indecent thoughts and are righteous believers."[1]

Al-Barāʾ ibn ʿĀzib (may Allah be pleased with him) said that the Messenger of Allah ﷺ said, "The destruction of this world is less significant to Allah than the killing of a single believer without just cause."[2]

---

1. Abū Hurayrah: Bukhārī, 2766, 6857; Muslim, 89 #145. See TM, 1590.
2. al-Barāʾ ibn ʿĀzib: Ibn Mājah, 2619 – with a sound chain. See: KBM, 2208.

A similar report comes from ʿAbd Allāh ibn ʿAmr (may Allah be pleased with him).[3]

‹The ḥadīths concerning this are so numerous that they reach the point of being considered mass-transmitted [*tawātur*] [and thus conveying knowledge that is sure to be true].[4]›

It is clear that murder is an enormity [*kabīrah*] and is associated with retribution in this world.

‹Allah Most High says, "But whoever kills a believer intentionally – his recompense is Hell, wherein he will abide eternally, and Allah has become angry with him and has cursed him and has prepared for him a great punishment" [Q4:93].[5]›

TYPES OF WRONGFUL KILLING

وهي ثلاثة.

There are three [types of wrongful killings].

DELIBERATE

[١] عمد: وهو قصد الفعل والشّخص بما يقتل غالبًا.

وهو موجب للقصاص، والدّيّة بدل عنه عند العفو، وتجب في ماله مغلّظة حالّة.

1. **Deliberate: one intends the act and the [targeted] individual while using something [i.e., a weapon or force] that is typically lethal.**

A reciprocal punishment is obligatory [for such an act].

3. ʿAbd Allāh bin ʿAmr: Tirmidhī, 1395. See: KBM, 2208.
4. al-Bughā, *Al-Tadhhīb,* 193 #1.
5. al-Bughā, *Al-Tadhhīb,* 193 #1.

An augmented indemnity[6] takes the place of the punishment when [the perpetrator is] pardoned; this indemnity is due immediately from his own property.

This is due to the hadith: "The survivors of a murder victim choose between the best of two: either [reciprocal] killing, or blood money."[7]

Pardoning is preferable, since Allah Most High says, "To forgo is nearer to piety" [Q2:237].

MISTAKEN AND SEMI-INTENTIONAL

[٢] وخطأ: وهو ما فقد فيه قصد أحدهما.

[٣] وشبه العمد: وهو قصدهما بما لا يقتل غالبًا.

ولا قصاص فيهما، ويجب في الأوّل دية مخمسّة مؤجّلة في ثلاث سنين، وفي الثّاني دية مغلّظة مؤجّلة، وكلاهما على العاقلة.

2. **Mistaken: either the act or target is not intended.**
3. **Semi-intentional: both the act and the target are intended, but with something [i.e., a weapon or force] that is not typically lethal.**

There is no reciprocal punishment for either of these two.

Allah Most High says, "It is not for a believer to kill a believer unless (it be) by mistake. He who hath killed a believer by mistake must set free a believing slave, and pay the blood-money to the family of the slain, unless they remit it as a charity" [Q4:92]. (Additional evidence is forthcoming.)

6 See "The Augmented Indemnity" on page 428 and "Blood Indemnity" on page 436.

7. Abū Hurayrah: Bukhārī, 6880; Muslim, 1355. See: TM, 1552.

The first type ["mistaken"] requires an indemnity divided into five portions and paid over three years.

It is reported that payment over three years agrees with the practice of ʿUmar, ʿAlī, Ibn ʿUmar, and ʿAbbās (may Allah be pleased with them all). No one objected to it, so there is consensus. Also, they (may Allah be pleased with them) would not have held that opinion in a matter such as this without them knowing it from the Messenger of Allah ﷺ. Imam al-Shāfiʿī (may Allah grant him His mercy) said, "I do not know of anything contradicting that the Messenger of Allah ﷺ decided that blood money is owed by the *ʿāqilah* [the perpetrator's male relatives] and paid over three years."[8]

This is when the complete indemnity is owed for killing a free male Muslim. The indemnity for killing a non-Muslim or for causing a miscarriage is owed in one year. The indemnity for killing a [Muslim] woman is owed over two years: 30 camels the first year, and the rest in the second.

When one-third or less of an indemnity is owed, it is owed in one year.

When more than one complete indemnity is owed (such as when both the victim's arms and both legs were severed), it is owed over six years.

The second type ["semi-intentional"] requires a deferred, augmented indemnity.

ʿAbd Allāh ibn ʿAmr (may Allah be pleased with him) said that the Prophet ﷺ said, "Semi-mistaken killing is killing with a whip or stick" – in one version: "for which [there is a blood money payment of] one hundred camels, of which forty should be pregnant with babies in their wombs."[9]

8. Al-Shāfiʿī, *Al-Umm,* 6:114.

9. Ibn ʿAmr: Ibn Mājah, 2627, Abū Dāwūd, 4547. See: TM, 1540.

The Prophet ﷺ said, "The blood money for semi-intentional killing is augmented like the blood money of intentional killing, though the killer is not [himself] killed."[10]

[The indemnity for] both [i.e., "mistaken" and "semi-intentional"] must be paid by the killer's *ʿāqilah.*

Abū Hurayrah (may Allah be pleased with him) said that two women from the Hudhail tribe fought each other. One of them threw a stone at the other and killed her and what was in her womb. They brought their case to the Messenger of Allah ﷺ. He ﷺ decided that the blood money owed for the dead woman's fetus would be a male or female slave, and that the blood money would be paid by the killer's *ʿāqilah.*[11]

The killing in the above event was semi-intentional and he ﷺ decided that the blood money would be paid by the *ʿāqilah.*[12] A fortiori, it is paid for a mistaken killing.

THE AUGMENTED INDEMNITY

والمغلظة: ثلاثون حقة، وثلاثون جذعة، وأربعون خلفة، أي حاملا.

The augmented indemnity consists of thirty *ḥiqqah,* thirty *jadhaʿah,* and forty pregnant camels.[13]

The Prophet ﷺ said, "Whoever kills deliberately is handed over to the guardians of the one killed. If they wish, they kill him; if they wish, they accept blood money. [The blood money] is thirty *ḥiqqah,* thirty *jadhaʿah,* and forty pregnant camels."[14] ‹Here the

---

10. ʿAmd ibn Shuʿayb from his father from his grandfather: Abū Dāwūd, 4565. See: TM, 1557.
11. Abū Hurayrah: Bukhārī, 5758; Muslim, 1681 #36. See: TM, 1563.
12. See "The ʿĀqilah" on page 406.
13. For definitions, see "Livestock" on page 151.
14. ʿAmr ibn Shuʿayb from his father, from his grandfather: Tirmidhī, 1387 – *ḥasan gharīb.* See: TM, 1555.

augmentation of the indemnity is its division into three groups.[15]›
Another version has: "The blood money [ʿ*aql*] for a semi-intentional killing is augmented like an deliberate killing."[16]

THE REDUCED INDEMNITY

والمخمّسة: عشرون حقّة، وجذعة، وبنت مخاض، وولد اللبون.

The reduced indemnity consists of twenty *ḥiqqah,* twenty *jadhʿah,* twenty *bint makhāḍ,* and twenty *walad labūn.*

Ibn Masʿūd (may Allah be pleased with him) said, "In mistaken [killings] there are twenty *jadhʿah,* twenty *ḥiqqah,* twenty *bint labūn,* twenty *ibn labūn,* and twenty *bint makhāḍ.*"[17] A ruling like this is not stated except when it is known to have come from the Prophet ﷺ since it is a quantity, and quantities cannot be determined based solely on one's own opinion.

The indemnity is reduced in that the livestock is divided into five age groups.

INDIRECTLY CAUSING DEATH

Causing or bringing about a condition [that results in death] is like direct involvement with respect to obligating the indemnity. Thus, just as the indemnity is owed for direct involvement (like when one person kills another), it is required for causing it (like by giving false testimony) or bringing about its condition (like digging a hole that someone stumbles into it, which leads to their death).

15. al-Bughā, *Al-Tadhhīb,* 198 #1.
16. Dāraquṭnī, 3144. See: TM, 1557.
17. Ibn Masʿūd: Abū Dāwūd, 4545; Ibn Mājah, 2631. See: TM, 1554.

INDIVIDUALS RESPONSIBLE FOR THE INDEMNITY

(فصل) [العاقلة]

والعاقلة: العصبات، الأصل والفرع.

The individuals who are responsible for paying the indemnity [the *ʿāqilah*] are one's male relatives: ancestors, and descendants.[18]

ولا يعقل فقير، ورقيق، وصبي، ومجنون، ومسلم عن كافر، وعكسه.

They do not include slaves, the poor,...

This is because the *ʿāqīlah* bear the burden for the sake of sharing [the financial responsibility], which the poor are unable to do.

...youths, or the insane.

A Muslim is not included [as part of the *ʿāqilah*] for a non-Muslim's killing, nor the opposite.

Because of the lack of mutual protection and assistance.

وعلى الغنيّ نصف دينار والمتوسّط ربعه ويعتبران آخر الحول.

The affluent must pay one-half a *dīnār,* while those of average wealth pay one-quarter.

This is the minimum amount that an affluent person is required to give as zakat assistance. Also, an affluent husband's spousal support is double that of a poor husband.

Nothing is taken from the poor.

18. See "Universal Inheritance" on page 308.

[The financial status of] both [the affluent and those of average wealth] is determined at the end of each year.

Because the payment is a type of cash assistance tied to lunar years, it is repeated annually.

RECIPROCAL PUNISHMENT

(فصل) [القصاص]

CONDITIONS OBLIGATING IMPLEMENTATION

إنّما يجب القصاص على البالغ العاقل المعصوم المكافيء.

Reciprocal punishment [*qiṣās*] is obligatory only when [the perpetrator] is mature and of sound mind,...

Reciprocal punishments are corporal punishments. Such punishments are not required except when a crime is committed. The actions of minors and the insane are not classified as crimes since their intention to commit maliciousness is not valid. Thus, they are not eligible to receive punishment, nor are they subject to reciprocal punishment when they kill – even if the crime appears to have been intentional.

...and the victim's life was sacrosanct and equal to [but not less than the killer's].

Women are killed for men, and men for women. Anas (may Allah be pleased with him) reported that a Jewish man who smashed a girl's head between two stones and killed her. The Prophet ﷺ ordered that his head be smashed between two stones.[19]

19. Anas: Bukhārī, 2413; Muslim, 1672 #15–17. See: TM, 1550.

SCENARIOS IN WHICH PUNISHMENT IS NOT IMPLEMENTED

فلا يقتل مسلم بكافر، وحرّ برقيق، ولا والد يقتل بولد، ولا لأجله.

A Muslim is not killed for killing a non-Muslim,...

ʿAlī (may Allah be pleased with him) said – in a saying attributed to the Prophet ﷺ: "A Muslim is not killed for [killing] a disbeliever."[20]

...nor is a freeman for killing his slave,...

Shāfiʿīs and Ḥanafīs agree that we do not amputate the limb of a freeman as a reciprocal punishment [for cutting off the limb of his slave]. A fortiori, we do not kill a freeman for killing his slave.

Ibn ʿAbbās (may Allah be pleased with him) said – in a saying attributed to the Prophet ﷺ: "A freeman is not killed for [killing] a slave."[21]

...nor is a parent for killing his child...

This is true even if it is intentional. The Prophet ﷺ said, "A father is not reciprocally killed for [killing] his son."[22]

Other ancestors have the same ruling as the father.

... – nor because of his child.

This could occur in some cases where the father kills a former slave whom his son had set free.

Equality at the time of injury is significant. If a *dhimmī* injures another *dhimmī* and the perpetrator enters Islam and the victim then dies, reciprocal punishment is still required because equality existed at the time of injury.

---

20. ʿAlī: Bukhārī, 6915. See: TM, 1545.
21. Ibn ʿAbbās: Dāraquṭnī, 3252; Bayhaqī, 15939. See: KBM, 2216.
22. ʿUmar: Tirmidhī, 1400; Ibn Mājah, 2662; Dāraquṭnī, 3276, 3277; Bayhaqī, 15963. See: KBM, 2217.

Sanctity at the time of injury and death is also significant. There is no liability for a Muslim who injures a *ḥarbī* [an individual who is at war with the Muslims] if the victim enters Islam [after being injured] and then dies from his injury or if the perpetrator leaves Islam after committing the act. However, if a Muslim injures another Muslim and then the victim leaves Islam but later returns and dies from his injury, there is liability for the blood indemnity but no reciprocal punishment.

NON-FATAL INJURIES

والأطراف كالنّفس، ويشترط فيها المماثلة، ولا تقطع صحيحة بشلّاء.

Injuries to limbs are akin to taking a life [in the above conditions]. Similarity is a condition [i.e., the limbs of the perpetrator must have the same name and be on the same side of his body as the limbs he injured]. A healthy limb is not severed for one that is paralyzed.

A healthy, functioning limb is not taken for one that it paralyzed. The meaning of reciprocal [*qiṣāṣ*] is "equivalency." There is no equivalency between a right and a left [limb or organ] in their utility, nor is there equivalency between a paralyzed and a healthy [limb or organ].

The size of the limb or organ is not significant.

COLLECTIVE MURDER

ويقتل جمع بواحد.

An entire group is killed for collectively murdering an individual.

This is when the action of each one of them, on his own, would have been fatal, whether the death resulted from blunt force, a sharpened edge, or both combined. This is because of the generality of the verse, "Whoso is slain wrongfully, We have given power unto his heir" [Q17:33] – meaning reciprocal punishment.

ʿUmar (may Allah be pleased with him) killed a group of five or seven people for one man whom they had killed by treachery. He said, "Had all the people of Ṣanāʿ gathered against him, I would have killed them all."[23] ‹This was reported from other companions without any objection, so it is consensus.›

This applies to co-conspirators who, individually, have caused injuries that would warrant reciprocal punishment. However, if one of them did not cause the injury deliberately, there is no reciprocal punishment [for him]. It is also necessary that the injury he caused not be immediately fatal, such as if one perpetrator cuts off a victim's hand and then his partner decapitates him: the latter would be deserving of reciprocal punishment but the former would not.

IF A SINGLE GUARDIAN PARDONS

وللولي عفو عن بعضهم على حصّته من الدّية باعتبار الرّؤوس.

The [victim's] guardian can pardon some of the perpetrators from the portion of the indemnity that they owe (by taking into account the number of participants).

If one guardian pardons, he reduces the other guardians' right to blood indemnity. ʿUmar was presiding over a similar case with Ibn Masʿūd at his side (may Allah be pleased with them both). ʿUmar asked Ibn Masʿūd for his opinion and Ibn Masʿūd said, "I opine that he [the victim's guardian] has saved him [one of the perpetrators] from being killed." ʿUmar slapped Ibn Masʿūd on the shoulder, and said, "A small sack, but full of knowledge!"[24]

---

23. Saʿid ibn al-Musayyib: Mālik (3246); Bayhaqī, 15973. See: BM, 8:404.
24. Qatādah: ʿAbd al-Razzāq, *Al-Muṣannaf,* 18187; al-Ṭabarānī, *Al-Muʿjam al-kabīr,* 9735.

NON-FATAL PERSONAL INJURIES

(فصل) [القصص في الشّجاج والقطع والكسر]

ولا قصاص في الشّجاج إلّا في الموضحة.

There is no reciprocal punishment for wounds to the face unless they cleaves flesh from the bone.

‹Allah Most High says, "...and for wounds retaliation [*qiṣāṣ*]..." [Q5:45].[25]›

The meaning of "retaliation" [*qiṣāṣ*] is equivalency. Equivalency is not achievable except with this type of wound.

ويجب القصاص في القطع من مفصل، لا في كسر عظام.

Reciprocal punishments are required for a limb severed at the joint...

This is because equivalency is possible here, in contrast to taking it from above or below the joint. Compensation [*ʿarsh*] is given for whatever is the difference.

... – but not for broken bones.

Equality is prescribed in reciprocal punishments for murder, so the guilty parties are likewise executed. Allah Most High says, "... And one who attacketh you, attack him in like manner as he attacked you..." [Q2:194]. ‹In the verse, "one who attacketh you," means "by fighting you in the Sacred Sanctuary", or "while making pilgrimage", or "during the inviolable months"; "...attack him in like manner as he attacked you..."– it is called "attack" because of the equivalent punishment's outward resemblance to the original crime.[26]›

However, an equivalent punishment is not implemented if it leads to something reprehensible, such as when the victim was

25. al-Bughā, *Al-Tadhhīb*, 197 #2.
26. al-Maḥallī and al-Suyūṭī, *Tafsīr al-Jalālayn*.

killed by magic, sodomy, or alcohol consumption. In that case, the perpetrator is executed by the sword and not in the way that he took the victim's life.

BLOOD INDEMNITY

(فصل) [الدّيات]

The word for blood indemnity "*diyāt*" is the plural of "*diyyah*." It is the obligatory compensation paid for killing or injuring an individual.

The legal foundation for blood indemnities [*diyāt*] is Allah Most High saying, "...then the blood-money must be paid unto his folk..." [Q4:92], as well as the instructions [from the Prophet ﷺ to] ʿAmr ibn Hazam (may Allah be pleased with him) and other reports mentioned within this section.

في النفس الكاملة لدى الموت مائة من غالب إبل البلد، أو إبل الجاني لا المعيب، ثمّ أقرب بلد ثمّ القيمة،

وللأنثى والمشكل النّصف، ولليهوديّ والنّصرانيّ الثّلث، وللمجوسيّ ونحوه [ثلث] الخمس.

The indemnity for taking a life [or its equivalent] is one hundred of the land's predominant [species of] camel,...

This is according to consensus and the verse cited above.

If the perpetrator already possesses another species of camels, those are used even if they are not predominant.

...or whatever [healthy,] defect-free camels the perpetrator has in his possession. Otherwise, it must be the predominant camel of the next closest land. [In the absence of the above, one must pay] their market value.

Originally, camels were used for payments. In their absence, their market value was used instead. The Prophet ﷺ appraised the *diyah* for villagers dwellers in camels. If the camels were expensive, he ﷺ raised the *diyah*'s value. And if they were cheap, he ﷺ lowered it.[27]

Half an indemnity is owed for females and hermaphrodites;...

[Muʿādh (may Allah be pleased with him)] said – in a report attributed to the Prophet ﷺ – that "A woman's blood money is half that of a man's."[28] The wisdom [*ḥikmah*] here is that blood money is a financial benefit and the Sacred Law has appraised the financial benefit of women to be half that of men – just as in an inheritance.

...one-third for Jews and Christians;...

Saʿīd ibn al-Musayyab (may Allah grant him His mercy) said, "ʿUmar (may Allah be pleased with him) made the blood money payment of Jews and Christians 4,000 [*dirhams*], and 800 [*dirhams*] for a Zoroastrian."[29]

...[one-third of] a fifth for Zoroastrians and their like.[30]

According to the old school, it is 800 *dirhams* [for a Zoroastrian], due to the previous hadith and due to another[31] ‹This is also narrated from ʿUthmān and Ibn Masʿūd, and it spread amongst the

27. ʿAmr ibn Shuʿayb from his father from his grandfather: Al-Shāfiʿī, *Al-Musnad,* p348; Nasāʾī, 4801. See: BM, 8:439.
28. Muʿadh: Bayhaqī, 16305; Ibn Abī Shaybah, *Al-Muṣannaf,* 27497, 27505. See: BM, 8:442, 8:468.
29. Saʿid ibn al-Musayyib: Al-Shāfiʿī, *Al-Musnad,* p354; Dāraquṭnī, 3247, 3248, 3290, 3291, 3355, 3356; Bayhaqī, 16338. cf Tirmidhī's notes concerning 1413. See: BM, 8:443–4, 8:469, 8:489–90.
30. See Marrying a Non-Muslim Woman and The Jizyah Contract.
31. ʿUqbah: Bayhaqī, 16344. See: BM, 8:444; TM, 373.

Companions (may Allah be pleased with them) without any known objection, making it a consensus.[32]›

According to the new school, it is one-fifteenth [lit. two-thirds of one-tenth] of the blood money owed for a Muslim. ‹ʿUmar, ʿUthmān and Ibn Masʿūd (may Allah be pleased with them) reported the blood money owed for a Zoroastrian is two-thirds of one-tenth that of a Muslim. Therefore, it has become consensus.[33]›

THE BLOOD INDEMNITY FOR A FETUS

(فصل) [دية الجنين]

ويجب في الجنين الحرّ المسلم غرّة عبد أو أمة سليمًا من عيب يثبت الردّ مميّزًا لم يضعف بالهرم يساوي خمسًا من الإبل بدله إن فقد، ثمّ قيمتها، وفي الرقيق عشر قيمة أمّه.

The indemnity for causing the miscarriage of a free Muslim's fetus is the freeing of a male or female slave who is free from defects [severe enough] to justify its return [to the previous owner, if sold], who has reached the age of discernment and is not infirm from old age.

The Messenger of Allah ﷺ judged this way.[34]

The indemnity equals five camels in place of a slave if none is found.

It was reported from ʿUmar and Zayd ibn Thābit without any opposition. (May Allah be pleased with them both.)

Otherwise, the value of the camels [is owed].

The indemnity for causing the miscarriage of a non-Muslim's fetus is one-third what is owed for a Muslim's.

---

32. al-Bughā, *Al-Tadhhīb,* 200 #1.

33. al-Bughā, *Al-Tadhhīb,* 200 #1.

34. Abū Hurayrah: Bukhārī, 5758; Muslim, 1681 #36. See: TM, 1563.

The indemnity for causing the death of a slave's fetus is one-tenth the value of its mother.

The mother's value is assessed as though she were free of any defects.

If the fetus's father is a Muslim, the mother's value is appraised as though she were a Muslim.

The fetus is also assumed to have been fully formed and free of defects [prior to death], since any injuries could have been from whatever caused the miscarriage, and precaution is most suitable here.

[The amount is] analogous to the blood money owed for a free woman's fetus since that amount is estimated to equal one-tenth the blood money owed for the mother.

FACTORS AUGMENTING MISTAKEN KILLINGS

(فصل) [متي تغلّظ دية الخطأ]

وتغلظ دية الخطأ إذا قتل في الحرم أو في الأشهر الحرم، ذي القعدة وذي الحجة والمحرم ورجب، أو ذا رحم محرم.

The indemnity for a mistaken killing is augmented if the murder occurred in the Sacred Precinct or during one of the Sacred Months (Dhi l-Qaᶜdah, Dhi l-Ḥijjah, al-Muḥarram, or Rajab); or [if the victim] was one's close kin.

The Companions (may Allah be pleased with them) augmented the indemnity for these reasons. The Shāfiᶜī colleagues [*aṣḥāb*] asserted that this augmentation became well known and was agreed upon.[35]

Augmentation is not compounded when there are multiple reasons for augmentation, since this was not related from the Companions (may Allah be pleased with them) nor is it from the Sunnah.

---

35. Mujāhid: Bayhaqī, 16135. See: BM, 8:483.

INJURIES THAT REQUIRE A FULL BLOOD-INDEMNITY

(فصل) [مكمّلات دية النفس]

ويكمل دية النّفس في الثّنائيّ: كاليدين، والرّجلين، واللحيين، والأذنين، والعينين، والشّفتين، والأنثيين، وحلمتي المرأة وأسكتيها، وفي الأجفان الأربعة، واللسان وحركته، وذهاب البصر، والسّمع، والكلام، والشّم، والعقل، والذّكر، وإفضاء المرأة، والجلد، والذّوق، والمضغ، والحشفة، والإمناء، والإحبال، والتلذّذ بالجماع والطّعام.

The full indemnity owed for a life is also owed for the loss of both members of a pair (two hands; two legs; two jaw bones; two ears; two eyes; two lips; two testicles; a woman's two nipples; and both of her labia majora); and for the loss of the four eyelids; the tongue and its mobility; eyesight, hearing, speech, smell, soundness of mind; the penis; for tearing a woman [e.g., between her vagina and anus]; [tearing] the skin; [damaging the ability to] taste or the ability to chew; [tearing] the prepuce of the penis; causing the inability to produce sperm, the inability to become pregnant, or the inability to enjoy intercourse or food.

ʿAmr ibn Ḥazam (may Allah be pleased with him) said that the Messenger of Allah ﷺ wrote a document to the people of Yemen containing [rules of] inheritance, sunan, and blood money. He ﷺ sent it with ʿAmr Ibn Ḥazam. It included: "For [taking a] life, there is blood money of 100 camels; for a nose that has been cut off completely, there is the [full] blood money; for the tongue there is the [full] blood money; for two lips there is the [full] blood money; for the two testicles there is the [full] blood money; for the penis there is the [full] blood money; for the backbone [*ṣulb*] the [full] blood money, for the two eyes the [full] blood money]; for a single leg half the [full] blood money."[36]

---

36. ʿAmr ibn Ḥazam: Nasāʾī, 4853; Ibn Ḥibbān, 6559; Ḥākim, 1447. See: TM, 1553.

Other versions include "for a single hand is half the [full] blood money," "for the ear there is fifty camels,"[37] and "There is complete blood money for loss of hearing."[38, 39]

Limbs, senses, and abilities not mentioned in the hadith are considered analogous to the ones that are.

The blood money owed for a single finger or toe is one-tenth of the complete blood money, because of a hadith from ʿAmr ibn Shuʿayb, from his father, from his grandfather [ʿAbd Allāh ibn ʿAmr ibn al-ʿĀṣ] (may Allah be pleased with him) concerning it: "...and for every digit from the hand and foot are ten camels...."[40]

There is no difference between one digit and another. Ibn ʿAbbās (may Allah be pleased with him) reported that the Prophet ﷺ said, "This and this are the same"[41] – meaning the pinky and the thumb.

WOUNDS THAT CLEAVE FLESH FROM THE BONE

(فصل) [دية الموضحة والسّن]

وفي موضحة الحرّ نصف عشر دية صاحبها، وكذا في ظاهر سن متغّير أو بان فساد المنبت.

A wound that cleaves flesh from the bone of a victim [*mūḍiḥah*] who is free requires half of one-tenth of the [complete] indemnity [i.e., five camels for a free Muslim male].

37. ʿAmr ibn Ḥazam: Bayhaqī, 16220.
38. Muʿadh ibn Jabal: Bayhaqī, 16224.
39. Muʿādh (not ʿAmr): Bayhaqī, 16230. See: TM, 1553.
40. ʿAmr ibn Shuʿayb, from his father, from his grandfather [ʿAbd Allāh ibn ʿAmr ibn al-ʿĀṣṣ]: Abū Dāwūd, 4563–64; Nasāʾī, 4851. See: BM, 8:457.
41. Ibn ʿAbbās: Bukhārī, 6895. See: BM, 8:457.

This is because of the hadith of ʿAmr ibn Shuʿayb, from his father, from his grandfather [ʿAbd Allāh ibn ʿAmr ibn al-ʿĀṣ] (may Allah be pleased with him).[42]

The same is owed for causing a tooth to change color or clearly damaging its root.

This is because of the earlier hadith of ʿAmr ibn Ḥazam (may Allah be pleased with him).[43]

Five camels are *not* owed for breaking a tooth.

For a *ḥāshimah* (a wound that reaches the bone and breaks it), one-tenth of an indemnity is owed.

For a *jāʾifah* (a wound that reaches the inside of the body), one-third of an indemnity is owed.

For a *maʾmūnah* (a wound that reaches the membrane around the brain), one-third of an indemnity is owed.

For a *munaqilah* (a wound that moves bones after breaking them), one-tenth of an indemnity is owed. (This is according to consensus).

The above indemnities are based upon the hadith of ʿAmr Ibn Ḥazam (may Allah be pleased with him) and others. The letter that the Messenger of Allah ﷺ sent to ʿAmr ibn Ḥazam included: "For a head injury, one-third of the indemnity is paid; for a stab that penetrates the body, one-third of the indemnity; for a blow that breaks a bones or dislocates it, fifteen camels."[44]

---

42. ʿAmr ibn Shuʿayb, from his father, from his grandfather [ʿAbd Allāh ibn ʿAmr ibn al-ʿĀṣṣ]: Abū Dāwūd, 4566; Tirmidhī, 1390; Ibn Mājah, 2655; Nasāʾī, 4852; al-Bayhaqī, 16195, 16279. See: TM, 1559.

43. ʿAmr ibn Ḥazam: Nasāʾī, 4853; Dāraquṭnī, 3482; Ibn Ḥibbān, 6559; Ḥākim, 1447. See: TM, 1554.

44. ʿAmr ibn Ḥazam: Abū Dāwūd, 4564; Nasāʾī, 4853, 4857; Dāraquṭnī, 3480; Bayhaqī, 16191, 16207, 16216, 16219; Ḥākim, 1447; al-Bazzār, 261. See: TM, 1554.

APPRAISAL

(فصل) [الحكومة]

وفيما لا مقدّر فيه الحكومة: وهي جزء نسبته إلى دية النّفس، نسبة نقصها من قيمته لو كان رقيقًا بصفاته.

An appraisal [*ḥukūmah*] is made for any injury that does not have a particular punishment [associated with it].

An appraisal is owed for injuries to nonfunctional parts of the body. Examples include a paralyzed hand, an extra digit, a male's nipples, and the like.

The appraisal is a portion of the complete indemnity and is proportionally equal to the reduction in the person's market value if he were a slave with the same injuries.

Suppose the victim's value is estimated to have been ten [units of currency, for example] before the injury and nine afterwards. The difference is one-tenth, so he is owed one-tenth of an indemnity.

BLOOD INDEMNITY FOR SLAVES

(فصل) [دية الرّقيق]

وفي الرّقيق القيمة، وما ضمن من الحرّ بالدّية ضمن منه بالقيمة أو بالحكومة فيما نقص.

The indemnity for killing a slave is the slave's value.

This is because a slave is a type of property – like all other properties [its value is used].

Whatever is compensated for a free person via an appraisal is compensated for a slave – according to his value or an appraisal based on the loss [in his value].[45]

MURDER ALLEGATIONS

(فصل) [القسامة]

The textual foundation for murder allegations [*qasāmah*] is from Sahl ibn Abī Ḥathmah (may Allah be pleased with him) who said, "ʿAbd Allāh ibn Sahl and Muḥayyiṣah ibn Masʿūd (may Allah be pleased with them) travelled to Khaybar when there was a [peace] agreement [between the Muslims and the Jews]. The two got separated amidst the date palms and Muḥayyisah later found ʿAbd Allāh ibn Sahl covered in blood, dead. He buried him and returned to Medina. Then Muḥayyisah and Ḥuwayyiṣah – the two sons of Masʿūd – and ʿAbd al-Raḥmān ibn Sahl [the brother of the victim] set out to meet with the Prophet ﷺ. ʿAbd al-Raḥmān began to speak but the Messenger of Allah ﷺ said to him, 'The greater first, the greater first' – meaning the older in age was to speak. So he remained quiet as the others spoke. He ﷺ then said, 'Do you swear with fifty oaths and claim the blood-money of your companion or the life of the murderer?' They said, 'O Messenger of Allah, it's an event we did not witness!' The Messenger of Allah ﷺ said, 'Will you acquit the Jews for fifty oaths?' They said, 'How can we take the oaths of people who are disbelievers?' So he ﷺ paid them the blood-money himself."[46]

45. See "Appraisal" on page 443.

46. Sahl ibn Abī Hathmah: Bukhārī, 6142; Muslim, 1669; Abū Dāwūd, 4520; Tirmidhī, 1422; Nasāʾī, 4712–3, 4716–7; Ibn Ḥibbān, 6009; Bayhaqī, 16431–5, 16450. See: See al-Shāfiʿī, *Al-Umm*, 7:157; BM, 8:509; cf TM, 1566.

تثبت القسامة في القتل بمحل لوث، وهو قرينة لصدق المدّعي، كأن تفرّق جمع عن قتل، فيحلف على قتل ادعاه خمسين يمينًا ويستحقّ الدّية.

Sworn allegations are established [as evidence] for murders if other evidence corroborates the accuser's claim,...

Something unique to killing is that it can be established by a sworn oath [from the accusers] when there is corroborating evidence. This is in contrast to all other allegations in which the oath is made by the accused. The basis for this is the hadith: "Evidence is required of the accuser and the oath is required from the one who denies it – except in murder allegations [*qassāmah*]."[47]

Corroboration can be circumstantial or spoken. Circumstantial corroboration includes finding the victim in a town or place inhabited solely by his enemies. Spoken corroboration includes testimony from one upright male or from someone whose testimony is not accepted for injurious crimes (such as women and children) in the form of "So-and-so killed so-and-so."

...like if a group [is seen] walking away from a murder victim, the survivor swears fifty oaths concerning the alleged murder[ers] and is then entitled to the indemnity.

The Prophet ﷺ said [in the hadith mentioned at the beginning of this section], "Will you acquit the Jews for fifty oaths?"[48]

The oaths are spread over the heirs of the victim according to their shares, since he ﷺ did not require other than fifty oaths from the group.[49]

---

47. ʿAmr ibn Shuʿayb from his father from his grandfather: Dāraquṭnī, 3190, 3191, 4507, 4508; Bayhaqī, 16445. See: BM, 8:513.
48. Sahl ibn Abī Hathmah: Bukhārī, 6142; Muslim, 1669; Abū Dāwūd, 4520; Tirmidhī, 1422; Nasā'ī, 4712–3, 4716–7; Ibn Ḥibbān, 6009; Bayhaqī, 16431–5, 16450. See: BM, 8:509; cf TM, 1566.
49. Sahl ibn Abī Hathmah: Bukhārī, 6142; Muslim, 1669. See: BM, 8:509; cf TM, 1566.

If the other heirs refuse to swear or are not present, the one requesting the indemnity fulfills the fifty oaths. If one of them returns, he makes half of the oaths. If a third returns, he makes one third of the oaths, and so forth.

EXPIATION FOR KILLING

(فصل) [كفارة القتل]

وفي قتل المعصوم كفارة مرتبة لكن لا إطعام.

Killing someone whose life is sacrosanct...

All life is sacrosanct except for that of a non-Muslim who is at war with Muslims, an apostate, an adulterer whom the court has sentenced to death by stoning, and anyone who Muslims are obliged to kill by military action.

Allah Most High says, "Whoever killed a believer..." [Q4:93] – which excludes aggressors against Islam.

The Messenger of Allah ﷺ said, "The blood of a Muslim is not permissible except in three [instances]: a married fornicator, a life for a life, and the one who abandons his religion and separates from the community."[50]

‹In this hadith, "a life for a life" refers to deliberate murder; "abandons his religion" means an apostate from Islam; and "the community" is the general community of Muslims.

Non-Muslims who are residents of the Islamic state [*ahl ul-dhimmah*] or who have been given amnesty [*musta'mīn*] are analogous to Muslims regarding the above. So are the young, the elderly, and even fetuses.[51]›

---

50. Ibn ʿUmar: Bukhārī, 6878; Muslim, 1676. See: TM, 1538.
51. al-Bughā, *Al-Tadhhīb*, 203 #1.

...requires an expiation that is in stages but does not include feeding [the poor].

Allah Most High says, "...He who hath killed a believer by mistake must set free a believing slave, and pay the blood-money to the family of the slain, unless they remit it as a charity. If he (the victim) be of a people hostile unto you, and he is a believer, then (the penance is) to set free a believing slave. And if he cometh of a folk between whom and you there is a covenant, then the blood-money must be paid unto his folk and (also) a believing slave must be set free. And whoso hath not the wherewithal must fast two consecutive months. A penance from Allah. Allah is Knower, Wise" [Q4:92].

‹In this verse, "slave" refers to both male and female; "remit it as a charity" means pardoning the killer; and "a folk between whom and you there is a covenant" refers to when the victim is from a community with whom the Muslims have an agreement (e.g., *dhimmah* or amnesty [*amān*]) and the victim is of their religion or is a Muslim.

Expiation is also required in a semi-intentional killing because it resembles a deliberate killing.›[52]

An expiation is required for a deliberate killing because of the report from Wā'ilah ibn al-Asqaʿ (may Allah be pleased with him): "We came to the Messenger of Allah ﷺ concerning a companion of ours who deserved Hell for murder. He ﷺ said, 'Emancipate a slave on his behalf...' (and in another version: 'He is to free a slave...') '...[and then] Allah will set a member of his body free from the Fire for every member of the slave's body.'"[53]

‹The scholars said that the Fire does not become obligatory except for deliberate killing, thus indicating the legal basis for the expiation. And an expiation for a mistaken killing is even more appropriate.[54]›

52. al-Bughā, *Al-Tadhhīb,* 204 #1.

53. Wā'ilah ibn al-Asqaʿ: Abū Dāwūd, 3964. See: KBM, 2315.

54. al-Bughā, *Al-Tadhhīb,* 204 #1.

RENEGADES

(فصل) [البغاة]

ويقاتل أهل البغي إذا كان لهم شوكة، وتأويل، ومطاع، بعد الإنذار، ولا يقاتل المدبّر ولا مثخنهم، وأسيرهم، ولا يغنم مالهم.

Those who rebel against the Imam are fought...

The foundation for the legal legitimacy of fighting Muslims who rebel against the Imam [*ahl al-baghī*] is Allah Most High saying, "And if two parties of believers fall to fighting, then make peace between them. And if one party of them doeth wrong to the other, fight ye that which doeth wrong till it return unto the ordinance of Allah; then, if it return, make peace between them justly, and act equitably. Lo! Allah loveth the equitable" [Q49:9]. Also, there is consensus amongst the Companions (may Allah be pleased with them) that rebels are to be fought.

‹As understood from the evidence, it is an obligation to fight the renegades – at the Imam's behest – when the rebellion is between two groups, so fighting them when the rebellion is against the Imam himself is even more appropriate.[55]›

'Arfajah (may Allah be pleased with him) said: "I heard the Messenger of Allah ﷺ say, 'Whoever comes to you when your affairs are united and tries to disrupt or disunite you is to be fought.'" And in another version: 'Whoever wants to disunite the affairs of this community while they are united, you are to strike him with the sword – no matter who he is.'"[56]

...if they pose a true physical threat,...

If they have the capability to oppose the Imam, such as by protecting themselves in a fortress, or taking over a Muslim land, then fighting them is necessary to repel their threat. They pose no real threat if they lack the capability to oppose the Imam.

55. al-Bughā, *Al-Tadhhīb,* 219 #1.

56. 'Arfajah: Muslim, 1852. See: TM, 1567.

...possess a reasonable explanation [for disobeying the Imam],...

Because if their explanation is indisputably false, they are treated as apostates – not as Muslim renegades. And because there is room for severity in matters that are certainly false.

...and have followers – but only after they have been warned.

It is permissible to fight them once they have been warned, just as ʿAlī (may Allah be pleased with him) did to the people of Nahrawān.[57]

Those who flee the battle, are wounded, or captured, are not executed.

The Prophet ﷺ said, "Those who flee are not pursued, and their wounded are not put to death."[58]

The renegades are not fought with fire, flood, or catapults if they have not used such weapons in their rebellion since the objective is to return them to obedience. However, if they do use them, it is permissible to use those same weapons against them.

Their property is not taken as spoils of war.

This is because they are Muslims.

Captured renegades are not released until they are no longer considered a threat. Once they are no longer a threat, their women and children are set free first. Then the men are released once they make a covenant not to return to fighting. They are not set free any earlier in order to break their morale.

Their legal judgments and collecting of zakat are affirmed if their actions agree with our judgments and they do not declare us [other

57. ʿAbd al-Razzāq, *Al-Muṣannaf,* 5962; Ibn Abī Shaybah, *Al-Muṣannaf,* 37929. See: BM, 8:550, 8:562.

58. Ibn ʿUmar: Ḥākim, 2662; Bayhaqī, 16755. See: KBM, 2337.

Muslims] permissible to kill. Another condition is that they pose a threat and have a [reasonable] justification for their rebellion.

THE SUPREME IMAM

(فصل) [الإمام]

CONDITIONS FOR SUITABILITY

شرط الإمام: كونه ذكرًا، حرًا، قرشيًّا، مجتهدًا، شجاعًا، ذا رأي وكمال أعضاء وسمع وبصر ونطق.

Suitability for the role of the Supreme Imam is conditional upon the person being
1. male,

Abū Bakrah (may Allah be pleased with him) reported that the Prophet ﷺ said, "A people who put a woman in charge of their affairs will not succeed."[59]

2. free,
3. from the tribe of Quraish,

Anas (may Allah be pleased with him) reported that the Prophet ﷺ said, "Imams are from Quraish."[60]

4. a *mujtahid*,[61]

The Imam should be well versed in the rulings pertaining to the Muslim community to know the legal rulings of various matters [and, thus, how to decide and legislate according to the Sacred Law].

---

59. Abū Bakrah: Bukhārī, 4425, 7099; Tirmidhī, 2262; Nasā'ī, 5388; al-Ḥākim, 4608; See TM, 1569, 1764.
60. Nasā'ī, Al-Kubrā, 5909; al-Ḥākim, 6962. See TM, 1570.
61 A *mujtahid* is someone who is qualified to employ legal reasoning to derive rulings in Sacred Law.

5. **astute,**
6. **possessing all of his limbs, hearing, eyesight, and speech.**

The Imam needs all of his faculties to properly govern and settle the various affairs of the Muslims.

The Imam must be a Muslim, male, responsible, and free; to be anything other than these is a deficiency.

وينعقد ببيعه أهل الحلّ والعقد، وباستخلاف الإمام، وبجعل الأمر شورى بين جمع، بالاستيلاء.

The Imam is installed in one of four ways:

1. **The people who enact and repeal community decisions [*ahl al-ḥall wa al-ʿaqd*] pledge their allegiance to him;**

Because they organize community affairs, the masses will follow their lead.

2. **he is appointed successor by the [previous] Imam;**

Abū Bakr appointed ʿUmar (may Allah be pleased with them both).

3. **he is selected by an appointed advisory group; or**

This is what ʿUmar (may Allah be pleased with him) ordered and ʿUthmān was eventually chosen.

4. **he seizes control by force.**

Leadership organizes society, even if those who gain power are sinful in doing so.

وينظر في أمر الرعية دينا ودنيا.

The Imam oversees the religious and temporal affairs of the people.

APOSTASY

(فصل) [الرِّدَّة]

Linguistically, the word for apostasy ["*riddah*"] means "reverting from one thing to another." Its legal meaning is found in the next section.

Apostasy is the most monstrous type of disbelief and therefore warrants the harshest penalty. May Allah protect us from it. Its foundation includes Allah Most High saying, "...whoso of you becometh a renegade from his religion..." [Q5:54], and the statement from the Prophet ﷺ: "Whoever changes his religion is to be killed."[62]

WHAT CONSTITUTES APOSTASY

الرِّدَّة قطع المسلم المكلف المختار الإسلام بنيّة أو قول كفر، أو فعل عنادًا، أو استهزاءً، أو اعتقادًا، كإلقاء مصحف بقاذورات، وقذف نبيّ، ولا شيء إن أسلم، ويقبل توبته حتى الزّنديق.

Apostasy is a [legally] responsible Muslim voluntarily removing himself from Islam, by means of intending to do so or by committing an act of disbelief in word or deed, whether rebelliously, or mockingly, or with conviction – such as placing a written Quran [*muṣḥaf*] in filth or accusing one of the prophets [peace be upon them one and all] of fornication. (Nothing is done [in the later case] if the accuser re-enters Islam.)

Apostasy also occurs by means of denying something that is necessarily known in Islam, such as Hajj being obligatory, and that wine and fornication are unlawful.

An apostate's repentance is accepted – even if he is a *zindīq*.

Allah Most High says, "Tell those who disbelieve that if they cease (from persecution of believers) that which is past will be forgiven

62. Ibn ʿAbbās: Bukhārī, 6922. See: TM, 1571.

them..." [Q8:38]. And due to the generality of the Prophet ﷺ saying, "And if they say [that there is no deity save Allah and that Muhammad is the Messenger of Allah], then their lives and property are inviolate to me except by a right of Islam and their accounting is upon Allah."[63]

A *zindīq* is someone who is irreligious, or who outwardly displays belief while inwardly disbelieving.

REPENTANCE

وتجب استتابته بلا مهل، فإن تاب بأن تلفّظ الشّهادتين، وبرىء من كلّ دين خالف الإسلام إن كان على دين يزعم أهله اختصاص الرّسالة بالعرب، وإلّا قتل.

The apostate must be given the opportunity to repent without delay.

It is obligatory to seek his repentance (through his return to Islam) before he is killed. Jābir (may Allah be pleased with him) said that a woman known as Umm Marwān had left Islam. The Prophet ﷺ commanded that Islam be presented to her [again] and ordered that she be killed if she did not repent.[64]

The apostate repents by pronouncing the two testimonies of faith [*shahādatayn*] and renouncing every religion besides Islam, including any claim that Islam was sent only to Arabs. If he refuses, he is executed.

The Prophet ﷺ said, "Whoever changes his religion is to be killed."[65]

---

63. Ibn ʿUmar: Bukhārī, 25; Muslim, 22. See: TM, 748.

64. Jābir: Dāraquṭnī, 3215. See: KBM, 2357.

65. Ibn ʿAbbās: Bukhārī, 3017, 6922; Abū Dāwūd, 4351; Tirmidhī, 1458; Nasāʾī, 4059–65; Ibn Mājah, 2535; Ibn Ḥibbān, 4475, 5606; Dāraquṭnī, 3182, 3200; Ḥākim, 6295; Bayhaqī, 16820, 16858, 16860, 16877, 18062. See: TM, 1571.

The Prophet ﷺ said, "The blood of a Muslim is inviolate except through one of three things..." and included "...one who forsakes his religion and separates from the community."[66]

Abū Mūsā al-Ashʿarī (may Allah be pleased with him) said that the Prophet ﷺ dispatched him to Yemen and later sent Muʿādh ibn Jabal (may Allah be pleased with him) after him. When Muʿādh arrived, he [Abū Mūsā] spread out a pillow for him and told him to descend [from his mount]. There was man in restraints beside him [Abū Mūsā]. He [Muʿādh] said, "What's this?" He [Abū Mūsā] replied, "He was a Jew. He entered Islam and then became a Jew [again]." He [Abū Mūsā] said, "Sit." He [Muʿādh] said, "I will not sit until he is killed, according to the decision of Allah and His Messenger" – [repeating it] three times. He [Abū Mūsā] then ordered that he [the apostate] be killed.[67]

‹An apostate is not buried in a Muslim graveyard since he has ceased being one of them. Allah Most High says, "And whoso becometh a renegade and dieth in his disbelief..." [Q2:217].[68]›

66. Ibn ʿUmar: Bukhārī, 6878; Muslim, 1676. See: TM, 1538.

67. Abū Mūsā: Bukhārī, 6923; Muslim, 1456. See: TM, 1573.

68. al-Bughā, *Al-Tadhhīb,* 224 #1.

11

PUNISHMENTS

كِتَابُ الْحُدُودِ

The phrase "*ḥadd*" means "to prevent." Some punishments are called a "*ḥadd*" for this reason, such as "the *ḥadd* for theft," which deters theft.

FORNICATION

(فصل) [الزّنا]

Fornication [*zinā*] is unlawful according to the consensus of all revealed religions.[1]

The legal basis [for the grave criminality of fornication] comes from Allah Most High saying, "The fornicator and the fornicator, scourge each one of them..." [Q24:2], and from the fact that he ﷺ stoned Māʿiz (may Allah grant him His mercy and be pleased with him). It also includes other well-known evidence.[2]

During Islam's early years, the punishment for fornication was imprisonment and chastisement, due to Allah Most High saying, "As for those of your women who are guilty of lewdness, call to witness four of you against them. And if they testify (to the truth of the allegation) then confine them to the houses until death take them or (until) Allah appoint for them a way (through new legislation)" [Q4:15]. Then the matter settled on the punishment of flogging and banishment for virgins and stoning for non-virgins.

1 According to Sacred Law, this includes Judaism, Christianity, Islam, and Zoroastrianism.

2. Ibn ʿAbbās: Bukhārī, 6824. See TM, 1583.

THOSE WITH THE CAPACITY TO REMAIN CHASTE

حدّ المحصن: وهو المكلّف الحرّ المصيب بنكاح صحيح الرّجم، بإيلاج فرج في فرج محرّم لعينه خال عن شبهة.

The punishment for someone who has the capacity to remain chaste [*muḥṣan*] (someone who is [legally] responsible, free, and has had intercourse within a valid marriage),...

It is not a condition that the person still be married. If the perpetrator is within the age of discernment but not yet an adult, he is disciplined in a manner that will prevent a repeat offense – even if he is immature or insane.

...who has inserted his penis into the vagina or anus [*farj*]...

The word "*farj*" refers to both a woman's vagina and the anus of either sex.

...of an individual with whom it is unlawful to have intercourse,...

This excludes cases in which intercourse is temporarily unlawful due to menstruation, lochia (postnatal bleeding), fasting, pilgrimage, or the like. There is no prescribed punishment for these instances since intercourse is not unlawful in itself. Rather, it is unlawful during menstruation and lochia due to the harm it causes, and unlawful during the other times because it violates the sanctity of worship.

...when the act is free of dubiousness;...

For example, having sex with his sister whom he owns as a slave [since ownership is a cause for dubiousness].

Ibn ʿAbbās (may Allah be pleased with them both) said, "When Māʿiz ibn Mālik (may Allah be pleased with him) came to the Prophet ﷺ [to confess to fornication], he ﷺ said, 'Perhaps you kissed, touched, or looked [at her].' But Māʿiz said, 'Nay, O Messenger of Allah ﷺ.' He ﷺ said – without using any euphemism, 'Did you have intercourse with her?' And [when Māʿiz indicated that he had] that is when he ﷺ ordered that Māʿiz be stoned."[3]

Partial ownership [of a slave] is an excuse for doubt, even if the act was committed with a Zoroastrian or a *maḥram*.

A marriage contract that is invalid according to consensus is not an excuse for doubt. Neither is a marriage contract with someone who became a *maḥram* via nursing, kin, or marriage.

Contracts of disputed validity are also an excuse for doubt, such as a marriage without the bride's guardian or any witnesses.

Another condition is that the person knew that it is unlawful. There is no prescribed punishment if they are new to Islam or were raised in the wilderness – far away from scholars – and did not know that it is unlawful. The prescribed punishment is obligatory, however, if they knew that fornication is unlawful but are ignorant of it requiring a prescribed punishment.

Another condition is that the act be committed consensually. There is no prescribed punishment for someone who was compelled to do so.

...is stoning [until death].

The Prophet ﷺ lapidated al-Ghāmidiyyah and Māʿiz ibn Mālik (may Allah be pleased with them).[4]

3. Ibn ʿAbbās: Bukhārī, 6824. See TM, 1583.

4. Buraydah: Bukhārī, 6825; Muslim, 1695 #22, 23; Abū Dāwūd, 4442; Nasāʾī, *Al-Sunan Al-Kubrā,* 7148; Dāraquṭnī, 3129; Bayhaqī, 16928, 16956, 16993. See: TM, 1539, 1588.

OTHER CATEGORIES OF FORNICATORS

و[حدّ] غيره جلد مائة وترغيب عام.

The punishment for other fornicators is a flogging of one hundred lashes and banishment for one year.

Allah Most High says, "The male and female fornicators, scourge ye each one of them (with) a hundred stripes. And let not pity for the twain withhold you from obedience to Allah, if ye believe in Allah and the Last Day. And let a party of believers witness their punishment" [Q24:2].

The Prophet ﷺ said, "Receive from me! Receive from me! Allah has ordained a way for them! When a virgin fornicates with a virgin, lash them one hundred times and banish them for a year. A non-virgin with a non-virgin receives one hundred lashes and stoning."[5]

‹In this verse, "And let not pity for the twain withhold you from obedience to Allah" means carrying out His orders and implementing His punishments; "their punishment" is the punishment being carried out upon them; and "party of believers…witness their punishment" is so encourage the believers to reflect, which would serve as a deterrent for them. The men and women mentioned in the verse are not married [non-*muḥṣin*] since it is already known that married individuals are stoned.[6]›

The place of exile must be at least as far away as the minimum distance allowed for shortening prayers [81 kilometers or 50 miles]. The purpose is to alienate the fornicators by putting them far from their families and homeland. When the distance is less than this, contact will still be possible so the alienation will not be complete.

Additional evidence for banishment includes the hadith narrated by Zayd ibn Khālid (may Allah be pleased with him) who said, "I heard the Messenger of Allah ﷺ command that those who

---

5. ʿUbādat ibn al-Ṣāmit: Muslim, 1690 #12–14; Abū Dāwūd, 4415, 4416; Tirmidhī, 1434; Nasāʾī, *Al-Sunan al-kubrā,* 7142–7144; Ibn Mājah, 2550. See: TM, 1574.

6. al-Bughā, *Al-Tadhhīb,* 206 #1.

fornicate and are not married be flogged one hundred times and banished for a year."[7]

‹Ibn Shihāb (may Allah grant him His mercy) said, "ʿUrwah ibn al-Zubayr informed me that ʿUmar ibn al-Khaṭṭāb (may Allah be pleased with him) exiled such a person, and this tradition is still valid."[8]›

A woman is not banished alone. Rather, she is sent away with her husband or a male relative. This is because Abū Hurayrah (may Allah be pleased with him) reported that the Prophet ﷺ said, "It is not permissible for a Muslim woman to travel a night's journey except accompanied by unmarriageable male kin."[9]

SLAVES

و[حدّ] الرّقيق نصفه.

A slave's punishment is half that of a freeman.

Allah Most High says, "...And if when they are honourably married they commit lewdness they shall incur the half of the punishment (prescribed) for free women..." [Q4:25]. ‹The verse means that if a slave girl fornicates, she receives half the punishment of a free woman: fifty lashes and banishment for half a year, whether she was married at the time or not. She is not stoned (and stoning is never a rational possibility for slaves) since stoning to death cannot be implemented halfway, and because one of its conditions is the ability to remain chaste, which is negated when one is a slave.

The verse mentions only female slaves but since male slaves are analogous to female slaves, the meaning applies to both.[10]›

Also, a male's status is diminished by his being a slave, so it is half that of a freeman – just like in marriage and during the waiting period.

7. Zayd ibn Khālid: Bukhārī, 2649. See: KBM, 2366.
8. al-Bughā, *Al-Tadhhīb*, 206 #1.
9. Abū Hurayrah: Muslim, 1339 #419. See TM, 1581.
10. al-Bughā, *Al-Tadhhīb*, 207 #3.

The punishment is carried out by the Sultan or his representative [once guilt has been established] in one of two ways:

[1] The perpetrator's admission (due to the hadith of Māʿiz[11]) – even if it is a single utterance. The Prophet ﷺ said to Unays (may Allah be pleased with him): "Go to this man's wife. If she admits it, stone her."[12]

[2] The testimony of four upright male witnesses. Allah Most High Says, "As for those of your women who are guilty of lewdness, call to witness four of you against them" [Q4:15].

The witnesses must testify to have [personally] seen the act – not just to have heard it – even if it is *shahādat al-ḥisbah.*

The punishment is not carried out on a woman while she is pregnant or nursing.

A punishment established by a confession can be retracted, since the Prophet ﷺ said in the hadith concerning Māʿiz (may Allah be pleased with him): "Perhaps you kissed. Perhaps you touched."[13]

ACCUSING A PERSON OF FORNICATION

(فصل) [القذف]

The phrase "*qadhf*" means "to cast." What is intended here is casting a shameful accusation of fornication.

The foundation for its punishment is Allah Most High saying, "And those who accuse honourable women but bring not four witnesses, scourge them (with) eighty stripes and never (afterward) accept their testimony..." [Q24:4].

---

11. Preceded. Bukhārī, 6825; Muslim, 1695 #22, 23; and others. See: TM, 1583–4.
12. Abū Hurayrah and Zayd ibn Khālid: Bukhārī, 6827; Muslim, 1697 #25. See: TM, 1582.
13. Ibn ʿAbbās: Bukhārī, 6824; Abū Dāwūd, 4427; Nasāʾī, *Al-Sunan al-kubrā,* 7130–1; Ibn Khuzaymah, 30; Dāraquṭnī, 3225–3227; Ḥākim, 8076; Bayhaqī, 16994. See: TM, 1583.

WHAT CONSTITUTES AN ACCUSATION AND ITS PUNISHMENT

إذا قذف مكلّف مختار - ليس بأصل - محصنًا جلد ثمانين.

When a [legally] responsible individual...

‹The prescribed penalty for a false accusation by a legally responsible adult is [corporal] punishment. Individuals who are immature or insane are not legally responsible, so there is no prescribed punishment for them, which is analogous to their legal status in regard to fornication.[14]›

Some books mention "adherent" instead of "responsible" since the punishment applies to Muslims, *dhimmīs*, apostates, and individuals given amnesty [i.e., those living under Muslim rule who must adhere to Sacred Law]. It does not include individuals at war with Islam.

...(other than a parent or ancestor)...

A father is not killed for killing his son (as mentioned previously[15]). A fortiori, he is not punished for accusing his son of fornication. All ancestors – male and female – are analogous to the father.

...willfully...

Someone acting under compulsion is not punished. The Prophet ﷺ said, "...and things you were compelled to do..."[16]

14. al-Bughā, *Al-Tadhhīb,* 209 #1.

15. See "Reciprocal Punishments" on page 431.

16. Ibn ʿAbbās: Ibn Mājah, 2044–5; Dāraquṭnī, 4351; Bayhaqī, 11454, 15094, 20013; Ibn Ḥibbān, 7219; Ḥākim, 2801. See: TM, 1486.

...accuses...

Examples include saying "You fornicator" or "You adulterer." Negating that someone is the son of the person known to be his father is an accusation against the mother.

If the phrase is not explicit, there is no punishment, unless the accuser admits that it was intended to indicate fornication.

...someone who has the capacity to remain chaste...

There is no prescribed punishment [for the accuser] if the accused is a slave or a non-Muslim.

Similarly, the accused must be mature and of sound mind. So there is no prescribed punishment for accusing a child or someone who is insane.

...of fornication [without presenting sufficient evidence], the accuser is flogged eighty lashes.

This is if the accuser makes an explicit accusation and cannot substantiate his claim.

Allah Most High says, "And those who accuse honourable women but bring not four witnesses, scourge them (with) eighty stripes and never (afterward) accept their testimony – They indeed are evil-doers..." [Q24:4].

Abū Bakrah and two others testified against al-Mughīrah. A fourth came to testify but would not confirm that he saw the actual act of penetration, so ʿUmar ordered that the three be flogged.[17] (May Allah be pleased with them.)

---

17. ʿAbd al-ʿAzīz ibn Abī Bakrah: Ḥākim, 5892. Abū ʿUthmān al-Nahdī: ʿAbd al-Razzāq, *Al-Muṣannaf,* 13566; al-Ṭabarānī, 7227; Bayhaqī, 20524; Ibn Abī Shaybah, *Al-Muṣannaf,* 28822. See: KBM, 2407.

SLAVES

والرّقيق على النّصف.

A slave's punishment is half that of a freeman.

Since the number of lashes can be halved, slaves receive half the punishment [forty lashes] because it is analogous to the punishment for fornication. Allah Most High says, "...they shall incur the half of the punishment (prescribed) for free women..." [Q4:25].

IF EVIDENCE IS PRESENTED

فإن أقام بيّنة بزناه أو عفى المقذوف سقط.

The punishment is waived if the accuser presents evidence of the fornication or if the accused pardons him.

This is because the punishment for spurious accusations of fornication is meant to repel the shame from the accused. This is solely an individual right [i.e., not a right owed to Allah Most High or society as a whole], so the punishment is waived if the accused pardons the accuser – just like with other individual rights. Similarly, the punishment is not carried out without the consent and insistence of the victim – just as with reciprocal punishments.

If a group is accused of fornication and some of them pardon the accuser, the rest still have the right to demand punishment since that right is established for each and every one of them – like guardianship for marriage.

Sheikh ʿIzz al-Dīn [ibn ʿAbd al-Salām] (may Allah grant him His mercy) said that when an accusation of fornication is made in private such that no one other than Allah and one's guardian angels hear it, the most apparent opinion is that it is not considered an enormity that prompts a prescribed punishment. This is because it is free of the harm of injuring another individual. Thus, one is not punished in the afterlife except for making a harmless lie.

IF THE ACCUSER MAKES A PUBLIC IMPRECATION

وكذا إذا لاعن كما مضى.

Similarly, [the punishment is lifted] if [the accuser] makes a public imprecation – as mentioned earlier.[18]

Because invoking Allah's curse upon oneself is the graver of the two, the punishment is averted.

ALCOHOL AND LIQUID INTOXICANTS

(فصل) [الشّرب]

Drinking intoxicants is among the enormities [in Sacred Law]. Allah Most High says, "O ye who believe! Strong drink and games of chance and idols and divining arrows are only an infamy of Satan's handiwork. Leave it aside in order that ye may succeed" [Q5:90]; and "Say: My Lord forbiddeth only indecencies, such of them as are apparent and such as are within, and sin..." [Q7:33]. This refers to alcohol, according to most scholars. There is consensus that its unlawfulness is based on the Quran, which the Sunnah then confirmed.

The consumption of alcohol was permissible in the early days of Islam. The [primary and] more fitting reason for its permissibility (according to *Al-Ḥāwī*) is the preservation of continuity in its ruling prior to Islam. The secondary reason is due to legislation concerning it (Allah Most High said, "And from the fruits of the palm trees and grapevines you take intoxicant and good provision..." [Q16:67]), and that it was later prohibited by consensus.[19]

18. See "Charging One's Wife With Adultery" on page 363.
19. al-Māwardī, *Al-Ḥāwi,* 13:376.

إذا شرب الملتزم المختار مسكر جنس بغير ضرورة، ضرب أربعين سوطًا للحرّ، وله أن يبلغه ثمانين تعزيرًا، ولا يحدّ بالرّيح.

When someone who is obliged to follow the law willfully drinks any sort of intoxicant...

The Arabic word "*khamr*" refers, literally, to grape juice when it becomes intoxicating. Does its literal sense apply to various types of *nabīdh* [a drink where water and a date or raisin is kept in a container until it ferments but is not yet intoxicating]? In *Al-Rawḍah,* Imam al-Nawawī (may Allah grant him His mercy) said that the majority of scholars say it does not.[20]

The ruling here applies to any liquid intoxicant, regardless of the source, name, or quantity. The Prophet ﷺ said, "I forbid you from small quantities of that which intoxicates in large quantities."[21] ʿĀʾishah (may Allah be pleased with her and her father) said that the Prophet ﷺ said, "Every drink that intoxicates is unlawful."[22]

Jābir (may Allah be pleased with him) said that the Prophet ﷺ said, "If a large quantity of a thing intoxicates, a small quantity is unlawful."[23]

...without necessity, he is flogged forty lashes, if a freeman.

Anas (may Allah be pleased with him) reported that "the Prophet ﷺ used to strike [the offender] forty times with shoes and palm branches [without leaves] for [consuming] wine. Abū Bakr would strike forty times, and ʿUmar eighty times [may Allah be pleased with them]."[24] All of these punishments are sunnah.

---

20. al-Nawawī, *Rawḍat al-ṭālibīn,* 10:168.
21. ʿĀmir ibn Saʿd from his father: al-Nasāʾī, 5608. See: TM, 1603.
22. ʿĀʾishah: Bukhārī, 242, 5585, 5586; Muslim, 2001 #67, #68.
23. Jābir: Abū Dāwūd, 3681; Tirmidhī, 1865 – *ḥasan gharīb*; Ibn Mājah, 3393; Ibn Ḥibbān, 5382; Ibn Ḥibbān, 5358. See: KBM, 2433; cf TM, 1603.
24. Anas: Muslim, 1706 #35–37. See: BM, 8:718; cf KBM, 2451; cf TM, 1607.

Anas (may Allah be pleased with him) said that he ﷺ would hit with palm fronds and sandals.[25]

A drunk was brought to the Prophet ﷺ; he ﷺ ordered that he be struck. Some struck him with their hands, with their sandals, and with their garments.[26]

Anas (may Allah be pleased with him) said that a wine drinker was brought to the Prophet ﷺ. He ordered twenty men to flog him, each one twice, with palm leaves and sandals.[27]

A slave is flogged twenty lashes because the number of lashes can be halved and a slave receives half of a freeman's punishment, which is analogous to his punishment for fornication.

[The judge] can increase the punishment to eighty lashes at his discretion.

An upright leader [Imam] may increase the punishment if he believes that it is in the best interest of the community [*maṣlaḥah*] and will serve as a deterrent – especially when drinking becomes common and its evil widespread. When ʿUmar [was the leader] and people lived near pastures and towns, he said [to the Companions], "What is your opinion concerning lashing for drinking?" Thereupon ʿAbd al-Raḥmān ibn ʿAuf said, "My opinion is that you make it the mildest prescribed punishment." Then ʿUmar would give eighty lashes.[28] None of the Companions (may Allah be pleased with them all) objected to this.

The punishment is not imposed except through a confession or testimony from two male witnesses.

---

25. Anas: Bukhārī, 6773, 6776; Muslim, 1706 #36. See: TM, 1604.
26. Abū Hurayrah: Bukhārī, 6777; Abū Dāwūd, 4477.
27. Anas: al-Bayhaqī, 17534. See: KBM, 2453, cf TM, 1604 – Muslim.
28. Anas: Muslim, 1706 #35–37; Ibn Ḥibbān, 4450. See: TM, 1607.

One is not punished for the smell [of alcohol].

Neither vomit nor the smell alcohol is sufficient proof of guilt since it is possible that the person drank it by mistake or was compelled to drink it.

THEFT

(فصل) [السّرقة]

Theft [*sariqah*] is means "covertly seizing another person's property and removing it from where it is secured."

The general foundation for its punishment is found in the Quran, Sunnah, and consensus. Allah Most High says, "As for the thief, both male and female, cut off their hands. It is the reward of their own deeds, an exemplary punishment from Allah. Allah is Mighty, Wise" [Q5:38].

ويقطع المكلّف بسرقة قدر ربع دينار خالص من حرز مثله، لا ملك له فيه، ولا شبهة – يده اليمنى من المفصل، فإن عاد فرجله اليسرى، فإن عاد فاليد اليسرى، فإن عاد فالرّجل اليمنى، فإن عاد عزر.

A [legally] responsible individual's hand is amputated for stealing an item valued at one-quarter of a pure *dīnār* [1.058 grams of pure gold]...

ʿĀʾishah (may Allah be pleased with her) said – in a statement attributed to the Prophet ﷺ – that "a thief's hand is cut off for one-quarter of a *dīnār* and above." And in another transmission of theirs, "A thief's hand is not cut off except for one-quarter of a *dīnār* and above."[29]

29. ʿĀʾishah: Bukhārī, 6789–6793; Muslim, 1684 #1–4. See: TM, 1592.

Ibn ʿUmar (may Allah be pleased with them both) said that "the Prophet ﷺ amputated for [the theft of] a shield valued at three *dirhams*,"[30] which at that time equaled one-quarter of a *dīnār*.

...from a place where similar items are secured,...

The Prophet ﷺ said about fruit that was hung up [to dry]: "Whoever steals any of it after it has been placed where dates are dried and its value has reached that of a shield, [his hand] will be amputated."[31] A shield's value at that time was estimated at one quarter of a *dīnār*.

...and which he does not co-own...

A partner stealing from shared capital would not be punished because of the possibility that the stolen portion actually belongs to him.

...nor can claim to own (even dubiously).

A son stealing from his father or a father stealing from his son would also not be punishable because of the possibility that one may be obligated to support the other.

The Prophet ﷺ said, "Ward off prescribed punishments from Muslims as much as you can. If there is an exit for him, clear his path. The Imam erring in pardoning is superior to his erring in punishing."[32]

---

30. Ibn ʿUmar: Bukhārī, 6795–97; Muslim, 1686 #6; Ibn Mājah, 2584; Abū Dāwūd, 4385; al-Tirmidhī, 1446; al-Nasāʾī, 4906–10; Ibn Ḥibbān, 4463. See: BM, 8:656.
31. ʿAbd Allāh ibn ʿAmr ibn al-ʿĀṣ: Abū Dāwūd, 4390; Nasāʾī, 4958–9; Dāraquṭnī, 4570; Ḥākim, 8151. See: TM, 1594.
32. ʿĀʾishah: Tirmidhī, 1424; Ḥākim, 8163. See: TM, 1593.

The thief's right hand [is amputated] at the [wrist] joint.

Allah Most High says, "As for the thief, both male and female, cut off their hands..." [Q5:38]. Ibn Masʿūd (may Allah be pleased with him) recited the verse "their right hands." This is supported by consensus.

That the hand is cut at the wrist is also according to consensus. ʿAmr ibn Dīnār (may Allah grant him His mercy) reported that ʿUmar (may Allah be pleased with him) would amputate a thief's hand at the wrist.[33]

This consensus is based on the hadith concerning the theft of the cloak of Ṣafwān ibn Umayyah (may Allah be pleased with him), which includes: "then he ﷺ commanded that the thief's hand be amputated from the wrist."[34]

If he steals a second time, his left foot [is amputated]. If he steals a third time, his left hand [is amputated]. If he steals a fourth time, his right foot [is amputated].

The Prophet ﷺ said concerning thieves: "If he steals, amputate his hand. Then if he steals, amputate his foot. Then if he steals, amputate his hand. If he then steals, amputate his foot."[35]

It is recommended to cauterize the wounds.

Guilt of theft is established by the testimony of two male witnesses – like all other punishments (with the exception of fornication) – or by the thief's confession, on the authority of his ﷺ statement, "Whomever we find with [the stolen] platter, I will carry out the [prescribed punishment in] the Book of Allah upon him."[36] Guilt is also established if the accused refuses to swear an oath [that he did not steal it].

---

33. ʿAmr ibn Dīnār: Bayhaqī, 17251. See: BM, 8:685.§
34. al-Dāraquṭnī, 3466. See: KBM, 2409.
35. Abū Hurayrah: Dāraquṭnī, 3392. See: BM, 8:671.
36. Ibn ʿUmar: Ḥākim, 8158; al-Shāfiʿī, *Al-Umm*, 6:149. See: KBM, 2416.

The thief is also liable for the stolen goods, due to him ﷺ saying, "The hand is responsible for whatever it takes until it returns it."[37]

When a group steals, every member's hand is amputated if each stole a[n amount equal in value to the] *niṣāb*. But if the total value of the goods stolen by the group equals the *niṣāb,* the punishment is not implemented.

If he steals a fifth time, he is given a discretionary punishment.[38]

The judge determines the manner of punishment (e.g., beating, imprisonment, exile) that will best prevent a repeated offense. Theft is a sin and since there is no prescribed punishment beyond the fourth offense, a disciplinary punishment is required.

HIGHWAY ROBBERY

(فصل) [قاطع الطّريق]

Those who commit highway robbery are referred to as "interceptors" [*qāṭiʿ al-ṭarīq*] because they prevent people from traveling safely due to fear of them.

The foundation for its punishment is Allah Most High saying, "The only reward of those who make war upon Allah and His messenger and strive after corruption in the land will be that they will be killed or crucified, or have their hands and feet on alternate sides cut off, or will be expelled out of the land. Such will be their degradation in the world, and in the Hereafter theirs will be an awful doom..." [Q5:33].

Most scholars consider this verse to have been revealed concerning highwaymen.

---

37. Al-Ḥasan from Samurah: Abū Dāwūd, 3561; Tirmidī, 1266 – *ḥasan ṣaḥīḥ*; Nasāʾī, *Al-Sunan al-kubrā,* 5751; Ibn Mājah, 2400; Ḥākim, 2302. See: TM, 1286.

38. See "Disciplinary Punishments" on page 473.

‹In the verse, they "make war upon Allah and His messenger" by fighting Muslims and "strive after corruption in the land" by blocking the roads.[39]›

ITS DEFINITION AND MINIMUM PUNISHMENT

قاطع الطريق إذا كان مسلمًا مكلفًا له شوكة وأخذ نصاب السّرقة قطعت يده اليمنى ورجله اليسرى، فإن عاد فيسراه ويمناه.

When a [legally] responsible, Muslim highwayman possessing a formidable force steals the minimum amount for the punishment for theft (one-quarter of a pure *dīnār* or 1.058 grams of pure gold), his right hand and left foot are amputated.

Although the verse cited above [Q5:33] appears to present disciplinary options, what is intended are different categories. This interpretation is supported by what Ibn ʿAbbās (may Allah be pleased with him) transmitted: "When they kill and steal property, they are killed and crucified. When they kill but do not take property, they are killed but not crucified. When they take property but do not kill, their opposite hands and feet are amputated."[40]

If the perpetrator transgresses again, his left hand and right foot are amputated.

39. al-Bughā, *Al-Tadhhīb,* 216 #5.
40. Ibn ʿAbbās: Al-Shāfiʿī, *Al-Umm,* 6:164; ibid., *Al-Musnad,* p366; Bayhaqī, 17313. See: KBM, 2440.

IF KILLING IS INVOLVED

وإن قتل عمدًا من يكافئه قتل حتمًا.

If the perpetrator deliberately kills someone who is equal to himself in status [according to the Sacred Law], his execution is mandatory.

This applies even if the victim's guardians pardon him.

IF KILLING AND THEFT ARE INVOLVED

وإن انضمّ إليه أخذ المال زيد صلبه ثلاثًا.

If the perpetrator kills and steals, he is also crucified [and left] for three [days].

His body is crucified after being washed, shrouded, and prayed upon (if he is Muslim) in order make an example of him and to publicize his fate. This is because of the seriousness of his crime and the enormity of his sin, and to deter others from doing the same.

The crucifixion lasts three days if the body does not begin decomposing. If it is feared that the body will change, it is removed beforehand.

WHEN ONLY SPREADING FEAR IS INVOLVED

فإن أخاف فقط عزر.

If the perpetrator only spreads fear [without stealing or killing],...

For example, he terrorizes people by blocking their path and threatening them.

...he is given a discretionary punishment.[41]

The authorities punish him in the manner that will best stop and deter him. If they choose imprisonment, it is preferable that it be done outside the perpetrator's locale in order to increase his alienation and its impact as a deterrent. He remains imprisoned until his repentance is evident and he has mended his ways, in order to safeguard public safety.

REPENTANCE BEFORE APPREHENSION

فإن تاب قبل القدرة عليه سقط الحد وأخذ الحق.

If the perpetrator repents before being apprehended, the punishment [specific to highway robbery] is cancelled,...

Allah Most High says, "Save those who repent before ye overpower them. For know that Allah is Forgiving, Merciful" [Q5:34].

...and he is held accountable for rights [owed to individuals, including personal injuries, stolen property, and other crimes against his victims].

He is still held accountable for crimes outside the context of highway robbery.

DISCIPLINARY PUNISHMENTS

(فصل) [التعزير]

The foundation for the disciplinary punishment [*taʿzīr*] – prior to consensus – is that Allah Most High says, "...As for those from whom ye fear rebellion, admonish them and banish them to beds apart, and scourge them..." [Q4:34].

---

41. See "Disciplinary Punishments" on page 473.

ويعزر في كلّ معصية لا كفارة لها، ناقصًا عن أدنى حدّه، وهو مضمون على العاقلة.

There is a disciplinary punishment [*ta*ʿ*zīr*] for every act of disobedience lacking an expiation.

This is because the prescribed punishments or expiations are adequate deterrents [for most sins]. An exception to this is intercourse during the daylight hours of Ramadan, for which both an expiation and a disciplinary punishment are required.

The *ta*ʿ*zīr* is less than the least prescribed punishment [of forty lashes].

Al-Nuʿmān ibn Bashīr (may Allah be pleased with him) said that the Messenger of Allah ﷺ said, "Whoever reaches [the level of] a prescribed punishment while [administering] a non-prescribed [disciplinary] punishment is among the transgressors."[42]

It is also possible for the authority to pardon crimes worthy of disciplinary punishments. The Prophet ﷺ said, "Forgive the virtuous when they slip, but not when they commit offenses that warrant prescribed punishments."[43]

The authority can also impose a disciplinary punishment even if the victim has pardoned the perpetrator. This is because the foundation of the punishment is according to the Imam or judge's discretion, so it is of no consequence if someone else waives it.

---

42. al-Nuʿmān ibn Bashīr: Bayhaqī, 17584. See: al-Māwardī, *Al-Ḥāwī al-kabīr,* 13:426, 13:438.

43. ʿA'ishah: Abū Dāwūd, 4375; Nasā'ī, *Al-Sunan al-kubrā,* 7254. See: BM, 8:730.

Discipline is a liability against the male relatives of the one who carried it out.

If discipline results in death, the male relatives of the one who carried it out are liable – whether the Imam, an instructor, husband, or father; or whether it was for a right owed to an individual or to Allah Most High. This is because the authority is commanded to discipline with the condition of a safe outcome.

SELF-DEFENSE

(فصل) [الصّيال]

Evidence for the permissibility of defending oneself [*ṣiyyāl*] is found in the hadith from Anas (may Allah be pleased with him) in which he relates that the Prophet ﷺ said, "Support your brother, whether he oppresses or is oppressed."[44] It is also found in Allah Most High saying, "…And one who attacketh you…" [Q2:194].

والصّائل يدفع بالأخف فالأخف ولو عن المال، ويجب عن البضع والمعاصي، والكافر عن النّفس، فإن أدى الدّفع إلى الهلاك فهدر.

One repels an attack using the least amount of force needed (then the second least) – even if the attack is upon one's wealth. It is obligatory to repel sexual assaults and acts of disobedience, and to defend oneself if physically attacked by a non-Muslim.

One must repel an animal, insane person, or non-Muslim if they attack one's person. One is not required to repel an attack from one of these three if it is against one's wealth [or property].

44. Anas: Bukhārī, 2444.

It is not obligatory to repel another Muslim's attack against one's person. The Prophet ﷺ said, "Be like the better of the two sons of Adam [peace be upon him]."[45,46]

It is obligatory to repel a sexual assault – in contrast to an attack on one's wealth – since unlawful intercourse is never permissible.

There is no liability if self-defense results in the attacker's death.

Saʿīd ibn Zayd (may Allah be pleased with him) reported that the Prophet ﷺ said, "Whoever is killed while protecting his property is a martyr. Whoever is killed while defending his family, his life, or his religion is a martyr."[47]

ANIMALS

(فصل) [دفع دابة]

ANIMALS ACCOMPANIED BY A HUMAN

ومن كان مع دابة أو دواب ضمن إتلافها.

Whoever accompanies one or more animals is liable for any damages they cause.

They are only liable if they were negligent in controlling the animal[s].

Its foundation is that the Prophet ﷺ decided that the owners of orchards are responsible for guarding them during the day, and animal owners are responsible for any damages caused by their livestock during the night.[48]

---

45. Abū Mūsā al-Ashʿarī: Ibn Mājah, 3961; Abū Dāwūd, 4259; Ibn Ḥibbān, 5962; Bayhaqī, 16800. See: TM, 1612.
46. See: Quran, 5:27–31.
47. Saʿīd ibn Zayd: Abū Dāwūd, 4772; Tirmidhī, 1421 – *ḥasan ṣaḥīḥ*; Nasāʾī, 4094–5; Ibn Mājah, 2580. See: TM, 1610–11.
48. Ḥarām ibn Muḥayyiṣah from his father and al-Barāʾ ibn ʿĀzib: Abū Dāwūd, 3569, 3570; Ibn Mājah, 2332; Nasāʾī in *Al-Sunan al-kubrā,*

UNACCOMPANIED ANIMALS

فإن كانت وحدها ضمن ليلًا فقط إن لم يفرط.

If the animal is alone [without its owner], its owner is liable only for what it damages during the night provided he was not negligent.

DESTRUCTIVE CATS

والهرّة المتلفة يضمن مالكها.

Owners of destructive cats are liable for their damages.

Cats that habitually consume someone else's birds and food should be restrained – but not killed. The same applies to other animals that cause harm.

LOOKING THROUGH A PEEPHOLE

(فصل) [رمي عين ناظر]

له رمي عين ناظر محرمة من ثقبة إذا لم يكن هناك محرمه وزوجته بنحو حصاة.

It is permissible to throw [any object] at someone's eye if he is looking through a peephole at one's or wife or female kin. If one's wife or female kin are not present where the voyeur is looking, one may only throw something [light], such as a pebble.

The Prophet ﷺ said, "If someone peeps into your house without your permission, and you throw a stone at him and destroy his eyes, there will be no blame on you."[49]

5755; Ibn Ḥibbān, 6008, Dāraquṭnī, 3314, Bayhaqī, 17682–3, 20365, Ḥākim, 2303. See: TM, 1619.

49. Abū Hurayrah: Bukhārī, 6888; Muslim, 2158. See: TM, 1615.

CIRCUMCISION

(فصل) [الختان]

والختان واجب بعد البلوغ، ويندب في سابعه، فإن ضعف عنه أخره إلى احتماله.

Circumcision is obligatory after adolescence.

Removal of the foreskin is obligatory for males, and removal of part of the clitoral hood is obligatory for females. Allah Most High says, "And afterward We inspired thee (Muhammad, saying): Follow the religion of Abraham, as one by nature upright..." [Q16:123], and circumcision was part of Abraham's religion (peace be upon him). ʿIkrimah (may Allah be pleased with him) said that Ibrāhīm (peace be upon him) circumcised himself, and that he (peace be upon him) did it when he was 120,[50] or 80,[51] or 70[52] years old.

Circumcision becomes obligatory with adolescence, since that is the age of responsibility.

It is recommended on the seventh [day after birth, not including the day of birth itself].

The Messenger of Allah ﷺ performed *ʿaqīqah*s for al-Ḥasan and al-Ḥusein (may Allah be pleased with them), and circumcised them on the seventh day [after their respective births]."[53]

If the individual is too weak [to endure it], it is delayed until he is able.

This ruling also applies to adults.

---

50. Abū Hurayrah: Ibn Ḥibbān, 6204, 6205, Ḥākim, 4022, 4023. See: TM, 1616.
51. Abū Hurayrah: Bukhārī, 6298; Muslim, 2370 #151. See: TM, 1616.
52. al-Māwardī, *Al-Ḥāwī al-kabīr,* 13:431.
53. Jābir: Bayhaqī, 17563.

12

JIHAD

كِتَابُ الجِهَادِ

The legal foundation for jihad is found in the Quran and Sunnah, which includes the following:

Allah Most High says, "Warfare is ordained for you, though it is hateful unto you; but it may happen that ye hate a thing which is good for you, and it may happen that ye love a thing which is bad for you. Allah knoweth, ye know not" [Q2:216].

‹In the verse, "...but it may happen that ye hate a thing which is good for you, and it may happen that ye love a thing which is bad for you," refers to the heart being inclined towards its lusts, which lead to its destruction, causing us to flee from those responsibilities that lead to our success. So perhaps in fighting – even if you may hate it – there is good since you will achieve victory and spoils of war, or martyrdom and its rewards; and perhaps in avoiding it – even though you may prefer it – there is evil since it contains humiliation, poverty, and being deprived of rewards.[1]›

Allah Most High says, "Go forth, light-armed and heavy-armed, and strive with your wealth and your lives in the way of Allah! That is best for you if ye but knew" [Q9:41].

‹In the verse, "light-armed and heavy-armed" means with or without vigor, whether strong or weak, or whether rich or poor. It is abrogated by the verse, "Not unto the weak nor unto the sick..." [Q9:91].[2]›

1. al-Maḥallī and al-Suyūṭī, *Tafsīr al-Jalālayn*.
2. Ibid.

The Prophet ﷺ said, "Verily! Setting out in the early morning or in the evening in order to fight in Allah's way is better than the world and what it contains."[3]

JIHAD IS AN ANNUAL OBLIGATION

هو كلّ سنّة مرّة فرض كفاية.

Jihad once each [lunar] year,...

The *jizyah* is taken from the non-Muslim subjects of the Islamic state [*dhimmī*s] once every lunar year in exchange for protection from hostility.[4] The portion of spoils owed to Muslim fighters is also distributed once each lunar year, so jihad must be waged at least once within that year – thought not against the *dhimmī*s, who are protected.

...is a communal obligation.

There is consensus that jihad is obligatory. The understanding that it is a communal obligation comes from Allah Most High saying, "Those of the believers who sit still, other than those who have a (disabling) hurt, are not on an equality with those who strive in the way of Allah with their wealth and lives. Allah hath conferred on those who strive with their wealth and lives a rank above the sedentary. Unto each Allah hath promised good, but He hath bestowed on those who strive a great reward above the sedentary..." [Q4:95]. Allah Most High mentions the superiority of "those who strive in the way of Allah" [*mujāhidīn*] but also promises a good reward for those who stay behind [due to illness]. If those who stayed behind were being negligent in their obligation to perform jihad, Allah would not have promised them a good reward.

3. Sahl ibn Saʿd al-Sāʿidī: Bukhārī, 2792, 2794, 2796; Muslim, 1880, 1881. See: KBM, 2493.

4. See "The Jizyah Contract" on page 494.

CONDITIONS OBLIGATING JIHAD

ولا يجب إلا على مكلّف حرّ ذكر بصير مستطيع.

It is only obligatory if someone is
1. [legally] responsible,

The obligation of jihad does not apply to children or the insane.

The Prophet ﷺ said, "The pen [that records deeds] has been lifted from three: a sleeper until he wakes, a boy until he reaches puberty, and a lunatic until he comes to reason."[5]

Ibn ʿAbbās (may Allah be pleased with them both) said, "The Messenger of Allah ﷺ scrutinized me on the battlefield on the Day of Uḥud. I was a fourteen-year-old boy and he ﷺ did not permit me [to participate]. He ﷺ then scrutinized me on the Day of Khandaq. I was fifteen years old and he ﷺ permitted me [to participate]."[6]

2. free,

The Prophet ﷺ would have slaves pledge Islam but not jihad. This is in contrast to freemen, who would pledge both.[7]

Also, slaves cannot participate because they are occupied with serving their owners.

3. male,

The Prophet ﷺ said, "Hajj is the jihad of the elderly, children, and women."[8]

ʿĀʾishah (may Allah be pleased with her) said, "I sought permission from the Messenger of Allah ﷺ for jihad. He ﷺ said,

---

5. ʿĀʾishah: Abū Dāwūd, 4398, 4401–3; Tirmidhī, 1423; Nasāʾī, 3432; Ibn Mājah, 2041; Ibn Ḥibbān, 142, 143; Ḥākim, 2350. See: TM, 1626.
6. Ibn ʿAbbās: Bukhārī, 2664; Muslim, 1868. See: KBM, 1577.
7. Majāshiʿ ibn Masʿūd al-Sulamī: Bukhārī, 2962; Muslim, 1863 #83, 84. See: KBM, 2500.
8. Abū Hurayrah: Nasāʾī, 2626. See: BM, 9:38, cf KBM, 2499.

'Your jihad is Hajj.' In another version [she said]: "O Messenger of Allah ﷺ, we consider jihad the most excellent of deeds. Should we [women] not perform jihad?" He ﷺ said, "You have the most excellent jihad: a Hajj that is accepted."[9]

‹ʿĀʾishah (may Allah be pleased with her) said, "I asked, 'O Messenger of Allah ﷺ. Shouldn't we [women] participate in battles and perform jihad with you?' He ﷺ said, 'You have the most excellent jihad and the most beautiful one: a Hajj that is accepted.'"[10]›

ʿĀʾishah (may Allah be pleased with her) also said, "I asked, 'O Messenger of Allah ﷺ, is it incumbent upon women to make jihad?' He ﷺ said, 'Yes, a jihad that includes no fighting: Hajj and Umrah.'"[11]

4. **can see, and**

Allah Most High says, "There is no blame for the blind, nor is there blame for the lame, nor is there blame for the sick (that they go not forth to war)..." [Q48:17].

5. **is able.**

Meaning one is able to walk or ride beyond the distance for shortening prayers.[12] Allah Most High says, "Not unto the weak nor unto the sick nor unto those who can find naught to spend is any fault (to be imputed though they stay at home) if they are true to Allah and His messenger..." [Q9:91].

Someone who has an outstanding debt that has come due cannot travel for jihad or for other reasons without permission from his lenders. ʿAbd Allāh ibn ʿAmr (may Allah be pleased with them both) narrated that the Prophet ﷺ said, "All sins are forgiven for

---

9. ʿĀʾishah: Bukhārī, 1520, 2784. See: TM, 1628.
10. ʿĀʾishah: Bukhārī, 1861. See: al-Bughā, *Al-Tadhhīb,* 226 #2.
11. ʿĀʾishah: Ibn Mājah, 2901. See: TM, 1042, 1627; KBM, 2499.
12. See "Shortening & Combining Prayers" on page 112.

martyrs except debts." One of his transmissions has: "Killing in the way of Allah expiates everything except debts."[13]

One must have permission from one's parents if they are Muslims. Jihad is a group obligation, whereas obeying one's parents is a personal obligation. ʿAbd Allāh ibn ʿAmr (may Allah be pleased with them both) said, "A man came to the Prophet ﷺ and asked his permission for jihad. He ﷺ said, 'Do you have parents?' He said, 'Yes.' He ﷺ said, 'For them you are to strive.'"[14]

If non-Muslims invade a frontier of Muslim-controlled territory, it is personally obligatory upon every able-bodied Muslim of that land to expend all efforts to defend it, and upon the Muslims of other lands [to assist then] if the number of Muslim residents does not suffice.

RULES OF ENGAGEMENT

HIRING DHIMMĪS TO PARTICIPATE IN JIHAD

The Imam can hire dhimmīs to participate in jihad or seek their assistance if he feels the Muslims will be safe from their treachery. The Prophet ﷺ sought assistance from the Jews of Banī Qaynuqāʿ after the Battle of Badr.[15] The Imam can do the same with slaves (with their owners' permission), and with adolescents.

13. ʿAbd Allāh ibn ʿAmr: Muslim, 1886 #119. See: TM, 1630.
14. ʿAbd Allāh ibn ʿAmr ibn al-ʿĀṣ: Bukhārī, 3004; Muslim, 2549 #5. See: TM, 1631.
15. al-Zuhrī: Abū Dāwūd, *Al-Marāʾsīl*, 281; Tirmidhī, 1558. See: BM, 9:72. MTM, 406; al-Juwaynī, *Nihāyat al-maṭlab*, 17:427.

HIRING MUSLIMS TO PARTICIPATE IN JIHAD

The Imam cannot hire Muslims to participate in battle because fighting becomes a personal obligation if they are present in the battle lines, and it is not permissible to give or receive wages for personal obligations.

KILLING WOMEN AND CHILDREN

It is not permissible to kill women or children since it is *ṣaḥīḥ* [rigorously authenticated] that the Prophet ﷺ forbade killing them.[16] But if they attack, it is permissible to retaliate.

It is not permissible to fire at the enemy's women and children out of fear that the enemy will flee to them [and use them as shields], when firing at the women and children could result in their death. But if the disbelievers use them as shields during fighting, it is permissible [to fire at them].

KILLING MONKS, FARMERS, ELDERLY MEN, AND THE WEAK

It is permissible to kill monks, farmers, elderly men, and the weak due to the general language of the verse "…slay the idolaters…" [Q9:5]. Also, Durayd ibn al-Ṣummah – who was said to be over 150 years old – was killed on the Day of Ḥunayn. The enemy had enlisted him to help plan the attack. The Prophet ﷺ did not object to him being killed.[17]

16. Ibn ʿUmar: Bukhārī, 3014, 3015; Muslim, 1744 #24–25. See: TM, 1634.
17. Abū Mūsā al-Ashʿarī: Bukhārī, 4323; Muslim, 2498 #165. See: BM, 7:348, 9:89.

USING CATAPULTS

It is permissible to use catapults against an enemy. He ﷺ used them against the people of Ṭā'if.[18] By analogy, it is permissible to launch fire or water at them – even if there are children, women, or Muslim captives among them – because the default assumption is that they would not be hit.

Al-Ṣaʿb ibn Jaththāmah (may Allah be pleased with him) reported that he passed by the Prophet ﷺ [who had been] asked about attacking pagan settlements at night when their women and children might be hit. The Prophet ﷺ replied, "They are part of them."[19]

SINGLE COMBAT

Single combat is permissible. (It is neither offensive nor unlawful.) It was done in the presence of the Prophet ﷺ without him objecting to it.[20] It is best that the person who engages in it is experienced and has the Imam's permission.

PRISONERS OF WAR

والنّساء والصّبيان إذا أسروا رقوا، والكامل يتخيّر فيه الإمام بينه والقتل والمن والفداء.

Women and children [of the enemy] who are captured [by Muslim forces] become enslaved.

They are enslaved by the very act of being captured, so they become property. The rulings related to them are the same as those of other captured property. (Textual evidence will follow.)

---

18. Thūr, *muʿḍilan*: Abū Dāwūd, *Al-Marā'sīl*, 335; Tirmidhī, 2762. See: BM, 9:93, 9:96; cf TM, 1636.
19. al-Ṣaʿb ibn al-Jaththāmah: Bukhārī, 3012. See TM, 1638.
20. ʿAlī: Abū Dāwūd, 2665. See: TM, 1642; cf TM, 1641.

[The fate of] mature males is left to the Imam's discretion. He can choose between

1. **enslaving,**
2. **executing,**
3. **freeing, or**
4. **ransoming them.**

All four options have been reported from the Prophet ﷺ.

‹Allah Most High says, "Now when ye meet in battle those who disbelieve, then it is smiting of the necks until, when ye have routed them, then making fast of bonds; and afterward either grace or ransom till the war lay down its burdens…" [Q47:4].

Ibn ʿUmar (may Allah be pleased with them both) said that [Banī] al-Naḍīr and [Banī] Qurayẓah fought [against the Prophet ﷺ]. The Prophet ﷺ exiled [Banī] al-Naḍīr and allowed [Banī] Qurayẓah to remain in their places along with whomever was with them, until [Banī] Qurayẓah fought [against the Prophet ﷺ]. In response, he ﷺ had their men executed and their women, children, and property distributed amongst the Muslims.[21]›

When Banī Qurayẓah was ready to accept his judgment, Saʿd ibn Muʿādh (may Allah be pleased with him) – who had been appointed mediator by the Prophet ﷺ – decreed that the men be killed.[22]

[During the Battle of Ḥunayn], the Muslims had taken some fighters from Hawāzin captive, so a delegation of Hawzānī Muslims came to the Prophet ﷺ and asked for the return of their captured tribesmen and seized property. He ﷺ interceded on their behalf and the captives were released.[23]

‹A Muslim raiding party returned from battle with captives, including a woman from Banī Fazārah. The Messenger of Allah ﷺ

21. Ibn ʿUmar: Bukhārī, 4028; Muslim, 1766 #62. See: al-Bughā, *Al-Tadhhīb*, 227 #3.
22. Abū Saʿīd al-Khudrī: Bukhārī, 3043; Muslim, 1768. See: KBM, 1580.
23. Ibn Shihāb: Bukhārī, 2307. See: BM, 7:347.

sent her to the people of Mecca as ransom for the Muslims who were being kept as prisoners in Mecca.[24]

The Prophet ﷺ accepted ransom for prisoners the Muslims had captured during the Battle of Badr.[25]›

ENTERING ISLAM PRIOR TO CAPTURE

ومن أسلم قبل الأسر، عصم نفسه، وماله، وصغار أولاده، لا زوجته.

Whoever [fights the Muslims] but enters Islam before being captured retains possession of his life and property, and his young children are protected from enslavement – though not his wife.

The Prophet ﷺ said, "I have been ordered to fight against people until they testify that there is none worthy of worship except Allah and that Muhammad is the Messenger of Allah, and until they establish the prayer and pay the zakat. And if they do that, they will have gained protection from me for their lives and property, unless [they commit acts that are punishable] in Islam, and then their reckoning will be with Allah."[26]

The Prophet ﷺ encircled Banī Qurayẓah. Thaʿlabah and Asayd (two sons of Saʿyah) entered Islam (may Allah be pleased with them all). Their submission to Islam protected their wealth and small children for them."[27]

Accepting Islam does not protect one's wife from enslavement since a woman is independent of her husband, and one's entering Islam occurs independently of her.

24. Salamah: Muslim, 1755 #46. See: al-Bughā, *Al-Tadhhīb,* 227 #3.
25. ʿUmar: Muslim, 1763 #58. See: al-Bughā, *Al-Tadhhīb,* 227 #3.
26. ʿUmar, Abū Hurayrah, and Ibn ʿUmar: Bukhārī, 25; Muslim, 22 #36. See: TM, 748, 907, 1572, 1647.
27. ʿĀṣim ibn ʿUmar ibn Qatādah, from a shaykh from Qurayẓah: Al-Shāfiʿī, *Al-Umm,*4:296, 7:388; Bayhaqī, 18263. See: BM, 9:125.

ABANDONED CHILDREN FOUND IN MUSLIM LANDS

ويحكم بإسلام الصّبي بسببه عند عدم أحد الأبوين، وكذا بوجدانه لقيطًا بدار الإسلام، وبكون أحد أبويه مسلمًا عند العلوق، وبإسلام أحدهما بعده.

A child is judged to be a Muslim if he is captured without either of his parents or is found abandoned within Muslim lands; [or], if one of his parents was a Muslim at the time of conception or entered Islam after conception.

‹This is because Islam dominates other attributes and precedence must be given to the welfare of the child and what is most beneficial to him. Since Islam is an attribute of wholeness, honor, and superiority [it is chosen for him].[28]›

The Messenger of Allah ﷺ said, "Islam is superior and should never be surpassed."[29]

FLEEING BATTLE

(فصل) [الانصراف]

ولا ينصرف من الصّف إلّا لعذر كزيادة على ضعف، وتحيّز إلى فئة.

One does not flee from the battle lines...

Allah Most High says, "O ye who believe! When ye meet those who disbelieve in battle, turn not your backs to them." [Q8:15]. ‹In the verse, "turn not your backs" means fleeing in retreat.[30]›

---

28. al-Bughā, *Al-Tadhhīb,* 229 #2.
29. ʿĀʾidh ibn ʿAmr al-Muzanī: Dāraquṭnī, 3620; Bukhārī: before 1354. See: TM, 1332, 1667.
30. al-Maḥallī and al-Suyūṭī, *Tafsīr al-Jalālayn.*

The Prophet ﷺ said, "Avoid the seven destructive things!" Fleeing from the battlefield was among those he mentioned.[31]

...except when excused to do so, such as when one is outnumbered two-to-one and needs to regroup.

Fleeing for those reasons is not unlawful. This is because of the negative implication when Allah Most High says, "Now hath Allah lightened your burden, for He knoweth that there is weakness in you. So if there be of you a steadfast hundred they shall overcome two hundred, and if there be of you a thousand (steadfast) they shall overcome two thousand by permission of Allah. Allah is with the steadfast" [Q8:66].

DESTROYING ENEMY PROPERTY AND ANIMALS

ويجوز إتلاف بنائهم وشجرهم بخلاف الحيوان لغير ضرورة.

It is permissible to destroy the enemy's buildings and trees...

Ibn ʿUmar (may Allah be pleased with them both) reported that the Messenger of Allah ﷺ burned down the trees of Bani al-Naḍīr and cut the trees of [a place called] al-Buwayrah. Thereafter, Allah revealed, "Whatsoever palm-trees ye cut down or left standing on their roots, it was by Allah's leave, in order that He might confound the evil-livers" [Q59:5].[32]

It is permissible when needed for victory or if there is no expectation that the Muslims will capture the land. If the Muslims are expected to capture it, it is recommended to leave the trees intact. This is because Abū Bakr (may Allah be pleased with him) forbade it.[33]

31. Abū Hurayrah: Bukhārī, 2766, 6857; Muslim, 89 #145. See TM, 1590, 1639.
32. Ibn ʿUmar: Bukhārī, 4031, 4884; Muslim, 1746 #29. See TM, 1643.
33. Ibn ʿAbbās: Bayhaqī, 18125–7; cf Al-Rāfiʿī, *Al-Sharḥ al-kabīr*, 11:422.

... – in contrast to destroying their animals without necessity.

This is because of the sanctity of the animals' lives. It is permissible to kill animals that are used in battle, since they are like instruments of war. And it is permissible to kill captured animals when it is feared that the enemy will recapture them, since killing them prevents a harm [to the Muslims].

Also, ʿAbd Allāh ibn ʿAmr (may Allah be pleased with him) reported that the Messenger of Allah ﷺ said, "There is no person who kills a small bird or anything larger without right, save that Allah will ask him about it." It was said, "O Messenger of Allah ﷺ, what does 'rightfully' mean?" He ﷺ said, 'That you slaughter it and eat it, and do not cut off its head and throw it aside.'"[34]

GIVING AMNESTY TO COMBATANTS

(فصل) [أمان الكفار]

ويصحّ من كلّ مسلم مكلّف مختار أمان حربيّ، وعدد محصور - لا أسير - بكلّ ما يفيد مقصوده، بشرط ألّا يزيد على أربعة أشهر.

It is valid for any [legally] responsible Muslim to willfully offer amnesty to an individual, non-Muslim enemy combatant or to a limited group.

A "limited group" might consist of ten or one-hundred people, for example. An individual Muslim cannot given amnesty to the entire population of a land or region, since it leads to voiding jihad in that area.

34. ʿAbd Allāh ibn ʿAmr: Nasāʾī, 4359, 4445; al-Ḥākim, 7574; al-Bayhaqī, 18128. See TM, 1654.

A imprisoned Muslim cannot [offer amnesty].

His offer of amnesty is not valid – even if he is not compelled – since he is under the control of non-Muslims and unaware of the [current] perspectives and [strategic] interests of [his fellow] Muslims.

The Prophet ﷺ said, "The protection granted by Muslims is one [i.e., equal]. Whoever violates a Muslim's covenant will have the curse of Allah, of his angels, and of all people upon him. Neither an obligatory nor a supererogatory act would be accepted from him as recompense on the Day of Resurrection."[35]

Slaves can offer amnesty. The Prophet ﷺ said, "The lowest of them is entitled to give protection on behalf of them."[36] Slaves are the lowest. A fortiori, non-slaves can also offer amnesty.

Women can also offer amnesty. The Prophet ﷺ said to Umm Hāniʾ (may Allah be pleased with her): "We have given protection to whom you gave protection, O Umm Hāniʾ."[37]

[Amnesty is offered] using any [phrase] that serves its purpose, provided that its duration does not exceed four months.

EMIGRATION FROM LANDS OF DISBELIEF

وتجب الهجرة من بلاد الكفر إن لم يمكنه إظهار دينه.

It is obligatory to emigrate from the lands of disbelief [*dār al-kufr*] if it is not possible for one to publicly display one's religion.

It is recommended to emigrate even if one can display it – out of fear of inclining towards the disbelievers' way of life – though it is not obligatory since one can publicly display it. Otherwise, it is obligatory.

35. ʿAlī: Bukhārī, 1870, 7300; Muslim, 1370 #467. See: TM, 1656.
36. ʿAmr ibn Shuʿayb from his father from his grandfather: Abū Dāwūd, 2751; Nasāʾī, *Al-Sunan al-kubrā*, 15913. See: cf KBM, 2574.
37. Umm Hāniʾ: Bukhārī, 3171; Muslim, 336 #82. See: KBM, 2575.

Allah Most High says "Lo! as for those whom the angels take (in death) while they wrong themselves, (the angels) will ask: In what were ye engaged? They will say: We were oppressed in the land. (The angels) will say: Was not Allah's earth spacious that ye could have migrated therein? As for such, their habitation will be hell, an evil journey's end; Except the feeble among men, and the women, and the children, who are unable to devise a plan and are not shown a way. As for such, it may be that Allah will pardon them. Allah is ever Clement, Forgiving" [Q4:97–99].

ʿAbd Allāh ibn al-Saʿdī (may Allah be pleased with him) said that the Prophet ﷺ said, "Emigration will not cease so long as disbelievers are fought."[38]

Jarīr ibn ʿAbd Allāh (may Allah be pleased with him) said that the Messenger of Allah ﷺ sent an expedition to Khathʿam. Some people [Muslims] sought protection by prostrating, and were hastily killed. When the Prophet ﷺ heard of this, he ordered half the blood money [*diyah*] be paid for them, and said: "I am not responsible for any Muslim who resides among polytheists." His Companions (may Allah be pleased with them) asked, "Why, Messenger of Allah?" He ﷺ said: "Their fires should not be visible to one another."[39]

Samurah ibn Jundub (may Allah be pleased with him) said that the Prophet ﷺ said, "Do not live among the idolaters and do not assemble with them, for whoever lives among them or assembles with them is similar to them."[40]

38. ʿAbd Allāh ibn al-Saʿdī: Nasāʾī, 4172–73; Ibn Ḥibbān, 4866. See: BM, 9:27; TM, 1657.

39. Jarīr ibn ʿAbd Allāh: Abū Dāwūd, 2645; al-Tirmidhī, 1604. See: TM, 1658; KBM, 2567.

40. Samurah ibn Jundub: al-Tirmidhī, before 1605; al-Ḥākim, 2627: *ṣaḥīḥ*; al-Bayhaqī, 18420. See: TM, 1659.

COMPENSATING NON-MUSLIM SPIES

(فصل) [إعطاء العلج]

وإن دلّ علج على قلعة ليعطى منها جاريّة وفتحنا بها، فله ،وإن نزلوا على حكم حاكم جاز، ويفعل الأحظّ للإسلام.

If a disbeliever points out a fortress's vulnerability [to the Muslims] desiring to receive a female slave as compensation, and the Muslims conquer that fortress as a result of his assistance, then he is entitled to his compensation.[41]

If the enemy surrenders the fortress according to an arbitrator's judgment, it is permissible [to give the disbeliever who pointed out its vulnerability his price] and [the leader] does whatever is in the best interest of Islam.

41. Ibn Mulaqqin explains that this is permissible because it is in the best interest of the Muslims and related to their welfare, so the compensation can even come from the Muslim treasury [*bayt al-māl*]. *Mukhtaṣar al-Tabrīzī,* 317.

THE JIZYAH CONTRACT

(فصل) [عقد الجزية]

The textual foundation for the *jizyah* contract – prior to consensus – is that Allah Most High says, "…until they pay the tribute [*jizyah*] readily, being brought low." [Q9:29]. And the Prophet ﷺ accepted the *jizyah* from the Zoroastrians of Hajar, and others.[42]

ELIGIBILITY

تعقد الجزية لمكلّف حرّ ذكر زعم التّمسّك بكتاب كالمجوسيّ، لم يعلم أن أصل آبائه اختار ذلك الدّين حين نسخ.

The *jizyah* contract is effected for a [legally] responsible, [non-Muslim], free male (such as a Zoroastrian), who claims to adhere to a book [of revelation],…

This is because of the universality of the verse in which Allah Most High says, "And [lawful to you in marriage] are the virtuous women of the believers and the virtuous women of those who received the Scripture before you (lawful for you) when ye give them their marriage portions and live with them in honour, not in fornication, nor taking them as secret concubines" [Q5:5]. And the Prophet ﷺ took *jizyah* from the Zoroastrians of Hajar.[43]

…and whose ancestors are not known to have chosen that religion after it was abrogated.

The *jizyah* is not taken from the insane because their lives are safe.

---

42. See: KBM, 2596; al-Māwardī, *Al-Ḥāwī al-Kabīr*, 14:308; al-Shīrāzī, *Al-Muhadhdhab*, 3:310; al-Rūyānī, *Baḥr al-madhhab*, 13:356; al-ʿUmrānī, *Al-Bayān*, 12:268.

43. ʿUmar: Bukhārī, 3157. See: TM, 1662.

It is also not taken from women or children because ʿUmar (may Allah be pleased with him) commanded his workers to not impose the *jizyah* on women or children.[44]

‹The *jizyah* is only taken from individuals who are legally responsible and potential combatants. This excludes women since they are not [typically] combatants, and similarly, slaves. Youth and the insane are also excluded since they are not legally responsible.›

THE AMOUNT OWED

وأقلّها دينار كلّ سنّة، وله أن يماكس، لا لسفيه، يزيد ضيافة المسلم المارّ، وتؤخذ برفق كسائر الدّيون، وإن مات في أثناء الحول، أو أسلم، أو جن، أخذ لما مضى.

The minimum amount of the *jizyah* is one *dīnār* [4.235 grams of pure gold] each year.

When the Prophet ﷺ sent Muʿādh (may Allah be pleased with him) to Yemen, he ﷺ ordered him to take one *dīnār* or its equivalent in garments from each mature male.[45]

[The Imam] can accept *jizyah* payments on a sliding scale [so the well-off pay more than the poor] – but not from a spendthrift.

This is based on the example of ʿUmar (may Allah be pleased with him), who imposed forty-eight *dirhams* on the affluent, twenty-four on the average, and twelve on the poor.[46] ‹The exchange rate at the time was one *dīnār* for ten *dirhams*.[47]›

44. Muʿādh: Bayhaqī, *Maʿrifat al-sunan,* 18552, 18553. See: TM, 1663.
45. Muʿādh: Tirmidhī, 623 – *ḥasan*; Nasāʾī, 2450–2; Ibn Mājah, 1803; Dāraquṭnī, 1935, 1937; Bayhaqī, 8287, 18643, 18667; Ibn Khuzaymah, 2268; Ibn Ḥibbān, 4886; Ḥākim, 1449. See: TM, 905, 1663.
46. Abū ʿAwn Muḥammad ibn ʿAbd Allāh al-Thaqafī: Bayhaqī, 18685. See: BM, 9:210; al-Māwardī, 14:299.
47. al-Bughā, *Al-Tadhhīb,* 234 #3.

[The Imam] can also insist that the *dhimmīs* accommodate Muslim travelers.

The Prophet ﷺ made a treaty with the people of Iliya for a *jizyah* payment of 300 *dīnārs* (taken from their three hundred men) and stipulated that they must also accommodate Muslims who pass by.[48]

Abū Hurayrah (may Allah be pleased with him) reported that the Messenger of Allah ﷺ said, "Hospitality extends for three days. Anything beyond this is charity."[49]

The *jizyah* is collected graciously, as are all other debts.

If someone dies during the year, enters Islam, or becomes insane, [the *jizyah* amount] is taken only for the time prior to their change in status.

OBLIGATIONS

ولا بدّ من التزامهم أحكام الملّة، ويبني دون بناء جاره المسلم، ويركب غير الخيل بإكاف عرضًا، ويلبس الغيار والزّنّار فوق الثّياب، ويتميّز في الحمام.

The *dhimmīs* must adhere to the rulings of their sect [by avoiding things their religion and Islam both consider unlawful, including theft, murder, and fornication].

The Prophet ﷺ stoned a male and female Jew for fornication.[50]

‹As for the things they do not believe to be unlawful: Sharīʿah law is not applied to them unless they bring a dispute to a Muslim judge, in which case he judges according to Sharīʿah Law.[51]›

48. Abū al-Huwayrith: Bayhaqī, 18678. See: BM, 9:196–98; cf TM, 1665.
49. Abū Hurayrah: Abū Dāwūd, 3749; al-Bayhaqī, 18692. See BM, 9:409; TM, 1665.
50. Ibn ʿUmar: Bukhārī, 6819; Muslim, 1699. See: KBM, 2377; al-Rūyānī, *Baḥr al-madhhab*, 13:10.
51. al-Bughā, *Al-Tadhhīb*, 234 #5.

The heights of the *dhimmīs*' buildings must be lower than those of their Muslim neighbors.

This is because of the hadith, "Islam is superior and is never surpassed."[52]

The height restriction is to prevent them from spying on Muslims in their private spaces.

If one buys a tall building, it is left as it is. If it falls into ruin, he cannot return it to a height that is higher or equal [to his Muslim neighbors].

They must ride mounts other than horses,...

Since horses are mighty.

...use a padded saddle, and ride side-saddle.

They are to dress distinctively with a sash over their clothes, and identify themselves in the public bath.

This is so they will not resemble ‹and be mistaken for› a Muslim.

RESTRICTIONS

ولا يوقر، ولا يصدر، ولا يبدأ بسلام، ويلجأ إلى أضيق الطّرق، ويمنع من إظهار منكر وإحداث بيع في دارنا،

وتبقي إن شرط، ويمنع من المقام في الحجاز، وكذا من سائر المساجد إلا بإذن.

***Dhimmīs* are not to be honored, introduced first, or greeted with "*al-salāmu ʿalaykum.*" They must keep to the sides of the streets.**

Abū Hurayrah (may Allah be pleased with him) reported that the Messenger of Allah ﷺ said, "Do not initiate [greetings of] peace

52. ʿĀʾidh ibn ʿAmr al-Muzanī: Bukhārī, 3:258 – *taʿlīqan*; Dāraquṭnī, 3620; Bayhaqī, 12155. See: TM, 1332, 1667.

with the Jews and Christians. When you encounter one of them on the road, force him to the narrowest part."[53]

They are barred from openly displaying anything objectionable,...

Including wine, bells, their beliefs concerning ʿĪsā (peace be upon him), and swine.

...and building places of worship in Muslim lands. [Existing places of worship] are allowed to remain, if stipulated [in the *jizyah* contract].

They are barred from residing in the Ḥijāz,...

ʿUmar (may Allah be pleased with him) said: "The Prophet ﷺ said, 'I swear to expel the Jews and Christians from the Arabian Peninsula so no one will be left except Muslims.'"[54]

...and similarly [from entering all] mosques – unless given permission.

‹Any Muslim's permission suffices.[55]›

TRUCES

(فصل) [الهدنة]

The foundation for truces [*hudnah*] (before consensus) comes from Allah Most High saying, "[O disbelievers], travel freely in the land four months..." [Q9:2], "And if they [the disbelievers] incline to peace, incline thou also to it..." [Q8:61]. Also, the Prophet ﷺ made a truce with Quraysh in the Year of Hudaybiyyah.

53. Abū Hurayrah: Muslim, 2167 #13; Tirmidhī, 1602, 2700; al-Bayhaqī, 18725. See TM, 1668.

54. ʿUmar: Muslim, 1767. See: TM, 1664.

55. al-Nawawī, *Rauḍat al-ṭālibīn*, 10:311.

يهادن الإمام ونائبه لمصلحة أربعة أشهر، ولضعف عشر سنين، لا بمال من غير خوف، وإن هادن على أن له الخيار في الفسخ متى شاء جاز، ويفي لهم بالشّرط الصّحيح إلى نقضهم، وبأمارته نبذ وأنذر.

The Imam or his deputy can make truces with the disbelievers – for the welfare of the Muslims – lasting up to four months or up to ten years, due to the weakness [of the Muslims].

Only the Imam or his representative can give amnesty to an entire land.

Amnesty was initially prohibited by the verse, "Then, when the sacred months have passed, slay the idolaters wherever ye find them..." [Q9:5]. It was then permitted for up to four months with the verse, "[O disbelievers], travel freely in the land four months..." [Q9:2].

The soundest opinion is that a truce between four months and one year is permissible, since that time is less than the duration of *jizyah*.

When the Muslims are weak (may Allah protect us!), a longer truce is permissible. This is because the Prophet ﷺ made truce for ten years with Suhayl ibn ʿAmr at Hudaybiyyah.[56]

Tribute is not paid [to the enemy] except out of fear. The Imam [or his deputy] may make a treaty that he can annul whenever he wishes.

He abides by the treaty and its valid conditions [and shows good will]until the enemy violates them.

Allah Most High says, "fulfil their treaty to them till their term" [Q9:4].

56. Al-Miswar ibn Makhramah and Marwān ibn al-Ḥakam: Abū Dāwūd, 2766. See: TM, 1669.

If they show signs of treachery, the Imam may break it off [preemptively] and warn the enemy [of the consequences].

Allah Most High says, "And if thou fearest treachery from any folk, then throw back to them (their treaty) fairly. Lo! Allah loveth not the treacherous." [Q8:58].[57]

And after fulfilling whatever rights the enemy is owed, the Imam escorts them to safety.

57. See al-Shāfiʿī, *Al-Umm,* 4:196.

13

HUNTING AND SLAUGHTERING

كِتَابُ الصَّيْدِ وَالْذَّبَائِحِ

The foundation for the rulings related to hunting and slaughtering is Allah Most High saying, "...But when ye have left the sacred territory, then go hunting (if ye will)..." [Q5:2], and "...Say: '(all) good things are made lawful for you...'" [Q5:4]. That which has been properly slaughtered is among the good things [mentioned in the verse]. The rulings also have a foundation in the Sunnah (as will come). And there is consensus concerning them as well.

SLAUGHTERING

(فصل) [الذّكاة]

Evidence that slaughtering [*dhakāh*] is of consideration comes in Allah Most High saying, "...saving that which ye make lawful (by the death-stroke)..." [Q5:3].

WHAT CONSTITUTES SLAUGHTERING

ذكاة الحيوان المأكول بالذّبح – في الحلق واللبة بتمام الحلقوم والمريء، ولو من كتابيّ بجارح، لا عظم، وغير المقدور بالعقر المزهق حيث كان.

An edible animal is [properly] slaughtered by cutting it (at the top of the throat or the base of the neck),...

ʿUmar (may Allah be pleased with him) said, "Slaughtering is at the top of the throat or the base of the neck."[1] ‹A similar report comes from Ibn ʿAbbās (may Allah be pleased with him).[2]› It is also attributed to the Prophet ﷺ.[3]

...and completely cutting the throat and esophagus...

The hadith from Rāfiʿ ibn Khadīj (may Allah be pleased with him) includes, "Tomorrow we hope or fear the enemy and we have no knives [for slaughtering animals]. Do we slaughter with reeds?" The Prophet ﷺ said, "Whatever causes blood to flow and Allah's name is mentioned over, eat – [but] do not use a tooth or a nail [to cut]. I will tell you why: as for the tooth, it is bone; as for the nail, it is the blade of the [non-Muslim] Ethiopians."[4]

It is not permissible to eat an animal killed by blunt force. When asked about prey [killed by] sticks, the Prophet ﷺ replied, "If it is killed by its [sharp] edge then eat, but if it was killed by its force then do not eat."[5]

...(even if by a Jew or Christian [*kitābī*]),...

Animals slaughtered by any other non-Muslims is not permissible to eat, since the general rule is that slaughtered meat is permissible from anyone whom we can marry, but not from whomever we cannot.

An exception [to this guideline is] a Jewish or Christian female slave, as marrying her is not permissible but it is permissible to consume meat she has slaughtered.

---

1. Bukhārī, 7:93; Bayhaqī, 19124. al-Muzanī, *Al-Mukhtaṣar,* 8:392.
2. Bukhārī, 7:93; Bayhaqī, 19122-3.
3. Bayhaqī, 19124.
4. Rāfiʿ ibn Khadīj: Bukhārī, 2488, 5503; Muslim, 1968. See: TM, 1673.
5. ʿAdī ibn Ḥātim: Bukhārī, 175; Muslim, 1929 #1–7; Abū Dāwūd, 2841; Nasāʾī, 4264. (Note: The hadith doesn't mention killing through blunt force.) See: TM, 1680.

Allah Most High says, "The food of those who have received the Scripture is lawful for you..." [Q5:5]. ‹What is meant by "food" is animals that have been slaughtered. This is explicit proof that meat slaughtered by the People of the Book is permissible for Muslims to consume, and that meat slaughtered by anyone else – including Zoroastrians, idolaters, and the like – is unlawful.[6]›

...with an implement (other than bone) that wounds.

This is because of the hadith of Rāfiᶜ ibn Khadīj (may Allah be pleased with him).[7] ‹Additionally, slaughtering using a bone or a tooth is painful for the animal.[8]›

An animal that one is unable to slaughter [in the manner mentioned above], is slaughtered by fatally wounding it however one can.

This is permissible out of necessity.

Rāfiᶜ ibn Khadīj (may Allah be pleased with him) said that the Prophet ﷺ captured camels and sheep as spoils of war and a camel fled. They didn't have a horse [to ride in pursuit] so a man shot it with an arrow and stopped it – i.e., it died – and the Messenger of Allah ﷺ said, "These animals are like wild beasts. If any of them does this [runs away], do just like this [shoot arrows at it]."[9]

---

6. al-Bughā, *Al-Tadhhīb,* 239 #1–2.
7. Preceded.
8. al-Bughā, *Al-Tadhhīb,* 238 #4.
9. Rāfiᶜ ibn Khadīj: Bukhārī, 5503, 5509; Muslim, 1968 #20. See: TM, 1673.

SAYING "*BISMI LLĀH*"

وتندب بالتسمية والاستقبال والسرعة.

It is recommended to say "*Bismi Llāh,*" face the animal towards the direction of prayer, and [slaughter it] quickly.

‹The complete method of slaughter is to sever the air passage [trachea], food passage [esophagus], and the two veins on either side of the neck [carotid arteries]. It is recommended to cut them all since it eases the passing of the spirit and so the act of slaughtering is a form of beneficence towards the animal.[10]›

Allah Most High says, "Eat of that over which the name of Allah hath been mentioned, if ye are believers in His revelations" [Q6:118]. As for "And do not eat of that upon which the name of Allah has not been mentioned..." [Q6:121], it refers to food that has been sacrificed to idols, as does "...and that which hath been dedicated unto any other than Allah..." [Q5:3]. One of these verses emphasizes this: "...for lo! it is abomination" [Q6:121]. And there is consensus that anyone who eats meat slaughtered by a Muslim who failed to mention Allah's name over it is not morally corrupt.

HUNTING WITH ANIMALS

وإذا أرسل بصير جارحة معلّمة على صيد، حلّ.

If someone who is not blind sends a trained predator against a game animal [and injures or kills it], it is permissible [to eat].

It is permissible to hunt using any animal with fangs (like lynxes or dogs), or birds with talons (like falcons and hawks). Allah Most High says, "They ask thee (O Muhammad) what is made lawful for them. Say: (all) good things are made lawful for you. And those beasts and birds of prey which ye have trained as hounds are trained, ye teach them that which Allah taught you; so eat of that which

10. al-Bughā, *Al-Tadhhīb,* 237 #1.

they catch for you and mention Allah's name upon it, and observe your duty to Allah. Lo! Allah is swift to take account" [Q5:4].

The predator must be trained so that when it is sent, it goes; when it is told to stop, it stops; if it kills the prey, it eats nothing from it; and it does the above repeatedly. When one of these conditions is not met, it is impermissible to eat the hunted animal's meat – unless it is found still alive and then slaughtered.

‹The foundation for these conditions includes the previous hadiths, along with the following hadiths:›

ʿAdī ibn Ḥātim (may Allah be pleased with him) said that the Prophet ﷺ said, "If you send a trained dog and mention the name of Allah, and it catches [its prey] and kills [it], then eat. If it eats of it then do not eat of it since it caught it for itself."[11]

Abū Thaʿlabah (may Allah be pleased with him) said that the Prophet ﷺ said, "If you hunt something with your untrained dog and are able to slaughter it before it dies, you may eat it."[12]

‹The hadith means reaching it while it is still alive and then slaughtering it.[13]›

AN ANIMAL'S FETUS

وذكاة الجنين ذكاة أمّه.

An unborn animal is slaughtered by slaughtering its mother.

It does not need to be slaughtered separately. The Prophet ﷺ said, "Slaughtering an unborn animal occurs by slaughtering its mother."[14]

---

11. ʿAdī ibn Ḥātim: Bukhārī, 5484; Muslim, 1929 #1–3. See: TM, 1680.
12. Abū Thaʿlabah: Bukhārī, 5488; Muslim, 1930. See: TM, 1681.
13. al-Bughā, *Al-Tadhhīb,* 238 #3.
14. Abū Saʿīd al-Khudrī: Tirmidhī, 1476 – *ḥasan*; Ibn Mājah, 3199; Ibn Ḥibbān, 5889; Dāraquṭnī, 4737, 4740; Ḥākim, 7110–12; Bayhaqī, 19492. See: TM, 1733.

Fish [i.e., aquatic creatures] do not need to be slaughtered. The Prophet ﷺ said, "Two unslaughtered animals are permitted to us: fish and locusts."[15]

PARTS SEVERED FROM LIVING ANIMALS

وما أبين من حيّ فهو ميّت إلا المسك وفأرته، وشعر المأكول.

Whatever is severed from a living animal is the same as something from an animal that was not [properly] slaughtered...

The Prophet ﷺ said, "Whatever is cut from a living creature is dead."[16] And there is consensus.

... – except for musk, musk pods, and hair [or fur, or feathers] from an edible animal.

Musk is according to consensus. Musk pods are analogous to an unborn animal and are pure only when separated while the animal is alive.

THE EID AL-AḌḤĀ SACRIFICE

(فصل) [التّضحيّة]

The foundation for the Eid sacrifice, prior to consensus, is that Allah Most High says, "And the camels! We have appointed them among the ceremonies of Allah..." [Q22:36], and "So pray unto

15. Preceded.

16. Abū Saʿīd al-Khudrī: Ḥākim, 7151, 7598. Another version reads, "Whatever is cut from a creature while it is alive is dead." [Abū Dāwūd, 2858; Tirmidhī, 1480, Dāraquṭnī, 4792–3; Ḥākim, 7150, 7152, 7597; Bayhaqī, 77, 78, 18924. See: TM, 127. And another, "Whatever is cut from creature while it is alive: what is cut is dead." [Ibn Mājah, 3216. See: TM, 127.] In these hadiths, "dead" means unslaughtered.

thy Lord, and sacrifice [*wa-nḥar*]…" [Q108:2]. According to the best-known opinion, "pray" refers to the Eid Prayer, and "sacrifice" [*wa-nḥar*] refers to the sacrifice of Eid. The Sunnah concerning it is *ṣaḥīḥ* and well known.

ELIGIBLE ANIMALS

يضحى بثني الإبل والبقر ويجزىء عن سبعة، والمعز وجذع الضأن.

Sacrifices [for Eid al-Aḍḥā]…

Anas (may Allah be pleased with him) said that the Prophet ﷺ offered as sacrifices two horned rams that were white in color with some black. He ﷺ slaughtered them with his own hand. He ﷺ mentioned the name of Allah over them, saying *"Allāhu akbar,"* and put his foot on their sides.

Slaughtering [on Eid al-Aḍḥā] is recommended; it is not obligatory unless one vowed to do it. He ﷺ said, "Whoever made a vow to obey Allah is to obey Allah."[17]

‹Thus, slaughtering for Eid al-Aḍḥā is recommended. Allah Most High says, "So pray unto thy Lord, and sacrifice," [Q108:2] – meaning pray the Eid prayer and slaughter your sacrifice.[18]›

…are made with a

1. **five-year-old camel or two-year-old cow (either one suffices for up to seven [individual sacrifices]);[19]**
2. **a one-year-old sheep; or**
3. **a two-year-old goat.**

17. ʿĀʾishah: Bukhārī, 6700. See: TM, 1749.
18. al-Bughā, *Al-Tadhhīb,* 242 #2.
19. Jābir: Muslim, 1318. See: TM, 1688.

DEFECTS THAT PRECLUDE ELIGIBILITY

ولا يجزىء فيها ما نقص لحمها.

[An animal] whose meat is reduced [due to sickness or defects] is ineligible [as a sacrifice].

Al-Barāʾ ibn ʿĀzib (may Allah be pleased with him) said that the Prophet ﷺ said, "Four are not permitted for Eid sacrifices: an animal that has lost sight in one eye, an animal that is clearly sick, an animal with a discernible limp, and an emaciated animal that has lost its marrow."[20]

ʿĀlī (may Allah be pleased with him) said, "The Messenger of Allah ﷺ ordered that we check the [sacrificial animal's] eyes and ears and not slaughter one that is cut from the front of its ears [*muqābalah*], or one that is cut from the back of its ears [*mudābirrah*], or one whose ears are split [*sharqāʾ*], or one with a hole made in its ears as a distinguishing mark [*kharqāʾ*]."[21]

ITS DESIGNATED TIME

ووقتها من طلوع الشّمس يوم العيد، ومضي قدر ركعتين وخطبتين خفيفات إلى آخر التّشريق، ولا بدّ من النّيّة.

The time [of sacrifice] begins on the Day of Eid, after the sun has risen, and enough time has passed to pray two prayer cycles [*rakʿatayn*] and give two short sermons.

20. al-Barāʾ ibn ʿĀzib: Abū Dāwūd, 2802; Tirmidhī, 1497 – *ṣaḥīḥ*; Nasāʾī, 4369, 4370, 4371; Ibn Mājah, 3144; Bayhaqī, 10246, 19097, 19099, 19100; Ibn Khuzaymah, 2912; Ibn Ḥibbān, 5919, 5921, 5922; Ḥākim, 1718, 7527. See: TM, 1692.

21. ʿĀlī: Abū Dāwūd, 2797; Tirmidhī, 1498; Nasāʾī, 4374; Ibn Mājah, 350–355. See: TM, 1693.

Al-Barā' ibn ʿĀzib (may Allah be pleased with him) reported that the Messenger of Allah ﷺ said, "The first thing we do on this day of ours is to offer the [Eid] prayer and then we return to perform our sacrifices. Whoever does so has acted in accordance our norms. Whoever slaughtered before the prayer has only offered meat to present to his family and that has nothing to do with rites."[22]

Its time continues until [sunset on] the last day of Tashrīq [the third day after Eid al-Aḍḥā].

Jubayr ibn Muṭʿim (may Allah be pleased with him) said that the Messenger of Allah ﷺ said, "All the days of Tashrīq are slaughtering days."[23]

One must make the intention [at the time of slaughter].

OPTIMAL MEASURES

والأفضل سبع من الغنم، ثمّ البدنة، ثمّ البقرة، وأن تكون سمينة بيضاء، وأن لا يزيل شعره وظفره في عشر ذي الحجة.

The best [animals] to [sacrifice, in order of preference are] seven sheep, then a camel, then a cow.

One sheep suffices for one person [or household]; a cow or a camel suffices for seven people.

Jābir (may Allah be pleased with him) said, "We slaughtered with the Messenger of Allah ﷺ at Ḥudaybiyyah: one camel for seven, and one cow for seven."[24]

---

22. al-Barā' ibn ʿĀzib: Bukhārī, 5545; Muslim, 1961 #7.
23. Jubayr ibn Muṭʿim: Ibn Ḥibbān, 3854; Dāraquṭnī, 4758; Bayhaqī, 10226, 19239, 19241, 19243. See: TM, 1696.
24. Jābir: Muslim, 1318. See: TM, 1688.

It is best if [the sacrificial animal] is fat and white.

It is best that [the person intending to slaughter] not cut or pluck his hair or trim his nails during the first ten days of Dhi al-Ḥijjah.

RECOMMENDED ACTS

وسنّ التّسميّة والصّلاة على رسول الله ﷺ، والاستقبال والتّكبير، والدّعاء بالقبول.

It is a sunnah [while sacrificing] to say "*Bismi Llāh*"; to offer prayers upon the Messenger of Allāh ﷺ; to face to direction of prayer; to say "*Allāhu akbar*"; and to supplicate for its acceptance.

It is recommended that the sacrificial animal or the person slaughtering it face the direction of prayer, as this is the best of directions and superior when performing good deeds.

GIVING AWAY THE MEAT

و[سّن] أكل لقمة - وتحرم من الواجب - والتّصدّق بالباقي، والكمال بالثلثين،
ويجب تمليك الفقير اللحم نيئًا أقلُ شيء، وجاز إطعام الغني لا تمليكه.

[It is recommended] to eat a small portion...

Allah Most High says, "And the camels! We have appointed them among the ceremonies of Allah. Therein ye have much good. So mention the name of Allah over them when they are drawn up in lines. Then when their flanks fall (dead), eat thereof and feed the beggar [*qāniʿ*] and the suppliant..." [Q22:36].

‹In the verse, "when their flanks fall (dead)," means when the sacrificial animals have fallen to the ground after being stabbed at the base of the neck. From that point on, one may eat from them;

"the beggar [*qāniʿ*]" refers to those who are needy yet satisfied with what they are given and do not ask [of men].[25]›

...(though it is unlawful if the sacrifice is obligatory)...

Vowing to sacrifice makes it obligatory. It is unlawful to eat from it since its legal status is analogous to the recompense for hunting [during Ḥajj].

Using the meat in any other way is analogous to eating it, so all of it must be given as charity. If one eats any part of it or makes other use of it, one must replace that portion with something similar or pay its value.

...and to give the rest away in charity, with two thirds being the optimum.

Allah Most High says, "...and feed the beggar and the suppliant..." [Q22:36].

It is required to give a minimal amount of raw meat to the destitute.

This is when the sacrifice is not obligatory. Otherwise, all of it must be given away.

It is permissible to feed the affluent – but not to give [the uncooked meat] to them.

Since the word "*qāniʿ*" in the verse [Q22:36] means "someone who is satisfied," [which includes the affluent, so one may feed them].

25. al-Bughā, *Al-Tadhhīb,* 246 #3.

SLAUGHTERING FOR A NEWBORN

(فصل) [العقيقة]

والعقيقة كالتّضحيّة من الولادة إلى البلوغ، وفي السابع أفضل، كما في التّسميّة وحلق رأسه.

للذّكر شاتان وللأنثى شاة، بلا كسر عظم، ويسنّ طبخه بحلو.

Slaughtering for a newborn [*ʿaqīqah*] requires the same conditions as a [typical] sacrifice. It can be performed anytime from the child's birth until adolescence, though is best to do it on the seventh day, just as it is to name the child and shave his head.

ʿĀʾishah (may Allah be pleased with her) said, "The Messenger of Allah ﷺ performed *ʿaqīqah*s for al-Ḥasan and al-Ḥusein (may Allah be pleased with them) on the seventh [day after their births] and named them. He commanded that their heads be shaved."[26]

Two sheep [are slaughtered] for a boy and one for a girl.

The Prophet ﷺ was asked about the *ʿaqīqah* and he said, "Two sheep are for males, one sheep is for females."[27]

Its bones are not broken and it is cooked in a sweet sauce.

[These symbolic gestures are meant] as optimistic forerunners to the lifelong well-being of the child.

---

26. ʿĀʾishah: Ibn Ḥibbān, 5311 and Ḥākim, 7588. See: TM, 1700.
27. ʿĀʾishah: Tirmidhī, 1513 – *ṣaḥīḥ*; Ibn Ḥibbān, 5310; Ḥākim, 7595. See also: Abū Dāwūd, 2834, 2835; Nasāʾī, 4218; Tirmidhī, 1516; Ibn Mājah, 3162; Ibn Ḥibbān, 5312; Ḥākim, 7595; Bayhaqī, 19336. See: TM, 1702.

LAWFUL AND PROHIBITED ANIMALS

(فصل) [بيان ما يحلّ من حيوان وما يحرم]

The foundation for the lawfulness and prohibition of certain animals includes Allah Most High saying, "They ask thee (O Muhammad) what is made lawful for them. Say: '(all) good things are made lawful for you...'" [Q5:4].

GENERAL GUIDELINES

كلّ حيوان استطابته العرب ولم يرد الشرع بتحريمه حلال، وعكسه حرام كما له ناب وظفر.

Every animal the Arabs [during the time of the Prophet ﷺ] considered wholesome...

The custom of the Arabs is given legal consideration since they are the ones who first received the Sacred Law. The Prophet ﷺ was one of them, and the Quran was revealed to them.

...and that the Sacred Law did not specifically declare unlawful, is lawful.

Allah Most High says, "...make lawful for them all good things [*ṭayyibāt*] and prohibit for them only the foul [*khabā'ith*]..." [Q7:157].

The opposite is unlawful, as is every animal with fangs...

Abū Tha'labah (may Allah be pleased with him) said that the Messenger of Allah ﷺ prohibited the consumption of every predator with fangs.[28]

28. Abū Tha'labah: Bukhārī, 5530; Muslim, 1931 #13–14. See: TM, 1719.

Animals forbidden because of fangs include wolves, lions, and dogs.

[The prohibition] does not include the hyena since there is an indemnity [*fidyah*] for killing it and indemnities are only owed for edible animals.

Jābir (may Allah be pleased with him) was asked whether hyenas are game. He said, "Yes." He was asked whether they are eaten. He said, "Yes." He was asked whether he heard it from the Messenger of Allah ﷺ. He said, "Yes."[29]

Dogs and cats are considered predators.

The ruling also applies to birds that hunt with their beaks.

All creatures that creep and crawl on the ground [*ḥasharāt*], which includes insects and reptiles, are inedible since they are disgusting. Locusts are an exception because the Prophet ﷺ said, "Two [types of] carrion are lawful for us: fish and locusts."[30]

Another exception is a type of desert lizard [Ar., *ḍabb;* Lat. *Uromastyx maliensis*]. This is because of a hadith about eating them.[31]

...and talons.

Ibn ʿAbbās (may Allah be pleased with him) said that the Messenger of Allah ﷺ prohibited the consumption of every predatory beast with fangs, and every bird with talons.[32]

Examples of other forbidden creatures include frogs (due to the prohibition of killing them).[33] Whatever is forbidden to kill has sanctity. Also, frogs are considered filthy.

[Other forbidden animals include] alligators (since they are filthy, harmful, and hunt with their fangs), [terrestrial] crabs,[34] and snakes.

29. Ibn Abī ʿAmmār: Nasāʾī, 2836; Ibn Mājah, 3236; Tirmidhī, 851; al-Ḥākim, 1662. See: TM, 1716.

30. Ibn ʿUmar: Ibn Mājah, 3218, 3314. See: KBM, 11.

31. Ibn ʿUmar: Bukhārī, 5536; Muslim, 1943 #39–41. See: TM, 1717.

32. Ibn ʿAbbās: Muslim, 1934. See: TM, 1721.

33. ʿAbd al-Raḥmān ibn ʿUthmān: Abū Dāwūd, 5269; Nasāʾī, 4355; Ḥākim, 5882, 8261; Bayhaqī, 9:317–318. See: TM, 3, 1707.

34. The prohibition excludes crabs that spend their entire lives in water.

ANIMALS THAT EAT URINE AND FECES

وتكره الجلالة حتى تطيب.

It is offensive to eat meat from an animal that feeds on urine and feces [*jalālah*] until it becomes wholesome.

Ibn ʿUmar (may Allah be pleased with them both) said, "The Messenger of Allah ﷺ forbade eating an animal that feeds on urine and feces [*jalālah*] and [consuming] its milk."[35]

ʿAbd Allāh bin ʿAmr (may Allah be pleased with them both) said, "The Messenger of Allah ﷺ forbade eating the meat or drinking the milk of animals that have fed on urine and feces [*jalālah*]. Nothing is carried on them except *udm,* and people do not ride them. [This is] until they are fed fodder for forty days."[36]

CONSUMING FORBIDDEN FOODS OUT OF NECESSITY

ويجب لخوف ومرض مخوف أكل الحرام.

It is obligatory for someone who fears dying from starvation or a fatal illness to eat things that are otherwise unlawful.

Allah Most High says, "...unless ye are compelled thereto..." [Q6:119].

‹In the verse: "unless ye are compelled thereto," means "eat of, since it is also permissible to," i.e., one is not barred from eating it out of necessity: what has been forbidden has been clarified and this is not among it.[37]

Allah Most High says, "Forbidden unto you (for food) are dead animals and blood and swineflesh, and that which hath been dedicated unto any other than Allah..." and then saying, "...Whoso is

35. Ibn ʿUmar: Abū Dāwūd, 3785; Tirmidhī, 1824; Ibn Mājah, 3189; Ḥākim, 2284. See TM, 1726.
36. ʿAbd Allāh ibn ʿAmr: Ḥākim, 2269; Bayhaqī, 19480. See TM, 1727.
37. al-Maḥallī and al-Suyūṭī, *Tafsīr al-Jalālayn.*

forced by hunger, not by will, to sin: (for him) lo! Allah is Forgiving, Merciful." [Q5:3].[38]›

The same applies to consuming what is forbidden for the sake of medical treatment. It is not permissible to ingest unadulterated alcohol since it is a poison rather than a medication. However, mixtures that include alcohol are permissible since their alcohol content has been [sufficiently] diluted.

38. al-Bughā, *Al-Tadhhīb,* 242 #1.

14

CONTESTS AND MARKSMANSHIP

كِتَابُ السَّبْقِ وَالرَّمِي

The foundation for the rulings on contests and marksmanship comes from the Quran and Sunnah. It includes Allah Most High saying, "Make ready for them all thou canst of (armed) force..." [Q8:60]. The Legislator ﷺ explained that the verse refers to marksmanship. The Prophet ﷺ said, "Surely, strength is in archery" three times.[1] Its foundation from the Sunnah is well known, and there is consensus concerning it. Al-Muzanī said that no one preceded al-Shāfiʿī in compiling a chapter on these subjects (may Allah grant them His mercy).

المسابقة جائزة فيما له حافر أو نصل ونحوهما بمال من أحدهما، ومنهما إن كان ثَمّ محلّل، مع علم المسافة.

Contests are permissible with every hoofed animal, marksmanship,...

The Messenger of Allah ﷺ held races from al-Ḥafyāʾ to Thaniyyat al-Wadāʾ using horses that had been trained for this purpose, and from Thaniyyah [al-Wadāʾ] to the mosque of Banī Zuraiq using horses that had not been trained. Ibn ʿUmar (may Allah be pleased with him and his father) was a contestant in the latter race.[2]

1. ʿUqbah ibn ʿĀmir: Muslim, 1917 #167. See: KBM, 2761.
2. Ibn ʿUmar: Bukhārī, 420, 2868, 2869; Muslim, 1870 #95. See: TM, 1735.

Such contests can be performed using any implements of war or whatever is useful for war. The Messenger of Allah ﷺ said, "There is no wager except for camels, horses, and marksmanship."[3]

‹The meaning of the hadith is that it is not permissible to take money from wagers except in the three contexts mentioned above, and provided that the conditions mentioned in the text are met.›

...and the like; with the wager coming from one of two participants or from both of them – if there is a [third] non-wagering participant,...

Abū Hurayrah (may Allah be pleased with him) reported that the Prophet ﷺ said, "Whoever enters a horse [in a race] against two other horses, not knowing whether it will win, is not gambling. But whoever enters a horse [in race] against two other horses, certain that it will win, is gambling."[4]

A contest in which every participant puts up a wager and has a chance to win or lose is not permissible – this is gambling, which is unlawful.

It is permissible when one of two participants puts up the wager, since it negates the form of gambling just mentioned. It is also permissible for the wager to come from a non-contestant, such as the Imam staking it from the Muslim treasury [*bayt al-māl*], or a private individual using his own money.

The introduction of a contestant who does not stake his own wager also removes it from being gambling.

...and provided that the distance is defined.

The distance must be defined (for races and marksmanship), as does whatever constitutes a "hit" (in marksmanship).

---

3. Abū Hurayrah: Abū Dāwūd, 2574; Tirmidhī, 1700; Nasā'ī, 3585, 3586, 3589; Ibn Mājah, 2878; Ibn Ḥibbān, 4690. See: TM, 1738.
4. Abū Hurayrah: Abū Dāwūd, 2579; Ibn Mājah, 2876; Ḥākim, 2536; Bayhaqī, 19770–71. See TM (1739).

15

OATHS AND VOWS

كِتَابُ الْأَيْمَانِ وَالنُّذُوْرِ

OATHS

(فصل) [الأيمان]

The foundation for the rulings on oaths is found in the Quran, such as Allah Most High saying, "And make not Allah, by your oaths, a hindrance..." [Q2:224]. Their foundation also includes well-known hadiths.

The Muslim community has consensus that oaths are binding, and that there is an expiation associated with violating them.

BINDING AND NON-BINDING OATHS

لا ينعقد اليمين إلّا من مكلّف مختار بالله تعالى، أو صفة له.

An oath is not binding unless it comes from someone who is [legally] responsible and who does it willfully by [mentioning] Allah Most High or one of His attributes.

‹An oath [*yamīn*] is a vow to tell the truth. It is so named because traditionally, an individual swearing to tell the truth would take hold of his companion's *yamīn* [right hand].[1]›

1. al-Bughā, *Al-Tadhhīb,* 252 #1.

Allah Most High says, "Allah will not take you to task for that which is unintentional in your oaths..." [Q2:225, Q5:89]. And he ﷺ said, "By Allah, I will fight the Quraysh" three times.[2]

The oath must be made willfully. An oath made under compulsion is not valid or binding. He ﷺ said, "Mistakes, forgetfulness, and what one is compelled to do have been lifted from my Community."[3]

An oath does not change the legality of the action one is swearing to perform. Saying "By God, I will not eat bread," does not make eating bread unlawful. Likewise, saying "By God, I will drink wine" does not make drinking wine permissible.

SWEARING TO GIVE AWAY ONE'S PROPERTY

ومن حلف ليتصدّقنّ بماله، خير بينه وبين كفارة اليمين.

Whoever swears to give his property away as charity must either do so...

One chooses between fulfilling what one swore to do (such as giving property as charity or performing a particular charitable deed), and making an expiation.

...or make an expiation for breaking his oath.

ʿUqbah ibn ʿĀmir (may Allah be pleased with him) said that the Messenger of Allah ﷺ said, "The expiation for [breaking] a vow is akin to the expiation for [breaking] an oath."[4]

---

2. ʿIkrimah, *mursil*: Abū Dāwūd, 3285–6; Ibn Ḥibbān, 4343; Bayhaqī, 19927, 19929, 19930. ʿIkrimah, *marfūʿ*: Ibn Ḥibbān, 4343; Bayhaqī, 19929. See: TM, 1741.
3. Abū Dharr: Ibn Mājah, 2043, 2045; Ibn Ḥibbān, 7219; Ḥākim, 2801 – and al-Dhahabī concurred. Al-Nawawī considered *ḥasan* in *Al-Rawḍah* (8:193). See: TM, 1486, 1542, 1576.
4. Uqbah ibn ʿĀmir: Muslim, 1645. See: TM, 1750.

CARELESSLY UTTERED OATHS

ومن سبق لسانه إلى لفظها من غير قصد فليس بيمين.

Thoughtlessly uttering a phrase with one's tongue is not an oath.

There is no expiation for this, nor is it a sin.

Allah Most High says, "Allah will not take you to task for that which is unintentional in your oaths. But He will take you to task for that which your hearts have garnered..." [Q2:225], "...the oaths which ye swear in earnest..." [Q5:89].

ʿĀ'ishah (may Allah be pleased with her) said, "This verse was revealed concerning statements such as 'No, by Allah,' and 'Yes, by Allah.'"[5]

SWEARING A COMPOUND OATH

والحلف على أمرين يتعلّق بهما.

Swearing to do two things entails performing them both.

[Performing just one of them] does not fulfill such an oath because the oath concerns the performance of [the combination of] both actions, not one or the other.

SWEARING NOT TO PERFORM AN ACT

والحلف على [ألّا ي]فعل شيء لا يحنث بفعل وكيله إلّا النّكاح.

If someone swears [not] to do something, the oath is not broken if his agent performs it – except for marriage.

Breaking an oath means failing to fulfill what is required by the oath. The oath would not be broken in the example given above because the one who swore the oath did not directly perform

5. ʿĀ'ishah: Bukhārī, 6286. See: TM, 1744.

the action, and actions are attributed to the person who directly performs them. Since he swore that he himself would not do it, someone else performing it did not break his oath.

EXPIATIONS FOR BROKEN OATHS

وكفارة اليمين مخيّرة بين عتق رقبة كالظّهار وإطعام عشرة مساكين كلّ مسكين مدّ حبّ - من غالب قوت بلده - وكسوتهم بما يسمّى كسوة، فإن عجز فصيام ثلاثة أيّام.

The expiation for breaking an oath is any one of the following: manumission of a Muslim slave (as with *ẓihār*);[6] feeding ten of the poor by giving each person one *mudd* [0.51 liters] of grain from the dominant foodstuff of his land; clothing ten poor persons, each with [a single article of] whatever is considered clothing; or, fasting three days (if one is incapable of the above).

Allah Most High says,"...The expiation thereof is the feeding of ten of the needy with the average of that wherewith ye feed your own folk, or the clothing of them, or the liberation of a slave, and for him who findeth not (the wherewithal to do so) then a three days' fast..." [Q5:89].

VOWS

(فصل) [النّذر]

The foundation for the rulings on vows is based on Allah Most High saying, "(Because) they perform the vow..." [Q76:7], well-known hadiths, and consensus. Al-Shāfiʿī (may Allah grant him His mercy) stated that vows are offensive because the prohibition against them is *ṣaḥiḥ,* so no good comes from them, and that they are to get the miserly to pay.

6. See "Likening One's Wife to One's Mother" on page 386.

BINDING AND NON-BINDING VOWS

النّذر التزام مكلّف مسلم قربةً لا مباحًا ومعصيةً.

A vow [*nadhr*] is when a [legally] responsible Muslim makes it binding upon himself to perform a virtuous act [*qurbah*]...

The foundation for the obligation to fulfill vows is found in the Quran, where Allah Most High mentions the attributes of the pious: "(Because) they perform the vow and fear a day whereof the evil is wide-spreading..." [Q76:7].

The Prophet ﷺ said, "Whoever vowed to obey Allah is to obey Him, and whoever vowed to disobey Him is not to disobey Him."[7]

If one makes a vow to pray, one must pray a minimum of two prayer cycles. If one vows to fast, one must fast a minimum of one day. If one vows to give charity, one must donate the minimal amount that is legally considered to be property. However, if one specifies a quantity in one's vow, then that is what is required to fulfill it.

– though not if the act is merely permissible [*mubāḥ*],...

The Prophet ﷺ said, "There is no [binding] vow except in that through which Allah's pleasure is sought."[8]

...or is an act of disobedience [*maʿṣiyah*].

7. Preceded.
8. ʿAmr ibn Shuʿayb from his father from his grandfather: Abū Dāwūd, 3273. See: KBM, 2812.

VOWS TO VISIT THE SACRED PRECINCT

وإتيان شيء من الحرم يوجب الحج أو العمرة.

Declaring that one will go to any part of the Sacred Precinct renders it obligatory to perform Hajj or Umrah.

If one vows to pray in a particular mosque, one need not pray in that mosque in order to fulfill one's vow, unless it is the Mosque of the Sacred Precinct [of Mecca] (due to its superiority and connection to rites), al-Aqṣā Mosque [in Jerusalem], or the Mosque of the Prophet ﷺ [in Medina]. Abū Hurayrah (may Allah be pleased with him) narrates from the Prophet ﷺ, who said: "Do not undertake a journey to visit any mosque except for three: this mosque of mine, the Mosque of the Sacred Precinct, and al-Aqṣā Mosque."[9] Because of this, the two other mosques resemble the Sacred Precinct in status.

9. Abū Hurayrah: Bukhārī, 1189; Muslim, 1397 #511–513. See: TM, 1758.

16

COURTS AND TESTIMONY

كِتَابُ الْأَقْضِيَةِ وَالشَّهَادَاتِ

JUDGMENTS AND ARBITRATION

The foundation for the rulings regarding judgements is found in verses of the Quran and in hadiths. The verses include Allah Most High saying "...and, if ye judge between mankind, that ye judge justly..." [Q4:58].

In one ḥadīth, the Prophet ﷺ said, "If the ruler [*ḥākim*] strives [*ijtahada*] but makes a mistake, he receives one reward. If he hits the mark, he gets two."[1]

ʿAlī (may Allah be pleased with him) said: "The Messenger of Allah ﷺ sent me to Yemen as a judge. I said, 'O Messenger of Allah, you send me while I am young and I know nothing about passing judgments?' He ﷺ said, 'Allah will guide your heart and keep your tongue true.' I never doubted a decision since."[2]

THEY ARE A COMMUNAL OBLIGATION

القضاء فرض على الكفاية، وقد يتعيّن.

Judgment is a communal duty and it can become a personal duty.

It becomes personally obligatory when one is the only qualified person in the land.

1. ʿAmr ibn al-ʿĀṣ: Bukhārī, 7352; Muslim, 1716 #15. See: TM, 1760.
2. ʿAlī: Abū Dāwūd, 3582; Tirmidhī, 1331; Bayhaqī, 20154, 20487. See: KBM, 2836.

CONDITIONS FOR JUDGES

وشرط القاضي أهليّة الشّهادات مع الكفاية والاجتهاد.

The conditions for being a judge are:

It is not permissible or valid for the authorities to appoint someone to who does not meet these conditions and it is a sin for an unqualified candidate to accept the appointment.

1. **being qualified to serve as a witness;**[3]

The judge must be a Muslim. This is because being Muslim is a condition for bearing witness. A fortiori, it is a condition for being a judge. Also, Allah Most High says, "…and Allah will not give the disbelievers any way (of success) against the believers…" [Q4:141].

The judge must be legally responsible and free. Someone who is a minor, insane, or a slave cannot be a judge since he is deficient.

The judge must be a male. It is not permissible for a woman to be a judge. Abū Bakrah (may Allah be pleased with him) said that the Prophet ﷺ said, "A people who make their ruler a woman will never thrive."[4]

The judge must be upright. Someone morally corrupt cannot look after his own child. A fortiori, he cannot be entrusted with being a judge.

2. **competency; and**

The judge must possess [some] hearing, eyesight, and speech. Someone who is totally deaf cannot differentiate between an affirmation and a negation. Someone who is completely blind cannot differentiate between the plaintiff and the defendant. Someone who is mute cannot execute rulings.

The judge should be active and alert so he is not deceived.

---

3. See "Witnesses" on page 534.
4. Abū Bakrah: Bukhārī, 4425. See: TM, 1764.

3. *ijtihād.*

It is not permissible to appoint someone who is ignorant of rulings, or who is a *muqallid* [a follower of a scholar's rulings without knowing their evidence]. *Taqlīd* is not permitted for issuing fatwas. A fortiori, it is not permitted when issuing judgments.

When these conditions are not found in a single individual – such as when the age is free of independent *mujtahid*s – the authorities who have power [to enforce the law] can appoint a *muqallid*. In such cases, the deficient judge's decisions are executed and enforced out of necessity and so that general welfare is not endangered.

DELEGATION

وله الاستخلاف عند الحاجة إلا أن ينهاه.

The judge is entitled to delegate when needed unless he was denied [the option to do so in his appointment].

ARBITRATION

والتّحكيم جائز – في غير الحدود – وإن كان هناك قاض.

Arbitration is permissible in matters not involving prescribed punishments, even if a judge is available.

This is conditional upon the individual being qualified to serve as a judge, since this occurred with a group of Companions (may Allah be pleased with them) without objection.

REMOVING JUDGES

(فصل) [انعزال القاضي]

وينعزل بالجنون والعمى، وذهاب الأهليّة، لا الإغماء، خلافًا للرّافعيّ.

[The judge] is removed if he becomes insane, blind, or loses [any other] qualifications. But he is not removed for losing consciousness – contrary to [the opinion of Imam] al-Rāfiʿī (may Allah grant him His mercy).[5]

ASSISTANTS TO THE JUDGE

(فصل) [بعض آداب القاضي]

ويتّخذ مزكّيًا وكاتبًا ومترجمًا ودرّة وسجنًا، ويندب له المشاورة.

The judge should have someone who evaluates witnesses, a scribe, a translator, a whip, and a jail. It is recommended that he consult with advisors.

He should not have someone who prevents people from entering while he is judging cases.

Abū Marham al-Azdī (may Allah be pleased with him) said: "I heard the Messenger of Allah ﷺ say, 'If the one whom Allah chooses to preside over the affairs of the Muslims withdraws from fulfilling their needs and their poverty, Allah will withdraw Himself from fulfilling his needs and poverty.'"[6]

---

5. al-Nawawī, *Rawḍat al-ṭālibīn*, 11:125; *Minhāj al-Ṭālibīn*, 337; al-Anṣārī, *Asnā al-maṭālib*, 4:111.

6. Abū Marham al-Azdī: Abū Dāwūd, 2948, Tirmidhī, 1332. See: KBM, 2857.

SOME ISSUES RELATED TO JUDGMENTS

(فصل) [بضع آداب القاضي]

AVOIDING CONFLICT OF INTEREST

ولا ينفذ حكمه لأصله وفرعه ورقيقه.

The judge's sentence is not carried out when it is for one of his ancestors, descendants, or slaves.

This is to prevent conflict of interest and bias.

GIVING EQUAL RESPECT TO PARTIES

وليسو بين الخصمين في الإكرام، وله رفع المسلم على الذّمّيّ.

He gives equal respect to both parties, though he can elevate a Muslim over a *dhimmī* [by raising the Muslim's seat].

The foundation for this is the narration from Umm Salamah (may Allah be pleased with her) in which the Prophet ﷺ said, "Whoever is tested with judging between people is to treat them equally: in his speech, his gestures, and his seating them," and "Whoever is tested with judging between people does not raise his voice against one litigant so long as he does not raise it against the other."[7]

7. Umm Salamah: Dāraquṭnī, 4466, 4467. See: BM, 9:595–60.

PRIORITY OF CASES

وقدم المسافر المستوفز، ثمّ المرأة، ثمّ السّابق، ثمّ بالقرعة بخصومه كالمفتي ومدرّس الفرض.

The judge gives priority to travelers who are in a hurry,...

In order to ward off harm from them.

...then to women,...

Because they tend to be shielded from public view.

...then to whomever arrived first,...

Because this is more fair.

...then by drawing lots amongst [the remaining] cases.

This is what Sacred Law has authorized for resolving impasse, such as when a man needs to choose which of his wives will accompany him on a trip.

[This prioritization of cases and impasse resolution] is equally applicable to muftis and those teaching obligatory knowledge.

MISTAKEN JUDGMENTS

(فصل) [نقض حكم القاضي]

[ونقض] الخطأ قطعًا وظنًّا بخبر الواحد وقياس جلي.

A mistaken judgment is overruled whether the mistake is certain or speculative via being based upon a singular report or manifest analogy.

Since *ijtihād* is acceptable when it does not contradict those and rejected when it does.

DESCRIPTION OF CLAIMS

(فصل) [الدّعوى]

وإذا جلس الخصمان بين يديه، فله أن يسكت، وله أن يقول: «ليتكلّم المدّعي»، فإن ادّعى صحيحة طالب خصمه بالجواب، فإن أقرّ ثبت، وإن أنكر فله أن يقول للمدعي: «ألك بيّنة؟»، وأن يسكت، فإن قال: «نعم، وأريد تحليفه» فله ذلك حلفه.

When the litigants are in front of the judge, he may remain silent or say, "The plaintiff is to speak."

The judge cannot advise the litigants on how to make a claim or a defense, or how to affirm or deny an accusation. This would show an inclination towards one litigant and harm towards the other, which is unlawful.

If the plaintiff presents a valid case, the judge demands that the defendant respond. If the defendant affirms [the claim against him], it becomes established. If he denies it, the judge may say to the plaintiff, "Do you have evidence?," or he may remain silent. If [the plaintiff] says, "Yes, and I want [the defendant] to swear an oath," the defendant must swear an oath [before the evidence is presented].

The Prophet ﷺ said, "[the burden of] proof [*bayyinah*] is with the one who is making the claim, and the oath [*yamīn*] must be taken from the one who rejects the claim."[8]

8. Ibn ʿAbbās: Tirmidhī, 1342; Bayhaqī, 21203. See: KBM, 2943; cf KBM, 2780.

JUDGMENT IN ABSENTIA

(فصل) [القضاء على الغائب]

والقضاء على الغائب جائز، ويحلف بعد البيّنة أن الحقّ ثابت في ذمّته، ويقضى من ماله.

It is permissible to judge someone who is absent.

Hind bint 'Utbah, the wife of Abū Sufyān (may Allah be pleased with them both) said, "O, Messenger of Allah [ﷺ]! Abū Sufyān is a miserly man and does not give me and my children adequate provisions for maintenance unless I take something from his possession without his knowledge. Is there any sin on me?" Thereupon the Messenger of Allah ﷺ said, "Take from his property what is customary and which may suffice you and your children."[9]

After providing proof, [the plaintiff] swears an oath that the right is owed to him. The debt is then paid from [the defendant's] wealth.

If a judge has ruled on a case related to an absent defendant and desires for that order to be carried out, he must send a written request to the judge under whose jurisdiction the defendant resides. The request must be attested to by two witnesses, who must later affirm its contents in the presence of the judge to whom the request was addressed.

DIVIDING PROPERTY

(فصل) [القسمة]

Umm Salamah (may Allah be pleased with her) said, "Two men who were disputing over an inheritance came to the Messenger of Allah ﷺ. They had no evidence other than their respective claims. The Prophet ﷺ said to them, 'I am a man, like you.' Thereupon, both the men wept and each of them said, 'This right of mine goes

9. Hind: Bukhārī, 5364, 7180; Muslim, 1714. See: TM, 1524, 1777, 1801; KBM, 2178.

to you.' The Prophet ﷺ then said, 'Now that you have done what you have done, divide up [your inheritance], aiming at what is right. Then draw lots, and let each of you consider what legitimately belongs to the other.'"[10]

ʿUbādat ibn al-Ṣāmit, Ibn ʿAbbās, and Abū Saʿīd al-Khudrī (may Allah be pleased with them all) reported that the Prophet ﷺ said, "Do not harm and do not reciprocate harm."[11]

Al-Mughīrah ibn Shuʿbah (may Allah be pleased with him) reported that the Prophet ﷺ forbade wasting wealth.[12]

يكفي قاسم لا مقوّم، ويجبر إن قسم بأجزاء متساوية الصفة، وكذا بتعديل - لا بردّ - ومهايأة، إن امتنعت القسمة.

A [single] partitioner suffices [for the division and allocation of property], but a [single] appraiser does not [as appraisals require two individuals].

A partner who refuses the [partitioner's] division [of the property] is forced [to comply] if the property is divided into segments with identical features [*ajzāʾ*] – or similarly, if it is divided into portions of equivalent value [*taʿdīl*] – but not by *radd*...

This is when the items are not identical (like different types of cloth) because there are different purposes and uses associated with each.

The first [division into identical segments (*ajzāʾ*)] occurs with things like seeds. The second [division into portions of equivalent value (*taʿdīl*)] occurs with land, when one-third of the land has the same value as the remaining two-thirds combined. The third type of division [*radd*] also occurs with land, when one edge of the land

---

10. Umm Salamah: Abū Dāwūd, 3584. See: TM, 1778.
11. ʿUbādat ibn al-Ṣāmit: Ibn Mājah, 2340. Ibn ʿAbbās: Ibn Mājah, 2341; Abū Saʿīd al-Khudrī: Ḥākim, 2345. See: TM, 1308, 1779.
12. Al-Mughīrah: Bukhārī, 1477, 2408, 5975, 7292); Muslim, 593 #12–14. See: TM, 1181, 1780.

has a tree. The first [type of division] is considered a partition in kind [*ifrāz*]. The other two are considered sales.

...or joint usufruct [*muhāya'ah*].

WITNESSES

(فصل) [صفات الشّاهد]

The foundation for the rulings regarding witnesses (prior to consensus) is Allah Most High saying, "...And call to witness, from among your men, two witnesses..." [Q2:282], and "...And have witnesses when ye sell one to another..." [Q2:282]. Both are commands indicating guidance [*amr irshād*] – not obligation. The evidence from Sunnah includes well-known hadiths.

شرط الشّاهد، ذكر، ناطق، مسلم، حرّ، عدل - ما باشر كبيرة موجبة حدّ، وما أصرّ على صغيرة ذو مروءة، تارك غير لائق به كإدامة سماع غناء وحرف دنية غير متّهم بجرّ ودفع وتغافل حيث يحتمل الغلط، ومبادرة قبل الطّلب، إلّا ما فيه حقّ مؤكّد لله تعالى كطلاق. وإن رأى المصلحة في التّستّر، ستر.

There are conditions for a witness. [One must be]

1. **male;**
2. **able to speak;**
3. **Muslim;**
4. **free;**
5. **upright...**

Testimony is not accepted from someone who is morally corrupt. Allah Most High says, "O ye who believe! If an evil-liver bring you tidings, verify it [*fa tabayyanū*]..." [Q49:6].[13]

13. In the verse: "verify," means to distinguish truth from lies. Another recitation has "investigate [*fa tathabbatū*]."

...– not having committed an enormity requiring a prescribed punishment [*ḥadd*], not persisted in committing a lesser sin...

‹Enormities [*kabāʾir*] are acts of disobedience for which severe threats have been mentioned in the Quran or Sunnah, indicating that whoever commits them is negligent in their religion. Examples include drinking wine, engaging in *ribā,* and accusing Muslim women of fornication. Allah Most High said concerning those who make accusations of fornication: "...and never (afterward) accept their testimony – They indeed are evil-doers; Save those who afterward repent and make amends. (For such) lo! Allah is Forgiving, Merciful" [Q24:4–5].

Lesser sins [*ṣaghāʾir*] are unlawful acts that do not fit the definition of enormities [*kabāʾir*]. Examples include looking at people in circumstances wherein it is not lawful to look at them, shunning a Muslim beyond three days, and the like.[14]›

... – adhering to the common standards of decorum [for observant Muslims of his time and place], and abstaining from things unsuitable for him – like habitually listening to singing or having an undignified profession;

Casting off common standards indicates a corrupt intellect, lack of care, or shamelessness. Either way, it voids any trust or reliance upon what he says.

6. not having ever been accused of
- **obtaining [a benefit] or warding [off harm];**

The basis for rejecting the testimony of someone who has been accused of either is his inherent bias and self-interest.

An example of obtaining a benefit is an inheritor testifying that his benefactor died before the wound healed, so he takes blood money.

14. al-Bughā, *Al-Tadhhīb,* 269 #2.

An example of warding off harm is when an individual has mistakenly taken a life and the family member responsible for paying the blood money on his behalf testifies that the witnesses to the killing are morally corrupt – just so they will not have to pay.

Testimony from one's enemy is not accepted. The Prophet ﷺ said, "Do not accept the testimony of a litigant or an enemy."[15]

- **heedlessness that could possibly lead to a mistake;**
- **rushing to testify before being asked – except when rights are emphatically owed to Allah Most High [*ḥaqq Allāh*], such as in a divorce.**

Testimony is not heard until the litigants request it, to prevent bias [*tuhmah*]. He ﷺ said, "...and they will give their witness without being asked to give their witness..."[16]

Exceptions to this include testimony related to fornication and all other rights owed to Allah Most High, since they do not have specific individuals who seek them. This is understood from the hadith, "Shall I not inform you who is the best witness? It is the one who produces his testimony before he is asked for it."[17]

If the witness believes that concealing [his testimony] would be better for the general welfare [of the Muslim community], he conceals it.

ويكفي في التّعديل «هو عدل»، وزيادة على ذلك تأكيد، ولا يقبل إلّا من ذي معرفة بالباطن.

"He is upright" suffices for vouching that a witness is upright. Anything more is emphasis. Vouching is not accepted except from someone who knows the subject's internal state.

15. Mālik, 2667; Abū Dāwūd, *Al-Marāsīl*, 396; Ibn Abī Shaybah, *Al-Muṣannaf*, 20823, 22855; Bayhaqī, 15365, 20861, 20865, 20866; ʿAbd al-Razzāq, *Al-Muṣannaf*, 15365. See: BM, 9:655.

16. ʿImrān ibn Ḥuṣayn: Bukhārī, 6428; Muslim, 2535 #214. See: TM, 1796.

17. Zayd ibn Khālid al-Juhanī: Muslim, 1719 #19. See: TM, 1797.

WHAT CONSTITUTES TESTIMONY AND EVIDENCE

(فصل) [الشّهادات]

RAMADAN

لا يحكم بشاهد إلّا في هلال رمضان.

A judgment is not based on [the testimony of] a single witness except for the new moon of Ramadan.

This is because of what preceded in the chapter on fasting. Also, Ibn ʿAbbās (may Allah be pleased with them) said that the Messenger of Allah ﷺ accepted the testimony of one man who claimed to have seen the new crescent moon of Ramadan, but did not accept the sighting [of the new [crescent] moon of Shawwāl] for ending the fast [of Ramadan] except from two individuals.[18] This hadith's chain of narrators [*sanad*] includes Ḥafṣ ibn ʿUmar al-Abulī (may Allah be pleased with him), who is a weak narrator.

‹The wisdom behind accepting a single witness to mark the beginning of Ramadan but two witnesses to signal its end (i.e. the beginning of Shawwāl) is out of being precautionary with regards to fasting, since it is less damaging to begin performing an act of worship prematurely than it is to end it prematurely.[19]›

FORNICATION

ولا [يحكم] بأربعة إلّا في الزّنا.

Nor [is a judgment based] on four except [in the case of] fornication.

Allah Most High says, "As for those of your women who are guilty of lewdness, call to witness four of you against them..." [Q4:15].

---

18. Ibn ʿUmar and Ibn ʿAbbās: Dāraquṭnī, 2148. See: al-Rūyānī, *Baḥr al-madhhab*, 3:241.
19. al-Bughā, *Al-Tadhhīb*, 272 #2.

‹The other verses related to the subject [Q24:4, 24:13] also indicate that the minimum number of witnesses for fornication is four males.[20]›

FINANCIAL MATTERS

و[يشهد] للمالِيِّ رجلان أو رجل وامرأتان.

Financial matters require two males, or a male and two females.

Two male witnesses are also required for manumission (freeing a slave), bequests, certain *ḥadd* punishments, and marriage.

Allah Most High says concerning divorce and returning a wife: "...take them back in kindness or part from them in kindness, and call to witness two just men among you, and keep your testimony upright for Allah..." [Q65:2], and "...when death draweth nigh unto one of you, at the time of bequest – two witnesses, just men from among you..." [Q5:106].

For other circumstances, the number of witnesses required is ascertained by analogy.

THINGS TYPICALLY KNOWN ONLY TO WOMEN

وما يختصّ بمعرفته النّساء أو لا يراه الرّجال غالبًا كولادة بذلك وبأربع نسوة.

Things that are typically known only to women and not typically seen by men (such as births) follow the same ruling [as the previous situations], or [require] four female [witnesses].

There must be four women, since two female witnesses equal one male witness.

‹Events of the same type [i.e., known only to women and not typically seen by men] that are not mentioned in the evidence [from Sacred Law] are considered analogous.

20. al-Bughā, *Al-Tadhhīb*, 271 #3.

The testimony of one woman is accepted for matters concerning herself. A fortiori, the testimony from both a man and two women is accepted. This is because the default in testimony is that it is done by men. And it is similar [in being accepted] if only men witness it.[21]›

A SINGLE MALE WITNESS ACCOMPANIED BY AN OATH

وما يثبت برجل وامرأتين يثبت برجل ويمين إلّا عيوب النّساء ونحوها.

Whatever is established by [the testimony of] a male and two females can also be established by one male [accompanied by] an oath...

The Prophet ﷺ pronounced a judgment on the basis of an oath and testimony from one [male] witness.[22]

‹This is accepted when the defendant refuses to swear an oath. For example, X claims that Y owes him. Y denies the claim and refuses to swear an oath. Thus, if X swears an oath affirming his claim, Y's refusal, when combined with X's oath, receives the status of two witnesses.

However, this is not accepted for prescribed punishments. For example, X accuses Y of stealing something of his that was worth the minimum value for requiring the prescribed punishment for theft (i.e. amputation). Y denies the claim and refuses to swear an oath. Thus, if X swears an oath affirming his claim, proof of the theft is established and Y is required to compensate X. However, this does not obligate the prescribed punishment.›

...(except for [physical] defects of females and the like).

---

21. al-Bughā, *Al-Tadhhīb,* 271 #1.

22. Ibn ʿAbbās: Muslim, 1712 #3; Abū Dāwūd, 3608; Ibn Mājah, 2370; Ibn Ḥibbān, 5073. Abū Hurayrah: Abū Dāwūd, 3610, 3611; Tirmidhī, 1343; Nasāʾī, *Al-Sunan al-Kubrā,* 5969; Ibn Mājah, 2368; Ibn Ḥibbān, 5073, Dāraquṭnī, 4489. See: TM, 1799.

WITNESSING WHAT ANOTHER WITNESSED

وتقبل الشّهادة على الشّهادة فوق مسافة العدوى في غير العقوبات، وفيها إذا كانت لآدميّ.

Witnessing what someone [else says they] witnessed is accepted for distances beyond those where one can expect help [*masāfah al-ʿudwā*] when it is not related to punishments – and it is accepted in things related to punishments if it is for a right owed to individual humans.

TESTIMONY FROM THE BLIND

(فصل) [شهادة الأعمى]

ولا تقبل شهادة الأعمى إلّا في التّرجمة والمضبوط، وفيما تحمّله قبل العمى، وفيما يشهد فيه بالاستفاضة، إذا تعيّن وإشارة، وهو النّسب والموت والوقف والعتق والولاء والنّكاح والملك.

Testimony from a blind witness is inadmissible except for

1. translations;

This is because clarifying and explaining the meaning of what litigants and witnesses say only requires the translator to hear and understand them, not see them.

2. when someone tells him something and he immediately takes the speaker by the hand in order to present him to the judge and testify as to what was said;

For example, when someone quietly mentions something to the blind person regarding a matter of legal significance (i.e., an admission, divorce, or the like) and he then takes that person by the hand to the judge and testifies about what he was told [it is admissible].

3. **things he witnessed before becoming blind;**

A condition for this exception is that he knows the identity of the people he is testifying for or against.

4. **things that are common knowledge – when he identifies [the person] and points [to them] – which are lineage, death, endowments, manumission, rights owed to the manumitter, marriage, and ownership.**

An example of ownership is an individual claiming to own an item when the ownership of that item is not disputed. The blind person may testify that the item is owned without specifying its owner. His testimony is accepted in such cases because they relate to facts that can be established by being spoken of to such an extent that they become common knowledge. Thus, hearing them directly is not required. Furthermore, because they persist over a long period of time, it is difficult to prove their origin, since those who were present then are now gone in most cases.

LAWSUITS

(فصل) [الدّعوات]

The foundation for this section on lawsuits [*daʿwāt*] is the hadith from Ibn ʿAbbās (may Allah be pleased with them both): "[the burden of] proof [*bayyinah*] is with the one who is making the claim, and the oath [*yamīn*] must be taken from the one who rejects the claim."

THE PLAINTIFF

المدّعي من يخالف قوله الظّاهر، والمدّعى عليه من يوافقه.

The plaintiff [*muddaʿī*] is the one whose statement contradicts apparent reality, and the defendant is the one whose word matches it [*mudaʿā ʿalayhi*].

WHAT CONSTITUTES A VALID LAWSUIT

ولا تصحّ الدّعوى إلّا من مطلق التّصرف فيما يدّعيه، وقد تسمع في غيره كدعوى الحسبة والمرأة النّكاح، ولا يصحّ دعوى مجهول إلّا في الوصية والإقرار بالمجهول ونحوهما، وأما ما سوى ذلك فلا بدّ من وصفها،

Lawsuits are not valid except from individuals who have the full right to manage and dispose of the property being contested.

Lawsuits may also be heard for other matters, such as regulatory claims, and a woman claiming marriage.

Nonspecific lawsuits are invalid except for bequests, admitting something nonspecific, and the like. Other than that, they must be unambiguously defined.

EVIDENCE AND OATHS

فإن كان مع المدّعي بيّنة سمعت، وإلّا فالقول قول المدّعى عليه مع يمينه، إلّا في القسامة، كما سلف، فإن نكل عنها ردّت على المدّعي، وقضي له، ولا يقضي بنكوله، فإن نكل صرفهما.

If the plaintiff possesses testimonial evidence, it is heard [and the judge acts according to it]. Otherwise, it is the defendant's word accompanied by his oath. An exception is when dividing property, as mentioned earlier.[23]

If the defendant refuses to swear an oath, the plaintiff is asked to swear an oath. If he does, the contested property is judged to be his.

A judgment is not made based on the plaintiff's refusal [to swear an oath]; if he does refuse, both parties [the case] are dismissed.

---

23. See "Dividing Property" on page 532.

CONFLICTING EVIDENCE

(فصل) [تعارض البيّنتين]

وإن تداعيا شيئا في يد أحدهما فالقول قوله، أو في أيديهما تحالفا وجعل بينهما، أو في يد ثالث وأقاما بيّنتين سقطتا.

If both parties claim ownership of something that one of them has in his possession, the word of the one who possesses it [combined with his oath] is relied upon.

This ruling is in accordance with the concepts of defaultness [*aṣl*] and presumption of continuity [*istiṣḥāb al-ḥāl*]. That a property is in one's possession makes it preponderant that one owns it, so long as there is no evidence to the contrary. This is because the default presumption is that the property did not enter into one's possession except through a legitimate cause.

If the contested item is in the possession of both parties, each swears an oath and the item is divided between them.

‹Each one of them swears an oath negating that it belongs to the other.[24]›

Abū Mūsā al-Ashʿarī (may Allah be pleased with him) said that two men came to the Prophet ﷺ claiming [ownership of] a camel or an animal. Neither had proof of ownership, so the Prophet ﷺ declared that the animal be shared between them.[25]

[If both parties claim ownership of something] that a third party possesses and each presents evidence, both claims are voided.

---

24. al-Bughā, *Al-Tadhhīb,* 268 #3.
25. Abū Mūsā al-Ashʿarī: Abū Dāwūd, 3613, 3615; Ḥākim, 7031–2 – *ṣaḥīḥ* chain; Bayhaqī, 21228, 21239. See: TM, 1804.

SWEARING OATHS

(فصل) [الحلف على الأفعال]

SWEARING AN OATH ABOUT ONESELF OR OTHERS

ومن حلف على فعل نفسه فعلى البتّ، أو غيره فكذا في الإثبات وإلّا فعلى نفي العلم.

Whoever swears an oath about his own actions [whether affirmative or negative] does so unequivocally.

One can make an absolute statement about oneself since one has comprehensive knowledge of one's own affairs.

[Whoever swears an oath about] another's actions also does so unequivocally – if the oath is an affirmation...

This is because of the ease of having observed and knowing that he is affirming.

...otherwise, he swears an oath denying knowledge [of their occurrence].

If one is negating someone else's action, one cannot swear with certainty since there is no way to be certain when it comes to negating someone else's actions. Rather, one says, "I do not know that so-and-so did that."

AUGMENTED OATHS

وتغلّظ اليمين فيما ليس بمال ولا يقصد به المال، كدعوى الدّم، وفي نصاب مال وفي دونه إن رآه القاضي.

Oaths are augmented when related to matters that are not financial or with the goal of finance – such as allegations related to blood [i.e. retaliation or indemnity], minimum amounts upon which money

is owed [*niṣāb al-māl*], and less than the minimal amounts – if the judge considers the oaths useful.

OATHS & DISPUTES

(فصل) [فائدة الأيمان]

واليمين يفيد قطع الخصومة في الحال لا براءة، فيحكم بقيام البيّنة بعده، ويتعدّد اليمين إذا توجّهت عليه لجماعة، ولو رضوا بواحدة.

Oaths serve to end disputes at the moment – not to establish innocence. A judgment can be made afterwards, when evidence is presented. Several oaths are taken when presented with a group – even if the claimants are satisfied with one.

TESTIMONY RELATED TO ACTIONS AND STATEMENTS

(فصل) [شروط قبول شهادة الأفعال أو أقوال]

ولا تجوز شهادة على فعل كغضب إلّا بإبصار، ولا على قول إلّا به وبسماعه.

It is not permissible to testify about an action (like theft) unless one saw it, nor about a statement except by seeing [who stated it] and hearing it.

WITNESSES RETRACTING TESTIMONY BEFORE JUDGMENT

(فصل) [رجوع الشّهود]

رجع الشّهود قبل الحكم امتنع، أو بعده وقبل استيفاء مال استوفي، أو عقوبة فلا، أو بعد الاستيفاء لم ينقض.

[If] witnesses retract their testimony before the judgment has been made, the judgment is averted.

[If they retract it] after the judgment but before what is owed has been paid, it is paid.

[If they retract it] before a punishment has been carried out, it is not carried out.

[If they retract it] after a punishment has been carried out, the judgment is not undone.

WITNESSES RETRACTING TESTIMONY AFTER JUDGMENT

(فصل) [عواقب الرّجوع]

ومتى رجع شهود المال بعد الحكم لزمهم، أو الطّلاق الثّلاث لزمهم مهر المثل ولو كان قبل الدّخول، أو شهود القتل بعده وقالوا: «تعمّدنا» فالقصاص وإلّا فالدّية.

When witnesses retract their testimony after a judgment related to finance, they [still] must pay the amount.

[Or if they do so in a matter related to] three-fold divorce, they must pay the bride the price given to women of similar status – even if the divorce occurred prior to consummation.

[Or if] murder witnesses [retract their testimony] after the sentence is carried out and the witnesses say, "We did it [i.e., gave false testimony] intentionally," they are given a reciprocal punishment. Otherwise they pay the blood indemnity.

TAKING RIGHTS

(فصل) [أخذ الحقوق]

ومن وجب له حقّ على منكر ولا بيّنة له، فله أن يأخذ جنس حقّه بغير إذنه، وكذا غيره عند الفقد.

If one makes an unsubstantiated claim that another owes him a right, and that other person doesn't deny the claim, one may take something similar to what one is owed without that person's permission. Likewise, one may take something of a different kind in its absence.

17

MANUMISSION

كِتَابُ الْعِتْقِ

The legal foundation for the liberation of slaves is Allah Most High saying, "(It is) to free a slave," [Q90:13] and "...and thou hast conferred favour..." [Q33:37], and in His commanding manumission as an expiation [for some sins]. Its foundation also includes well-known hadiths and consensus.

Abū Hurayrah (may Allah be pleased with him) reported that the Prophet ﷺ said, "If anyone frees a [Muslim] slave, Allah will free one of his limbs from the Fire for every limb that he freed – even his genitals for [the slave's] genitals."[1]

WHAT CONSTITUTES MANUMISSION

يصحّ إعتاق مالك جائز به، وتحرير، وفكّ رقبة، وكناية مع نيّة.

Manumission is valid from every slave owner who is entitled [to manage and dispose of his own property]...[2]

Freeing a slave is a type of transaction taking place while the transactor is alive, and it resembles giving a gift.[3] Thus, it is not valid from someone who is a minor, insane, or at war with Islam.

1. Abū Hurayrah: Bukhārī, 2517; Muslim, 1509 #22. See: KBM, 2958.
2. See "Suspension" on page 241.
3. See "Gifting" on page 270.

...using [words and phrases that are explicit, like] "manumission," "setting free," and "releasing,"...

These phrases are explicit [in Arabic] because they are customarily used only for manumission. The phrase "*fakku raqabah*" is explicit since it is mentioned in the Quran [Q90:13].

...or allusive phrases accompanied by intention.

Allusive phrases are those that imply surrender of ownership or indicate separation. For example [a slave owner may say]: "I have no authority over you," "You are a freed slave [*sāʾibah*] over whom I have no *walāʾ*," "You do not owe me any service," and the like.

CONTINGENT MANUMISSION

ويصحّ تعليقه على الصّفات والإخطار.

It is valid for manumission to be contingent upon the occurrence of certain conditions.

FREEING A PORTION OF A SLAVE

وإذا أعتق بعض عبده عتق كلّه.

The entire slave is set free, [even] if the owner frees a part of him.

FREEING A SHARE OF A CO-OWNED SLAVE

وإن أعتق شركًا له في عبد – وهو موسر بقيمته – سرى العتق إلى باقيه، وقوّم عليه نصيب شريكه يوم العتق.

When a slave's co-owner frees his share of the slave and has enough to pay the remaining value, the manumission extends to the rest

[of the slave], so the co-owner must pay the value of his partners' shares on the day of manumission.

The Prophet ﷺ said, "Whoever frees his share of a slave and has sufficient wealth to cover the remaining price of the slave is to have an honest man estimate the slave's value, and then give his partners their share and free the slave. Otherwise [if he does not have enough], he frees whatever portion he owned."[4]

Freeing a portion of a shared slave extends to the entire slave. A fortiori, it extends to the entirety of a slave one owns completely.

POSSESSING ONE'S ANCESTOR OR DESCENDANT

ومن ملك أصوله أو فروعه عتق عليه.

When one takes possession of one's ancestor or descendant, [that relative] is automatically set free.

The foundation for this with respect to parents is that the Prophet ﷺ said, "A son does not repay his father unless he were to find him enslaved, purchase him, and then set him free."[5]

The foundation with respect to children is that Allah Most High says, "And they say: The Beneficent hath taken unto Himself a son. Be He Glorified! Nay, but (those whom they call sons) are honoured slaves" [Q21:26]. The verse indicates that if they are slaves they cannot be children, thus negating ongoing ownership of a child.

Other means of acquiring ownership are considered analogous to buying goods or property, and receiving a gift or an inheritance.

Automatic manumission also occurs if someone comes to own a portion of either parent (or of a descendant) through his own volition. Automatic manumission does not happen if ownership was acquired through inheritance.

---

4. Ibn ʿUmar: Bukhārī, 2522; Muslim, 1501 #1, 47. See: TM, 1809.
5. Abū Hurayrah: Muslim, 1510 #25; Tirmidhī, 1906; Nasāʾī, *Al-Sunan al-kubrā,* 4876, Ibn Mājah, 3659. See: TM, 1812.

Descendants are considered analogous to ancestors, since they are both part of one another. A child (the branch) is like part of the father (the root). Just as a root cannot be owned by a part of itself, it cannot own part of itself.

WALĀʾ

(فصل) [الولاء]

WHO IS ENTITLED TO WALĀʾ

ومن عتق عليه رقيق فولاؤه له، ثمّ لعصبته الأقرب فالأقرب.

Whoever frees a slave is entitled to *walāʾ*.

Walāʾ [a right associated with manumission] is permanently acquired by virtue of manumission and cannot be removed or forfeited. *Walāʾ* means the former owner inherits from his slave if the slave has no free heirs.

The Prophet ﷺ said, "Indeed, *walāʾ* belongs to the manumitter."[6]

Then, [in the manumitter's absence, the inheritance goes to] his universal inheritors, in order of nearness.

‹The manumitter is entitled to the same rights and responsibilities that universal inheritors (like brothers and fathers) are entitled to through lineage. These include inheritance, guardianship for marriage, liability for blood money, and the right to demand it.[7]›

The Messenger of Allah ﷺ said, "*Walāʾ* is an interweaving just as lineage is an interweaving."[8][9]

---

6. ʿĀʾishah: Bukhārī, 6752; Muslim, 1504 #8, 14. See: TM, 1353, 1814, 1819.
7. al-Bughā, *Al-Tadhhīb,* 276 #3.
8. Ibn ʿUmar: Ibn Ḥibbān, 4950; Ḥākim, 7990 – *ṣaḥīḥ* chain; Bayhaqī, 12381, 21433, 21435–8. See: TM, 1433, 1815.
9. See also"Universal Inheritance" on page 308.

WOMEN DO NOT INHERIT WALĀʾ

ولا ترث امرأة ولاء إلّا من عتيقها أو منتميًا إليه كما سلف.

A woman does not inherit *walāʾ* except from a slave she [herself] set free or from someone related to him, or through his own act of manumission [*walāʾ*] – as previously mentioned.[10]

WALĀʾ IS NOT TRANSFERABLE

ولا يصحّ بيع الولاء ولا هبته.

It is not valid to sell *walāʾ* or to give it as a gift.

Ibn ʿUmar (may Allah be pleased with him) said "The Messenger of Allah ﷺ forbade selling *walāʾ* or giving it as a gift."[11]

TADBĪR

(فصل) [التّدبير]

There is consensus concerning the permissibility of *tadbīr*.

WHAT CONSTITUTES TADBĪR

التّدبير تعليق العتق بموته، فيعتق بعده من الثّلث.

***Tadbīr* is when a slave owner makes manumission contingent upon his death, whereupon his slave is set free from [the top] one-third of the estate.**

This is after his funerary expenses and debts are paid. *Tadbīr* is a voluntary donation contingent upon death, so it resembles a bequest, which is taken from the top third.

---

10. See page 309.
11. Ibn ʿUmar: Bukhārī, 2535; Muslim, 1506 #16. See: KBM, 2966.

Ibn ʿUmar (may Allah be pleased with him) said that the Prophet ﷺ said, "The *mudabbar* is from the [top] third of the estate."[12]

RETRACTION

وله الرّجوع عنه بالفعل.

It is permissible for the owner to retract it.

So long as the master remains alive, the *mudabbar* slave is the same as a fully owned slave: the master can manage and dispose of him by selling him, giving him as a gift, and the like.

Jābir ibn ʿAbd Allāh (may Allah be pleased with them both) said, "A man stipulated that a slave he owned would be freed after his death. Later, when he was in need [of funds], he took the slave to the Prophet ﷺ and said, 'Who will buy him from me?' Nuʿaym ibn ʿAbd Allāh (may Allah be pleased with him) bought him for such and such price, and [the man] gave [the slave] to him."[13]

PARTIAL TADBĪR

ويجوز في البعض من غير سراية.

Partial manumission upon death is valid, and it does not automatically extend to the whole.

KITĀBAH

(فصل) [الكتابة]

The linguistic root of "*kitābah*" is "joining things together." Legally, it is manumission contingent upon compensation.

Its foundation is the Word of Allah Most High: "…write it for them if ye are aware of aught of good in them…" [Q24:33], in addition to well-known hadiths and consensus.

---

12. Ibn ʿUmar: Ibn Mājah, 2514; Dāraquṭnī, 4263; Bayhaqī, 21573–4. See: TM, 1817.
13. Jābir: Bukhārī, 2141; Muslim, 997. See: TM, 2976.

IT IS CONDITIONALLY RECOMMENDED

والكتابة مستحبة عند طلب القوي الأمين بنجمين فصاعدًا.

[It is recommended for an owner to accept his slave's request to buy his freedom [*kitābah*] if [the slave is] trustworthy, strong [and capable of earning a livelihood];...

Imam al-Shāfiʿī (may Allah grant him His mercy) said that "good in them" in the verse [Q24:33] refers to a slave's trustworthiness and capacity to earn.[14]

...[the amount is] to be paid in at least two installments.

VOIDING THE CONTRACT

وهي جائزة من جهته فله تعجيز نفسه وفسخها متى شاء ولازمة من جهة سيّده.

The contract is non-binding for the slave. He can declare himself unable [to proceed with the purchase] and cancel it whenever he wishes. [But it is] binding upon his master.

Since the purpose of this contract is to safeguard his slave's welfare, it is binding upon the master to accept it because the slave is his responsibility.

WAIVING A PORTION OF THE PRICE

وعليه أن سخط عنه جزءًا وهو أولى أو يدفعه إليه.

[The master] must waive a portion of [the stipulated price] (which is best); or give [the slave] that amount.

---

14. al-Shāfiʿī, *Al-Umm,* 8:32.

This is to make it easier for the slave to complete the transaction. Allah Most High says, "…and bestow upon them of the wealth of Allah which He hath bestowed upon you…" [Q24:33].

The master must give the slave the minimum amount that is considered property, since no amount has been transmitted.

IMMEDIATE CONSEQUENCES

ولا يعتق ما بقي عليه شيء منها، ويملك بها التّصرف بما فيه التّنميّة أو تبرّعاته بالإذن.

[The slave] is not set free so long as any installment remains.

The Prophet ﷺ said, "The slave buying back his freedom [*mukātab*] is a slave so long as a single dirham remains of his contract."[15]

Through the contract, the slave possesses the right to manage and dispose of his own property: he may either invest it in ways that lead to increased wealth[16] or give it away – with his master's permission.

UMMAHĀT AL-AWLĀD

(فصل) [أمّهات الأولاد]

The legal foundation for the rights of female slaves who have borne their master's child [*ummahāt al-awlād*] includes the hadith in which the Prophet ﷺ speaks of Māriyyah bint Shamʿūn – who had given birth to his son Ibrāhīm (may Allah be pleased with them both) – saying, "Her son set her free."

15. ʿAbd Allāh ibn ʿAmr: Abū Dāwūd, 3926; Ḥākim, 2863. See: KBM, 2982.
16. He is restricted, however, to engaging in transactions that are likely to bring about an increase in the overall value of his property.

HOW IT IS ATTAINED

من أتى بظاهر تخطيط علقت من السّيّد عتقت بموته من رأس المال.

If a slave owner impregnates his slave and she gives birth to something resembling a human being, [she becomes an *umm walad* and] upon his death, is set free from the top [portion] of the estate.

The textual foundation for these rulings is the Prophet ﷺ saying, "Any slave woman who gives birth to her master's child is free upon his death."[17]

Her child will also be free, as will any children she bears thereafter, regardless of who their father is. Her children become free – just as she does – after her master dies, since children follow their mothers with respect to their freedom.

If a husband impregnates his wife and she is someone else's slave, the child belongs to her master. This is because the mother belongs to the master, so her child has her legal status.

If a slave becomes pregnant after having sex with a man who mistakenly thought she was his own slave or his free wife, and she gives birth to the child, the child is free and the father must pay its value to her owner.

If a man buys his former wife who had borne his child while they were married, she does not automatically become his *umm walad*.

CONSEQUENCES RELATED TO HER

وله التّصرف بغير ما يزيل الملك.

Her owner can continue to manage her [e.g., time and services] so long as it does not negate his ownership.

Although he cannot sell her or transfer ownership, he can set her free.

17. Ibn ʿAbbās: Ibn Mājah, 2515; Dāraquṭnī, 4236; Ḥākim, 2191. See: KBM, 2989.

Ibn ʿUmar (may Allah be pleased with them both) reported: "Her owner enjoys her so long as he lives."[18]

The Prophet ﷺ said, "An *umm walad* is not sold or given as a gift. She is set free upon her master's death."[19]

CONSEQUENCES RELATED TO HER CHILD

ويتبعها ولدها بعده.

Afterwards, her child's fate follows hers.

Once her status as *umm walad* is established, any subsequent child she bears will be set free when the master dies, including children from other marriages and those born out of wedlock. Additionally, these children cannot be sold.

COMPELLING HER TO MARRY

ويزوّجها جبرًا على ما صحّحه الرّافعيّ وجزم الشّافعيّ في «الأمّ» بأنه لا بدّ من رضاها كالمكاتبة.

Her owner can compel her to marry him, according to what Imam al-Rāfiʿī considered valid.[20] But Imam al-Shāfiʿī wrote decisively in *Al-Umm* that she must consent – just as with the contract to buy back one's freedom. (May Allah grant them His mercy.)[21]

18. Ibn ʿUmar: Dāraquṭnī, 4247, 4250; Bayhaqī, 21764–7. See: TM, 1823.
19. Ibn ʿUmar: Dāraquṭnī, 4246, 4247, 4249, 4250; Bayhaqī, 21763–5, 21769, 21795, 21804. See: KBM, 2992.
20. al-Rāfiʿī, *Al-Sharḥ al-kabīr,* 13:588; al-Nawawī, *Rawḍat al-ṭālibīn,* 12:311.
21. al-Shāfiʿī, *Al-Umm,* 5:9, 5:233; al-Muzanī, *Al-Mukhtaṣar,* 8:443.

11

CLOSING

الخَتَمُ

وليكن هذا آخر كلامنا وبالله التّوفيق والحمد لله الّذي هدانا لهديه وما كنا لنهتدي لولا أن هدانا الله. تمّ بحمد الله وعونه وحسن توفيقه وأفضل صلواته وسلامه على سيّدنا محمد وآله.

These will be our final words: Success is only through Allah and all praise is for Him, Who has brought us to His guidance. We would never have been guided had Allah not guided us. Praise Allah, for it has been accomplished through His assistance and excellent [granting of] success. And may His most sublime prayers and salutations be upon our Master Muhammad and his family.

A

CROSS-REFERENCES

The table below lists all of the sections in this book, along with the first page for each corresponding section from Ibn Mulaqqin's other fiqh books. This will enable readers to easily locate specific references mentioned in the book, and find additional commentary. This should be especially useful since my three primary sources follow slightly different orders.

The abbreviations after the first column are as follows:

KF *Khulāṣat al-fatāwī*
MT *Mukhtaṣar al-Tabrīzī*
UM *ʿUjālat al-muḥtāj*

CHAPTER/SECTION TITLE	KF	MT	UM
I PURIFICATION	1:189	25	63
Water	1:189	25	65
Confusing Pure and Filthy Water	1:251	36	70
Containers	1:261	47	72
The Toothstick	1:301	55	97
Ablution Invalidators	1:318	56	74
Actions Unlawful Due to Minor Ritual Impurity	1:329	60	79
Obligatory Actions of Ablution	1:264	47	90
Recommended Actions of Ablution	1:294	51	102
Wiping Over Khuffs	1:279	49	110
Relieving & Cleaning Oneself	1:312	57	85
The Purificatory Bath	1:345	97	114

CHAPTER/SECTION TITLE	KF	MT	UM
Actions Unlawful Without Major Ritual Purity	1:332	66	115
Recommended Baths	2:259*	67	
FIlth and I645ts Removal	1:215	39	122
Dry Ablution	1:353	70	131
Menstruation, Postnatal & Irregular Bleeding	1:395	74	149
Actions Unlawful Due to Menstruation & Lochia	1:332	78	150
2 PRAYER	1:439	84	160
Times	1:440	84	160
Conditions Obligating Prayer	1:450	83	173
Recommended Prayers	1:545:	106	286
Denying Its Obligation & Neglecting Its Performance	2:40*	85	409
Prerequisites for Prayer	1:470	100	225
Essential Elements of Prayer	1:480	90	189
Actions Recommended Before & During Prayer	1:460	101	175
Differences Between Men & Women During Prayer	1:527*		
Invalidators of Prayer	1:520	96	241
Quantity of Prayer Elements			
Forgetfulness During Prayer	1:533	97	225
Times Wherein Prayer is Unlawful	1:456	108	169
Congregational Prayer	1:554	108	293
Shortening & Combining Prayers	1:595	111	342
Friday Prayer	1:630	113	356
The Two Eids	2:220	106	388
The Eclipse Prayer	2:30	107	399
The Drought Prayer	2:36	107	403
Prayer During Peril	2:5	112	380
Clothes	2:12	46	384
3 FUNERALS	2:41		
Preparing for Death	2:42	115	411
Funerary Preparations	2:44	115	415
The Funeral Bath	2:46	116	415
Funeral Shrouds	2:53	117	420
The Funeral Prayer	2:63	117	425
Burial	2:67	119	437

CHAPTER/SECTION TITLE	KF	MT	UM
Crying Over The Deceased	2:73	119	442
Offering Condolences	2:73	119	441
4 ZAKAT	2:79	123	362
Properties Subject to Zakat	2:103		
Livestock	2:79		462
Camels	2:79	123	463
Cows	2:90	125	470
Sheep	2:91	125	470
Mixed Flocks	2:119		
Gold & Silver	2:94	125	483
Agriculture & Fruit	2:97	128	477
Trade Goods	2:103	126	487
Mines & Treasure	2:94	129	487
Conditions Obligating Zakat	2:108	123	502
Zakāt al-Fiṭr	2:145	129	495
Eligible Recipients	4:137	131	1140
Voluntary Charity		133	1155
5 FASTING	2:155	137	519
Conditions and Invalidators	2:155	137	519
Intercourse in Ramadan During the Daytime	2:177	139	545
Issues Related to Fasting	2:180	139	538
Voluntary Fasting	2:186	142	550
Spiritual Retreat	2:188	142	556
6 PILGRIMAGE	2:207	147	567
Conditions for Being Obligatory	2:218	148	571
Integrals of Hajj	2:239	149	636
Integrals of Umrah	2:230	158	637
Obligatory Acts of Hajj	2:231	154	580
Recommended Acts of Hajj	2:258	159	639
Entering Iḥrām	2:262	159	587
Things Unlawful During Pilgrimage	2:290	162	644
Omitting Standing on ʿArafah	2:235		666
Expiations	2:341	164	660
The Expiation for Intercourse	2:308	165	649
Visiting the Grave of the Prophet ﷺ			635
7 SALES AND OTHER TRANSACTIONS	2:343		780
Sales	2:343	171	670

CHAPTER/SECTION TITLE	KF	MT	UM
Unlawful Gain	2:380	189	681
Choosing to Rescind	2:431	176	698
Various Issues Related to Sales	2:524	188	729
Ordering Goods	2:551	194	742
Personal Loans	2:586	199	751
Contractual Disagreement	2:541	193	735
Slaves Who Have Permission to Trade	2:528	194	738
Offering Collateral	2:591	199	755
Suspension	3:5	209	786
Settlement	3:55	218	798
Property-Related Settlement	3:62	220	803
Assignment of Debt	3:75	221	810
Providing Surety of Payment	3:85	225	815
Surety of Physical Presence	3:91	227	820
Partnerships	3:109	230	827
Commissioning Others	3:117	235	832
Admissions	3:157	242	850
Lending	3:213	247	869
Deposits for Safekeeping	4:97	311	1111
Wrongfully-Taken Property	3:233	251	879
Preemption	3:269	184	893
Financing a Profit-Sharing Venture	3:297	255	910
Watering Crops for a Stipulated Portion	3:319	262	920
Renting Goods & Hiring Services	3:335	259	927
Wages	3:383	265	1019
Reclamation & Use of Unclaimed Resources	3:391	267	947
Water Rights	3:408		957
Endowments	3:411	271	960
Gifts	3:453	275	981
Found Items	3:461	278	994
Foundlings	3:477	283	1008
8 INHERITANCE AND BEQUESTS	3:501	292	1037
The Estate	3:502	294	1037
People Who Always or Never Inherit		304	1050
Preventers of Inheritance	3:548	296	1064
Shares	3:505	298	1044

CROSS-REFERENCES

CHAPTER/SECTION TITLE	KF	MT	UM
Universal Inheritance	3:518	302	1060
Bequests & Executors	4:5	305	1078
Tribute & Spoils of War	4:117	314	1123
9 MARRIAGE AND DIVORCE	4:161	321	1161
Rulings Unique to the Prophet ﷺ	4:162		
Issues Related to Marriage	4:186	323	1161
Looking at Members of the Opposite Sex	4:190		1167
Engagement	4:200		1185
The Marriage Contract	4:204	324	1194
The Bride's Guardians	4:215	325	1211
Those Barred From Being Guardians	4:225	328	1214
Suitability	4:236		1232
A Husband's Rights	4:316		
Compelling Women to Marry	4:217	327	1204
Unmarriageable Women	4:243	321	1248
Marrying a Non-Muslim Woman	4:265	322	1260
An Individual Spouse Entering Islam	4:267	331	1265
Spousal Defects Permitting Annulment	4:291	330	1277
Providing a Wife for One's Father	4:322	361	1284
The Wife's Marriage Payment	4:337		1292
Amenity Payment	4:378	331	1308
The Wedding Feast	4:384	331	1311
Giving Wives Equal Time	4:391	332	1320
Disobedience	4:408	335	1328
Release for Compensation	4:411	335	1331
Divorce	4:453	335	1345
Taking Back One's Wife	4:551	341	1389
Forswearing One's Wife	5:5	345	1398
Likening One's Wife to One's Mother	5:21	347	1406
Charging One's Wife With Adultery	5:52	353	1418
Establishing Paternity		355	1864
The ʿIddah Waiting Period	5:71	342	1430
Mourning	5:81		1441
Keeping to One's Residence	5:107		1445
Ensuring Lack of Pregnancy	5:119	344	1451
Wet-Nursing	5:131	356	1487
Spousal Support	5:149	357	1475
Supporting Relatives	5:173	360	1488
Nursing One's Child	5:181		1490

CHAPTER/SECTION TITLE	KF	MT	UM
Supporting Slaves, Animals & Non-Movable Properties	5:196		1497
Custody	5:183	363	1491
Issues Related to Custody	5:193	373	1495
10 INJURIOUS CRIMES	5:201	367	1500
Types of Wrongful Killing	5:236	367	1542
The ʿĀqilah	5:229	375	1588
Reciprocal Punishments	5:308	367	1516
Non-Fatal Personal Injuries	5:288	371	
Blood Indemnity	5:240	372	1549
A Fetus's Blood Indemnity	5:247	373	1590
Factors Augmenting Mistaken Killings	5:224	374	1550
Things that Complete a Blood-Indemnity	5:264	376	1565
Wounds That Cleave Flesh from the Bone	5:276	377	1524, 1555
Appraisal	5:315	378	1573
Blood Indemnity for Slaves		373	1575
Murder Allegations	6:401	380	1597
Expiation for Killing	2:181	378	1593
Renegades	5:381	381	1607
The Supreme Imām			1612
Apostasy	5:393	382	1615
11 PUNISHMENTS			1632
Fornication	5:409	383	1620
Accusing a Person of Fornication	5:39	351	1631
Alcohol & Liquid Intoxicants	5:487	393	1656
Theft	5:433	387	1633
Highway Robbery	5:471	391	1651
Disciplinary Punishments	5:496	396	1661
Self-Defense	5:509	398	1665
Animals	5:518	398	1674
Looking Through a Peephole	5:514	399	1668
Circumcision	5:507	56	1671
12 JIHAD	5:525	403	1678
It Being a Yearly Obligation	5:525	403	1678
Conditions for Being Obligatory	5:520	403	1680
Rules of Engagement	5:535	406	1685

CHAPTER/SECTION TITLE	KF	MT	UM
Prisoners of War	5:555	407	1690
Fleeing Battle	5:552	407	1689
Destroying Enemy Property and Animals	5:549	408	1690
Giving Amnesty to Combatants	6:5	409	1700
Emigration from Lands of Disbelief			1701
Compensating Non-Muslim Spies	6:14	317	1702
The Jizyah Contract	6:22	411	1704
Truces	6:59	409	1717
13 HUNTING AND SLAUGHTERING	6:69	418	1723
Slaughtering	6:69	418	1723
Sacrifices for Eid al-Aḍḥā	6:99	415	1736
Slaughtering for a Newborn	6:120	417	1743
Lawful and Prohibited Animals	6:123	413	1746
14 CONTESTS AND MARKSMANSHIP	6:149	419	1759
15 OATHS AND VOWS	6:173	423	1769
Oaths	6:173	423	1769
Vows	6:227	426	1788
16 COURTS AND TESTIMONY	6:243	431	1797
Regarding Judges and Arbitration	6:243	431	1797
Removing Judges	6:252	432	1802
Assistants to the Judge	6:259		1806
Some Issues Related to Judgments	6:263	432	1809
Mistaken Judgment	6:271		1809
Description of Claims	6:273	434	1812
Judgment In Absentia	6:359		1815
Dividing Property	6:451	437	1821
Witnesses	6:300	436	1827
What Constitutes Testimony and Evidence	6:330	432	1638
Testimony from the Blind	6:329		
Evidence	6:429		1849
Conflicting Evidence	6:441		1820
Swearing Oaths	6:424		1855
Oaths & Disputes	6:427		1856
Testimony Related to Actions	6:424	435	1840
Witnesses Retracting Testimony Before Judgment	6:381		1846

CHAPTER/SECTION TITLE	KF	MT	UM
Witnesses Retracting Testimony After Judgment	6:382		1846
Taking Rights			1849
17 MANUMISSION	6:477	438	1867
What Constituted Manumission	6:477	439	1867
Walāʾ		440	1876
Tadbīr	6:501	444	1879
Kitābah	6:511	441	1885
Ummahāt al-Awlād	6:553	433	1899

B

PERSONS MENTIONED IN THE TEXT

Basic information about persons mentioned in this book is provided below to facilitate locating them in more comprehensive biographical works, and to differentiate Companions, Successors, and later scholars. Entries are in alphabetical order, ignoring the initial "al-" and diacritics. Each begins with the person's name and lineage, usually followed by their Hijri dates of birth and death (in parentheses, if known), and then brief biographical information. Most honorifics have been omitted for the sake of brevity, so readers are encouraged to add them as they read through the book.

al-ʿAbbās ibn ʿAbd al-Muṭṭalib ibn Hāshim (d. 77) was the paternal uncle of the Prophet ﷺ. He died at 88 years of age.

ʿAbd Allāh ibn ʿAbbās ibn ʿAbd al-Muṭṭalib, Abū al-ʿAbbās (-3–68) was the son of the Prophet ﷺ's paternal uncle and nephew of one of his ﷺ wives. The Prophet ﷺ asked Allah to endow him with wisdom, understanding of the religion, and comprehension of the Quran. He saw Jibrīl (peace be upon him) twice. He was 13 years old when the Prophet ﷺ passed away. Despite ibn ʿAbbās's young age, ʿUmar ibn al-Khaṭṭāb sought his counsel. He lost his eyesight at the end of his life and died in Ṭā'if.

ʿAbd Allāh ibn ʿAbd al-Raḥmān ibn al-Faḍl, Abū Muḥammad al-Dārimī (181–255) was a great hadith master, exegete, and legist whose esteemed book of sunan is held above Ibn Mājah's *Sunan* in reliability by several scholars.

ʿAbd Allāh ibn ʿAmr ibn al-ʿĀṣ, al-Sahmī, al-Qurashī was a Companion who possessed vast knowledge, memorized the Quran, and was devoted to worship. He asked for and received permission from the Prophet ﷺ to record hadith.

ʿAbd Allāh ibn Buḥaynah (see ʿAbd Allāh ibn Mālik)

ʿAbd Allāh ibn Mālik ibn Buḥaynah ibn al-Qishb, Abū Muḥammad (d. >50). An affiliate of Banī al-Muṭallib.

ʿAbd Allāh ibn Masʿūd ibn Ghāfil, al-Hudhalī, Abū ʿAbd al-Raḥmān (d. 32) was an early convert to Islam and an emigrant to both Abyssinia and Medina. He is one of the companions in whom the Prophet ﷺ would confide secrets. ʿUmar assigned him to oversee the courts and the Muslim treasury in Kūfa. He died in Medina, having aged more than sixty years.

ʿAbd Allāh ibn Qays ibn Sālim, Abū Mūsā al-Ashʿarī (d. 52) was an early convert to Islam who emigrated to Abyssinia. During ʿUmar's caliphate, he was appointed governor of Baṣra.

ʿAbd Allāh ibn Saʿd al-Anṣārī was a Companion who participated in conquering al-Qādisiyah.

ʿAbd Allāh ibn al-Saʿdī al-Qurashī was a Companion. His father is said to be ʿAmr ibn Waqdān.

ʿAbd Allāh ibn Sahl was a Companion who was found murdered near Khaybar.

ʿAbd Allāh ibn Shubramah (d. 144) was the illustrious Imam and jurist of Iraq and judge of Kūfa. He narrated hadiths from numerous Companions.

ʿAbd Allāh ibn ʿUmar ibn al-Khaṭṭāb, Abū ʿAbd al-Raḥmān (d. 73) was born one year before the revelation began. He and his father entered Islam in Mecca, while he was young. He was known for his knowledge, piety, and scrupulousness, in both his personal actions and when giving legal judgments. He died in 73 AH at the age of 84.

ʿAbd Allāh ibn ʿUthmān, Abū Bakr ibn Abī Quḥāfa al-Ṣiddīq (d. 13) was a life-long Companion of the Prophet ﷺ and the first adult male to enter Islam. Many entered Islam through him, including ʿUthmān ibn ʿAffān, Ṭalḥa ibn ʿUbaydullāh, al-Zubayr ibn al-ʿAwwām, Saʿd ibn Abī Waqqāṣ, and ʿAbd al-Raḥmān ibn ʿAwf. He died in Medina on Tuesday night (eight days before the end of Jumāda al-Ākhira) in the year 13 AH, between the Sunset and Night Prayers. He was 63 years old. His wife Asmāʾ ibn ʿUmays washed him, and ʿUmar prayed the Funeral Prayer over him. He was buried next to the Prophet ﷺ in his daughter ʿĀʾishah's house.

ʿAbd Allāh ibn Zayd ibn ʿĀṣim ibn Kaʿb al-Anṣārī al-Māzanī, Abū Muḥammad (d. 63) was a Companion credited with killing Musaylimah the Liar. He was martyred in Ḥirrah.

ʿAbd Allāh ibn al-Zubayr ibn al-ʿAwwām al-Qurashī al-Asadī, Abū Bakr or **Abū Khubayb** (d. 73) was the first child born to the Emigrants in Medina. He was appointed caliph and served for nine years until his murder at Dhi al-Juḥfah.

ʿAbd al-Karīm ibn Muḥammad ibn ʿAbd al-Karīm, Abū al-Qāsim al-Rāfiʿī (557–623) was one of the greatest Shāfiʿī legal scholars ever. He died in Qizwīn.

ʿAbd al-Mālik ibn ʿAbd al-ʿAzīz, Ibn Jurayj (d. 150), an affiliate [mawlā] of the Umayyads, was known as a superior, trustworthy hadith narrator and legist. He narrations appear in the six canonical hadith collections.

ʿAbd al-Raḥmān ibn ʿAuf ibn ʿAbd al-Ḥārith ibn Zuhrah al-Qurashī (d. 32) was an early convert to Islam and one of the ten Companions promised Paradise. His accomplishments are well known.

ʿAbd al-Raḥmān ibn Ṣakhr, Abū Hurayrah (d. 57) received his nickname "Abū Hurayrah" because of a cat he carried in his sleeve. He entered Islam late during the year of Khaybar (7 AH). After his conversion, he spent as much time as possible with the Prophet ﷺ and became one of the greatest hadith narrators from among the Companions. More than eight hundred Companions and Successors narrated from him, including Ibn ʿAbbās, Ibn ʿUmar, Jābir, Anas, and Wathila ibn al-Asqaʿ. Among the supplications that the Prophet ﷺ made on his behalf was "O God! Make Your little servant Abū Hurayrah and his mother beloved to Your believing servants."

ʿAbd al-Raḥmān ibn Yaʿmar al-Dīlī, Abū al-Aswad was a Companion who lived in Kūfa and reportedly died in Khurāsān.

ʿAbd al-Raḥmān ibn Yasār, Ibn Abī Laylā (d. 83) was among the senior Successors in Kūfa. He narrated hadiths from ʿAlī ibn Abī Ṭālib, ʿUtmān ibn ʿAffān, Abī Ayyūb al-Anṣārī, and others.

ʿAbd al-Raḥmān ibn al-Zabīr ibn Bāṭā al-Quraẓī al-Madanī was a Companion who divorced his wife Umaymah thrice.

ʿAbd al-Razzāq ibn Hammām, al-Ṣanʿānī, Abū Bakr (126–211) was a renowned hadith master who memorized approximately 17,000 hadiths in his lifetime. His most famous work is his *Muṣannaf fī al-ḥadīth,* published in eleven volumes.

ʿAbd al-Wāḥid ibn Ismāʿīl ibn Aḥmad ibn Muḥammad al-Ruwyānī (415–501) was a Shāfiʿī legist and esteemed scholar of fiqh and jurisprudence. He once said that if all of Imam al-Shāfiʿī's works were to be burned, he would be able to dictate them from memory.

Abū Ayyūb al-Anṣārī (see Khālid ibn Zayd)

Abū Bakr al-Ṣiddīq (see ʿAbd Allāh ibn ʿUthmān)

Abū Bakrah (see Nufayʿ ibn al-Ḥārith)

Abū Baṣrah al-Ghaffārī (see Ḥumayl ibn Baṣrah)

Abū Dardāʾ (d. 32) was a companion known by this agnomen (Dardāʾ was his daughter). He was the last of his household to enter Islam. Knowledgeable and wise, he was one of the Companions who gave legal opinions. He resided in Greater Syria and died in Damascus.

Abū Dāwūd (see Sulayāan ibn al-Ashʿath)

Abū Dharr (see Jundub ibn Junāda)

Abū Ḥāmid al-Ghazālī (see Muḥammad ibn Muḥammad)

Abū Ḥanīfa (see al-Nuʿmān ibn Thābit)

Abū Ḥumayd al-Sāʿidī (d. 60) was a well-known Companion who fought in military campaigns, starting with Uhud.

Abū Hurayrah (see ʿAbd al-Raḥman ibn ibn Ṣakhr)

Abū Mūsā al-Aʿsharī (see ʿAbdullāh ibn Qays)

Abū Qatādah (see al-Ḥārith ibn al-Ribʿī)

Abū Rāfiʿ al-Qibṭī was a freed slave of the Prophet ﷺ. There is disagreement whether his first name was Ibrāhīm, Aslam, Thābit, or Hurmuz. He died during ʿAlī's caliphate.

Abū Saʿīd al-Khudrī (see Saʿd ibn Mālik)

Abū Saʿīd ibn al-Muʿallā (d. 73) was a Companion, although there is disagreement about his name and lineage.

Abū Sufyān (see Ṣakhr ibn Ḥarb ibn Umayyah)

Abū Ṭalḥa (see Zayd ibn Sahl)

Abū Thaʿlabah (d. 75) was a Companion, though scholars differ regarding his name and his father's name.

Abū Umāmah ibn Sahl (see Asʿad ibn Sahl)

Abū al-Zubayr (see Muḥammad ibn Muslim)

ʿAdī ibn Ḥātim ibn ʿAbd Allāh ibn Saʿd al-Ḥashraj al-Ṭāʾī, Abū Ṭurayf (d. 68) was a well-known Companion who participated in conquering Iraq. He was 120 years old when he died.

Aḥmad ibn ʿAlī ibn Thābit, Abū Bakr al-Baghdādī (392–463) was a historian, hadith master, and the most important early codifier of the hadith sciences. When his death drew near, he gave away all of his property and declared his works an endowment for all Muslims. His wrote more than 56 works, including *Tarīkh Baghdād, Al-Nukhalaʾ, Al-Kifāya fī ʿilm al-riwāya, Taqyīd al-ʿilm,* and *Sharaf aṣḥāb al-ḥadīth*. He died in Baghdad in 463 AH.

Aḥmad ibn ʿAmr ibn ʿAbd al-Khāliq, al-Baṣrī, Abū Bakr al-Bazzār (210–292) was a hadith master who transmitted hadiths in Isfahan, Baghdad, Egypt, Mecca, and Ramla. He later compiled these narrations into his *Musnad*.

Aḥmad ibn Ḥanbal (see Aḥmad ibn Muḥammad)

Aḥmad ibn Muḥammad ibn Ḥanbal al-Shaybānī, Abū ʿAbd Allāh (164–241) was the founder of the Ḥanbalī school of law, the epitome of hadith masters, and champion of the Sunnah. Imam al-Shāfiʿī said, "I have left no one in Baghdad with more understanding and knowledge, or who is more scrupulous and ascetic than Aḥmad ibn Ḥanbal."

Aḥmad ibn Shuʿayb ibn ʿAlī, al-Nasāʾī, Abū ʿAbd al-Raḥmān (215–303) was the esteemed Shāfiʿī and Mālikī hadith master and author of many works. His *Sunan* is one of the six major hadith compilations. It applies the most rigorous criteria for authenticity among them, after the two *Ṣaḥīḥ*s.

ʿĀʾisha bint Abī Bakr al-Ṣiddīq (d. 57) was the third and youngest wife of the Prophet ﷺ and one of the Mothers of the Faithful. Al-Dhahabī said she was "absolutely the most knowledgeable woman in the Ummah, or rather, among humankind." Al-Suyūṭī called her "comprehensive in her knowledge, unique in her understanding, and a *mujtahidah* – indeed the epitome of learning and teaching." She was the daughter of Abū Bakr al-Ṣiddīq, the Prophet ﷺ's successor and dearest friend. Her mother was Umm Rūmān, daughter of ʿAmir ibn Uwaymir. Lady ʿA'ishah was known for her eloquence and knowledge of religious matters, medicine, and Arab lore. She was 19 years old when the Prophet ﷺ passed away.

ʿAlī ibn Abū al-Ṭālib, Abū al-Ḥasn (d. 40) was the fourth Rightly Guided Caliph and first male youth to embrace Islam. He was the nephew and son-in-law of the Prophet ﷺ and fought alongside him ﷺ in every battle except for Tabūk, during which the Prophet ﷺ instructed him to look after his own family instead. He was appointed caliph in 35 AH, after ʿUthmān's assassination. He was stabbed during Ramadan and died three days later in Kūfa, at the age of 63. He was caliph for four years and nine months.

ʿAlī ibn Muḥammad ibn Ḥabīb, Abū al-Ḥasan al-Māwardī (364–450) was the eminent Shāfiʿī Imam who was given authority over the Baghdad courts. During the ʿAbbāsid caliphate of al-Qā'im bi-amri-llāh, he was appointed chief justice. The term "māwardī" refers to one who sells rose water. His many works include *Al-Hāwī* and *Al-Aḥkām al-sulṭāniyyah*. He died in Baghdad.

ʿAlī ibn ʿUmar ibn Aḥmad, Abu al-Ḥasn, al-Ḥāfiẓ, al-Dāraquṭnī (306-385) was a well-known hadith master.

ʿAmmār ibn Yāsir ibn ʿĀmir ibn Mālik, Abū al-Yaqẓān (d. 37) was a freed slave of Banī Makhzūm who was among the early converts to Islam. He fought alongside ʿAlī ʿat Ṣiffīn and was martyred.

ʿAmr ibn ʿAuf ibn Zayd ibn Milḥah, Abū ʿAbd Allāh al-Muzanī was an early convert to Islam. He died in Medina towards the end of Muʿāwiyah's rule.

ʿAmr ibn Dīnār, Abū Muḥammad al-Jumḥī (45–146) was one of the greatest scholars of his age and the shaykh of the Sacred Precinct.

ʿAmr ibn Hazam ibn Zaynd ibn Lawdhān al-Anṣārī (d. > 50) was a Companion who participated in the Battle of the Trench and in subsequent battles.

ʿAmr ibn Salamah ibn Nafiʿ al-Jurmī, Abū Burayd was a Companion of the Prophet ﷺ who lead his people in prayer when he was only six or seven years old, since he was the most learned in Quran among them.

ʿAmr ibn Shuʿayb ibn Muḥammad ibn ʿAbd Allāh ibn ʿAmr ibn al-ʿĀṣ (d. 108) was a Companion of the Prophet ﷺ.

Anas ibn Mālik ibn al-Nuḍr (d. 91) was the Prophet ﷺ's servant for ten years, then moved to Baṣra during the caliphate of ʿUmar in order to teach. He died in Baṣra at the age of 103 – the last of the Companions to pass away. He left behind 100 offspring.

ʿArfajah ibn Shurayḥ al-Ashjaʿī was a Companion, though scholars differ concerning his father's name. He settled in Kūfa.

al-Asadī (see Qays ibn al-Ḥārith)

Asʿad ibn Sahl ibn Ḥunayf al-Anṣārī, Abū Umāmah (d. 100) was a Companion who was known by his agnomen. He saw the Prophet ﷺ but didn't learn directly from him ﷺ. He was 92 when he died.

Asayd ibn Saʿyah, along with his brother Thaʿlabah, was among the Jews of Medina who entered Islam.

Aṣḥamah ibn Abḥar al-Najāshī was the king of Ḥabshah and is counted amongst the Companions. The Prophet ﷺ led a funeral prayer in absentia [*ṣalāt al-ghāʾib*] on his behalf when he died.

Asmāʾ bint Abī Bakr al-Ṣiddīq, Umm ʿAbd Allāh (d. 73) was the elder sister of ʿAʾishah and one of the earliest converts to

Islam. She married al-Zubayr ibn ʿAwwām in Mecca and bore his son ʿAbd Allāh in Medina. She died in Mecca at the age of 100 – ten days after her son was killed.

Asmāʾ bint Shakal al-Anṣāriyyah was one of the Companions.

ʿAtāʾ ibn Abū Rabāḥ Aslam (27–115) was one of the Meccan Successors and an illustrious legist. He died in Mecca at the age of 88.

al-Baghawī (see Al-Ḥusayn ibn Masʿūd)

Al-Barāʾ ibn ʿĀzib ibn al-Ḥārith ibn ʿAdī al-Anṣāri al-Awsī (d. 72) was a Companion of the Prophet ﷺ who lived in Kūfa. He was deemed too young for the Battle of Badr, as he was the same age as Ibn ʿUmar.

Barīrah ibn Ṣafwān was a freed slave of ʿAʾishah. She died during the caliphate of Yazīd ibn Muʿāwiyah.

Birwaʿ bint Wāshiq, al-Rawwāsiyyah al-Kilābiyyah was the wife of Hilāl ibn Murrah. Both were Companions.

Al-Bayhaqī, Aḥmed ibn Ḥusein ibn ʿAlī (384–458/994–1066) was one of the most influential Imams of hadith.

Al-Bazzār (see Aḥmad ibn ʿAmr)

Bilāl ibn Rabāḥ al-Ḥabashī (d. 20) was the Prophet ﷺ's muezzin and an early convert to Islam. He performed his last call to prayer after the Prophet ﷺ passed away and remained in Medina until the armies left for Sham. He joined them and later died in Damascus.

Al-Bukhārī (see Muḥammad ibn Ismāʿīl)

Busrah bint Ṣafwān ibn Nawfal was a Companion and among the earliest emigrants to Medina.

Al-Dāraquṭnī (see ʿAlī ibn ʿUmar)

Al-Dāramī (see ʿAbd Allāh ibn ʿAbd al-Raḥmān)

Dāwūd ibn al-Ḥuṣṣayn al-Umawī, Abū Sylaymān (d. 53) was a master of fiqh and a trustworthy narrator – although not when it comes to ʿIkrimah.

Dhu l-Yadayn, Khirbāq ibn ʿAmr was a Companion.

Ḍirār ibn Mālik ("al-Azwar") ibn Aws (d. 11) was a Companion who was known for his poetry, horsemanship, and bravery.

Ḍubāʿah bint al-Zubayr ibn ʿAbd al-Muṭṭalib al-Ḥāshimiyyah was the daughter of the Prophet ﷺ's paternal uncle.

Al-Dūlābī, Muḥammad ibn al-Ṣabbāḥ, Abū Jaʿfar (150–227) was a narrator from whom Imam Aḥmad took hadith.

Fāṭimah al-Zahrāʾ (-18–11) was the daughter of the Prophet ﷺ and Khadījah bint Khuwaylid. She married ʿAlī in 2 AH and went on to be the mother of al-Ḥasan, al-Husein, Umm Kalthūm, and Zaynab. She died six months after the Prophet ﷺ passed away.

Fāṭimah bint Abi Ḥubaysh, al-Asadiyyah was a Companion. Her father's name was Qays ibn al-Muṭṭalib.

Ghaylān ibn Salamah (d. 23) was a pre-Islamic sage and poet.

al-Ghazālī (see Muḥammad ibn Muḥammad)

Ḥabībah bint Abī Tajrāh was a Companion of the Prophet ﷺ.

Ḥabbān ibn Munqadh ibn ʿAmr ibn ʿAṭiyyah was a Companion who suffered from a head injury.

Habbār ibn al-Aswad ibn al-Muṭṭalib (d 15) wrote seditious poetry against the Prophet ﷺ but later repented and accepted Islam when the Muslims conquered Mecca.

al-Ḥākim (see Muḥammad ibn ʿAbdullāh)

Ḥafṣ ibn ʿUmar al-Ubulī was a weak narrator of hadiths, though al-Dāraquṭnī compiled some of his narrations.

Ḥafṣā bint ʿUmar ibn al-Khaṭṭāb (d. 45) was a wife of the Prophet ﷺ and Mother of the Faithful. She died during the month of Shaʿbān at 60 years of age.

Hālah bint ʿAuf al-Zuhriyyah was the sister of ʿAbd al-Raḥmān ibn ʿAuf and wife of Bilāl, according to Imam al-Rāfiʿī in his book concerning suitable marriages.

al-Ḥārith ibn al-Ribʿī ibn Buldamah, Abū Qatādah, al-Salamī al-Madini (d. 54) was a Companion who fought in a number of battles, starting with Uḥud, though his participation in Badr is not authenticated.

Al-Ḥasan ibn ʿAlī ibn Abī al-Ṭālib, al-Hāshimī al-Qurashī (3–50) was the grandson of the Prophet ﷺ and the fifth Caliph.

Ḥawayyiṣah ibn Masʿūd ibn Kaʿb was a Companion who fought at Uḥud and in all others battles.

Hilāl ibn Umayyah was a Companion of the Prophet ﷺ.

Hind bint Abī Umayya Suhayl ibn al-Mughīra, Umm Salamah (d. 59) was a Mother of the Faithful. She died at age 84.

Hind bint ʿUtbah ibn Rabīʿah ibn ʿAbd al-Shams (d. 14) was the wife of Abū Sufyān and mother of Muʿāwiyah. She fought against the Muslims during the Battle of Badr. She and her husband entered Islam when Mecca was conquered.

Ḥudhayfa ibn al-Yamān (d. 35 or 36) was the protector of the Prophet ﷺ's secrets. Both he and his father (Ḥusayl ibn Jābir) emigrated to the Prophet ﷺ sometime near the Battle of Badr. He died in Madā'in, in modern day Iran, some forty days after ʿUthmān was assassinated.

Ḥumayl ibn Baṣrah ibn Waqqāṣ, Abū Baṣrah al-Ghaffārī was a Companion of the Prophet ﷺ who resided and died in Egypt.

al-Ḥusayn ibn Masʿūd, Abū Muḥammad, Abū Muḥammad al-Baghawī (d. 516) was a Shāfiʿī legist, hadith master, and exegete. He is the author of *Al-Tahdhīb fī fiqh al-Imām* *al-Shāfiʿī* in four large tomes, an emendation of al-Qāḍī Ḥusayn's *Al-Taʿlīqa,* and from which al-Nawawī frequently quotes in his *Rawḍat al-ṭālibīn.*

Al-Husein ibn ʿAlī ibn Abī Ṭālib, al-Hāshimī, Abū ʿAbd Allāh (d. 61) was the grandson of the Prophet ﷺ. He was martyred on the Day of ʿAshūrā', at the age of 56.

Huzail ibn Shiraḥbīl al-Azdī al-Kūfī was a Successor and is considered a trustworthy narrator.

Ibn ʿAbbās (see ʿAbd Allāh ibn ʿAbbās)

Ibn Abī Laylā (see ʿAbd al-Raḥmān ibn Yasār)

Ibn ʿAbd al-Barr (see Yūsuf ibn ʿAbd Allāh)

Ibn ʿAbd al-Salām ʿAbd al-ʿAzīz ibn ʿAbd al-Salām ibn Abī al-Qāsim ibn al-Ḥasan al-Sulamī al-Dimashqī, ʿIzz al-Dīn and Sulṭān al-ʿUlimā' (577–660/1181–1262) was a Shāfiʿī legist, and a master of jurisprudence and hadith. He was born, raised, and educated in Damascus. Known for his courage, he never failed to command the right and forbidding the wrong. He died in Cairo.

Ibn Ḥabīb was a scholar whose works are the sources of the legislative history that appears in this book.

Ibn Ḥibbān (see Muḥammad ibn Ḥibbān)

Ibn Kajj, Abū al-Qāsim Yūsuf ibn Aṃad al-Dīnawarī (d. 145) was a judge, eminent scholar, prolific author, and shaykh of the Shāfiʿīs. A student of Abī al-Ḥisayn ibn al-Qaṭṭān and an attendee at al-Dārakī's assemblies, he was considered exemplary in memorizing the *madhhab*. He was murdered on the 27th night of Ramadan.

Ibn Khuzaymah (see Muḥammad ibn Isḥāq ibn Khuzaymah)

Ibn Mājah (see Muḥammad Ibn Yazīd)

Ibn Masʿūd (see ʿAbd Allāh ibn Masʿūd)

al-Miqdād ibn al-Aswad al-Kindī, Ibn ʿAmr ibn Thaʿlabah ibn Mālik (d 33) was a Companion who died at 77 years of age.

Ibn al-Mundhir (see Muḥammad Ibn Ibrāhīm)

Ibn al-Qaṭṭān, Aḥmad ibn Muḥammad ibn Aḥmad ibn al-Qaṭṭān (d. 359) was a Shāfiʿī legist and author of works in jurisprudence and its methodologies. He died in Baghdad, the city of his birth.

Ibn al-Rifʿah (645–710) was an Egyptian Shāfiʿī scholar whose many works include *Kifāyat al-nabīh fī sharḥ Al-Tanbīh*.

Ibn al-Ṣalāḥ (see ʿUthmān ibn ʿAbd al-Raḥmān)

Ibn Shihāb (see Muḥammad ibn Muslim)

Ibn ʿUmar (see ʿAbd Allah ibn ʿUmar)

ʿIkrimah, Abū ʿAbd Allāh (27–107) was a freed slave of Ibn ʿAbbās and one of the great legists of Mecca. He was also an extensive traveler.

ʿImrān ibn Ḥuṣayn.

Ismāʿīl ibn Yaḥyā ibn Ismāʿīl, Abū Ibrāhīm al-Muzanī (175–264) was a student of Imam al-Shāfiʿī in Egypt. An ascetic, scholar, and mujtahid, he was known for the strength of his arguments. Concerning him, Imam al-Shāfiʿī said, "Al-Muzanī is my madhhab's champion," and "If he were to debate Satan, he would defeat him."

Jābir ibn ʿAbd Allāh ibn ʿAmr (d. 74) was one of the most prominent Companions and a transmitter of many hadiths. He died in Medina at age 94, having been one of the last remaining Companions.

Jābir ibn Samurah ibn Junādah al-Suwāʾī (d. 70) was a Companion and a Companion's son. He lived and died in Kūfa.

Jarīr ibn ʿAbd Allāh ibn ʿAmr ibn Ḥarām al-Anṣārī al-Salamī (d. > 70) was a Companion and son of a Companion who participated in 19 military campaigns. He died in Medina at the age of 49.

Kaʿb ibn Mālik ibn ʿAmr (d. 50) was a Companion and poet who used his unrivaled eloquence for the sake of the Prophet ﷺ. He was one of the three who stayed back from the Battle of Tabūk. His repentance and its acceptance is recorded in the Quran [9:118]. He died at the age of 77.

Kaʿb ibn ʿUjrah al-Anṣārī al-Madinī, Abū Muḥammad (d. 51) was a well-known Companion who participated in all of the battles. He resided in Kūfa, where he died at approximately 75 years of age.

Khabbāb ibn al-Arat ibn Jandalah ibn Saʿd al-Tamīmī, Abū ʿAbd al-Raḥmān (d. 37) was among the earliest converts to Islam, for which he was tortured. He participated in the Battle of Badr and in other battles and later died in Kūfa.

Khālid ibn Zayd, Abū Ayyūb al-Anṣārī (d. 50) was among the senior Companions who participated in the Battle of Badr. He hosted the Prophet ﷺ upon his arrival in Medina. Years later, he died during a military campaign.

al-Khaṭīb Abū Bakr al-Baghdādī (see Aḥmad ibn ʿAlī ibn Thābit)

Kulayb ibn Manfaʿah al-Ḥanafī narrated one hadith related to piety from his father or grandfather, which is recorded in Abū Dāwūd's *Sunan* and al-Bukhārī's *Tarīkh*.

Laqīṭ ibn Ṣabirah ibn ʿAbd Allāh was a well-known Companion.

Laylā bint Qānif al-Thaqafiyyah was a Companion.

Māʿiz ibn Mālik al-Salamī was a Companion who was stoned to death for fornication during the Prophet ﷺ's time.

Mālik ibn Anas (93–179) was the great Imām of Medina and founder of the school of jurisprudence that bears his name. He authored *Al-Muwaṭṭāʾ* in response to Caliph Manṣūr's request for a book of Prophetic traditions. Years later, Caliph Hārūn al-Rashīd ordered Mālik to come and relate hadith to him, to which Mālik replied: "Knowledge is something that is sought, not brought." Imam al-Shāfiʿī, his student, said of him: "Mālik is Allah's proof over His creation."

Mālik ibn al-Ḥuwayrith, Abū Sulaymān al-Laythī (d. 74) was a Companion. He passed away in Baṣrah.

Maʿqil ibn Sinān ibn Muṭahhir al-Ashjaʿī (d. 63) was a Companion who settled in Medina, then Kūfa. He was later martyred at Ḥirrah.

Maʿqil ibn Yasār ibn ʿAbd Allāh (d. > 60) was a Companion whose narrations appear in the six major hadith collections.

Māriyyah bint Shamʿūn al-Qibṭiyyah, Umm Ibrāhīm (d. 16) was a gift to the Prophet ﷺ from the ruler of Alexandria, in 7 AH. He ﷺ set her free when she gave birth to Ibrāhīm.

Manfʿah was a Companion of the Prophet ﷺ.

Al-Māwardī (see ʿAlī ibn Muḥammad)

Maymūnāh ibn al-Ḥārith ibn Ḥazan al-Hilāliyyah (d. 61) was one of the Mothers of the Faithful. The Prophet ﷺ married her in 7 AH, after she was widowed. She was the last woman to marry him ﷺ, and the last of his wives to survive him ﷺ. By the time she passed away (at age 80), she had transmitted over 76 hadiths.

Al-Miswar ibn Makhramah ibn Nawfal, Abū ʿAbd al-Raḥmān (2–64) was a Companion, as was his father.

Muʿādh ibn Jabal ibn ʿAmr ibn Aws al-Anṣārī al-Khazrajī, Abū ʿAbd al-Raḥmān (d. 18) was among the most eminent Companions. He participated in the Battle of Badr and other conflicts that followed. His knowledge of legal rulings and Quranic exegesis was of the highest order.

Muʿāwiyah ibn al-Ḥakam al-Sulamī was a Companion of the Prophet ﷺ who settled in Medina.

Al-Mughīrah ibn Shaʿbah ibn Masʿūd ibn Muʿtib al-Thaqafī, Abū ʿAbd Allāh (-20–50) was a Companion.

Muḥammad ibn ʿAbdullāh, al-Ḥākim Abū ʿAbd Allāh (321–405) was an acclaimed hadith scholar and legist. His more famous works include *Al-Mustadrik ʿalā al-ṣaḥīḥayn* and *Maʿrifat ʿulūm al-ḥadīth*. The latter is one of the first books concerning hadith sciences.

Muhaṃmad ibn Abī Laylā (see Muḥammad ibn ʿAbd al-Raḥmān)

Muḥammad ibn ʿAbd al-Raḥmān ibn Abī Laylā Yasār (74–148) was appointed judge in Kūfa for 33 years, where he passed away.

Muḥammad ibn Ḥibbān ibn Aḥmad ibn Ḥibban ibn Muʿādh ibn Maʿbad, Abū Ḥātim (d. 354) was the illustrious and scholarly Imam and Shaykh of Khurasān; a hadith master and historian; and the author of many famous works.

Muḥammad ibn Ibrāhīm ibn al-Mundhir, Abū Bakr (242–319) was a Shāfiʿī legist, mujtahid, and the chief scholar of Mecca in his time. He remained in Mecca until his death.

Muḥammad ibn Idrīs ibn al-ʿAbbās, Abū ʿAbd Allāh al-Shāfiʿī (150–205) was the great legist and founder of the school bearing his name. As a youth, he excelled in marksmanship, language, poetry, and the history of the Arabs. He then took to fiqh and hadith, becoming qualified to give religious verdicts by the time he was fifteen years old. Imam Aḥmad praised him saying, "The likeness of al-Shāfiʿī to other people is as the likeness of the sun to the earth." His works include *Al-Umm, Al-Musnad, Faḍā'il Quraysh, Ādāb al-qāḍī,* and others. He died in Egypt.

Muḥammad ibn ʿĪsā ibn Sawra al-Tirmidhī, Abū ʿĪsā (d. 279) was the blind hadith master, author of *Al-Jāmiʿ*, and the most brilliant of al-Bukhārī's students after Muslim.

Muḥammad ibn Isḥāq ibn Khuzaymah ibn al-Mughīrah (233–311) was a Shāfiʿī master of hadith.

Muḥammad ibn Ismāʿīl ibn Ibrāhīm, al-Bukhārī, Abū ʿAbd Allāh (194–257) was the hadith master of his generation. He analyzed over 600,000 hadiths in compiling his *Ṣaḥīḥ*, which is the soundest book in Islam after the Quran.

Muḥammad ibn Muḥammad ibn Muḥammad ibn Aḥmad, Abū Ḥāmid al-Ghazālī, Hujjat al-Islām (450–505) was an eminent Shāfiʿī legist, Sufi, and theologian. His works include *Iḥyā ʿulūm al-dīn, Tahāfūt al-falāsifa, Al-Muṣṭaṣfā fī ʿilm uṣūl al-fiqh, Al-Wasīṭ,* and *Al-Iqtiṣād fī al-itiqād.*

Muḥammad ibn Muslim ibn ʿAbd Allāh ibn Shihāb al-Zuhrī, Abū Bakr (58–124) was a Successor who is credited as the first to have recorded hadith. A consummate hadith master and faqīh, he memorized 1,200 hadiths and organized them into a *muṣannaf*.

Muḥammad ibn Muslim ibn Tadrus al-Asadi, Abū al-Zubayr (d. 128) was a Successor who had reached nearly 80 years of age at the time of his death.

Muḥammad ibn Yazīd, Abū ʿAbdullāh Ibn Mājah (209–273) was a great hadith master, legist, and Quranic exegete. His *Sunan* is one of six major collections of hadith.

al-Mujaziz al-Mudlijī, Ibn Aʿwar ibn Jaʿdah ibn Muʿādh was a Companion and a *qāʾif* – an individual adept at determining lineage via physical resemblances.

Muḥayyiṣah ibn Masʿūd ibn Kaʿb a-Khazrajī, Abū Saʿd was a Companion and the brother of ʿAbd Allāh ibn Masʿūd and Ḥuwayyiṣah, whom he preceded in entering Islam.

Muʿmar ibn ʿAbd Allāh ibn Nāfiʿ ibn Naḍlah was a Companion.

Muṣʿab ibn ʿUmair ibn Hāshim ibn ʿAbd Manāf, al-Qurashī (d. 3) was an early convert to Islam. He emigrated to Ḥabshah, then to Medina and was the first to lead Friday Prayers there. He was martyred at the Battle of Badr.

Muslim ibn al-Hajjāj ibn Muslim al-Qushayrī, al-Naysābūrī, Abū al-Hussein (204–261) was the most brilliant student of al-Bukhārī. His *Ṣaḥīḥ* is the third soundest book in Islam after the Quran and al-Bukhārī's *Ṣaḥīḥ*.

Al-Muzanī (see Ismāʿīl ibn Yaḥyā ibn Ismāʿīl)

Nāfiʿ, Abu ʿAbd Allah (d. 117) was the freed slave of Ibn ʿUmar.

Nufayʿ ibn al-Ḥārith ibn Kaladah ibn ʿAmr al-Thaqafī, Abū Bakrah (d. 51 or 52) was a Companion who entered Islam in Ṭā'if. He later resided and died in Baṣrah.

Al-Najāshī (see Aṣḥamah ibn Abḥar)

Al-Nasā'ī (see Aḥmad ibn Shuʿayb)

Al-Nawāwī (see Yaḥyā ibn Sharaf)

Nuʿaym ibn ʿAbd Allāh, al-Nahhām was a Companion.

Al-Nuʿmān ibn Bashīr ibn Saʿd ibn Thaʿlabah, al-Anṣārī al-Khazrajī (d. 65) was killed in Homs at the age of 64. He and his parents were all Companions.

al-Nuʿmān ibn Thābit ibn Zūwṭa, al-Taymī, al-Kūfī, Abū Ḥanīfah (80–150) was the great legist and founder of the school bearing his name. He was known for his noble character, sound intellect, and beautiful appearance. Imam al-Shāfiʿī praised him saying: "All scholars depend on Abū Hanīfah in fiqh."

Qatāda ibn Duʿāma ibn Qatāda, Abū al-Khaṭṭāb (61–118) was the hadith master and exegete of his age. He was blind. Imam Aḥmad said, "Qatāda has the best memorization of all in Baṣra." He died in Wāsiṭ from the plague.

Qays ibn ʿĀṣim ibn Sinān ibn Khālid al-Minqarī (d. circa 20) was a Companion who was famous for his foresight and discernment. He resided in Baṣrah.

Qays ibn al-Ḥārith ibn Ḥadhdhār al-Asadī (or, al-Ḥārith ibn Qays) was a Companion of the Prophet ﷺ.

al-Rāfiʿī (see ʿAbd al-Karīm ibn Muḥammad)

Rāfiʿ ibn Khadīj ibn Rāfiʿ ibn ʿAdī al-Ḥārithī al-Awsī al-Anṣārī (d. 73 or 74) was a Companion who participated the Battle of Uḥud and the Battle of the Trench.

Rifaʿah ibn Simwāl al-Quraẓī was a Companion of the Prophet ﷺ.

Al-Rumayṣāʾ bint Milḥān ibn Khālid ibn Zayd ibn Ḥarām, Umm Sulaym (d. circa 30) was the mother of Anas ibn Mālik.

Al-Rūyānī, Muḥammad ibn Hārūn, Abū Bakr (d. 307) was a hadith master who authored a *musnad* and books of fiqh.

Al-Rūyānī (see ʿAbd al-Wāḥid ibn Ismāʿīl)

Al-Ṣaʿb ibn Jaththāmah ibn Qays al-Laythī (d. 25) was a Companion known for his bravery.

Sabaiʿah ibn al-Ḥārith al-Aslamiyyah was a Companion.

Saʿd ibn Abī Waqqāṣ (see Saʿd ibn Mālik)

Saʿd ibn Mālik ibn Sanān, al-Khazrajī, al-Anṣārī, al-Khudrī, Abū Saʿīd (d. 74) was a Companion who narrated many hadiths. He died at 84 years of age.

Saʿd ibn Mālik ibn Wahb (d. 55) was an early convert to Islam. He converted through Abū Bakr al-Ṣiddīq. He was the first to launch an arrow in jihad and was one of ten Companions who were promised Paradise while they were still alive. During ʿUmar's caliphate and part of ʿUthmān's, he was responsible for managing the city of Kūfa. He died on his property, outside of Medina and was carried to Medina for burial in Baqīʿ.

Saʿd ibn Muʿādh ibn al-Nuʿmān ibn Imriʾ al-Qays (d. 5) was a Companion who fought at Badr. He was struck by an arrow during the Battle of the Trench and died a month later, after deciding the fate of Banī Qurayẓah.

Ṣafwān ibn ʿAssāl al-Murādī was a Companion of the Prophet ﷺ who settled in Kūfa.

Ṣafwān ibn Umayyah ibn Khalaf ibn Wahb (d. 41) was a Companion of the Prophet ﷺ.

Sahl ibn Abī Ḥathmah (b. 3) was a junior Companion who died during Muʿāwiyah's caliphate.

Sahl ibn Saʿd al-Khazrajī al-Anṣārī (d. 91) was a Companion who lived approximately 100 years.

Al-Sāʾib ibn Abī al-Sāʾib, Ṣayfī ibn ʿĀʾidh ibn ʿAbd Allāh ibn ʿUmar ibn Makhzūm was a Companion who was a business partner of the Prophet ﷺ prior to Islam.

Saʿīd ibn al-Musayyib ibn Ḥazn ibn Abū Wahb, Abū Muḥammad (d. 94) was one of the seven great jurists of Medina. He was born two years after ʿUmar was appointed caliph. His character was the synthesis of fiqh, hadith, abstinence, and scrupulousness. Among the Successors, he was the most knowledgeable concerning ʿUmar's judgements. He died in Medina.

Saʿīd ibn Zayd ibn ʿAmr ibn Nufayl al-ʿAdawī al-Qurashī, Abū al-Aʿwar (-22–51) was one of the ten Companions who were promised Paradise. He fought in all battles except for Badr. He was born in Mecca and died in Medina.

Sahl ibn Saʿd ibn Mālik (d. 91) was the last of the Companions to die in Medina.

Ṣakhr ibn Ḥarb ibn Umayyah ibn ʿAbd al-Shams ibn ʿAbd Manāf, Abū Sufyan (-57–33) was among the Meccan opposition leaders when Islam first emerged. He entered

Islam in 8 AH, on the day Mecca was conquered, thus redeeming himself.

Salamah ibn ʿAmr ibn Sinān ibn al-Akwaʿ (d. 74) was a Companion who fought in several battles in Africa and elsewhere. He died in Medina.

Ṣāliḥ ibn Khawwāt ibn Jubay ibn al-Nuʿmān al-Anṣārī was a Successor and a trustworthy narrator. His father was a Companion.

Al-Ṣammāʾ bint Busr was a Companion. It is said her name was Buhaynah.

Samurah, Abū Maḥdhūrah (d. 59) was a Companion with a pleasing voice. The Prophet ﷺ taught him the Call to Prayer and used him as a muezzin.

Samurah ibn Jundab ibn Hilāl al-Fazārī (d. 58) was a Medinan Companion of great courage. He passed away in Baṣrah.

Al-Shāfiʿī (see Muḥammad ibn Idrīs)

Shurayḥ ibn Hāniʾ ibn Yazīd al-Ḥārithī (d. 78) was one of ʿAlī's companions. He was martyred in Sajistan.

Sufyān ibn Saʿīd ibn Masrūq al-Thawrī, Abū ʿAbdullāh (d. 161) was the premier hadith master, jurisprudent, and devotee of his time. He, along with Abū Ḥanīfah, was the chief representative of the Kūfa School. Aḥmad called him an "Imam par excellence." Ibn al-Mubārak said, "I learned from eleven hundred shaykhs – none better than Sufyān."

Sufyān al-Thawrī (see Sufyān ibn Saʿīd ibn Masrūq)

Suhayl ibn ʿAmr ibn ʿAbd al-Shams (d. 18) was a powerful Qurayshi orator and delegate. The Muslims captured him during the Battle of Badr and then ransomed him. He represented the people of Mecca in the pact of Ḥudaybiyah and entered Islam when Mecca was conquered. Later, he died of the plague.

Sulaymān ibn al-Ashʿath ibn Shidād, al-Azdī, al-Sajistānī, Abū Dāwūd (202–275) was an Imam in jurisprudence, hadith, and other sciences. A student of Imam Aḥmad, he authored many works, most notably his *Sunan,* which is one of the six canonical hadith collections.

Sulaymān ibn Yasār, Abū Ayyūb (34–107) was a free slave of Maymūnah, Mother of the Faithful. Born during the caliphate of ʿUmar, he became one of the seven great legists of Medina.

Surāqah ibn Mālik ibn Jaʿshum al-Mudlijī al-Kinānī (d. 24) was a skilled tracker in the Days of Ignorance, so Abū Sufyān sent him to track the Prophet ﷺ when he ﷺ made hijrah to Medina. He entered Islam in 8 AH.

Ṭalḥah ibn ʿUbayd Allāh ibn ʿUthmān al-Taymī al-Qurashī, Abū Muḥammad (-28–36) was among the first eight to enter Islam and one of the ten who were promised Paradise.

Ṭāriq ibn ʿAbd Allāh al-Muḥārabī was a Companion who settled in Kūfa. He transmitted two or three hadiths.

Thābit ibn Qays ibn Shimmās al-Khazrajī al-Anṣārī (d. 12) was a Companion who participated in the Battle of Uḥud and subsequent battles. He was martyred during the caliphate of Abū Bakr.

Thaʿlabah ibn Saʿyah al-Quraẓī, along with his brother Asayd, was among the Jews who entered Islam.

Al-Tirmidhī (see Muḥammad ibn ʿIsā)

ʿUbādat ibn al-Sāmat ibn Qays, Abū al-Walīd (d. 34) was a Companion whom ʿUmar sent to Greater Syria as a judge and teacher. He resided in Ḥams, then moved to Palestine. He died at the age of 72.

Ubay ibn Kaʿb (d. 19) was among the scribes of the Revelation. He and five other companions memorized the entire

Quran during the Prophet ﷺ's lifetime, but he was the most skilled at reciting it. He died in Medina.

ʿUbayd Allāh ibn ʿAbd Allāh ibn ʿUtbah ibn Masʿūd, Abū ʿAbd Allāh (d. 98), the mufti of Medina and one of its seven legists, was among the most knowledgeable of Successors and a reliable hadith narrator. He died in Medina.

Umāmah bint Zaynab (Umāmah bint Abī al-ʿĀṣ) was the granddaughter of the Prophet ﷺ, whom he would carry while he prayed.

ʿUmar ibn ʿAbd al-ʿAzīz ibn Marwān ibn al-Ḥakam (61–101) is sometimes considered the fifth of the Rightly Guided Caliphs. He was a man of great knowledge, a hadith master, ascetic, and *mujtahid*. His mother was Laylā bint ʿĀṣim ibn ʿUmar ibn al-Khaṭṭāb, Umm ʿĀṣim. He was known for his fairness, abstinence, and Godfearingness. In 99 AH, he succeeded Sulaymān ibn ʿAbd al-Malik as caliph.

ʿUmar ibn al-Khaṭṭāb, Abū Ḥafṣa (d. 23) was the second of the Rightly Guided Caliphs who was known for his fairness, judiciousness, and strength. He was the first caliph to be given the title "Commander of the Faithful," the one who established the Hijrah-based calendar, the first to collect the Quran into one volume, and the first to gather the Muslims for Tarāwīḥ Prayer. He was murdered while leading the Dawn Prayer. He was 63 years old and had been caliph for ten and a half years. He was buried in ʿAʾishah's home, near the Prophet ﷺ.

Umm ʿAṭiyyah, Nusaybah bint Kaʿb al-Anṣāruiyyah was a Companion who resided in Medina and later, Buṣrah.

Umm Hāniʾ bint Abī Ṭālib al-Ḥāshimiyyah, Fākhitah (d. > 40) was the sister of Caliph ʿAlī and narrator of 46 hadiths, though historians disagree about her first name. She entered Islam the year Mecca was conquered and outlived her brother, who was assassinated in 40 AH.

Umm Hishām bint Ḥārithah ibn al-Nuʿmān al-Anṣāriyyah was a Companion of the Prophet ﷺ.

Umm Kalthūm (d. 9) was the daughter of the Prophet ﷺ and Khadījah bint Khuwaylid. She immigrated to Medina with the Prophet ﷺ's family in 2 AH. She married ʿUthmān ibn ʿAffān in 3 AH and remained so until her death.

Umm Salamah (see Hind bint Abī Umayya)

Umm Sulaym (see al-Rumayṣāʾ bint Milḥān)

Umaymah bint al-Ḥārith was a Companion and the wife whom ʿAbd al-Raḥmān ibn al-Zabīr divorced three times before marrying Rifāʿ.

ʿUmrah bint Ḥabbān al-Sahamiyyah was the narrator of a hadith from ʿAʾishah, though it is not clear whether she was the daughter of Ḥabban or Ḥayyan.

ʿUmrān ibn Ḥuṣain ibn ʿUbayd, Abū Nujayd (d. 52) was among the scholars of the Companions. He embraced Islam in 7 AH and served as a judge in Kūfa. He died in Buṣrah.

Unays al-Aslamī was a Companion who was mentioned in a hadith concerning fornication.

ʿUqba ibn ʿAmr ibn Thaʿlaba, Abū Masʿūd was a Companion who resided in Kūfa and died during the caliphate of ʿAlī ibn Abī Ṭālib.

ʿUrwa ibn al-Zubayr ibn al-ʿAwwām, Abū ʿAbd Allāh (22–93) was one of the seven great legists of Medina. He was erudite, righteous, generous, and a trustworthy narrator. He abstained from engaging in the dissensions [*fitan*] of his time. He died in Medina.

Usāmah ibn Zayd ibn Ḥārith, Abū Muḥammad (-6–54) was the son of an early convert, so he was raised as a Muslim. The Prophet ﷺ loved him as much as he loved his own grandsons al-Ḥasan and al-Ḥusayn. He narrated 128 hadiths.

Ibn ʿAsākir wrote that the Prophet ﷺ chose him to lead an army that included Abū Bakr and ʿUmar.

ʿUthmān ibn ʿAbd al-Raḥmān ibn ʿUthmān, Abū ʿAmr Ibn al-Ṣalāḥ (d. 643) was a great Shafiʿī legist and hadith scholar. He served as a teacher at Dār al-Ḥadīth in Damascus, where he dictated what has become one of the classic manuals on hadith sciences.

ʿUthmān ibn ʿAffān, Abū ʿAbdullāh (d. 35) was the third of the Rightly Guided Caliphs and among those who were famed for reciting the entire Quran in a single prayer cycle. He married two of the Prophet ﷺ's daughters (Ruqayyah and Umm Kalthūm) and was thus nicknamed "he of the two lights." He assembled and distributed the *muṣḥaf,* which he had recited in its entirety before the Prophet ﷺ's death. During his tenure as caliph, Armenia, Caucasia, Khurāsān, Kirmān, Sijistān, Cyprus, and much of North Africa were added to the dominion of Islam.

ʿUwaymir ibn Abī al-Abyaḍ al-ʿAjalānī was a Companion who was also said to be ʿUwaymir ibn al-Ḥārith ibn Zayd.

Wāʾil ibn Ḥujr ibn Saʿd ibn Masrūq al-Ḥaḍramī, Abū Hunaydah (d. 50) was a Companion of Yemeni royalty. He resided in Kūfa.

Wāʾilah ibn al-Asqaʿ ibn Kaʿb ibn ʿĀmir (-22–83) was among the poor companions who lived under the awning in the Mosque of the Prophet ﷺ. He was the last of the Companions to die in Damascus.

Yaḥyā ibn Maʿīn ibn ʿAwn ibn Ziyād, Abū Zakariyā (125–223) was a master of hadith and narrator analysis. He lived in Baghdad and died in Medina while making Hajj.

Yaḥyā ibn Sharaf al-Ḥūrānī al-Nawawī, Abū Zakariyā (631–676) was the great Imam of Shāfiʿi fiqh and hadith, known for his piety and asceticism. He authored several books.

Yaʿlā ibn Umayyah ibn Abī ʿUbaydah (d. 37) was a Companion who was also known as Yaʿlā ibn Munyah, after his mother or paternal grandmother.

Yūsuf ibn ʿAbd Allāh ibn Muḥammad ibn ʿAbd al-Barr ibn ʿĀṣim, Abū ʿUmar (378–463) was the renowned Andalusian Mālikī scholar, Quran and hadith master, and historian.

Zayd ibn Arqam al-Khazrajī al-Anṣārī (d. 68) was a Companion. He fought alongside the Prophet ﷺ 17 times and transmitted 70 hadiths. He died in Kūfa.

Zayd ibn Khālid al-Juhanī (d. 78) transmitted 81 hadiths. He died in Medina at 85 years of age.

Zayd ibn Sahl ibn al-Aswad ibn Ḥarām, Abū Ṭalḥa (d. 31) was a Companion who died at the age of 77.

Zayd ibn Thābit al-Ḍaḥḥāk ibn Zayd ibn Laydhān (d. 45) was one of the Prophet ﷺ's scribes. He was among the legists of the Companions, and the most learned concerning inheritance laws. During the caliphate of Abū Bakr, he participated in the compilation and recording of the Quran. Later, during the caliphate of ʿUthmān, he assisted in copying it. He died in Medina, at the age of 56.

Zaynab (d 8) was the Prophet ﷺ's eldest daughter. Her husband was Abū al-ʿAṣ – her maternal cousin with whom she had Umāmah. She entered Islam and immigrated six years before her husband.

Zaynab ibn Jaḥsh al-Asadiyyah (-33–20) was a Mother of the Faithful. The Prophet ﷺ married her after Zayd ibn Ḥārithah divorced her. She transmitted 11 hadiths.

DETAILED TABLE OF CONTENTS

المُحْتَوَيَاتُ المُفَصَّلَةُ

PREFACE, IX

INTRODUCTION, 1
Obligatory Doctrinal Knowledge, 2

1 PURIFICATION, 5
Water, 6
Confusing Pure and Filthy Water, 10
Containers, 11
The Toothstick, 12
Other Sunnas of the body, 13
Ablution Invalidators, 13
Actions Unlawful Due to Minor Ritual Impurity, 16
Obligatory Actions of Ablution, 17
Doubts about purification, 20
Recommended Actions of Ablution, 20
Wiping Over Khuffs, 24
Duration, 24
Conditions for validity, 26
Invalidators, 27
Relieving & Cleaning Oneself, 28
Facing the direction of prayer, 29
Places where relieving oneself is offensive, 30
Entering and exiting the lavatory, 31
The Purificatory Bath, 34
When it is necessary, 34
Obligatory acts, 36
Recommended acts, 37
Actions Unlawful Due to Major Ritual Purity, 39
Recommended Baths, 41

Filth and its removal, 44
Liquid intoxicants, 44
That which exits from the private parts, 45
Living animals, 46
Dead animals, 48
Hair and bones, 48
Washing due to dogs or pigs, 49
Removing other types of filth, 49
Vinegar and tanning of animal skins, 50
Dry Ablution, 50
Conditions, 51
Obligatory actions, 52
Recommended actions, 54
Invalidators, 54
It is repeated for each obligatory act, 55
Splints and bandages, 55
In the absence of water or earth, 56
Menstruation, Postnatal & Irregular Bleeding, 57
Menstruation, 57
Purity, 58
Pregnancy, 59
Postnatal bleeding, 60
Irregular bleeding, 61
Actions Unlawful Due to Menstruation & Lochia, 64

2 PRAYER, 66
Prayer Times, 67
Conditions Obligating Prayer, 72
Recommended Prayers, 74
Recommended in congregation, 74
Emphasized rawātib, 75
Non-Emphasized rawātib, 76
Emphasized supererogatory prayers, 78
Maximum number of voluntary prayers, 80
Repudiating Prayer And Neglecting Its Performance, 81
Prerequisites for Prayer, 83
Nakedness During Prayer, 87
Essential Elements of Prayer, 89
Actions Recommended Before And During Prayer, 95
Prior to prayer, 95
During the prayer, 97

Differences Between Men & Women During Prayer, 107
Invalidators of Prayer, 109
Quantities of Prayer Elements, 111
Forgetfulness During Prayer, 111
Omitting an obligatory act, 111
Omitting a lesser recommended act, 112
Omitting an emphatically recommended act, 112
Doubting performance or number of prayer elements, 113
Its proper place within the prayer, 114
Times During Which Prayer is Unlawful, 115
Congregational Prayer, 117
Shortening & Combining Prayers, 120
Shortening, 120
Combining, 122
Friday Prayer, 124
Who is obligated to attend, 124
Conditions for its performance, 125
Obligatory elements, 126
Recommended acts, 128
The Two Eids, 131
Their rulings, 131
Their performance, 131
Customary litanies, 132
The Eclipse Prayers, 133
The Drought Prayer, 135
Prayer During Peril, 137
Clothing, 140

3 FUNERALS, 141
Preparing for Death, 141
Funerary Preparations, 141
The Funeral Bath, 143
Funeral Shrouds, 144
The Funeral Prayer, 145
Burial, 147
Crying over the deceased, 148
Offering condolences, 149

4 ZAKAT, 150
Properties subject to zakat, 151
Livestock, 151
Camels, 152

Cows, 154
Sheep, 155
Mixed Properties, 156
Flocks, 156
Money, 156
Gold & Silver, 157
Minimum Amounts, 157
What is Owed, 158
Jewelry, 158
Agriculture & Fruit, 159
The minimum amount, 159
What is owed, 159
Conditions, 160
Trade Goods, 160
Mines & Treasure, 161
Conditions Obligating Zakat, 162
Zakāt al-Fiṭr, 164
Eligible Recipients, 165
Categories of recipients, 165
Minimum distribution, 167
Ineligible recipients, 167
Voluntary Charity, 169

5 FASTING, 170
Conditions and Invalidators, 171
Conditions obligating the fast of Ramadan, 171
Conditions for Ramadan being valid, 172
Invalidators, 172
Intention, 174
Recommended actions, 175
Days Unlawful to Fast, 176
Intercourse in the Daytime During Ramadan, 178
Issues Related to Fasting, 179
The deceased who owes fasts, 179
The elderly and those unable to fast, 180
Pregnancy, illness, and travel, 180
Voluntary Fasting, 181
Recommended fasting days, 181
Offensive fasting days, 183
Spiritual Retreat, 184
It is a Sunnah, 184

Conditions for a valid retreat, 184
Invalidators, 185
Conditions for the one intending retreat, 185
Interruption of consecutive performance, 185

6 PILGRIMAGE, 187
Conditions Obligating Pilgrimage, 189
Integrals of Hajj, 191
Integrals of Umrah, 195
Obligatory Acts of Hajj, 196
Recommended Acts of Hajj, 201
Entering Iḥrām, 203
Things Unlawful During Pilgrimage, 205
Omitting Standing at ʿArafah, 210
Expiations, 211
The Hadi Sacrifice for omitting non-integral obligation, 211
The expiation for shaving and using luxuries, 212
The expiation for being restrained, 213
The expiation for killing game, 214
The expiation for intercourse, 215
The location for expiation, 216
Visiting the Grave of the Prophet ﷺ, 216

7 SALES AND OTHER TRANSACTIONS, 217
Sales, 217
Conditions for validity, 217
Non-Muslims buying the Quran or a Muslim slave, 222
Separating a mother from her child, 222
Unlawful Gain, 223
Goods subject to unlawful gain, 223
Transactions involving a single usurious category, 224
Transactions involving different usurious categories, 225
Exchanging meat for animal products, 226
Choosing to Rescind, 227
During the transaction, 227
Stipulating return, 228
Defective goods, 229
Various Issues Related to Sales, 231
Fruit and crops, 231
Taking possession, 231
Ordering Goods, 233

Conditions for the goods, 233
Conditions for the transaction, 234
Personal Loans, 235
Contractual Disagreement, 236
Slaves Who Have Permission to Trade, 237
Offering Collateral, 237
Goods offerable as collateral, 238
Transactions on collateral, 239
Upkeep and liability, 239
Releasing collateral, 240
Suspension, 241
People who are suspended from transactions, 241
Settlements, 246
Property-related settlements, 247
Thoroughfares, 247
Walls, 248
Development, 249
Assignment of Debt, 249
Providing Surety of Payment, 251
Surety of Physical Presence, 254
Partnerships, 255
Conditions for valid partnerships, 256
Profit and loss, and liability, 257
Partnership nullifiers, 257
Commissioned Transactions, 258
Conditions for commissioners and agents, 258
The blind, 259
Youth and slaves, 259
Conditions for commissioned transactions, 260
What voids or invalidates the contract, 261
The Agent, 262
Admissions, 262
Who can convey an admission, 263
Retractions, 263
Miscellaneous issues, 264
Null Admissions, 264
Attributions of paternity, 265
Lending, 266
Conditions for lenders and borrowed items, 267
Liability, 268
Open-ended or time-limited loans, 268

Sub-Lending, 268
Disagreements, 269
Deposits for Safekeeping, 269
Wrongfully Seized Property, 270
Preemption, 273
Financing a Profit-Sharing Venture, 276
Watering Crops for a Portion of the Yield, 278
Renting Goods & Hiring Services, 280
Wages, 282
Reclamation and Use of Unclaimed Resources, 283
Water Rights, 285
Endowments, 286
Gifts, 288
Withdrawing a gift, 290
Life and survivor grants, 290
Found Items, 291
Foundlings, 293

8 INHERITANCE AND BEQUESTS, 295
The Estate, 297
Claims against the estate, 297
Reasons for inheritance, 298
Male heirs, 298
Female heirs, 299
People Who Always or Never Inherit, 299
Preventers of Inheritance, 300
Shares, 302
Universal Inheritance, 308
Bequests & Executors, 310
Tribute & Spoils of War, 314
Tribute, 314
Spoils of war, 315

9 MARRIAGE AND DIVORCE, 318
Rulings Unique to the Prophet ﷺ, 318
Issues Related to Marriage, 322
Who should marry, 322
Characteristics desirable in a bride, 323
Looking before engagement, 324
Maximum number of wives, 324
Intercourse with slaves, 325
Marrying minors and those with diminished capacity, 326

Male slaves, 327
Looking at Members of the Opposite Sex, 327
Adult males and unrelated adult women, 327
Sexual partners, 329
Close relatives and other adult males, 329
Slaves and eunuchs, 330
Beardless youths, 330
Between women, 330
Women and unrelated adult males, 331
Touching what is unlawful to see, 331
Engagement, 332
The Marriage Contract, 333
Elements and conditions for a valid contract, 333
Women cannot engage directly in the contract, 334
The witnesses, 335
When the bride is a dhimmī or a slave, 335
The Bride's Guardians, 336
Those Barred From Being Guardians, 337
Those stripped of guardianship, 337
When guardians reject a woman's selection without right or are absent, 338
Suitability, 339
Factors for Suitability, 339
Consenting to marry a less than suitable groom, 340
A Husband's Rights, 341
Compelling Women to Marry, 342
Unmarriageable Women, 344
Blood relation, 344
Marriage, 345
Nursing, 346
Sisters and aunts, 346
Triply-divorced former wife, 347
A fifth wife, 347
A freeman marrying a second slave, 347
A slave marrying a third wife, 348
Shighār, 348
Temporary marriage, 348
Marrying a Non-Muslim Woman, 349
Idolatresses and revelationless women, 349
Jewish and Christian women, 349
Apostate women, 351

Freemen marrying slaves, 351
An Individual Spouse Entering Islam, 352
Marriage between non-Muslims, 354
Spousal Defects Permitting Marriage Annulment, 354
Providing a Wife for One's Father, 356
The Wife's Marriage Payment, 357
It is recommended, 357
What is valid as a payment, 358
Ownership and establishment, 359
The bride's right to its disposal, 360
When the payment is halved, 360
Withholding its payment, 361
Disagreements concerning payment, 361
When the wife declines specifying an amount, 362
Invalid or unstated amounts and mahr al-mithl, 362
What is owed for invalid or dubious intercourse, 362
Guardians cannot waive it, 363
Amenity Payment, 364
The Wedding Feast, 365
Holding the feast, 365
Attending the feast, 365
Throwing and collecting sweets, 366
Giving Wives Equal Time, 367
Travel, 369
New brides, 369
Disobedience, 370
A disobedient wife, 370
A harmful or negligent husband, 371
Arbitration, 371
Release for Compensation, 372
Unlawful, innovated divorce, 375
Sunnah divorce, 377
Neither of the above, 378
Maximum number of divorces for freemen, 378
Number of divorces for slaves, 379
Exceptions and contingencies when pronouncing divorce, 379
Pronouncement of divorce prior to marriage, 380
Doubts about occurrence or number of divorces, 380
Giving a woman the option to pronounce divorce, 381
Divorcing part of a woman, 382
Taking Back One's Wife, 382

Forswearing One's Wife, 385
Likening One's Wife to One's Mother, 386
Charging One's Wife With Adultery, 389
Establishing Paternity, 393
The Waiting Period, 394
Widows, 395
Non-Widows, 396
Slaves, 398
Support during the waiting period, 398
Mourning, 400
Remaining in One's Residence, 401
Ensuring Lack of Pregnancy, 402
Wet-Nursing, 405
Conditions for preventing and nullifying marriage, 405
Spousal Support, 407
Definition and basis, 407
Obligatory amounts, 408
Waived for disobedience, 410
Inability to provide, 410
Supporting Relatives, 411
Nursing One's Child, 414
Supporting Slaves, Animals And Immovable Property, 415
Slaves, 415
Livestock, 416
Property development, 416
Negligent owners, 417
Milking, 417
Custody, 417
Issues Related to Custody, 421

10 INJURIOUS CRIMES, 424
Types of Wrongful Killing, 425
Deliberate, 425
Mistaken and semi-intentional, 426
The augmented indemnity, 428
The reduced indemnity, 429
Indirectly causing death, 429
Individuals Responsible For The Indemnity, 430
Reciprocal Punishment, 431
Conditions obligating implementation, 431
Scenarios in which punishment is not implemented, 432

Non-fatal injuries, 433
Collective murder, 433
If a single guardian pardons, 434
Non-Fatal Personal Injuries, 435
Blood Indemnity, 436
The Blood Indemnity for a Fetus, 438
Factors Augmenting Mistaken Killings, 439
Injuries That Require A Full Blood-Indemnity, 440
Wounds that cleave flesh from the bone, 441
Appraisal, 443
Blood Indemnity for Slaves, 443
Murder Allegations, 444
Expiation for Killing, 446
Renegades, 448
The Supreme Imam, 450
Conditions for suitability, 450
Apostasy, 452
What constitutes apostasy, 452
Repentance, 453

11 PUNISHMENTS, 455
Fornication, 455
Those with the capacity to remain chaste, 456
Other categories of fornicators, 458
Slaves, 459
Accusing a Person of Fornication, 460
What constitutes an accusation and its punishment, 461
Slaves, 463
If evidence is presented, 463
If the accuser makes a public imprecation, 464
Alcohol and Liquid Intoxicants, 464
Theft, 467
Highway Robbery, 470
Its definition and minimum punishment, 471
If killing is involved, 472
If killing and theft are involved, 472
When only spreading fear is involved, 472
Repentance before apprehenSion, 473
Disciplinary Punishments, 473
Self-Defense, 475
Animals, 476

Animals accompanied by a human, 476
Unaccompanied animals, 477
Destructive cats, 477
Looking Through a Peephole, 477
Circumcision, 478

12 JIHAD, 479
Jihad Is An Annual Obligation, 480
Conditions Obligating Jihad, 481
Rules of Engagement, 483
Hiring dhimmīs to participate in jihad, 483
Hiring Muslims to participate in jihad, 484
Killing women and children, 484
Killing monks, farmers, elderly men, and the weak, 484
Using catapults, 485
Single combat, 485
Prisoners of War, 485
Entering Islam prior to capture, 487
Abandoned children found in Muslim lands, 488
Fleeing Battle, 488
Destroying Enemy Property and Animals, 489
Giving Amnesty to Combatants, 490
Emigration from Lands of Disbelief, 491
Compensating Non-Muslim Spies, 493
The Jizyah Contract, 494
Eligibility, 494
The amount owed, 495
Obligations, 496
Restrictions, 497
Truces, 498

13 HUNTING AND SLAUGHTERING, 601
Slaughtering, 501
What constitutes slaughtering, 501
Saying "Bismi Llāh," 504
Hunting with animals, 504
An animal's fetus, 505
Parts severed from living animals, 506
The Eid al-Aḍḥā Sacrifice, 506
Eligible animals, 507
Defects that preclude eligibility, 508

Its designated time, 508
Optimal measures, 509
Recommended acts, 510
Giving away the meat, 510
Slaughtering for a Newborn, 512
Lawful and Prohibited Animals, 513
General guidelines, 513
Animals that eat urine and feces, 515
Consuming forbidden foods out of necessity, 515

14 CONTESTS AND MARKSMANSHIP, 517

15 OATHS AND VOWS, 483
Oaths, 519
Binding and non-binding oaths, 519
Swearing to give away one's property, 520
Carelessly uttered oaths, 521
Swearing a compound oath, 521
Swearing not to perform an act, 521
Expiations for broken oaths, 522
Vows, 522
Binding and non-binding vows, 523
Vows to visit the Sacred Precinct, 524

16 COURTS AND TESTIMONY, 525
Judgments and Arbitration, 525
They are a communal obligation, 525
Conditions for judges, 526
Delegation, 527
Arbitration, 527
Removing Judges, 528
Assistants to the Judge, 528
Some Issues Related to Judgments, 529
Avoiding conflict of interest, 529
Giving equal respect to parties, 529
Priority of Cases, 530
Mistaken Judgments, 530
Description of Claims, 531
Judgment In Absentia, 532
Dividing Property, 532
Witnesses, 534
What Constitutes Testimony and Evidence, 537

Ramadan, 537
Fornication, 537
Financial matters, 538
Things typically known only to women, 538
A single male witness accompanied by an oath, 539
Witnessing what another witnessed, 540
Testimony from the Blind, 540
Lawsuits, 541
The plaintiff, 541
What constitutes a valid lawsuit, 542
Evidence and oaths, 542
Conflicting Evidence, 543
Swearing Oaths, 544
Swearing an oath about oneself or others, 544
Augmented oaths, 544
Oaths & Disputes, 545
Testimony Related to Actions and Statements, 545
Witnesses Retracting Testimony Before Judgment, 545
Witnesses Retracting Testimony After Judgment, 546
Taking Rights, 547

17 MANUMISSION, 548
What Constitutes Manumission, 548
Contingent manumission, 549
Freeing a portion of a slave, 549
Freeing a share of a co-owned slave, 549
Possessing one's ancestor or descendant, 550
Walāʾ, 551
Who is entitled to walāʾ, 551
Women do not inherit walāʾ, 552
Walāʾ is not transferable, 552
Tadbīr, 552
What constitutes tadbīr, 552
Retraction, 553
Partial tadbīr, 553
Kitābah, 553
It is conditionally recommended, 554
Voiding the contract, 554
Waiving a portion of the price, 554
Immediate consequences, 555
Ummahāt al-Awlād, 555

BIBLIOGRAPHY

المَصَادِرُ وَالمَرَاجِعُ

ʿAbd al-Razzāq, *Al-Muṣannaf* ("ʿAbd al-Razzāq"). Edited by Ḥabīb al-Raḥmān al-ʿAẓamī, 2nd edition. Beirut: Al-Maktab al-Islāmī, 1403AH.

Abū Dāwūd, Sulaymān bin al-Ashʿath al-Sajisānī. *Al-Marāsīl*. Edited by Shuʿayb al-Arnāʾūṭ. Beirut: Muʾassisah al-Risālah, 1408AH.

———. *Al-Sunan* ("Abū Dāwūd"). Edited by Muḥammad Muḥya al-Dīn ʿAbd al-Ḥamīd. Beirut: Dār al-Fikr, n.d.

Aḥmed, *Al-Musnad* ("Aḥmed"). Edited by Shuʿayb al-Arnāʾūṭ, ʿĀdil Murshid, et al. Beirut: Muʾassisah al-Risālah, 2001/1421.

al-Anṣārī, Zakariyā. *Asnā al-maṭālib fi sharḥ Rawḍ al-ṭālib*. n.a.: Dār al-Kitāb al-Islāmī, n.d.

al-Baghdādī, Abū Bakr Aḥmad bin ʿAlī al-Khaṭīb. *Al-Jāmiʿ li-akhlāq al-rāwī wa ādāb al-sāmiʿ*. Edited by Maḥmūd al-Ṭaḥḥān. Riyadh: Maktabat al-Maʿārif, n.d.

al-Bayhaqī, Aḥmed bin al-Ḥussein. *Al-Sunan al-kubrā* ("Bayhaqī"). Edited by Muḥammad ʿAbd al-Qādir ʿAṭā. Beirut: Dār al-Kutub al-ʿIlmiyyah, 2003/1424.

———. *Shuʿab al-īmān*. Edited by ʿAbd al-ʿAlī ʿAbd al-Ḥamīd Ḥāmid, et al. Riyadh: Maktabat al-Rushd, 2003/1423.

———. *Aḥkām Al-Qurʾān li-l-Shāfiʿī*, 3rd ed. Cairo: Maktabah al-Khānjī, 1994/1414.

al-Bazzār, Abū Bakr Aḥmed bin ʿAmr, *Al-Baḥr al-zakhkhār (Al-Musnad)* ("Bazzār"). Edited by Maḥfūẓ al-Raḥmān Zayn Allāh, ʿĀdil bin Saʿd, Ṣabrī ʿAbd al-Khāliq al-Shāfiʿī. Medina: Maktabat al-ʿUlūm wa-l-Ḥikam, 1988–2009.

al-Bukhārī, Muḥammad bin Ismāʿīl Abū ʿAbd Allāh. *Al-Adab al-mufrad*. Edited by Muḥammad Fuʾād ʿAbd al-Bāqī. 3rd ed Beirut: Dār al-Bashāʾir al-Islāmiyyah, 1989/1409.

———. *Al-Jāmiʿ al-ṣaḥīḥ al-mukhtaṣar min umūr rasūli Llāh ﷺ wa sunanihi wa ayyāmihi (Ṣaḥīḥ al-Bukhārī)* ("Bukhārī"). Edited by Muḥammad Zuhayr bin Nāsir al-Nāṣir. n.a.: Dār Tawq al-Najāh, 1422AH.

al-Dārамī, Abū Muḥammad ʿAbd Allāh bin ʿAbd al-Raḥmān. *Musnad al-Dāramī (Sunan al-Dāramī)* ("Dārami"). Edited by Ḥussein Sulaymān Asad al-Dārānī. n.a.: Dār al-Maʿrifah li-l-Nashr wa-l-Tawzīʿ, 2000/1412.

al-Dāraquṭnī, Abū al-Ḥasan ʿAlī bin ʿUmar. *Sunan al-Dāraquṭnī* ("Dāraquṭnī"). Edited by Shuʿayb al-Arnāʾūṭ, et al. Beirut: Muʾassisah al-Risālah, 2004/1424.

al-Ghazālī, Abū Ḥāmid Muḥammad bin Muḥammad al-Ṭūsī. *Al-Wasīṭ fi-l-madhhab*. Edited by Aḥmad Maḥmūd Ibrāhīm, Muḥammad Muḥammad Tāmir. Cairo: Dār al-Salām, 1417AH.

al-Haytamī, Aḥmed bin ʿAlī bin Ḥajar. *Tuḥfat al-muḥtāj sharḥ Al-Minhāj*. Beirut: Dār Iḥyā al-Turāth al-ʿArabī, 1983/1357.

al-Ḥākim, Abū ʿAbd Allāh Muḥammad. *Al-Mustadrak ʿalāl al-Ṣaḥīḥayn* ("Ḥākim"). Edited by Muṣṭafā ʿAbd al-Qādir ʿAṭā. Beirut: Dār al-Kutub al-ʿIlmiyyah, 1990/1411.

al-Ḥākim, Abū ʿAbd Allāh Muḥammad. *Maʿrifat ʿulūm al-ḥadīth*, ed al-Sayyid Muʿzam Ḥussein. Beirut: Dār al-Kutub al-ʿIlmiyyah, 1997/1397.

Ibn ʿAbd al-Barr, Abū ʿUmar Yūsuf bin ʿAbd Allāh. *Al-Kāfī fī fiqh ahl al-madīnah*, 2nd edition. Riyadh: Maktabat al-Riyāḍ al-Ḥadīthiyyah, 1980/1400.

Ibn ʿAbd al-Barr, Abū ʿUmar Yūsuf bin ʿAbd Allāh. *Al-Tamhīd li mā fi Al-Muwaṭṭa' min al-asānīd*. Edited by Muṣṭafā bin Aḥmed al-ʿAlawī and Muḥammad ʿAbd al-Kabīr al-Bikrī. Morocco: Wizārat ʿUmūm al-Awqāf wa al-Shu'ūn al-Islāmiyyah, 1387AH.

Ibn Abī Shaybah, Abū Bakr ʿAbd Allāh bin Muḥammad. *Al-Kitāb al-muṣannaf fi al-aḥādīth wa-l-athār* ("Ibn Abī Shaybah"). Edited by Kamāl Yūsūf al-Ḥūt. Riyāḍ: Maktabat al-Rushd, 1409AH.

Ibn ʿAdī, Abū Aḥmad al-Jurjānī. *Al-Kāmil fī ḍuʿafā' al-rijāl*. Edited by ʿĀdil Aḥmad ʿAbd al-Mawjūd and ʿAlī Muḥammad Muʿawwaḍ. Beirut: Dār al-Kutub al-ʿIlmiyyah, 1997/1418.

Ibn al-Mundhir, Abū Bakr Muḥammad bin Ibrāhīm. *Al-Awsaṭ fi al-sunan wa-l-ijmāʿ wa-l-iktilāf*. Edited by Abū Ḥammād Ṣaghīr Aḥmed Muḥammad Ḥunayf. Riyāḍ: Dār Ṭayyibah, 1985/1405.

———. *Al-Ijmā'*. Edited by Fu'ād ʿAbd al-Munʿim Aḥmad. n.a.: Dār al-Muslim li-l-Nashr wa-l-Tawzīʿ, 2004/1425.

Ibn Ḥajar, Abū al-Faḍl Aḥmed bin ʿAlī al-ʿAsqalānī. [*Al-*]*Talkhīṣ al-ḥabīr fī takhrīd aḥādīth al-Rāfiʿī al-kabīr*. Beirut: Dār al-Kutub al-ʿIlmiyyah, 1989/1419.

Ibn Ḥazm, Abū Muḥammad ʿAlī bin Aḥmed, *Al-Maḥallā bi-l-āthār*. Beirut: Dār al-Fikr, n.d.

———. *Marātib al-ijmāʿ fi-l-ʿibādāt wa-l-muʿāmalāt wa-l-iʿtiqādāt*. Beirut: Dār al-Kutub al-ʿIlmiyyah, nd.

Ibn Ḥibbān, Muḥammad al-Bustī and al-Amīr ʿAlā' al-Dīn ʿAlī bin Balbān al-Fārasī. *Al-Iḥsān fī taqrīb Ṣaḥīḥ Ibn Ḥibbān* ("Ibn Ḥibbān"). Edited by Shūʿayb al-Arnā'ūṭ. ʿAmmān: Mu'assisat al-Risālah, 1988/1408.

Ibn al-Jawzī, Jamā al-Dīn Abū al-Faraj ʿAbd al-Raḥmān. *Zād al-masīr fī ʿilm al-tafsīr*. Edited by ʿAbd al-Razzāq al-Mahdī. Beirut: Dār al-Kutub al-ʿIlmiyyah, 1422AH.

Ibn Kathīr, Abū al-Fadā' Ismāʿīl bin ʿUmar. *Tafsīr Al-Qur'ān al-ʿaẓīm*. Edited by Sāmī bin Muḥammad Salāmah. n.a.: Dār Ṭayyibah li-l-Nashr wa-l-Tawzīʿ, 1999/1420.

Ibn Khuzaymah, Abū Bakr Muḥammad bin Ishāq. *Ṣaḥīḥ Ibn Khuzaymah* ("Ibn Khuzaymah"). Edited by Muḥammad Muṣṭafā al-ʿAẓamī. Beirut: Al-Maktab al-Islāmī, n.d.

Ibn Mājah, Abū ʿAbd Allāh Muḥammad bin Yazīd al-Qizwīnī. *Sunan Ibn Mājah* ("Ibn Mājah"). Edited by Muḥammad Fū'ād ʿAbd al-Bāqī. Aleppo: Dār Iḥā' al-Kutub al-ʿArabiyyah, n.d.

Ibn Mulaqqin, Sarāj al-Dīn Abū Ḥafṣ ʿAmr bin ʿAlī. *Al-Badr al-munīr fī takhrīj al-aḥādīth wa-l-āthār al-wāqiʿah fi Al-Sharḥ al-kabrī*. Edited by Muṣṭafā Abū al-Ghayẓ, ʿAbd Allāh bin Sulaymān and Yāsir bin Kamāl. Riyadh: Dār al-Hijrah li-l-Nashr wa-l-Tawzīʿ, 2004/1425.

———. *Tuḥfat al-muḥtāj ilā adillat Al-Minhāj*. Mecca: Dār Ḥarrā', 1406AH.

———. *Khulāṣat Al-Badr al-munīr*. Riyāḍ: Maktabat al-Rushd li-l-Nashr wa-l-Tawzīʿ, 1989/1410.

Ibn Ṣalāh, ʿUthmān bin ʿAbd al-Raḥman Abū ʿAmr. *Sharḥ mushkil Al-Wasīṭ*. Edited by ʿAbd al-Munʿim Khalīfah Aḥmed Bilāl. n.a.: Dār Kunūz Ishbīliyā li-l-Nashr wa-l-Tawzīʿ, 2011/1432.

al-Isnawī. *Tadhkirat al-nabīh fī taṣḥīḥ Al-Tanbīh*. Edited by Muḥammad ʿUqlah Ibrāhīm. Beirut: Mu'assisah al-Risālah, 1996.

al-Jamal, Sulaymān bin ʿUmar. *Futūḥāt al-wahhāb*. n.a., n.d.

Mālik bin Anas. *Al-Mudawwana al-kubrā*. Beirut: Dār al-Kutub al-ʿIlmiyyah, 1994/1415.

———. *Al-Muwaṭṭa'* ("Mālik"). Edited by Muḥammad Muṣṭafā al-ʿAẓamī, 8 vols. Abu Dhabi: Mu'assisah Zāyad bin Sulṭān Āl Nahyān li-l-ʿAmāl al-Khayriyyah wa-l-Insāniyyah, 2004/1428.

al-Māwardī, ʿAbū al-Ḥasan ʿAlī bin Muḥammad. *Al-Ḥāwī al-kabīr fī fiqh madhhab al-Imām al-Shāfiʿī*. Beirut: Dār al-Kutub al-ʿIlmiyyah, 1999/1419.

———. *Al-Nukat wa-l-ʿuyūn* (*Tafsīr al-Māwardī*). Edited by al-Sayyid Ibn ʿAbd al-Maqṣūd bin ʿAbd al-Rahīm. Beirut: Dār al-Kutub al-ʿIlmiyyah, n.d.

Muslim bin al-Ḥajjāj. *Al-Musnad al-ṣaḥīḥ al-mukhtaṣar bi-naql al-ʿadl ʿan al-ʿadl ilā rasūl Allāh* ﷺ ("Muslim"). Edited by Muḥammad Fuʾād ʿAbd al-Bāqī. Beirut: Dār Iḥyāʾ al-Turāth, n.d.

al-Muzanī, Islmāʿīl bin Yaḥyā bin Ismāʿīl. *Mukhtaṣar al-Muzanī,* printed as appendix to *Al-Umm*. Beirut: Dār al-Maʿrifah, 1990/1410.

al-Nasāʾī, Abū ʿAbd al-Raḥmān Aḥmed bin Shuʿayb. *Al-Mujtabā* ("Nasāʾī"). Edited by ʿAbd al-Fattāḥ Abū Ghuddah, 2nd ed. Aleppo: Maktab al-Maṭbūʿāt al-Islāmiyyah, n.d.

———. *Al-Sunan al-kubrā*. Edited by ʿAbd al-Ghaffār Sulayman al-Bandārī. Beirut: Dā al-Kutub al-ʿIlmiyyah, n.d.

———. *ʿAmal Al-Yaum wa-l-Lalalah*. Edited by Fārūq Ḥammādah. Beirut: Muʾassisah al-Risālah, 1406AH.

al-Nawawī, Yaḥyā bin Sharaf. *Al-Majmūʿ sharḥ Al-Muhadhdhab*. Beirut: Dār al-Fikr li-l-Ṭibāh wa-l-Nashr, n.d.

———. *Rawḍat al-ṭālibīn*. Edited by Zuhary al-Shāwīsh. Beirut: Al-Maktab al-Islāmī, 1991/1412.

———. *Al-Minhāj sharḥ Ṣaḥīḥ Muslim bin al-Ḥajjaj*, 2nd ed. Beirut: Dār Iḥyāʾ al-Turāth, 1392AH.

al-Qurṭubī, Abū ʿAbd Allāh Muḥammad bin Aḥmed. *Al-Jāmiʿ li-aḥkām Al-Qurʾān*. Edited by Aḥmed ʿAbd al-ʿAlīm al-Bardūnī, 2nd edition. Cairo: Dār al-Kutub al-Miṣriyyah, 1964/1384.

al-Rāfiʿī, ʿAbd al-Karīm bin Muḥammad. *Al-ʿAzīz sharḥ Al-Wajīz* (*Al-Sharḥ al-kabīr*). Edited by ʿAlī Muʿawwiḍ and ʿĀdil ʿAbd al-Wujūd, 1st edition. Beirut: Dār al-Kutub al-ʿIlmiyyah, 1997/1417.

———. *Al-Muḥarrar.* Edited by Muḥammad Ḥasan Ismāʿīl. Beirut: Dār al-Kutub al-ʿIlmiyyah, 2005.

al-Rūyānī, Abū Bakr Muḥammad bin Hārūn. *Musnad al-Ruyānī.* Edited by Aymān ʿAlī Abū Yamānī. Cairo: Muaʾassisah Qurṭubah, 1416AH.

al-Rūyānī, Abū al-Maḥāsin ʿAbd al-Wahhāb. *Baḥr al-madhhab fī furūʿ madhhab al-imām al-Shāfiʿī*. Edited by Ṭāriq Fatḥī al-Sayyid. Beirut: Dār al-Kutub al-ʿIlmiyyah, 2009.

al-Shāfiʿī, Muḥammad bin Idrīs bin ʿAbbās bin ʿUthmān bin Shāfiʿ bin ʿAbd al-Muṭallab. *Al-Musnad*. Beirut: Dār al-Kutub al-ʿIlmiyyah, 1400AH.

———. *Al-Umm*. Beirut: Dār al-Maʿrifah, 1990/1410.

———. *Ikhtilāf al-ḥadīth* (printed as an appendix to *Al-Umm*). Beirut: Dār al-Maʿrifah, 1990/1410.

al-Shīrāzī, Abū Isḥāq Ibrāhīm bin ʿAlī. *Al-Muhadhdhab fī fiqh al-Shāfiʿī*. Beirut: Dār al-Kutub al-ʿIlmiyyah, n.d.

al-Ṭabarānī, Sulaymān bin Aḥmed bin Ayyūb bin Muṭīr. *Al-Muʿjam al-awsaṭ*. Edited by Ṭāriq ʿIwaḍ Allāh Muḥammad. Cairo: Dār al-Ḥaramayn, n.d.

———. *Al-Muʿjam al-kabīr*. Edited by Ḥamdī al-Salafī, 2nd ed. n.a.: Maktabat al-ʿUlūm wa-l-Ḥikam, n.d.

———. *Al-Muʿjam al-ṣaghīr*. Edited by Muḥammad Shakūr Maḥmūd al-Ḥājj Amrīr. Beirut: al-Maktab al-Islāmī & Dār ʿAmmār, 1985/1405.

al-Ṭabarī, Muḥammad bin Jarīr bin Yazīd. *Jāmiʿ al-Bayān fī ta'wīl Al-Qur'ān*. Edited by Aḥmed Muḥammad Shākir. Beirut: Mu'assisah al-Risālah, 2000/1420.

al-Tirmidhī, Muḥammad bin ʿĪsā bin Sawrah bin Mūsā. *Al-Sunan* ("Tirmidhī"). Edited by Aḥmed Muḥammad Shākir, et al, 2nd edition. Cairo: Sharikah Maktabah wa Maṭbaʿah Muṣṭafā al-Bābī al-Ḥalabī, 1975/1395.

al-ʿUmrānī, Abū al-Ḥussein Yaḥyā bin Abī al-Khayr bin Sālim. *Al-Bayān fī madhhab al-Imām al-Shāfiʿī*. Edited by Qāsim Muḥammad Nūrī. Jeddah: Dār al-Minhāj, 2000/1421.

Also from Islamosaic

Hadith Nomenclature Primers

Ibn Juzay's Sufic Exegesis

Infamies of the Soul And Their Treatments

Hanbali Acts of Worship

The Accessible Conspectus

The Encompassing Epistle

The Refutation of Those Who Do Not Follow the Four Schools

Etiquette With the Quran

The Ultimate Conspectus

Sharḥ Al-Waraqāt

Supplement for the Seeker of Certitude

ISLAMOSAIC

www.islamosaic.com

Made in the USA
Middletown, DE
12 September 2023

38417764R00373